Inclusive Welfare

Solikin M. Juhro • Ferry Syarifuddin • Ali Sakti

Inclusive Welfare

On the Role of Islamic Social-Public Finance and Monetary Economics

Springer

Solikin M. Juhro
Macroprudential Policy Department
Bank Indonesia
Jakarta, Indonesia

Ferry Syarifuddin
Islamic Economics and Finance Department
Bank Indonesia
Jakarta, Indonesia

Ali Sakti
Islamic Economics and Finance Department
Bank Indonesia
Jakarta, Indonesia

ISBN 978-981-96-0053-3 ISBN 978-981-96-0051-9 (eBook)
https://doi.org/10.1007/978-981-96-0051-9

This work was supported by Bank Indonesia Institute.

This Springer imprint is published by the registered company Springer Nature Singapore Pte Ltd.
The registered company address is: 152 Beach Road, #21-01/04 Gateway East, Singapore 189721, Singapore

"This book is unique. It explains how achieving welfare in Islam uses the perspective of two sectors, namely the public finance sector and the monetary sector. From the perspective of these two sectors, this book explains the principles and tools of Islamic economics in achieving welfare. The book also succeeds in explaining the relationship between the two sectors and welfare in the current context with information on its practice by several institutions and several countries. The issues explained in this book are very relevant amid the global campaign for inclusive, sustainable development. The information presented in this book is an alternative paradigm to the modern economy that has been trying to achieve prosperity for the world's population for years. Through Islamic Public Finance and Islamic Monetary principles and tools, Islamic Economics provides alternative strategies and policies that the authorities or other related institutions can implement to achieve prosperity. Congratulations to the authors; this book is an essential and significant contribution to knowledge."
—*Prof. Kabir Hasan,* University of New Orleans, USA. The 2016 IDB Prize Winner in Islamic Banking and Finance

"In conventional macroeconomics, public (fiscal) and monetary policies are two main stabilization policies, i.e. policies to achieve stable trajectories for real activities and inflation. While these policies are well acknowledged within Islamic economics, their implementation must align with principles of Islam and have societal welfare as its core agenda. This book brings the Islamic perspectives in the discussion and formulation of fiscal and monetary policies. Through scientific research and approach, it demonstrates how the two policies are integral to development strategies and shared prosperity of a nation via more equal income distribution and engagement in productive activities. Framing the issues in the context of the modern economy, the book serves as a must read and reference for crafting policies in solving pressing issues of the present. My congratulations to the authors for this outstanding contribution. And to all, happy reading."
—*Prof. Mansor Ibrahim,* INCEIF, Malaysia

"This book consists of two interrelated parts, i.e. exploration of the role of Islamic social-public finance on ameliorating prosperity in the

economy and social sector, and examination of the role of Islamic monetary economics. As such, the book contributes meaningfully to the literature of Islamic Monetary Economics and Social Welfare. It is presented in thirteen clearly written and comprehensive chapters, covering philosophical foundation, basic concepts and theories, lesson learned from multi-country practices, as well as policy implications. I am therefore glad to recommend this book to academia including students, regulator, business players, and other stakeholders related to Islamic economic and financial discipline."
—*Prof. Hermanto Siregar,* IPB University and Perbanas Institute, Indonesia

Governor's Remarks

Over time, the dynamics of Islamic economic and financial knowledge and practices have evolved. The presence of Islamic financial institutions and development of Islamic finance have endured in response to societal needs for financial services in accordance with sharia principles. The public sector, through government agencies, and the private sector continue to synergise and maintain an ecosystem for the Islamic economy and finance conducive to create equitable welfare for all.

The public sector is generally accepted and believed to serve the community. Currently, however, the public sector, as managed by the government, cannot achieve its goals alone, thus requiring the support of a social sector, including *zakat, infaq, sadaqah,* and *waqf* (ZISWAF). The social sector, therefore, complements the public sector, in particular serving those languishing at the bottom of the pyramid, which is also consistent with religious teachings concerning the equitable distribution of wealth and income. ZISWAF offer a means to distribute wealth and ensure inclusiveness for all social strata while enabling the productive flow of individual wealth and property. Islam encourages public participation in building social resilience through ZISWAF, thereby maintaining social balance and stability while naturally reducing economic inequality.

Islamic social-public finance requires integration with the monetary sector, especially in relation to Islamic monetary policy. The monetary sector is necessary to regulate the money supply and facilitate the equitable distribution of income by maintaining a seamless flow of money and preventing the hoarding of idle funds. In other words, the monetary system aims to support the intermediation function and create an efficient allocation of finance and resources.

The monetary authority plays a key role in implementing and transforming an optimal Islamic financial system. Pursuant to its mandate, Bank Indonesia performs a critical role in strengthening and developing the conventional and Islamic financial systems, including the development of innovative Islamic monetary instruments. In conjunction with relevant stakeholders, Bank Indonesia develops the Islamic economy and finance based on economic values, along with equitable, transparent, and productive Islamic finance, managed in accordance with good governance principles.

The publication of *Inclusive Welfare: On the Role of Islamic Social-Public Finance and Monetary Economics* represents a concrete step for Bank Indonesia in discharging its central bank duties and responsibilities to support the development of the sharia economy and finance in supporting sustainable economic development by strengthening research and education on the Islamic economy and finance. Consequently, our hope is that Islamic economics and finance, from the perspective of the public, social, and monetary sectors, can be better understood in theory and in practice to promote inclusive welfare and achieve prosperity in this world and the hereafter.

Bank Indonesia, Jakarta, Indonesia
30 October 2024

Perry Warjiyo

Senior Deputy Governor's Remarks

The dutiful goal of every country is to realise quality welfare for its people. To that end, various efforts are taken in the form of broad development policies facilitated through three sectors, namely the private sector, public sector, and social sector. The existence of the Islamic social sector is prerequisite knowledge to greater understanding regarding the scope and application of Islamic economics. This is also in pursuance of Islamic rules and principles, which advocate a life of prosperity and welfare (*falah*) in this world and the next.

Within the Islamic economic system, the social sector plays a significant role supporting current developmental efforts. The robust growth of Islamic social finance institutions serving the asset management needs of Muslim communities in accordance with sharia law is gradually complementing Islamic financial services for all social strata in Indonesia. Islamic commercial finance is adequately serving the needs of medium and large enterprises, while Islamic social finance reaches the poorest of the poor, those languishing at the bottom of the pyramid, as well as supermicro (nano) enterprises. The economic implications of the social sector foster the production of goods and services to be utilised by the community, thereby boosting individual and collective satisfaction within the community. Furthermore, the social sector also facilitates the equitable distribution of wealth and income.

Achieving equitable wealth-income distribution and *falah* in this world and the hereafter through Islamic social-public finance requires the support and synergy of the monetary sector. The role of the government, specifically the monetary authority or central bank, is incontrovertible. Seeking to achieve the goals more effectively, broad policy synergy is required, encompassing Islamic social-public finance and monetary economics. Islamic monetary policy is responsible for regulating the money supply, oriented towards maintaining macroeconomic stability and protecting the equitable distribution of income. Islamic monetary policy, therefore, can help to achieve *falah*, interpreted as achieving quality welfare in this life and the next. In this case, prosperity not only alludes to stronger economic growth; it also implies that the benefits of stronger economic growth are enjoyed by all levels of society.

Inclusive Welfare: On the Role of Islamic Social-Public Finance and Monetary Economics presents well-researched material for the Islamic finance industry to integrate the Islamic financial system and strengthen Islamic finance as a catalyst ameliorating social welfare.

Last but not least, we wish to extend our highest appreciation to the authors and various parties who have contributed to the completion of this book. May God Almighty bless us and enlighten our steps towards a better future.

Bank Indonesia, Jakarta, Indonesia
30 October 2024

Destry Damayanti

Foreword

Praise to Allah SWT, the most Knowing, who provides opportunities for all humans to learn to place science in Islamic perspective as evidence of God's truth among which are economic activities to improve the maslahah of Ummah.

In its application, modern economics gives various ways to fulfil human satisfaction as long as they have access or ability to manage economic resources. Infrastructure, facilities, and technological advances which make life easier are proof of modern economic development. It is no wonder that these parameters altered the economic behaviour of each individual with the paradigm of market forces (capitalism), individual satisfaction (individualism), and materialism. Consequently, economic chaos often occurs, in the form of economic crises as well as social chaos. Economic splendour does not encourage individuals to be more social such as prioritising the value of camaraderie and kinship; instead, it drives individuals to be greedy.

Whereas according to Islamic teachings, it is essential for an economic system to possess a strong ideology and moral values that harmonise idea and action, practice and goal, work and wish, and also deed and aspiration. Moral values are not solely based on individual activities, but also collective interactions. Moreover, moral values and practices are able to lead people to put the common good ahead of their own interest by not living lavishly and paying zakah and other social funds that reflect the Islamic social and public finance.

In the development of the Islamic economy, the Islamic social and public finance sector needs to be integrated with the Islamic monetary sector. Islamic monetary sector does not only concern itself with monetary regulation, but also addresses the alignment and harmonisation between the monetary sector and the real sector as the main core of Islamic economics is the real sector, whereas the monetary sector is the driver of the real sector's development. The continuity and harmony of these two will lead to a more stable economy. The practice of using money and its types also contributes to building a stable monetary system.

Hence, this book takes an approach that focuses on exploring the characteristics and applications of Islamic economics in the original manner combined with comparisons to conventional applications, as well as observing the extent of Islamic social and public finance's dynamics that occurs in several regions in Indonesia. Additionally, this book will comprehensively explain the theory of Islamic monetary economics, including the past, the present, and the future of money, and also the extent of Islamic monetary policy implementation in several countries. This book also provides a number of perspectives on issues in Islamic monetary economics in the original manner and conventional applications.

The drafting, publishing, and dissemination of the book *Inclusive Welfare: On the Role of Islamic Social-Public Finance and Monetary Economics* is one of Bank Indonesia's concrete forms of support in providing information and input for Islamic financial industry players and monetary authorities. The issuance of this book is hopefully able to become a reference for all related parties and sparks our enthusiasm to further contribute to the development of the Islamic financial industry and Islamic monetary economics.

Bank Indonesia Institute, Jakarta, Indonesia
30 October 2024

Yoga Affandi

Preface

Different countries implement a variety of endeavours to achieve public welfare. This is consistent with the principles and rules of Islam that strongly advocate for people to live in equitable prosperity in this life and the hereafter. Well-being is achieved by upholding the principles of *Maqasid Syariah*. This represents a common thread in the economic activities undertaken, namely to help Muslims and the wider community achieve equitable welfare to be enjoyed by all social strata.

The public sector supports the role of the market as the main sector that functions to distribute wealth and income. From an Islamic perspective, the equitable distribution of wealth and income is not left to the private sector in its entirety. Intervention is necessary through incentives for community groups lacking market access, such as via the use of *zakat* instruments. Islam, therefore, has its own mechanism in the social sector, with a focus on the poor and needy (*duafa*).

In the social sector, Islam places *zakat* as a religious obligation to sustain underprivileged community groups through purchasing power and market access. In addition to *zakat*, other instruments are also used to achieve equitable welfare, namely *infaq*, *sadaqah,* and *waqf.* Though often viewed as a complementary sector to support commercial finance, the social sector in the Islamic economic system is a significant proponent of current development, as evidenced by the institutional growth of Islamic social finance that serves community asset management needs in accordance with Islamic law.

The COVID-19 pandemic has accelerated the development of digital finance, which has resulted in several benefits, such as corporate establishment, corporate financial performance improvement, and resilience. Scholars also confirm the driving effect of digitalisation, in particular digital finance, on economic growth. Islamic Social Finance (ISF), which is based on Islamic principles, also has the potential to benefit from digitalisation, which could increase its scope and optimise its potential.

The nature of digital technology that can induce efficiency, transparency, redundancy avoidance, and access widening is symmetrical with the objective and principles of ISF act in Indonesia. Digitalisation can help reduce unbanked people and alleviate inequality, which could ease the ISF collection, especially in Indonesia with its large Muslim population and potential for ISF's funds utilisation. However, implementing digitalisation in ISF requires high investment costs and raises concerns around cyberattack, data privacy, and legal frameworks. In addition, digitalisation is heavily reliant on electrical sources and Internet coverage, which could pose risks and create a digital divide, particularly in remote areas. Alternatives technologies that can be utilised for ISF digitalisation are artificial intelligence (AI), blockchain, cloud computing, big data, QR code, and digital platform.

In the modern era, the social sector is increasingly emerging as complementary to the public sector in serving the community, particularly the underprivileged. The economic implications of the social sector tend to manifest by increasing the production of goods and services that can be utilised by the community. Furthermore, the social sector also facilitates the orderly and equitable distribution of wealth and income. Islamic economic activity involving movements between sectors and stakeholders demonstrates that the concept of economics from an Islamic perspective proscribes idle money, namely funds that are not allocated to productive activities.

The Islamic social-public finance sector cannot achieve inclusive welfare by itself. Support from the monetary sector is also necessary to support the fair and impartial distribution of income through Islamic social-public finance. To that end, the role of the monetary authority, specifically the central bank, is crucial. Islamic monetary policy serves to regulate the money supply based on Islamic values in pursuit of *falah*, defined as welfare, or well-being, in this world and the next.

The practices of Islamic economics and finance are comparatively different from the conventional economic system, particularly the financial system. Financial transactions in Islam require an underlying transaction, including trade-based transactions and profit-sharing transactions, thus establishing a close relationship between the financial sector and real sector. Financial sector development is only possible based on commensurate real sector development. Meanwhile, the monetary system, including monetary policy, aims to support the intermediation function of financial institutions. The financial sector cannot develop separately, however, instead relying on real sector activities to drive growth. Such interlinkages constitute an important factor when trying to understand monetary mechanisms in the Islamic financial system. The expectation, therefore, is stable growth in the long term.

Various explanations and dynamics concerning the Islamic economy, role of Islamic social-public finance, and Islamic monetary sector support towards inclusive welfare must be discussed in depth. It has become essential to understand the role of the Islamic financial system in greater detail, including the economic contribution of Islamic social-public finance and Islamic monetary policy. In addition, it is important to understand the dynamics of Islamic social-public finance and Islamic monetary policy in terms of development strategies for the various instruments, institutions, regulations, and other supporting infrastructure including digitalisation.

Inclusive Welfare: On the Role of Islamic Social-Public Finance and Monetary Economics was written to spur further development of Islamic economic and financial concepts and practices, particularly in terms of Islamic social-public finance and Islamic monetary policy support. The book has a number of objectives across different aspects. From an academic perspective, the book aims to foster frontier thinking and concepts that advance scientific ideas and teaching materials relating to the Islamic financial system, particularly the role of Islamic social-public finance and Islamic monetary economics. From a policy perspective, the book explores and develops discussions that support public policy innovation, thereby providing comprehensive understanding of policy theories and practices in the Islamic financial system. From a practical perspective, the book is expected to contribute by increasing knowledge and understanding concerning the application and scope of the Islamic economic system. This will confer various benefits to the readers.

Jakarta, Indonesia
30 October 2024

Solikin M. Juhro
Ferry Syarifuddin
Ali Sakti

Acknowledgements

Inclusive Welfare: On the Role of Islamic Social-Public Finance and Monetary Economics explains the Islamic financial system holistically and comprehensively from the perspective of Islamic social-public finance as well as Islamic monetary economics. The elucidation of Islamic social-public finance and its relation to monetary economics is engrossing and consequential for the public to know as a material consideration when implementing modern policies of the sharia economy and finance. From an Islamic standpoint, Islamic social-public finance and Islamic monetary economics are implemented with the goals of safeguarding equitable distribution to achieve the ultimate goal of effective policymaking. To that end, both financial systems require knowledge of Islamic economic principles and theories (Islamic monetary economics and Islamic social finance) and the full support of the institutions and regulators tasked with protection.

The book would have been impossible if not for the massive contributions provided by various credible and competent parties in Islamic economics and finance. The contributors are from various backgrounds, including academics, practitioners, and policymakers. We would like to express our utmost appreciation to all contributors who have helped in the completion of this book.

First, we would like to thank Perry Warjiyo, Governor of Bank Indonesia, and Mr. Dodi Budi Waluyo, Deputy Governor of Bank Indonesia (2018–2023), for their tireless support, motivation, and direction during the process of compiling this book. Second, to Bank Indonesia Institute Department Head, Dr. Yoga Affandi, and The Research Center Head, Dr. Iman Gunadi, for their kind support to publish this book. Third, we thank Prof. Mansor Ibrahim and Dr. Irfan Syauqi Beik for their assistance in terms of line editing and proofreading the manuscript of this book, thereby ensuring the quality of the writing.

Fourth, we also express our appreciation and gratitude to those who helped deepen the substance and knowledge in the completion of this book as resource persons and discussion partners, adding invaluable data and information. We thank those who helped enrich the trove of scientific knowledge as resource persons, fulfilling field data and information, namely Prof. Azam Noer Achsani, Prof. Hermanto Siregar, Dr. Leo Herlambang, Dr. Bayu Arie Fianto, Drs.Ec. Suherman Rosyidi, M.Com., Prof. Munawar Ismail, Dr. Israk Ahmadsyah, Dr. Shabri Abd. Majid, Dr. Rahmatina Awaliah Kasri, Dr. Ahmad Juwaini, Dr. Raditya Sukmana, and Dr Heri Sudarsono.

Furthermore, we would also like to thank the resource persons who became discussion partners in the field survey as an integral component of this book, including Prof. Dr. Munawar Ismail (Brawijaya University), Dr. Leo Herlambang (Islamic Economics and Business Lecturer Forum), Dr. Bayu Arie Fianto (Airlangga University), Dr. Raditya Sukmana (Airlangga University), Drs.Ec. Suherman Rosyidi, M.Com. (Airlangga University), Jauhari Sani (Al Falah Social Fund Foundation), Dr. Mugiyati (UIN Sunan Ampel), Dr. Ahmad Djalaluddin (UIN Malik Ibrahim Malang), Dr. Arief Hoetoro (Brawijaya University), Dr. Asfi Manzilati (Brawijaya University), Dr. Idah Zuhroh (Muhammadiyah University Malang), Dr. Hastin Umi Anisah (Lambung Mangkurat University), Dr. Ahmad Greece (Lambung Mangkurat University), Muhammad Luthfi Alfin (Rumah Zakat Banjarmasin), Dr. Muhaimin (UIN Antasari), Dr. Sukarni (UIN Antasari), Ahmad Rifani, S.E., M.M. (LAZISMU South Kalimantan), Dr. Muhammad Hudaya (Lambung Mangkurat University), Syahrituah Siregar, S.E., M.A. (Lambung Mangkurat University), Ari Syantoso, M.Sc. (UNISKA Muhammad Arsyad al-Banjari), Rahmadi Aulia (PT Mitra Aulia Indonesia), M. Yusuf Syahputra (Region-A Duafa Partner Cooperative), Sayed Muhammad Husen (Baitul Mal Aceh), Dr. Israk Ahmadsyah (UIN Ar-Raniry), Dr. Zaki Fuad (UIN Ar-Raniry), Dr. Shabri Abd. Majid (Shia Kuala University), Dr. Eddy Gunawan (Shia Kuala University), Dr. Iskandarsyah Madjid (Shia Kuala University), Amri bin Abdullah (Grameen Replica Aceh), Dr. Hafas Furqani (UIN Ar-Raniry), Dr. Ahmad Akbar Susamto (Gadjah Mada University), Cahyono (LAZISMU DIY), Dr. Dimas Bagus Wiranata Kusuma (Muhammadiyah University Yogyakarta), Hj. Mursida Rambe (KSPPS BMT Beringharjo), Mohammad Bekti Hendrie Anto, S.E., M.Sc. (Islamic University of Indonesia), Ust. Muhammad Jazir ASP (Jogokariyan Mosque Yogyakarta), Yuli Utami, S.E.I., M.Ec. (Muhammadiyah University Yogyakarta), Dr. Juliana (Indonesia University of Education), Herlyanti (Hijau Lestari NGO), Elis Solihat (Hihau Lestari NGO), Koharudin Saefulloh (Baitul Mal itQan), Dr. Sofyan Al Hakim (UIN Sunan Gunung Djati), Nur Efendi (CEO of Rumah Zakat), and Dr. Cupian (Padjadjaran University).

We would also like to thank the assistant researchers from the Bank Indonesia Institute, Maudy Mishfanny S.E., Camilla Nur Azima, M.Sc., Danis Nurul Yunita, S.Pd., M.Sc., and Yodi Izharivan, M.Sc., for overseeing the preparation of this book since the beginning. The determined work of research assistants was crucial for the literature study and when compiling the various kinds of information necessary in the preparation of this book.

The authors would also like to give special mention concerning the professional language editing provided by Matthew L. Burrows.

Hopefully, this book entitled *The Role of Islamic Social-Public Finance and Monetary Economics* will endure as a charitable contribution by all those involved towards advancing Islamic economics. In addition, we hope that the enthusiasm shown by the contributors in the preparation of this book can provide broad benefits to all readers.

Jakarta, 30 October 2024

Solikin M. Juhro
Ferry Syarifuddin
Ali Sakti

Contents

List of Figures

List of Tables

Chapter 1
Introduction

1.1 Welfare from an Islamic Perspective

Each country has its own vision or aspirations to realise public welfare and prosperity. Authorities in different jurisdictions implement various initiatives, in the form of broad development policy, to achieve economic and social welfare. In general terms, **welfare** refers to a state of well-being where individuals or communities experience good health, prosperity, and peace. This broad concept encompasses both physical and mental health, economic stability, and overall quality of life. This term reflects an ideal state where societal systems and policies aim to enhance the overall well-being of individuals and communities. Referring to this understanding, the state of welfare should be improving, where every effort of public and government policy will be attempted to improve welfare in a complete dimension. In other words, welfare has an inclusive dimension where a system is built so that benefits and services that help public meet economic, social, educational, and health needs that are important for the continuity of life.

The realisation of the desired welfare, therefore, is not "pareto" (non-Pareto optimal) in nature. Non-Pareto optimal condition implies that the achievement or improvement of a person's welfare will not reduce the welfare of others; in contrast to the Pareto optimal condition, where the improvement in the welfare of a person or group will certainly reduce the welfare of other people or groups. In fact, the inclusive welfare is also intended to create a more just and cohesive society by addressing the needs of marginalised and vulnerable groups and to ensure that no one is left behind, creating a more equitable and supportive system for all individuals in society.

The spirit of inclusive welfare explored above is inherent to Islamic teachings and sharia law, which strongly encourage adherents to live in global prosperity, fairly and equitably (*falah*), in this life and the hereafter in accordance with *Maqasid Syariah*. In Islam, Iman Al Ghazali stated that the goal of sharia in Islam is to ameliorate welfare through the protection of faith (*din*), protection of life (*nafs*),

S. M. Juhro et al., *Inclusive Welfare*, https://doi.org/10.1007/978-981-96-0051-9_1

protection of mind (*aql*), protection of lineage (*nasl*), and protection of property (*maal*). Similarly, in economic terms, the goal is to help all social strata achieve prosperity fairly. Based on the principles of *maqasid syariah*, Islamic guidance covers four aspects of economic and business activity, namely ethical, moral, social, and religious aspects, which aim to increase proportionally and equitably for the greater good of the community as a whole. Therefore, the philosophical foundation of the Islamic financial system expands beyond financial and economic aspects merely to maximise profit, thus differentiating it from the conventional financial system that focuses on economic and financial aspects to maximise profit.

It is important to understand that *maqasid syariah* represents the strategic aspects of the Islamic economic and financial framework, playing a critical role as the foundation of economic and financial activities as well as business transactions. The presence of financial aspects (maintaining property (*hifz al-mal*)) in *maqasid syariah* and economic activity brings benefits as the honourable goal of sharia. Such a goal affords value to finance, banking, trade, and all business transactions. The implementation of *maqasid syariah* increases financial performance and trade, while building fairness in the business community and amongst the public in general. Furthermore, the achievement of sharia goals in business transactions presents happiness and satisfaction and meets the economic needs of the public.

Currently, various parties are striving towards equitable prosperity and inclusive welfare that is enjoyed by all social strata. Nevertheless, such efforts appear suboptimal, thus making welfare difficult to achieve. It is unequivocal that large swathes of people continue to live in poverty around the world, particularly in developing/poor countries. Poverty remains an overarching global issue and a significant problem in all countries. For decades, global campaigns have sought to end poverty, as contained in the Millennium Development Goals (MDGs). The MDGs were eight international development goals for the year 2015 that were established following the Millennium Summit of the United Nations in 2000, following the adoption of the United Nations Millennium Declaration. All 191 United Nations member states, and at least 22 international organisations, committed to help achieve the Millennium Development Goals by 2015 as follows: (i) to eradicate extreme poverty and hunger; (ii) to achieve universal primary education; (iii) to promote gender equality and empower women; (iv) to reduce child mortality; (v) to improve maternal health; (vi) to combat HIV/AIDS, malaria, and other diseases; (vii) to ensure environmental sustainability; and (viii) to develop a global partnership for development. On the issue of poverty, the MDGs targeted to halve, between 1990 and 2015, the proportion of people living in poverty. That target was achieved 5 years ahead of schedule in 2010. In general, the major successes of the MDGs include lifting more than 1 billion people out of extreme poverty (since 1990), more than halving child mortality (since 1990), more than halving the number of out-of-school children (since 1990), and reducing HIV/AIDS infections by nearly 40% (since 2000).

Despite alleviating poverty, the number of people globally still living in extreme poverty remains high. As the challenge becomes more onerous moving forward, the international community continued the MDG campaign, which ended in 2015, with the newest initiative, known as the Sustainable Development Goals (SDGs). The SDGs are a collection of 17 interlinked global goals set up by the United Nations General Assembly in 2015, involving 193 member states and civil societies globally. The SDGs are parts of UN Resolution A/RES/70/1 of the United Nations General Assembly, namely "Transforming our world: the 2030 Agenda for Sustainable Development", otherwise known as the 2030 Agenda. Paragraph 54 of UN Resolution A/RES/70/1 of the United Nations General Assembly, dated 25th September 2015, contains the SDG and targets. The SDGs cover social and economic development issues, including poverty, hunger, health, education, global warming, gender equality, clean water and sanitation, affordable and clean energy, urbanisation, the environment, and social inclusion. The 17 individual goals are as follows:

1. **No Poverty**: Inclusive economic growth is required to provide sustainable employment and promote equality.
2. **Zero Hunger**: The food and agricultural sectors offer key solutions for development as the centre of hunger and poverty eradication.
3. **Good Health and Well-Being**: Ensure healthy lives and promote well-being for all at all ages, which is critical for sustainable development.
4. **Quality Education**: Provide quality education as the foundation to improve lives and ensure sustainable development.
5. **Gender Equality**: Gender equality is not only a fundamental human right but a prerequisite for a peaceful, prosperous, and sustainable world.
6. **Clean Water and Sanitation**: Clean and accessible water for all is an important part of the world we want to live in.
7. **Affordable and Clean Energy**: Energy is critical for nearly all the main challenges and opportunities.
8. **Decent Work and Economic Growth**: Sustainable economic growth requires conditions that allow for decent work.
9. **Industry, Innovation, and Infrastructure**: Investment in infrastructure is critical to achieve sustainable development.
10. **Reduce Inequality**: To reduce income inequality, universal policies are required in principle based on the needs of disadvantaged and marginalised populations.
11. **Sustainable Cities and Communities**: To create a future where cities provide opportunities for all, with access to basic services, energy, housing, transportation, and more.
12. **Responsible Production and Consumption**: Ensure sustainable consumption and production patterns.
13. **Climate Action**: Climate change is a global challenge affecting everyone everywhere.
14. **Life Below Water**: Management of this essential global resource is a key feature of a sustainable future.
15. **Life on Land**: Sustainably managing the forests, combating desertification, halting and reversing land degradation and halting biodiversity loss.

16. **Peace, Justice, and Strong Institutions**: Access to justice for all and building effective, accountable, and inclusive institutions at all levels.
17. **Partnership for the Goals**: Revitalising the global partnership for sustainable development.

Based on estimations made in 2015 in Table 1.1, 10% of the global population lives on less than USD1.90 per day compared with 11% in 2013. The figure has fallen 36% since 1990. In 2015, 736 million people lived on less than USD1.90 per day. Two regions, East Asia and the Pacific (47 million people living in extreme poverty) as well as Europe and Central Asia (7 million people living in extreme poverty) have reduced extreme poverty to less than 3%. More than half of the extreme poor live in sub-Saharan Africa. In fact, the number of people living in extreme poverty in sub-Saharan Africa has risen by nine million, where more than 413 million people lived on less than USD1.90 per day in 2015. If that trend continues, forecasts indicate that by 2030, nearly 9 in 10 extremely poor people will live in sub-Saharan Africa. Globally, most of the extreme poor live in rural areas with low education, working in the agricultural sector and under 18 years old. Based on current global growth projections, the pace of poverty alleviation is insufficient to achieve the target of ending extreme poverty by 2030.

Unfortunately, the latest projections suggest that without any significant change, the global community will not eradicate extreme poverty by 2030 as those left in extreme poverty become increasingly difficult to reach, often living in vulnerable countries and remote areas. It has become critical to find a solution to this problem as we move towards 2030. With increasing extreme poverty and a concentration of wealth and power in the hands of a few, economic inequality is widening.

Looking more closely, the emergence of the MDG and SDG global commitments demonstrated a new paradigm in the strategy to overcome poverty. Previously, poverty eradication strategies were indirect in nature, offering incentives to large industries to stimulate the development of other economic sectors. This was known as trickle-down economics, based on the economic proposition that cutting taxes for businesses and the rich would enable wealthy owners to invest in the short term, thus with broader benefits trickling down to middle- and working-class citizens in the long term. This strategy is extolled by critics of supply-side economic policy, such as Reaganomics. Although the substance is the same, supply-side theory generally supports lower taxes for all, while trickle-down theory targets tax cuts for the rich. According to both strategies, however, the distribution of wealth and income relies on market forces or private sector mechanisms, where the success of advanced sectors will trickle down to underdeveloped sectors.

Trickle-down effect theory as a development strategy is now derided as ineffective. Instead of ameliorating the living standards of the poor, the strategy has supported the emergence of business conglomerates with far-reaching tentacles. Initially, large industrial corporations were expected to revive the business environment, particularly targeting micro and small enterprises as well as the poor, but large corporations have instead spread their business wings end to end, incorporating downstream and upstream processes. Market mechanisms in the private sector have

Table 1.1 Global poverty

	Survey coverage (%)		$1.90: headcount ratio (%)		$1.90:number of poor(mil)		$3.20: headcount ratio (%)		$3.20:number of poor(mil)		$5.50: headcount ratio (%)		$5.50:number of poor(mil)	
Region	Oct 2017	Apr 2018	Oct 2017	Apr 2018	Oct 2017	Apr 2018	Oct 2017	Apr 2018	Oct 2017	Apr 2018	Oct 2017	Apr 2018	Oct 2017	Apr 2018
East Asia and Pacific	96.5	97.7	3.7	3.6	73.9	73.2	17.6	17.6	354	352	42.6	42.5	855	853
Europe and Central Asia	90.7	90.7	2.2	1.6	10.4	7.7	6.8	5.8	32.8	27.7	14.9	14.1	72.1	67.8
Latin America and the Caribbean	91.7	91.6	4.9	4.5	30.1	27.8	11.6	11.3	71.0	69.5	27.3	27.1	167	166
Middle East and North Africa	78.0	77.7	2.3	2.7	8.3	9.6	13.1	14.5	47.1	52.0	40.8	42.7	146	153
South Asia	98.3	98.1	14.7	15.1	249	257	52.0	52.6	883	894	83.2	83.5	1414	1418
Sub-Sharan Africa	49.6	69.1	41.0	42.3	390	401	66.5	67.5	633	639	85.0	85.2	809	807
Other High Income Economies	68.9	76.1	0.6	0.6	6.5	6.4	0.9	0.9	9.7	9.5	1.5	1.5	15.9	15.9
World total	84.9	88.8	10.7	10.9	769	783	28.3	28.6	2031	2044	48.4	48.7	3479	3481

Source: World Bank, April 2018 & PovcalNet

failed to have maximum impact on raising the living standards of the poor. The MDG and subsequent SDG campaigns championed by United Nations member states acknowledge the weaknesses of the trickle-down strategy. Therefore, MDG and SDG campaigns call for greater government involvement and commitment through policy discretion to alleviate poverty.

In the case of Indonesia, BPS-Statistics Indonesia (2018) published data indicating 26.58 million people in September 2017 living below the poverty line, down 1.18 million from 27.76 million one year earlier. Although the number of people who live in poverty in Indonesia has continued to track a downward trend, the total population increased to 261.9 million in 2017 from 258.7 million in 2016, implying a 3.2 million increase in the reporting period.

A comparison between the number of people living in poverty and total population in Indonesia implies that the decline is not necessarily a corollary of an effective poverty alleviation program but actually because the percentage of poor people against total population has stagnated. Between 2014 and 2017, the poverty rate in Indonesia never fell below 10%. In fact, the poverty rate in 2016 stood at 10.86% and then 10.64% in 2017. The 0.22% decline from 2016 to 2017 is considered insignificant, especially when taking population growth into consideration.

Such a phenomenon points to ineffective public and private sector poverty alleviation programs in Indonesia. In the 2018 State Revenue and Expenditure Budget (APBN), the government earmarked Rp283.7 trillion for poverty alleviation and to support low-income earners, up 3.65% on the previous year. Of the total allocation, Rp25.5 trillion was apportioned to the National Health Insurance (JKN) plan for 92.4 million poor people as well as food assistance totalling Rp20 trillion. In the private sector, a survey confirmed that Rp105.4 trillion of social funds (including *zakat*, *sadaqah*, charity, donations, grants, et cetera) was accumulated in Indonesia in 2014. Nevertheless, the actual figure was much higher, as evidenced by *zakat* potential totalling Rp270 trillion per year.

Fundamentally, the economy according to Islam is based on market mechanisms in the private sector (Salama, 1995). Market mechanisms as the main economic interaction are illustrated in the story of how *Rosullullah* rejected requests for price intervention at Medina market when prices soared. Intervention was instead achieved through incentives for the poor without access to the market. In essence, the religious obligation of *zakat* under sharia law maintains public purchasing amongst the poor and needy (*duafa*). *Zakat* also demonstrates the government's role and position as *zakat* manager within an economy. Therefore, Islam has its own mechanisms in the social sector, mechanisms that specifically target *duafa*. The social sector in Islam places *zakat* as an essential instrument to sustain income, purchasing power and market access amongst the poor and needy. Furthermore, *zakat* reflects the orientation of public policy in Islam, which focuses or prioritises *dhuafa* in the economic development strategy. Finally, the obligatory *zakat* mechanism within an economy demonstrates a relative policy focus on the demand side.

In addition to *zakat* and other similar obligatory instruments, Islam also recognises voluntary instruments, such as infaq, sadaqah, and waqf. Moreover, the Islamic social system has other teachings and advantages in its application, namely budget discipline. In terms of *zakat* management, the guidelines are unambiguous, where *zakat* funds are collected from the wealthy (*muzaki*) and distributed to eight categories of recipient (*mustahiq*). Waqf social fund management is similar, where the waqf funds are donated by the owner (*waqif*) to the manager (*nazhir*) to provide benefits for the community. If the *waqif* makes a special request for the funds, such as building a clinic, school, or something similar, the *nazhir* is required to oblige. Instruments of Islamic social finance provide a different style of budget management than what is currently available in the modern world. The definitive allocation of *zakat* and waqf assets shows that such instruments naturally tend towards disciplined and transparent management in their use.

From a contemporary application perspective, the function and task of government has continued to evolve, implying larger state spending as a consequence and requiring new revenues, such as taxes, to maintain the government's role. This differs from *zakat*, the function of which is clearly defined for eight categories of recipient using unproductive or unutilised assets, thus discouraging members of the community from hoarding assets, instead using their wealth for the benefit of others in need. Nevertheless, *zakat* implementation in a government system that eschews Islamic principles, such as in Indonesia, creates different opinions concerning who should manage the funds. One school of thought opines that the government authority should be responsible for *zakat* management, while the opposing opinion states that *zakat* management is the responsibility of the individual. Such opposing opinions concerning tax and *zakat* imply that the revenues of both have failed to reach potential, leading to ineffective government action to eradicate poverty and create prosperity for all. Consequently, problems have arisen from the pros vs cons arguments, namely that as citizens there is only the need to pay tax without paying *zakat* because the functions are considered the same, and vice versa. This has also undermined the potential of both revenue streams.

Currently, the social sector's role in the Islamic economic system to support development is regarded as significant, although conditions in reality are not aligned, with the social sector relegated to merely complementing and supporting Islamic commercial finance. The growth of Islamic social finance institutions to serve Muslims and manage wealth in accordance with sharia law is slowly complementing sharia financial services targeting all social strata in Indonesia. In general, the Islamic commercial finance sector tends to serve medium and large enterprises, while the sharia microfinance sector serves micro and small enterprises. Finally, Islamic social finance targets the poorest of the poor (*duafa*) and the supermicro (nano) economy.

To accelerate Islamic social finance (ISF), digitalisation has played one of the key developments of ISF. Thus far, with covid-19 pandemic as a catalyst, digital finance has developed more rapidly. Digitalisation brings several benefits such as financial performance improvement, corporate establishment, and stability. Furthermore, scholars are also confirming the driving effect of digitalisation, in particular digital finance, on economic growth. Despite the impacts on corporate and macroeconomic, it is not impossible that digitalisation could have a positive impact on ISF. In brief, ISF, e.g. *zakat, infaq, alms, and waqf*, is a financial system based on Islamic principles and aims to promote inclusive welfare. This remarkable potential could be attained for developing countries if implemented accordingly.

Digitalisation to the end has increased the scope of ISF and further optimised its potential. Correlation between digitalisation and financial inclusion has also been reported by Aziz et al. Mohd Nor et al. argue that the usage of technology, such as blockchain, could support Islamic social finance if there is a proper socialisation and education. Following the same spirit, the enthusiasm of Muslim to implement digitalisation within ISF is already reported by Usman et al. Moreover, it is explained that digitalisation has important role in reducing unbanked people by providing accessibility, which could ease the ISF collection.

According to modern economic theory, the economy is divided into two main sectors, namely the private sector and public sector. The private sector supplies the goods and services demanded by the public commercially, including shoes, motor vehicles, travel, finance, and so on. The public sector supplies the goods and services demanded by the public yet not provided commercially by the private sector due to a lack of intrinsic economic value, including roads, bridges, airports, city parks, and so on. Faridi (1983) stated that Islam has a third economic sector, namely the social sector. In the social sector, the main players are individuals, who provide goods and services for other individuals on a voluntary basis through instruments such as infaq, sadaqah, and waqf. In addition, the public sector under the Islamic economic system is based on a unique mechanism in accordance with sharia law. The existence of the Islamic social sector is imperative to understand the scope and application of the Islamic economic system.

1.2 Integration of Public and Social Finance Towards Welfare

In essence, there are distinctive characteristics in economic activity towards realising welfare and prosperity from an Islamic perspective. Based on the principle that Allah SWT created mankind on the earth to always believe and worship Him and implement that faith in every facet of life, and with Islamic moral values and sharia principles, mankind is encouraged to achieve happiness on earth and the hereafter, including through economic activity. The principle of the afterlife, or hereafter, makes the principles of Islam from an economic perspective unique. If *falah* is the goal in Islam, then utilising the resources bestowed by Allah SWT, including wealth and property, will also be different. The freedom afforded to mankind by Allah SWT in the pursuit, management, and utilisation of wealth and property must be in line with the religious values and teachings of Islam. Therefore, economic activity under Islam stretches beyond private sector markets and the public sector to include the social sector. In this case, the social sector encompasses the social activities of the public (potentially in conjunction with the government) that are obligatory, such as *zakat*, and voluntary, such as *infaq*, *waqf sadaqah,* and *qardul hasan*. The goal is to

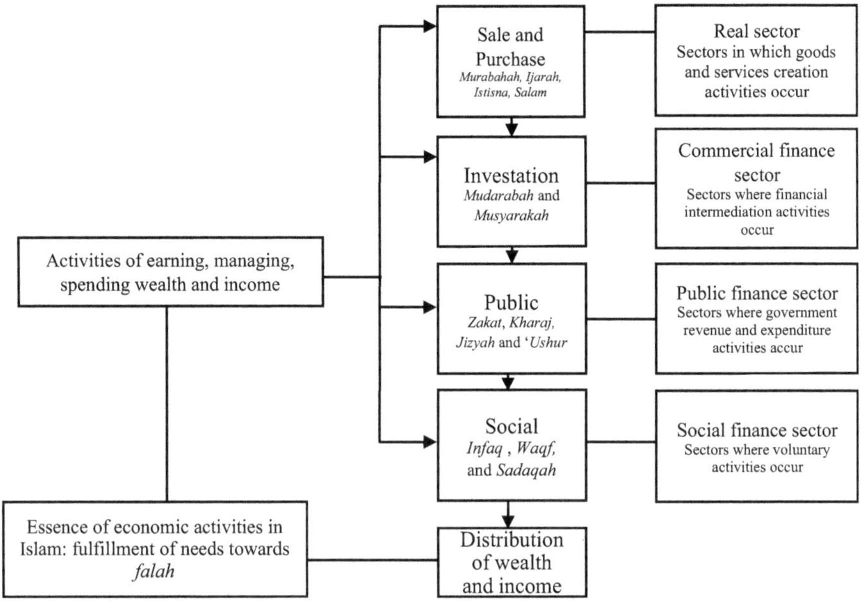

Fig. 1.1 Essence and scope of economic activities in Islam. Source: Created by Author

meet the needs of the poor and needy using *zakat, infaq, sadaqah,* and *waqf* (ZISWAF) instruments. The scope of economic activities under Islam is presented in Fig. 1.1.

The importance of the government's role in the economy stems from the government's mandate under Islam to maintain Islamic norms and values in society through the authority to make policies, including economic affairs. Siddiqi (1996) stressed that the public cannot be organised or regulated based on Islamic principles without using the government as a medium. In Islam, a number of regulations are only effective if implemented, regulated, and supervised by the government. In the economy, for example, *zakat* implementation and *riba* prohibition are only effective through firm government regulation.

In the modern era, the social sector is gaining recognition and prominence as complementary to the public sector (government) in serving the public, particularly the poor and needy (*duafa*). The economic implications of the social sector will stimulate the production of goods and services for the benefit of society. Therefore, public satisfaction is expected to increase. Furthermore, the social sector remains a viable conduit for equitable income and wealth distribution.

Such arguments are consistent with early or classical Islamic philosophy, where the public and social sectors were inextricably linked as one. According to Islam, *zakat, infaq, sadaqah,* and *waqf* (ZISWAF) are considered fiscal instruments, managed by the state. Nowadays, however, the ZISWAF sector has become separate, regarded as the social sector. In this case, *zakat* is considered an integral part of fiscal policy because the role of *zakat* is clearly defined to safeguard the basic needs

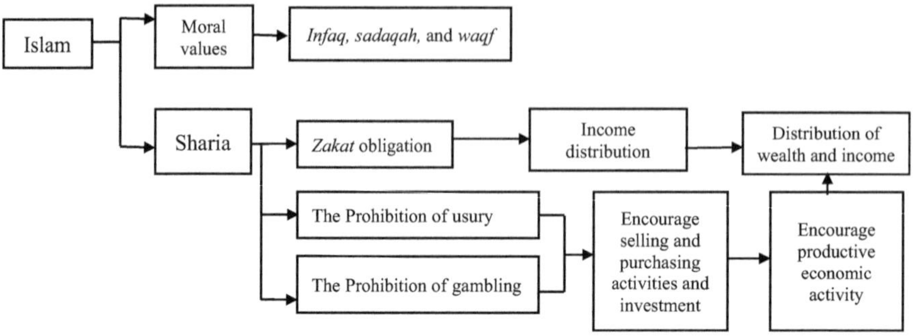

Fig. 1.2 Focus of Islamic economy. Source: Created by Author

of society, particularly the poor and *fakir*. Metwally (1996) found that *zakat* has a net positive economic benefit as it stimulates investment and prevents the hoarding of wealth, thus contributing to the macroeconomy. Once *zakat* potential has been optimised, Muslims will no longer go without the basic necessities.

Many have argued that *zakat* suppresses consumption and saving. This may be true in the short term from the perspective of the *zakat* payer (*muzakki*). In accordance with Islamic principles, however, *zakat* funds are used to guarantee the basic necessities, thus in fact increasing demand. This is certainly true among *zakat* recipients (*mustahiq*) and, therefore, should be the object of analysis because *zakat* functions to help the *mustahiq* not the *muzakki*. Furthermore, the demand that increases is demand for basic goods and services, which are unquestionably consumed by the public. In the short term, the prices of goods and services may increase, yet in the medium and long term, the basic goods/services industry would expand, with the markets receiving demand-side stimuli, implying more attractive markets. Consequently, more competitors would enter the market, leading to competitive prices as supply increases. As a result, market prices would experience corrections and return to previous levels. From a macro perspective, market movements due to *zakat* intervention would foster national economic growth and even GDP per capita, which would have a massive benefit for all, not only *mustahiq*.

Social sector instruments also have specific economic implications. Moral values (*akhlak*) and Islamic law (sharia) significantly influence the economic application of Islamic social instruments. Concerning morals and sharia law, both aspects are considered important instruments in achieving the goals of the Islamic economy, namely the equitable distribution of wealth and income. That is what ensures the Islamic economy is considered an economic system which prioritises the poor and needy because *duafa* must rightfully be the focus of equitable wealth distribution. This concept is explained in Fig. 1.2 as follows:

In Islam, all activities undertaken by mankind must be based on the rules set forth in the al-Qur'an and Hadith. Both sources of Islamic teachings encourage mankind to behave based on good morals in accordance with sharia law as a representation of individual faith. When translated into economic concepts, through sharia law, Islam unequivocally defines the obligations and acts forbidden by God, namely the religious obligation of *zakat* for all Muslims who meet the necessary criteria of wealth (*nisab*) to help the needy as well as the forbidden practices of *riba* and *maysir* (gambling). *Riba* and *maysir* are forbidden in the Islamic economy to ensure wealth remains in the real sector. In a conventional economy where *riba* and *maysir* are permitted, for example, money tends to concentrate in the financial sector as a commodity for profit. In Islam, using money as a commodity to generate income and profit without real goods/services to be traded is forbidden. Therefore, by prohibiting *riba* and *maysir*, economic activity in the real sector, such as trade and investment, is nurtured, thus reflecting productive economic conditions and creating the equitable distribution of income and wealth. Simultaneously, the religious obligation of *zakat* plays a similar role in terms of safeguarding the direct distribution of income and wealth to the poor and needy.

Complementing the goals of sharia law, good morals are also a prerequisite for accelerating the distribution of wealth and income in an economy. Greater levels of individual faith, as reflected in good morals, increase the possibility of successfully carrying out religious guidelines that are not obligatory. For example, if *zakat* is an obligatory instrument for all Muslims who meet the necessary criteria of wealth, such individuals are also more likely to pay infaq, sadaqah, and waqf along with other social instruments given greater religious understanding and empathy for others. Therefore, *zakat*, *infaq*, *sadaqah,* and *waqf* (ZISWAF) are instruments of Islamic social finance that have a direct impact on wealth and income distribution through *duafa* empowerment.

Based on those arguments, the goals and concepts of the Islamic economy, namely the realisation of orderly economic activity in the real sector and goods/ services markets, are a prerequisite of quality welfare for all. In that context, the Islamic economy also embraces the Circular Flow of Islamic Economic Activity as befitting the conventional economy, where the role of all stakeholders to achieve the goals of the Islamic economic system is clearly defined. This concept is explained in Fig. 1.3 as follows:

Similar to the flow of conventional economic activity, the Islamic economy also involves various stakeholders, including households, corporations, and the government. Each stakeholder has its own role and contribution towards achieving the goal of economic activity. As explained previously, the goal of Islamic economic activity is to safeguard the flow of goods and services in the real sector. Certainly, the flow of money is an inherent part of that. This is what differentiates the conventional and Islamic economic systems, where goods and services are the focus of economic activity rather than money, which only functions as an intermediary or exchange instrument to facilitate the flow of goods and services. Chapra (1985) tried to explain such a concept that full employment is created when all stakeholders in an economy are producing goods and services. This implies that the level of economic involvement in the Islamic economy is critical.

Therefore, the Islamic economic system is replete with numerous channels to facilitate the velocity of money between sectors and stakeholders, thus reflecting the concept in Islam that forbids idle money and the hoarding of wealth, rather than distributing money for productive purposes. In other words, Islam encourages the

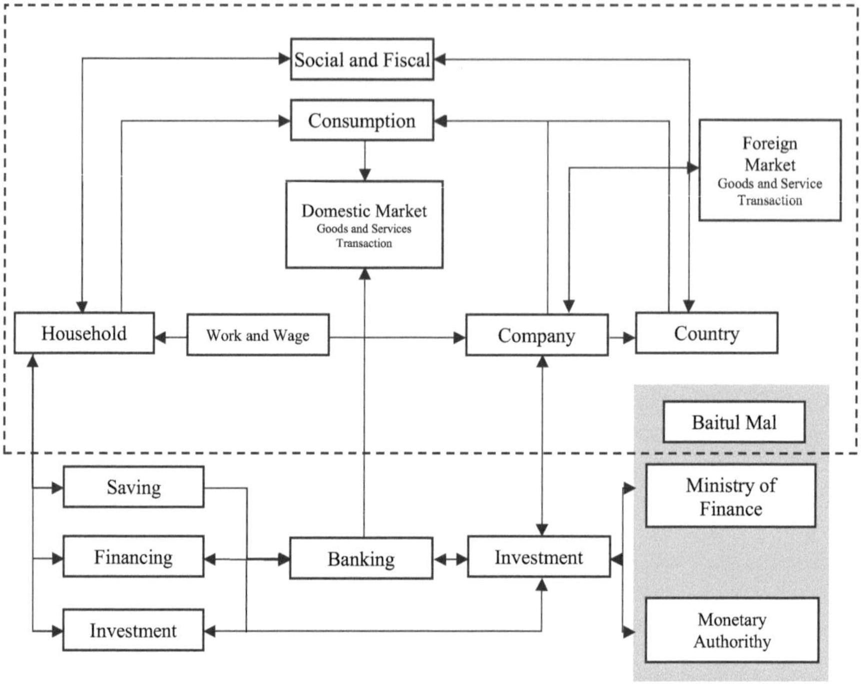

Fig. 1.3 Circular flow of Islamic economic activity. Source: Created by Author

presence of markets that are always available for producers to supply and consumers to maintain demand. Therefore, the real sector is constantly maintained at a level where economic activity thrives by safeguarding trade or the interaction between supply and demand. This concept is explained in the quantity of money theory and, if applied to the Islamic economy, the velocity of money in the economy will accelerate as the level of stakeholder faith increases.

Based on such conditions, households, corporations, and the government mobilise their resources towards the (domestic) goods and services market. In Islamic social finance, it is necessary to observe the circular flow of Islamic economic activity in the blue dashed line. Households produce services (work) to receive incentives in the form of wages that can be spent on the consumption of goods and services produced in the domestic market. Households with income and wealth beyond consumption needs are required to channel the excess into the financial sector for the purposes of saving, lending, or investing. Excepting those three motives, households with excess resources are obligated to pay *zakat* and encouraged to pay *infaq*, *sadaqah*, *waqf* and similar instruments to the state through *Baitul Mal* as social and fiscal instruments in the Islamic economy.

From a corporate perspective, money is channelled to the household sector as consumption of the services produced by households and also channelled to the domestic goods and services markets as consumption of capital. Both corporate production factors (household services and capital goods) are used by businesses to produce goods and services for the domestic market. Excess income generated by businesses from profit must be reinvested into the social or fiscal sectors, or as investment in the financial sector. The flow of money into the fiscal and social sectors is the moral responsibility of doing business and generating a profit to pay *zakat* to the state through *Baitul Mal*. In addition, specific to the corporate sector, another market is available to trade goods and services, known as the international market, where such transactions are identified as exports and imports.

Based on conventional theory, there are potential revenues for the state from export–import activity as customs duties, which are considered a fiscal instrument. According to Islam, however, the concept of customs duties is fundamentally not permitted or recommended, with the practice strictly forbidden during the time of *Rosullullah* due to racketeering connotations. During the time of the caliphate, however, after the passing of *Rosullullah*, specifically during the reign of Umar bin Khattab, the practice was legalised based on the principles of reciprocity. During that period, international Muslim traders were taxed to enter and trade in another country. In response, Umar bin Khattab applied a similar practice for foreign traders wishing to enter and trade in the caliphate. Caliph Umar expanded the scope of *ushr* to include this type of border trade tax as a fiscal instrument. If that concept was applied in the modern day, a system of reciprocity would be required similar to the Umar bin Khattab caliphate. State revenues from the household and corporate sectors would be re-channelled to resourceless households and thus enable economic participation, at least for the consumption of basic necessities or at most to participate in the production of goods and services for the domestic market.

1.3 Role of the Monetary Sector

Support of the monetary sector is required to ensure the equitable distribution of income through Islamic social-public finance. The role of government, the monetary authority, or central bank, in particular, is vital in this case. Broad policy synergy, encompassing Islamic social-public finance and monetary economics, is essential to achieve the desired goals. Islamic monetary policy plays a key role in the circulation of money, which must be oriented towards creating and maintaining macroeconomic stability, while ensuring the equitable distribution of income. Therefore, Islamic monetary policy supports the achievement of *falah* or quality prosperity, and thus inclusive welfare. Such prosperity not only elevates economic growth but also ensures economic equality.

The etymology of the term monetary stems from the Latin word *moneta*, or money. Therefore, monetary economics is the science of all things relating to money and its impact on economic and financial activity. The scope of discussion on monetary economics includes analysing money and its functions, the institutions responsible for printing and regulating the circulation of money as well as monetary policy that aims to achieve economic development goals. In modern economic practice, money not only serves as a medium of exchange, unit of account, and store of value, but the existence of interest rates has also positioned money as a commodity to be traded via a diverse range of financial products. Money as a commodity has itself created markets within the financial sector, such as the money market, capital market, foreign exchange market, and derivatives market. In addition, the role of authorities, for instance the central bank, has become dominant in terms of managing the monetary sector. Central banks or monetary authorities execute the function of printing and circulating currency, regulating the payment system and formulating monetary policy to achieve monetary targets and stimulate stronger economic growth. In general, monetary policy uses various monetary instruments to control total money supply towards price and exchange rate stability.

In a conventional financial system, where the mechanisms work based on the principles of interest, monetary mechanisms also function based on interest. As previously elaborated, interest positions money as a tradable commodity, thus creating its own markets that are influenced by the financial products transacted therein, such as the money market, capital market, and foreign exchange market. Such characteristics imply a financial sector separate and parallel to the real sector, comprising two markets, namely goods and services as well as labour. By allowing *riba* and *masyir*, the financial sector operates in a vacuum, absent the dynamics influencing the real sector, and vice versa, which is known as "decoupling". Under certain conditions, in fact, large disparities between total money supply in the financial sector and the real sector can emerge. Total money supply is like the two sharp edges of a dagger, where excess money supply can create inflation and insufficient money supply can impede economic growth. In that context, monetary policy is oriented towards maintaining adequate money supply to avoid the adverse impacts on price stability and economic growth.

From an Islamic economic perspective, however, economic and financial practices are comparatively different, particularly in the financial sector. By prohibiting *riba* and speculative practices (*masyir*), the financial sector is unable to operate as an independent entity. Islamic finance requires underlying transactions based on trade or profit sharing. Therefore, all Islamic financial transactions depend on real sector activity. Consequently, there is an intimate relationship between the real sector and financial sector. The financial sector will only develop as the real sector develops because the financial sector is positioned to support real sector activity. Technically, Islamic finance acts as an intermediary between investors and productive business sectors in the economy when such investors are not conducting activities directly in productive businesses. The reverse is also true, namely that the financial sector facilitates people with the aspirations, skills, and time to perform productive business activity yet lack sufficient capital. Fundamentally, therefore, the financial sector executes the mission of the Islamic economy, which is to maintain the orderly distribution and flow of economic resources (including money), prevent idle resources and the hoarding of wealth, and ensure everyone can benefit from the economic resources available.

As such, the overarching economic issue is not the scarcity of economic resources but orderly wealth and income distribution. By prohibiting *riba* and *maysir*,

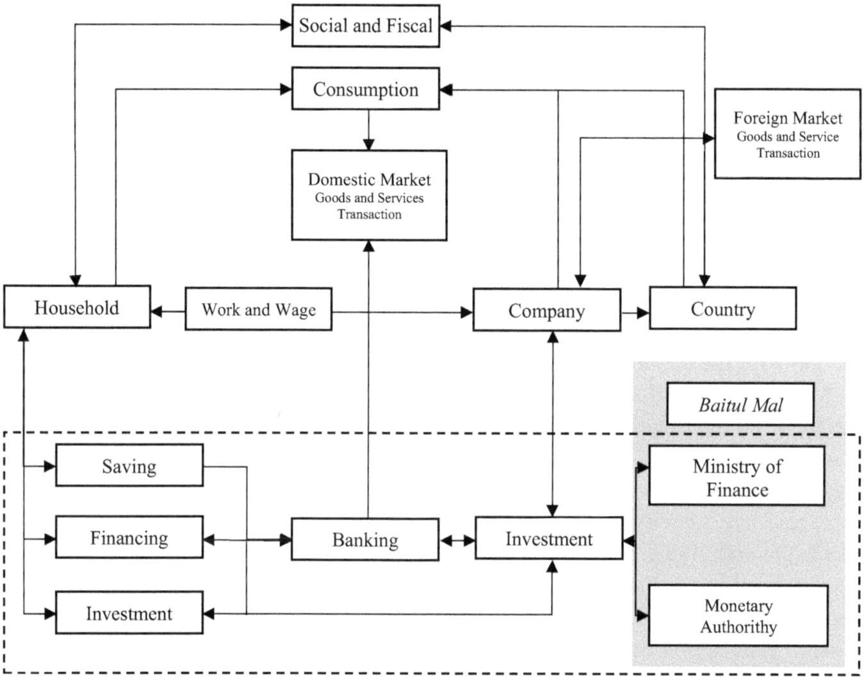

Fig. 1.4 Resource allocation in an Islamic economy. Source: Darsono et al. (2017)

investors can only generate profit from their funds through productive activity in the sector. If an investor has not the time, risk appetite, nor expertise, an intermediary financial institution is available to disburse the funds to a manager based on contracts in accordance with Islamic principles, such as profit sharing.

The monetary system and monetary policies therein aim to support the intermediation function of financial institutions. During periods of excess money supply that can create inflation, the monetary authority has the policy option to provide channels for the funds to investment activities or projects in the productive sector, including investment projects initiated by the government, private entities, or the central bank as the monetary authority (refer to Fig. 1.4).

Fundamentally, therefore, financial activities and monetary policy support real sector activity as the primary economic sector. Currently, the main challenge is implementing Islamic principles and values in their entirety in a monetary system. Indonesia is tackling that challenge by embracing a dual monetary system, consisting of conventional and Islamic systems (Juhro et al., 2018).

In addition, the rejection to prohibit *riba* and *masyir* has led to a disconnect between the financial sector and real sector. In other words, the financial market has created a separate market in the economic system. Therefore, the financial sector can no longer develop in a vacuum, linkages with the real sector are required. Interlinkages between the financial sector and real sector are critical to understanding monetary mechanisms within the Islamic financial system, thus leading to stable economic growth in the long term, where money supply growth is commensurate with growth in the real sector and does not create excessive inflation.

How to weigh the needs and obligations of economic activity? According to conventional wisdom in the literature, economics is the science that studies human behaviour in meeting unlimited needs using limited resources, thus leading to the phenomenon of scarcity. Owing to scarcity, existing resources must be managed efficiently. Therefore, the main issues in conventional economics are scarcity and efficiency (Samuelson & Nordhaus, 2009). That definition illustrates the underlying philosophy of economics, which stigmatises the economy that prioritises meeting individual needs, including the individual person or corporation. The individual perspective leaves economic motivation consistent with achieving individual satisfaction with the quantitative parameters of goods and services.

Meanwhile, the disparity between unlimited needs and limited resources forms the basis of the conclusion that the overarching economic problem is scarcity of resources. In addition, the focus on "limited resources" demonstrates that the issue of limited (scarce) economic resources is material for every human individual. Therefore, resource scarcity forms the basis of all individual economic activity. In fact, that is the underlying assumption of various economic theories. The more resources accumulated by an individual, the more satisfied that individual would become. In their economic behaviour, each individual will thus strive fully to achieve the highest level of satisfaction by acquiring the desired resources.

On the other hand, however, from an Islamic perspective, economics not only focuses on meeting needs yet also considers the afterlife dimension. An orderly economy aims to ensure that mankind can fulfil their main obligations as servants of God, namely to worship Him without the hindrance of economic problems. Economics in Islam is not about maximising satisfaction by accumulating as many resources as possible, yet utilising those resources to help others in need. In addition, the economy is strongly influenced by the belief that the world and everything in it was created by God in sufficient abundance for mankind.

This is contained in the teachings of Allah SWT, in al-Qur'an as follows:

اَلَمْ تَرَوْا اَنَّ اللّٰهَ سَخَّرَ لَكُمْ مَّا فِى السَّمٰوٰتِ وَمَا فِى الْاَرْضِ وَاَسْبَغَ عَلَيْكُمْ نِعَمَهٗ ظَاهِرَةً
وَّبَاطِنَةً ۗوَمِنَ النَّاسِ مَنْ يُّجَادِلُ فِى اللّٰهِ بِغَيْرِ عِلْمٍ وَّلَا هُدًى وَّلَا كِتٰبٍ مُّنِيْرٍ

Do you not see that Allah has made subject to you whatever is in the heavens and whatever is in the earth and amply bestowed upon you His favors, [both] apparent and unapparent? But of the people is he who disputes about Allah without knowledge or guidance or an enlightening Book [from Him]. (QS. Luqman [31]: 20).

Therefore, the main problem in Islamic economics is not scarcity, such as in conventional economic wisdom. According to Islamic economics, the overarching issue is the orderly flow and distribution of economic resources in order to prevent the hoarding of economic resources or wealth. In this context, Islamic law that forbids *riba* (interest) and *maysir* (speculation or gambling) fundamentally prevents the hoarding of wealth or resources amongst certain individuals because interest affords money a price and creates financial markets that are independent of the real sector. Furthermore, financial market development has led to the emergence of speculative financial products, such as secondary markets and derivative markets. As a consequence, investors are drawn to the financial markets rather than investing in the real sector to produce goods and services. The multiplication and concentration of money in financial markets due to profit from *riba* and *masyir* ultimately lead to sectoral imbalances between the real sector and financial sector because through such mechanisms the financial market can operate and develop without commensurate real sector growth. Al-Qur'an unequivocally forbids *riba*, as is written in the following verse:

ٱلَّذِينَ يَأْكُلُونَ ٱلرِّبَوٰاْ لَا يَقُومُونَ إِلَّا كَمَا يَقُومُ ٱلَّذِى يَتَخَبَّطُهُ ٱلشَّيْطَٰنُ مِنَ ٱلْمَسِّ ۚ ذَٰلِكَ بِأَنَّهُمْ قَالُوٓاْ
إِنَّمَا ٱلْبَيْعُ مِثْلُ ٱلرِّبَوٰاْ ۗ وَأَحَلَّ ٱللَّهُ ٱلْبَيْعَ وَحَرَّمَ ٱلرِّبَوٰاْ ۚ فَمَن جَآءَهُۥ مَوْعِظَةٌ مِّن رَّبِّهِۦ فَٱنتَهَىٰ فَلَهُۥ مَا
سَلَفَ وَأَمْرُهُۥٓ إِلَى ٱللَّهِ ۖ وَمَنْ عَادَ فَأُو۟لَٰٓئِكَ أَصْحَٰبُ ٱلنَّارِ ۖ هُمْ فِيهَا خَٰلِدُونَ

> Those who consume interest cannot stand [on the Day of Resurrection] except as one stands who is being beaten by Satan into insanity. That is because they say, "Trade is [just] like interest." But Allah has permitted trade and has forbidden interest. So whoever has received an admonition from his Lord and desists may have what is past, and his affair rests with Allah. But whoever returns to [dealing in interest or usury]—those are the companions of the Fire; they will abide eternally therein. (QS. Al-Baqarah [2]: 275)

Al-Qur'an also reminds that *riba* does not bring additional benefits in the eyes of Allah:

وَمَآ ءَاتَيْتُم مِّن رِّبًا لِّيَرْبُوَا۟ فِىٓ أَمْوَٰلِ ٱلنَّاسِ فَلَا يَرْبُوا۟ عِندَ ٱللَّهِ ۖ وَمَآ ءَاتَيْتُم مِّن زَكَوٰةٍ تُرِيدُونَ
وَجْهَ ٱللَّهِ فَأُو۟لَٰٓئِكَ هُمُ ٱلْمُضْعِفُونَ

> And whatever you give for interest to increase within the wealth of people will not increase with Allah. But what you give in zakah, desiring the countenance of Allah—those are the multipliers. (QS. Ar Rum [30]: 39).

Islamic economic principles are presented in Fig. 1.5. By forbidding *riba* and *masyir*, investors are left with no other option to generate income from economic activity except through productive business activities, such as the production of goods and services in the real sector, which encourages money to flow to the real sector and stimulate trade and investment activities, thus distributing wealth and income. The Islamic financial system requires appropriate devices in the form of instruments and policies to maintain the flow of money to the real sector and prevent the concentration of idle funds due to impediments in the intermediation mechanism. When the flow of money is impeded or idle funds are allowed to accumulate in the economy, price instability will follow.

Meanwhile, the main role of the financial system is to facilitate the efficient allocation of financial resources and real resources for various purposes and targets (Iqbal & Mirakhor, 2007). The real sector will determine the rate of return for

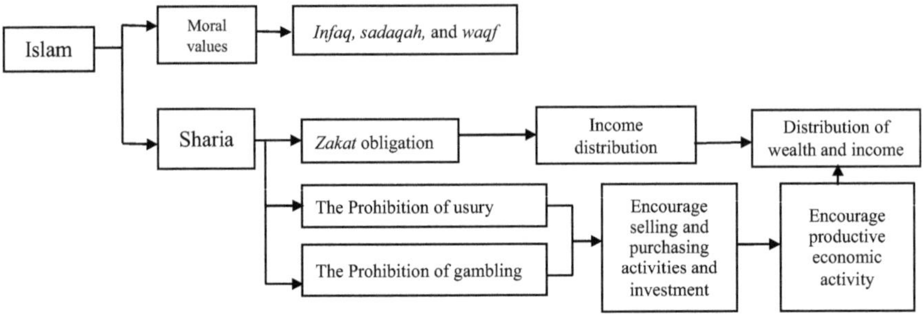

Fig. 1.5 Islamic economic principles. Source: Compiled by the authors

investors in the financial sector. Islamic economics applies the principle that investment activity in the real sector and rate of return on investment are determined by actual productivity in the real sector. In addition to the real sector, economic growth also requires financial sector support. The financial sector has emerged as a consequence of the complex economy, providing a channel for real sector development and economic growth. The Islamic finance sector consists of several Islamic financial institutions, including banks, the capital market, insurance, pension funds, finance companies, microfinance institutions, pawnbrokers, and foreign exchange markets.

From a broader perspective, the Islamic economic system fundamentally strives to prevent human economic issues by providing middle ground between two extremes, namely capitalism and communism (Huda, Idris, Nasution, & Wiliasih, 2013). Islamic economics ensures that resources are equitably distributed to meet human needs in the present and hereafter (*falah*). The comprehensive application of Islamic economics leads to the equitable distribution of wealth and income from those with wealth to those without through *zakat*, *infaq*, *sadaqah,* and *waqf* (ZISWAF) instruments. Beyond that, forbidding *riba* and *maysir* stimulates trade and investment as productive activities in the real sector.

Therefore, Islamic economics did not emerge in reaction to conventional economics, Islamic economics has been present since Islam originated on Earth and is an integral part of the human life system that cannot be separated from Islam. In addition, the implementation of Islamic economics may be considered an integral part of worship. Nevertheless, the application of Islamic economics remains an onerous challenge in various countries. First, the development of financial instruments without applying interest rates. Second, the development of an interest-free monetary system (Khan & Mirakhor, 1989).

Islam acknowledges the importance of a financial system that regulates funds transfers from the wealthy to the needy, thus achieving the efficient and targeted allocation of funds. Of course, in addition to transferring capital, risk is also transferred to the owner and bearer of capital. In an Islamic financial system, funds are disbursed directly and indirectly. The distribution of Islamic financial institutions depends on the target and provider of funds at each respective institution. More specifically, the Islamic financial system is divided into three major sectors as follows: (1) commercial/private sector; (2) public sector; and (3) social sector. The main role of the Islamic financial system is to create the efficient allocation of finance and resources. The Islamic financial system is the part of an economy that provides financial services through financial institutions in accordance with Islamic principles. Islamic financial institutions conduct business in compliance with sharia principles. Currently, Islamic financial institutions comprise bank and nonbank financial institutions (insurance, pawnbrokers, mutual funds, capital market, sharia rural banks, and *baitul maal wat tamwil*).

Financial institution practices emerged during the period of *Rosullullah* until the Abbasid Caliphate, although financial institutions were not explicitly established. The primary functions of such institutions were as follows: (1) receive cash deposits; (2) guarantee money or extend financing in the form of *mudharabah, musyarakah, muzara'ah,* and *musaqah*; and (3) provide remittance services. The term *fiqh* also emerged at that time and is suspected of influencing the technical terms of modern banking, such as *qardh*, which refers to an interest-free loan in credit parlance. In addition, the terms *suq* and *suquq*, which in Arabic mean market, evolved into a medium of exchange and were transferred into English and changed to mean check or cheque in French.

Terms for specific financial institutions, such as bank, were not known during that era, yet sharia principles were applied to the functions. During the period of *Rosullullah*, the intermediary function was executed for funds transferred from one person to another with the same vision. Nevertheless, institutions known as banks emerged during the Abbasid Caliphate. Banking developed after the emergence of different currencies containing various precious metals, together with the advent of currency exchange expertise, known as *naqid, sarraf,* and *jihbiz*, as the forerunners of money changers.[1]

Financial institutions, banks in particular, play an important and strategic role in turning the wheels of economy, with various Muslim countries establishing financial institutions based on Islamic principles. Malaysia, for example, in the mid-1940s, opened an interest-free bank. Now, Malaysia is endowed with one of the largest Islamic banking industries based on assets worldwide, totalling USD799 million, placing it within the top 10 globally (IFSB, 2020). Towards the end of the 1950s, Pakistan also began to open interest-free rural banks. In 1963, Egypt established the Mit Ghamr Local Saving, which was welcomed by farmers and other rural dwellers but government intervention ended the endeavour. In 1967, Mit Ghamr was taken over by the Central Bank of Egypt (Alharbi, 2015). In addition to Malaysia, Pakistan and Egypt, Indonesia, as the most populous Muslim country, established a nascent Islamic economy by inaugurating the first sharia bank in 1992, namely Bank Muamalat.

[1]During the Abbasid Caliphate, banking became popular under the Government of Khalifah Al-Muqtadir (908-932 M). Meanwhile, *suq* (cheques) were already widely used as a payment instrument. The history of Islamic banking credits Saefudaulah al-Hamdani as the first person to issue a cheque for clearing purposes between Baghdad, Iraq, and Aleppo.

Although there are financial institutions acting as a bridge between the owner and manager of funds, there remain constraints to the seamless distribution and circulation of the funds. Economic resources should be available to all social strata. Friction in this economic sector causes stagnation in the real sector and other sectors are unable to fully enjoy the benefits. For example, if there is full employment in an economy and capacity is full yet excess money still exists, idle money will result. Such conditions are likely to cause inflation. To avoid higher inflation caused by excess money on the supply side, the supply and demand of money should be re-synchronised. Money supply must be adjusted to the needs of the rural sector to avoid excess supply.

Departing from the capitalism model that states economic activity is free and all activities are at the whim of market mechanisms, including price setting, in an Islamic economy, the government must intervene when there is the inequitable distribution of economic resources. Therefore, monetary policy was created to regulate the monetary system through the monetary authority. In general, monetary policy regulates total money supply in order to achieve monetary targets, such as price and exchange rate stability. What is prioritised in the conventional system, where price stability is regulated by controlling money supply that is fundamentally dominated by the demand side, in Islam, money supply management not only considers the demand perspective but also the position of supply. In this case, printing money balances the flow of money between sectors with excess money and those with insufficient money or requiring additional supply, thus avoiding the concentration of money or idle funds. Therefore, the government must intervene and absorb Currency Outside Banks (COB), for instance through *zakat*, *waqf*, and other institutions that can facilitate development projects in the real sector, including government, private, community, and central bank projects.

Ultimately, the culmination of successful economic development can be measured by a solid and prosperous real sector with the optimal support of the financial sector. In this case, the financial sector can execute a sound and balanced intermediation function. Academically, such conditions refer to the workings of an effective monetary policy transmission mechanism. Therefore, the role of the monetary sector in the Islamic financial system can be recapitulated as follows: (i) assist the financial system to maintain the orderly flow of economic resources, in this case money supply; (ii) prevent the concentration of idle funds in the economy. Idle funds can occur at the community, corporate, and government levels when businesses in the real sector and the financial system are unable to absorb excess money; and (iii) maintain adequate money supply for the needs of real sector activity. The application of monetary policy in accordance with sharia principles will also stimulate economic activity based on Islamic principles. By applying sharia principles, the financial system will allocate resources to the appropriate sectors and distribute wealth to ameliorate welfare inclusively.

1.4 About This Book

Various explanations and dynamics concerning the Islamic economy and role of Islamic social-public finance and monetary economics to promote inclusive welfare as mentioned above require deeper discussion. As such, it is essential to know in greater detail the role of Islamic social-public finance and monetary economics for the economy as well as the dynamics, including the development strategy, instruments, institutions, regulations, and other supporting infrastructure. Therefore, the discussion in this book focuses on two parts. The first part explores the role of Islamic social-public finance to ameliorate prosperity in the economy and social sector, while the second part examines the role of Islamic monetary economics.

The book begins with a theoretical comparison of the public sector and Islamic social sector as well as the reality of current applications, while outlining the diverse challenges and opportunities to build a better Islamic economy. In addition, recommendations for future development are also provided. In the second part of the book, the role of monetary economics is explored. In general, the discussions presented in the second half of the book cover several dimensions, namely the concept of money from an Islamic perspective, the implications of sharia principles in the financial or monetary concept, including policy tools and monetary policy, Islamic monetary economic practices in several countries as well as the challenges and prospects of Islamic monetary economics moving forward.

Literature concerning the Islamic financial system is incomplete, particularly concerning the role of Islamic social-public finance and monetary economics, enriched with the perspective of the Indonesian economy and implementation therein, making this a highly anticipated book. Therefore, there are three overarching goals associated with publishing this book.

First, academically, to generate frontier thinking and stimulate scientific development, while providing teaching materials concerning the Islamic financial system, particularly the role of Islamic social-public finance and monetary economics. The book is expected to enrich reference materials concerning the theories, concepts, and practices of monetary economics based on sharia principles as teaching materials for professors and students, specifically postgraduate students reading Islamic economics.

Second, from a policy perspective, to enrich the discussion and support public policy innovation. To that end, the book identifies the challenges, opportunities, and recommendations concerning the direction of economic development policy, specifically regarding the future role of the Islamic economy and finance. This book provides comprehensive understanding concerning the policy theories and practices in the Islamic financial system based on the aspects of philosophy, economic role, institutions, instruments, regulations, and infrastructure as well as the implications or impact on the economy.

Third, from a practical standpoint, to contribute and complement current understanding concerning the application and purview of the economic system in Islam, including popular topics such as Islamic banking and microfinance. Therefore, this book is a vehicle to increase understanding and insight for practitioners, stakeholders, and regulators.

Based on those goals and contributions, the scope of target readers is broad, including tertiary students, regulators, practitioners, business players, and all stakeholders of Islamic economic and financial development.

The book is divided into 13 chapters. The first few chapters in part one of the book explore the conception, philosophy, and fundamental theories underlying the role, implications, and practices of Islamic social-public finance towards prosperity and inclusive welfare. **Chapter 2** presents the dimensions and fundamental concepts of the Islamic economy and finance, focusing on Islamic financial institutions and the role of the state. A brief discussion is also presented regarding how Islamic social-public finance intersects with other Islamic financial institutions, such as banks, microfinance institutions, and others. How the relationship between sectors influences the efficiency and effectiveness of the Islamic social-public sectors, as well as the implications, is also discussed in this part. **Chapters 3** and **4** develop the fundamental theories underlying social-public finance from the conventional and Islamic perspectives. Although the first part of the book provides a comprehensive outline of social-public finance from an Islamic perspective, a theoretical review of conventional social-public finance is required and explored to allow the readers to compare and contrast the differences between the two perspectives, thereby highlighting the advantages of social-public finance in Islam. Furthermore, both economic systems are explored to demonstrate why the application of Islamic social-public finance is urgently required.

The subsequent three chapters focus on the practical dimension. **Chapter 5** discusses the economic implications when instruments of Islamic social-public finance are practised, particularly from a contemporary perspective. The chapter also presents the implications of social-public financial instruments from a conventional perspective as a comparison. **Chapter 6** explores the history of Islamic social-public finance in the Islamic world, focusing on ideal practices during the period of *Rosullullah*, the Rashidun Caliphs and the Caliphate. This chapter is expected to provide the readers greater understanding of social-public finance practices in Islam from their inception. **Chapter 7** discusses in greater detail the practices and impact of Islamic social-public finance in several regions of Indonesia, thus enriching the readers' knowledge concerning the advantages of the *zakat* absorption and distribution system along with other social funds that could be adopted in other regions. In addition, how Islamic social-public finance can be applied in practice globally and in Indonesia is also explored in detail, starting with a broad outline of the motivation behind the emergence of Islamic social-public finance in the modern era, along with the roles and application in several countries. The discussion moves on to explain institutional aspects, services, existing regulations and laws as well as the infrastructure available to achieve success in this sector in Indonesia.

The second part of the book presents the role and relevance of the monetary sector from a framework approach, monetary economic theories as well as the Islamic financial system and real practices. **Chapter 8** explains the framework approach to Islamic monetary economics, discussing the concepts of conventional economics as a framework for issues concerning Islamic monetary economics. The discussion begins with the flow of funds from the revenue and expenditure sides and the concept of IS-LM balance in Islam. The theory of market imperfection and financial instability is subsequently discussed along with the role of the monetary authority in the Islamic economy, including supporting policies and regulations from the central bank to create a prosperous monetary and financial system for the public. **Chapter 9** outlines the basic theories and important aspects of money, including the history of money and classifications or types of money. Of no less importance is the theory of money demand and supply, highlighting the contrary teachings of the conventional and Islamic perspectives. The chapter also explains in depth the Islamic point of view concerning money and how money should be used.

Chapter 10 is particularly substantive because it presents the essence of money based on the variables that influence and are impacted, namely inflation, exchange rates, and interest rates. The discussion not only focuses on the nature of money itself yet also reflects the extent to which a country can successfully maintain currency stability, at home and internationally, including inflation and exchange rates. Inflation reflects how stable the value of money is domestically by looking at general changes in prices. Meanwhile, the exchange rate illustrates the stability of domestic money against foreign currencies. In general, the exchange rate is calculated as the ratio of a domestic currency to a foreign currency, such as the United States dollar (USD). The nature of exchange rates is also discussed in this chapter, namely how money has been used to create a system known as interest rates. Currently, interest rates are ingrained in all aspects of the economy, particularly the monetary and financial sectors. In fact, interest rates are an instrument of monetary control regulated by the central bank in each jurisdiction. On the other hand, Islam takes a different perspective by prohibiting *riba*. True Islam forbids interest rates in the economy as *haram*. Therefore, the chapter also explains alternative interest-free monetary system controls.

Chapter 11 discusses the relationship between investment, finance, and the monetary sector in Islam. As we know, interest rates are forbidden as an instrument under Islamic law, yet such tools are still in use, even in countries with a Muslim-majority population. This is because conventional economic wisdom believes that interest rates play an important role not only in the monetary sector but also in the real sector. The role of interest rates in the real sector, according to conventional economic wisdom, is indirect, instead affecting the level of investment. In Islamic economics, however, investment (real sector) is an integral part of the financial and monetary sectors. The financial sector is necessary for the real sector to facilitate business financing, and similarly, the financial sector can only develop as the real sector develops. Interaction between the financial sector and real sector is regulated under a monetary system framework.

Closing the second part of the book, **Chap. 12** discusses monetary policy practices under Islam. The chapter provides an in-depth discussion of why there is such urgency for Islamic monetary economics and how far Islamic monetary economics has evolved and developed. The discussion also covers the Islamic monetary policy framework from a different perspective than conventional monetary policy or a dual financial system. Real contemporary Islamic monetary economic practices in various countries are explored, not only in Indonesia but also Malaysia, Iran, Saudi Arabia, Sudan, and Bahrain.

At the end of the book, the **Epilogue** in Chap. 13 covers the current challenges and opportunities facing all economic players through the monetary and financial sectors, as well as the policy implications for all public policymakers to ensure inclusive welfare is achieved. As mentioned in the opening part of the book, the context of the discussion is the presence and role of money. Therefore, the epilogue is a reflection concerning the role of the gold money as well as money development and innovation, such as technological disruption. Currently, electronic money and digital currencies are developing with rapidity, including digital money issued by private entities (cryptocurrency) and central banks (Central Bank Digital Currency). This provides no tangible reason, however, to feel the application of Islamic principles is more complex. Muslims are naturally inclined to review financial innovations based on Islamic principles. Finally, to optimise the realisation of quality welfare, the portrait and potential of Islamic social-public finance to create new sources of economic growth are explored along with the salient issues concerning sustainable development through the green economy and financing.

In closing, this is a living document. The authors are aware that the material in this book will be adjusted to current needs and developments over time in terms of public policy practices and recommendations from readers and teachers in line with the issues developing in the public space and academic community. To that end, comments, recommendations, and suggestions from the readers are warmly welcomed to help hone the contents of this book. Hopefully, this book not only meets the needs of readers wishing to obtain deeper understanding concerning the salient aspects of social-public finance and monetary economics from an Islamic perspective, but also expands our scientific knowledge.

References

Alharbi, A. (2015). Development of the Islamic Banking System. *Journal of Islamic Banking and Finance, 3*(1), 12–25.

Chapra, M. U. (1985). *Towards a just monetary system* (Vol. 8). International Institute of Islamic Thought (IIIT).

Darsono, S. A., Darwis, A., Suryanti, E. T., & Astiyah, S. (2017). *Dinamika Produk dan Akad Keuangan Syariah di Indonesia.* PT RajaGrafindo Persada.

Faridi, F. R. (1983). *Theory of fiscal policy in an Islamic State. Journal of King Abdulaziz University: Islamic Economics, 1*(1).

Huda, N., Idris, H. R., Nasution, M. E., & Wiliasih, R. (2013). *Ekonomi Makro Islam: Pendekatan Teoritis.* Kencana Prenada Media Group.

IFSB. (2020). *PSIFI's Data.* Dipetik April 7, 2020, dari Islamic Financial Services Board. https://www.ifsb.org

Iqbal, Z., & Mirakhor, A. (2007). *An introduction to Islamic finance: Theory and practice.* Wiley.

Juhro, S. M., Darsono, S. F., & Sakti, A. (2018). *Kebijakan Moneter Syariah dalam Sistem Keuangan Ganda: Teori dan Praktik.* Tazkia Publishing.

Khan, M. S., & Mirakhor, A. (1989). The financial system and monetary policy in an Islamic economy. *Journal of King Abdulaziz University: Islamic Economics, 1*, 39–57.

Metwally, M. (1996). Attitude of Muslims Towards Islamic Banks in a DualBanking System. *American Journal of Islamic Finance, 6*, 11–17.

Salama, A. A. (1995). *Fiscal policy of an Islamic state. Readings in Public Finance in Islam* (Edited by Mahamoud A. Gulaid & Mohamed Aden Abdullah), Islamic Research and Training Institute (IRTI). IDB.

Samuelson, P. A., & Nordhaus, W. D. (2009). *Economics* (19th ed.). McGraw Hill.

Siddiqi, M. N. (1996). *Role of the state in the economy: An Islamic perspective*. The Islamic Foundation.

Chapter 2
Islamic Economic and Financial System

2.1 Introduction

According to conventional teaching, the economic system represents a group of institutions established by the public that agree to implement end-to-end economic activities, which include the management of resource allocation, production of goods and services as well as distribution of income and wealth. On the other hand, the Islamic economic system is based on sharia principles that are permanent, eternal, and timeless, which comprehensively influences socio-economic behaviour from end to end. Nevertheless, there are slight conceptual differences in the Islamic economic system in terms of determining the laws and rules. The Islamic economic system was designed and regulated by Allah SWT, as set forth in the Al-Qur'an and Hadith, covering all possible aspects. Even the economic policies instituted are based on prevailing sharia principles, for instance limited intervention by the authorities in economic activity. The Islamic economic system was built using various tools in accordance with Islamic principles, including the institutions and rules.

The Islamic economic system has existed since long before the inception of conventional economic ideas, such as capitalism and socialism that exist today. The Islamic economy is an inherent feature of Islamic history, stretching further back than the profits and messengers prior to the Prophet Muhammad SAW. Nonetheless, modern Islamic economic theory began to emerge in the 1970s (Juhro et al., 2019). To fully understand the Islamic economic system, an in-depth review of the main characteristics is required from the Al-Qur'an and Hadith. Islamic principles teach that economic activity requires a clear goal, healthy transactions, dynamism, and pro-growth orientation. A healthy economic system can be achieved through rules, institutions, operational activities, and social behaviour in accordance with sharia principles.

The overarching foundation of all actions by Muslims is the prostration of everything in the universe to Allah SWT. Therefore, this includes all economic

S. M. Juhro et al., *Inclusive Welfare*, https://doi.org/10.1007/978-981-96-0051-9_2

activities, including trade, debt, investment, and associations. The economic goal of mankind must be founded on compliance and obedience as servants of God. As such, the values and principles followed must be in line with His guidance as set forth in the Al-Qur'an and Hadith. In addition, the Islamic economic system is endowed with specific social finance characteristics in the form of *zakat* obligations to facilitate wealth and income distribution in the community. The Islamic economic system remains an integral part of the religion, with each production, distribution, and consumption activity based on Islamic philosophy and sharia law. In addition, all decision-making is based on prevailing Islamic norms. It can be concluded, therefore, that the Islamic economic system is oriented towards quality welfare (*falah*). The principle of quality welfare is achieved based on protecting the Islamic legal doctrine of *maqasid syariah*, covering five key aspects, namely the protection of faith, life, mind, lineage, and property. Everything that has meaning in the preservation of those five aspects is known as *maslahah* and anything that detracts from them is known as *mafsadah*.

There exists a disparate framework to the Islamic economic perspective. The conventional economic system was built on the principle that an individual has unlimited needs, yet resources are finite, thus leading to the problem of scarcity. On the other hand, the Islamic economic system emphasises quality welfare for the entire community. Collectively, resources in Islam are unlimited, as written in the Al-Qur'an, verse 29 of surah Al-Baqarah as follows:

هُوَ الَّذِيْ خَلَقَ لَكُمْ مَّا فِى الْاَرْضِ جَمِيْعًا ثُمَّ اسْتَوٰٓى اِلَى السَّمَاۤءِ فَسَوّٰىهُنَّ سَبْعَ سَمٰوٰتٍۗ وَهُوَ بِكُلِّ شَيْءٍ عَلِيْمٌ ۝

> It is He who created for you all of that which is on the earth. Then He directed Himself to the heaven, [His being above all creation], and made them seven heavens, and He is Knowing of all things. (Q.S. Al-Baqarah [2]: 29).

The verse above can be interpreted that Allah provides sustenance to all of humankind, in this case resources. Allah has provided all resources on earth to support life and it is the purpose of man to utilise such resources wisely. Thus, resources from an Islamic perspective are not finite but unlimited. The important point, therefore, is how humans can allocate and distribute resources amongst themselves. Starting with production, how can humans produce goods or services to generate value-added and benefits for consumption by other humans? Regarding the activity between production and consumption, namely distribution, how can distribution be implemented to achieve the equitable and optimal allocation of resources?

Therefore, because the conventional economic system is oriented from the perspective of each respective individual, the overarching problem that emerges is how each person can utilise limited resources optimally to achieve satisfaction and meet the needs of each individual. In contrast, the Islamic economic system is oriented towards society in general, therefore the main issue is how to allocate and distribute unlimited (abundant) resources for the optimal benefit of all equitably to achieve quality welfare (*falah*) for all. To that end, the economic system does not reject the optimal use of resources at the individual level as long as the resources are not used to meet unlimited individual needs. In Islam, each individual is permitted to utilise resources optimally for the self and everyone else. Meanwhile, the concept of justice is the overriding principle in every aspect of human life, including the economy. In fact, the principle of justice is the main highlight as the target of the Islamic economic system. Islam teaches persistence, a clear goal, structured plan, and generous disposition. Therefore, with all efforts undertaken by the individual, he has the right to receive compensation for those efforts. The achievement of economic equity is expected to minimise economic disparity between different social strata, thus eliminating division and segmentation due to socio-economic disparity.

The main sector in the Islamic economic system is the real sector, where core economic activities are undertaken, such as trading, investing, and associating. Notwithstanding, the financial system also has an important role to play. The financial system supports real sector activity. Although Allah provides sustenance to all of humankind, it is irrefutable that not all individuals can fully realise their opportunities and not all individuals have equitable access to resources. This is where the financial sector has a role to play, by creating equitable access to resources to meet basic life necessities in the real sector. Nevertheless, the financial sector in Islam is unable to exist independently of the real sector, rather serving as a facilitator for actors wishing to transact in the real sector and as an intermediary to improve the real sector. Therefore, the real sector and financial sector must exist synchronously (Juhro et al., 2019).

The financial system has a significant impact on economic sustainability in a country. Financial system independence and stability are prerequisites and must be maintained because if not, the deleterious economic impact is extensive, comprehensive, and all-encompassing. Financial system independence is essential to avoid dependence upon another country or even prevent a form of modern-day colonialism.

Financial system stability is equally important because eventually financial system instability will lead to myriad other problems. The empirical evidence points to this such as the Global Financial Crisis (GFC) in 2007–2008. Triggered by a financial system shock in the United States (US) stemming from the subprime mortgage debacle, the cost of failure was exorbitant. The shock spread with rapidity through contagion to other countries, quickly evolving into an international financial crisis. The crisis became one of the largest since the Great Depression in the 1930s. The GFC in 2007 precipitated the closure of 323 banks in advanced economies during the period from 2008–2010. A decade earlier, a financial crisis befell Asia in 1997–1998. Preceded by an exchange rate crisis in Thailand, conditions spread quickly to Indonesia, prompting a severe economic and banking crisis. In contrast, achieving financial system stability depends on the degree of economic development. Therefore, it can be concluded that between the economic system, level of economic development, and financial system of the country lies a mutually reinforcing relationship.

2.2 Institutional Arrangements of the Islamic Economic System

The ideal institutional framework of an economic system covers every institution, every rule within the institutions and the enforcement of those rules. In Islam, the structure of the framework is regulated by Allah, with the overarching goal of creating justice and quality welfare (*falah*). To that end, a set of rules is clearly required.

Rules play an important role in the running of an institution, namely: (a) to harmonise universal individual behaviour in the execution of economic activity, (b) to determine acceptable behavioural norms, and (c) to create uniform individual behaviour concerning the possible conditions that will transpire. Rules can determine the most appropriate individual behaviour when facing alternative choices and actions. In addition, rules create boundaries around what is acceptable and does not interfere with life or social order, both for other individuals and the environment. Comprehensive rules are formed starting with production, exchange, distribution, redistribution, consumption, and market behaviour.

Public support is required to enforce rules and achieve social equality effectively, thus building awareness to obey the rules. Such rules must be internalised by every individual as a framework for implementing economic activity. Public obedience to rules is directly proportional to successful outcomes. In addition, public compliance to rules prevents conflicts, reconciles differences, and accommodates cooperation between individuals. Ultimately, this will enforce social integration and public unity, thus maintaining social order.

Institutionally, the core of the Islamic economic system covers the following facets (Iqbal & Mirakhor, 2007).

Individual Ownership Rights

Humans have a natural tendency to want to own something for their efforts or actions. Therefore, Islam governs individual ownership of an asset, covering the rights, duties, authority, and obligations associated with that asset. Furthermore, the main principles of ownership according to Islam can be explained as follows:

1. Allah SWT is the owner of each and everything, and everything belongs to Him. Humans are only entrusted as temporary holders of assets and wealth to fulfil their duties and obligations to Allah in worship. This is bestowed upon humans with specific conditions, for instance when working and conducting business.
2. Collective rights are ascribed to shared resources.
3. Individuals are free to determine the production of goods and services in accordance with the resources owned, including labour and natural resources, yet without interfering with the shared (collective) resources.
4. There are three ways a person can obtain ownership rights over an asset: (i) create the asset using the resources and labour owned, (ii) transfer of ownership from another individual through exchange activity. It can be concluded, therefore, that ownership of an asset can be obtained through work. For humans, work is not

only a means to meet needs and desires, more than that, work is the inherent duty and obligation of mankind, and (iii) transfer of ownership through giving, including inheritance and gifts.

5. Not all humans have the same access rights to natural resources, yet the human right to manage and utilise resources is not relinquished. Each individual has the right to apply creativity and manage natural resources, as long as this is done wisely.
6. The natural resources available must be allocated equitably, and not allowed to accumulate amongst specific groups. Every individual has the same right to produce goods and services in line with their individual capacity. In addition, every individual has the same right to transact in the market fairly without infringing on the rights of others.
7. All individuals are forbidden from damaging, destroying, or abusing assets in violation of the law.

Although Islamic teachings stipulate that each individual must have the same right to utilise resources, in reality humans have specific and unique characteristics, including in terms of resource management. Not all individuals are given the same ability to manage the resources available. In addition, not all individuals are blessed with the same abilities and strengths. The grace of Allah is different in each individual. As is written in Al-Qur'an, verse 165 of surah Al-An'am as follows:

وَهُوَ الَّذِيْ جَعَلَكُمْ خَلٰۤىِٕفَ الْاَرْضِ وَرَفَعَ بَعْضَكُمْ فَوْقَ بَعْضٍ دَرَجٰتٍ لِّيَبْلُوَكُمْ فِيْ مَآ اٰتٰىكُمْۗ اِنَّ رَبَّكَ سَرِيْعُ الْعِقَابِۖ وَاِنَّهٗ
لَغَفُوْرٌ رَّحِيْمٌ ࣖ

> And it is He who has made you successors upon the earth and has raised some of you above others in degrees [of rank] that He may try you through what He has given you. Indeed, your Lord is swift in penalty; but indeed, He is Forgiving and Merciful. (Q.S. Al-An'am [6]: 165).

Therefore, there will be groups of individuals who can produce more goods and services and have more wealth than others. Consequently, Islam emphasises the principle of sharing from those with excess wealth to those in need. Sharing with others is the responsibility and obligation of all individuals, especially individuals with excess wealth.

Besides ownership rights of a specific asset, each individual is also bound by the duties and responsibilities of owning an asset, including the obligation to share with others and the environment. In Islam, it is believed that the wealth of an individual is owned, in part, by those in need. This is written in the words of Allah, verse 19 of surah Adh-Dhariyat as follows:

وَفِيْٓ اَمْوَالِهِمْ حَقٌّ لِّلسَّاۤىِٕلِ وَالْمَحْرُوْمِ

> And from their properties was [given] the right of the [needy] petitioner and the deprived. (Q.S. Adh-Dhariyat [51]: 19).

In addition, there is the obligation to maintain and not break or destroy assets/ property or the environment. To break something is considered commensurate to breaking shared ownership rights. The rights and responsibilities governed in Islamic teachings ultimately aim to achieve equitable welfare and prosperity.

Agreements (Contracts)

An economic system is part of the social order. As such, the individuals therein interact mutually through economic transactions. Such transactions between individuals are accommodated through various forms and types of agreement or *akad* (contract) in Islamic economic vernacular. Contracts aim to bind the transacting parties to a shared goal within a specified period. The concept of contracts is a characteristic of the Islamic economic system. Contracts are not only part of the law and rules of executing a transaction of exchange, yet also a form of human obedience to the principles and rules determined by Allah.

Contracts play a crucial role within a sharia-based economic system. It is unjustifiable to have a transaction between two parties without a contract when the transaction is initiated. When transacting, Islam states that each contract is fundamentally sound from a legal standpoint, providing the contract contains no special provisions that are forbidden.

Contracts also play another important role, namely to minimise potential misunderstandings between the transacting parties and to avoid any ambiguity concerning the rights and responsibilities of each party. The Islamic economic system is based on solid principles and explicit contracts between the transacting parties, which is why it is considered more reliable.

This does not imply, however, that Islam is not a dynamic religion in the face of increasingly complex economic systems. In fact, the opposite is true. Ulema and Islamic economists constantly review innovations that can be applied to modern contracts, thus adjusting to the complexity of the system and human needs in the contemporary era.

Trust

In Islam, trust is a critical element of developing social capital. In addition, trust forms the foundation of the relationship between humans and Allah. When performing economic transactions, it is important for the transacting parties to trust in their partners. On the other hand, for a party wishing to initiate a transaction, it is important to foster a feeling of responsibility (trust) to ensure mutual trust flourishes between the transacting parties.

The aspect of trust also ties in closely with the previous aspect, namely contracts. To garner trust within a transactional relationship, compliance to the jointly agreed contract is absolute. This is an important characteristic of realising a healthy economy. Trust and agreements have a mutually reinforcing relationship. Without mutual trust, contracts are difficult to agree. And to garner a feeling of trust, a binding contract is required.

Risk Sharing

Every transaction that will generate profit is also accompanied by risk. Profit is only created when there are possible liabilities and risks. The higher the profit, the greater the risk of loss. Therefore, the principle of risk sharing in Islam is important to achieve justice for the transacting parties.

Not only are the risks distributed between the transacting parties, so too are the profits. Profit and risk sharing is determined in the agreement between transacting parties based on the obligations, roles as well as time and labour contributions of each respective party.

Market Conduct

Society requires markets to facilitate the exchange transaction process. Market transactions are based on mutual agreement. In addition, rules are required to maintain harmony in the market and among participants. Markets also rely on institutions tasked with market supervision and oversight. Such supervisors have the obligation to ensure fair price setting, thus avoiding the need for intervention.

Market participants must adhere to the principles of healthy competition. Each individual has the right to sell any product in the market, providing no harm is caused to another other party or the environment. Moreover, each individual has the right to purchase any product as required. Therefore, supply and demand in the market is a natural process based on fair prices and free from intervention.

Islam encourages its adherents to compete equally and productively. This is written in the Al-Qur'an, verse 148 of surah Al-Baqarah as follows:

وَلِكُلٍّ وِّجْهَةٌ هُوَ مُوَلِّيْهَا فَاسْتَبِقُوا الْخَيْرٰتِ ۗ اَيْنَ مَا تَكُوْنُوْا يَأْتِ بِكُمُ اللّٰهُ جَمِيْعًا ۗاِنَّ اللّٰهَ عَلٰى كُلِّ شَيْءٍ قَدِيْرٌ

> For each [religious following] is a direction toward which it faces. So, race to [all that is] good. Wherever you may be, Allah will bring you forth [for judgement] all together. Indeed, Allah is over all things competent. (Q.S. Al-Baqarah [2]: 148)

Verse 148 implies that humans are required to compete in good deeds. This principle forms the basis of the market structure and market competition, namely perfect market competition.

The institutional structure of the market is built on five foundations, namely, property rights, free information, trust, contracts as well as the right not to be disturbed by others and the obligation not to disturb others. Built on such solid foundations, uncertainty, risks, and transaction costs are minimised, facilitating a cooperative market transaction process with minimal barriers.

Concept of Work

Work in Islam has a broader meaning than is typically taught under conventional economic theories. Work is the most important activity that must be undertaken by humans in their lifetime. In fact, Al-Qur'an describes the concept of work in verse 469 using various kinds of Arabic diction, thus demonstrating the importance of work in Islam. Work is given special importance in Islam to the extent that it is considered an act of worship itself, inseparable from the faith dimension. Islam firmly discourages idle, unproductive, and futile activities.

Work is the right and obligation of every individual. Each individual has the right to work as desired, providing it does not conflict with Islamic principles. And when an individual has secured the profession they desire, they are obligated to work in the job to which they are entrusted to the best of their ability.

Islam does not recognise different degrees of human division from wealth. The distinguishing factor is ability and effort in work, whether working for oneself or for Allah, because Islam upholds justice, implying humans will reap results based on the effort exerted.

Islam eschews laziness, idleness, and unproductiveness. In fact, individuals with physical or mental disabilities are actively supported to engage in productive activities similar to the public in general. This is underpinned by the principle that all individuals have the same opportunity and freedom to access resources. Nevertheless, there are specific conditions that may cause certain individuals to have greater abilities or limitations than others, either physically or mentally.

Concept of Wealth

Islam encourages society to strive fully and utilise the resources bestowed by Allah to provide useful assets/wealth. Wealth is important for humans in their lives to achieve their goals. Humans have a natural tendency to view wealth as something desirable. Therefore, Islam encourages the pursuit of wealth in an honest and morally acceptable way. The quality and quantity of wealth owned are directly proportional to the efforts exerted by the individual.

Based on Islamic principles, wealth is not the ultimate goal in life, yet merely a tool to facilitate life. Wealth can be obtained through resources processed via productive work to produce something useful. Each process must be executed in accordance with sharia principles. When wealth is accumulated in violation of Islamic principles, greed and misery will ensue.

Greed as it exists in humans creates socio-economic problems. The accumulation or hoarding of wealth amongst certain groups exacerbates social inequality. This is clearly in contradiction of Islamic principles that prioritise quality welfare and economic equality, which can be achieved through the equitable distribution of wealth, amongst others. Wealth distribution is of upmost importance in the Islamic economic system, which is in line with the goal of the Islamic economy to achieve quality welfare (*falah*). That goal is the shared responsibility of every person on earth.

Islam explicitly forbids the hoarding of wealth. This can be overcome via social finance mechanisms, such as *zakat*, *infaq*, *sadaqah,* and *waqf* (ZISWAF). In addition, Islam increases the equitable distribution of wealth based on Islamic principles that forbid humans from excess. Excess leads to greed. Therefore, the implementation of social finance must be balanced with public awareness to avoid excessive consumption and distribute wealth optimally.

Basically, the concept of wealth in Islam can be concluded as follows:

1. Humans are required to seek productive wealth in accordance with halal values.
2. Wealth is not the ultimate goal in life, yet merely a tool to facilitate life, especially in the worship of Allah.
3. Wealth must be distributed equitably amongst all social strata.
4. Social finance plays a vital role in optimising wealth distribution.

Role of the State

The core of an economic system is the production, distribution, and consumption of wealth and income from economic resources. State intervention is required to run such a complex system. Optimising the role of government to ensure seamless and orderly mechanisms depends on the prevailing trends in the national and international economies. A crisis, for instance, can demonstrate the level of strategic success or failure of government policies instituted (Juhro et al., 2019). The role of government also depends on the economic system adopted in a country, namely socialist-communist, capitalist, or a combination.

The economic systems outlined above are better known as conventional economic systems. The economic system according to Islam, however, has different characteristics, stretching beyond worldly social aspects to integrate the spiritual and social dimensions. Therefore, the ultimate target of the economic system is not in pursuit of individual interests but the collective interest of the people. This is the important role of the state, namely to determine and apply rules in accordance with Islamic principles in the implementation of the economic system.

The state has a crucial task to create social order, achieve the planned goals, create equitable prosperity for all (materially and spiritually), as well as establish and enforce rules in accordance with sharia principles. Most importantly, the state must ensure justice and fairness are upheld across all social strata to maintain social order.

In the economic transaction process, the government must safeguard equitable opportunities, freedoms, and accessibility for all to the resources available. When freedom and opportunities are available, the equitable distribution of productivity, assets, and wealth is achieved. In addition, the government is responsible for providing the infrastructure and facilities required by the community to perform economic transactions.

The state also has an important role to play in terms of maintaining market order and harmony. The government must ensure that each individual is free to trade in the market. In addition, the role of market supervisor is also the duty and responsibility of the government. Nevertheless, market intervention by the government is forbidden according to Islamic teaching, except during market disruptions, such as those caused by dishonesty or large-scale disasters.

Though the government guarantees each individual has the same opportunities and freedoms, in practice individuals may be unable to actualise the opportunities afforded. Naturally, asset and wealth distribution are not maximised. In this case, the government is required to minimise potential gaps, for instance by optimising and leveraging social finance.

Reducing social inequality and alleviating poverty are the overarching duties of government. Islam considers most poverty as a corollary of suboptimal wealth sharing from individuals with more to those with less (Iqbal & Mirakhor, 2007). In terms of poverty eradication, in addition to the role of government, the commitment of those entrusted with comparatively more wealth than others is also required. Therefore, the government must contribute to ensure the optimal transfer of ownership from individuals with excess wealth to indigent people.

The government is required to formulate economic policies specific to the respective goals. In summary, there are four main goals of government. *First*, to guarantee that each individual has the same access to the resources available. *Second*, to ensure that each individual has the same opportunities and freedoms to use and manage those resources. *Third*, to oversee market conditions and transactions, ensuring equitable exchange and justice. *Fourth*, to ensure the transfer of some wealth from individuals with excess to those in need.

In the execution of duties, the government has the right to claim some of the community's resources as a source of state income, for instance through taxes. This is to ensure the government can effectively discharge its mandate. In addition, the government is also entitled to borrow, if required, providing no elements of *riba* are involved.

2.3 Islamic Financial System

2.3.1 Conception and Principles

The existing financial system embraced by economists and conceived based on conventional economic theories attracts criticism from Islamic economists. Based on conventional economics, society is considered individualistic and rational in its decision-making. Therefore, public prosperity and development are achieved by prioritising the satisfaction of each respective individual. This clearly conflicts with Islamic teachings, where humans are considered social beings with a natural tendency to help each other. Furthermore, since the 2007–2008 global crisis, studies concerning the relationship between Islamic values and ethics and the financial system have increased and matured. This is important to achieve optimal financial system stability. In addition, the incorporation of Islamic religious values into financial system practices can restrain the darker side of human nature, including greed, ego, individualism, and dishonesty.

The Islamic financial system is built on the foundation of *maqasid syariah* (the meaning and goals are justified and required by Islamic law), with the achievement of equitable prosperity (*falah*) at its core. In essence, the goal is to increase *maslahah* (benefits) and prevent *mafsadah* (harm or loss). According to *maqasid syariah*, humans are commanded to protect faith, life, mind, lineage, and property based on priority. Therefore, the financial system implications are that each individual has the right to own property (in any form), providing it has not been acquired using falsehood or deception (*bathil*), or harms another person. For example, transactions containing elements of *riba, maysir,* or *gharar* are strictly forbidden. This is prohibited within the Islamic financial system, which upholds the principles of honesty, integrity, justice, and welfare *(falah)* for all as well as balance in life.

Implementation of an Islamic financial system creates a financial system as the backbone of the real sector. The relationship between the real and financial sectors is directly interdependent, thus preventing sectoral imbalances and avoiding financial crises.

Islam upholds the values of justice and honesty, particularly in matters involving the interests of the Muslim community. Therefore, transparency and accountability in every transaction are critical to achieve those values in terms of Islamic financial system practices. It must be inculcated in every individual that only Allah is the true owner of everything, humans are merely *khalifah* (caliphs or leaders) entrusted as representatives of Allah to maintain and manage that which is bestowed by Allah in accordance with the Al-Qur'an and as-Sunnah. As such, individuals are responsible for everything they have.

Fundamentally, implementation of an Islamic financial system is based on Islamic values, the purview of which forbid *riba* and *maysir*, and oblige *zakat* almsgiving. The principles of Islamic finance will be explored in more depth in a separate chapter. Based on the description in previous paragraphs, however, there is a clear distinction between the Islamic financial system and conventional financial system, namely that individualism is controlled within an Islamic financial system through the application of Islamic values and principles, while conventional teaching considers humans as rational beings and prioritises self-interest. In addition, the goal of an Islamic financial system is *falah.*

A financial system facilitates the direct or indirect transfer of funds (finance) from individuals with excess funds to those requiring additional funds based on simple or complex transactions. The direct transfer of funds occurs when an investor and fund manager performs a transaction without an intermediary, for instance if an investor purchases a security directly from a fund manager. Meanwhile, indirect funds transfers involve an intermediation process between the investor and borrower through a bank. In addition to allocating funds directly through a capital market and indirectly through financial intermediaries, the Islamic financial system also has a fund allocation mechanism for the goal of quality welfare through social and public institutions. The financial system contains various elements, including financial institutions, markets, instruments, infrastructure, products, services, practices, and transactions.

In general, financial systems can be categorised into two distinct forms, namely market-based industry and bank-based industry. In a market-based industry, the financial system is dominated by capital market activity. Most economies with this type of financial system are advanced, with well-developed capital markets. On the other hand, a bank-based industry represents a financial system where the banking sector commands a dominant market share. The banking sector dominates financial transactions, including fund disbursements and lending, in developing economies.

Capital markets in emerging economies continue to grow and develop. Globally, however, the bank-based industry remains dominant.

In addition to the aforementioned classification, a financial system can be categorised as conventional or Islamic. The clearest distinction between the two is the application of Islamic principles and values in Islamic financial system practices, which are not applied in a conventional financial system. The most tangible implication is that a conventional financial system uses interest (*riba*) as a reference to determine the rate of return. According to Islamic teaching, however, interest rates are considered *riba* and, therefore, haram under sharia law. Consequently, the Islamic financial system uses a profit-sharing approach to determine the rate of return. Islamic financial transactions apply specific contracts, broadly classified as *tijari* and *tabarru*, which will be discussed in the following chapter.

A financial system that applies Islamic principles enjoys a close relationship with the real sector, which prevents the accumulation or hoarding of wealth and property in the hands of a few. According to Islamic law, the financial sector only functions to support the real sector, as the protagonist turning the wheels of economy. This is a specific characteristic of Islamic finance. There is no doctrine in Islam stating that the financial sector is more dominant than the real sector. In fact, it is the financial sector that supports real sector activity. It can be stated, therefore, that the main characteristic of the Islamic economy, in essence, is support for real sector activity by an orderly financial sector.

One of the core activities of Islamic finance is investment. Investment is an integral part of productive real sector activity. The main purpose of the financial sector is to create conditions conducive to effective and efficient funds transfers and mobilisation between lenders and borrowers. According to Islam, the financial system not only operates in accordance with its role, yet must also comply with Islamic norms and values, explained as follows (ISRA, 2015):

1. **Freedom to Transact**

   Allah ensures convenience for humans to maximise their servitude to Allah. In the Al-Qur'an, Allah does not comprehensively detail aspects of worship, such as *shalat* (prayers), *zakat* (almsgiving), and *shaum* (fasting), instead focusing on *muamalah*. The ratio of verses that discuss worship and *muamalah* is approximately 10:90. In terms of *muamalah*, the legal and fundamental basis of *muamalah* is *mubah* (permitted). All legal transactions are permitted, unless explicitly forbidden in verse. It can be concluded, therefore, that Islam affords individuals the freedom to perform any transaction. Freedom, however, implies responsibility and limitations, providing the transactions are not explicitly forbidden in verse.

2. **Eradication of *Riba, Gharar,* and *Maysir***

   Riba includes unjust, exploitative gains or compensation without accompanying effort or risk. *Riba* is an additional gain in a financial transaction that is not justified. *Riba* is the predetermined addition or excess that exceeds the total loan/debt allocated through certain provisions relating to a specific period. *Gharar* means uncertainty. *Gharar* typically occurs when a definitive transaction becomes uncertain, such as the sale of what is not present. *Maysir* is gambling or speculation, namely expecting a profit based on wishful hopes of future gain by mere chance. *Riba, Gharar,* and *Maysir* are absolutely forbidden in Islam and considered as acquiring gains by falsehood or deception (*bathil*).

3. **Prohibition of Price Manipulation and Intervention**

   In essence, prices are formed by the interaction between supply and demand. All forms of intervention, therefore, including by the regulator, are not permitted in Islam. Markets must remain subject to the laws of supply and demand. Nevertheless, certain conditions permit price intervention by the regulator, such as to recover from market imbalances or unhealthy competition. For instance, hoarding or profiteering (*ihtikar*) by unscrupulous sellers of goods during periods of scarcity to obtain higher prices or driving up prices by creating artificial demand (*bai'najasy*). Under such circumstances, the government is permitted to intervene to restore healthy market conditions.

4. **Opportunity to Transact at Fair Prices**

   As explained previously, prices are formed based on supply and demand forces. There are certain cases, however, where prices are formed based on an estimation. In those cases, discrepancies can emerge between the fair price and the actual price quoted in a transaction. A fair price is achieved through perfect interaction between supply and demand without interference. Meanwhile, the transaction price can be formed as a result of authorised intervention by the government.

5. **Accurate and Balanced Information**

   Information is critical in a transaction between two or more parties. The availability and accessibility of complete and unambiguous information is the inalienable right of all parties in a transaction. Detailed and comprehensive information cover the transactions and markets, including market prices, estimated value of goods, quality of goods, contracts, and others. All market transactions must consider all relevant information, thus emphasising the importance of market institutions to remain transparent and accountable. Information must be delivered clearly to transactional parties and interpreted based on the same understanding by transactional parties. Transparency in the delivery of information builds trust among transacting parties. Asymmetric and abstruse information cause misunderstanding and can erode trust in the transacting parties. In Islam, it is unacceptable for one or more parties to be misrepresented or have an incorrect perception. Furthermore, Islam strictly forbids the concealment of important information that could lead to information asymmetry.

6. **Free from Harm/Loss**

   For transactions between two parties, both parties must ensure the contract does not create a gain for one at the expense of the other, including harm to others and the surrounding community. Transactions that cause harm/losses are forbidden in Islam.

7. **Cooperation and Brotherhood**

   Cooperation, brotherhood, and solidarity are values upheld in Islam. Islam encourages humans to help one another in kindness. Fair transactions are considered acts of kindness permitted for mutual benefit. In fact, when a dispute or conflict emerges in a contract, it must be resolved in a familial way.

The structures of Islamic and conventional financial systems are similar. Within an Islamic financial system there are institutional arrangements, accompanied by banks and nonbank financial institutions, financial markets, financial instruments, and financial system infrastructures. Notwithstanding, there is a fundamental difference from the conventional financial system, namely that all financial system elements must be implemented and operated based on Islamic principles and values as commanded in the Al-Qur'an and Hadith, and independent reasoning (*ijtihad*) by clerics. The institutional arrangements, as well as financial institutions, markets, instruments, and infrastructure are discussed in more detail in the following subsection.

2.3.2 Financial Instruments and Contracts

All economic activity in Islam proceeds under an agreement based on a specific contract. Financial instruments can also be categorised as agreements. The agreement clearly stipulates the terms and conditions as well as the risks of the associated financial instrument.

Financial instruments encompass all products traded in the financial sector, including those from financial institutions and financial markets. Therefore, financial sector instruments are fairly diverse. Furthermore, with the advancement of information technology, instruments are becoming more innovative and simpler to trade. Consequently, players in the financial system have a greater abundance of choices for investment diversification and sources of capital. Financial instrument/product innovation within a conventional financial system is easier to facilitate because it is not subject to absolute Islamic rules and laws.

To innovate or create new Islamic financial instruments, however, a series of reviews by Islamic scholars and economists is required to establish whether the financial product may be launched publicly. Therefore, the contracts used are the most important and inextricable part of a financial instrument. One contract may be used for a variety of financial instruments and, similarly, one type of instrument may apply various contracts.

The fundamental considerations on whether a contract is permitted or not is written in the Al-Qur'an, verse 275 of surah Al-Baqarah as follows:

وَاَحَلَّ اللّٰهُ الْبَيْعَ وَحَرَّمَ الرِّبٰوا

... But Allah has permitted trade and has forbidden interest ... (Q.S. Al-Baqarah [2]: 275)

That is why *riba* is absolutely forbidden for Islamic financial transactions, both directly and indirectly. Allah has actually made it easier for Muslims to perform transactions in accordance with Islamic principles. Fundamentally, Allah has made transactions lawful (*mubah*), unless forbidden in verse (Al-Qur'an and Hadith). Therefore, all transactions are permitted unless forbidden in Islam. The practices that Islam prohibits do not outnumber those that Islam permits.

The Islamic financial system has core contracts that contain Islamic financial instruments therein. Based on the function and purpose, Islamic financial instruments can be categorised into four types as follows (Iqbal & Mirakhor, 2007):

1. **Transactional Contract**
   This instrument accommodates real sector transactions, for example exchanging or trading goods/services. Exchange activity in the real sector is the underlying of this instrument, including the exchange of goods or services for other goods or services (barter) or the exchange of goods or services using money. This exchange can be settled using cash or deferred arrangement.
2. **Financial Contract**
   This instrument facilitates funding activity for production in the real sector through the allocation of credit or financing. In addition, the instrument also serves as a bridge between investors and business managers, primarily in the form of a cooperation agreement.
3. **Intermediation Contract**
   This instrument facilitates the intermediation function, while also supporting the previous two instruments, making fee-based financial services possible to support economic activity in the real sector.
4. **Social Welfare Contracts**
   This instrument accommodates individuals wishing to share and help the local community towards achieving equitable welfare and prosperity for all. In addition, this instrument helps to minimise social inequality.

Figure 2.1 illustrates which contracts are used to underlie the aforementioned financial instruments and transactions.

Based on the specific orientation towards profit, contracts in Islam are generally categorised into two groups (Fig. 2.2). *First*, a gratuitous *tabarru'* contract is a not-for-profit agreement, which facilitates social-oriented financial services without any specific consideration in return. *Tabarru'* contracts cover deposit and loan services as well as social-oriented funds. The most common example of a *tabarru'* contract is a *qardh* (debt) contract.

Second, a compensational *tijarah* contract is a for-profit agreement that is sharia compliant. For example, a trade contract. *Tijarah* contracts are subdivided into two categories, namely Natural Certainty Contract (NCC) and Natural Uncertainty Contract (NUC). NCC has contractual certainty rather than a profit-sharing basis, for example price and value assurance in a trade contract or in a lease agreement, product assurance, and cost of the lease. On the other hand, NUC contains contractual uncertainty based on a profit-sharing scheme. The uncertainty stems from the profit-sharing system based on business profit, which cannot be accurately predicted or determined until the end of the agreement period. *Mudharabah* is the most popular example.

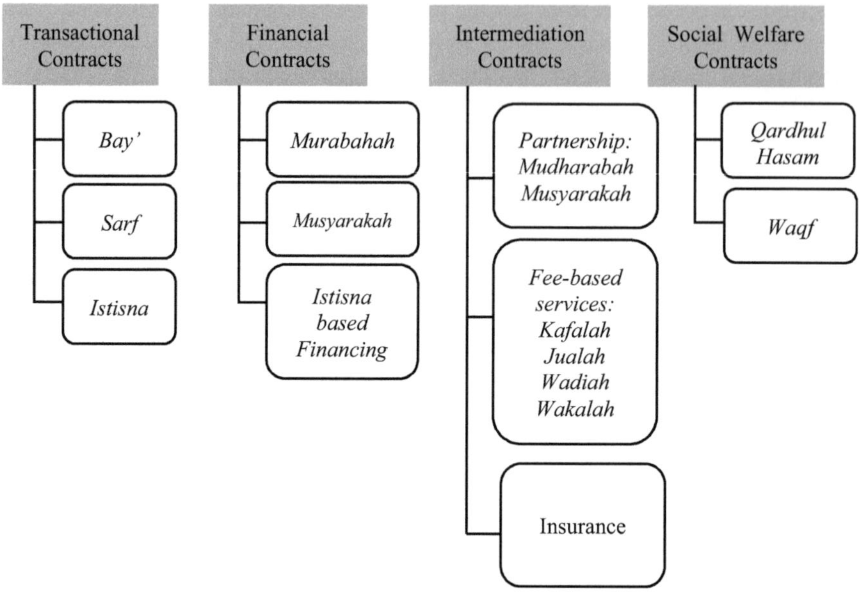

Fig. 2.1 Contracts for each type of Islamic financial instrument (Transactional contracts; financial contracts; intermediation contracts; social welfare contracts). Source: Created by Author

NCC must be executed with certainty, while NUC contains an element of uncertainty. A Natural Certainty Contract practised with uncertainty will become invalid (*bathil*) due to the element of *gharar* (contractual uncertainty) contained within. Similarly, a Natural Uncertainty Contract cannot be practised with certainty due to the inherent speculative (*maysir*) actions and elements of *riba* thus contained.

The flowchart of Islamic financial contracts explained above can be illustrated as follows. The contracts can be implemented for Islamic financial products in an Islamic financial system through financial institutions and financial markets.

2.3.3 Policy Authority and Regulator

(a) Financial System Authority

The financial system is regulated by an authority that oversees, regulates, and maintains financial system stability because a financial system is complex and depends on trust. In addition, there is high potential for moral hazard and adverse selection in a financial system because of information asymmetry and systemic risk. In Indonesia, the financial system authorities comprise Bank Indonesia (BI), Financial Services Authority (OJK), and Indonesia Deposit Insurance Corporation (IDIC). In the 1945 Constitution, Bank Indonesia played a crucial role in terms of regulating and supervising the monetary, financial, and payment systems. Meanwhile, OJK and

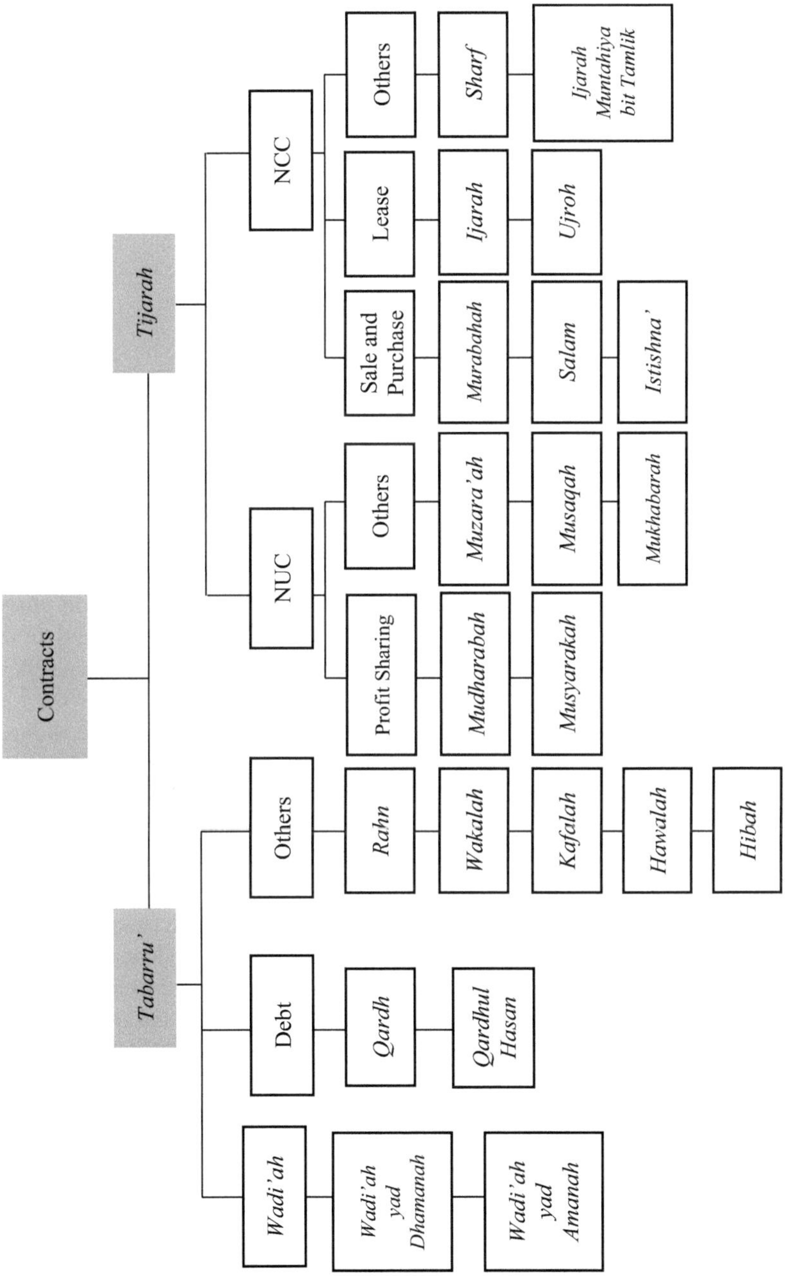

Fig. 2.2 Classification of Islamic financial contracts. Source: Darsono et al. (2017)

IDIC are regulated pursuant to prevailing laws with a more limited scope of authority at the microprudential level in relation to individual financial institutions.

The institutional arrangements of an Islamic financial system are comparable to the conventional system yet reflect the specific characteristics of the Islamic financial system, involving a Sharia Board. The jurisdiction of the Islamic financial system authority is more or less the same as conventional authorities, namely to regulate, supervise, and formulate policies relating to financial institutions, yet must be implemented in accordance with Islamic principles. In addition, an Islamic financial system entails specialised institutions to manage social finance, including *zakat, infaq, sadaqah,* and *waqf* (ZISWAF).

(b) Central Bank

In general, the overarching duties of a central bank are to maintain monetary stability, financial system stability (macro and microprudential), and a seamless payment system. Likewise, in an Islamic economy, the central bank is entrusted as the Islamic monetary authority, Islamic macroprudential authority, Islamic microprudential authority, and payment system authority. Stability is something that must be regulated and maintained with utmost urgency, including at the systemic level. In the event of a monetary system shock, for instance excessive inflation or rupiah depreciation, economic uncertainty and instability will ensue. Disruptions to financial system stability can lead to financial crises and if the payment system is disrupted or default occurs, the risks that emerge are very serious and can destabilise the payment system and even the economy.

In Indonesia, the legal framework of the central bank is regulated in accordance with Act Number 23 of 1999 concerning Bank Indonesia, as amended by Act Number 6 of 2009 (Bank Indonesia Act). The BI Act also stipulates the monetary controls in the form of open market operations (OMO), setting the discount rate and reserve requirements as well as regulating loans or financing. In the latest amendment, monetary controls in accordance with Islamic principles are also elucidated.

Development of the Islamic economy in Indonesia, including Islamic banking, is an inextricable part of Bank Indonesia's role and service. Indonesia currently embraces a dual financial system, comprising the conventional and Islamic financial systems, like other countries, such as Malaysia, Pakistan, Qatar, and others. Meanwhile, in countries with a full-fledged Islamic financial system, the central bank is also full-fledged Islamic central bank, discharging its function and duties in accordance with Islamic principles, such as in Iran and Sudan.

In Indonesia, the central bank implements a range of strategic measures and policies to create a conducive, competitive, efficient, and prudent Islamic banking industry. Islamic banking development is expected to advance the real sector through profit-sharing financing that targets micro, small, and medium enterprises (MSME) and ultimately alleviates poverty and reduces income inequality. Bank Indonesia applies the following paradigms to its Islamic banking development policies and measures:

1. The same treatment of conventional and Islamic banks.
2. A market-driven approach to product and network development.
3. Phased and sustainable regulatory and infrastructure development.
4. Policymaking based on governance and compliance with sharia law, while applying universal values.

(c) Financial Services Authority (OJK)

In Indonesia, plans to establish an autonomous authority mandated with financial services sector supervision and independent from the central bank were originally drawn up in 1999. Only in 2011, however, was the Financial Services Authority (OJK) established in accordance with Act Number 21 of 2011. As stipulated in the OJK Act, OJK is an independent body and free from interference from other parties that have the function, duty and authority of regulation, supervision, examination, and investigation concerning all matters relating to financial institutions.

OJK replaced the central bank function of maintaining stability through the supervision of financial institutions, including banks and nonbanks. Previously, the function of supervising nonbanks had been mandated to the Ministry of Finance. Considering that Indonesia embraced a dual financial system, in terms of the function to maintain microprudential stability, OJK oversaw all financial institutions, encompassing conventional and Islamic. OJK was established with the following salient roles and goals:

1. Implement fair, regulated, transparent, and accountable financial institution activity in the financial services sector.
2. Create and maintain stable and sustainable financial system growth.
3. Protect the interests of consumers and the public.
4. Protect the national interest, namely human resources, management, control and ownership in the financial services sector with consideration to aspects of globalisation.

Based on that vision, OJK shouldered the burden of stimulating financial services sector activity in Indonesia to ensure domestic competitiveness was maintained internationally.

OJK is an autonomous body, independent of the government and free from government interference. Notwithstanding, OJK coordinates with the government to ensure the regulations and policies instituted are aligned and in synergy with the government and fiscal policy. Therefore, OJK welcomes representatives from each respective authority in an ex-officio role to coordinate, cooperate, and harmonise policies amongst authority stakeholders, particularly in terms of fiscal, monetary, and financial services policy. This aims to create and maintain a national economic system free from conflict between the respective authorities.

(d) Indonesia Deposit Insurance Corporation (IDIC)

The Indonesia Deposit Insurance Corporation (IDIC) is an independent, transparent, and accountable legal authority. Based on Act Number 24 of 2004 concerning the Indonesia Deposit Insurance Corporation, in the execution of duties and function, IDIC is responsible directly to the president. The main role and duties of IDIC are to guarantee customer deposits in the banking industry, encompassing the conventional and Islamic banking industries.

Urgency to establish IDIC actually emerged during the monetary crisis in 1997–98. During that crisis, customer trust in the banking sector retreated drastically. In fact, bank runs became a common occurrence, creating bank panic and leaving the banking sector reeling from illiquid conditions. No banks were spared, even big banks. As a corollary of the crisis, 16 banks shuttered their doors permanently. The government took subsequent measures to fully guarantee customer deposits in the banking industry through Presidential Decree (Kepres) Number 26 of 1998, which was superseded by the Banking Act (Number 10) of 1998. The Banking Act explicitly clarified the importance of establishing a deposit guarantee corporation.

All banks in Indonesia, including conventional and Islamic banks, are mandatory IDIC members, thus incurring an initial membership fee as a percentage of paid-up capital and a premium due each semester as a percentage of the average monthly balance of total deposits each period. For conventional banks in Indonesia, deposit instruments include demand deposits, term deposits, certificates of deposit, savings deposits, and other similar instruments. On the other hand, the scope of deposits guaranteed by IDIC at Islamic banks includes *wadi'ah* demand deposits, *wadi'ah* savings deposits, *mudharabah* savings deposits, and *mudharabah* term deposits.

In terms of guaranteeing customer deposits, IDIC has the following jurisdiction:

1. Setting the premium rate and collecting the guarantee premiums from banks.
2. Setting and collecting the initial registration and membership fees.
3. Managing the premium funds collected from participants.
4. Collecting data concerning customer deposits, bank soundness, bank financial reports, and bank inspection reports.
5. Reconciling, verifying, and confirming the data.
6. Setting the requirements, procedures, and regulations for claim payments.

Meanwhile, the primary functions of IDIC to maintain financial system stability, particularly in the banking industry, are as follows:

1. Formulate and set deposit guarantee program implementation policy.
2. Implement the deposit guarantee program.
3. Set, formulate, and implement policies to create and maintain banking system stability.
4. Formulate, set and implement resolution policy for the failure of non-systemic banks.
5. Manage the failure of systemic banks.

(e) Sharia Board

Specific to the Islamic financial system, the Sharia Board is a specialised institution, independent and tasked with formulating fatwa (legal opinion), given by a qualified jurist, concerning the activities implemented by Islamic financial institutions in terms of product innovation, contracts, services, businesses as well as operating activities. This is done to ensure Islamic financial institutions, including banks and nonbanks, are not in violation of Islamic law, values, or principles.

Sharia Board in Indonesia

In Indonesia, the highest Sharia Board in charge of *muamalah* jurisprudence, specifically in terms of the economy, finance, and banking, is the National Sharia Board of the Indonesian Council of Ulama (DSN-MUI). As of 2019, DSN-MUI had formulated 125 fatwa concerning economic and financial practices in Indonesia. Several factors underlie the urgency of establishing DSN-MUI in Indonesia as follows:

1. Fostering the application of Islamic principles in the economic and financial systems of Indonesia.
2. Actualising the aspirations and opinions of Muslims to create a universal rule for the economy and finance in accordance with Islamic law.
3. Providing a vehicle for ulema to review, study, and coordinate various issues in the economy and finance more effectively and efficiently. Therefore, *muamalah* jurisprudence in Indonesia would remain within the corridor of Islamic law.

DSN-MUI status as an autonomous body independent of the central bank and government affords greater credibility and public trust when issuing fatwa concerning Islamic economic and financial practices in Indonesia. In turn, Islamic financial institutions are also more trusted by the public because an independent board is overseeing all halal aspects. This minimises public concerns over participating in a financial sector that is vulnerable to usury or *riba*. Therefore, DSN-MUI has the following primary tasks:

1. Review the latest issues concerning the Islamic economy and finance.
2. Analyse, review, and evaluate product or contract innovations submitted by financial institutions.
3. Formulate fatwa concerning the operational activities of Islamic banks and nonbank financial institutions.
4. Issue fatwa concerning the practices of Islamic banks and nonbank financial institutions.

Meanwhile, DSN-MUI has the following primary functions:

1. Supervise products and innovation as practised by Islamic financial institutions to avoid violations of Islamic principles and values. In practice, therefore, Islamic financial institutions cannot deviate from sharia law.

2. Research and review towards the creation of new fatwa in line with the development of Islamic financial products.
3. Recommend DSN-MUI members for the Sharia Supervisory Board (DPS) at each Islamic financial institution to ensure institutional practices are not in violation of Islamic law.
4. Issue warnings and reprimands to Islamic financial institutions found in violation of the guidelines published by DSN-MUI. If ignored, DSN-MUI is authorised to recommend sanctions to the relevant authority.

(f) *Zakat, Infaq, Sadaqah,* and *Waqf* (ZISWAF) Boards

Zakat, infaq, sadaqah, and *waqf* (ZISWAF) boards are authorised to regulate Islamic social finance in Indonesia based on prevailing laws and regulations. In general, there are two centralised institutions that regulate ZISWAF at the national level. *First*, the National Amil Zakat Board (BAZNAS), which functions to plan, implement, and regulate the collection, management, distribution, and utilisation of *zakat, infaq,* and *sadaqah*. *Second*, there is a separate institution that regulates, manages, and develops waqf assets, namely the Indonesia Waqf Board (BWI).

BAZNAS

BAZNAS is a non-structural, autonomous, and independent government institution under the Ministry of Religious Affairs and responsible to the president. The main role of BAZNAS is to collect and distribute *zakat, infaq,* and *sadaqah* nationally. BAZNAS was established in accordance with Presidential Decree of the Republic of Indonesia Number 8 of 2001. This was subsequently amended by Act Number 23 of 2011 concerning *Zakat* Management. *Zakat* laws stipulate that BAZNAS is authorised for *zakat* management nationally.

BAZNAS has established Regional Amil Zakat Boards (BAZDA) at the provincial as well as regency/city administrative levels to optimise its duties and responsibilities. In addition, other Amil Zakat Institutions (LAZ) have also been established in the private sector. Nevertheless, existing BAZDA and LAZ are obligated to report their *zakat, infaq, sadaqah,* and other social finance management activities to BAZNAS.

BAZNAS, BAZDA, and LAZ work in synergy to collect, manage, distribute, and utilise ZIS funds in accordance with their respective authority. When discharging their function, all *zakat* institutions are obligated to apply Islamic law, trust, accountability, justice, utility, integration, and legal assurance.

Indonesia Waqf Board (BWI)

In addition to BAZNAS, which is mandated to manage *zakat, infaq,* and *sadaqah* (ZIS) funds, the Indonesia Waqf Board (BWI) is a specialist institution entrusted to manage waqf funds in Indonesia. BWI was established as an independent institution to collect, manage, and develop waqf assets in Indonesia. Waqf receive separate government support and attention, as evidenced by the Waqf Act (No. 41) of 2004. BWI is responsible for developing Indonesian waqf nationally and internationally. Furthermore, BWI is expected to maximise the economic potential and benefits of waqf assets for quality welfare and well-being.

According to the Waqf Act, Paragraph 1 of Article 49 stipulates the jurisdiction and duties of BWI as follows:

1. Mentor waqf asset managers (*nazhir*) on managing and developing waqf assets, which is crucial to optimise *waqf* asset development.
2. Manage and develop *waqf* assets nationally and internationally.
3. Approve and/or licence changes in the designation or status of waqf assets.
4. Dismiss and replace *nazhir*.
5. Approve the exchange of *waqf* assets.
6. Provide advice and recommendations to the government concerning *waqf* policymaking.

2.4 Islamic Financial Institutions

The business of financial institutions involves managing funds from individuals with a surplus to those with a deficit. Financial institutions play a key role as actors turning the wheels of the real sector. Without financial institutions, the flow of funds between individuals with a surplus and those with a deficit is less efficient. In general, financial institutions can be classified into two broad groups, namely banks and nonbanks. Banks are dominant with larger assets than other financial institutions. In addition, financial institutions can also be classified based on Islamic law, namely conventional and Islamic financial institutions.

Islamic financial institutions consist of various types of institutions like the conventional system. Notwithstanding, the fundamental principles, contracts/agreements, mechanisms, and implications between Islamic financial institutions differ from conventional financial institutions. Nonbank financial institutions include the capital market, mutual funds, insurance, pawnbrokers, cooperatives, pension funds, and finance companies. Nevertheless, there are specialised Islamic financial institutions without equivalent in the conventional system, such as Islamic microfinance institutions, namely *Baitul Maal wat Tamwil* (BMT). In addition to commercial financial institutions, Islamic teaching is renowned for social finance, comprising *zakat*, *infaq*, *sadaqah*, and *waqf* (ZISWAF) as well as other instruments of social finance.

The primary function of financial institutions is financial intermediation, namely the efficient and effective allocation of resources, as well as secure and orderly payments, asset management, and risk management. Moreover, to achieve financial intermediation efficiency, financial institutions have more comprehensive functions, as illustrated in Fig. 2.3. One indicator of success in the Islamic financial system is

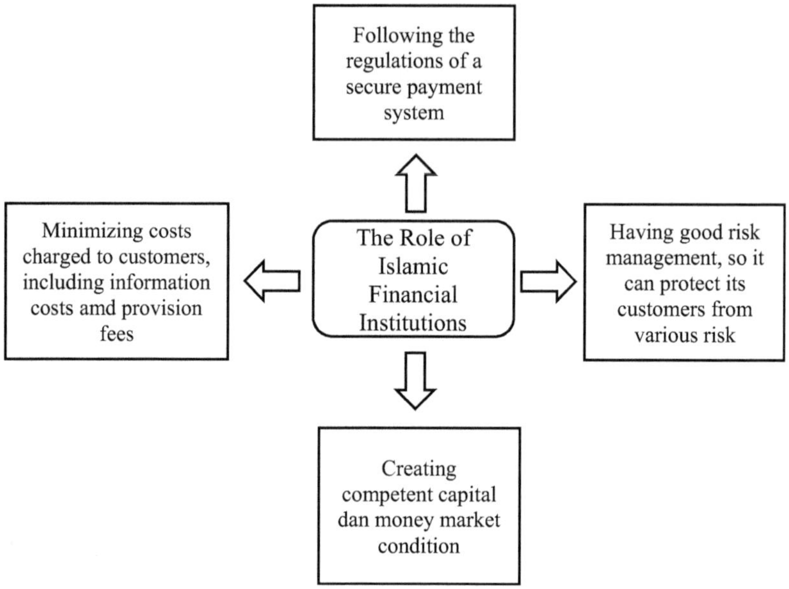

Fig. 2.3 Function of Islamic financial institutions. Source: Simorangkir (2014)

the effectiveness and efficiency of financial intermediation through financial markets and financial institutions (such as banks). Financial intermediation is the hallmark of the overall financial system.

Fundamentally, the primary goal of financial institutions in the Islamic financial system is to maintain the accurate flow of funds between individuals with a surplus and those with the deficit because, in Islam, the economic goal is to achieve justice, balance, and the equitable distribution of income (Fig. 2.4). Therefore, it is essential to operate financial institutions within the corridor of Islamic principles and values.

Financial intermediation in the Islamic financial system has specific characteristics that differentiate it from conventional intermediation, elucidated as follows (Iqbal & Mirakhor, 2007):

1. **Profit and loss sharing mechanism**. In a conventional financial system, the return on investment is based on a specific predetermined period. Therefore, the profit for the investor and intermediary institution (bank for example) is fixed and not determined by fluctuations in real profit generated from productive economic activity in the real sector. This contradicts sharia principles, where the return on investment is not predetermined. The return depends on the amount of profit generated at the end of the agreement period. Therefore, the task of financial intermediaries in Islam is not to determine a fixed return but to motivate business players and increase productivity because Islamic intermediary institutions focus on the return in the real sector. Therefore, the return available to financial intermediaries and investors depends on the real profits generated in the real sector.

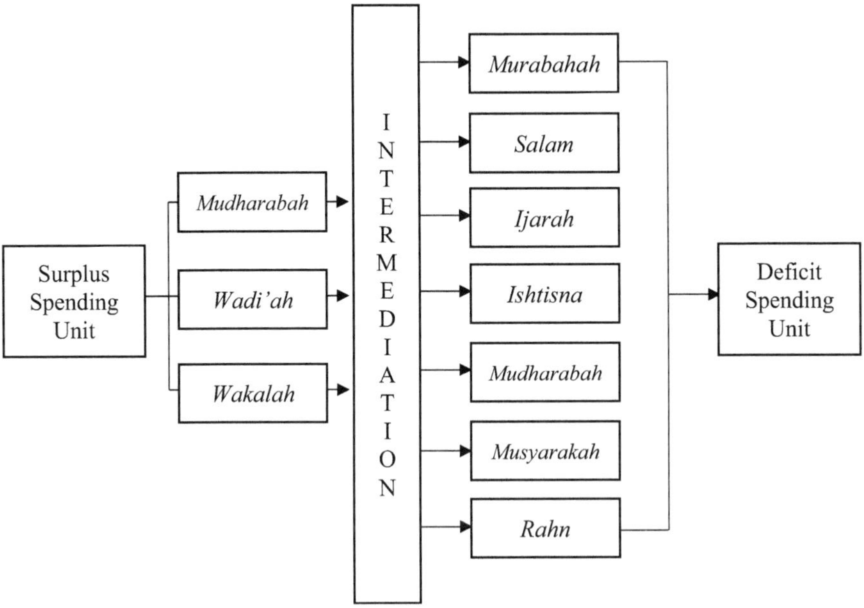

Fig. 2.4 Islamic financial intermediation process. Source: Created by Author

2. **Asset/liability management**. The application of Islamic principles in the financial system minimises asynchrony on the asset and liability sides of the financial reports due to the lack of a predetermined rate with a fixed return at the start of the agreement. Therefore, financial bookkeeping is more accurate and in keeping with real conditions.
3. **Sharia institutions**. Sharia institutions are a specific characteristic of the Islamic financial system, which exist to ensure all operating activities remain within the sharia corridor. Sharia institutions consist of ulema, sharia experts, and economists. Each new instrument or product to be launched by a financial intermediary must be approved by a sharia institution.
4. **Strict oversight**. Agreements concerning Islamic financial transactions are based on long-term relationships. Therefore, the supervision of businesses funded by financial intermediaries is carried out regularly and periodically to optimise output in the real sector.

2.4.1 Banks

The banking industry is still the mainstay for the public to conduct transactions in the financial sector, including deposits and loans/financing. Banks are also the primary actor in financial intermediation, especially in developing economies where capital market activity is underdeveloped. It is not surprising, therefore, that the banking sector is the primary source of funding in the community. In addition, the banking industry commands the largest share of total assets in the financial sector. Consequently, the stability and reliability of the banking sector is a crucial concern in the financial system.

The primary functions of banks include intermediation, liquidity, payment systems, and as a media of monetary policy transmission. Banking activity to collect funds from individuals with a surplus for disbursement to those experiencing a deficit is implemented via the intermediation function. The funds collected belong to individuals and the bank acts as a manager. Therefore, the bank is responsible for maintaining the liquidity of private funds for when the funds are needed.

The bank intermediation function has an inherent advantage for the financial system compared with direct mechanisms as follows. *First*, the funds transfer process is simpler and more efficient for both parties, particularly those with limited time and knowledge concerning financial transactions. *Second*, high transaction volume minimises the transaction cost. *Third*, direct transactions between two parties can increase information asymmetry to the potential detriment of one party, with the intermediation function thus minimising asymmetric information and creating more efficient information costs between both parties. *Fourth*, by transacting through an intermediary, the channelled funds are diversified and more variative, thus mitigating the risks associated with direct financial transactions.

Indonesia embraces a dual banking system, comprising Islamic banking and conventional banking. The establishment of Islamic banks in Indonesia is based on Act Number 10 of 1992 concerning Islamic Banking. The law states that Islamic banks are defined as interest-free institutions operating based on profit-sharing principles. In addition, the law formed the legal foundation for the establishment of the first Islamic bank in Indonesia, namely Bank Muamalat.

The position of Islamic banks was strengthened in 2008 for the development of Islamic banking in Indonesia. The position was strengthened through promulgation of Act Number 21 of 2008 concerning Islamic Banking, as an amendment to the previous law. In the same year, a severe global financial crisis caused by the conventional financial system fuelled the urgency of Islamic banking development. In fact, the conventional financial system was exposed as not resilient, or vulnerable, to financial crises.

Islamic banks were established in Indonesia with the hope of stimulating real sector activity (trade, investment, and other activities) by managing deposits and disbursing funds to businesses under the auspices of Islamic principles and values. Underlying sharia banking practices in Indonesia were the Islamic values to prohibit *riba* (interest), *maysir* (speculation), and *gharar* (uncertainty), while forbidding any profit-taking based on *bathil* (falsehood or dishonesty). Those values are applied to achieve quality welfare and well-being *(falah)*.

As mentioned, Islamic banks have specific characteristics that differentiate them from conventional banks, namely contractual relationships. At Islamic banks, there are unambiguous contracts that are ready to use, for example *wadi'ah*, *mudharabah*, *murabahah*, *ijarah*, and so on. This is because *riba* is forbidden in Islam. Each contract has its own respective characteristics and features yet, fundamentally, most sharia-compliant contracts lean towards equity-based financing. Islamic financial contracts can be classified into the following groups:

1. Equity-based contracts, such as *mudharabah* dan *musyarakah.*
2. Sales contracts, such as *murabahah*, *salam*, dan *istishna'.*
3. Leasing contracts, such as *ijarah.*
4. Other contracts, including *kafalah*, *wakalah*, *rahn*, dan *ju'alah.*

Islamic banking transactions use an equity-based system. Therefore, depositors are not guaranteed a fixed rate, rather a profit-sharing percentage. If the business activities of the bank generate a profit, the depositor will receive a portion of those profits and vice versa, if the bank incurs losses, the customer will also share the burden of those losses. Banks are forbidden from charging interest on customer financing, instead preferring a profit and loss sharing scheme.

Furthermore, the application of Islamic principles in banking practices prevents the solicitation of predetermined returns on investments placed by a customer at a bank. Departing from conventional banks where the return and principal are predetermined and guaranteed in the agreement, Islamic banks apply a percentage of the profit and loss sharing scheme after the funds are used for business activity. As the total profit cannot be accurately ascertained before the business activity has been conducted, the total return will depend on the profits generated from real activity.

As an intermediary institution, Islamic banks conduct business on the fund surplus and deficit sides. Banks collect funds and receive funding sources from customers with surplus funds and disburse funds to those experiencing a deficit. This is illustrated in Fig. 2.5, with a description of the characteristics and contracts used presented in Table 2.1.

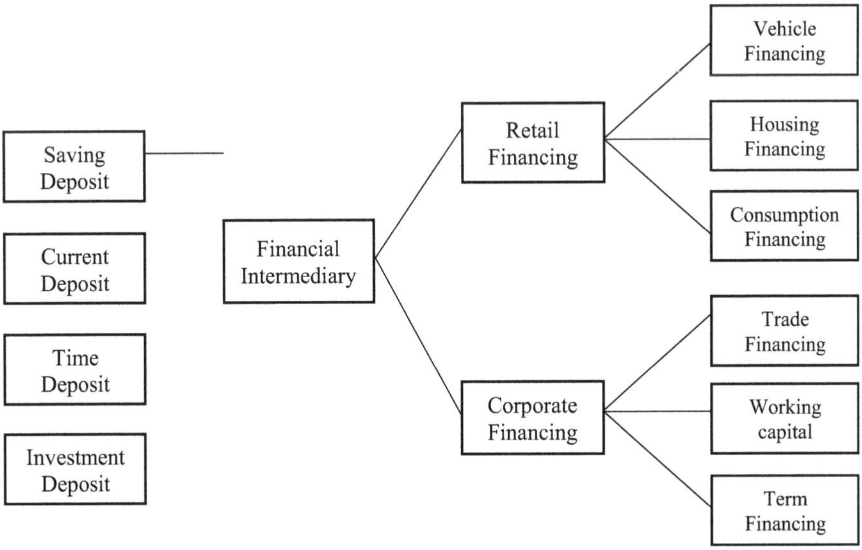

Fig. 2.5 Classification of Funding Sources and Financing at Islamic Banks. Source: ISRA (2015)

Table 2.1 Definitions of Islamic financial contracts

Contract type	Contract	Description
Tabarru'	*Wadi'ah* (Deposit)	*Wadi'ah yad dhamanah:* a safekeeping or deposit contract with a repayment guarantee. The depositary guarantees the return of the deposited property.
		Wadi'ah yad amanah: a pure deposit contract
	Debt	*Qardh*: debt or loan that must be returned
		Qardhul hasan: a gratuitous contract, where the borrower is not obliged to return the loan if unable to do so
	Others	*Rahn*: pawn contract
		Wakalah: agency contract
		Kafalah: guarantee contract
		Hawalah: transfer of debt contract
		Hibah: gift or grant
Tijari Natural Uncertainty Contract (NUC)	Profit Sharing	*Mudharabah*: a financing contract in which the owner entrusts a certain amount of capital to the manager
		Musyarakah: a joint partnership contract where capital is entrusted and managed by each party based on agreed proportions
	Others	*Muzara'ah*: a sharecropping partnership on agricultural land between the landowner and farmer, where the agricultural inputs and cultivation costs are contributed from the cultivation of that land
		Mukharabah: a sharecropping partnership on agricultural land between the landowner and farmer, where the agricultural inputs and cultivation costs are contributed by the landowner
		Musaqah: a simpler *muzara'ah* contract, where the farmer is responsible for maintaining the agricultural land
Tijari Natural Certainty Contract (NCC)	Lease	*Ijarah*: lease contract
		Ujroh: service remuneration or fee or wage
	Trade	*Murabahah*: a trade contract with a predetermined mark up or margin
		Salam: a trade contract in which advance cash payment is made for goods to be delivered at a future date, yet the goods specification is already set
		Istishna: a trade contract for goods to be delivered at a future date and payment based on specific terms
	Others	*Sharf*: foreign currency exchange contract
		Ijarah al muntahiyah bit tamlik: lease contract that is terminated with a trade contract

The aforementioned savings instruments are used by banks to collect funds from those with a surplus as part of the source of funds of commercial banks. Banks provide diverse savings instruments based on the preferences, needs, and goals of each individual.

Savings deposits and demand deposits have similar characteristics, including no maturity date and unrestricted customer deposits and withdrawals. In addition, there is no or a low minimum account balance. The types of contracts applicable to savings deposits and demand deposits are also the same, namely *mudharabah, wadi'ah yad dhamanah,* and *qardh.* The main difference between the two is that savings deposits are typically in the form of cash, while demand deposits are a type of checking account with a special cash security facility. In addition, demand deposit customers receive a cheque book and multifunction card.

In addition to demand deposits and savings deposits, other sources of bank funds include term deposits and investment deposits. Term deposits apply a specific agreement period, thus restricting the individual from depositing or withdrawing funds at any time before maturity. Investment deposits are available to individuals seeking a more competitive return. Notwithstanding, a more competitive rate of return also increases the risk of incurring losses. Therefore, individuals considering investment deposits must be prepared to face all possible consequences. The various classifications regarding sources of Islamic bank funds are presented in Table 2.2.

After discussing the various sources of funds available to Islamic banks from individuals with surplus funds, the focus now is on disbursing those funds to individuals experiencing deficit funds. This section explains the different characteristics and underlying principles of disbursing funds in accordance with sharia law. In general, banks have two main targets, namely individuals (retail) and businesses (corporate). Therefore, fund disbursements are also divided into two types, namely retail and corporate financing, based on the business scale of the customer. This does not mean, however, that an individual customer is not eligible to receive corporate financing and vice versa, retail financing may be extended to businesses.

The figure above summarises the different classifications of fund disbursements by Islamic banks. Starting with retail financing, the focus is on disbursing funds to individual customers rather than corporate entities. In addition, retail financing tends to involve more detailed, narrow, and specific requirements. The different types of retail financing offered by Islamic banks are similar to conventional banks, spanning three categories, namely automotive financing, housing financing, and personal financing.

A more detailed explanation of the characteristics and contracts available for the three types of retail financing is presented in Table 2.2. Moving on to corporate financing, the focus is on helping business owners and entrepreneurs meet their business needs. Corporate financing consists of trade financing, working capital financing, and term financing. A detailed description of corporate financing is presented in Table 2.2.

From the tables above, it can be concluded that Islamic banking products are already sufficiently diverse to meet consumers' deposit and financing needs, yet with the expectation that Islamic banking will continue to develop and innovate moving forward.

The presence of Islamic banks in various countries, and Indonesia specifically, has important and significant economic implications, including the financial sector and real sector, as follows:

Table 2.2 Classification of funding sources and financing

Instrument	Characteristic	Contract
Source of funds		
Saving Deposit	1. No or low minimum account balance. 2. No restrictions on customer deposits or withdrawals. 3. No maturity date.	1. *Mudharabah* 2. *Wadi'ah Yad Dhamanah* 3. *Qardh*
Demand Deposit	1. Checking account with cash deposit security facilities. 2. Cheque book and multifunction card. 3. No restrictions on customer deposits or withdrawals.	1. *Mudharabah* 2. *Wadi'ah Yad Dhamanah* 3. *Qardh*
Term Deposit	1. Customer agrees to deposit funds for a predetermined period. 2. Withdrawals restricted to end of predetermined period.	1. Commodity *Murabahah* 2. Unrestricted *wakalah* investment 3. General *mudharabah* investment
Investment Deposit	Having the opportunity for more competitive return, but having risk of loss from the business activity.	1. *Wakalah bi istitsmar* 2. *Mudharabah*
Retail financing		
Automotive Financing	Financing for the purchase of a motor vehicle.	*Ijarah muntahiyah bittamlik*
Housing Financing	Housing financing facility offered by specialised Islamic banks to individuals.	1. Parallel *Istishna'* 2. *Ijarah* 3. *Bay' bitsaman ajil* 4. *Musyarakah mutanaqishah*
Personal/Individual Financing	Financing facilities for customers requiring funds yet not for a specific object, such as a house or motor vehicle.	1. *Rahn* 2. *Bay' al-'inah* 3. *Bay' tawarruq*
Corporate financing		
Trade Financing	Provides capital for trade activity.	1. *Mudharabah* 2. *Musyarakah*
Working Capital Financing	For short-term business/operating activities.	1. *Mudharabah* 2. *Musyarakah*
Term Financing	For long-term business/operating activities.	1. *Mudharabah* 2. *Musyarakah*

Source: ISRA (2015)

1. Promote a competitive financial system and maintain price stability. *Maysir* is prohibited in the financial markets, ensuring the financial system is more resistant and resilient to economic shocks.
2. Create alignment between the financial sector and real sector by providing liquidity based on the actual needs of the real sector. Therefore, the liquidity gap between the financial sector and real sector is narrowed, while strengthening real sector productivity and lowering inflation.

3. Provide alternative financial institutions, markets, and instruments for individuals seeking sharia-compliant financial institutions, markets, and instruments.
4. Create balanced growth and economic equality to ensure those towards the bottom of the pyramid feel the benefits through Corporate Social Responsibility (CSR) and ZISWAF in the Islamic banking industry.

2.4.2 Nonbank Financial Institutions

1. **Insurance**
   According to OJK, insurance is a financial transaction between the insured and insurer, where the insured is required to pay a premium for the guarantee of compensation for the risk of unforeseen loss, death, damage, or loss of expected profit. Insurance companies are required to provide claims on the losses incurred by the insured. In general, insurance can be classified into two groups as follows (Darsono et al., 2017):
   (a) General Insurance. Consisting of property insurance, accident insurance as well as property and accident insurance.
   (b) Life Insurance. Consisting of health insurance, annuity insurance, disability insurance, and life insurance. Life insurance covers and guarantees the material welfare of the insured party's family. Upon the death of the insured, the insurance company is responsible for paying the policy benefits to the beneficiary as a lump sum or in instalments based on the contract agreement.

In addition to Islamic banking, which has developed rapidly in Indonesia, Islamic insurance is also gaining popularity amongst the public. Islamic insurance was first established in Indonesia in 1994 with the formation of PT Syarikat Takaful Indonesia, after the first Islamic bank, Bank Muamalat, was set up. Syarikat Takaful Indonesia was indeed established to strengthen the position of the first Islamic bank in Indonesia because Islamic banking practices inescapably require the services of an insurance company, especially one based on Islamic teachings and principles.

In general, the foundations and main principles of Islamic insurance are similar to other Islamic financial transactions, with *riba, gharar* (uncertainty), and *maysir* (speculation/gambling) as well as *zalim* (cruelty or unjust acts of exploitation) forbidden, which means behaving in such a way that does not harm or exploit another person in pursuit of personal gain.

Islamic insurance, known as *takaful* in Arabic, is based on the main principle of mutual solidarity and cooperation as well as risk sharing. Future potential risks are shared by all insured participants based on a cooperative system of reimbursement. Therefore, insurance companies do not bear the risk of the insured as in the case of conventional insurance yet are limited to act as the manager of insurance funds.

In Islamic insurance, the participants are required to pay a premium; however, the insurance company cannot use those premiums as a source of funds. The premiums are used as a contribution for mutual risk sharing among the participants. The sources of funds for insurance companies are discussed in more detail in subsequent paragraphs. The operational activities of Islamic insurance are based on a unique mechanism that differs significantly from conventional insurance.

Premium payments by insurance participants are divided into two types of contract, namely voluntary/social contracts based on donations and *mudharabah* contracts. *Ta'awun* premiums are a contribution made by the participants to share their mutual risk. In the event an insured participant experiences loss or damage, the claim is paid from the pooled premium fund. In addition, the pool of funds may also be allocated to pay a fee or *ujroh* for the insurance management services provided by the insurance company. *Ujroh* is recognised as insurance company revenue. In addition to the premium fund used to compensate losses experienced by the participants, the premium fund can also be used for business activities or investment based on a *mudharabah* contract. Nevertheless, the premium cannot be repaid to a participant upon leaving the insurance partnership.

By using a *mudharabah* contract, the insurance company is permitted to channel *mudharabah* premium funds to business activity in the real sector or invest in the real sector or financial sector in pursuit of profit. Any proceeds are recognised as a source of insurance company funds. In addition, insurance participants will also receive a share of the profits realised from the business activity. Funds paid to a *mudharabah* contract are returned to the participant upon leaving the insurance partnership.

2. **Pawnbrokers**

   In general, pawnbroking activity includes transactions to obtain sources of funds by pledging assets as security. Pawnbroking regulations in Indonesia are based on Government Regulation Number 10 of 1990, dated 10th April 1990. More than 95% of pawnbroking transactions in Indonesia are performed by a state-owned enterprise (BUMN) known as Perusahaan Umum (Perum) Pegadaian. The core activity is extending loans to customers who have pledged personal effects, typically in the form of gold, jewellery, vehicles, and electronic devices, as security on the loan. In addition, however, pawnbrokers also offer the following services:

   (a) **Disbursing Loans**

   The loans disbursed by Perum Pegadaian consist of consumer loans and productive loans. Consumer loans are extended to customers as employees with a fixed monthly salary, thus allowing the repayments to be deducted at source from the monthly salary. Consumer loans are not restricted to the purchase of a specific object. Meanwhile, productive loans are used to develop a project based on a cooperation agreement with the proceeds shared between the pawnbroker and customer.

(b) **Appraisal Services**

In addition to extending credit secured using personal effects, Perum Pegadaian also offers appraisal services concerning the validity, authenticity, and quality of the property; the actual value of the property; total price of the property and selling price. A fee is charged to the customer for such services.

(c) **Safe Deposit Box Facilities**

This facility is available to customers who feel uncomfortable leaving valuable items in an empty house due to travel plans. For a fee based on value and duration, customers can secure such items in a safe deposit box.

(d) **Gold Counter Galeri 24**

As the name suggests, the Gold Counter is a jewellery store, specialising in gold, silver, gems, and others, owned by Perum Pegadaian. The authenticity and quality of the precious metals sold are guaranteed.

Similar to other financial institutions, Islamic pawnbrokers already exist in Indonesia. Ulema permit *rahn* based on a hadith that *Rasulullah* bought food on credit from a Jew and gave His steel armour as collateral towards the seller. In Indonesia, *rahn* is permissible based on DSN-MUI Fatwa Number 25/DSN-MUI/III/2002, dated 26th June 2002, which clarifies that *rahn* transactions are permitted.

Islamic pawnbroking offers an alternative source of funds to banking. The advantage of pawnbroking over banking is that pawnbrokers can facilitate smaller sources of funds over shorter tenors than the banking industry. In addition, the return period is not specifically stated, with repayment based on the customer's capacity. Upon maturity, if the customer is unable to repay the loan, an extension fee is another option. Therefore, pawnbroking is more reliable and affordable to those towards the bottom of the pyramid.

The goals of Islamic pawnbroking are as follows:

(a) Help members of the community obtain loans based on less burdensome requirements.
(b) Protect the community from loan sharks that charge exorbitant interest rates.
(c) Avoid illegal pawnbroking practices, informal loans, and other dangerous lending practices.
(d) Implement government economic policies and programs by providing funding based on *rahn* contracts.

In practice, Islamic pawnbroking does not charge interest to the customer for profit. An administration fee or *ujroh* is charged, however, along with a safe deposit box fee.

3. **Mutual Funds**

The mutual fund industry comprises nonbank financial institutions with a primary focus on portfolio investment. The mutual fund mechanism is attractive, especially for ordinary people without adequate resources to transact in the capital market in terms of available time, funds, or knowledge concerning the capital market and money market. Mutual fund companies collect funds from investors, which are managed by an investment manager and invested in various types of portfolio in the capital market and money market. In Indonesia, supervision of the mutual funds industry was the preserve of the Capital Market and Financial Institution Supervisory Agency (Bapepam-LK) until 2012, when the function was transferred to the Financial Services Authority (OJK).

Mutual funds benefit from the following advantages:

(a) Diverse investment portfolios. Funds raised through mutual funds can be channelled to various investment portfolios in the money market and capital market.
(b) Members of the public can diversify investment portfolios in the money market and capital market without in-depth or comprehensive knowledge.
(c) Lower transaction costs due to large transactions.

Islamic mutual funds are present in Indonesia, with the first Islamic mutual fund product issued in 1997, known as Danareksa Syariah, by the Capital Market and Financial Institution Supervisory Agency (Bapepam-LK) as a safe investment platform for Muslims in accordance with sharia law. In general, the mechanism of Islamic mutual funds is the same as conventional mutual funds. The only difference is that the instruments must be issued in accordance with Islamic principles, not contain *riba* and avoid speculation. Islamic mutual funds have a number of advantages over conventional funds as follows:

(a) Income from Islamic mutual funds is set aside and channelled to *zakat maal.*
(b) Investment is restricted to sharia-compliant instruments.
(c) The Sharia Supervisory Board (DPS) maintains sharia compliance in Islamic mutual fund practices.

The vision and goals of Islamic mutual funds are to grow asset value in the long term, thus generating sustainable income in accordance with Islamic principles.

4. **Pension Funds**

The pension funds industry consists of financial institutions that collect and manage a portion of income throughout the working life to provide retirement income. Pension funds fall under two categories based on ownership, namely government (public) pension funds and private pension funds. Based on implementation, however, pension funds consist of the following:

(a) Financial Institution Pension Funds (FIPF), namely a pension fund founded and managed by a financial institution, specifically a bank or insurance company, which is available to employees and independent workers. Specific to employees, this type of pension fund can be combined with an independent corporate pension fund program.
(b) Employer Pension Funds, namely a pension fund founded and managed by an employer to provide retirement funds for the employees. This is usually done by the employer.

(c) Benefit-based Pension Fund, namely a pension fund managed by an employer, where participation is limited and tied to the employer's profit.

In addition to conventional pension fund practices, Islamic pension funds are becoming more popular. Islamic pension funds are managed in accordance with Islamic principles and rules to maintain welfare in retirement. FIPF continue to dominate Islamic pension funds in Indonesia, managed by the following financial institutions: Bank Muamalat Indonesia, Allianz, and Manulife.

5. **Finance Companies**

The main activity of finance companies is to provide financing in the form of cash or capital goods. Nevertheless, the source of funds allocated to financing is not collected directly from individuals through deposits. Finance companies consist of the following types:

(a) **Consumer Finance Company**. The core activity of a consumer finance company is disbursing financing for the purchase of goods as required by the customer, with repayment in instalments.
(b) **Leasing**. Leasing involves two parties, namely the lessee and lessor. In practice, leasing is an agreement where the lessee utilises an asset leased by the lessor at a specific lease rate over a predetermined period. Common assets that are leased include real estate, other property, vehicles, and other equipment.
(c) **Factoring**. Factoring is a financial transaction in which a business sells a portion of its accounts receivable to a third party (known as a factor). Once the Accounts Receivable have been purchased, all claims are taken over by the factor.

In addition to conventional finance companies, Islamic finance companies have emerged in Indonesia. Islamic finance companies undertake similar core activities as conventional finance companies yet are based on Islamic principles as guidelines in accordance with sharia law. Islamic finance companies use specific contracts permitted in Islam in their operating activities. Similar to other Islamic financial institutions, Islamic finance companies must have a Sharia Supervisory Board (DPS) to maintain all activities and practices within the corridor of Islamic law and principles.

6. **Microfinance Institutions**

Microfinance institutions have a different type of urgency than only disbursing financing and loans to micro enterprises. The goal of microfinance institutions is local economic empowerment and independence. To that end, microfinance institutions provide public consultancy services to improve specific useful skills for the development of micro enterprises. Such skills include teamwork, bookkeeping, management, and self-confidence, which will help micro enterprises level up and develop independently.

As the customers of microfinance institutions are micro business owners, the loan procedures, requirements, and approval process are less complicated with smaller transactions and shorter maturities predominating.

Microfinance institutions are categorised based on the level of formality as follows:

(a) Formal microfinance institutions, which are the most formal of the microfinance institutions, legally incorporated by the government. In addition, the operational activities are supervised by the government. Examples of formal microfinance institutions include BRI Unit Desa, Bank Dagang Bali, KURK from East Java, LPD Bali, and others.
(b) Semi-formal microfinance institutions, which are not formed or owned by banks but are legally registered and licensed by the relevant authorities. Examples include the Bank Relationship Development Project with non-governmental groups, Micro Loan Project, as well as village unit and savings and loans cooperatives.
(c) Informal microfinance institutions, which are not formed or owned by banks nor legally registered and licensed by the relevant authorities. Examples include social gatherings involving informal credit and saving schemes (*arisan*).
(d) Islamic Microfinance Institutions are beginning to emerge in Indonesia based on Islamic principles. The goal of Islamic microfinance institutions is to ensure those towards the bottom of the pyramid wishing to start a business or currently starting a business avoid the trap of unscrupulous loan sharks. Examples of Islamic microfinance institutions include cooperatives, non-governmental organisations (NGOs), and *Baitul Maal wa Tamwil.*

7. ***Baitul Maal wa Tamwil***

Baitul Maal wa Tamwil, abbreviated to BMT, is a specific type of Islamic microfinance institution. In addition, BMT is also considered an Islamic cooperative. BMT only conducts financial transactions based on Islamic principles. In Indonesia, the first BMT was established in 1984 in Bandung, namely BMT Teknosa.

BMT performs two core functions based on the name of the institution itself, *baitul mal* and *baitul at-tamwil. Baitul mal* functions to manage social funds, such as *zakat*, *infaq*, and *sadaqah* (ZIS). As a *baitul mal*, BMT is responsible for optimally distributing social funds in accordance with Islamic rules. Meanwhile, *baitul at-tamwil* functions to develop assets through investment or other productive business activities based on Islamic rules. *Baitul at-tamwil* aims to increase economic productivity and quality amongst micro, small, and medium enterprises (MSME) through capital financing.

BMT has the following targets:

(a) Grow and develop productive micro and small enterprises.
(b) Ameliorate the standard of living and quality of life for those towards the bottom of the pyramid.
(c) Alleviate poverty and the inequitable distribution of income.
(d) Increase access to capital for those towards the bottom of the pyramid.

BMT provides equality of opportunity for all social strata to obtain capital from financial institutions. Therefore, not only do large enterprises have easy access to capital from financial institutions, so too do small businesses. In terms of diversity, financial institutions in Indonesia offer a wealth of variety. The task, therefore, is to optimise the practices of such financial institutions.

2.5 Financial Markets and Infrastructures

In short, a financial market is a medium where parties with surplus capital can meet parties with deficit funds to transact. Through this forum, all kinds of financial claims are transacted or traded based on specific methods. In addition, a financial market also facilitates risk management and transformation as well as the addition of capital. Fundamentally, a financial market aims to create and maintain balance regarding the prices of financial instruments.

Based on whether there is an intermediary in the transaction between parties, financial markets can be classified into two types. *First*, a direct financial market has no intermediary, with direct transactions in the capital market, money market, and derivative market. *Second*, an indirect financial market involving an intermediary in the form of a bank or nonbank financial institution.

In addition to conventional financial markets, there are Islamic financial markets. Conceptually, Islamic and conventional financial markets are similar, except Islamic financial markets and practices are based on Islamic values, principles, and teachings that forbid the use of contracts containing elements of *riba, gharar,* and *maysir.* Furthermore, the instruments tradable in Islamic financial markets are halal and permitted in Islam.

In general, Islamic financial markets can also be classified into two types, namely direct and indirect Islamic financial markets. Fundamentally, the understanding of both types of Islamic financial market is equivalent to conventional financial markets despite a subtle difference. Direct Islamic financial markets only recognise the Islamic capital market and Islamic money market. The derivative market is excluded from the Islamic model because derivative market products contain elements of *riba, gharar,* and *maysir*, which are absolutely forbidden in Islam.

2.5.1 Capital Market

A capital market is a forum bringing together parties with surplus capital (investors) and parties needing funds through the trade of securities, primarily in the long term. Stock and bond instruments are traded in capital markets.

A stock is a type of security that indicates the holder has a proportionate ownership in the issuing company. A company must be publicly listed to issue stock (public company). Stocks are issued and subsequently traded through an exchange, including physically (on exchange) and electronically (over the counter).

When a stock is purchased, the buyer automatically has a proportionate ownership in the issuing company. The return on the stock comes from two sources, namely a dividend and a capital gain. A dividend is a sum of money paid by a company to its shareholders out of its profits. A dividend will be paid regularly providing the investor is still a shareholder of the company. Legally, a dividend is paid at the issuing company's discretion, not a fixed interval. Meanwhile, a capital gain is the profit earned on the sale of stock that has increased in value over the holding period. A capital gain is realised when the investor also functions as a stock trader.

On the other hand, a bond is also a type of security that is issued and traded through an exchange, including physically (on exchange) and electronically (over the counter). Bonds can be issued by the government and corporate sector. What differentiates the ownership of a bond or stock is that a bondholder (investor) will receive a debt acknowledgement from the issuer. The issuer is obligated to repay the nominal amount on the maturity date. The yield is the rate of return received in the form of a coupon or discount paid at a regular interval.

Similar to the development of other types of Islamic finance, Islamic capital markets have also flourished. Islamic capital market practices, such as trading securities in the form of Islamic stocks or bonds (sukuk), operate under Islamic principles. Securities based on *riba, maysir,* and *gharar* are strictly forbidden in the Islamic capital market. In addition, predetermined profits agreed upon in advance are not a permitted practice in the Islamic capital market.

The Islamic capital market complies with several principles as follows:

1. Transactions containing *riba, gharar,* or *maysir* are forbidden absolutely.
2. The profit and rate of return on an amount of capital deposited are not predetermined.
3. The flow of investment funds in the form of securities and loans are interest free.
4. Market information is transparent and accessible to all participants (symmetric).

In Indonesia, regulations concerning the Islamic capital market were strengthened by DSN-MUI Fatwa Number40/DSN-MUI/X/2003, dated 4th October 2003, concerning the Capital Market and General Application Guidelines for Sharia Principles in the Capital Market. The fatwa regulates the investment product requirements necessary for sharia-compliant status as follows:

1. Transactions must not contain the following elements:

   (a) Prohibited under Islam, namely *riba, maysir, gharar,* and *zhulm*, which in practice include insider trading, *bay al-ma'dun* and *bay najashy*.
   (b) Investing in companies with a larger debt owed to conventional financial institutions than capital at the time of transaction.
   (c) Margin trading and *ihtikar* (hoarding).
   (d) Disseminate misinformation to gain from a transaction.

2. The business, commodity, and/or service must not be forbidden according to Islam as follows:

    (a) Conventional bank and nonbank financial institutions associated with *ribawi* items.
    (b) Producers, distributors, and sellers of haram food and beverages, including pork, animals with fangs and birds of prey as well as alcoholic (*khamr*) beverages.
    (c) Producers, distributors, and sellers of goods/services to the detriment of mankind, for example cigarettes.
    (d) Gambling businesses or any games that contain gambling.

    Islamic capital market instruments include the following:

1. **Islamic Shares**

    Islamic shares must not contain elements of speculation, *gharar* and *riba*. In addition, an Islamic securities company must comply with specific requirements for Islamic stock status. The following companies cannot be categorised as Islamic securities companies (ISRA, 2015):

    (a) *Ribawi* financial institutions, namely banks and nonbank financial institutions operating using interest-based instruments (*riba*).
    (b) Selling goods or services forbidden under sharia law, for example pork, alcohol, and prostitution as well as brokers trading in violation of Islamic principles.
    (c) *Maysir* practices, such as gambling, lottery, and casino games.
    (d) Producers and distributors of tobacco because tobacco is a raw material of cigarettes.

In addition to the businesses outlined above, there are several types of business which remain the topic of debate concerning compliance with sharia law as follows:

    (a) Entertainment that could potentially contain elements forbidden in Islam, for example hotels, cinema, and karaoke.
    (b) Weapons and defence.

2. **Islamic Bonds or Sukuk**

    A sukuk is a direct asset ownership interest of an underlying asset. The return is a lease payment or profit sharing of the underlying asset. Meanwhile, the principal payment stems from the sale of the ownership rights of the sukuk asset. Sukuk are divided into two classifications based on issuer, namely government sukuk, or Government Sharia Securities (SBSN), and corporate sukuk.

    SBSN were launched in 2008. For the government, SBSN represent a source of funds to develop public infrastructure projects. On the other hand, corporate sukuk are issued by private companies to bolster capital.

3. **Islamic Mutual Funds**
   Conventional mutual funds remain the benchmark for Islamic mutual funds. Notwithstanding, the foundation of sharia-compliant mutual funds refers to Islamic principles. Transactions between investors (*shohibul maal*) and investment managers (*mudharib*) are based on *mudharabah* contracts with investment managers permitted to allocate the investment funds only to Islamic securities.

2.5.2 Money Market

The money market functions to bring together investors to execute business activities through primarily short-term financing mechanisms dominated by financial institutions. Securities in the money market are traded electronically or over the counter. Money market instruments include repurchase agreements, commercial papers, and promissory notes. The money market is also used to invest as project financing in the short term, providing capital to companies requiring quick access to funding sources for projects.

Recently, the Islamic money market has also become more established as a means to trade short-term Islamic financial instruments in accordance with Islamic principles. In general, the Islamic money market has the same concepts and goals as the conventional money market, yet with different contracts used and instruments traded.

The Islamic money market plays an important role as facilitator of Islamic financial institutions, particularly Islamic banks, to develop portfolios and funding sources in the near term. Islamic financial institutions focus on short-term funding for the following reasons:

1. Short-term investment is required to contain liquidity risk in the event of unexpected customer fund withdrawals and to anticipate the risk of loss in long-term projects.
2. Through short-term investments, customer funds are not idle. Furthermore, the return is realised within a short period, allowing the bank to grant a bonus to the customer in the form of a reward.
3. Most funds collected by banks are short term in nature. Therefore, banks use short-term instruments to manage such funds considering the funds could potentially be withdrawn in relatively short order.

In Indonesia, Islamic money market instruments consist of two broad categories as follows:

1. Sharia Interbank Money Market (PUAS), as a source of short-term funds between Islamic banks used to meet liquidity obligations.
2. Bank Indonesia Sharia Securities (SBIS), previously known as Bank Indonesia Wadi'ah Certificates (SWBI). SWBI were based on *wadi'ah* contracts and available daily. SBIS are based on *jualah* (auction) contracts with a maturity of one month and weekly auctions.

2.5.3 Foreign Exchange and Derivatives Markets

The foreign exchange (forex) market is an over-the-counter (electronic) market for the trading of currencies. The market facilitates unrestricted buyers and sellers in terms of scope and time. The global decentralised nature implies the forex market is the most open and efficient. It is also the largest and most liquid, facilitating spot, forward, future, and swap transactions. The Islamic perspective of the foreign exchange market is elucidated in DSN-MUI Fatwa Number 28/DSN-MUI/III/2002 concerning the Trading of Currencies (*Al-Sharf*). In Islam, spot transactions in the foreign exchange markets are permitted.

Meanwhile, the derivatives market is the financial market for derivatives of stocks, bonds, term deposits, loans, and foreign currencies. The derivatives market fluctuates in response to the corresponding underlying asset. Derivatives are traded physically (on exchange) and electronically (over the counter), yet with rapid technological advancement OTC trading has become dominant. As derivative markets have developed, speculation has increased. In fact, issues in the derivatives market in 2007 prompted the subprime mortgage debacle in the United States, which spread rapidly into a severe global crisis.

According to Islamic teaching, the derivatives market is forbidden due to elements considered haram in Islam, such as *riba* and *gharar*. In addition, *maysir,* or speculative trading, is a primary characteristic of the derivatives market. Meanwhile, it has been shown that the derivatives market has an adverse effect on the overall financial system, as evidenced by the global financial crisis in 2007–2008, which was triggered by issues in the derivatives market.

2.5.4 Financial System Infrastructure

Financial system infrastructure is the entire underlying foundation supporting the financial system to enable an orderly and stable function, including the institutions, regulations, standards, networks, technology, and information in the financial sector. The quality of infrastructure influences financial system efficiency and risk management effectiveness. In the Islamic financial system, financial infrastructure maintains sustainability, nurtures the development process, fosters Islamic financial system globalisation, and stimulates rapid growth of the financial services industry, while supporting intermediation and Islamic financial markets. Thus far, Islamic infrastructure remains a duplicate of conventional financial infrastructure with some specific characteristics, including the Sharia Supervisory Board (DPS), Sharia Arbitration Board, and Associations of Islamic Finance.

Islamic financial infrastructure is categorised as hard infrastructure and soft infrastructure. Hard infrastructure includes the supporting physical infrastructure, including specific bodies and institutions, while soft infrastructure pertains to governance. What is considered hard or soft infrastructure is explained in the following subsections:

Hard Infrastructure

Before discussing infrastructure specific to the Islamic financial system, the discussion focuses more broadly on the infrastructure featured generally in financial systems, both conventional and Islamic as follows:

1. **Authorities**
   The highest regulatory and supervisory institution for the overall financial system.
2. **Regulation**
   Rules and standards formulated by the authorities to discharge the function as overall financial system regulator and supervisor.
3. **Exchange**
   An organised market where tradable securities are bought and sold via the capital market, including stocks and bonds/sukuk.
4. **Custodian**
   A specialised financial institution responsible for maintaining and safeguarding physical and electronic securities transaction activity.
5. **Guarantee Institution**
   A specialised financial institution responsible for protecting against risk of loss among market participants.

Hard infrastructure specific to the Islamic financial system is categorised as national or international. Hard infrastructure at the national level in Indonesia is described as follows:

1. **Sharia Supervisory Board (DPS)**
   An autonomous institution independent of government or private sector interference formed by the Indonesian Council of Ulama (MUI). DPS is present in every Islamic financial institution to create and maintain sharia compliance. The status of DPS is bolstered by the regulatory support of Bank Indonesia Regulation (PBI) Number 6 of 2004, Article 27.
2. **National Sharia Arbitration Board (BASYARNAS)**
   An autonomous and independent institution mandated with mediation and dispute settlement between transacting parties in a financial institution.
3. **Accounting Standards Board**
   An institution responsible for formulating and setting accounting standards in accordance with Islamic principles. In Indonesia, the Institute of Indonesian Chartered Accountants (IAI) serves this role through Financial Accounting Standards (SAK).
4. **Islamic Financial Associations**
   An association of similar players in the financial industry, for example the Indonesia Sharia Bank Association (ASBISINDO), Indonesia Sharia Insurance Association (AASI), Indonesia BMT Association (ASBINDO) as well as the Indonesia Sharia Accounting and Finance Association (AAKSI).

5. **Professional Certification Institute (LSP)**
   An institution authorised to certify certain professions. Professional certification strengthens the competitiveness of the Islamic finance industry in terms of HR quality.
6. **HR Capacity Building Institutions**
   Institutions established to mould competent human resources for the Islamic finance industry, able to compete with human resources in the conventional financial industry, namely the International Centre for Development in Islamic Finance—Indonesia Banking Development Institute (ICDIF-LPPI).

Meanwhile, hard infrastructure at the international level is described as follows:

1. **Islamic Development Bank (IDB)**
   IDB was established in 1975 by the Organisation of the Islamic Conference (OIC). IDB is a multilateral development bank (MDB), with a focus on quality social and economic development in member countries and Muslim communities worldwide, delivering impact at scale. Towards the achievement of that goal, IDB actively implements the following activities:

   (a) Providing capital through sustainable and long-term financing structures for development projects in member countries.
   (b) Managing funds to help other Muslim communities outside IDB member countries.
   (c) Providing education and financial training to member countries towards self-determination and socio-economic sovereignty.
   (d) Fostering international trade among member countries to help promote international trade products.
   (e) Providing training and education to member countries concerning development activities in accordance with Islamic principles.

2. **Accounting and Auditing Organisation for Islamic Financial Institutions (AAOIFI)**
   Established in 1991 and based in Bahrain, AAOIFI is the leading international not-for-profit organisation primarily responsible for development and issuance of accounting and financial standards for the global Islamic finance industry.
3. **Islamic Financial Services Board (IFSB)**
   IFSB serves as an international standard-setting body of regulatory and supervisory agencies that have a vested interest in ensuring the soundness and stability of the Islamic financial services industry. IFSB members consist of financial institution stakeholders, including regulatory and supervisory authorities (central banks) and representatives of financial institutions.
4. **International Islamic Financial Market (IIFM)**
   IIFM was established based on the collective initiative of Indonesia, Malaysia, Sudan, Brunei Darussalam, and Bahrain in conjunction with IDB. IIFM implements the following core tasks:

(a) Deepening the Islamic capital market and money market.
(b) Focusing on standardisation and developing Islamic financial structures, instruments/products, contracts, and infrastructure.
(c) Formulating guidelines and increasing cooperation between Islamic financial institutions.
(d) Creating secondary markets for Islamic financial instruments/products.

5. **Islamic International Rating Agency (IIRA)**

   IIRA is an independent institution with two goals and a primary vision. *First*, to be a credit rating role model and reference in Islamic finance. *Second*, to nurture financial markets at the regional level by disseminating entity profiles as a basis for investment decision-making.
6. **Islamic Development Bank Institute (IsDB)**

   Established in 1981 as the Islamic Research and Training Institute (IRTI), the Institute was renamed in April 2021 as the IsDB Institute with three core tasks to advance Islamic economics and finance worldwide. *First*, perform pioneering research relating to issues in the Islamic economy, finance, and banking to develop models and applications based on Islamic principles. *Second*, provide training to stakeholders or agents of development in member countries to achieve equitable economic development. Third, provide information services as required to advance the Islamic economy, finance, and banking.
7. **General Council for Islamic Banks and Financial Institutions (CIBAFI)**

   CIBAFI is an international non-profit organisation founded in 2001 by the Islamic Development Bank (IDB) located in Bahrain. The main task of CIBAFI is to develop and accelerate promotional and branding activities for the Islamic financial services industry, including financial institutions and instruments/products.
8. **Training and Education Centres**

   Institutions that provide training and education for staff and stakeholders connected with the Islamic financial services industry to build the capacity and quality of human resources (HR) in the industry. Each jurisdiction has its own Training and Education Centres.
9. **International Islamic Liquidity Management Corporation (IILM)**

   Established on 25th October 2010, headquartered in Kuala Lumpur, Malaysia, and with diverse membership comprising central banks, monetary authorities, and financial institutions, IILM is an international organisation established by central banks and a multilateral organisation to create and issue sharia-compliant financial instruments and facilitate effective cross-border Islamic liquidity management. IILM provides short-term Islamic financial instruments/products with maturities of 3 to 6 months.
10. **International Islamic Centre for Reconciliation and Commercial Arbitration (IICRA)**

    Similar to the National Sharia Arbitration Board (BASYARNAS) in Indonesia, IICRA was established in the United Arab Emirates in 2004 as an independent international non-profit organisation.

11. **Liquidity Management Centre (LMC)**
    Incorporated in July 2002 in Bahrain, LMC plays an active role providing short-term sharia-compliant investment instruments to financial institutions to deepen the interbank money market internationally.

Soft Infrastructure
Without a physical presence, soft infrastructure is financial system governance, from management to regulation. According to Simorangkir (2014), soft infrastructure consists of five aspects as follows:

1. **Appropriate Regulatory and Supervisory Framework**
   Designed in such a way as to maintain financial system stability, the regulatory and supervisory framework is based on Islamic rules. Regulation and supervision are implemented through various rules governing the Islamic financial system, for example the activities of Islamic financial institutions, the establishment of Islamic financial institutions, issues concerning products and contracts as well as dispute settlement.
2. **Transparent Information**
   Information concerning business activities, financial conditions, performance, and risk management at a financial institution must be transparent to ensure the information can be used to assess, evaluate, and make investment decisions. Qualitative and quantitative information must be accountable, accurate, timely, honest, and relevant as well as easy to use and interpret.
3. **Solid Risk Management Framework**
   The risk management framework covers the policies, procedures, and structures in a financial institution concerning risk management. The framework begins with risk identification, risk assessment, risk mitigation and formulating risk management strategies at conventional and Islamic financial institutions. Risk management at a financial institution must identify, measure, and supervise the risks that may emerge from each transaction in the financial system.
4. **Dynamic and Innovative Sharia Framework**
   The sharia framework covers the regulation, supervision, governance, and processes of operational activities in an Islamic financial institution in order to maintain sharia compliance. Islamic principles and rules (*Al-Qur'an, Hadiths,* and *Ijtihad*) underlie formulation of the sharia framework. Islamic principles do not impede or curtail the innovation of Islamic financial products/instruments, instead providing impetus for innovation and creation to advance a contemporary and dynamic Islamic financial system in the era of technology. The opportunity to innovate Islamic financial products remains massive considering that the legal foundation of Islamic jurisprudence is *mubah* (permitted), providing there is no legal justification against it. This implies that more types of financial transaction are permitted in Islam than those that are forbidden.
5. **Effective Corporate Governance**
   Corporate governance covers the procedures and methods by which a financial institution is regulated and managed by senior management. Corporate governance pervades every aspect and every individual of the institution. Effective

corporate governance leads to good governance in the financial system, which is important to maintain public trust in financial institutions and the financial system as a whole. Without good corporate governance, public trust in financial institutions will be eroded, leading to issues in the financial system, for example liquidity shortfalls.

The Role of Digitalisation to Accelerate Islamic Social Finance

1. Background

   As a developing country with a large population, poverty is still an issue in Indonesia. The changes in Indonesia's poverty rate between March 2019 and September 2022. Based on that data, it is known that during the Covid-19 pandemic, there was an increase of poor people in Indonesia. As of September 2022, the rural poverty rate has decreased back to the pre-pandemic level. In contrast, the poverty rate in urban areas has not dropped to the pre-pandemic level. The total number of poor people in rural and urban areas in September 2022 was 26.36 million people. This means that 9.57% of Indonesians have an average monthly per capita expenditure below the poverty line. In addition, the disparity between poor people in urban and rural areas is also high.

   Limited aid funds mobilisation for underprivileged community is one of the factors that cause high poverty, though it is needed in order to maximise distribution and redistribution of wealth so as to improve welfare. Low financial literacy could also affect a person's financial wellness (Zhang & Chatterjee, 2023). Digitalisation can be used to address the causes of poverty. Rahayu et al. stated that technology can effectively improve financial literacy. Rosele et al. also reported that digitalisation is needed to improve the effectiveness of collecting and distributing aid to the poor.

   Thus far, with Covid-19 pandemic as a catalyst, digital finance has developed rapidly. Digitalisation brings several benefits for companies such as financial performance improvement, increased resilience to external shocks, and increased risk-taking behaviour. Furthermore, scholars are also confirming the driving effect of digitalisation, in particular digital finance, on economic growth. In addition to its impact on companies and macroeconomics, digitalisation could also have a positive impact on Islamic Social Finance (ISF). At brief, ISF, e.g. zakah, infaq, alms, and waqf, is a finance based on Islamic principle that aims to promote inclusive welfare.

   Digitalisation to the end has increased the scope of ISF and further optimise its potential. Correlation between digitalisation and financial inclusion has been reported by Aziz et al. Mohd Nor et al. argue that the usage of technology such as blockchain could support ISF if there is a proper socialisation and education. Following the same spirit, the enthusiasm of Muslim to implement digitalisation within ISF is already reported by Usman et al. Moreover, it is explained that digitalisation has an important role in reducing unbanked people by providing accessibility, which could ease the ISF funds collection. This remarkable potential could be attained for developing countries if it is implemented accordingly.

On the broader view, ISF digitalisation carries both benefits and drawbacks within its implementation. ISF brings solution for socio-economic problem. For instance, zakah could alleviate inequality by increasing purchasing power of mustahiq. Furthermore, the underutilised ISF potential, followed by most Muslim population creates a potential for ISF development in Indonesia. However, there will be a high upfront investment cost to implement such technology. Besides, digitalisation means exposure to cyberattack, which becomes a threat in managing ISF fund.

Despite numerous studies that discuss about ISF, to the best of my knowledge, there are few studies that further assess ISF as a whole. Several studies only focus on waqf implementation (Ari & Koc, 2021; Darus et al., 2017) and zakah performance (Ammani et al., 2014; Hayeeharasah et al., 2013). Moreover, to the best of my knowledge, there is no study that further assesses digitalisation on ISF. One study that shares some similarities came from Usman et al. However, their study only covers the willingness to use fintech in the context of Islamic philanthropy, not a further strategy for ISF digitalisation.

(a) Islamic Social Finance Digitalisation: Benefits and Drawbacks

Due to the nature of digitalisation, it is obvious that digitalisation encourages financial inclusion. Moreover, ISF aims to alleviate poverty and inequality, which is commonly found within rural and remote area. To that end, digitalisation is amplifying ISF in terms of financial inclusion and poverty/inequality alleviation. In addition, digitalisation is radically changing the business process, including in financial sector, to become more transparent, efficient, and effective.

In analysing opportunities, the impact of digitalisation could be amplified by the abundant Muslim population. This is because Indonesia is considered as the most Muslim population country worldwide. Furthermore, ISF has gained a traction from numerous scholars, which is expected to ease ISF digitalisation. Last but not least, Indonesia has a great potential of zakah utilisation. In 2021, the total combined potency of zakah and waqf is amounting to 500 trillion IDR or equal to 32 billion USD. As for comparison, these amounts are equal to half of 2021 Indonesia's GDP.

However, digitalisation brings several consequences. Despite these benefits, implementing digital ISF requires a high investment cost. This includes but not limited to brand new infrastructure, IT helpdesk, server, and so on. Aside from this, digitalisation raises cyberattack issues, thus consumers worry about companies using their data for commercial purposes without consent. As data are being increasingly commoditised, some institutions may see this as an opportunity to exploit user data, and expecting them to ignore it. Turning to legal issue, since digitalisation is considered as a new thing for several countries, their legal framework has not been created. Following der Meulen, 81 percent of legal departments are unprepared for digitalisation. To that end, cost related to legal construction is considered due to the massive reformation within legal framework.

Following the same spirits, digitalisation has several inherent risks. Since digitalisation is closely related to internet, risk of cyberattack is imminent. The same goes with energy resources, digitalisation is heavily relying on electrical sources, which implies that electrical outage will disrupt its operation. Adding a relevancy, digitalisation demands a well-structured internet coverage area to become optimal. Meanwhile, Indonesia is considered as an archipelago country, which there will be numerous remote areas that may not be covered by internet. To that end, digital divide becomes an inherent risk for ISF digitalisation.

(b) The Role of Technology on Islamic Social Finance Digitalisation

Generally speaking, the application of digital technology is aligned with the objectives and principles of ISF act in Indonesia. The nature of digital technology that can induce efficiency, transparency, redundancy avoidance, and access widening is symmetrical with the objective of zakah act that aims to increase efficiency and effectivity of ISF operation and services as well as enlarge the impact of ISF for poverty alleviation and public welfare. Adopting Lai et al. and OECD, alternatives financial technologies that will be analysed in this study are artificial intelligence (AI), blockchains, cloud computing, big data, QR code, and digital platform.

(i) Artificial Intelligence (AI)

Briefly stated, AI is a computer-based system that performs activities that generally require intelligence. The use of AI could overcome system-related vulnerability in a much better and faster way than human. AI is modelled around some algorithms that can better tackle cybersecurity, providing greater value to customers, improving employee productivity, and so on. Algorithm itself is a series of actions to solve problems. The approach to creating algorithms that automatically improve through experience and without significant human intervention is called machine learning, which falls under the sub-category of AI. Machine learning can be used to reveal patterns in large and diverse data.

Following Sarea et al., AI is useful in Islamic finance industry due to the development of information technology for automating processes. This technology is able to support the formation of new business models in the form of financial service automation. The role of AI in finance industry is generally divided into five types, namely predictive analysis, natural language processing (NLP) to understand human language, image recognition, and anomaly detection in transactions. With NLP, it is no longer necessary to physically visit an office because virtual services are already available. Hence, the existence of AI will drive the evolution of business.

Recently, several examples have emerged in the Islamic finance sector, such as online Islamic banking, Islamic insurance (e-Takaful), charity sector, endowment (e-Waqf), Islamic levy (e-Zakah), and other

Islamic financial institutions across Muslim and non-Muslim countries. Another application in non-profit is to improve fundraising by using AI and machine learning. Essentially, AI is capable of providing a more in-depth understanding of data patterns. By factoring in unique relationships with each supporter, AI could predict likely behaviours down to the individual level. Then, these insights will be used to improve fundraising, in this context zakah, infaq, sadaqah, and waqf, through smarter segmentation. Referring to the previous explanation, it is known that the benefits offered by AI are in line with the goals of ISF, therefore it is possible for AI to supports the application of Islamic principles.

Eligible zakah receiver should provide evidence of their needs (proof of need) in the form of text or media. The system then uses machine learning, natural language processing (NLP), and digital image processing to analyse the information. The system will go through a verification process to ensure that the needs meet the eligibility criteria, then it will be classified into appropriate categories. Once verified, *muzakki* can view the proof of needs information and select zakah receiver they wish to support from the dashboard. AI is utilised to suggest potential zakah receiver based on the *muzakki*'s past support history. *Muzakki* have the option to transfer funds directly to the chosen zakah receiver or if the zakah receiver does not have a linked bank account with the platform, the zakah platform will receive the funds and it will be delivered by the zakah platform's representative to the chosen beneficiary.

(ii) Blockchain

Blockchain is a sequence of blocks, which holds a list of completed transaction records like conventional public ledger. Following Zheng et al., blockchain is immutable, which means that transaction data cannot be tampered once it's packed into the blockchain. Businesses that require high reliability and honesty can use blockchain to attract customers. Moreover, blockchain is distributed so as to avoid single point of failure situations. Transactions on blockchain are executed based on smart contract rules. As for smart contract, it could be executed by miners automatically once the contract has been deployed on the blockchain.

In the context of ISF, when the waqf institution conducts fundraising through the blockchain system, the waqf institution will issue a smart contract containing rules about waqf projects to be carried out. The smart contract must be approved in advance by the waqf authority. Once approved, the smart contract will be placed in the waqf blockchain system. *Waqif* who have registered in the wakaf blockchain ecosystem can choose the desired waqf project and then the waqf money will be forwarded to the waqf institution through a fund manager to be managed. All stages in the wakaf blockchain can be seen by anyone in the ecosystem, so that the implementation of the principles of accountability and transparency will be better maintained.

The best practice in managing waqf fund by using blockchain technology is coming from Finterra company. Finterra is one of the tech start-up companies headquartered in Singapore, they have been developing blockchain technology for managing waqf funds based on crowdfunding system. In utilising blockchain technology, Finterra creates a waqf chain platform where there are several parties involved in the ecosystem of the chain, namely, platform providers, waqf institutions, waqf authority, and donors. All parties must be registered and have access to the platform. Other service offered by Finterra is blockchain consulting, such as token, software, and blockchain system development.

Other implementation of blockchain in crowdfunding can be done by connecting all stakeholders in one blockchain platform that uses a cryptocurrency called CharityCoin (CC) as a medium of exchange. These coins could be bought using either fiat money or cryptocurrency. The stakeholders in the blockchain network consist of donors, beneficiaries with wallet, and organisation as the intermediary for donations directed for beneficiaries without wallet. Beneficiaries with wallet are beneficiaries who regularly receive a specific amount of donations, such as a government-owned welfare institutions and religious charities. Beneficiaries without wallet are parties who only need help at certain times, such as during a natural disaster. In this case, an example of an organisation that delivers funds to beneficiaries without wallet is a non-profit organisation. The benefits of blockchain-based crowdfunding are donors can track their donations easily through mobile application or website, transactions cannot be changed, only the government as a supervisor could monitor transactions on the platform, and the cash flow of CharityCoin is self-sustainable by using exchange fee, transaction fee, and smart contract deployment fee which is a fixed percentage of donations raised through the contract.

Donors could donate in two ways. First, donors donate CharityCoin directly to beneficiaries with wallets, after a successful transaction is recorded in the block, donors will receive a token which contains a successful transaction message. The second way is donors donate CharityCoin to the registered organisation, then the organisation will exchange CharityCoin into fiat money to be given to people in need who do not have a cryptocurrency wallet. After the money is given, the donor will receive a token in the form of a successful transaction message along with an image or scanned receipt as a proof.

(iii) Cloud Computing

Following Qian et al., cloud computing is a kind of computing technique where IT services are provided by massive low-cost computing units connected by IP networks. Similarly, according to the

Regulation of The Ministry of Communication and Informatics of the Republic of Indonesia Number 5 of 2000 regarding Private Scope Electronic System Providers, cloud computing is a model that provides network access to a shared set of configurable computing resource such as networks, servers, storage, application, and services. Cloud computing possesses characteristics of easy to use, distributed, and on-demand. Moreover, it can be provisioned rapidly with a minimal management and services.

Three types of services provided in cloud computing are Infrastructure as a Service (IaaS), Platform as a Service (PaaS), and Software as a Service (SaaS). Companies that do not have enough computing resources can use IaaS which offers storage, server, and network services that are available online. Some of IaaS providers are Microsoft Azure, IBM Softlayer, and Google Compute Engine. Following, PaaS offers a platform or environment that allows developers to build, test, launch, and manage applications using a built-in software components, thus eliminating the cost of purchasing software licenses, infrastructure, and other resources. Examples of PaaS providers are Microsoft Azure, IBM Bluemix, and Google App Engine.

SaaS offers services in the form of applications or software that can be accessed through a website without having to do any installation, such as Dropbox to store data, G Suite to improve the productivity of company activities, social media, namely Instagram, Facebook, and so on. SaaS advantages compared to building an application on PaaS are more efficient, affordable, and practical because SaaS provides an application that has met the user's needs. For instance, if a business owner would like to simplify his business management, he can use applications such as enterprise resource planning (ERP), customer relationship management (CRM), warehouse management and these applications are also customisable according to user needs.

Cloud computing services often utilise a multi-tenancy system in which tenants who have similar needs will share system software. This makes cloud computing services more affordable, as explained by Usman et al., who stated that implementing cloud computing technology could further develop ISF with economies of scale. In the context of ISF, economies of scale means that the increase of funds collected is not followed by an increase in cost for cloud computing technology, because cloud computing has high scalability of IT investment and minimises management cost. In addition, Weaver also argues that enhanced security, increased compliance, improved data management, advanced scalability, and improved sustainability are obtained through cloud computing.

This technology could be implemented for ISF concern. Similar to previous example, Finterra operates using cloud computing to provide cloud-based financial services. This platform uses internet as a centre for managing, storing data, and applications. This technology allows users to gain access to or run programs via computers and internet networks without installation, hence promoting efficiency and practicality.

ISF could use SaaS service for website hosting, implementing customer relationship management to enhance marketing, employing email management to improve marketing effectiveness, and automating accounting records through a cloud-based accounting software that offers integration with popular payment gateways. In addition, ISF can take advantage of using a pre-built platform developed by SaaS providers to accelerate the launch of its application. All of the data generated from platform, finance, and marketing activities will be stored on storage service.

(iv) Big Data

Big data refers to large sets of complex data, both structured and unstructured which traditional processing techniques and/or algorithms are unable to operate on. It aims to reveal hidden patterns and has led to an evolution from a model-driven science paradigm into a data-driven science paradigm. Miskam and Eksan discussed the application of big data for decision-making in Islamic financial institutions. As mentioned earlier, understanding customer habits can help Islamic financial institutions to provide more personalised services to the customers. Big data not only helps to understand the behaviour of customers but also helps to prevent fraud and other financial crimes. Big data is also capable of assisting in auditing, reporting, and compliance issues, which will ultimately reduce overhead cost.

One example of using big data is the integration of zakah report into an agreed zakah management platform to create a national report and database. Mustahik database integration is one of the benefits of a unified and integrated zakah management system which can avoid redundant distribution, prevent inequality disbursement between regions, and become a baseline of performance measurement or policymaking. This aligns with Ahmed statement that the performance of zakah institution to combat poverty hinges on the information exchange, with which the zakah institution can gain trust from the customer and increase its credibility.

It is important to form a web-based national-centred data system that all stakeholders can access to optimise the management of ISF. At present, there is no platform that consolidates data from all ISF instruments in Indonesia. As shown in Fig. 1.5, Islamic Social Finance platform is at the centre, as the source of all ISF's data. The initial phase of big data technology implementation involves collecting and preprocessing data, where information is obtained from the platform and prepared for analysis. The data that has been gathered will be analysed in order to make data-driven decisions such as to pinpoint areas of needs where ISF programs could have the most impact, develop new features or products by identifying customer preferences, improve donation collection by doing targeted marketing campaign, and maximise the impact of ZISWAF funds. Regular evaluation of the Islamic social finance platform's performance will be conducted regularly to enhance its processes over time.

(v) QR (Quick Response) Code

QR (Quick Response) Code is a type of 2D barcode that typically has a square shape and is made up of black data modules on a white background (Shaik, 2021). It is a type of optical tag that is capable of storing various types of data. The data contained in QR code could be decoded quickly and with a high level of speed by scanning it with a machine or with smartphone's camera. The data contained in the QR code can be used to encode files, linking to a website, displaying videos, making mobile payments, and connecting to social network (Jathar et al., 2019). Due to its convenience and swiftness, QR code is quickly being accepted as a means of payment for mobile transactions.

One of the most common uses of QR code in Islamic social finance is for ZISWAF payment. QR code enables more efficient and convenient payment method as users are no longer required to carry cash or manually typed the account numbers. Tagoranao et al. found evidence that by placing QR code in some strategic locations, the waqf and zakah funds collection has increased by six times as a result of the cashless contributions made by individuals through the QR code.

Donors can scan the QR code using mobile banking or e-wallet applications on their mobile phones. Then, information about the bank account of the intended ISF organisation will appear. Donors will transfer the donation money to the organisation's bank account. Next, the app will submit a transfer request to the bank used by the ISF organisation and the money will be sent to the ISF organisation's account. If the money is successfully sent, there will be a notification to the donor that the payment has been successful.

(vi) Digital Platform

A digital platform can be defined as a technological structure that links organisations to the platform, allowing them to gather, combine, and compute information within the platform. It provides an efficient way for businesses to interact with information quickly, decrease information asymmetry, and lower expenses related to searching for resources and conducting transactions. Digital platform allows users to easily access many types of products aggregated in digital platform anytime and anywhere.

Islamic Social Finance platform must adhere to sharia principles in providing. Digital platform in the context of Islamic social finance has made operations, coordination, and consolidation within organisations easier and more efficient. It has also improved communication among donors, partners, and beneficiaries. In addition, digital platform also promotes transparency of ISF and increases donors interest in donating. Donors will give their donations to the platform that can be accessed through a website or mobile application. The donation will be given to the beneficiaries, then the ISF platform will provide a report on the donation to the donors.

One example of using digital platform in the context of Islamic social finance is a crowdfunding platform. Ethis is a world's leading crowdfunding platform that adheres to sharia principles. Ethis enables investors to invest in sustainable projects that have a real impact on society and environment. Fundraising for these projects is done using *mudarabah* and *istisna* contracts.

(vii) Existing Islamic Social Finance Platform

The following information will explain one example of Islamic social finance platform that is currently operating, namely Blossom Finance. It is a platform that offers sukuk investments in sustainable development projects using a sharia-compliant investment model. Blossom Finance partners with Indonesian *Baitul Maal wa Tamwil* (BMT), an Islamic microfinance cooperative that provides free savings accounts and finances underprivileged micro-entrepreneurs who are unable to access conventional banks due to high bank fees and lack of access. A distinctive feature of BMT is its unique customer service which involves visiting their members during convenient hours so the members do not have to spend time away from their businesses. The funds from investors will be used by cooperatives to reduce poverty by funding microbusinesses.

Blossom Finance employs SmartSukuk token, which uses smart contracts on the Ethereum blockchain to standardise and automate the legal, accounting, and payment aspects of conventional sukuk offerings. This token will enhance the efficiency and expand the reach of sukuk issuance on a global scale. SmartSukuk token follows the ERC20 protocol, a widely accepted standard in the industry which enables it to be traded globally on many public cryptocurrency platforms.

Initially, investors invest their capital in the portfolio managed by Gernas, a licensed Indonesian cooperative, under the *Mudaraba* Investment Agreement. In return, investors will receive a monthly profit sharing generated by the portfolio. The portfolio is comprised of at least 125 seasoned asset-backed murabaha financings, so it has lower risk since seasoned financings indicate stable performance over time. As for the profit-sharing ratio (*nisbah*) for investors is between 65% and 80% depending on the tenure selected. Smart contracts are programmed to enforce contract rules regarding payments and transfer of ownership. This means that when the institution makes payments, the smart contract rules will automatically distribute the funds back to the SmartSukuk token holders, eliminating the need for conventional banks or intermediaries.

Next, Gernas channels the investors' capital to verified service providers which have undergone strict scrutiny, review, and approval process by Blossom. Following, the service partners proceed to provide financing to small and micro businesses by purchasing raw materials or equipment using a *murabaha* (cost plus) basis and these assets are added to the portfolio. The service partners then submit reports regarding the portfolio and beneficiaries' performances, as well as the impacts every month to Blossom. After that, Blossom will provide the investor with monthly reports on the performance and impact of their investment. Upon maturity, the portfolio manager is obliged to repay 100% of the invested capital, after subtracting any losses from defaults that were not covered by the gross profits. On the other hand, Blossom will earn between 20% and 35% of the investors' profits depending on the tenure chosen by the investors. Blossom does not profit from any additional payment fees. However, bank transfer and currency exchange fees will be charged by third parties.

References

Ammani, S. A., Abba, S. A., & Dandago, K. I. (2014). Zakah on employment income in Muslim majority states of Nigeria: Any cause for alarm?. International Conference on Accounting Studies, 18–19 August 2014. Kuala Lumpur. *Procedia – Social and Behavioral Sciences, 164*, 305–314.

Ari, I., & Koc, M. (2021). Towards sustainable financing models: A proof-of-concept for a waqf-based alternative financing model for renewable energy investments. *Borsa Istanbul Review, 21*, S46–S56.

Darsono, S. A., Darwis, A., Suryanti, E. T., & Astiyah, S. (2017). *Dinamika Produk dan Akad Keuangan Syariah di Indonesia*. PT RajaGrafindo Persada.

Darsono, S. A., Suryanti, E. T., Astiyah, S., & Darwis, A. (2017). *Masa Depan Keuangan Syariah Indonesia*. Tazkia Publishing dan Bank Indonesia.

Darus, F., Huda, N., Shukri, A., Yusoff, H., Ramli, A., Zain, M. M., & Abu Bakar, A. A. (2017). Empowering social responsibility of Islamic organizations through Waqf. *Research in International Business and Finance, 42*, 959–965.

Hayeeharasah, F., Sehvises, S., & Ropha, H. (2013). The Timeline of Zakah. *Procedia – Social and Behavioral Sciences, 88*, 2–7.

Iqbal, Z., & Mirakhor, A. (2007). *An introduction to Islamic finance: Theory and practice*. Wiley.

ISRA. (2015). *Sistem Keuangan Islam: Prinsip dan Operasi*. International Shari'ah Research Academy for Islamic Finance.

Juhro, S. M., Syarifuddin, F., Sakti, A., & Suryanti, E. T. (2019). *Keuangan Publik dan Sosial Islam: Teori dan Praktik*. PT Rajagrafindo Persada.

Simorangkir, I. (2014). *Pengantar Kebanksentralan: Teori dan Praktik di Indonesia*. PT RajaGrafindo Persada.

Zhang, Y., & Chatterjee, S. (2023). Financial Well-Being in the United States: The roles of financial literacy and financial stress. *Sustainability*, *15*, 4505.

Chapter 3
Philosophical Foundation and Underlying Principles of Islamic Finance

3.1 Introduction

In practice, Islamic finance is based on contracts agreed and approved in accordance with Islamic principles and rules. Contracts of Islamic finance contain several critical elements, including the transacting parties, type of contract, and object of the contract. A contract demonstrates the transfer of an object from one of the transacting parties to another transacting party, or recipient, with legal consequences for the object exchanged between both parties. The object of the contract is the subject that is agreed in the contract, to which contractual law is applied. The object of the contract must be lawful, possible, and ascertainable. The type of contract is the form of the agreement between both transacting parties, with different types of contracts obligating different legal consequences. Based on type, financial transaction contracts can be classified into two categories, namely profit-oriented and social-oriented contracts.

Commercial finance is profit oriented, facilitating trading, leasing, and investing, for example. In Islam, commercial-oriented contracts are known as *tijari*. Commercial finance is evolving as the overall economy becomes more complex. Under sharia law, the commercial finance sector operates in an interest-free environment, instead applying profit and risk sharing principles for capital and sales contracts as a replacement for interest. As public demand for commercial finance products has grown, commercial finance institutions have become more innovative and diverse. The products of Islamic commercial finance are distinguishable based on the underlying contract, namely *mudharabah, musyarakah, murabahah, salam, istishna,* and others.

On the other hand, social finance refers to social-oriented (*ihsan*) financial transactions for mutual benefit (*ta'awun*) rather than profit-oriented contracts. Such transactions do not necessitate an exchange or transfer of ownership of a specific asset. In practice, social finance is facilitated using *tabarru'* contracts, as an inherent part of the Islamic financial system. Social finance has a significant role in the overall

S. M. Juhro et al., *Inclusive Welfare*, https://doi.org/10.1007/978-981-96-0051-9_3

economy through the distribution and allocation of economic resources, the purview of which includes collecting *zakat, infaq, sadaqah,* and *waqf* (ZISWAF) funds. Social finance is the manifestation of Islamic economic system implementation.

The overarching goal of Islamic social finance is to achieve quality welfare for all, particularly from an economic perspective. More specifically, Islamic social finance aims to ameliorate the standard of living amongst those towards the bottom of the pyramid. Consequently, the equitable distribution of income and wealth can be achieved more quickly. Though the equitable distribution and allocation of income will be achieved naturally through market forces, productivity, performance, and the environment, it is undeniable that marginalised communities are plagued by economic inequality and limited economic access. Therefore, social finance is required to improve economic accessibility, particularly for indigent people. In addition, Islamic social finance contributes to strengthening government welfare programs towards equitable prosperity for all. Social finance can minimise the social costs borne by the population, including education, health, transportation, and other social services through the proceeds of non-profit-oriented social investment.

Though several weaknesses persist in the institutional practices of Islamic finance, Islamic financial institutions are expected operate in accordance with Islamic principles.[1] That way, there is greater potential for success in supporting the economy, particularly the monetary sector. Al-Jarhi (2004) found significant monetary policy implications if Islamic banks can avoid interest-based transactions. In addition, proper implementation of Islamic banking will also impact the monetary system, particularly in terms of credit management and development, for example. Credit expansion is meant to be directly proportional to growing demand for assets and commodities, which has a direct correlation with aggregate supply and demand. Therefore, financing disbursed by Islamic financial institutions, such as Islamic banks, will accelerate economic growth and lower inflation. On the other hand, the monetary authority will monitor real growth as the basis underlying monetary policymaking to achieve price and financial stability, along with an optimal pace of growth. Consequently, economic success is measured based on the ability to create and maintain price stability and optimal growth, thus achieving equitable prosperity.

[1]Islamic finance is not completely free from criticism, where the existence, mechanisms, and function of Islam are still debated amongst Islamic historians, experts, and economists. Nevertheless, this idea is also refuted by other Islamic economists, including Al-Qardhawi (2005), who found that prevailing conditions, political conflicts, government corruption, arbitrary authorities, behaviour that deviates from Islamic law and human greed (consumption and capitalism) have left the institutional practices of Islamic finance far from their actual function. Al-Qardhawi (2005) added that this negative phenomenon is also a function of national or social cyclicality. On the other hand, the application of *zakat*, forbidding of *riba* in trade and leasing activities as well as the presence of social institutions, such as *Baitul Mal, Al Hisbah,* and others, continues in line with Islamic teachings (Al-Qardhawi, 2005).

3.2 Philosophical Foundation and Underlying Principles of Islamic Finance

Islamic finance is an integral part of the Islamic economy, dealing with the regulation, utilisation, and management of wealth. Finance influences the pace of economic growth. In addition, finance is the main source of economic strength, particularly in the real sector. Islamic finance has characteristics distinct from conventional finance, the philosophical foundation, and underlying principles of which adhere to Islamic (sharia) law.

3.2.1 Philosophical Foundation of Islamic Economy and Finance

Studying the philosophical foundation of the Islamic economic and financial system requires a look back to the emergence of the Islamic religion. Islam first emerged on earth during the lifetime of the Prophet Muhammad SAW, born in the Year of the Elephant or 571 CE, appointed a messenger by Allah SWT in 611 CE and died in 632 CE, though Islamic teachings date back further to earlier profits. Therefore, Islamic economics and finance are as old as the religion itself, far outdating modern economic theories, such as capitalism and socialism, which are dominant in the present day. Notwithstanding, modern theories of Islamic economics and finance have been developed since the 1970s.

Understanding the philosophical foundation of the Islamic economy and finance requires an appreciation of the underlying principles (ontology) of Islamic religious teachings, namely the Al-Qur'an as well as the traditions and practices (*Sunnah*) of Rasulullah SAW (Asutay, 2007). Al-Qur'an is the central religious text of Islam, containing the divine messages and revelations of Allah SWT, as revealed to the Prophet Muhammad SAW, while *Sunnah Rasul* is a collection of religious teachings for life and worship as a reference for Muslims as contained in the Hadiths. Therefore, the philosophical foundation of the Islamic economy and finance is grounded in the teachings contained in Al-Qur'an and the Hadiths, as practised during the time of Rasulullah SAW and the Islamic caliphs.

According to Al-Qur'an and the Hadiths, every aspect, or the code, of every Muslim's life is aligned with Islamic principles and values, namely sharia. Economic activity in Islam is also regulated by Al-Qur'an and *Sunnah* as part of Islamic jurisprudence. *Muamalah* is a part of traditional Islamic jurisprudence (*fiqh*) that deals with the instructions of Allah SWT and teachings of Rasulullah SAW, covering all interactions between people, including trade transactions. Notwithstanding, Al-Qur'an does not explicitly describe the economy from an Islamic perspective, instead offering instructions and prohibitions that essentially advise humans towards honest and true commerce, while forbidding deception and *riba*.

Trade and avoiding riba are implied in the Al-Qur'an, verse 275 of surah Al-Baqarah as follows:

اَلَّذِيْنَ يَأْكُلُوْنَ الرِّبٰوا لَا يَقُوْمُوْنَ اِلَّا كَمَا يَقُوْمُ الَّذِيْ يَتَخَبَّطُهُ الشَّيْطٰنُ مِنَ الْمَسِّۗ ذٰلِكَ بِاَنَّهُمْ قَالُوْٓا اِنَّمَا الْبَيْعُ مِثْلُ الرِّبٰواۘ وَاَحَلَّ اللّٰهُ الْبَيْعَ وَحَرَّمَ الرِّبٰواۗ فَمَنْ جَاۤءَهٗ مَوْعِظَةٌ مِّنْ رَّبِّهٖ فَانْتَهٰى فَلَهٗ مَا سَلَفَۗ وَاَمْرُهٗٓ اِلَى اللّٰهِ ۗوَمَنْ عَادَ فَاُولٰۤىِٕكَ اَصْحٰبُ النَّارِ ۚ هُمْ فِيْهَا خٰلِدُوْنَ

Those who consume interest cannot stand [on the Day of Resurrection] except as one stands who is being beaten by Satan into insanity. That is because they say, "Trade is [just] like interest."" But Allah has permitted trade and has forbidden interest. So whoever has received an admonition from his Lord and desists may have what is past, and his affair rests with Allah. But whoever returns to [dealing in interest or usury]—those are the companions of the Fire; they will abide eternally therein. (Q.S. Al-Baqarah [2]: 275)

Islam also promotes honest and true trade and forbids deception at the expense of others, as written in verse 29 of surah An Nisaa:

يٰٓاَيُّهَا الَّذِيْنَ اٰمَنُوْا لَا تَأْكُلُوْٓا اَمْوَالَكُمْ بَيْنَكُمْ بِالْبَاطِلِ اِلَّآ اَنْ تَكُوْنَ تِجَارَةً عَنْ تَرَاضٍ مِّنْكُمْ ۗ وَلَا تَقْتُلُوْٓا اَنْفُسَكُمْ ۗ اِنَّ اللّٰهَ كَانَ بِكُمْ رَحِيْمًا

O you who have believed, do not consume one another's wealth unjustly but only [in lawful] business by mutual consent. And do not kill yourselves [or one another]. Indeed, Allah is to you ever Merciful. (Q.S. An Nisaa [4]: 29)

Islam also unequivocally and categorically commands Muslims towards the religious duty or obligation of *zakat* almsgiving, which is still considered an instrument of worship with a beneficial economic role. In fact, based on the concept of the Islamic moral economy, *zakat* is considered a beneficial instrument and characteristic of the Islamic economic system. The importance of *zakat* is represented by the large number of Qur'anic verses containing instructions concerning mandatory *zakat* contributions, next in importance only to prayer (*shalat)*, as written in verse 277 of surah Al-Baqarah as follows:

اِنَّ الَّذِيْنَ اٰمَنُوْا وَعَمِلُوا الصّٰلِحٰتِ وَاَقَامُوا الصَّلٰوةَ وَاٰتَوُا الزَّكٰوةَ لَهُمْ اَجْرُهُمْ عِنْدَ رَبِّهِمْۚ وَلَا خَوْفٌ عَلَيْهِمْ وَلَا هُمْ يَحْزَنُوْنَ

Indeed, those who believe and do righteous deeds and establish prayer and give zakah will have their reward with their Lord, and there will be no fear concerning them, nor will they grieve. (Q.S. Al Baqarah [2]: 277)

The rationale that the Islamic economic system must refer to its fundamental ontology is also supported by modern Islamic economists through a concept known as the Islamic moral economy.[2] Based on this concept, Navqi (1994) explained that the Islamic economy is an economic system based on the principles and ethics found in Islamic teachings. Furthermore, the principles and ethics in Islam are contained in

[2]The Islamic moral economy is derived from the moral economy concept, where an economic system must be founded on the positive principles and values of societal culture.

their entirety in Al-Qur'an and the Hadiths. In general, therefore, the concept of an ethical or moral economy states that all economic activities must contain social values and equity, as taught in Islam.

In terms of the literature, Asutay (2007) stated that the norms and ethics in Islam are already integrated into all aspects of life, including economic activity. Therefore, the Islamic economy can be interpreted as a system that is an inherent part of the religion, where the activities therein, such as production, consumption, and distribution, are performed from an Islamic viewpoint and each decision is made in line with prevailing Islamic norms, which is a necessary alternative to other economic systems.

Similar to Islamic banking, Islamic finance specifically was initially a representation of the current concept of the Islamic moral economy. Based on Islamic principles and values, however, the scope of the Islamic economy stretches beyond financial and banking practices to encompass broad-based empowerment across all social strata, social aspects, and sustainable development. The Islamic moral economy is a human-centred economic concept that prioritises social aspects, justice, and equality. This definition implies that the economic system as taught in Islam focuses on human welfare as an entity representing the people by safeguarding equitable access to achieve prosperity. Therefore, philanthropic instruments in Islam, including *zakat, infaq, sadaqah,* and *waqf* (ZISWAF), are critical variables of the Islamic economy and finance.

Such is also the case with other sectors, namely Islamic microfinance, the capital market, and halal industry. Ideally, the Islamic financial sector must be developed with an aim to empower and stimulate the local economy by creating new entrepreneurship.

Based on that explanation, it may be concluded that the scope of the Islamic economy comprises activities founded on achieving the salvation, happiness, and well-being of Islamic man (*Homo Islamicus*), known as *falah*. In Islam, *falah* is defined as happiness in this world and the next. Such happiness is subsequently translated to mean a condition that can be achieved if a person's wants and needs are fulfilled materially and spiritually. *Falah* must be achieved through *mashlahah* (welfare for the self and others) without creating *mafsadah* (anything that is harmful and destructive).

The position of the economy in Islam is illustrated in Fig. 3.1 as follows:

By building the philosophical foundation of the Islamic economy based on the concept of the Islamic moral economy, Islamic economists such as Umar Chapra, Mohammad Nejatullah Siddiqi, Syed Nawab Haider Naqvi, Kurshid Ahmad, Sirageldin, and Mehmet Asutay have formulated axioms referring to Islamic teachings founded on the understanding that, ideally, the Islamic economy is an ethical economy, where each policy taken considers all aspects of human life, as taught in Islam. Each axiom is described and explained as follows:

1. ***Tawhid***

   Tawhid, meaning the absolute oneness or unification of God Almighty, is the indivisible oneness concept of monotheism in Islam. Accordingly, Allah SWT is

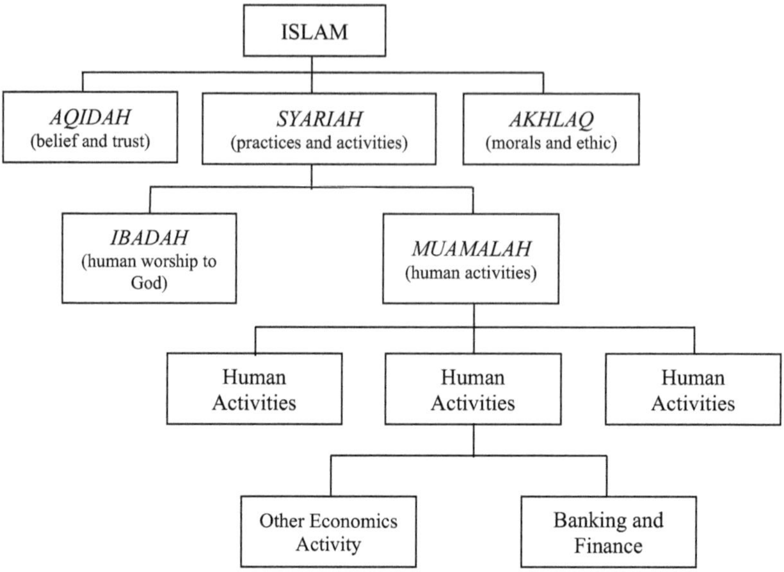

Fig. 3.1 Position of economy and finance in Islam

the progenitor of all things and owns everything, without exception. Based on this foundation, humans believe that the Prophet Muhammad SAW is a messenger of God on earth (*risalah*) and that there is life after death (the afterlife or *akhirah*). Therefore, humans also understand to live all aspects of their lives based on the instructions and revelations of God (Al-Qur'an) and Sunnah Rasulullah (Hadiths), and that life on earth is temporary with eternal life after death.

Consequently, everyone is equal in the eyes of God, with all activities thus based on the ethics and values of Islam, and all humanity acknowledging justice and equity to create quality welfare.

2. ***'Adalah***

'Adalah means balance, equilibrium, or justice. Departing from the *Tawhid*, which reflects the vertical relationship between people and God, *'Adalah* represents the horizontal relationship between people. This principle leads us to understand that God created people as social beings not individuals, with everyone granted the same rights and access to the resources bestowed by God. Therefore, the equitable distribution of resources (income) must be strived towards. When *Tawhid* and *'Adalah* are well implemented, life on earth will be fulfilled, where everyone can meet their individual needs and joint prosperity, which is known as *al hayah at-tayyibah*.[3]

[3] Ahmad, K. (2003). The Challenge of Global Capitalism. In J. H. Dunning (Ed.), Making Globalisation Good: The Moral Challenges of Global Capitalism. Oxford: Oxford University Press.

3. ***Rububiyyah***
   Simply, *rububiyyah* means divinity. This philosophical foundation of Islam explains that everything created on earth by Allah SWT is perfect and within its own system. Like natural law, everything needs to reach perfection over time, meaning that humans, animals, plants, and others have the right to grow, develop, and improve. As with development, kindness and perfection must be considered along with future sustainability. In practice, therefore, the Islamic economy does not permit marginalisation or the lack of opportunity to develop the self sustainably. Another common example is the integrity of the environment, where Allah SWT created the heavens and the earth, and all that is between them, perfect in every way and bestowed to man to manage fairly and equitably. When nurturing economic growth, mankind must consider the integrity of the environment to ensure the benefits are not only felt in the present but also for generations to come (sustainability).
4. ***Tazkiyah***
   Tazkiyah is an Arabic-Islamic term meaning sanctification and development. This implies that in the development process, humans must engage in purification of the self to ensure all developmental activities remain in line with the original goals, values, and aspirations. For example, individuals must avoid arrogance, greed, and other negative traits when performing economic activity.
5. ***Khilkiyya***
   Khilkiyya means affirmed behaviour. This axiom refers to improving all aspects in the growth process, including attitude. In Islamic economics, therefore, an individual must also focus on self-improvement over time.
6. ***Ikhtiyar* and *Hurriyah***
   Referring to free will, this axiom implies that Allah SWT fundamentally bestows free will upon mankind to choose based on needs and desires. In Islamic economics, market systems clearly apply, and individuals are free to express their respective preferences yet also adhere to the principle of *Tazkiyah*, by avoiding harm to others.
7. ***Fard***
   Meaning responsibility, every human being must understand that each respective individual is responsible for every decision and action taken. In Islamic economics, everyone is responsible for each other through sensitivity to the social environment.
8. ***Haqq***
   In this case, *haqq* means right. Each person has the right to develop and grow with the consequence of *fard*, or responsibility. Furthermore, each person's rights must be upheld in accordance with the principles of *amanah, tazkiyah,* and *rububiyyah.*
9. ***Amanah***
   Meaning entrusted by God or the trust from God, man was placed on earth by Allah SWT as His vicegerent. With the freedom bestowed to grow and develop, individuals are responsible for that role. Therefore, in the context of the Islamic economy, individuals are required to work hard and perform every economic

activity to the best of their ability to achieve a maximal and most beneficial outcome, while remaining accountable in the eyes of Allah SWT.

10. ***Islah***

    Islah is to reform, in the sense to improve. Through this philosophical foundation, Islam demands constant improvement over time and modernisation. In Islam, modernisation is not forbidden providing the principles and values contained in Al-Qur'an and the Hadiths are not violated. When performing economic activity, therefore, self-improvement and self-adjustment are required through a reformation (*islah*) process, to innovate, develop, and find better, more civilised and fairer ways over time in an effort to modernise.

11. ***Khilafah***

    Khilafah is the individual's role as God's vicegerent on earth. This axiom implies that at every stage of life and in all activities, individuals must remember their responsibility to Allah SWT and the mission bestowed by Allah SWT towards universal prosperity. Therefore, the Islamic economy urges individuals to strive towards kindness, prosperity, and quality welfare for the self and others (social aspect), accountable to Allah SWT.

12. ***Ukhuwah***

    Meaning brotherhood, the axiom *Ukhuwah* in the context of the Islamic economy requires individuals to grow and develop economically through brotherhood, solidarity, and cooperation. This is inextricably linked to the human as a social being because people on earth are not alone but live together in brotherhood and extended families side-by-side. The equitable distribution of welfare is more important than individual prosperity.

13. ***Maqasid Syariah***

    From an Islamic perspective, the economy is founded on the higher objectives of Islam, namely *Maqasid Syariah*. Al Ghazali formulated five goals of sharia, namely the protection of faith (*din*), protection of life (*nafs*), protection of mind (*aql*), protection of lineage (*nasl*), and protection of property (*maal*).

Based on the concepts and axioms outlined above, the economy according to Islam not only focuses on physical, material, and individual development, yet prioritises creating and maintaining quality welfare at the macro level. Furthermore, Darsono et al. (2017, b) explained that *mashlahah* as oriented in Islam is achieved through balance (equilibrium) by mankind. In Islam, equilibrium is the traditions and practices (*sunnah*) of Rasulullah SAW that constitute an exemplary model for moderate Muslims (*ummatan wasathan*) to follow.

3.2.2 Elements of Maqasid Syariah

Essentially, *Maqasid Syariah* are the higher objectives of the rules of sharia law in Islam. All statutes of sharia law, including economic activity, have a universal final objective, namely to achieve happiness and glory on earth and in the afterlife (*falah*). Such happiness and glory are not artificial, which would cause suffering, but true happiness and glory. In practice, the objectives of the Islamic economy involve micro and macro aspects as well as the dimensions of this world and the hereafter.

Falah, or salvation, may be achieved if the life lived creates the conditions required to meet the needs of human life fairly, equitably, and in equilibrium. To that end, *Maqasid Syariah* must be implemented properly and in order of priority. *Maqasid Syariah* contains five basic and universal necessities or priorities for humans to achieve true happiness in this world and the next as follows:

1. **Protection of Faith or Religion (*din*)**
   The most important need of every human being, namely guidelines to lead a good and true life. The guidelines are in the form of religion (*din*), Islam specifically. Islam provides guidance, belief, rules, and procedures to live a good life in line with moral values. Religion must remain the utmost priority for humans to determine all actions taken in life. Compliance to that which is forbidden or ordered by Allah SWT is expected of every Muslim. In terms of the economy, the implications are to absolutely avoid anything forbidden in Islam, namely *riba, gharar,* and *maysir.*
2. **Protection of Life (*nafs*)**
   The second priority after religion is the protection of life (*nafs*). This extends to meeting all needs with respect to maintaining the existence of life and avoiding anything that causes death. In the economy, this means trading honestly and remaining trustworthy to meet the basic human needs, such as sustenance, clothing, and shelter.
3. **Protection of Mind/Intellect (*'aql*)**
   Islam also includes the mind or intellect as part of the basic human needs, as demonstrated by the emphasis in Islam that commands the pursuit of knowledge (*thalabul 'ilm*). Humans require knowledge to understand the teachings of Islam as contained in Al-Qur'an and the Hadiths. Consequently, humans can fully comprehend how to live their lives and avoid life's difficulties. The economic implications mean that humans have a clear mind and sufficient knowledge to implement and enforce the Islamic economy within their environment or country.
4. **Protection of Family/Lineage (*nasl*)**
   Progeny play an essential role in maintaining the generational continuity of an individual. This need has an urgency to maintain the continuous existence of an individual and surrounding community. For instance, if an Islamic economist dies yet is survived by a child, that child can take up the struggle of his parent. Therefore, the role of an individual is not lost upon their death and perpetual charity can continue.
5. **Protection of Property (*maal*)**
   It is undeniable that property or wealth is a critical aspect of human life, not only in this life but also in the hereafter. Without sufficient wealth, life is more difficult, in terms of meeting both worldly and religious needs. On earth, wealth is required to meet the basic human needs of sustenance, clothing, shelter, education, transportation, and other basic needs, providing this is not wasteful or

excessive. In terms of worship, wealth is required, for example, to purchase prayer essentials, meals for *sahur* and to break the fast, the cost of study, constructing worship facilities, and so on. In addition, various forms of worship require wealth or property in implementation, such as *zakat, infaq*, *sadaqah,* and *waqf* (ZISWAF) as well as the Hajj pilgrimage.

3.2.3 Underlying Principles of Islamic Finance

Based on the current literature, the underlying principles of Islamic finance are as follows:

1. **Belief in Divinity**

   Allah SWT created the heavens and the earth, and all that is between them, for worship to Him, for obeying all His commands and for leaving behind all that He forbids. In this context, His commands not only relate to individual worship and religion, but also cover all aspects of human life and activity. Muslims are required to believe that the orders commanded by Allah SWT must be obeyed literally and substantially.

   Not only is the relationship between humans and Allah SWT the Creator, known as *habluminallah*, important, but also the relationship between humans, known as *habluminnannas*, covering all aspects of social life, including economic and financial transactions. As servants of God, humans require guidance on how to live the *habluminallah* and *habluminnannas* aspects of their lives. Such guidance is required to ensure true happiness in this life and the next.

   The virtue of achieving welfare not only on earth but also in the afterlife changes one's perspective concerning the use of income, including transactional activity in the financial sector, such as the rejection of greed and wealth created through speculation. Consequently, humans are more introspective and prioritise prudence when transacting.

   By upholding the values of creed and morality, and adhering to sharia law, human behaviour becomes oriented more towards prosperity on earth and in the afterlife. In relation to wealth, for example, if an individual receives more income, consumption should not increase, with the additional income instead used for investment or saving purposes. Investment aims to increase and facilitate the circulation of wealth to avoid idle funds. In addition, when investing, the individual eschews speculation, which contains *maysir*, by prioritising investment in the real sector.

   Further to investment and saving, an individual oriented towards prosperity in the afterlife tends to allocate a portion of wealth to social causes, including mandatory *zakat* obligations as well as voluntary *infaq*, *sadaqah,* and *waqf*. Most importantly, wealth is spent as required not desired. Through behaviour in accordance with Islamic teachings and strong faith, the equitable distribution of income and wealth can be achieved. This describes the behaviour of *Homo Islamicus* or Islamic Man.

2. ***Riba* Forbidden**

The nucleus of Islamic finance is based on the absolute prohibition of the payment or receipt of loans or debt and profit from interest (riba). Islamic finance refers to certain conditions where financial institutions and individuals must meet relevant Islamic principles. The conditions were created in such a way as to ensure that financial activities and transactions do not contain riba, gharar, and maysir or other forbidden elements, which can create economic imbalances, as evidenced by various financial crises and issues stemming from contamination by haram elements (Ayub, 2009).

According to Islam, money has no intrinsic value but is a measure of value only and not valuable in and of itself. It is a medium of exchange or a unit of measurement but not a tradeable asset. Therefore, any form of money management or income that uses money to generate more money through fixed or variable, simple or compounding returns, as well as low or high interest rates (riba), is absolutely forbidden under sharia.

Etymologically, riba derives from the Arabic word meaning growing, developing, or increasing. This does not mean, however, that Islam forbids all forms of growth or increase, only in the context of riba, which implies surplus value without counterpart. Riba emerges when the certainty of something uncertain is predetermined. For example, when party A extends capital to party B at a predetermined rate of return agreed and approved by both parties that must be repaid by party B, where neither party knows for certain whether the business venture will generate a profit or not, how much profit or even a loss. In general, there are two principal forms of riba as follows:

(a) **Riba Nasi'ah**

Nasi'ah translates as waiting, delaying, or suspending. The term riba nasi'ah means an additional return on a debt arising due to the period between the disbursement and repayment of the loan. Islam strictly forbids an additional return/profit on a loan, even though the lender must wait for the repayment. All forms of predetermined additional return on a loan are forbidden, including fixed and variable returns as well as gifts. The prohibition is absolute, with no further debate or difference of opinion between Islamic scholars.

(b) **Riba Fadhl**

Riba fadhl relates to trade, exchange, business, and other transactions between interest-bearing commodities. During the period of Rasul, such commodities included gold, silver, wheat, salt, dates, and barley. Nowadays, gold and silver are equivalent to money, while the other commodities are considered basic necessities. Over time, however, such commodities have been overgeneralised to all commodity groups, and over time, the commodities traded have become more diverse and innovative. In terms of the generalised commodities, debate continues amongst Islamic jurists (fuqaha) as experts in fiqh. According to Imam Hanafi and Imam Hanbali, all tradable goods have the potential for riba fadhl. In contrast, Imam Syafi'i states that only food commodities have the potential for riba fadhl. Meanwhile, Imam Maliki added that riba fadhl could emerge from edible goods and storable goods that do not experience significant change over time. In addition to the opinions of the Islamic jurists (fuqaha) mentioned, the minority Mazhab Zhahiri school stated that the potential for riba fadhl is limited to the six commodities mentioned by Rasulullah SAW, no more no less.

Riba fadhl emerges in the simultaneous exchange of unequal quantities or qualities of a given commodity, giving one party an advantage over the other. In addition, the exchange of interest-bearing goods could give rise to riba fadhl if the transaction is not settled on the spot, unless specific contracts are used that do not violate Islamic principles. The practice of riba fadhl eliminates the purity, equity, and honesty of the transaction. Therefore, the exchange of commodities must apply the same measurement standards to avoid riba fadhl in the transaction. Furthermore, Rasulullah SAW did not advocate the practice of bartering due to the complexity of evaluating a fair value for two different commodities. This is where money has a role to play, by creating a level playing field for the exchange of goods.

The principles of the Islamic economy aim squarely at achieving economic justice and equity for all. All forms of deception and exploitative activities are absolutely forbidden in Islam, including riba fadhl, to uphold justice and eliminate deceitfulness in economic activity.

The concept of riba fadhl is harder to understand than riba nasi'ah. Caution and vigilance concerning riba fadhl must be improved. Riba fadhl encompasses all forms of deceit and injustice in all economic transactions, including financial, business, and other transactions that seek to profit at the expense of others. Moreover, riba fadhl has the potential to impede healthy business competition.

In business, the involvement of different parties directly necessitates legally binding terms and conditions stipulating the implementation and rights to the proceeds in order to avoid riba for the investor, bank, and borrower (Ayub, 2009). The regulation and calculation of financial activity, in terms of business, trade of goods and services as well as other financial activities, refers to specific contracts permissible by Islamic law, namely mudharabah, musyarakah, murabahah, ijarah, istisna, salam, rahn, and so on.

3. **Investment is not Haram**

The flow of money from individuals with a surplus to those with a deficit is considered investment activity. In accordance with Islamic law, money is not tradable, money has no intrinsic value but is only a measure of value. Therefore, investment in the real sector with tangible transactions based on underlying assets is prioritised. The main orientation of investment lies in equitable welfare and social justice by maximising profit-sharing principles, thus avoiding a dichotomy between the real and monetary sectors. In other words, the key to the Islamic economy is real sector activity.

4. **Risk Sharing**

Fundamentally, Islam prioritises an equitable system of quality welfare for all human interactions on earth, including economic interactions. Business activity is the spearhead of the financial sector and equitable business is achieved through fair profit and risk sharing.

Losses are anticipated based on the risks borne by all business partners, including the investor and fund manager. Risk sharing aims to increase transactional transparency and accountability, promote honesty and accountability, create trust amongst transacting business partners or financial institutions (such as banks) and their customers, increase prudence in the decision-making process, and maximise profit based on halal strategies within the Islamic legal corridor.

Islam not only focuses on risk or loss sharing, but also seeks to derive profit from muamalah activity providing elements forbidden in Islam are not involved. Sharia principles evaluate capital performance fairly, while providing an equitable return to the investor. It is important to note that profit is not generated by an additional amount over the principal of a loan or debt, rather a portion of the investment capital. Calculating profit based on capital is not forbidden because the determinants are a natural consequence of the principal business or investment transaction.

The profit-sharing proportions are determined based on obligations and risk sharing, including losses and precautionary measures as well as returns on ownership by determining the capital, price of goods, services, and benefits. This is highly recommended for all business activities in the real sector (Ayub, 2009). Verse 275 of surah Al-Baqarah in the Al-Qur'an explains the restrictions on improperly calculating returns, risk sharing as well as licensing issues for trade under muamalah Islamic jurisprudence as follows:

اَلَّذِيْنَ يَأْكُلُوْنَ الرِّبٰوا لَا يَقُوْمُوْنَ اِلَّا كَمَا يَقُوْمُ الَّذِيْ يَتَخَبَّطُهُ الشَّيْطٰنُ مِنَ الْمَسِّۗ ذٰلِكَ بِاَنَّهُمْ قَالُوْٓا اِنَّمَا الْبَيْعُ مِثْلُ
الرِّبٰواۘ وَاَحَلَّ اللّٰهُ الْبَيْعَ وَحَرَّمَ الرِّبٰواۗ فَمَنْ جَاۤءَهٗ مَوْعِظَةٌ مِّنْ رَّبِّهٖ فَانْتَهٰى فَلَهٗ مَا سَلَفَۗ وَاَمْرُهٗٓ اِلَى اللّٰهِۗ وَمَنْ عَادَ
فَاُولٰۤىِٕكَ اَصْحٰبُ النَّارِۚ هُمْ فِيْهَا خٰلِدُوْنَ

Those who consume interest cannot stand [on the Day of Resurrection] except as one stands who is being beaten by Satan into insanity. That is because they say, "Trade is [just] like interest."" But Allah has permitted trade and has forbidden interest. So whoever has received an admonition from his Lord and desists may have what is past, and his affair rests with Allah. But whoever returns to [dealing in interest or usury]—those are the companions of the Fire; they will abide eternally therein. (Q.S. Al-Baqarah [2]: 275)

The verse explains that profit obtained from trade is halal (permitted), but riba is haram (forbidden), implying that all business and trade activities driven by financial activity in the economy are permitted providing there are real underlying assets and the equitable sharing of risk.

5. **Financing based on Real Assets**

In Islamic finance, extending debt is part of the virtue of social-oriented activity rather than profit-oriented activity (commercial). It is also seen as transferring funds from one hand to another with full payment guarantees yet without an additional return to the lender (creditor). Therefore, extending debt is not considered the main activity of Islamic financial institutions, including Islamic banks. No profit is received from extending debt. Consequently, the primary activity of Islamic banking seeks to foster business activity.

Islamic banks generate profit from entities conducting productive business and create returns for the depositors, investors, or financiers. In addition, Islamic banks are permitted to receive funding or fees for the operating activities and services provided. This represents part of the efforts to reduce speculation and excessive credit growth, while simultaneously growing the economy, particularly the real sector as the heart of the economic system.

By complying with the fundamental principles of Islamic finance, financial institutions, the government, and all other relevant parties will obey the law and remain impartial to others. This is intended to achieve the goals of Islamic finance (falah) as follows:

(a) Creating and maintaining healthy financial and monetary system conditions in an interest-free environment, while developing financial activities in accordance with Islamic principles.
(b) Achieving quality welfare for all through the equitable distribution of income and wealth as well as the distribution of productive resources and production outcomes for entrepreneurs and capital investors. According to the following Qur'anic verse, adequate resources on earth are guaranteed for mankind:

إِنَّ هَٰذَا لَرِزْقُنَا مَا لَهُ مِن نَّفَادٍ

Indeed, this is Our provision; for it there is no depletion. (Q.S. Sad [38]: 54)

Based on economic understanding from an Islamic perspective, the scarcity of resources is not an issue, with the focus instead considering the orderly and equitable distribution of resources amongst all social strata.

From a financial perspective, human welfare is based on productivity and the distribution of resources, production, instruments, institutions and markets for trade, investment and business purposes. In addition, optimal economic development and growth are measured based on the stable value of money (domestically and internationally) and reducing unemployment by providing full employment opportunities for the community.

3.3 Sharia Law and Islamic Morals in Islamic Finance

3.3.1 Tijari *and Commercial Finance*

It is important to emphasise that all financial sector activities must be accompanied by underlying activities in the real sector (business/trade). This is a concept vehemently supported in Islam, as confirmed in the Hadith as follows:

عَنْ رِفَاعَةَ بْنِ رَافِعٍ - رضى الله عنه - أَنَّ اَلنَّبِيَّ - صلى الله عليه وسلم -سُئِلَ: أَيُّ اَلْكَسْبِ أَطْيَبُ؟ قَالَ: {
عَمَلُ اَلرَّجُلِ بِيَدِهِ, وَكُلُّ بَيْعٍ مَبْرُورٍ} رَوَاهُ اَلْبَزَّارُ، وَصَحَّحَهُ اَلْحَاكِمُ. 1 .

Narrated Rifa'a bin Rafi' (RA):

The Prophet (ﷺ) was asked, 'What type of earning is best?' He replied, "A man's work with his hand and every transaction which is free from cheating or deception". [Reported by al-Bazzar; al-Hakim graded it Sahih (authentic)]

The canonical Hadith collection clearly shows that Islam prioritises business activity as a source of livelihood. In fact, the best income is said to derive from trade/business. Furthermore, the legal foundation of *muamulah* is *mubah* (permitted), unless explicitly forbidden. Consequently, the proportion of transactions permitted in Islam is much larger than those forbidden. It can be concluded, therefore, that Islam affords individuals the freedom to perform any transactions or activities, providing they are not unequivocally forbidden.

Islamic finance applies the concept of *tijarah* in *muamalah*. *Tijari* is profit-oriented activity based on trade/commerce contracts. *Tijari* contracts consist of the following types:

(a) **Sales/Trade Contract**

A contract of sale is permitted to stipulate a margin incurred by the buyer based on mutual agreement between the buyer and seller. In addition, cashless trade is also permitted providing the quantity and quality of the object of the transaction is clearly stipulated from the beginning. Examples of sales contracts include *bai' bitsaman ajil* (deferred payment) as well as *bai' as-salam* and *bai' al istishna* (purchase order).

(b) **Profit-Sharing Contract**

A form of cooperation used when two or more entities agree to work together. In general, profit-sharing contracts comprise two types, first. Namely *musyarakah* or cooperation in the form of a joint venture partnership, where both parties agree to inject capital (contributing the same or different shares). The investor is also permitted but not required to manage the business, which must be agreed and stipulated at the time of the agreement. Second, *mudharabah,* a profit-sharing contract in which the investor entrusts a certain amount of capital to the business.

(c) **Lease Contract**

Lease transactions are facilitated using *ijarah* contracts. The object of an *ijarah* contract can be a commodity or service. According to *ijarah* contracts, the lessor reserves the right to set a fee or *ujroh* to cover the leasing services of the good or service provided.

(d) ***Ju'alah* Contract**

A *Ju'alah* contract is one in which one of the parties offers a specified compensation to anyone who will achieve a determined result in a known or unknown period.

(e) **Hybrid *Tijari* Contract**

There are several forms of *tijari* mechanisms that differ slightly from the other contracts. First, *ijarah muntahiyah bit tamlik* is a lease contract that becomes a sales contract at the end of the agreement. Second, *mudharabah musytarakah* is a combination of *mudharabah* and *musyarakah*, namely a profit-sharing contract in which the entrepreneur includes his capital in the business he is running. Third, is a *musyarakah mutanaqisah* contract of partnership between two parties that becomes a sales contract at the end of the agreement.

Based on the concept of *tijari* and the underlying principles of Islamic finance already elaborated, Islamic commercial finance must comply with the following principles:

(i) *Riba* (Interest) Forbidden

In essence, Islamic teachings aim to achieve equity for all Muslims covering all aspects, including humanitarian, social, political, gender, socio-economic, and economic. In totality, more Qur'anic verses are dedicated to ways of living a better life than rules of worship to Allah SWT. This shows that Allah SWT revealed the path for humans to live their best and most equitable life.

Furthermore, Islam places great emphasis on economic equality and justice, while vigorously opposing anything that could detract from the value of justice, such as the acquisition of wealth through falsehood or deception (bathil). This is explained in Al-Qur'an, verse 29 of surah An-Nisa as follows:

يٰٓاَيُّهَا الَّذِيْنَ اٰمَنُوْا لَا تَأْكُلُوْٓا اَمْوَالَكُمْ بَيْنَكُمْ بِالْبَاطِلِ اِلَّآ اَنْ تَكُوْنَ تِجَارَةً عَنْ تَرَاضٍ مِّنْكُمْ ۗ وَلَا تَقْتُلُوْٓا اَنْفُسَكُمْ ۗ
اِنَّ اللّٰهَ كَانَ بِكُمْ رَحِيْمًا

O you who have believed, do not consume one another's wealth unjustly but only [in lawful] business by mutual consent. And do not kill yourselves [or one another]. Indeed, Allah is to you ever Merciful. (Q.S. An Nisaa [4]: 29)

Allah SWT absolutely forbids humans from taking profit through falsehood or deception (bathil). One of the central principles of Islamic economics is the implementation of that verse by forbidding riba. The prohibition of riba is fundamental to Islamic economic teaching. At its core, riba is additional profit in a financial transaction obtained without counterpart business activity. Riba is considered the main cause of inequality and the inequitable distribution of wealth.

(ii) *Maysir* (Speculation) Forbidden

Maysir is defined as gambling on games of chance. Like riba, Allah SWT explicitly and categorically forbids maysir in Al-Qur'an, verse 90-91 of surah Al-Maidah as follows:

يٰٓاَيُّهَا الَّذِيْنَ اٰمَنُوْٓا اِنَّمَا الْخَمْرُ وَالْمَيْسِرُ وَالْاَنْصَابُ وَالْاَزْلَامُ رِجْسٌ مِّنْ عَمَلِ الشَّيْطٰنِ فَاجْتَنِبُوْهُ لَعَلَّكُمْ تُفْلِحُوْنَ

اِنَّمَا يُرِيْدُ الشَّيْطٰنُ اَنْ يُّوْقِعَ بَيْنَكُمُ الْعَدَاوَةَ وَالْبَغْضَاۤءَ فِى الْخَمْرِ وَالْمَيْسِرِ وَيَصُدَّكُمْ عَنْ ذِكْرِ اللّٰهِ وَعَنِ الصَّلٰوةِ
فَهَلْ اَنْتُمْ مُّنْتَهُوْنَ

O you who have believed, indeed, intoxicants, gambling, [sacrificing on] stone alters [to other than Allah], and divining arrows are but defilement from the work of Satan, so avoid it that you may be successful. Satan only wants to cause between you animosity and hatred through intoxicants and gambling and to avert you from the remembrance of Allah and from prayer. So will you not desist? (Q.S. Al-Maidah [5]: 90–91)

Maysir is also defined as any activity relating to gambling or betting, where the winner of the bet acquires the wealth or property of the loser. The primary reason for forbidding *maysir* is because the winnings are obtained at the expense of another, which could potentially lead to disputes amongst the populace. In addition, the previous Qur'anic verse also states that betting distances the gambler from God.

(iii) *Gharar* (Uncertainty) Forbidden

Etymologically, *gharar* literally means risk, uncertainty, or hazard. In practice, *gharar* is a financial transaction that contains an element hidden to one party resulting in a financial loss to that party. In addition, *gharar* also refers to the sale of what is not present, where one party in an agreement may be unable to settle his obligations, for example a seller who cannot deliver the object of the transaction due to a lack of ownership rights. There are no specific Qur'anic verses that explicitly forbid *gharar*, although proof (*dalil*) of *gharar* is found in verse 29 of surah An-Nisa, stating that it is forbidden to devour the wealth of others through falsehood and deception (*bathil*). Islamic jurists and experts in *fiqh* (*fuqaha*) agree that *bathil* covers all illegal and unjust elements of financial transaction agreements. In this context, *gharar* is considered *bathil* because it leads to the acquisition of another's wealth through cruelty or unjust acts of exploitation, oppression, and wrongdoing (*zalim*). *Gharar* is forbidden for the good of all transacting parties because the practice is likened to purchasing something without knowing what it actually is or the Indonesian idiom "*membeli kucing di dalam karung*" (to buy a cat in a sack).

Gharar erodes the values of justice and equity in a financial transaction. When a transaction is contaminated by *gharar*, one or both parties may incur losses. Such practices are forbidden in Islamic financial transactions, as stated in the Hadith of Rasulullah SAW as follows:

وَعَنْهُ أَنَّ رَسُولَ اللَّهِ صَلَّى اللَّهُ عَلَيْهِ وَسَلَّمَ مَرَّ عَلَى صُبْرَةِ طَعَامٍ فَأَدْخَلَ يَدَهُ فِيهَا فَنَالَتْ أَصَابِعُهُ بَلَلًا فَقَالَ: «مَا هَذَا يَا صَاحِبَ الطَّعَامِ» قَالَ: أَصَابَتْهُ السَّمَاءُ يَا رَسُولَ اللَّهِ قَالَ: «أَفَلَا جَعَلْتَهُ فَوْقَ الطَّعَامِ حَتَّى يَرَاهُ النَّاسُ مَنْ غَشَّ فَلَيْسَ مني» . رَوَاهُ مُسلم

He said that God's Messenger once came upon a heap of grain, and when he put his hand into it his fingers felt some dampness, so he asked the owner of the grain how that came about. On being told that rain had fallen on it he said, "Why did you not put the damp part on the top of the grain so that people might see it? He who deceives has nothing to do with me".[4]

[4]Mishkat al-Masabih 2860, in book reference: book 11, hadith 98

There are generally three types of *gharar* acknowledged by Islamic jurists. First, *gharar* because the seller does not have full ownership rights of the object of the transaction, implying that the seller may not be able to supply the object. Second, *gharar* because of inadequate or inaccurate information concerning all aspects of the transaction, such as the characteristics, value, type, quality, and quantity of the object. This may be an attempt to deceive the other party. Third, *gharar* due to ambiguous contracts/agreements, such as combining two prices into the same contract. For instance, a seller and buyer agree to transact an object, the value of which at the time of agreement is Rp100,000, but in the following period the buyer must pay Rp150,000.

(iv) Hoarding Forbidden

In essence, Allah SWT has already revealed the intricacies of wealth ownership and distribution. Allah SWT strictly forbids the hoarding of wealth, including idle and unproductive funds. In this context, wealth is money or other capital, such as land and buildings. According to verse 34 of surah At-Taubah, Allah SWT said:

يٰٓاَيُّهَا الَّذِيْنَ اٰمَنُوْٓا اِنَّ كَثِيْرًا مِّنَ الْاَحْبَارِ وَالرُّهْبَانِ لَيَأْكُلُوْنَ اَمْوَالَ النَّاسِ بِالْبَاطِلِ وَيَصُدُّوْنَ عَنْ سَبِيْلِ اللّٰهِ ۗوَالَّذِيْنَ
يَكْنِزُوْنَ الذَّهَبَ وَالْفِضَّةَ وَلَا يُنْفِقُوْنَهَا فِيْ سَبِيْلِ اللّٰهِ ۙفَبَشِّرْهُمْ بِعَذَابٍ اَلِيْمٍۙ

O you who have believed, indeed many of the scholars and the monks devour the wealth of people unjustly and avert [them] from the way of Allah. And those who hoard gold and silver and spend it not in the way of Allah - give them tidings of a painful punishment. (Q.S. At-Tawbah [9]: 34)

Islam vehemently upholds the values of justice and equity for all. If an excess of wealth is hoarded in the hands of a few, this is to the detriment of others living without abundance or even in a deficit. Excessive wealth should be used for productive investment purposes as business capital or distributed towards prosperity and welfare through *zakat, infaq,* and *sadaqah*.

This was emphasised during the period of Caliph Omar, stating that:

Whoever has money, let him invest it, and whoever has land, let him cultivate it.

Business and investment are necessary to facilitate the seamless transfer of capital from individuals with a surplus to those with a deficit. In addition, the seamless distribution of wealth creates justice and equity as the overarching goals of the Islamic economy.

3.3.2 **Tabarru** *and Social Finance*

1. Concept of *Tabarru*

Contrasting *tijari, tabarru* is a non-profit or social-oriented mechanism, which can be categorised as follows:

(a) Two types of loan contact, *qardh* (loan) dan *qardhul hasan* (benevolent loan).
(b) Two types of deposit contract known as *wadi'ah*. *Wadi'ah yad amanah* is a pure deposit contract, where the deposited funds are restricted and cannot be used for any activity, including business in the real sector. On the other hand, *wadi'ah yad dhamanah* is a safekeeping or deposit contract, where the funds can be used for specific business purposes.
(c) Other *Tabarru* Contracts

Other *tabarru* contracts have their own distinct characteristics and mechanisms, including *wakalah* agency contracts, *hawalah* transfer of debt contracts, *rahn* pawn contracts, and *kafalah* guarantee contracts. These contracts typically refer to certain services, accompanied by a specific return, which are subsequently known as *tabarru* containing *ujroh* (a fee) and become new contracts, such as *wakalah bil ujroh*, *kafalah bil ujroh*, and *hawalah bil ujroh*.
(d) Social-Oriented Contracts

Contracts with social-oriented mechanisms towards social welfare and prosperity. This mechanism is regulated in Islam through obligatory *zakat* almsgiving and encouraging voluntary *infaq, sadaqah, waqf,* and other donations.

2. *Zakat* Obligations

As one of the pillars of Islam, *zakat* is a religious duty for all Muslims. Several Qur'anic verses command Muslims to undertake *zakat* as a religious duty, including verse 103 of surah At-Taubah as follows:

خُذْ مِنْ اَمْوَالِهِمْ صَدَقَةً تُطَهِّرُهُمْ وَتُزَكِّيْهِمْ بِهَا وَصَلِّ عَلَيْهِمْۗ اِنَّ صَلٰوتَكَ سَكَنٌ لَّهُمْۗ وَاللّٰهُ سَمِيْعٌ عَلِيْمٌ

Take, [O, Muhammad], from their wealth a charity by which you purify them and cause them increase, and invoke [Allah 's blessings] upon them. Indeed, your invocations are reassurance for them. And Allah is Hearing and Knowing. (Q.S. At-Taubah [9]: 103).

That verse contains the word "take", implying almsgiving is not merely a recommendation but a firm command, calling for sincere and intentional almsgiving as a form of worship to Allah SWT. In addition, the verse also states that *zakat* will cleanse and purify the individual. In this context, to cleanse means cleansing man's excessive love for his property, thus avoiding internal afflictions, such as greed and hoarding of wealth. Meanwhile, to purify means enriching the positive attributes of mankind, such as eternal gratefulness and awareness that a portion of all wealth belongs to others and ownership must be transferred. *Zakat* facilitates the flow of wealth from individuals with a surplus to those with a deficit, thus contributing to the goal of the Islamic economy, namely the orderly and equitable distribution of economic resources.

Zakat, therefore, has two dimensions, namely as a form of worship and a socio-economic dimension, to achieve quality economic welfare for those in need. *Zakat* is characterised by specific attributes. First, there are certain periods to pay *zakat*, for instance *zakat fitrah* during the holy fasting month of Ramadan prior to the Eid-ul-Fitr prayers. Second, concerning the *zakat* on wealth (*maal*), payment is made upon achieving the minimum threshold of wealth (*nishab*) for a specific period (*haul*), typically one year. Third, *zakat* payments are limited to eight categories of people (*asnaf*) who qualify to benefit from *zakat* funds, as revealed by Allah SWT in verse 60 of surah At-Taubah as follows:

اِنَّمَا الصَّدَقٰتُ لِلْفُقَرَاۤءِ وَالْمَسٰكِيْنِ وَالْعَامِلِيْنَ عَلَيْهَا وَالْمُؤَلَّفَةِ قُلُوْبُهُمْ وَفِى الرِّقَابِ وَالْغَارِمِيْنَ وَفِيْ سَبِيْلِ اللّٰهِ وَابْنِ السَّبِيْلِۗ
فَرِيْضَةً مِّنَ اللّٰهِ ۗوَاللّٰهُ عَلِيْمٌ حَكِيْمٌ

> Zakah expenditures are only for the poor and for the needy and for those employed to collect [zakah] and for bringing hearts together [for Islam] and for freeing captives [or slaves] and for those in debt and for the cause of Allah and for the [stranded] traveler - an obligation [imposed] by Allah. And Allah is Knowing and Wise. (Q.S. At-Taubah [9]: 60).

Zakat funds are allocated to eight categories of *asnaf*, including the indigent, poor, and needy, who require assistance to boost income. In the long term, the consistent implementation of *zakat* obligations will ameliorate the standard of living amongst the *dhuafa*.

3. Voluntary *Sadaqah, Infaq*, Gifts/Grants, and *Waqf*

   In addition to obligatory *zakat* almsgiving, Muslims also have other instruments at their disposal to disburse funds for social purposes, consisting of *infaq, sadaqah,* grants, and *waqf.* Such instruments are not compulsory but highly recommended in the traditions and practices of the Prophet Muhammad (*sunnah*) according to Islamic teachings. Furthermore, such instruments are unrestricted in terms of the recipients, providing the funds are not used for sinful acts of disobedience to God's commands. Despite the voluntary and social commonalities, the instruments also have their own distinct characteristics. *Infaq* refers to all spending or disbursements made by Muslims for the greater good, simply to please God without asking for any favour or hoping for a return. *Sadaqah* is a voluntary charity allocation for the greater good. All forms of kindness or benevolence intended to please Allah SWT can be categorised as *sadaqah*.

   According to Act Number 41 of 2004 concerning *Waqf, waqf* is an inalienable charitable endowment under sharia law for a specific period or in perpetuity for religious purposes or general welfare and prosperity. *Waqf* assets have economic value and benefits in the long term. In general, *waqf* assets are immovable, such as land or buildings. More recently, however, cash *waqf* has risen to prominence. Finally, grants encompass all forms of gifts given to another party.

3.4 Legal and Moral Implications of Islam in Economic and Financial Activity

3.4.1 Legal Implications of Tijari Muamalah

The diverse needs of mankind to create wealth and property are an important component of life, with humans recommended to seek wealth for the sake of survival. In Islam, the process of seeking and acquiring wealth has inherent ethics to which Muslims must comply. All efforts to seek wealth must be justified according to Islamic teachings, which prioritise self-employment and actualisation through *muamalah* using *tijari* contracts.

The overarching goal of civil acts or commercial transactions (*muamalah*) based on *tijari* contracts is to seek profit. This is permitted in Islam providing the activities apply legal and halal contracts, avoid *riba, gharar,* and *maysir*, and do not hoard wealth. *Muamalah* in Islam emphasises close and direct interlinkages between the financial sector and real sector.

Economic and financial activities that are in line with Islamic principles absolutely avoid *riba* in its entirety to ensure transactions are equitable to all parties. According to conventional economics, *riba* is reflected in the application of interest. In Islam, however, profit and loss sharing mechanisms substitute interest.

In addition to *riba*, the Islamic economy also forbids elements of *maysir* in economic and financial activity. According to Islamic economics, *maysir* disrupts the fair and normal price setting system. Fundamentally, the Islamic economy provides a viable solution to economic activities that only benefit a few by aligning the financial and real sectors, which forcibly changes the public mindset and behaviour concerning economic activity.

Economic behaviour will evolve in a better direction through Islamic economics with a focus on productive economic activity in the real sector. The economic goal of mankind is to survive, while acquiring profit and power. Notwithstanding, the Islamic economy adds the dimension of faith to economic activity, leading to equitable economic sustainability for all social strata. Furthermore, economic activity is no longer merely profit-oriented, yet seeks to meet the public interest (*maslahah*). Therefore, core economic activity is synonymous with productive economic activity in the real sector, thus obviating the need to generate income in the financial sector without underlying activity in the real sector.

One of the main activities justified in the productive economic sector is profit-seeking through trade. In terms of trade, profit is considered both urgent and crucial, generated by a margin between the selling price and cost of goods sold. In Islam, margin is permitted due to the inherent risks and efforts involved, with margin thus considered compensation for the efforts exerted and the potential risks faced.

In addition to trade, investment is also a core activity to seek profit while avoiding *riba*. The return on investment is generated as a rate of return on business conducted in the real sector. Nevertheless, investment must also apply specific contracts permitted in Islam as follows (Darsono et al., 2017, b):

1. *Mudharabah*. A profit-sharing contract in which the investor entrusts a certain amount of capital to the business.
2. *Musyarakah*. A joint financing partnership contract where capital is entrusted and managed by each party based on agreed proportions.

3.4.2 Legal Implications of Tabarru Muamalah

The primary objective of any government should be to meet the minimum living standards of the citizenry. This will guarantee human survival for life on earth (clothing, sustenance, and shelter) and in the afterlife (worship). This is achievable by maximising implementation of *tabarru muamalah*.

Zakat, infaq, and *sadaqah* have their own distinct roles to play in a country's economy. *Zakat* almsgiving can ensure economic activity runs at a level sufficient to safeguard minimum living standards for all residents by meeting basic primary needs. On a deeper level, *zakat* also contributes to macroeconomic growth by nurturing investment, while preventing miserly behaviour and the hoarding of assets. During a crisis, *zakat* instruments protect the economy from further deterioration by maintaining public purchasing power. From a monetary perspective, *zakat* can also drive the velocity of money and, thus, stimulate real sector growth.

Departing from *zakat, infaq* and *sadaqah* are utilised more for development programs to alleviate poverty. *Infaq* and *sadaqah* focus on not only meeting the basic necessities for life, but also raising the overall standard of living. If implemented optimally and sustainably, this will increase the level of aggregate demand and nurture economic growth.

The implication of *tabarru* instruments, comprising *zakat, infaq, sadaqah,* and *waqf* (ZISWAF), instils the quality of generosity as well as concern for the problems faced by others. As stated in verse 2 of surah Al-Maidah of Al-Qur'an, humans are recommended to cooperate in righteousness and piety, not in sin and aggression.

وَلَا تَعَاوَنُوْا عَلَى الْاِثْمِ وَالْعُدْوَانِ ۖوَاتَّقُوا اللّٰهَ ۗاِنَّ اللّٰهَ شَدِيْدُ الْعِقَابِ

> ... And cooperate in righteousness and piety, but do not cooperate in sin and aggression. And fear Allah; indeed, Allah is severe in penalty. (Q.S. Al-Maidah [5]: 2)

Tabarru contracts are also used in Islamic banking in the form of *qardhul hasan* products to provide capital to micro and small enterprises through a gratuitous contract where the borrower is not obliged to return the loan if unable to do so. Such products are also available to customers in dire need of funds yet unable to liquidate internal funds for specific reasons.

References

Al-Jarhi, M. (2004). The philoshophy of Islamic Banking and Finance. *MPRA Paper.*

Al-Qardhawi, Y. (2005). *Distorsi Sejarah Islam.* Pustaka Al Kautsar.

Asutay, M. (2007). A political economy approach to Islamic economics: Systemic understanding for an alternative economic system. *Kyoto Bulletin of Islamic Area Studies, 1-2*, hlm. 3-18.

Ayub, M. (2009). *Understanding Islamic Finance: A-Z Keuangan Syariah*. PT Gramedia Pustaka Utama.

Darsono, S. A., Darwis, A., Suryanti, E. T., & Astiyah, S. (2017). *Dinamika Produk dan Akad Keuangan Syariah di Indonesia*. PT RajaGrafindo Persada.

Darsono, S. A., Suryanti, E. T., Astiyah, S., & Darwis, A. (2017). *Masa Depan Keuangan Syariah Indonesia*. Tazkia Publishing dan Bank Indonesia.

Chapter 4
Basic Theory of Islamic Social-Public Finance

4.1 Introduction

In general, economics is defined as the branch of knowledge concerned with studying human behaviour in terms of selecting and creating prosperity. Economics can also be defined as a scientific discipline studying how humans manage limited resources to make better decisions (Mankiw, 2014). In that context, understanding the motivation to consume and produce is beneficial when trying to comprehend the overall concept of the economy because the economic foundations determine what will be built thereupon. Between the two conflicting economic concepts that have emerged over the past century, namely capitalism and socialism, capitalism has become the dominant economic concept adopted by most countries. According to Adam Smith (1776), the capitalist economy is built on prevailing economic behaviour to overcome the issue of meeting needs. Smith (1776) opined that capitalism is built on individual needs to acquire material wealth based on sentiment, feeling, and desires. The morals underlying economic values are a constant and consistent community response to individual behaviour. It can be concluded, therefore, that the capitalist economy is at once individualistic and materialistic.

Based on such an underlying philosophy, not surprisingly economics is always associated with the overarching issue in life, namely resource scarcity. This limitation creates imbalances between unlimited human needs and finite resources. Human needs manifest in the form of consumption, while needs are met through the production and distribution process. Consequently, economics, as the branch of knowledge concerned with the production, consumption, and transfer of wealth, was born. Nevertheless, three fundamental questions emerged in economics due to finite resources, which relate closely with production, consumption, and distribution activities (Mankiw, 2014) as follows:

1. **What to produce?**
   Determining what to produce is a salient issue in an economy, which is inextricably linked to the limited supply (scarcity) of resources. Slight

S. M. Juhro et al., *Inclusive Welfare*, https://doi.org/10.1007/978-981-96-0051-9_4

miscalculations when determining what to produce can incur massive losses, potentially bankrupting a producer. On the other hand, this could also lead to public losses in a region if the goods and services produced are not utilised. Such conditions are a major cause of resource profligacy. This problem mainly concerns the types and quantities of goods/resources that must be produced in accordance with the needs of the local community or globally.

2. **How to produce?**

   The second key issue of the modern economy is how to produce. The choices include using capital goods, labour, resources, or other factors of production. If a producer has determined and decided what to produce, the next step is to think about how to produce. Production methods for a product/service involve combining the resources or factors of production required. By applying economic principles, producers primarily pursue efficiency and effectiveness in the production process. In addition, there are several fundamental considerations and questions when seeking to improve the production process, including "will the production methods used create environmental degradation?" or "what is the impact of production on the environment and surrounding communities?" Such questions must be addressed by producers when determining the most appropriate production methods.

3. **For whom to produce?**

   This issue is not only concerned with to whom the goods produced should be marketed, but who else will benefit. The production of goods and services not only focuses on the consumers who will consume those goods and services. In fact, production activity is advantageous to many other parties. Through production activity, workers can receive wages, suppliers of raw materials have an outlet to sell, investors can receive interest on the capital, owners of land and buildings can receive rent and entrepreneurs can receive a profit on the sales of the product. Therefore, the question of "for whom to produce" also relates closely to who will enjoy income and benefit from production activity. This also concerns how to distribute the final goods or income equitably to avoid gaps and sowing discontent between owners of production factors.

Several economists have added one more fundamental question, namely "how are these decisions made?" where the control and ownership of production factors is the overriding issue. In the modern era, a diverse range of entities can undertake production activities, including the government, private sector, individuals, and corporations. Each entity will produce in accordance with its expertise and specialisation. Consideration of the producers is important because each has its own advantages that can lead to better production (Blanchard, 2018).

The underlying philosophy of the conventional economy and finance has continued to evolve over time and is thus regarded as the basic theories and concepts of economics that underlie economic practices today. In practice, however, the economy often fails to achieve the expected goals, hence necessitating government intervention even though this can sometimes trigger government failures in the economy. In this context, the philosophical foundation of the Islamic economy and finance has emerged and is driving the evolution of Islamic economics in the modern era. The Islamic economy boasts principles and ethics taken directly from Al-Qur'an and the Hadiths, emphasising that each economic or *muamalah* activity must contain social values and justice. Using *zakat* instruments to achieve equitable welfare is not only a religious obligation for Muslims, such instruments also play a key economic role. This is in line with the Islamic moral economy as a human-centred economic concept that prioritises social aspects, justice, equity, and equality. The definition implies an economic system, as taught in Islam, that places strong emphasis on welfare for humans as the entity representing "*umat*" by guaranteeing equitable access to achieve such prosperity. The core substance of such issues will be explored in depth in this chapter, particularly in terms of the philosophical foundation and purview of the conventional Islamic economy and finance as well as Islamic social-public finance.

4.2 Conventional Social-Public Finance

4.2.1 Scope of Conventional Economy

In general, the purview of conventional economics encompasses the microeconomy and macroeconomy. Microeconomics is the branch of economics concerned with the economic behaviour of individuals and the markets where the individuals exist, while macroeconomics is the branch concerned with aggregate economic variables, such as national output and growth, interest rates, unemployment, and inflation. Though both branches are closely related, they are principally very different, with each addressing different economic questions and issues (Mankiw, 2014).

More specifically, microeconomics deals with consumer, corporate, worker, and investor behaviour in the product market along with the market production factors in an economy. With finite income, consumers are faced with consumption decisions concerning the goods and services required to meet living standards and maximise satisfaction/utility. On the other hand, producer behaviour concerns the decision of what to produce based on limited factors of production and minimising costs to maximise profit. One production factor is labour, where workers are also consumers in the product market, and workers must decide how to allocate their finite time between work and other activities. Meanwhile, investors must apportion their limited resources and take investment decisions to maximise returns. The relationship between such individuals in the product market and market production factors is illustrated in the following diagram.

In a perfectly competitive market, equilibrium is achieved when supply equates to demand. In practice, however, there is often a surplus or deficit of products in the market, which serves to disrupt equilibrium. Under such conditions, market intervention by the government is available through taxes, subsidies, and so on. The

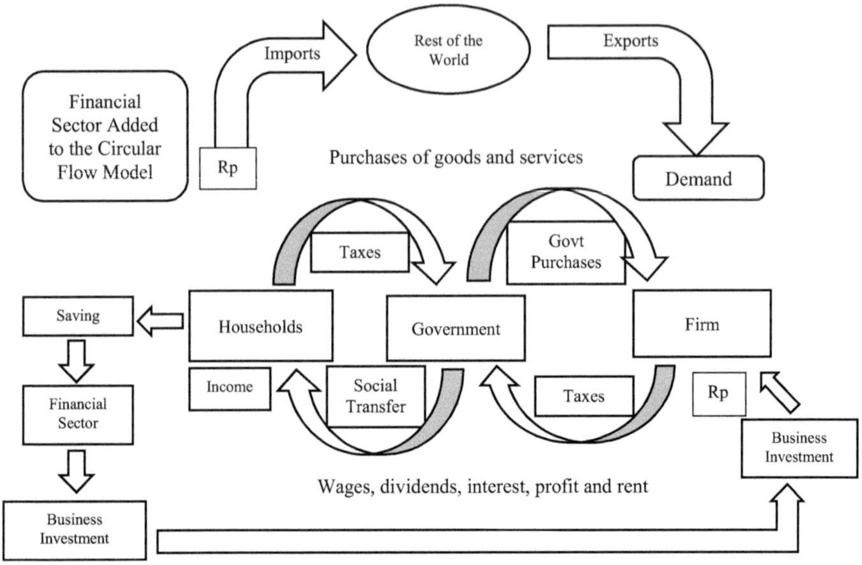

Fig. 4.1 Circular flow model, including financial sector. Source: https://www.tutor2u.net/economics/reference/circular-flow-of-income-and-spending

different forms and timing of government intervention are explained in the following subchapter.

On the other hand, macroeconomics seeks to explain aggregate economic changes that influence public, corporate, and market behaviour. Macroeconomic discussions involve diverse concepts and variables. According to Blanchard (2018), however, three main topics dominate macroeconomics, namely national income (and components thereof, including aggregate consumption, investment, government expenditure, exports and imports), unemployment, and inflation. Those three topics relate closely to the government's role as an intermediary in the flow of goods/services in an economy.

An open economy is formed from the flow of internal/domestic income—consisting of households, firms, and the government—and the flow of external/international income from exports and imports. In the circular flow of domestic income, households purchase goods and services from firms, which also pay households in the form of wages, salaries, dividends, interest, profit, and rent. In addition, households pay taxes to the government which are used to purchase goods/services from firms. Businesses also pay taxes to the government, which are used to provide social transfers, in the form of subsidies, etc., to households. When international trade occurs, as a distinct characteristic of an open economy, exports and imports are included in the circular flow of income.

Figure 4.1 illustrates the circular flow model in an open economy when the financial sector is included. A financial system emerges when there are surplus units (groups with surplus funds, for instance households with savings) and deficit units (groups with deficit funds, for instance firms requiring investment funds). In this case, savings are considered an injection into the economy and investments are seen as leakages or withdrawals. Businesses use investment in the production process, the outcome of which is used by households, the government, and external sector.

Based on that description, the government clearly plays an important role in the economy and precipitated the development of public economics, which includes the discipline of public finance. Public economics is the study of government (public sector) policy in the economy through the lens of economic efficiency and equity, including the rationale and forms of government intervention and the economic impact. In terms of analysis, both disciplines combine the principles and analysis tools of the microeconomy and macroeconomy. The government's role and scope of public economics are explained in the following section.

4.2.2 Government Role in Government Failure in the Economy

The government is required to play an active economic role in the public interest. This is a mercantilist mindset prevalent in the seventeenth and eighteenth centuries (Stiglitz, 1988). Classical economics according to Smith (1776) put forward the notion of the invisible hand, arguing that free individuals operating in a free economy, making decisions that are primarily focused on their self-interest, logically take actions that benefit society as a whole. That process occurs within a market mechanism, where the interest of society is served via commercial interactions. Mutual needs will create reduction processes if the value of a good or service exceeds the production costs. Therefore, the distribution of wealth and income is dominated by the private sector. In reality, however, the role of government to ensure a more optimal distribution of wealth and income is determined by prevailing trends in the global and national economy. A crisis, for example, will expose the success or failure of the government's crisis response protocol.

The role of government is also influenced by the predominant government system and ideology, as well as the history, socio-political development, and economic issues faced (Stiglitz & Rosengard, 2015). In Cuba and North Korea, for instance, the government plays a dominant role in controlling the economy, influenced by a socialist-communist ideology. This model is known as a socialist-communist economic system. Conversely, in the United States, countries in Western Europe and most other countries in the world, influenced by freer and more dynamic economic, legal and social mindsets (from mercantilism and laissez-faire economics to the Great Depression that saw the birth of Keynesian economics), the government plays a more balanced role with the public and private sectors driving the economy. This model is commonly known as a mixed economic system, combining aspects of both capitalism and socialism.

From an historical perspective, in terms of the mixed economic system, as embraced by most countries currently, the Great Depression in 1929 was the seminal moment when modern concepts and theories concerning the role of government intervention in the economy were born. The massive collapse of economies in the United States and Europe created awareness that (private) markets cannot be left unattended because market failure will inevitably ensue. Nevertheless, can government intervention in the economy resolve all issues immediately or ensure the success of all government programs? Of course not, this depends on numerous factors, implying that government failures can still occur.

In the context of public economics, government failures imply economic efficiencies caused by government intervention. According to Williamson (2005), the term "government failures" was first coined by Ronald Coase (1964, in Williamson, 2005) when he compared the actual and ideal regulatory systems, where discourse concerning regulatory systems actually distanced economists from thinking about optimal means of production. Other examples of government failures include the crowding out of private investment through higher interest rates as a corollary of increasing government borrowing to fund higher government spending. It can be said, therefore, that government failures occur when government intervention in the economy leads to an inefficient allocation of resources and stifles economic prosperity. Uniquely, government failures often emerge from efforts to resolve market failures that instead create a different set of problems (Pettinger, 2018).

Stiglitz and Rosengard (2015) gave four reasons concerning government failure in achieving its goals: (i) limitations on government information; (ii) limited government control over public reaction to each government program implemented; (iii) limited government control over bureaucracy; (iv) potential government limitations caused by a dynamic political process.

According to Pettinger (2018), however, government failures can arise from many causes as follows:

(a) Lack of Incentives

Players in the public sector are not motivated by profit (non-profit motives). As workers and managers are not incentivised to improve services and cut costs, inefficiencies can emerge. For instance, the public sector is more vulnerable to surplus staff. Furthermore, the government may be reluctant to dismiss civil servants due to the political cost associated with unemployment.

(b) Bad Information

Politicians may have bad information concerning the types of services provided. In addition, politicians may not be experts in their particular department, instead focusing on their political ideology, yet they are responsible for taking decisions concerning public economic issues.

(c) Political Interference

Economic decisions are often taken for short-term political gain. Consequently, for example, it is not uncommon for politicians to take decisions to maintain unproductive workers rather than create a healthy economy.

(d) Inconsistency
New government administrations typically lead to changes in political initiatives and approaches rather than maintaining the existing approach that may have been economically more advantageous in the long term.

(e) Moral Hazard
An example of moral hazard is when the government offers to guarantee all bank deposits to protect the financial system. This may unintentionally lead to excessive risk appetite as the banks know they will be bailed out by the government.

(f) Regulatory Capture
This typically occurs when a regulatory agency created to act in the public interest instead advances the commercial concerns of an industry or sector, thereby damaging the public interest.

(g) Unintended Consequences
Policies to alleviate poverty through subsidies, for example, that instead create dependence among the recipients.

(h) Special Interest Groups
When the government offers temporary special incentives to certain groups, such as tax holidays for specific businesses, which are subsequently difficult to remove politically and administratively because the special interest groups have become reliant on the incentives, leading to reluctance and adverse impacts.

4.2.3 Scope of Conventional Social-Public Finance

Public finance is the study of the role of the government in the economy. It is the branch of economics that assesses government revenue and government expenditure and the adjustment of both to achieve the desired goals (Gruber, 2010). Meanwhile, the public financial management system relates to resources, the allocation of resources, and expenditure management (resource utilisation).

Similar to economics in general, public finance is based on four fundamental questions that focus on choices relating to the public sector, the role of government, and the way government influences decisions made in the private sector. According to Stiglitz, the four questions are as follows:

(a) **What to produce?**
Public goods or private goods?

(b) **How to produce?**
Through the public sector, by the government or transferred to the private sector?

(c) **For whom to produce (and the relevant policies)?**
Taxes will affect individual spending to differing degrees. A diverse government policy program will influence diverse groups also.

(d) **How are decisions based on those questions taken?**
Must take into consideration all relevant mutually affecting factors.

According to Gruber (2010), the scope of public finance deals with the when, the how, the what, and the why of government intervention as follows:

1. **When should the government intervene in the economy?**

   In terms of economic activity, the buying and selling of goods and services, or trade, is considered efficient when both parties benefit, in other words one of the parties is not left worse off and the other better off. Through a microeconomic lens, the most efficient market is one in perfect competition. Perfect market competition is considered the best condition to maximise profit for all individuals in the market. Second, a perfectly competitive market achieves supply and demand equilibrium, where equality between supply and demand can absorb all production and consumption.

   In reality, however, there are always excesses and shortages in terms of production and consumption. This affects the cost price and selling price. Therefore, producers will lower production when demand retreats or is below the amount of goods produced. Similarly, consumers will reduce consumption when market supply is low due to higher prices.

   (a) **Market Failure**

   Adjustments in supply and demand by producers and consumers create market equilibrium. In practice, however, the efficiency gains available through market equilibrium are difficult to achieve, so real markets are never perfect. Market failure is used to describe the failure of achieving such market efficiency, with equilibrium created in the market instead leading to inefficiency.

   The health insurance market provides a good example of such inefficiencies, where there is high supply from various companies and also high demand. In the health insurance market, particularly in the United States, individuals without health insurance make up the minority, accounting for just 17.2% in 2007. That minority does not disrupt market mechanisms in terms of supply or prices. Notwithstanding, when an individual decides to opt out of health insurance, the individual becomes more susceptible to illness due to a lack of vaccines and so on. If that individual subsequently falls ill, the virus could spread to others who are also unvaccinated. Consequently, such individuals incur larger expenses, while suffering a loss of productivity and performance. This example shows how one individual's economic decision can detrimentally impact others, which is known as negative externalities, namely a cost that is suffered by a third party as a consequence of an economic transaction. Negative externalities demonstrate that ostensibly sound market conditions in terms of efficiency through supply and demand equilibrium do not necessarily reflect social inefficiencies, hence the need for government intervention.

   Through government intervention, market efforts to maximise efficiency are not only addressed at the individual or firm level, but also from a more general macro perspective to ensure the benefits are felt by all. In the case of the health insurance market in the United States, the government intervenes to provide free vaccines to low-income families. Consequently, measles cases have declined drastically, showing that government intervention can maximise social efficiency.

(b) **Redistribution**

In addition to reducing and overcoming market failure, income and resource redistribution are another important aspect. In general, economic goals include maximising income, benefit, and utility at the macro and micro levels. From a macro perspective, however, economic growth and development are often achieved at the expense of economic equality.

All countries compete to achieve advancement and growth by expanding the economy. Notwithstanding, how and to whom the economy is divided is rarely prioritised. Consequently, efforts to enlarge the economy create conditions where only a handful of individuals receive the lion's share of the economic spoils, while the majority go without.

Through government intervention, however, economic inequality can be addressed and alleviated through regulation, subsidies, and taxation, which redistribute income and other resources from those with a surplus to those with a deficit. Nonetheless, the redistribution of income and resources can also create inefficiencies through suboptimal policymaking that leaves certain individuals worse off and, thus, less productive.

2. **How does the government intervene?**

Government intervention can take many forms and be implemented in many ways as follows:

(a) **Taxation and Subsidies on Private Sales or Purchases**

By enforcing taxes and subsidies, the government can reduce and overcome market failure through price mechanisms. Through taxes, the government can raise the price of an overproduced product to lower production. Conversely, the government can lower the price of an underproduced product to increase production through subsidies.

(b) **Restricting or Forcing Private Sales or Purchases**

The government can restrict sales or purchases of an overproduced product by limiting total sales or purchases. In addition, the government can force sales or purchases of an underproduced product.

(c) **Providing Public Goods**

The government can provide public goods with broad benefits to achieve a level of consumption that maximises social welfare and prosperity.

(d) **Public Financing of Private Goods**

The government can influence consumption by financing the private sector to produce goods at the desired or required level.

3. **What is the impact of intervention?**

Intervention has direct and indirect impacts. The direct impact is the predictable effect of government intervention if the individual does not change their response to the intervention. Meanwhile, the indirect impact emerges when an individual changes his or her response to the intervention, which is not due to the individual itself or the characteristics of the individual.

4. **Why does the government intervene?**

   The government intervenes not only to mitigate or reduce market failure or safeguard economic equality, but also because each policy made or decision taken influences the political landscape and, hence, the broader economic climate or conditions.

   After government intervention, the potential for government failure emerges, as described in previous sections. Government failure has triggered widespread discourse regarding a third sector, otherwise known as the voluntary sector or social sector. Coined by Etzioni (1973, in Corry, 2010), the third sector is defined as a distinct alternative sector that counterbalances the government sector (first sector) and private sector (second sector). The third sector is considered a bridge between the public and private sectors, thus minimising not only government failures but also market failures.

   Various operational definitions for the third or social sector have emerged from Etzioni's initial findings. The UK Government, for instance, uses the social sector to categorise similar organisations that are distinct from the two other economic sectors, namely the public sector and private sector. According to Ridley-Duff and Seanor (2008, in Corry, 2010), an economy conceptually has three sectors, namely the public sector, private sector, and third sector. The third or social sector is established voluntarily by individuals pursuing social or community-based goals. Though not explicit, it is in this context that the term "social finance" has emerged theoretically and conceptually.

   Fundamentally, social finance is concerned with the expenditure and revenue activities of organisations in the third or social sector. Revenues originate from various sources, including donations from the public, private sector and occasionally contributions from the government. Various fundraising methods are used to attract funds. On the other hand, social sector spending is usually based on the vision and mission of the associated organisation, which is influenced by public values and community norms. It is common for social organisations to pursue a vision and mission in line with the religious beliefs embraced by its members.

4.3 Social-Public Finance in Islam

4.3.1 Scope of Islamic Economy

It is undeniable that public perception of the Islamic economy is dominated by *riba* and non-*riba* transactions at a financial institution, such as a bank, rather than how to trade and conduct business honestly and fairly. Such conditions imply that comprehension of the Islamic economic system is limited to banking and the financial sector. This is understandable considering the modern concept of the Islamic economy emerged from the banking sector, which is notable due to its inherent conflict with Islamic principles and teachings by applying an interest-based system.

Based on the principles and axioms elaborated previously, it is evident that Muslim behaviour to wealth is critical to achieve *falah* or salvation and well-being. According to Islam, everything in the world belongs to Allah SWT, thus to man possessions are merely entrusted. As stated by Adhiwarman Karim, money in Islam is a public good based on the flow concept, while capital is a private good based on the stock concept,[1] as a departure from the conventional perspective where money and capital are treated as private goods. Under a conventional system, therefore, it can be said that wealth is an asset belonging to an individual providing the ownership process does not violate prevailing laws and regulations.

Currently, however, the Islamic social sector has emerged through the collection and utilisation of religious social funds, such as *zakat, infaq, sadaqah,* and *waqf* (ZISWAF), which is understood as part of the broader scope of the Islamic economic system. Previously, philanthropic sectors were considered a part of worship for Muslims. Now, however, various academic studies have shown that the Islamic social sector has significant potential as an agent of economic development, establishing the sector's importance in the Islamic economy. In practice, the ZISWAF sector is not only part of the economic system from an Islamic perspective but also offers a distinct advantage over the conventional economic system.

It can be concluded, therefore, that the core of the Islamic economy is trade as an economic activity and the social sector. The question that emerges is how to position a sharia-compliant financial system at the heart of the Islamic economy as the most prominent sector of the Islamic economy? To understand and address this issue, the Islamic economy must be understood constructively through the teachings of Islam as revealed in Al-Quran and the Hadiths, similar to the previous chapter on the philosophical foundation of the Islamic economy.

Based on Al-Quran and the Hadiths, Allah SWT created mankind to live on earth as caliphs with everything necessary provided to support human life. Based on the principle that Allah SWT is God Almighty, it is important to believe that everything on earth was bestowed in sufficient abundance by Him for all, from generation to generation. This is written in several verses of Al-Quran as follows:

[1] Adiwarman Azwar Karim, Islamic Economy: A Macroeconomic Study, The International Institute of Islamic Thought Indonesia (IIIT Indonesia), 2002, pp.19–22.

ءَاَنْتُمْ اَشَدُّ خَلْقًا اَمِ السَّمَاۤءُ ۚبَنٰىهَاۗ (27)

رَفَعَ سَمْكَهَا فَسَوّٰىهَاۙ(28)

وَاَغْطَشَ لَيْلَهَا وَاَخْرَجَ ضُحٰىهَاۖ(29)

وَالْاَرْضَ بَعْدَ ذٰلِكَ دَحٰىهَاۗ(30)

اَخْرَجَ مِنْهَا مَاۤءَهَا وَمَرْعٰىهَاۖ(31)

وَالْجِبَالَ اَرْسٰىهَاۙ(32)

مَتَاعًا لَّكُمْ وَلِاَنْعَامِكُمْۗ(33)

Are you a more difficult creation or is the heaven? Allah constructed it. He raised its ceiling and proportioned it. And He darkened its night and extracted its brightness. And after that He spread the earth. He extracted from it its water and its pasture, And the mountains He set firmly. As provision for you and your grazing livestock. (Q.S. An-Nazi'at[79]: 27–33)

هُوَ الَّذِيْ خَلَقَ لَكُمْ مَّا فِى الْاَرْضِ جَمِيْعًا ثُمَّ اسْتَوٰٓى اِلَى السَّمَاۤءِ فَسَوّٰىهُنَّ سَبْعَ سَمٰوٰتٍ ۗوَهُوَ بِكُلِّ شَيْءٍ عَلِيْمٌ ࣖ

It is He who created for you all of that which is on the earth. Then He directed Himself to the heaven, [His being above all creation], and made them seven heavens, and He is Knowing of all things. (Q.S. Al-Baqarah [2]: 29)

وَابْتَغِ فِيْمَآ اٰتٰىكَ اللّٰهُ الدَّارَ الْاٰخِرَةَ وَلَا تَنْسَ نَصِيْبَكَ مِنَ الدُّنْيَا وَاَحْسِنْ كَمَآ اَحْسَنَ اللّٰهُ اِلَيْكَ وَلَا تَبْغِ الْفَسَادَ فِى
الْاَرْضِ ۗاِنَّ اللّٰهَ لَا يُحِبُّ الْمُفْسِدِيْنَ

But seek, through that which Allah has given you, the home of the Hereafter; and [yet], do not forget your share of the world. And do good as Allah has done good to you. And desire not corruption in the land. Indeed, Allah does not like corrupters. (Q.S. Al-Qasas [28]: 77)

الْبَيْعُ اِنَّمَا قَالُوْٓا بِاَنَّهُمْ ذٰلِكَ الْمَسِّۗ مِنَ الشَّيْطٰنُ يَتَخَبَّطُهُ الَّذِيْ يَقُوْمُ كَمَا اِلَّا يَقُوْمُوْنَ لَا الرِّبٰوا يَأْكُلُوْنَ اَلَّذِيْنَ
ۗاللّٰهِ اِلَى وَاَمْرُهٗٓ سَلَفَۗ مَا فَلَهٗ فَانْتَهٰى رَّبِّهٖ مِّنْ مَوْعِظَةٌ جَاۤءَهٗ فَمَنْ الرِّبٰواۗ وَحَرَّمَ الْبَيْعَ اللّٰهُ وَاَحَلَّ الرِّبٰواۘ مِثْلُ
خٰلِدُوْنَ فِيْهَا هُمْ ۚالنَّارِ اَصْحٰبُ فَاُولٰۤىِٕكَ عَادَ وَمَنْ

Those who consume interest cannot stand [on the Day of Resurrection] except as one stands who is being beaten by Satan into insanity. That is because they say, "Trade is [just] like interest." But Allah has permitted trade and has forbidden interest. So whoever has received an admonition from his Lord and desists may have what is past, and his affair rests with Allah. But whoever returns to [dealing in interest or usury]—those are the companions of the Fire; they will abide eternally therein. (Q.S. Al-Baqarah [2]: 275)

Those Quranic verses imply that Allah SWT as creator of man has bestowed everything necessary for life on earth in the form of abundant resources. As caliphs, humans are commanded to manage those resources using the intellect given to ensure sufficiency across generations. The intergenerational dimension is important to highlight because the seventh verse of Al-Qashash reveals that humans are forbidden from harming or damaging the earth. This verse implies that humans are forbidden from excess and must consider the needs and rights of others.

Thus, the meaning can be construed that humans are indeed ordered to utilise everything on earth to support life. This can be achieved through production to increase the value added of resources to be consumed by humans. In a broader context based on economic concepts, this includes the distribution process via exchange between producers and consumers using a barter mechanism or other media of exchange, such as currency. This is the salient point of the Islamic economy, namely the real sector, which initially focused on meeting decent living standards yet has become synonymous with trade activity.

Based on those Quranic verses, it is important to understand that Islam initially taught the concepts of capitalism. This form of capitalism, however, differed considerably from that practised by occidental countries, namely by justifying the trade of capital and assets. During the life of Rasulullah SAW, He lived as a trader, even using capital lent by His wife Khadijah. Through mutual trust, the success of the Prophet Muhammad SAW as a trader was exemplary. That was the initial concept of capitalism that has morphed over time due to a lack of Islamic morals and ethics. This is emphasised in the seventh verse of Al-Qashash, namely that although humans were created to worship Allah SWT as the creator, humans are also forbidden from neglecting their worldly affairs and interests as their rights.

The seventh verse of Al-Qashash also explains that humans must be kind to each other, which is interpreted based on humans as social beings. According to this concept, all efforts to seek happiness and prosperity on earth must also consider the welfare and interests of others. To that end in Islam, humans are instructed to fulfil religious *zakat* almsgiving obligations and increase *infaq, sadaqah,* and *waqf* donations. This is an integral part of social concepts in Islam, which absolutely condemns injustice and commands humans to share. Emphasis on paying attention to onc another is also implied in the words of Rasulullah SAW as follows:

حَدَّثَنَا مُحَمَّدُ بْنُ كَثِيرٍ قَالَ: أَخْبَرَنَا سُفْيَانُ عَنْ عَبْدِ الْمَلِكِ بْنِ أَبِي بَشِيرٍ عَنْ عَبْدِ اللهِ بْنِ الْمُسَاوِرِ قَالَ: سَمِعْتُ ابْنَ
عَبَّاسٍ يُخْبِرُ ابْنَ الزُّبَيْرِ يَقُولُ: سَمِعْتُ النَّبِيَّ صلى الله عليه وسلم يَقُولُ: لَيْسَ الْمُؤْمِنُ الَّذِي يَشْبَعُ وَجَارُهُ جَائِعٌ.

Ibn ’Abbas informed Ibn az-Zubayr, “I heard the Prophet, may Allah bless him and grant him peace, say, ’He is not a believer whose stomach is filled while his neighbor goes hungry[2]

Returning to the previous question, what is the financial sector’s position in Islam? Continuing the former explanation that Islam prioritises trade in the real sector, it is clear that real sector activity occurs due to disparate access to resources, which naturally tends towards exchange. Such conditions show that although Allah SWT bestowed everything necessary for mankind on earth, not everyone has the same

[2] Al-Adab Al-Mufrad 112, in-book reference: book 6, Hadith 0.

access to resources. This encapsulates how the economy in Islam comprises the trade or commercial sector and social sector, which aims to create equitable access to resources and everything else related to fulfilling life's necessities.

Disparities in opportunities and access are what necessitate the financial sector. Differences in purchasing power caused by a lack of access to resources are overcome through the financial sector. It can be seen here, therefore, that construction of the economic mindset in Islam is different to the conventional mindset. Islam does not recognise the financial sector, instead focusing on the real sector, with the financial sector merely serving as a medium to invigorate the real sector, with both sectors operating conjointly. On the other hand, in a conventional system, the financial sector and real sector are two independent industries. Money, therefore, functions merely as a medium of exchange in Islam, contrasting the conventional system where money has become a commodity, which is forbidden as *riba* in Islam.

Historically and over time, like the conventional system, the financial sector in Islam has bifurcated into commercial finance and public finance. Nevertheless, the social sector as mentioned previously, namely ZISWAF, where most potential is dominated by cash, has developed into Islamic social finance. In Islam, public finance and social finance are the salient topics of this book and will be discussed at length in subsequent chapters. First, the scope of public finance and social finance in Islam is explored.

4.3.2 State Supervision of Economic Activity in Islam

In the *fiqh* economy of Umar Radhiyallahu Anhu based on Islamic jurisprudence, the *hisbah* (accountability) system of upholding community morals embraced several important goals for general economic activity as follows:

1. **Ensuring Rule-based Economic Activity**

   External supervision, through *hisbah*, is a critical element due to inherent weaknesses of individual supervision by Muslims when performing economic activity as producers or consumers. Supervision functions to prevent negligence by economic players and maintain the following economic rules:

   (a) Sharia-compliant economic activity, which forbids Muslims from engaging in haram economic activity irrespective of the potential profit. This includes ensuring the products and methods used to generate profit do not violate Islamic rules. As exemplified by Umar, who sent his companions to expel ignorant market patrons, even striking those sitting idly for not knowing sharia law. Umar stated, "do not trade in our market unless you are knowledgeable because the ignorant will devour *riba*, whether on purpose or not". (Associating the impact of *riba* with the microeconomy).

(b) Combating Deception

Small behaviours are often underestimated by economic players and can have harmful consequences for consumers, the distribution of foreign exchange and spending, as well as the ability to produce and expand the economy. Combating and eliminating all forms of deception are critical for production because producers cannot compete without considering the production outcomes, while striving to improve the quality of goods and services.

2. **Creating Peace and Security**

Peace and security are prerequisites to realise an investment climate conducive to economic growth. Umar and his companions secured the markets in Medina to prevent crime and wickedness amongst traders. In a contemporary economic context, maintaining a conducive investment climate is achieved through the realisation of investment projects and maintaining economic stability, including inflation within the target corridor, fiscal sustainability with a manageable budget deficit, tight interest rates to dampen short-term rupiah exchange rate volatility, and a healthy level of government debt.

3. **Maintaining the Public Interest**

This includes maintaining supporting infrastructure for economic activity by prioritising welfare for all citizens, implementing checks, protecting from idle people, and distancing from anything harmful, which could impact a seamless production and distribution process.

Regulating market transactions implies supervising transactions that may lead to unhealthy competition. In general, *hisbah* in an economy aims to create prosperity and prevent harm. The form of supervision depends on the circumstances, place, and conditions.

4.3.3 Scope of Islamic Social-Public Finance

Islam guarantees individual freedoms. Concerning *muamalah*, Islam also consistently applies that principle by safeguarding a free market in terms of supply and demand, which influences price formation in the market. Islam allows market forces to determine production, consumption, distribution, and other economic activity in line with prevailing conditions, providing such activities do not violate sharia law or Islamic principles. Therefore, Islam naturally embraces an economic system built on market mechanisms and market forces free from government control or intervention over prices. In fact, this was explicitly stated by the Prophet Muhammad SAW, as leader, when requested to intervene after market prices experienced inflation, stating:

حَدَّثَنَا مُحَمَّدُ بْنُ بَشَّارٍ حَدَّثَنَا الْحَجَّاجُ بْنُ مِنْهَالٍ حَدَّثَنَا حَمَّادُ بْنُ سَلَمَةَ عَنْ قَتَادَةَ وَثَابِتٍ وَحُمَيْدٍعَنْ أَنَسٍ
قَالَ غَلاَ السِّعْرُ عَلَى عَهْدِ رَسُولِ اللَّهِ صلى الله عليه وسلم فَقَالُوا يَا رَسُولَ اللَّهِ سَعِّرْ لَنَا . فَقَالَ " إِنَّ اللَّهَ
هُوَ الْمُسَعِّرُ الْقَابِضُ الْبَاسِطُ الرَّزَّاقُ وَإِنِّي لأَرْجُو أَنْ أَلْقَى رَبِّي وَلَيْسَ أَحَدٌ مِنْكُمْ يَطْلُبُنِي بِمَظْلَمَةٍ فِي دَمٍ
وَلاَ مَالٍ " . قَالَ أَبُو عِيسَى هَذَا حَدِيثٌ حَسَنٌ صَحِيحٌ

Narrated Anas:

Prices became excessive during the time of the Messenger of Allah (ﷺ), so they said: 'O Messenger of Allah! Set prices for us!' So he said: 'Indeed Allah is Al-Musa'ir, Al-Qabid, Al-Basir, Ar-Razzaq. And I am hopeful that I meet my Lord and none of you are seeking (recompense from) me for an injustice involving blood or wealth.[3][Abu 'Eisa said:] This Hadith is Hasan Sahih.

Notwithstanding, even Rasulullah SAW intervened and regulated the economy when issues or losses arose from economic activity. It is indeed nearly impossible to find a market system that genuinely creates justice for all parties. This is due to asymmetric information amongst economic players and the natural human tendency to maximise profit. Fundamentally, welfare gaps can also occur as a corollary of disparate access to economic activity, leading to the inequitable distribution of income.

Seeking to overcome such conditions, a system to balance the economy is required and, in this case, the government authority is the most likely candidate. This is known as the public policy sector. To discharge this function, a specific budget is required, the management (revenue and expenditure) of which is known as public finance. That is how the public finance sector emerged in response to overcome disparities in public access to the economy.

In Islam, the scope of social-public finance is explained based on the principles and values revealed in Al-Qur'an and the Hadiths. The explanation begins with one of the goals of sharia (*maqasid syariah*), namely to guarantee the lives of all Muslims, implying that the life of a Muslim is the responsibility of the individual. This concept is also supported by Al-Shatibi (in Siddiqi, 1996), who argues that in Islam, the individual is responsible and obliged to strive towards fulfilling his own life. Nevertheless, Siddiqi (1996) stated that the basic necessities for life on earth are already guaranteed. This is linked to the Islamic principle stating that Allah SWT created man on earth with sufficient resources to sustain life, implying that life is guaranteed by the Creator and humans need only exert themselves to acquire it. Furthermore, humans were created on earth as caliphs or vicegerents. Such status places the burden of responsibility on humans to manage all the resources bestowed by Allah SWT to be enjoyed from generation to generation.

Based on the concept of *maqasid syariah*, religion is the primary goal concerning the creation of mankind on earth. Siddiqi (1996) explained the significance of religion as the primary goal of life on earth, namely to worship Allah SWT in accordance with the precepts revealed in Al-Qur'an and the Hadiths. To that end, individuals must have strength and capability, which can be achieved once the basic

[3]Jami` at-Tirmidhi 1314, in-book reference: book 14, Hadith 117.

necessities have been met. Therefore, it is reasonable that the basic needs of individuals must be guaranteed, for which only the government has the power and authority to achieve. This is where the concept of public finance was conceived, with the government or state required to manage its finances or resources to create justice and equity for all citizens. Therefore, Siddiqi (1996) also concluded that meeting the basic needs or necessities of life by the government is considered *fardu kifayah* or a communal obligation, yet if discharged by only one Muslim, the remaining Muslims are freed from the responsibility before God.

In Islam, in addition to public policy, the reallocation and redistribution of economic resources can be achieved using *zakat, infaq, sadaqah, waqf* (ZISWAF), and other social instruments. Social finance plays a role in complementing and strengthening the government's target of public finance policy. Nevertheless, the social finance sector typically emerges and is operated by and for the community, implying that social finance is a bottom-up initiative of the community.

Fundamentally, therefore, the scope of social-public finance in Islam differs little from conventional public finance in the contemporary era, particularly in terms of the instruments used on the revenue side.

Under the Islamic economic system, the dominance of fiscal policy in the real sector is clearly perceptible, as reflected in how Islamic fiscal instruments dictated economic discussions amongst classical Islamic economists. Furthermore, the central religious text of Islamic teachings, Al-Qur'an, states that in the Islamic economy the *zakat* fiscal mechanism is a prerequisite.

There are several fiscal instruments as tools of the state to run the economy towards spiritual and material prosperity, including those required under sharia law and those performed in accordance with the authority of the state. *Zakat* is an example of a fiscal instrument required under sharia law, while instruments under the authority of the state determine the enforcement, magnitude, and object of fiscal instruments, including *kharaj, jizyah, ushur* and other similar tax instruments.

From a conventional perspective, two institutions provide mechanisms that address the issue of allocating and distributing economic resources, namely the markets and the government. The markets maintain the allocation and distribution of economic resources through supply and demand forces, motivated by profit. Meanwhile, the government is a complementary institution that intervenes in cases of market failure to serve the economic needs of the people. Nevertheless, the markets and market forces tend to dominate economic allocation and distribution.

From an Islamic perspective, the existence of a third sector addresses the issue of allocating and distributing economic resources, namely the voluntary sector. This complementary sector is a consequence of sharia law concerning *zakat, infaq, sadaqah, waqf* (ZISWAF), and other instruments. According to Faridi (1983), the structure of the voluntary sector is similar to the private sector, where the existing mechanisms depend on parties external to the government, such as the accumulation of *infaq, sadaqah,* and *waqf.*

In terms of the goal, however, the voluntary sector is identical to the public sector, namely public prosperity and welfare. In fact, the voluntary sector specifically facilitates those towards the bottom of the pyramid to actively access the economy

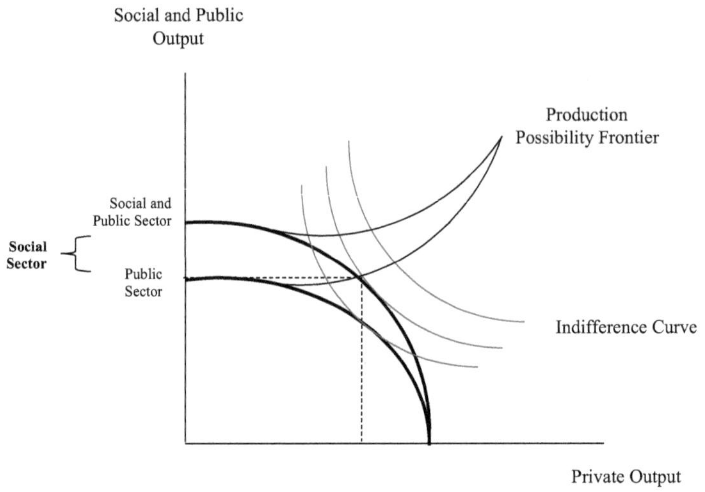

Fig. 4.2 Public, private, and social sectors. Source: Faridi (1983), modified further by authors

based on a moral understanding (akidah and akhlak) of Islamic teachings. In other words, the scale of the voluntary sector rests on faith. Furthermore, the presence of the voluntary sector is a consequence of implementing sharia law, which is absent from the conventional economic system (Fig. 4.2).

The normal allocation and distribution of economic resources via market mechanisms are determined by productivity, performance, and the environment. It is important to understand, however, that certain social groups will naturally lack economic access given limitations in terms of productivity, performance, or environmental support, such as age (too old or too young), physical or mental disabilities, or other factors. Such limitations restrict economic access or may even force certain individuals out of the economy, where access was once possible. Therefore, it is the government's role to maintain accessibility through *zakat* regulations and other instruments in the public sector. What is the role of the third sector or social sector?

The social sector plays a complementary role by strengthening the targets of government policy through community-based initiatives (similar to the private sector) using *infaq, sadaqah, waqf,* and other similar instruments. While some argue that management is still centralised under the government, from an initiator perspective, this mechanism distinguishes the sector from the other two. Furthermore, the social sector is also a variable of social investment in the macroeconomy, where a larger social investment will offset the social cost borne by the community. Social costs include school fees, healthcare costs, and other costs incurred in relation to social services. The social costs are offset because all public service facilities are constructed using social investment funds, including health facilities and schools built using *waqf* funds, along with other facilities such as mosques, bridges, roads, markets, and so on. Cumulatively, therefore, development of the three economic sectors (private, social, and public) will increase economic satisfaction in the community.

Underlying Principles of Islamic Public Finance

Public finance, as practised throughout the history of Islamic civilisation, was established based on the revelations found in Al-Qur'an and the Sunnah. Nevertheless, Al-Qur'an and the Sunnah do not explicitly describe how public finance is achieved in Islam. Based on the instructions and commands relating to public finance; however, the principles of Islamic public finance can be derived. Furthermore, the implementation of Islamic public finance was exemplified during the life of the Prophet Muhammad SAW and Khulafaur Rasyidin. The principles of Islamic public finance are as follows:

(a) Based on an unambiguous foundation, namely an Islamic social and ethical philosophy (sources of sharia law), rather than a financial process in the hands of those with power.
(b) Public prosperity and economic growth are the overarching focus of public finance policies in Islam.
(c) Public funds, primarily from *zakat*, are mandated to create public prosperity and the equitable distribution of income amongst all social strata.
(d) Voluntary donations from prosperous Muslims, primarily in the form of *waqf* assets, are an important source of public financing.
(e) Islam permits the imposition of new taxes and debt if justified (under emergency conditions).

Public policy in Muslim countries focuses on several aspects. First, to meet the basic needs of all citizens from an economic, moral, and religious perspective. The authority mandated to each individual to execute government activity must be fully utilised for public prosperity, extending beyond merely the economic dimension to include other sharia goals. Public finance is an intermediary serving those needs. Second, the state must also focus on fulfilling other social obligations for the community. According to Al-Ghazali, the authorities must provide assistance to communities impacted by disaster, famine, hunger, and other suffering. An-Nawawi stated that social obligations include the eradication of hunger by providing sustenance and clothing as required. Realistically, however, the social obligations of the state also take into consideration the financial conditions of *Baitul Mal*. Third, the government is obligated to provide public goods. Again, according to Al-Ghazali, the production of public goods is *fard al-kifayah*. To avoid production disputes, the government must provide without incurring direct costs on the populace. Public goods that must be provided by the state include agricultural infrastructure projects.

Instruments of the Islamic Public Sector

Instruments of the Islamic public sector are obligatory under sharia law and available to the government as budget revenue. Utilising *zakat*, *kharaj*, *jizyah*, and other similar instruments, the government can fund development or contribute to meeting community needs.

1. ***Zakat***

Literally, the word *zakat* is derived from the Arabic verb *zaka* meaning "to improve, to purify, and to increase" or "purity" in Aramaic. Those meanings signify the function of *zakat* itself. Therefore, *zakat* collected from those with surplus wealth (*muzakki*) will grow, cleanse, and purify the remainder of their wealth. The economic mechanism that explains the development process is when *zakat* is appropriately applied in the economy. That was the objective when writing this chapter, to explain how *zakat* transmission influences economic performance.

Similar to other rules and instruments Allah SWT has applied to all aspects of human life, there are two primary functions, namely to provide benefit to the individual (*nafs*) and the collective (*jama'i*). In this case, *zakat* also has two economic functions. First, as a means of worship that brings benefit to the individual (*nafs*) as the *zakat* payer (*muzakki*) and benefit to the collective (*jama'i*) for those in the community applying the *zakat* system. Furthermore, the words of Allah SWT reveal that *zakat* will cleanse and purify the *muzakki*, with cleansing in this sense implying that *zakat* will cleanse the soul of miserliness and greed. This is because mankind's love for wealth must heed the warnings of Allah SWT in the Al-Qur'an.

وَاِنَّهٗ لِحُبِّ الْخَيْرِ لَشَدِيْدٌ

And indeed he is, in love of wealth, intense. (Q.S. Al 'Adiyat [100]: 8)

Meanwhile, the goal of *zakat* to purify implies that *zakat* will sanctify the soul and enrich kindness. *Zakat* is a constant reminder to those with surplus wealth that others also have a rightful claim on some of that wealth. The aspects of sanctification and kindness ensure *zakat's* contribution as an instrument that provides benefit to the collective (*jama'i*). With tenderness and kindness, individuals can offer their wealth to others in need. In other words, *zakat* forces (in a binding and sanctionable way) humans to interact with other humans. The interaction is between humans with surplus wealth and those with deficit funds.

As explained in the previous Quranic verse, *zakat* will multiply human wealth. The implications of multiplying wealth through *zakat* must be observed through a collective (*jama'i*) lens, because that way the collective function of *zakat* will clearly be felt. The actual multiplication process is explained in more detail in the following subchapter, yet to briefly illustrate the collective function of *zakat*, it is important to note that *zakat* increases market demand and, thus, stimulates economic growth. Demand is increased as the economy accommodates the *duafa*, thus increasing the number of market players on the demand and supply sides in line with population growth. The distribution of *zakat* to the needy serves as income and increases purchasing power. In other words, *zakat* provides access to the economy, especially if the state provides facilities for recipients to actively engage as market actors on the supply side.

Zakat is an original system and instrument of the Islamic economic system, which distributes wealth to the needy, based on the belief that contained in all wealth is the right to a portion for the poor and needy (eight types of *asnaf*).

إِنَّمَا الصَّدَقٰتُ لِلْفُقَرَاۤءِ وَالْمَسٰكِيْنِ وَالْعَامِلِيْنَ عَلَيْهَا وَالْمُؤَلَّفَةِ قُلُوْبُهُمْ وَفِى الرِّقَابِ وَالْغَارِمِيْنَ وَفِيْ سَبِيْلِ اللّٰهِ
وَابْنِ السَّبِيْلِۗ فَرِيْضَةً مِّنَ اللّٰهِ ۗوَاللّٰهُ عَلِيْمٌ حَكِيْمٌ

> Zakah expenditures are only for the poor and for the needy and for those employed to collect [zakah] and for bringing hearts together [for Islam] and for freeing captives [or slaves] and for those in debt and for the cause of Allah and for the [stranded] traveler—an obligation [imposed] by Allah. And Allah is Knowing and Wise. (Q.S. At Taubah [9]: 60)

Although the command or mechanism of *zakat* was revealed in the earlier chapters of Al-Qur'an in Mecca (*Makiyah*), *zakat* was only effectively and comprehensively implemented 18 months later or 2 years after *Hijrah*. In other words, *zakat* was first implemented in Medina. During that period, it was customary for *mustahiq* to receive one dirham per day to meet their needs, which was equivalent to the wages of an unskilled labourer.

There are two existential reasons for *zakat* in life for the individual or collective, namely worship and economic reasons. In terms of worship, *zakat* is a variable or measure of obedience to Allah SWT. Therefore, *zakat* is a religious obligation or duty for all Muslims who meet the necessary criteria of wealth (*nisab*). Economic reasons imply that *zakat* is a primary variable in maintaining socio-economic stability. Through *zakat*, economic sustainability is maintained, while preserving social harmony between humans, market participants as well as the poor and wealthy.

In addition to *zakat*, the Islamic economy offers several similar instruments with broader uses for public finance, namely *kharaj, jizyah, ushr,* and *ghanimah.* Such instruments provide state income for development programs. The obligatory instruments are *zakat*, *kharaj, jizyah,* and *ushr.*

Therefore, it is important to classify sources of state income, considering the origins and expenditure goals, because income from each category must be maintained and managed separately (Tables 4.1, 4.2, 4.3, and 4.4). The main sources of *Baitul Mal* income are as follows:

Table 4.1 Objects of obligatory 2.5% zakat payment

Zakatable assets	Nisab	Prerequisite condition
1. Gold 2. Silver 3. Cash 4. Merchandise 5. Mining goods (minerals)	*Zakat* is imposed if the goods reach the minimum limit of 200 dirhams or 5 uqiyya silver or 20 dinars (1 dinar is equal to 4.25 g of gold and 1 dirham is equal to 2975 g of silver; so the nisab is 86 g of gold or 595 g of silver)	Payments are made after the *zakat* assets settle for one hijri year. However, the conditions for mining goods (minerals) are not clear enough.

Source: Hasanuzzaman (1991)

Table 4.2 Objects of obligatory 5% and 10% zakat payment[a]

Zakatable assets	Nisab	Prerequisite condition
1. Agricultural Goods (dates, wheat, corn, grapes, etc.)	*Zakat* is imposed if the goods reach a total production of 5 wasqs (1 wasqs equals 60 sha' equals 2176 kg; so the nisab is 652.8 kilograms)	Payment is made at harvest time
2. Olive oil		

[a]10% for rain-watered agricultural land or other production costs. 5% for irrigated arable land

Table 4.3 Objects of obligatory 20% zakat payment

Zakatable assets	Nisab	Prerequisite condition
1. Found treasure 2. Hidden treasure (Treasure)	There is no nisab	Payment is made when you get the item

Table 4.4 Livestock zakat

Animal	Nisab	*Zakat*
Goat/Sheep	40	1
	30	1 Male Adult
Cow/Buffalo	40	2 Male Adults
	5	1 Goat/Sheep
Camel	25	Mature Camel

2. ***Kharaj***

Kharaj is a type of individual Islamic tax on community-owned productive agricultural land and its produce under Islamic law. In certain cases, the state reserves the right to confiscate potential land abandoned by the owner to obtain benefit. The state also has the right to determine the amount of tax based on prevailing economic conditions. According to such characteristics, *kharaj* is a reliable fiscal instrument for the government to support national development programs.

Hasanuzzaman (1991) explained that land tax falls into two categories, namely *ushr* and *kharaj*. *Ushr*, or a religious tithe, was paid on land located on the Arabian Peninsula obtained generationally or through conquest. Meanwhile, *kharaj* was levied upon the lands of conquered provinces outside the Arabian Peninsula. Abu Yusuf argued that all Muslim-owned land was *ushr* land, while foreign land reconciled by the population and under the responsibility of Muslims was *kharaj* land. In other words, *kharaj* refers to a tax levied by Muslim rulers on their non-Muslim subjects, while Muslim landowners paid *ushr*, a religious tithe, on their land.

Notwithstanding, there are other definitions of *kharaj*. In the literature, Abidin Ahmad Salama (1995) explains *kharaj* in more detail, with different definitions during different periods of Islamic state power. According to Salama (1995), *kharaj* refers to a tax levied on idle land irrespective of a Muslim or non-Muslim

Table 4.5 Kharaj in Iraq during Umar bin Khattab Caliphate

Standard	*Kharaj*
One bushel of wet wheat	2 Dirhams
One bushel of wet corn	4 Dirhams
One bushel of wet grapes	5 Dirhams
One bushel of wet chrome wood	10 Dirhams

landowner, with the levy adjusted according to the land area owned. During that period, productive arable land was no longer subject to *kharaj* tax. That model was prevalent from the reign of Umar bin Khattab to the Abbasid Caliphate led by El Mahdi. Since the time of El Mahdi, however, the concept of *kharaj* has undergone significant change, with the tax levied on the agricultural produce harvested from the land using a profit-sharing system between the government and landowner. In fact, the rate of taxation also varied according to the conditions of the farmer and his harvest. During the cultivation process, for example, if a farmer encountered irrigation constraints or inclement weather that detrimentally impacted the harvest, the rate of taxation or profit sharing for the government would be reduced. This policy was used to reduce the burden on landowners or farmers created by harvest failures in terms of quality or quantity.

Based on the two definitions of *kharaj* outlined above, there are different economic consequences of implementation. The concept of *kharaj* levied on idle land would encourage the community to produce actively, particularly the agricultural sector, thus increasing the production and supply of agricultural produce and lowering market prices. In addition, such a policy would minimise idle assets, which are not recommended or even forbidden in Islam.

Classifying land based on its contribution to the state, Abu Ubaid put forward three classifications. First, Muslim-owned land, namely *ushr* land. Second, land reconciled by the population and under the responsibility of Muslims with a predetermined (*kharaj*) tax, namely *kharaj* land. Third, land acquired through conflict.

Quthb Ibrahim Muhammad (2002) explained that determining the rate of *kharaj* (land tax) was based on the following variables:

(a) **Land Type**

Fertile land allows crops to flourish, with larger harvests than degraded land.

(b) **Crop Type**

Some crops command higher prices than others, therefore the type of crop also determines the rate of *kharaj*.

(c) **Land Management**

Kharaj levied on land with high maintenance costs is lower than *kharaj* levied on (low cost) rainfed arable land.

Quthb Ibrahim Muhammad (2002) provided historical sample data concerning how *kharaj* standards were set under the Caliphate of Umar bin Khattab in Iraq during that period (Table 4.5).

According to Hasanuzzaman (1991), although Islam recognises individual freehold rights on land, certain conditions will make an individual relinquish those land rights. Hasanuzzaman put forward six conditions for when a landowner may transfer or give up his land rights as follows:

(a) Temporary land ownership rights awarded by the state, implying that the rights will return to the state upon completion of the leasehold or other specific conditions. This occurred when Umar bin Khattab retook land ownership rights in Egypt upon the death of the owner.
(b) The state enacts new laws (amendments) concerning the apportionment of public land.
(c) The owner leaves land idle for a given period. In this case, Quthb Ibrahim Muhammad (2002) discovered regulations enforced under the Caliphate of Umar bin Khattab stipulating that if an individual makes productive use of idle land, the land will belong to that person, but if that land is abandoned for a period of 3 years, the ownership rights are lost.
(d) The owner is unable to pay the agreed levy to the state as a condition of ownership rights. This occurred in the case of Hilal Bani Muta'an, who entered into an agreement with Rasulullah SAW.
(e) An urgent state interest to appropriate certain land ownership rights. This occurred in the case of residents from Najran and Fadak during the reign of Umar bin Khattab.
(f) In the public interest or for the greater good, land ownership can be sequestered by the state, as in the case of the Nabawi Mosque expansion project in Medina.

Concerning land issues, Quthb Ibrahim Muhammad (2002) disclosed that the government can also manage land given by the community for protection. Plots of land under the protection of the government are known as *Al Hima*, the utilisation of which must be in the public or state interest, namely for defence, security, poverty alleviation, and so on.

In a modern economic context, *kharaj* is an important instrument in the receipt of development capital. Innovative fiscal policy using *kharaj* as a reference is essential in the modern economy. For instance, how to address individuals without access to productive land but sufficient income? Perhaps it would be more *maslahah* or beneficial if innovative tax policy could apply this analogous *kharaj* approach rather than *zakat* because *kharaj* distribution is broader and freer than *zakat* distribution, which is tied to eight categories of *asnaf*. Nevertheless, interpretation of sharia justification concerning *kharaj* would have to be agreed as well as its application in the modern economy. Consequently, the targeted implementation of this instrument could be maximised for the state.

3. **Jizyah**

Jizyah (poll tax) is paid by non-Muslim citizens who have the means to pay it to their Muslim rulers. Historically, based on classical Islamic economics

Table 4.6 Jizyah under Umar bin Khattab

Standard	Jizyah
High income	48 Dirhams
Medium income	24 Dirhams
Low income	12 Dirhams

Source: Majid Khadduri (1955)

Table 4.7 Jizyah rate in Egypt (103 Hijriah)

Jizyah mandatory land area	Jizya in dinar
95	230
5	7 $^1/_6$
7	17
15	38 ½
7	20 ½
5	13
12	25 $^1/_6$
14	108 $^2/_3$

Source: Hasanuzzaman (1991)

literature, this tax was levied on non-Muslim men. Nevertheless, the old, people with disabilities, the mentally ill and individuals with economic constraints (no livelihood) were exempt from paying this tax. In fact, under certain circumstances, the state was responsible for meeting the basic needs of non-Muslims, providing the population was willing to live under an Islamic government. This is linked to the primary function of the government, as explained previously, namely to meet the basic needs of the population. Therefore, under an Islamic government and economic system, the fulfilment of basic needs is not restricted only to the Muslim population.

Majid Khadduri and Hasanuzzaman as well as several prominent classical Islamic economists from history stated that *jizyah,* averaging 2 dinar, was levied on each non-Muslim adult male. Such males were categorised as non-Muslim *Dzimmah*, known as *dzimmi*. Etymologically, the roots of *dzimmah* are defined as agreement and protection, implying that *dzimmi* were those who agreed to be protected under an Islamic government. There are several opinions concerning the amount of *jizyah* to be levied on *dzimmi*, as presented in Tables 4.6 and 4.7 taken from Majid Khadduri and Hasanuzzaman. The variation stems from the amount of *jizyah* that must be paid in Egypt, which was not explicitly stated, whereas the levy elsewhere averaged 2 dinar per head.

As additional clarification, Hasanuzzaman stated that Islamic economic history has shown a general *kharaj* rate of 1 dinar per 4 aroura, as a measure of land during that era. Hasanuzzaman also showed how Islam views land ownership and management rights as important economic factors. Land was considered the most productive factor of production, with ownership and management rights thus important economic factors. Therefore, Islam pays close attention to land ownership and management rights.

4. ***Ushur***

Ushur was a border trade tax levied on commercial merchandise that was imported across the border to a Muslim country. Today, this is known as customs duties. According to Umar bin Khattab, this was a reciprocal tax, applied at the same rate as the trading partner country. Therefore, there is a difference between *ushur* and *ushr*. *Ushr* is more accurately defined in terms of the *kharaj* discussion above. On the other hand, according to Hasanuzzaman, *ushur* (plural of *ushr*) was a 10% levy on the value of goods (possibly of one dirham per transaction) traded prior to the emergence of Islam, with *ushur* officials known as *ashir*. Several hadiths mention that Rasulullah SAW outlawed the practice of *ashir*. Under Umar bin Khattab, however, the practice returned to regulate international economic relationships with non-Muslim countries and create prosperity, the principles and form of which were not the same as *ashir* prior to Islam. According to Hasanuzzaman, Abu Ubayd stated the practice of *ashir* was replaced with *zakat* by Rasulullah SAW, with *ushur* thus only levied on Harbi (infidels hostile to Islam) as well as *dzimmi* (non-believers not hostile to Islam). *Ushur* was levied at 10% for Harbi traders, 5% for *dzimmi* traders, and 2.5% for Muslim traders (*zakat*).

A portion of ulema stated that *usyur* should not be levied on Muslim traders. The application of this system can prevent economic impotence amongst Muslim traders in their own country caused by the dumping of products or domination and prevalence of systems instituted by non-Muslim traders.

Political Impact of *Ushur* (Customs Duties) in the Contemporary Era

An Islamic government can reap political benefits from *usyur* towards the realisation of various international economic goals as follows:

(a) Import restrictions by raising the *usyur* rate on specific goods deemed undesirable or lowering (eliminating) *usyur* to motivate imports of goods considered necessary for Muslim welfare. Notwithstanding, unwise import decisions for Muslims concerning all forms of consumer goods will drive believers towards other economies or economic systems, yet the spread of Western products could infiltrate Muslim regions and possibly introduce other lifestyles or fashions for Muslims.
(b) A means to stimulate trade between Islamic countries by waiving *usyur*. This will motivate trade and import activities concerning products required by Muslims, thereby triggering a macro effect in the economy. The largest advantages afforded by international trade are in the hands of Muslims in Islamic countries.
(c) Protecting the rights of Muslim traders and offering protection from reciprocal relationship requirements with non-Muslim countries. The benefits are achieved through the application of equivalent *muamalah* principles, namely that Islamic countries are required to apply trade regulations to non-Muslim countries as such regulations are applied to Muslim traders.
(d) Realising the goals of *da'wah* from *usyur* politics, namely the political activity of calling people to embrace Islam. Islamic countries can teach *usyur* to traders

in non-Muslim countries, providing an opportunity to proselytise Islam in the host country.

(e) Islamic countries can determine and adjust the number of imported products from non-Muslim countries providing the policy helps to realise general welfare for Muslims and protect the production of products flourishing in Muslim regions.

(f) Eliminating the problem of double taxation in the conventional economy that currently restricts trade and hikes consumer prices by charging *usyur* once per year.

(g) Attracting international investors to Muslim countries by lowering *usyur* as a special citizenship right. During the reign of Umar bin Khattab, officials lowered *usyur* to 5% from 10% for Ahlul Harbi traders living in Muslim regions for a minimum of 1 year, the same rate as *dzimmah*.

(h) Restricting the movement of non-Muslim traders in Muslim regions. Such restrictions serve to promote Muslim innovation to fill the gaps. This allows Muslim traders to trade without competition from non-Muslim traders and create welfare for themselves and Muslims in general.

(i) Contributing to state income in Islamic countries because Muslims pay *zakat* and non-Muslims pay *usyur* (tax) in addition to other property and wealth requirements determined by the government for the citizens of Islamic countries.

Ibn Khaldun emphasised that tax enforcement and exemption must take place in accordance with sharia law, such as *sadaqah*, land tax, *kharaj, jizyah,* and others. In his epistemology, Ibn Khaldun illustrated how tax influences incentives and productivity. He concluded that the most important factor of business is lightening the tax load as much as possible to stimulate business activity and guarantee larger after-tax profits.

"When taxes and customs tariffs are light, people are incentivised to actively conduct business. Furthermore, business will also progress, bringing greater satisfaction to the people due to low taxes. Government will receive higher tax revenues due to a larger tax base because of the low taxes". Ibn Khaldun also analysed the effect of government failures in terms of tax handling, such as lower taxes on government spending, which was subsequently discussed by Keynes, "lower tax income is also caused by lower government spending". Accumulating tax revenue or not spending tax revenue appropriately will reduce total money available for civil servants in the form of wages and have a multiplier effect on total private spending.

5. ***Ghanimah***

Ghanimah is state income in the form of wealth taken by force from an enemy in times of war. In other words, the spoils of war. In a modern context, *ghanimah* is equivalent to confiscated items. The use of money originating from *ghanimah* is regulated in writing in the Al-Qur'an, Al-Anfal:41, for five groups of recipients.

وَاعْلَمُوْٓا اَنَّمَا غَنِمْتُمْ مِّنْ شَيْءٍ فَاَنَّ لِلّٰهِ خُمُسَهٗ وَلِلرَّسُوْلِ وَلِذِى الْقُرْبٰى وَالْيَتٰمٰى وَالْمَسٰكِيْنِ وَابْنِ السَّبِيْلِ اِنْ كُنْتُمْ
اٰمَنْتُمْ بِاللّٰهِ وَمَآ اَنْزَلْنَا عَلٰى عَبْدِنَا يَوْمَ الْفُرْقَانِ يَوْمَ الْتَقَى الْجَمْعٰنِۗ وَاللّٰهُ عَلٰى كُلِّ شَيْءٍ قَدِيْرٌ

And know that anything you obtain of war booty—then indeed, for Allah is one fifth of it and for the Messenger and for [his] near relatives and the orphans, the needy, and the [stranded] traveler, if you have believed in Allah and in that which We sent down to Our Servant . . . (Q.S. Al-Anfal [8]: 41)

Four-fifths of *ghanimah* are distributed to combat soldiers (Mujahideen), with one-fifth going to the religious obligation known as *khums* (refer to explanation of khums). Hasanuzzaman defined *ghanimah* as an immovable object captured by a Muslim army in battle. The different ways *ghanimah* was distributed are noteworthy. *Nafal* is the reward granted by a state leader or field leader to a Mujahideen fighter as part of the *ghanimah* spoils, the total of which is above average. *Nafal* can be distributed without a prearranged agreement by the state. There is also *Salab*, or personal objects captured by a soldier from a fallen foe. Finally, there is a *Safi'*, which are objects personally selected by the leader from *ghanimah* for himself.

6. ***Khums***

Khums is literally one-fifth, referring to the religious obligation of giving one-fifth of the spoils (*ghanimah*) of a military expedition justified by sharia law to the state of Islam, which may be used by the state for development programs. In Al-Qur'an, Al-Anfal: 41 explains the use of *khums* as state revenue.

وَاعْلَمُوْٓا اَنَّمَا غَنِمْتُمْ مِّنْ شَيْءٍ فَاَنَّ لِلّٰهِ خُمُسَهٗ وَلِلرَّسُوْلِ وَلِذِى الْقُرْبٰى وَالْيَتٰمٰى وَالْمَسٰكِيْنِ وَابْنِ السَّبِيْلِ اِنْ كُنْتُمْ
اٰمَنْتُمْ بِاللّٰهِ وَمَآ اَنْزَلْنَا عَلٰى عَبْدِنَا يَوْمَ الْفُرْقَانِ يَوْمَ الْتَقَى الْجَمْعٰنِۗ وَاللّٰهُ عَلٰى كُلِّ شَيْءٍ قَدِيْرٌ

And know that anything you obtain of war booty—then indeed, for Allah is one fifth of it and for the Messenger and for [his] near relatives and the orphans, the needy, and the [stranded] traveler . . . (QS. Al-Anfal[8]: 41)

Based on that Quaranic verse, the use of revenue from *khums* is clearly designated, which is the same as the use of state funds originating from *fay'* (refer to explanation of *fay'*).

7. ***Fay'***

According to Muhammad Nejatullah Siddiqi, *fay'* is state income other than *zakat*. Therefore, this includes *kharaj, jizyah, ghanimah*, *ushr,* and other incomes from commercial businesses owned by the government (for instance, state-owned enterprises). This definition is considered a more contemporary economic construct, differing from conditions during the period of Rasulullah SAW.

Abidin Ahmad Salama (1995) mentioned that state income originates from *Al Mustaglat* (government investment). This source of income is considered a new source introduced by Walid bin Abdul Malik, who established a new government department responsible for state investment.

Meanwhile, Hasanuzzaman defined *fay'* based on the interpretation of Rasulullah SAW, namely as the collective wealth of Muslims derived from the taxation of conquered peoples (not through war or the battlefield), and subsequently owned and managed by the state of Islam. Therefore, *fay'* contains elements of *ghanimah* and non- *ghanimah,* while *ghanimah* itself contains *khums* (one-fifth) and four-fifths for the Mujahideen.

مَآ اَفَاۤءَ اللّٰهُ عَلٰى رَسُوْلِهٖ مِنْ اَهْلِ الْقُرٰى فَلِلّٰهِ وَلِلرَّسُوْلِ وَلِذِى الْقُرْبٰى وَالْيَتٰمٰى وَالْمَسٰكِيْنِ وَابْنِ السَّبِيْلِۙ كَيْ لَا يَكُوْنَ
دُوْلَةً ۢ بَيْنَ الْاَغْنِيَاۤءِ مِنْكُمْۗ وَمَآ اٰتٰىكُمُ الرَّسُوْلُ فَخُذُوْهُ وَمَا نَهٰىكُمْ عَنْهُ فَانْتَهُوْاۚ وَاتَّقُوا اللّٰهَ ۗاِنَّ اللّٰهَ شَدِيْدُ الْعِقَابِۘ

And what Allah restored to His Messenger from the people of the towns—it is for Allah and for the Messenger and for [his] near relatives and orphans and the [stranded] traveler—so that it will not be a perpetual distribution among the rich from among you. And whatever the Messenger has given you—take; and what he has forbidden you—refrain from. And fear Allah; indeed, Allah is severe in penalty. (Q.S. Al-Hasyr [59]: 7).

As explained previously, the use of *fay'* is identical to *khums* as components of *ghanimah*. In the modern context, *fay'* and *khums* funds, as intended by Allah SWT, Rasul and His companions, are interpreted as state revenue, with the government maintaining the right to determine use. Based on those three sources, the use of *fay'* and *khums* is based on the priority scale of existing development programs.

8. **Special Taxes (*Nawaib*)**

This tax is levied depending on (transitory) economic conditions based on the state's prerogative to determine the rate of tax to apply. For example, when *zakat* and *fay'* funds are insufficient to meet the primary function of government, namely to fulfil the basic needs of the citizenry, this tax can be levied on the rich. It is important to remember that this policy is conditional and incidental based on the financial conditions of the state in terms of meeting its obligations. This implies that *nawaib* is complementary to the other more common economic instruments available to an Islamic state.

In a contemporary economic context, where the economic condition of many countries in the Islamic world is suboptimal, the mechanism of the obligatory *zakat* system is not operating as originally intended and, thus, *zakat* is no longer able to fulfil the state function of meeting the basic needs of the population, especially if other state revenues are in a similar situation. Consequently, the imposition of special taxes may provide an effective exit strategy (even if motivated by conventional fiscal system rationale). Therefore, in a transition state such as this, it is considered wise for Islamic states to apply tax mechanisms with characteristics similar to fiscal instruments in the Islamic economy.

9. **Other Islamic Public Sector Instruments**

State revenues may also originate from other variables, such as inheritance, confiscated items, fines, grants, or gifts from other Islamic states, *himma* and conditional assistance from other countries and international financial institutions.

From the explanation of other fiscal instruments, it is important to understand that each instrument has its own respective characteristics in terms of the collection (revenue for the state) and utilisation (expenditure for the state). In terms of collection, there are regulated fiscal instruments, which are applied to specific objects with predetermined sanctions applicable to those who do not fulfil their payment obligations, as in the case of *zakat*, *kharaj*, *jizyah*, and *ushur*. In the case of *zakat*, collection is a religious duty only from Muslims who meet the necessary minimum criteria of wealth (*nisab*). Meanwhile, conditional instruments are also available in the form of *khums*, special taxes, *fay'*, and others. The use of such instruments is determined by the prevailing economic conditions in a country, for example a prolonged crisis or when a sizeable portion of the population cannot meet their basic needs. Under such circumstances, the collection of special taxes is permitted by sharia law, but only from the rich.

4.4 Social Sector Instruments

Islam overcomes poverty by touching upon humanitarian aspects as well as acknowledging the inalienable rights of others through a social welfare system. Social security or *takaful ijtimai* refers to the obligation of Muslims to others in need by covering and realising their needs, caring for them and avoiding harm befalling them. Social security also refers to the right of an employee to receive protection if disaster prevents gainful employment and protection for his family while at work or after death.

The most comprehensive words of the Prophet concerning social security are as follows:

وعن أبي موسى رضي الله عنه قال: قال رسول الله صلى الله عليه وسلم " المؤمن للمؤمن كالبنيان
يشد بعضه بعضًا" وشبك بين أصابعه . ((متفق عليه)) .

Abu Musa (May Allah be pleased with him) reported:

Messenger of Allah (ﷺ) said, "The relationship of the believer with another believer is like (the bricks of) a building, each strengthens the other." He (ﷺ) illustrated this by interlacing the fingers of both his hands [Al-Bukhari and Muslim].[4]

Therefore, poverty cannot be treated merely by transferring ownership but through the expression of individual solidarity, sincere intentions, and a sense of love, until the essence of *takaful* is aligned with the command to unite Allah SWT, faith, and piety in oneness and refrain from falling into *Saqar* hell for ignoring the rights of people in need.

[4] Riyad as-Salihin 222, in-book reference Introduction, Hadith 222

مَا سَلَكَكُمْ فِيْ سَقَرَ(42)

قَالُوْا لَمْ نَكُ مِنَ الْمُصَلِّيْنَۙ(43)

وَلَمْ نَكُ نُطْعِمُ الْمِسْكِيْنَۙ(44)

> [And asking them], "What put you into Saqar?" They will say, "We were not of those who prayed, Nor did we used to feed the poor." (Q.S. Al-Muddassir [74]: 42–44).

The importance of *takaful* makes this system the responsibility of all elements, namely the individual, the community, and the government. At an individual level, the responsibility is *fardhu'ain* (obligatory) for individuals who are able to support others as blood relatives to meet their basic needs and protect them from harm. The government is also required to protect the needy directly through funds from *Baitul Mal* or indirectly through the community if the *ulil amri* (government) fails to carry out its social security obligations. From the words and actions of Umar, the role of the state is to force those who can take care of those in need.

Infaq, *sadaqah,* and waqf are voluntary donations by the community for the good of the community in pursuit of the pleasure of Allah SWT alone. For the state, however, such instruments are utilised in the national interest to facilitate state development projects and improve public welfare.

In keeping with the traditions and practices (*Sunnah*) of the Prophet Muhammad, *infaq* is an obligatory disbursement, along with *zakat*, *kafarat*, and other similar instruments. Meanwhile, *infaq sunah* includes *infaq* disbursed to indigent Muslims, natural disaster donations, humanitarian *infaq*, and others.

Departing from the common understanding of *sadaqah* as any form of benevolence or righteousness with the intention of pleasing Allah SWT, *sadaqah* can also be in the form of property or wealth similar to *zakat* or *infaq* or, indeed, not in the form of property, for instance helping someone else in need, smiling, removing obstacles on the road or any other forms of kindness.

If the faith of the people is strong, it is possible (likely even) that state revenue from such voluntary variables would exceed other mandatory instruments, providing the production factors are maximised. In the case of *waqf*, with public ownership in perpetuity, a larger *waqf* endowment implies a smaller social cost that must be borne by the people in their economy because *waqf* is linked to public functions as required by sharia law. According to Ahmed Faridi, revenue from voluntary donations has a positive correlation with the level of faith among the citizenry, where greater faith implies higher state revenue which can be channelled into further state development. Therefore, it is important for the government or state to consider the level of faith among the people to create an established, sustainable, and growing economy. Hence, it is natural that in an Islamic economy, tools and policies that can maintain or, preferably, nurture faith must be facilitated or implemented directly by the state. This is another point that distinguishes the Islamic economic system from the conventional.

Fiqh economist Umar RA outlined the most salient areas to achieve social security as follows:

1. ***Fakir* and Poor**

   In this subchapter, it is important to discuss the difference between the two and the current discord between ulema. Both groups are entitled to receive *zakat*, while paying due consideration to the specific requirements for the blessings and amount given to both.

   "It is not that poor people do not have wealth; the poor includes those who have jobs yet insufficient income to meet their needs". An individual has the right to receive *zakat* if his wealth is less than *auqiyah* (equivalent to 40 dirham) or less than two heads of goat.

   If applied to the present day, particularly in Indonesia, the criteria used by the National Amil Zakat Board (BAZNAS) for *zakat* distribution is in accordance with the Syafi'i and Maliki school of thought (*mazhab*), namely that *fakir* do not have access to income and cannot meet their basic needs, while the poor have access to income but insufficient to meet half of their basic needs. In nominal terms, the poverty line for Indonesians according to BPS-Statistics Indonesia in March 2018 averaged Rp401,220 per capita per month, calculated based on food and non-food aspects. Therefore, Indonesian citizens earning less than the poverty line are eligible to receive *zakat* or other social welfare assistance.

   Based on that calculation, the eligibility requirements will differ at different times and in different cities. Also, how is it possible to test the integrity of the beneficiaries of social funds? Under the governments of Umar and other caliphs, inspections were often performed. Umar even regularly mingled among his subjects incognito to see for himself the real conditions in his community rather than waiting for such information to arrive. Such inspections are very conceivable in the present day through coordination, integrity, and synergy with leaders of community-centred local government.

2. **Widows and Orphans**

   The evidence of Umar's concern for widows is reflected in his words just a few days before his passing "Indeed, if Allah SWT saves me, I will leave the widows of Iraq so that they will never need anyone else after me". This was based on the belief that Islam provides safeguards and guarantees for widows and orphans, such as *jihad fi sabililah* or "for the sake of Allah SWT", by bearing the cost of living.

   There are also practical reasons for protecting the lives of orphans, namely by taking care of them and paying them attention, protecting their property and safeguarding their development to ensure they become productive members of the community and can secure gainful employment. In terms of developing the property of orphans, Umar said "Trade the property of orphans so they are not consumed by *zakat*". That command encouraged the *muzzaki* (those obliged to play *zakat*) and wealth managers to develop their businesses to ensure the *zakat* issued is the result of profit and not capital.

3. **Sick and Disabled**

   Umar's concern for the sick is portrayed in the story of when he travelled to Sham and passed a group of Christians stricken with leprosy. He ordered *zakat* be distributed for their basic needs. Another example was when Umar sent a slave to guide a blind person after it was discovered he had left Friday prayers at the mosque of Rasulullah SAW.

Another example of protecting the disabled occurred when Umar observed one of the Yarmuk War veterans using his left hand to eat. After repeated reprimands, the veteran revealed his amputated limb, to which Umar immediately enquired "Who helps you with your *wudhu* ablutions? Who washes your clothes? Who does this and that?" Umar then ordered he be given a servant and five camels as a form of *zakat* for his quality welfare.

4. **Progeny of Mujahideen**

   Umar's guarantees to the family and progeny of Mujahideen were evidenced by his willingness to cover their obligations until they returned home from *jihad*.

5. **Prisoners of War**

   Any Muslim captured as a prisoner of war was unencumbered from the obligations of *Baitul Mal*.

6. **Slaves**

   During the reign of Umar, slaves were purchased, freed from enslavement, and subsequently given two sacks of wheat every month as social security.

7. **Neighbours**

   Islam affords special rights to neighbours and denies faith to those who are full while thy neighbour is hungry.

8. **Criminals**

   The government is obliged to provide social security for criminals in the form of basic sustenance.

9. **Indebted Persons (*Gharim*)**

   People in debt due to the destruction of other's property by mistake or through forgetfulness are also considered *gharim*. Islam helps *gharim* through *zakat*.

10. **Traveller or Wayfarer (*Ibnu Sabil*)**

    Al-Qur'an provides social security to travellers by treating them well, providing *zakat* rights, *ghanimah, fay'*, and other special guarantees, such as water and shelter, guest rights, and transportation.

11. **Abandoned Children**

    The proliferation of abandoned children due to economic hardship or adultery is a social issue stemming from weak religious understanding and the destruction of moral values. Umar stated that abandoned children are free from external control, free to form social relationships with those who can take care of them and eligible to receive social security from *Baitul Mal*.

12. ***Dzimmi***

    Social security was also afforded by Islam to *dzimmi*, as non-Muslims living in an Islamic state with legal protection from Allah SWT and Rasulullah SAW, in the form of *zakat* and exemption from *jizyah*. On the other hand, they were obliged to receive and entertain guests for 3 days to the best of their ability.

The social security system in Islam stands on the solid foundation of faith and moral principles, which will never be reflected in any other system than Islam. The willingness of every Muslim to take care of his brothers and sisters manifests in the face of parsimony and miserliness, strengthening family ties and maintaining a close-knit cell as the nucleus of the community, namely the family. Therefore, the social security political system applied by Umar reflects the beauty and justice of *takaful* under Islam. A flexible system with broad purview to cover all the needs of any individual, however diverse or new in form, will have the following substance in practice:

(a) The awareness of Umar as a leader concerning the magnitude of responsibility towards each individual in the community.
(b) Individual's understanding of their limitations in fulfilling state obligations and the responsibility of the state to protect the weak.
(c) Intelligent politics by Umar by providing something that is sufficient.

The same applies to the mechanisms for using such funds. There are instruments where the use of funds is restricted and regulated as well as those that are unrestricted or free. Instruments that are restricted and regulated must refer to the instructions determined through sharia deliberation, for example *zakat* instruments, the use of which is limited to eight groups of *mustahiq*. On the other hand, the use of unrestricted fiscal instruments implies that the accumulated funds collected from these instruments can be used broadly in the context of state development, depending on the current development priorities (refer to the discussion on public expenditure policy). For example, *fay'* funds that are absolute or unrestricted.

The discipline of managing funds from these types of Islamic fiscal instruments appears quite prominent, which demonstrates how the economy in Islam is concerned about ensuring and maintaining all individual and collective interests, which can automatically maintain social stability in Islamic society. Under such circumstances, therefore, the individual and collective community can play their roles and functions as servants of Allah SWT, namely through pious worship for maximum result. Indirectly, this characteristic reinforces the opinion that each fiscal instrument has its own respective "shooting target" in the Islamic economy. This discipline was also implicitly expressed by the companions of Ali bin Abi Thalib when responding to the questions of Umar bin Khattab's friends concerning the insistence of other friends at that time who demanded Umar utilise Ka'bah jewellery to finance war. Ali bin Abi Thalib stated the following:

4.5 Government Policy and Fiscal System in Islam

4.5.1 Role and Function of Government

After providing a brief history of public finance in Islam, the core discussion on the principles of Islamic public finance is explored in this section. Before diving into the principles of Islamic public finance, the role and function of government from an Islamic perspective must be explained. The government remains the most important actor in both conventional and Islamic public finance. The government's influence in collecting, managing, and distributing economic resources to the community is very powerful. Though the role and function of government from an Islamic perspective have many similarities to those in a conventional economic sense, the characteristic differences between the two warrant further discussion from an Islamic standpoint.

By definition, the state is a group of people with a leader (law) and territory, coming together with the same vision and goals. The state is the highest institution that explains, regulates, and oversees human interactions therein. For the people, the state is a tool to achieve their life goals collectively. In Islam, state institutions are inseparable from the collective concept that permeates the moral and sharia foundation of Islam. The concepts of *ukhuwah* (brotherhood), *tawsiyah* (proselytising), and caliphate are the foundations upon which Islamic institutions are developed in the form of state. Based on those concepts, a country that is also equipped with sharia regulations is expected to comprehensively serve all needs.

Imam Ghazali stated that religion provides the foundation or principles, while power, in this case the state, is the guardian of that foundation or principles. Therefore, there is symbiotic mutualism as a mutually beneficial and reinforcing relationship. On the one hand, religion provides a foundation for the state to act in the interests of its people towards quality welfare. On the other hand, the state represents a tool for religion to spread and ensure it is practised correctly and efficiently. Nejatullah Siddiqi stressed that society cannot be organised or regulated using Islamic principles unless utilising the state as a medium. Indeed, Islam also contains various regulations that only the government of a country can implement effectively, such as mechanisms for *zakat*, regulations to prohibit *riba*, as well as the implementation of Islamic criminal law (*hudud*).

The importance of the role of state in the effective implementation of sharia principles across every aspect of human life was also mentioned by Yusuf Qardhawy in his book entitled Fikih Daulah. Yusuf Qardhawy revealed that existence of the state is expected to maintain and develop the message of Islam, including faith and order, worship and morals, life and civilisation, so that all sectors of human life can operate in balance and harmony, both materially and spiritually. It is also important to understand that discussions concerning the state in Islam refer to an ideal Islamic state in the world environment. The Islamic state should not be divided by territorial boundaries. When Islam is the foundation of the state, all interests are automatically under the auspices of this state. That assumption forms the basis of the discussion in this chapter. Muslims are assumed to dominate the state, with the economic policies, in terms of financial and social management, therefore influenced by this assumption.

It is undisputable that what the Prophet Muhammad SAW did after the liberation of Mecca in managing Islamic society and the spread of Islam itself were deeds more commonly associated with political action. In other words, at that time the Islamic community of Medina-Mecca was gradually organised into a framework known as a state. Fundamentally, Rasulullah SAW carried out the mission of monotheism by prospering the people of the world and the hereafter in all aspects of life, while spreading the teachings of *rahmatan lil a'lamin* in accordance with the mission he carried to all corners of the world. It is not surprising, therefore, that in his function as head of state, Rasulullah SAW strived hard to maximise all efforts so that mankind prospered, economically, politically, legally, and culturally.

Politically, the function of state as practiced by Rasulullah SAW established relations with other countries without disregarding the mission of monotheism by sending diplomatic envoys to disseminate Islamic teachings to the leaders of other countries around the world. Economically, Rasulullah SAW implemented the *zakat* mechanism and abolished the practice of *riba* in economic activity. As an institution, *Baitul Mal* played a significant role in terms of implementing state development programs led by Rasulullah SAW. In fact, regulations concerning the population did not go unnoticed by the state, including the rights and responsibilities of non-Muslim citizens in social life.

Faridi said that in modern economic theory, there are two main economic sectors based on the actors, namely the private sector and public sector (government). The government and private sector in the economy function to resolve distribution problems in the market. Price equilibrium was first achieved in the private sector through a supply and demand mechanism. Nevertheless, when the equilibrium price requires correction, the public sector is expected to intervene. In the Islamic economy, according to Faridi, the existence of a third sector that complements the existing private and public sectors, namely a voluntary sector that is not motivated by material gain, becomes significant in terms of maintaining macroeconomic balance.

In broad terms, the function of state as proposed by Dr. Yusuf Qardhawi is divided into the following two parts:

1. **The state function to guarantee the basic needs of the people**

   The first function implies that the state must provide or maintain the basic needs of society. For those who have attained a certain level of wealth (*muzzaki* and non-*muzakki/mustahiq*), the state can ensure an appropriate level of supply to maintain fair and affordable prices of basic necessities. For the less fortunate (*mustahiq*), the state is responsible for providing basic needs free of charge. In essence, this function aims to reinforce the faith of the population. By meeting the basic needs, the transcendental relationship between humans and Allah SWT can be maintained. Acts of worship are not disrupted by external factors beyond the control of each respective individual. Therefore, the inability of an individual to meet their basic necessities, which could impede worship, must be overcome through collective activity, as the responsibility of the state.
2. **State function to educate and nurture society**

   According to this function, the purview of the state is to provide quality infrastructure, regulations, institutions, human resources, and knowledge. Therefore, complete and comprehensive (*syaamil mutakammil*) knowledge correlates positively with the preservation and improvement of faith as mentioned in the first function of state above. With such characteristics of knowledge, it is also hoped that economic growth and economic development can be accelerated, referring to better physical growth and the quality of sharia law in its applications, both in the context of individual and collective activities. It is important to note that this function ensures the community plays a role not only as users of the economic system, yet also as creators and the backbone of the economic system. Therefore, a successful education and nurturing process is expected to maintain the strength of the system and maximise the social benefits conveyed by the economic system (in the context of humans as users of the system).

The definition of basic needs that must be fulfilled by the state in this case is dynamic, evolving with the economic conditions of the country. It is possible that certain items may at one time be considered a secondary need, before becoming a basic need at a later date. Anas Zarqa (1980) classified basic needs into two groups, namely necessities and needs. Zarqa also opined that the state should be able to meet the needs of its citizens to achieve a decent standard of living beyond fulfilling the basic necessities.

In general, those two functions, therefore, aim to maintain and increase public faith and the underlying foundation of economic development. From an Islamic perspective, the parameters of economic success are not dominated by the advancement of physical development, yet by the collective closeness of the community to Allah SWT.

Meanwhile, according to Hasanuzzaman, the full panoply of state functions aims to ensure that justice and balance in the community are maintained as follows:

(a) **Policymaking and Legislation**

As the authority of the state, policymaking and legislation are expected to suppress inefficiency and discrimination. Policies and legislation provide freedom and opportunities for all citizens to improve their morality and spirituality, social equality, and economic advancement.

(b) **National Defence**

National defence as a state duty is inevitable. In this case, Islam not only defends the state physically, yet also defends the message of Islam normatively. Therefore, the national defence function is closely intertwined with the state function to maintain international relations.

(c) **Education and Books**

The virtues of science and knowledge along with their further development are revealed in Al-Qur'an and the Sunnah. Accordingly, the state is a central medium in facilitating the transfer and development of knowledge. In this way, established science is expected to trigger a multiplier effect for the development of all functions of the state.

(d) **Moral and Social Development and Oversight**

It is imperative that an Islamic state habitually maintains sharia principles in the lives of all citizens. Oversight and amelioration of social-moral society is a fundamental task of the state. The key concept is *amar ma'ruf nahi munkar* (Q.S. Ali Imran: 104). This function is achieved by state institutions known as *Al Hisbah*, which are discussed in more depth as a subsequent topic.

(e) **Law Enforcement, Maintaining Order, and Islamic Criminal Law (*hudud*)**

In line with the aforementioned state functions, namely the responsibility for maintaining physical and moral order and discipline, unambiguous and legally binding law enforcement is required, accompanied by the appropriate consequences and oversight. Therefore, the citizens are legally protected in terms of their rights and responsibilities under an Islamic framework.

(f) **Public Welfare**

In this case, the state functions as a catalyser for the residents to achieve quality welfare. The state is responsible for maximising resource empowerment to achieve the greatest quality of welfare for its citizens. In addition, the state is also responsible for providing vital facilities to the citizenry, including sustenance, clothing, shelter, healthcare, and other basic needs. In fact, if the state has sufficient resources to fund citizens wishing to get married, it is the state's obligation to fulfil that duty. This function aims to maintain and improve faith in the community and eliminate economic barriers that could potentially disrupt the relationship between humans and Allah SWT.

(g) **International Relations**

According to Hasanuzzaman, in addition to maintaining good relations with other countries, the state can use diplomatic missions to monitor potential resistance or conspiracies seeking to destroy the Islamic state.

Nejatullah Siddiqi classified the functions of state into three categories as follows:

1. **Functions that are the duty of sharia**

   These functions of state are specifically revealed in Al-Qur'an and the Sunnah and justified by Islamic jurists (*fuqaha*). These functions do not depend on social change in society, for example defence, public order, prohibition of *riba*, and implementation of *zakat*.
2. **Derived functions of sharia based on *ijtihad* in contemporary situations**

   The function of state in this category is derived from the analogous arguments based on Al-Qur'an and the Sunnah, which are highly dependent on circumstances (place and time), for instance the state function to protect the environment from social ills.
3. **Functions assigned by the community to the state through the *shura* (parliament)**

   The function of state in this category is a community "request" through a mechanism justified by sharia law, in this case the authority of the *shura* (parliament), for instance the function to provide public facilities, such as electricity, clean water, and affordable housing.

In the literature, several Islamic economists have affirmed that one of the specific functions of the state is printing the legal tender of the country. Under the leadership of Ali bin Abi Thalib, the first Islamic money was printed by the state through *Baitul Mal*. Before Islamic countries printed their own money (prior to Ali bin Abi Thalib), other currencies were used as legal tender, dominated by the gold dinar from the Byzantine Empire and the silver dirham from the Sassanian Kingdom.

Several common threads run through the three functions of the state in an Islamic economy as discussed. The Islamic economic system, which is distinctive in terms of the philosophy, paradigms, principles, and application, also has a unique definition concerning the function of state in the economic mechanism. In broad terms, it can be concluded that the state has two primary functions, namely stabilisation and development of the geographical frontier (such as national defence) as well as the ideological frontier, which includes socio-moral functions and economic functions that aim to maintain and increase the belief and faith of all citizens.

In the literature, a key reference used to elucidate the rights and obligations of the state (government) to its citizenry is contained in the opinion of Abu Ubaid (2009) as follows:

1. Trusted/Trustworthy
2. Governing according to the rules of Islamic law
3. Responsible/accountable
4. Fair
5. Diligent without procrastination
6. Serving the community

In return, the obligations of the citizenry to the government include the following:

1. Heed orders from the government
2. Obey the government
3. Responsive to the government

Islamic jurists (*fuqaha*) in the classical era understood the importance of the government's role (Table 4.8). Therefore, several *fuqaha* have systematically recorded the tasks of state, including Imam Al-Ghazali, Imam Al-Mawardi, and Ibnu Khaldun, recapitulated as follows:

Al-Ghazali

The role of the state in ensuring protection to the citizenry covering the five components of *maqasid syariah* as follows:

1. Religion/faith (*dien*)
2. Life (*nafs*)
3. Mind (*aql*)
4. Lineage (*nasl*)
5. Property (*maal*)

Al-Mawardi

The tasks of the state are as follows:

1. Protection of faith
2. Law enforcement and stability
3. Maintaining Islamic state borders
4. Availability of an environment conducive to economic activity

Table 4.8 Tasks of state according to Fuqaha

Islamic jurists realised how important the role of government is. Therefore, some of the jurists who have written down the tasks of the state systematically include Imam Al-Ghazali, Imam Al-Mawardi, and Ibn Khaldun. The opinions of each of the *fuqaha* are summarised in the table below:
Al-Ghazali The government has duties to provide protection to the community in 5 components of *maqasid syariah*, including: 1. Preservation of Faith (*Dien*) 2. Preservation of Life (*Nafs*) 3. Preservation of Intellect (Aql) 4. Preservation of Lineage (*Nasl*) 5. Preservation of Wealth (*Maal*)
Imam Mawardi Duties of the government, among others: 1. Protection of faith 2. Law enforcement and stability 3. Maintenance of Islamic state borders 4. Availability of an environment conducive to economic activity 6. Availability of public administration, justice, and law enforcement 6. Collecting income from the available sources and increasing income by imposing new taxes as required 7. Utilising funds to implement the objectives and obligations of the state
Ibnu Khaldun The government has various tasks, including: 1. Protecting society from its enemies 2. Enforcing the law and ensuring public stability to avoid hostility and the destruction of property 3.Overseeing general issues involving *muamalah* life and transactions 4. Supervising the printing of currency to avoid disorderly exchange

Source: Summarised from various sources

5. Availability of public administration, justice, and law enforcement
6. Collecting income from the available sources and increasing income by imposing new taxes as required
7. Utilising funds to implement the objectives and obligations of the state

Ibnu Khaldun

The government is tasked as follows:

1. Protecting society from its enemies
2. Enforcing the law and ensuring public stability to avoid hostility and the destruction of property
3. Overseeing general issues involving *muamalah* life and transactions
4. Supervising the printing of currency to avoid disorderly exchange

Source: Summarised from various sources

The government is the main institution in realising the state's goals. From an Islamic perspective, those goals encapsulate normative behaviour to achieve quality welfare. For example, the government of an Islamic state must protect society and maintain the religion, enforce the law based on Al-Qur'an and the Sunnah, as well as create and maintain economic stability by minimising duplicity in the markets, et cetera. Of the various goals that must be realised by an Islamic government, there are two overarching roles from an Islamic perspective (Askari et al., 2015:225), namely: (i) policymaking to ensure private sector interests do not deviate from the public interest, and (ii) oversight to create and provide incentives to all parties.

The private sector is oriented differently from the public sector by placing profit as the overarching goal (profit-oriented). To maximise profit, the private sector often prioritises actions that are contrary to the goals of the state, in the use of natural resources for example. The private sector will endeavour to secure the cheapest raw materials by exploiting natural resources, which is starkly in conflict with the state's role to create sustainable development. Thus, the government is required to make policies governing the utilisation of natural resources to regulate private sector interests and remain in harmony with the state/public interest. From an Islamic standpoint, the interests that must be aligned not only relate to this life but also the hereafter. For example, the government is responsible for policies concerning the implementation of Hajj and Umrah pilgrimages to avoid irregularities for those wishing to undertake a pilgrimage, thus creating harmony with the public interest for pilgrims seeking protection when performing religious duties.

In addition, the government also plays a supervisory role to create incentives in various areas. For instance, the government is responsible for enforcing and supervising the law both from a conventional and Islamic perspective. Government actions can provide incentives to economic actors to produce and consume without fear of deception by a third-party. That production and consumption process will increase economic dynamism. Similar to its policymaking role, however, the supervisory purview of an Islamic government also encompasses religious matters, such as religious aberration.

In the modern context, an Islamic government has several functions that must be discharged, including government functions that are similar to conventional public finance despite significant differences in the objectives and policy instruments. The state functions are as follows:

1. **Allocation Function**

   The allocation function is a function of government to allocate resources in the economy. This function is derived from market failures in terms of effectively and efficiently allocating resources, necessitating government intervention in the allocation of economic resources in the community. For example, the markets may be unable to provide sufficient basic staples to the wider community, such as rice or corn, because the production of other goods and services with a higher selling value takes precedence. Under such conditions, the government has an obligation to intervene in the economy, providing incentives to the private sector to produce the goods and services required by the broader community or government through its business lines. State-owned enterprises also produce the goods and services required by the public. Therefore, the government is obliged

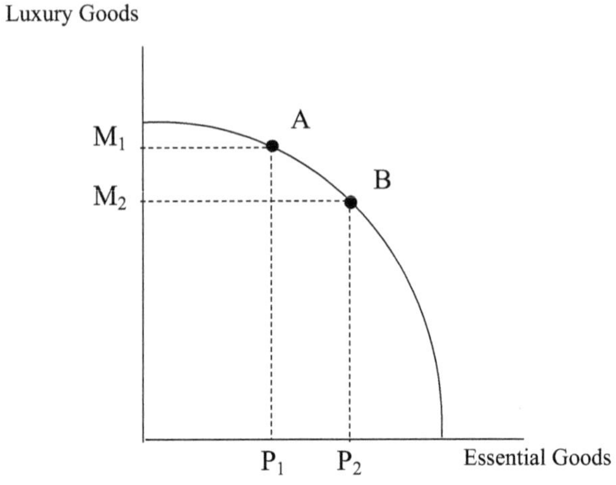

Fig. 4.3 Allocative efficiency between luxury goods and essential goods. Source: Faridi (1983)

to correct market failures arising from the ineffective and inefficient allocation of goods and services.

Allocative efficiency generated by the private sector's efficiency through market mechanism filters. In Fig. 4.3, combined production along the Production Possibility Frontier (PPF) line is a condition of efficiency because all available resources have been used to produce two groups of goods. Only by relying on the market will allocation move towards efficiency of existing market demand (Point A in Fig. 4.3). Meanwhile, the government wants the allocative efficiency created as a form of social allocative efficiency, assuming that closer to Point B is social allocative efficiency of private demand. The government, therefore, must orient allocative efficiency towards the inclinations of society.

In Islam, there are commands that explicitly regulate the allocation function of government. Several of these commands or orders include the prohibition of actions that cause market imperfections, such as monopolistic behaviour (*ikhtikar*), dumping to lower prices below the market price (*siyasah al-ighraq*), deception (*tadlis*), and so on.[5] Market imperfections will undermine the efficiency and effectiveness of allocating goods and services, leading to deadweight loss and supernormal profit. Referring to Fig. 4.3, the emergence of market imperfections will prevent the production of goods and services from reaching the PPF line due to idle resources. Therefore, the prohibition of various actions that can cause market imperfections by the government is indicative that allocative efficiency is the desired condition.

There are also *Fardu Kifayah* commands to produce public and quasi-public goods. The private sector is unable to allocate public goods and services due to the non-excludable and non-rivalry characteristics (with quasi-public goods only having one of those two characteristics), such as the national armed forces, roads,

[5]Refer to HR. Muslim No. 1605; HR. Abu Dawud No. 1765, among others.

lighthouses, et cetera. In the absence of private sector actors willing to produce such goods, while from an Islamic perspective there are explicit orders that public goods must be produced, allocation is therefore a government function.

2. **Distribution Function**

   The distribution function deals with how the government distributes resources to the public. The distribution function complements the allocation function of government resources due to a strong correlation on the income side. An allocation function reliant merely on market mechanisms will lead to inefficiencies, or lack social allocative efficiency, while a distribution function reliant purely on market mechanisms will lead to large income gaps and disparities. In economic systems that rely on market mechanisms, asset ownership is critical for economic players. Through asset ownership, economic players can generate income through renting, selling, and producing. Unfortunately, economic assets are dominated by higher income individuals, with market mechanisms thus leading to the inequitable distribution of income.

   Through various policies and instruments, the state is obliged to create social justice, including equitable income distribution. In terms of conventional public finance policy, the primary policy instrument used to regulate income distribution is income tax. Income tax is levied on individuals with income exceeding a specific threshold, which is subsequently channelled to the wider community through various government programs. From an Islamic perspective, income distribution is also a government concern. Revelations not to monopolise or hoard wealth in the hands of certain groups are explicitly contained in Al-Qur'an.[6] As the entity authorised to enforce the commands contained in Al-Qur'an and the Hadiths, the government is responsible for issuing policies to ensure such commands are executed. The main instrument of the distribution function is *zakat*. As an income distribution instrument, the *zakat* mechanism is clearer than taxation because it is levied on individuals meeting the necessity criteria of wealth (*nisab*) and distributed to the eight *asnaf* categories who qualify to benefit from *zakat* funds.

   In addition to *zakat* instruments, the prohibition of *riba* is another command concerning the distribution of wealth from an Islamic perspective. Normally, *riba* is charged on debt by increasing the principal. This practice ensures one transacting party will receive additional benefits without any risk born in the economy. Consequently, the impact on the transacting parties is to increase the income gap because one party is always guaranteed an income. The prohibition of transactions containing elements of *riba* also shows that Islam supports equitable income distribution. The government is obligated, therefore, to prohibit *riba* to realise fair and equitable income distribution.

3. **Stabilisation Function**

   The government's stabilisation function in terms of conventional public finance relates closely with the government's economic function. The

[6] Refer to Q.S. Al-Hasyr (59): 7.

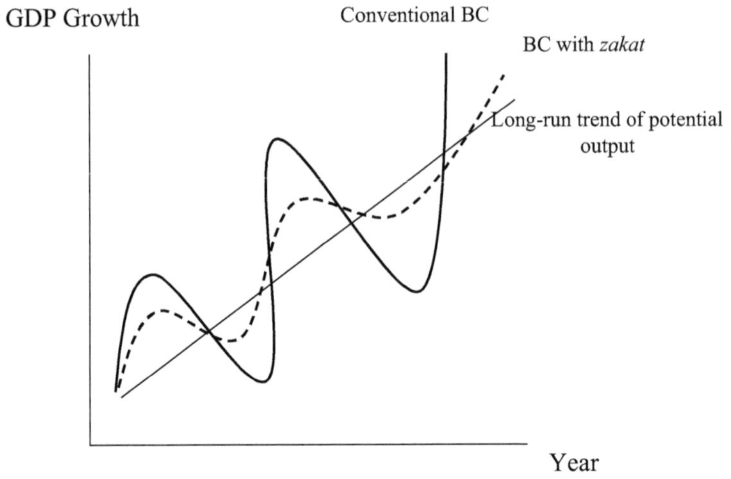

Fig. 4.4 The role of zakat in economic stability. Source: Authors

government is obligated to run the economy at full employment. When an economy experiences a recession, the government must use countercyclical policies, such as expansive fiscal and monetary policies, to rebalance the economy. Meanwhile, if inflation in the economy becomes too high, the government must use procyclical policies, such as contractive fiscal and monetary policies, to bring the economy back to full employment. In addition, the government is also required to protect the economy from internal and external sources of instability.

From an Islamic perspective, the government stabilisation function extends beyond the economy to include social aspects, politics, security, and so on. Stability across those various aspects is prerequisite to creating quality welfare. In economics, conventional and Islamic public finance are required to stabilise economic conditions, often known as the business cycle, yet the stabilisation instruments differ in scope. Under a conventional system, the government predominantly uses fiscal policy to increase stability, while *zakat* is dominant in an Islamic system. Figure 4.4 illustrates the differences between business cycles with and without *zakat* instruments. Assuming no government intervention, the conventional business cycle will follow market activities fully, with the economy experiencing high booms and deep recessions. This is an undesirable situation for economic actors due to the high level of uncertainty. Using *zakat* instruments, however, *zakat* collection increases during a boom period as a consequence of higher private income. *Zakat* payments will thus prevent the economy from overheating. After the funds have been collected during a boom period, *zakat* payments are subsequently distributed during a recession to the poor and needy who may have lost employment. Consequently, business cycle fluctuations are dampened under an Islamic system.

4.5.2 *Fiscal System in Islam*

The characteristics of the Islamic economy differ from the conventional economy. In a conventional sense, the economy is divided into the private sector and public sector, but the Islamic economy has an additional third sector, known as the voluntary sector. The third sector encompasses all individual and collective activities in the social interest, including philanthropic activities (*sadaqah*), public empowerment, production of public goods, et cetera (Faridi, 1983).

In general, the characteristics of the private and public sectors are not dissimilar to the conventional economy, with different instruments and broader goals because the Islamic economy also considers the hereafter. On the other hand, however, the third sector is specific to the Islamic economy and not recognised in the conventional sense. In Islam, the third sector is associated with the various duties to perform social activities, such as *zakat, infaq, sadaqah, waqf* (ZISWAF), and so on. Such activities have created their own sector, which functions like other existing sectors. Furthermore, the third sector also differentiates and distinguishes the fiscal system in Islam from the conventional fiscal system (Faridi, 1983). Based on the third sector model in the Islamic economy developed by Faridi (1983), the interactions of the third sector within the Islamic fiscal system are illustrated in Fig. 4.5.

Each sector has separate and collaborative allocation, distribution, and stabilisation functions. Nevertheless, each sector will act in accordance with the respective economic characteristics and roles. The private sector is profit oriented,

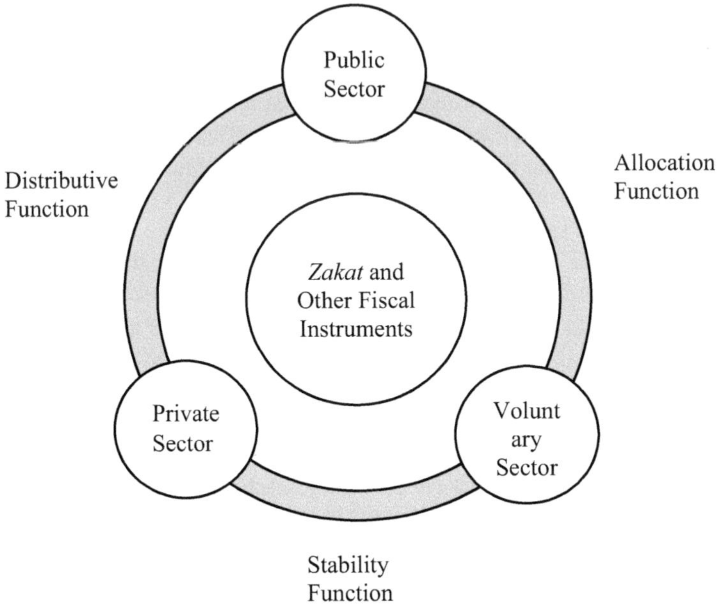

Fig. 4.5 Islamic Fiscal System. Source: Authors

the public sector is oriented towards public welfare, and the third sector is oriented towards social welfare. Collaboration between those three sectors will produce dynamic and complementary functions.

The resource allocation function within an economy is not merely beholden to market mechanisms in the private sector or instruments of public finance, such as taxes, as occurs in the conventional fiscal system, yet can be integrated with the third sector through social funds, such as *zakat, infaq,* and *sadaqah*. As elucidated previously, when limited to a combination of private and public sectors only, the allocation function produced by market mechanisms in the private sector is often mistargeted due to market demand with the option for correction by the public sector. By combining the three sectors in an Islamic economy, however, the third sector serves to help the government allocate resources to those in need. The third sector does not suffer the same bureaucratic constraints as the public sector and directly reflects social needs, thus perfecting the allocation function when the private sector fails to reach social allocative efficiency and the public sector faces limitations in terms of corrective instruments.

The Islamic economy is also more dynamic in meeting demand for public goods. The private sector is reluctant to produce non-excludable and non-rivalrous public goods, thus relying on the public sector. Notwithstanding, the government itself also faces constraints in terms of funding, manpower, time and area, meaning that not all public goods can be fulfilled by the public sector. It is common to observe in developing countries that public goods and quasi-public goods, such as roads, clean water facilities, mass transportation, and so on, are not available or underdeveloped. Here, the third sector could play a crucial role in helping the government provide public goods and quasi-public goods as required by the community. There are instruments, such as *waqf*, that are naturally in the public interest, thus making the magnitude of the third sector in the economy directly proportional to the production of public goods and quasi-public goods in society.

Figure 4.6 shows optimal intersectoral allocative efficiency in the Islamic economy. Private sector output is plotted on the x axis, with public and third sector output on the y axis. There are differences between the characteristics of output produced by the private sector and that of the public and third sectors, where the output produced by the private sector tends to focus on goods and services that generate higher profits, while the goods produced by the public and third sectors are goods and services needed by the community. If the preference for goods and services desired by the community is illustrated by the S curve, the intersection between S2 and the PPF curve is the social allocative efficiency, with the allocation of goods and services produced by the private sector totalling x and the goods and services produced by the public and third sectors totalling y. The additional allocation from the third sector makes the allocative efficiency reach the point of social allocative efficiency rather than merely relying on the public sector, whose allocation may not reach the point of social efficiency.

In a conventional economy, the distribution function can be executed by either the private sector or public sector. The private sector distributes income through market mechanisms to those with access. Meanwhile, the public sector can distribute

Fig. 4.6 Optimal intersectoral allocative efficiency in the Islamic economy. Source: Faridi (1983)

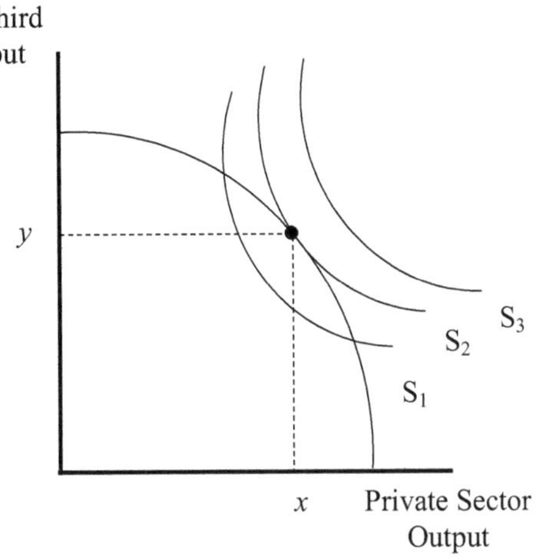

income via the market through economic intervention policy or by circumventing the market and providing direct assistance (transfer payments) to those in need. Nonetheless, the combination of both sectors is often ineffective, as can be seen in many countries around the world where the Gini ratio, as a measure of income inequality, is comparatively high. In an Islamic economy, the distribution function is assisted by a third sector oriented towards quality welfare.

Equitable income distribution is the overarching goal of the third sector, using *zakat* as the primary instrument. *Zakat* is collected directly from those with surplus wealth and distributed those with a deficit. In addition, *zakat* is also imposed on unproductive or idle assets in the community. A combination of both mechanisms helps create a broader flow of wealth and income distribution in the Islamic economy. *Waqf*, as another instrument of the third sector, is also oriented towards reducing social income inequality. The proceeds of *waqf* assets are used fully in the public interest.

Fundamentally, the stabilisation function in the economy is the primary responsibility of the public sector. The government has an obligation to ensure the seamless functioning of the economy. In the Islamic economy, however, the presence of a third sector reinforces the public sector's role in maintaining economic stability. If the public sector uses fiscal and monetary policies to maintain stability from a macro purview, the third sector uses social fund instruments to maintain economic stability with a narrower purview. In a recession, for example, more people will lose a portion or all of their income, thus the third sector plays a role in helping such people through various instruments, including *zakat, sadaqah,* and *waqf* proceeds. Social funds can be used to contain the risk of economic fluctuations and stabilise conditions to a limited extent. In addition, *zakat* instruments can also be used by the public sector as a fiscal policy to stabilise conditions. During a boom period, a portion of the proceeds from *zakat* must be saved to ensure that when the economy begins to show signs of recession, the funds can be distributed to the public and, thus, stabilise conditions.

4.5.3 Public Expenditure Policy

Based on sharia law as contained in Al-Qur'an and the Hadiths concerning the management of funds from various sources, including *zakat, kharaj, jizyah, ushur, fay'* or special taxes, as well as other revenues from voluntary sources, such as *infaq, sadaqah, himma, and waqf*, public expenditure policy in Islam has unique characteristics. The most obvious characteristic is the massive attention paid to spending on the poor and needy (*duafa*). Accommodating those towards the bottom of the pyramid is a key characteristic of the Islamic economy and is quite different from the modern conventional economy.

In a conventional economic system, economic reliance on domestic and foreign sources of financing or debt, as well as taxation is clear.

Based on Table 4.9, the servicing of government debt has the potential to burden the state budget, particularly routine expenditures. Such conditions will evidently exacerbate pressures on the development budget or other routine expenditures and government savings because the government prioritises the servicing of external debt. Under a conventional system, the application of interest on loans means the amount of debt that must be repaid is the current debt expense plus the interest payments. In his book on Islamic macroeconomics, Adiwarman Karim explains the differences in the formula as follows:

All state revenue innovations that are in accordance with sharia law, in terms of expenditure policies, should refer to the characteristics of Islamic public spending. That way, the characteristics stipulated in sharia law will be maintained, with the expectation of more precise and effective targeting. Such characteristics will further strengthen the opinion of Islamic economists that the main function of the state is to guarantee the basic needs of society, which essentially maintains public faith in God. By overcoming economic barriers in daily life, society can function maximally as a servant of Allah SWT. In other words, without economic constraints, as common barriers faced by almost everyone and motivating human behaviour, all individuals will be able to worship Allah SWT to the fullest.

Mohammed Nejatullah Siddiqi argues that the amount and subject of public expenditure in a country embracing an Islamic economic system are not fixed but relate to the functionality of the state. Before describing the characteristics of public expenditure, Siddiqi classified three state functions as follows:

1. Permanent functions of state based on sharia law
2. Functions of state derived from sharia law as determined by *ijtihad* based on the current situation
3. Functions of state at a particular time and situation based on the will of the people through a *shura* (parliamentary) decision

Therefore, public expenditure policy refers to those classifications of state function. In addition, Siddiqi proposed expenditure posts based on the first state function as follows:

Table 4.9 Recapitulation of state revenue and expenditure budget (APBN) 2019

		Description (trillion rupiah)	2016 LKPP	2017 LKPP	2018 Outlook	2019 State budget
A	State revenue		1555.9	1666.4	1903.0	2165.1
	I	Domestic revenue at the national (APBN) level	1546. 9	1654.7	1897. 6	2164.7
		1. Tax receipt	1285.0	1343.5	1548.5	1786.4
		Tax Ratio	0.01	0.01	11.57	12.22
		a.I. PPh Migas	666.2	646.8	761.2	894.4
		2. State non-tax revenue at the national level	262.0	311.2	349.2	378.3
	II	Hibah	9.0	11.6	5.4	0.4
B	State expenditure		1864.3	2007.4	2217.3	2461.1
	I	Central Government Expenditure	1154.0	1265.4	1453.6	1634.3
		1. Expenditure K/L	684.2	765.1	813.5	855.4
		2. Non-expenditure K/L	469.8	500.2	640.2	778.9
	II	Regional transfer and village funds	710.3	742.0	763.6	826.8
		1. Regional transfer	663.6	682.2	703.6	756.8
		2. Village funds	46.7	59.8	60.0	70.0
C	Primer equilibrium		(125.6)	(124.4)	(64.8)	(20.1)
D	Surplus/(Deficit) Budget (A-B)		(308.3)	(341.0)	(314.2)	(296.0)
	% Surplus/(Deficit) Budget to GDP(A-B)		(2.49)	(2.51)	(2.12)[a]	(1.84)
E	Budget financing		334.5	366.6	314.2	296.0
	Debt financing		403.0	429.1	387.4	359.3
	Investment financing		(89.1)	(59.8)	(65.7)	(75.9)
	Lending		1.7	(2.1)	(6.5)	(2.4)
	Loan obligations		(0.7)	(1.0)	(1.1)	(0.0)
	Other financing		19.6	0.4	0.2	15.0

Source: Ministry of Finance
[a]Outlook in term I report and in end of the year is estimed below 2.0% to GDP

1. National defence
2. Law and order
3. Justice
4. Basic needs
5. *Da'wah* (proselytising) and international diplomacy to bring the Islamic message to the world
6. *Amal Ma'ruf Nahi Munkar* (enjoining good and forbidding wrong)
7. Public administration/regulation
8. Fulfilling social obligations in cases of private sector/market failure

Meanwhile, Siddiqi proposed expenditure posts based on the second state function as follows (Table 4.10):

Table 4.10 Public expenditure policy

Income	Recipient
Zakat	*Fakir. Miskeen. Ibnussabil. Fisabilillah. Gharimin.* Servant. *Muallaf. Amil.*
Fay'	Allah SWT. Rasullullah SAW. Rasullullah brethren. orphans. poor people. *Ibnussabil*
Khums (1/5 *Ghanimah*)	Allah SWT. Rasullullah SAW. Rasullullah brethren. orphans. poor people. *Ibnussabil*
Kharaj	Depending on the priority of the country
Jizyah	Depending on the priority of the country
Ushur	Depending on the priority of the country
Hibah/Hadiah	Depending on the priority of the country
Infaq-Sadaqah	Depending on the priority of the country
Waqf	Depending on the Contract (*Akad*) & Needy People
Tax	Whole society (Depending on the priority of the country)
4/5 *Ghanimah*	*Mujahidin* (soldier)

1. Environmental protection
2. Providing public needs/facilities
3. Scientific books
4. Economic development and capital formation
5. Subsidies targeting specific private subsectors
6. Spending on stabilisation policy

Finally, expenditure posts based on the third state function include all expenditures issued by the state or government under specific circumstances based on the urgent needs of the community.

Siddiqi's opinion is consistent with the arguments put forward by F. R. Faridi concerning the social sector, which plays a role when the private sector is unable to perform its function through market forces to fulfil the needs of the community. Notwithstanding, Siddiqi places Faridi's social sector in the function of state because, in its application, the social sector is considered more efficient when managed by the state or at least under state supervision and control.

State expenditure is influenced strongly by the function of the Islamic state itself. In accordance with the state functions discussed previously, state expenditure can comprise social welfare, education and books, infrastructure, defence and security, *da'wah* and *fikrah* (proselytising and propaganda), and so on. Several budgeting aspects of the Islamic state must be understood because Islam has unique characteristics in terms of state revenue and expenditure. In terms of state expenditure, the economic instruments available to the state to finance economic development in the context of executing state functions are categorised into two groups, namely restricted expenditures and unrestricted expenditures. Restricted expenditures originate from specific revenue instruments that require the use of accumulated funds for specific recipients (objects or projects), such as *zakat, khums,* and *waqf.* In the

Table 4.11 State Revenue and Expenditure Budget in Islam

Revenue	
Regulation type	Expenditure
Zakat	Basic Needs
Kharaj	Social Welfare
Jizyah	Book and Education
Ushur	Infrastructure (Public Facility)
Voluntary Type	*Da'wah* Islam
Infaq-Sadaqah	Country Administration
Waqf	Defence and Security
Hibah	Ataya (A year or half year Pension Fund)
Conditional Type	Arzaq (Monthly Pension Fund)
Khums	
Tax (*Nawaib*)	
BUMN Profit (*Mustaghlah/Fay'*)	
Others	

Source: Developed from the APBN Table, State Revenue and Expenditure Budget

specific case of *zakat*, according to sharia law, the collected funds can only be distributed to the eight *asnaf* groups or *mustahiq* (Table 4.11).

Daulah Islamiyah Al Madinatul Munawwarah: Period of Rasulullah SAW and Khulafaur Rasyidin, Adiwarman A. Karim, ISEG-UNPAD module, 1997.

In the past, *zakat* was distributed directly on the spot after levying taxes. Many accounts have been retold of how the companions of Rasulullah SAW tasked with collecting *zakat* would be left with nothing except their own entitled share because all the *zakat* collected would be distributed immediately to the *mustahiq*. This may have been because the exigencies of the time made on the spot distribution a viable option. This demonstrates the local nature of *zakat* distribution, implying that the *zakat* alms collected in one region would be distributed first to meet the needs of the local *mustahiq*, before any residual funds were collected centrally.

Hasanuzzaman (1991) revealed that in addition to distributing *zakat* to the eight *asnaf* groups, the main expenditures using funds accumulated in the *Baitul Mal*, according to historical literature, were pension payments (*ataya* and *arzaq*), allowances and wages for civil servants, defence programs and development programs. In the case of pension funds, there were two types, namely *ataya*, which are annual or biannual pension payments, and *arzaq*, which are monthly pension payments (Table 4.12).

The policy of providing allowances in the form of pensions during the era of Umar bin Khattab was also subject to criticism from other companions. One companion, Hakim bin Nizam, argued that if allowances were given *ad infinitum*, it would change the productive nature of some people. For example, a trader could lose enthusiasm to trade due to a reliance on such allowances. This mindset manifested during the Abbasid era, when the state stopped providing such allowances and benefits.

Table 4.12 Fixed Pensions during Era of Umar bin Khattab

Recipient	Dirham per person
Rasulullah's Wife	12.000
Rasulullah's uncle and grandson	5.000
Alumni Badar	5.000
Alumni Uhud	4.000
Abyssinia Migrant	4.000
Migrant before Makkah liberation	3.000
Alumni Badar Children	2.000
Muallaf in Makkah liberation	2.000
Anshar's Children	2.000
Muslim in Syria and Iraq	200–2.000
Mujahid in Qadisiyya	2.000
Mujahid who conquer Qubulla	2.000
Who joined the Hudaybiyya Agreement	2.000
Makkah resident except Muhajirin	600–700
Yaman resident	700
Women	200–500
The newborn	100
Muallaf Persian landlord	2.000
Orphans	100

Source: Hasanuzzaman (1991)

Regarding state expenditure, Umar bin Khattab once instructed a governor in Egypt, Amr bin Ash, to spend one third of state funds received from sources other than *zakat* on public infrastructure development.

The discussion on state spending was also elaborated in more detail in the previous chapter in terms of fiscal policy in an Islamic economy. It is important to understand that state expenditure is inseparable from sharia law and the contemporary needs permitted by sharia law, as explained by Muhammad Nejatullah Siddiqi. The exemplary behaviour of Rasulullah SAW and his companions as well as various Islamic leaders represent a valuable reference. At least, such behaviour can be used as inspiration when formulating state expenditure policy considering the economic complexities and public problems that exist in every era. That way, the Islamic economy will not be seen as a static system, which can stifle the local economy. Islam is perfect, including the economic guidance it provides. Just in terms of state expenditure policy, Islam provides a rich space to offer policy solutions and improvisation to realise the most appropriate and effective policies for maximum effect. Furthermore, the orientation towards spiritual satisfaction is maintained in the Islamic economic system.

In the modern economy, a state revenue and expenditure budget could adopt the balanced-budget concept applied in the *Baitul Mal*, namely to ensure balance between the expenditures and revenues. Although debt is permitted, Islam does not recommend it. In terms of state financial management, Rasulullah SAW managed the state revenue and expenditure budget prudently, effectively, and efficiently, with budget deficits a rare occurrence despite frequent wars. In contrast, the economic arguments put forward by Yuswar Zainul Basri and Mulyadi Subri show the concept of a balanced state revenue and expenditure budget to be spurious, where the budget deficit is always covered by the component of foreign loans, which triggers growth of the debt burden and interest payments that continue to compound.

In Islam, however, the fiscal policy presented by Imam Al-Ghazali (1990) is an instrument to achieve the goals of sharia, including protecting the faith, life, mind, lineage, and property. Those five aspects are framed by *masaqid*, which is the foundational basis of government expenditure policy to determine priority scales. Commitment to Islamic values and the application of *maqasid shariah* will help reduce indecision in terms of government expenditure policy because the criteria for establishing priorities are already there (Chapra, 2000).

Islamic jurists (*fuqaha*) have put forward six principles concerning a priority scale for state expenditure to support the formation of *maqasid,* while ensuring effectiveness and efficiency are a rational and consistent basis for every economic actor, particularly in terms of state decision-making, as follows:

(a) Government expenditure policy must adhere with the rules of *maslahah.*
(b) Avoiding *masyaqqah* (difficulties, fatigue, exhaustion, and hardship) and *mudharat* should take precedence over making improvements.
(c) Individual *mudharat* is a valid reason to avoid *mudharat* on a more general scale.
(d) Individual sacrifices can be made and individual interests can be sacrificed in order to avoid losses and sacrifices on a more general scale.
(e) *Al-giurmu bil gunni* is a rule that states those who benefit must be prepared to bear the burden. In other words, those who wish to profit must be prepared to bear a loss.
(f) *Maa la yutimmu al waajibu illa bihi* is a rule stating that something must be erected, and without the necessary supports cannot be built, therefore, those supports are obligatory.

According to Umer Chapra, a Muslim government must minimise borrowing, which can be achieved if the government enforces strict discipline in terms of expenditure programs, taking into account the aforementioned rules to avoid overspending.

The following discussion materials are important to recognise the fundamental characteristics of the Islamic financial and fiscal systems in an Islamic economy:

(a) Broad economic expedience based on full employment and an optimal level of economic growth.
(b) Socio-economic justice, coupled with the equitable distribution of income and quality welfare.

(c) Stability in the value of money that allows the medium of exchange to be used as a unit of calculation, a fair benchmark in deferring payments and a stable exchange rate.
(d) Effective invoicing of all services is typically expected from the banking system.

As discussed previously, the state is entrusted to maintain the provisions of sharia law (as revealed by Allah SWT), thus ensuring optimal functions. Therefore, state expenditure policy must consider the targets outlined by sharia law, as reflected in the function of sharia law to maintain human life. Al Shatibi explains this concept well, namely that sharia must take care of basic (*druri*), tertiary (*haji*), and complementary (*tahsini*) human needs. More specifically, the basic human needs are faith (*din*), life (*nafs*), mind (*aql*), lineage (*nasl*), and property (*mal*).

Urgency of Social Security

Poverty is the largest problem in life because it engenders other issues, including hunger, disease, ignorance, and the underdevelopment of civilisation, while potentially eroding the faith and morals of Muslims. This could tarnish Islamic *izzah*, which fundamentally deals with the distribution of wealth.

Islam views poverty as a disaster or calamity that must be overcome and asks Allah SWT for protection from its evil, as typified by the prayer of the Prophet Muhammad "O Allah SWT, I seek refuge in You from disbelief and poverty". Among the various ways established by Islam to alleviate poverty are calls for work and simplicity in spending. In fact, wealth is distributed by establishing rights for the poor to the wealth of the rich through *zakat, sadaqah sunnah,* and other instruments in the social security system, which are also developed in the productive sector. This can also help prevent a country from sinking into a debt crisis or economic collapse from entanglement in debt politics.

State Debt

In the contemporary economy, debt is understood to be a ubiquitous instrument commonly applied by all countries to meet their state expenditure needs in the form of external debt or domestic debt. It is also important to note that in today's economy, debt as a development policy not only arises to meet the need for funds beyond state revenues yet is also due to massive prevalence in the world economy. Therefore, any country will inevitably find it difficult to extricate itself from debt conditions or avoid debt. The main fiscal instruments of Islam have been described above, now it is time to explore the concept of debt or state debt in Islam.

Unequivocally, Islam strongly advocates avoiding debt individually and collectively (the state). In the context of the state, there are situations where an Islamic state must proselytise and use propaganda (*fikrah*) as part of its international diplomatic mission. The prerequisites of such a function include an independent Islamic state with high integrity. How could it be possible to discharge this function of state optimally when there is a lack of sovereign independence and integrity caused by an accumulation of external debt? In conclusion, sources of debt must be avoided when financing state development programs. If debt is unavoidable, it is better obtained from a fellow Muslim country, providing domestic financing is no longer sufficient.

Concerning a financial deficit, the state has various options to cover expenditure. In fact, through development of the modern Islamic economy, several innovations have emerged to help finance economic development. It is becoming popular to finance state economic development programs using instruments involving public–private partnerships, such as Islamic bonds that essentially facilitate joint financing in the form of investment or trading schemes based on *mudharabah, murabahah, salam,* or *istisna* certificates. This is also expected to create state independence, fiscal independence specifically.

4.6 Role of Economic Institutions

The state has several institutions that play a significant role in facilitating economic activity as follows:

4.6.1 Baitul Mal

Based on classical Islamic economics literature, *Baitul Mal* (treasury house) is a central and concrete institution of the state. According to the literature concerning classical Islamic civilisation and economics, the *Baitul Mal* mechanism is inextricably linked to the function of the caliph as head of state, namely that the decisions concerning *Baitul Mal* as well as the institutional policies are predominantly the preserve of the caliph.

Together with the caliph, *Baitul Mal* discharges the functions of state, beyond economic aspects to include all facets of life, including social aspects. Essentially, *Baitul Mal* functions to manage state finances using funds accumulated from various revenue sources, including *zakat, kharaj, jizyah, khums, fay'*, and others, to execute socio-economic development programs, national defence and security, and proselytism through international diplomacy as well as any other state development program.

In a modern economic context, the *Baitul Mal* institution is known as the Department of Finance—Treasury House of the State, responsible for implementing economic policies through development divisions, creating currency, building economic infrastructure as well as receiving, managing, and distributing development funds, et cetera. Nowadays, the development of social and public financial management institutions has been divided into various more complex institutions to prevent economic crises. For example, Indonesia has Bank Indonesia as the central bank, responsible for regulating the monetary system, such as safeguarding money supply, monitoring exchange rate indicators, and maintaining financial system stability. Meanwhile, the Ministry of Finance develops various fiscal indicators to explore the impact of suboptimal taxation, risk in the SBN market, and other policies that will affect potential state financial growth or deficit. The Financial Services

Authority (OJK) serves as the microprudential authority, responsible for monitoring the health of individual financial institutions, banks, nonbanks, and the capital market.

In terms of social finance, Indonesia has institutions such as the National Amil Zakat Board (BAZNAS) and Indonesia Waqf Board (BWI) to manage the collection and distribution of social funds, including *zakat, infaq, sadaqah,* and *waqf* (ZISWAF), as independent state institutions established in accordance with prevailing laws and regulations.

The function and existence of *Baitul Mal* were explicitly mentioned during the time of Rasulullah SAW and the subsequent caliphs after His passing. In concrete terms, however, the *Baitul Mal* institution emerged during the reign of Umar bin Khattab, when the distribution of collected funds underwent a change. At that time, *Baitul Mal* was centralised in the capital city of Medina, with branches in each province of the Islamic caliphate.

During the time of Rasulullah SAW until the leadership of Abu Bakar, the collection and distribution of *zakat* funds and other levies were carried out simultaneously, implying the immediate distribution of funds after collection and obviating the need for officers to bring any surplus funds to deposit in *Baitul Mal.* During the reign of Umar bin Khattab, however, the collection of funds became so large that the decision to set aside a portion for unforeseen circumstances was taken. Consequently, *Baitul Mal* was officially instituted with the intention of managing those deposited funds.

During the time of Umar bin Abdul Azis, the organisational and operational hierarchy of *Baitul Mal* was divided into several departments based on the revenues received as state treasury. Therefore, the department handling *zakat* was different from those managing *khums, jizyah, kharaj,* and so on.

Yusuf Qaradhawi (1988) divided *Baitul Mal* into four divisions based on the revenues received in a classical Islamic context as follows:

1. Department for *sadaqah* (*zakat*)
2. Department for taxes and tributes
3. Department for *ghanimah* and *rikaz*
4. Department for assets of unknown inheritance or severed inheritance rights (due to homicide, for instance)

Such arrangements were also expressed by Ibnu Taimiyyah, who divided the administration of state finances into several *Baitul Mal* departments known as Diwan (councils) as follows:

1. Diwan al Rawitab, functioning to administrate the salaries and honoraria of civil servants and army personnel.
2. Diwan al Jawali wal Mawarits al Hasyriyah, functioning to manage poll tax (*jizyah*) and heirless property.
3. Diwan al Kharaj, functioning to levy *kharaj.*
4. Diwan al Hilali, functioning to collect monthly taxes.

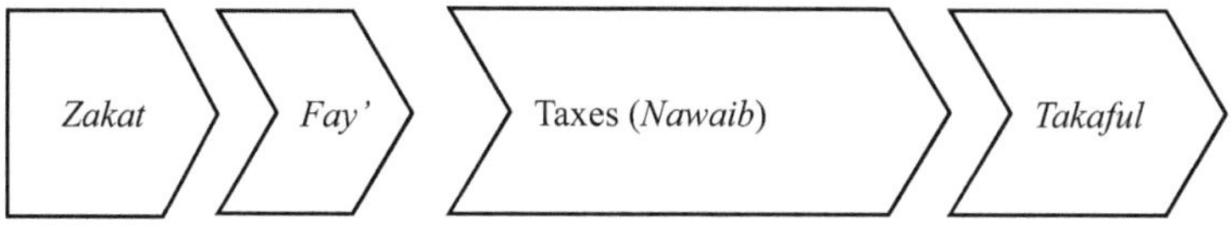

Fig. 4.7 Stages of State Finance in Islam. Source: Authors

In essence, the development of institutions and policies in Islamic economics does not adhere to standard regulations unless stipulated in sharia law. Regarding the collection and utilisation of state revenues, the formation of departments and policies depends on the economic development or condition of the country at the time. This implies that the development of economic institutions and policies is not tied to what previous leaders have implemented. Based on contemporary conditions, the role of *ijtihad* is to determine the orientation and form of economic institutions and policies.

Referring to Yusuf Qardhawi and his explanation about *Baitul Mal* operations, one of the policies for managing state revenues when there are insufficient funds in the *sadaqah* (*zakat*) department, whose function is to meet the basic needs of the citizenry, is to utilise funds from other departments, such as the tax and tribute department. In the classical Islamic period, however, this was achieved through a debt scheme, implying that the debt must be repaid to the tax and tribute department once sufficient funds have been collected in the *sadaqah* (*zakat*) department. The stages of utilising state financing have been explained previously, where the main source of state finance is *zakat*, followed by *fay'* and taxes. If a shortage still persists, the state can implement a *takaful* scheme where all assets are collected by the state and distributed equally (Fig. 4.7).

According to historical data, *Baitul Mal* at the time of caliph Ali bin Abi Thalib also functioned to print currency in circulation (dinar and dirham), indicating that *Baitul Mal* also functioned as a monetary authority responsible for determining money supply. With the complexity of the modern monetary sector, regulation by *Baitul Mal* is not merely limited to money supply, yet also encompasses the supervision and regulation of capital flows through investment and trade activities undertaken by Islamic financial institutions in the economy. Therefore, a specialised division in charge of the monetary sector is also required in the organisational structure of *Baitul Mal*.

With the economic complexity that pervades today's modern economy, the organisational structure of *Baitul Mal* may change. Notwithstanding, the basic function as mandated by sharia law, namely to fulfil the basic needs of the community, must remain the overarching purpose. Based on the complexity of the modern economy, the function of *Baitul Mal* includes economic policymaking in the real and monetary sectors, in addition to the more natural role of policymaking in the social sector. Real sector policies include determining the rate of tax and distribution, and determining the organisational hierarchy of *Baitul Mal*, while monetary policies deal with creating money and managing money supply. At the dawn of Islam, this role was largely dominated by the caliphs, yet the ever-increasing complexity of the modern economy would make this role ineffective in the hands of just one leader.

The organisational mechanism of *Baitul Mal* is expected, however, to discharge that function.

The regional scope of *Baitul Mal* is also a consideration when developing the organisational structure. As a state economic institution, *Baitul Mal* applies the concept of decentralisation. The relationship between the central and regional elements regarding the collection and distribution of funds must be based on sharia law and the priority scale of local economic development. For example, *zakat* funds must first be used to meet the needs of local *mustahiq* in the area where the funds were collected, with any residual funds subsequently distributed to surrounding areas in need. Nonetheless, this can also be achieved through centralisation, where the central *Baitul Mal* is responsible for the distribution of accumulated funds, with a portion, half or all the *zakat* funds surrendered to the central *Baitul Mal.*

Baitul Mal Manager (*Amil*)

The management of funds collected by *Baitul Mal* is a sensitive issue, thus requiring professional managers with high moral and technical integrity. Managerial dishonesty or the mismanagement of funds erodes the popularity of the *Baitul Mal* institution, thus sowing seeds of distrust regarding state leadership because *Baitul Mal* is considered an institutional pillar of the country.

The existence of *Baitul Mal* is a logical consequence of the professional management entrusted to *zakat* managers (*amil*), yet also reflects the scope of Islam, which is defined as a religion and government, Al-Qur'an and power, implying that the institution is responsible for discharging the functions of government and powers of state. Therefore, the government must also manage state revenues, encompassing those revenues regulated by sharia law as well as the revenues obtained based on prevailing conditions. The state requires an institution that collects, manages, and distributes funds in the interest of the state, including funds regulated by sharia law and also the current development priorities of the time.

The portion of *zakat* funds allocated to *zakat* managers (*amil*) clearly falls within the framework of state income. According to Imam Al Ghazali in The Revival of the Religious Sciences (*Ihya Ulumuddin*), the portion of *zakat* funds allocated to *amil* is based on necessity, with necessity here defined as an intrinsic element of the *amil* function and the basic needs of the *amil* himself. Anas Zarqa classified such needs of the *amil* into two types, namely the basic needs for survival and the needs for a decent life.

4.6.2 Al Hisbah: *Market Supervisory and Judicial Institution*

Markets are a central institution of the economy, even considered the heart of the economy. In the Islamic economy, the market is a medium or catalyst for the circulation of economic resources amongst individuals. To ensure the market functions in line with Islamic principles, where the benefits are distributed maximally and quality welfare is felt by all within the system, strong oversight is a prerequisite. In this case, Islam has its own market mechanism, known as the *Hisbah* institution.

1. **Definition of *Al Hisbah***

   A unique characteristic, and simultaneously the original form of the Islamic economic system, is the existence of economic supervisory and judicial institutions, particularly market supervisors that have existed since the time of Rasulullah SAW, known as *Al Hisbah*. This topic has not featured in many studies conducted by contemporary Islamic economists, yet various sources of classical economics mention the role of this institution and its urgency in economic mechanisms.

   Existence of the *Al Hisbah* market authority institution demonstrates how the Islamic economy views the importance of the market in terms of economic activity. The market is the heart of the economy and utilised by individuals to achieve welfare globally, while maintaining the position of every human being to ensure safety and maximise worship to Allah SWT. With the adverse consequences that can also arise from economic activity in the market, market oversight is a prerequisite to ensure the goals can be achieved.

2. **History of *Al Hisbah***

   A further discussion or indeed a book is needed concerning the role of the *Al Hisbah* institution, particularly with the contemporary economic structure that is considerably more complex than in the past. Therefore, an *Al Hisbah* mechanism or structure more suited to the modern economy is required. The institution is central to ensuring the seamless running of the economy in the market, as well as maintaining sharia principles and rules in implementation.

   In his article, Ahmed Sobhi Mansour explores in greater depth the history of the first *Al Hisbah* institution. Institutionally, he argues, *Al Hisbah* did not exist during the time of Rasulullah SAW, the caliphs or Umayyad dynasty. It is important to note, however, that the environmental conditions during the time of Rasulullah SAW, the caliphs and Umayyad dynasty were quite different. Those differences influenced all national decisions concerning the governing of the country, including the state's attitude towards the function of *Al Hisbah*.

   During the time of Rasulullah SAW and the caliphs, when the leadership role was central and government democratic, numerous policies were motivated by broad welfare priorities. Meanwhile, during the Umayyad and Abbasid caliphates, violence was a more prominent characteristic due to the dynastic style of government, including betrayal stemming from envy and dissatisfaction, as well as enemies of the state. Consequently, various policies issued during those periods were motivated by maintaining or consolidating power, which is where the institutionalisation of *Al Hisbah* is thought to have begun. It is natural, therefore, that *Al Hisbah* was more of a political institution than a socio-economic institution. Ahmed Sobhi Mansour found that during the Umayyad caliphate, the government seemed to justify its power by exploiting the strength of fatwas issued by the ulema. Concerning the Abbasid caliphate, with the same intention, the leaders promoted slogans as the official family heirs of Rasulullah SAW, with the right to rule as caliphs. It was during the Abbasid era that *Al Hisbah* was first formally institutionalised at the state level.

Though the *Al Hisbah* institution was not officially recognised as a systemic institution of the state during the time of Rasulullah SAW and the caliphs, the inherent functions were unequivocally implemented by the state under the auspices of Rasulullah SAW or the caliphs directly, or indirectly by companions appointed by Rasulullah SAW or the caliphs, known as a *muhtasib*.

There are many accounts of how Rasulullah SAW, in his function as state leader, visited the market to supervise all activities, including trade, debt, profit sharing, and the distribution of goods and services.

وَعَنْهُ أَنَّ رَسُولَ اللَّهِ صَلَّى اللَّهُ عَلَيْهِ وَسَلَّمَ مَرَّ عَلَى صُبْرَةِ طَعَامٍ فَأَدْخَلَ يَدَهُ فِيهَا فَنَالَتْ أَصَابِعُهُ
بَلَلًا فَقَالَ: «مَا هَذَا يَا صَاحِبَ الطَّعَامِ» قَالَ: أَصَابَتْهُ السَّمَاءُ يَا رَسُولَ اللَّهِ قَالَ: «أَفَلَا
جَعَلْتَهُ فَوْقَ الطَّعَامِ حَتَّى يَرَاهُ النَّاسُ مَنْ غَشَّ فَلَيْسَ مني» . رَوَاهُ مُسلم

He said that God's Messenger once came upon a heap of grain, and when he put his hand into it his fingers felt some dampness, so he asked the owner of the grain how that came about. On being told that rain had fallen on it he said, "Why did you not put the damp part on the top of the grain so that people might see it? He who deceives has nothing to do with me".[7]

Rasulullah SAW also appointed companions as holders of the office of *Al Hisbah* (*muhtasib*), as did subsequent caliphs (Khulafaur Rasyidin). After the liberation of Mecca, Rasulullah SAW appointed Sa'id bin "Ash bin Umayyah as *muhtasib* of the Mecca market. Moreover, Rasulullah SAW also appointed a female *muhtasib* by the name of Samra" binti Nuhaik al-Asadiyah.

The existential rationale for the *Al Hisbah* institution as a market supervisor also stems from the argument that market participants tend to behave deceptively, including lying to sell their wares at the market.

حَدَّثَنَا أَبُو سَلَمَةَ يَحْيَى بْنُ خَلَفٍ حَدَّثَنَا بِشْرُ بْنُ الْمُفَضَّلِ عَنْ عَبْدِ اللَّهِ بْنِ عُثْمَانَ بْنِ خُثَيْمٍ عَنْ إِسْمَاعِيلَ بْنِ
عُبَيْدِ بْنِ رِفَاعَةَ عَنْ أَبِيهِ عَنْ جَدِّهِ أَنَّهُ خَرَجَ مَعَ النَّبِيِّ صلى الله عليه وسلم إِلَى الْمُصَلَّى فَرَأَى النَّاسَ
يَتَبَايَعُونَ فَقَالَ " يَا مَعْشَرَ التُّجَّارِ " . فَاسْتَجَابُوا لِرَسُولِ اللَّهِ صلى الله عليه وسلم وَرَفَعُوا أَعْنَاقَهُمْ
وَأَبْصَارَهُمْ إِلَيْهِ فَقَالَ " إِنَّ التُّجَّارَ يُبْعَثُونَ يَوْمَ الْقِيَامَةِ فُجَّارًا إِلاَّ مَنِ اتَّقَى اللَّهَ وَبَرَّ وَصَدَقَ " . قَالَ أَبُو
عِيسَى هَذَا حَدِيثٌ حَسَنٌ صَحِيحٌ . وَيُقَالُ إِسْمَاعِيلُ بْنُ عُبَيْدِ اللَّهِ بْنِ رِفَاعَةَ أَيْضًا [13].

Narrated Isma'il bin 'Ubaid bin Rifa'ah:

From his father, from his grandfather, that he went with the Messenger of Allah (ﷺ) to the Musalla, and he saw the people doing business so he said: 'O people of trade!' and they replied to the Messenger of Allah (ﷺ) turning their necks and their gazes towards him, and he said: Indeed the merchants will be resurrected on the Day of judgement with the wicked, except the one who has Taqwa of Allah, who behaves charitably and is truthful". [Abu 'Eisa said:] This Hadith is Hasan Sahih. And they also say Isma'il bin 'Ubaidullah bin Rifa'ah.

Ahmed Sobhi Mansour argues that the function of *Al Hisbah* is essentially supervising Muslims to not violate sharia law that protects the greater good, while simultaneously safeguarding the rights and dignity of each individual Muslim. According to Ahmed Sobhi Mansour, *Al Hisbah* was officially founded to

[7] Mishkat al-Masabih 2860, in book reference: book 11, hadith 98.

legalise the suppression of traitorous rebel groups who disrupted government stability during the Abbasid dynasty, functioning as a supervisor and judge of all community behaviour. Based on such historical data, the office of *Al Hisbah* was fundamentally not limited to the functions of an economic institution, yet was more closely represented in the contemporary context by the national police and judiciary. Ahmed Sobhi Mansour also pointed out that the position of *muhtasib* was voluntarily rather than a salaried civil servant. Upon the institutionalisation of *Al Hisbah*, however, the *muhtasib* became a state official bound to the interests of the state.

3. **Function of *Al Hisbah***

   The function of *Al Hisbah* is indeed that of a market supervisory body but from the application and historical data, the function is much broader. *Al Hisbah* is more accurately referred to as a market authority institution because *Al Hisbah* not only overseas market activities, yet also functions to provide facilities and infrastructure, as well as prosecuting market players in violation of sharia principles. Al Mawardi states that *Al Hisbah* functions to restore good when it fades and prevent evil when it emerges. The purpose of market power during Umar's reign was to discharge the market supervision function, thus ensuring fair and just transactions, avoiding irregularities and collecting property from the market in accordance with *Baitul Mal* policy, while protecting the rights of all transacting parties. Such oversight aimed to create perfect competition of supply and demand naturally.

   In his book Ibnu Taimiyah concerning *Al Hisbah*, Rabah briefly mentions that the institutional function is to prevent wrongdoing. Therefore, *Al Hisbah* is not only an economic institution, but the purview also extends to judicial matters, similar to the contemporary police. Based on a study conducted by Hafas Furqani (2002), the functions of *Al Hisbah* are as follows:

   (a) **Overseeing the weighing scales, measures, and prices**

   In the contemporary economic context, *Al Hisbah* also oversees the standards or parameters that determine (through a general agreement permitted by the market) the quality, quantity and halal status of goods and services, or even a business unit, in Islamic economic activity. Though Islamic market mechanisms are free-market mechanisms, *Al Hisbah* still has to monitor general price fluctuations, particularly the prices of staple goods and essential services, to ensure instability is not created that could disrupt macroeconomic activity. In other words, the institution reinforces the government's role in terms of meeting the basic needs of the community, which has a significant impact on the socio-political stability of the country.

   (b) **Overseeing forbidden trade, *riba, maysir, gharar,* and deception**

   Aligning and harmonising economic activity with sharia law is the preserve and function of the *Al Hisbah* institution. In addition to providing guidance and clarification concerning economic activity, sharia law also contains restrictions on its implementation, such as trade mechanisms and contracts, payments and settlement, the objects traded and relevant information, which are applied in order to ensure justice.

(c) **Overseeing halal, health, and cleanliness in the community**

Maintaining the cleanliness and integrity of economic interactions, *Al Hisbah* not only ensures that economic transactions run in accordance with sharia law, but also guarantees that goods are traded in pursuance of Islamic principles.

(d) **Arranging the Market Layout**

Seeking to ensure seamless and orderly market transactions, considering the freedom of all parties to participate, as well as the cleanliness, health, rights, and obligations of all entities, *Al Hisbah* has the authority to regulate the layout or arrangement of the market. This includes providing all facilities necessary to support economic activity in the market, including street lighting, waste disposal, sanitation and irrigation, lodgings for adventitious merchants, and so on.

(e) **Settling Disputes and Injustice**

As discussed previously, the state functions to maintain socio-economic stability based on sharia law. Therefore, *Al Hisbah* has the authority to intervene and settle disputes and injustice that threaten the harmonious relationships of market participants, socially and economically, such as in the case of a market participant unwilling to repay debt despite adequate capacity. In such a case, *Al Hisbah* has the authority to coerce the debtor into paying the outstanding obligations along with additional penalties upon refusal to pay.

(f) **Implementing Market Intervention**

The free-market mechanism is recognised and upheld in Islam based on the assumption that the market is fair. If, under such conditions, however, market prices soar as a corollary of disaster, epidemic or other force majeure, and that threatens the basic needs of the community, the state, through *Al Hisbah*, may intervene, set prices, and establish sufficient product reserves. In the context of contemporary Indonesia, the Indonesian Bureau of Logistics (Bulog) fulfils a similar function.

(g) **Punishing Violations**

In addition to providing guidance, clarification, and boundaries on economic activity, sharia law also explicitly stipulates the punitive consequences for violating sharia, with *Al Hisbah* functioning to ensure the punishments are meted out.

In conclusion, *Al Hisbah* is not only responsible for market oversight but also to provide the facilities and infrastructure necessary for the markets to flourish in accordance with sharia law. Therefore, *Al Hisbah* is duty-bound to provide roads, lighting, bridges, lodgings, et cetera. According to Chapra, *Al Hisbah* obviates the need for market intervention through *Baitul Mal* or other institutions due to its maximised role in maintaining market stability physically and in line with sharia law. Notwithstanding, *Al Hisbah* cannot discharge its function arbitrarily, which could lead to injustice.

In addition to the functions of market supervisor and facilitator of market activities, *Al Hisbah* is also part of the judiciary. Structurally, the judiciary in

Islam is divided into three branches, namely *Al Mazaalim, Al Qadha,* and *Al Hisbah*, as government institutions (defined by Ibnu Taimiyyah). *Al Hisbah* is the lowest level of judicial institution, directly responsible for adjudicating infractions witnessed first-hand by the *muhtasib*. *Al Qadha* is tasked with judiciary responsibilities requiring statements, oaths, witnesses, and evidence. Finally, *Al Mazaalim* is responsible for handling higher risk cases, such as state officials who have interfered with market mechanisms.

Under a conventional system, however, this supervision mechanism rarely features systematically in the discussion and when it does, it is not institutionally part of the larger conventional economic framework. This demonstrates how the role of sharia, as an economic paradigm, significantly shapes the architecture of the Islamic economic system, which is absolutely disparate from the conventional economic system.

4. **Structure of *Al Hisbah***

As stated by Ahmed Sobhi Mansour, holders of the office of *Al Hisbah* (*muhtasib*) fundamentally operate on a voluntary basis, yet institutionalisation established the position of *muhtasib* as an intrinsic part of the state apparatus. Ultimately, the role was not limited to market overseer, with the purview extending to administrative and other tasks for *Al Hisbah* and the incumbent *muhtasib*.

In response to the broader scope of work and complexity of the markets, *Al Hisbah* developed in terms of organisational structure as well as internal–external task management. Mirroring the evolution of *Baitul Mal, Al Hisbah* the organisation had to adapt to increasingly integral and complex market trends as the market authority. For reasons of institutional efficiency and effectiveness, *Al Hisbah* can play a centralised or decentralised role based on prevailing economic conditions.

The market authority, *Al Hisbah*, must coordinate with *Baitul Mal*, the economic authority, to create and maintain an orderly market based on sharia principles that also supports the country's economic development goals. When inflationary pressures in the market become so intense that the basic needs of the citizenry are threatened, for instance, *Al Hisbah* can offer recommendations to *Baitul Mal* in terms of market intervention.

During the reign of Umar, market oversight and transaction rules were applied with the following goals:

(a) **Free Entry and Exit**

Free entry and exit as well as perfect competition cannot be achieved unless the barriers are removed. Economic actors enjoy the freedom to enter and exit the market as well as transfer production factors between economic activities based on fluctuations in the supply and demand of goods. Umar stated, therefore, that traders in the free market can select a place to trade without limitation by specific buildings or kiosks as a sign of ownership.

Quoting Umar, "the market adheres to the rules of the mosque, namely that whoever arrives first can keep that place until he has finished trading for the day and returns home".

Such rules, however, cannot be applied to the contemporary economy due to the diverse range of goods containing harmful or flammable chemicals that require special storage. The key takeaway, therefore, is that if a person can display his wares without the need to construct a permanent space, such places may be used freely by anyone.

(b) **Promotion and Propaganda**

There is no issue in Islam with merchants promoting their wares as long as the promotional efforts are based on honesty, trust, and integrity, leading to something beneficial and oriented towards successful investments.

(c) **Hoarding**

Hoarding (*ikhtikar*) is the largest barrier to regulating competition in Islamic markets. Hoarding merchandise can inflate prices and have an adverse effect on fluctuations in supply and demand. More broadly, hoarding is the biggest cause of economic crises due to monopolistic production and trade. Islamic economics views monopolies in terms of individuals, producers, and sellers. If goods are held that could threaten the public interest with the aim of inflating prices, this is considered monopolistic behaviour in Islam. On the other hand, conventional economics views monopoly based on the number of buyers and sellers, such as when there is only one company producing and selling certain goods in the market.

(d) **Trade Intermediaries (Middlemen)**

The law concerning trade intermediaries is prescribed consistently among Muslims without any difference of opinion. While recognising the importance of middlemen, leaving them unregulated could lead to a dereliction of duties through deception and monopolistic behaviour, thus killing competition and creating price instability. Furthermore, the arbitrariness of some intermediaries could intensify inflationary pressures.

Umar's message, "show them to the market, show them the way and tell them the price," aims to reduce the number of middlemen and lower marketing costs, which prevents hoarding.

5. **Monitoring of Prices**

Prices are considered the best indicator of livelihood because prices influence the value of currency. In fact, higher prices are the biggest indicator of inflationary pressures because when inflation occurs, prices rise sharply and reduce the value of currency. This is a key trigger of the imperilments associated with economic growth.

Unsurprisingly, Islam considers rising prices to be calamitous and caused by the sins of man, with Rasulullah SAW, as leader, unwilling to intervene and determine prices. Notwithstanding, price intervention by Umar bin Khattab did not contradict the reluctance of Rasulullah SAW because Umar did not limit

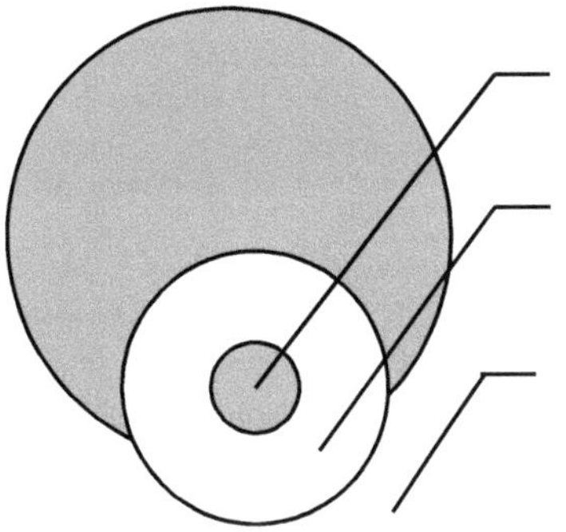

Fig. 4.8 Losses incurred from selling below normal prices

certain selling prices according to the intended textual meaning. Instead, Umar asked the traders to sell at the market price. This policy also has an economic implication that selling goods below the normal price intentionally without any acceptable reason can harm the economy (Fig. 4.8):

Monopolistic behaviour in the form of dumping is widespread amongst non-Muslim companies selling products to Muslim countries at low prices to eliminate the competition and control the economy in the long run. This shows that Umar's attitude to price setting did not allow price fixing or monopolies. In the event of a monopoly, however, the government would require traders to sell their wares at fair market prices.

References

Al-Ghazali, I. (1990). *Ihya Ulumuddin*. Jilid 2. Asy Syifa.

Askari, H., Iqbal, Z., & Mirakhor, A. (2015). *Introduction to Islamic Economics: Theory and application*. Wiley.

Blanchard, O. (2018). On the future of macroeconomic models. *Oxford Review of Economic Policy, 34*(1-2), 43–54.

Chapra, M. U. (2000). *Towards a just monetary system.* (I. A. Basri, Trans.). Gema Insani Press.

Corry, O. (2010). Defining and theorizing the third sector. In *Third Sector Research* (pp. 11–20). Springer.

Faridi, F. R. (1983). *Theory of fiscal policy in an Islamic State*. *Journal of King Abdulaziz University: Islamic Economics, 1*(1).

Furqani, H. (2002). *Institusi Hisbah: Studi Model Pengawasan Pasar dalam Sistem Ekonomi Islam. Skripsi S1 Jurusan Muamalat*. Fakultas Syariah UIN Syarif Hidayatullah.

Gruber, J. (2010). *Public finance and public policy* (3rd ed.). Worth Publisher.

Hasanuzzaman. (1991). *Economic functions of an Islamic State (The early experience)*. The Islamic Foundation.

Khadduri, M. (1955). *War and Peace in the Law of Islam*. The Johns Hopkins University Press.

Mankiw, N. G. (2014). *Principles of economics*. Cengage Learning.

Muhammad, Q. I. (2002). *Kebijakan-kebijakan Ekonomi Umar bin Khattab*. Azzam.

Pettinger, T. (2018). Government failures. dalam https://www.economicshelp.org/microessays/market-failure/government-failure/

Qaradhawi, Y. (1988). *Hukum Zakat*. Pustaka Litera Antar Nusa.
Salama, A. A. (1995). *Fiscal policy of an Islamic state. Readings in Public Finance in Islam* (Edited by Mahamoud A. Gulaid & Mohamed Aden Abdullah), Islamic Research and Training Institute (IRTI). IDB.
Siddiqi, M. N. (1996). *Role of the state in the economy: An Islamic perspective*. The Islamic Foundation.
Smith, A. (1776). *The wealth of nations*. Bantam Classics (Reprint ed.).
Stiglitz, J. E. (1988). *Economics of the public sector*. W.W. Norton & Company.
Stiglitz, J. E., & Rosengard, J. K. (2015). *Economics of the public sector: Fourth international* (Student ed.). WW Norton & Company.
Williamson, O. E. (2005). The economics of governance. *American Economic Review, 95*(2), 1–18.

Chapter 5
Economic Implications of Islamic Social-Public Finance

5.1 Introduction

The discussion in previous chapters has implicitly shown that Islamic social-public finance innovation encourages philanthropy, as described in Al-Qur'an as follows:

وَمَآ اٰتَيْتُمْ مِّنْ رِّبًا لِّيَرْبُوَا۠ فِيْٓ اَمْوَالِ النَّاسِ فَلَا يَرْبُوْا عِنْدَ اللّٰهِ ۚوَمَآ اٰتَيْتُمْ مِّنْ زَكٰوةٍ تُرِيْدُوْنَ وَجْهَ اللّٰهِ فَاُولٰۤىِٕكَ هُمُ الْمُضْعِفُوْنَ

> And whatever you give for interest to increase within the wealth of people will not increase with Allah. But what you give in zakah, desiring the countenance of Allah—those are the multipliers. (Q.S. Ar Rum [30]: 39).

It is important to note that innovation only thrives in a competitive, open, and egalitarian environment. Innovation can also develop rapidly within a culture of creativity and solution-based traditions supported by dynamism. Innovation is nurtured by the wealth of information and knowledge disseminated to all stakeholders. Therefore, fostering conditions conducive to individual and philanthropic innovation is necessary.[1] Ultimately, the urge to donate enables anyone to be useful and kind to others, thus strengthening the fabric of humanity.

In the spirit of philanthropy, nearly 200 representatives of various donor agencies, grantmakers, philanthropic organisations and associations as well as centres for philanthropic studies and development from 56 countries around the world gathered at the WINGSForum 2010 in the Philippines. Established 10 years ago, the

[1]Philanthropy is an awareness to donate and the desire to promote the welfare of others. Philanthropy may stem from spiritual awareness, yet can also arise from the call of humanity or because of seeking a meaningful life and participating in the creation of better lives. Philanthropic resources come from individual donations and corporate donations in the form of corporate social responsibility (CSR), as well as several large philanthropists such as Bill Gates, Warren Buffett, and other billionaires, who not only act as donors but also set up foundations, including the Gates Foundation, as grantmakers to fund various humanitarian programmes implemented by different organisations.

S. M. Juhro et al., *Inclusive Welfare*, https://doi.org/10.1007/978-981-96-0051-9_5

Worldwide Initiatives for Grantmaker Support (WINGS) is a community of thought leaders and changemakers who are committed to ensuring philanthropy reaches its fullest potential as a catalyst for social progress. The WINGS secretariat previously moved from Asia to Europe and America yet is currently more permanently located in Brazil. The WINGSForum is the pre-eminent global conference on philanthropy and grantmaking, offering a rare opportunity for a unique collection of philanthropy associations, support organisations, funders, and academics from all regions of the world to network, learn from each other, and deeply explore how philanthropy can make an ever-greater contribution to social impact and civil society building. Entitled Innovation and Impact: The Role of Grantmaker Associations in Changing Society, the WINGSForum in 2010 discussed several topics, including: how to make change through innovation and impact, efforts to create regulations and support for philanthropic development, the need to develop a philanthropy handbook, the role of leadership and collaboration in philanthropic development, and how to realise good governance for philanthropic development.

Over time, the philanthropic movement has become a pillar of the third sector, or the public sector, by strengthening the position of civil society between two other forces, namely the government and private sector. In addition, the philanthropic movement represents part of the efforts to create a balanced life between rich and poor, between men and women, and between young and old. Philanthropic development increases significantly when innovation is encouraged to create new works and ideas, motivated to find new ways of developing organisations and programmes as well as finding new breakthroughs and problem-solving solutions to the existing challenges and barriers. Innovation will maintain the sustainability of philanthropic efforts as well as future developmental leaps moving forward.

The spirit of generosity and the presence of philanthropic efforts are aligned with Islamic philosophy, particularly in the social-public dimension. Therefore, the global emergence of Islamic economics and finance, including social-public finance, offers an alternative to existing conventional economic systems. As with most alternatives, Islamic social-public finance exists to offer a better system of quality public welfare. This chapter elucidates the implications of Islamic social-public finance, particularly from a socio-economic perspective in the lives of ordinary Indonesians. The discussion in this chapter also covers the implications of various aspects of Islamic social-public finance, ranging from the (mandatory and voluntary) instruments to the institutions, especially those currently operating in Indonesia.

5.2 Utilisation of *Zakat*

5.2.1 Zakat *to Alleviate and Overcome Poverty*

Zakat, infaq, sadaqah, and *waqf* (ZISWAF) are social funds as taught by Islam and practised by Muslims. *Zakat* is an obligatory instrument of Islamic social finance, while *infaq, sadaqah*, and *waqf* are voluntary. Though *zakat, infaq*, and *sadaqah*

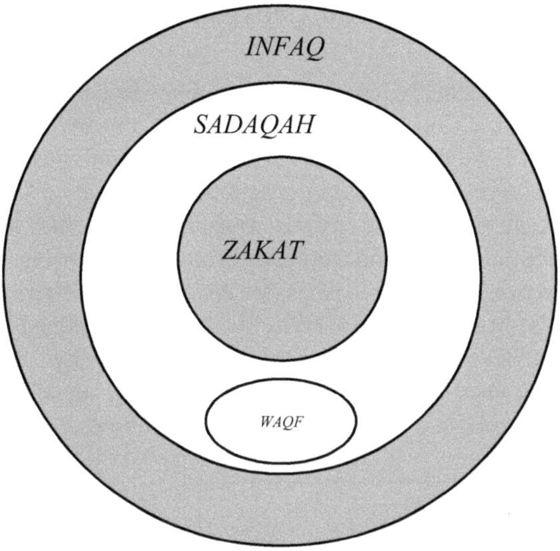

Fig. 5.1 Relationship between Zakat, Infaq, Sadaqah, and Waqf. Source: Created by Author

constitute Islamic social funds, their allocation entails an economic dimension that affects the welfare of Muslims.

Zakat is an expenditure or donation with specific usage requirements and regulations (*nisab, haul*, rate, and recipients), representing a specific portion of wealth that must be donated annually by Muslims who meet the necessary criteria (*nisab*) for the benefit of the poor and needy in the Muslim community. As one of the five pillars of Islam, *zakat* is an obligatory religious duty and the primary economic means for establishing social justice, while directing Muslims towards prosperity and security.

Infaq encompasses all expenditures or gifts made by an individual, for good or evil. Al-Qur'an identifies *infaq fi sabilillah* (*infaq* in the way of Allah SWT—*infaq* for good) and *infaq fi sabilit thagut* (*infaq* in the way of the devil—*infaq* for evil). Meanwhile, *sadaqah* includes all material and non-material benevolent charitable offerings. On the other hand, *waqf* is an inalienable charitable endowment in perpetuity, typically involving a building, plot of land, or other assets for Muslim religious or charitable purposes with no intention of reclaiming the assets. *Waqf* is prioritised for productive purposes to generate income or profit to be used for charitable ends in the interest of the community (Fig. 5.1).

Some Muslims still practice *zakat, infaq, sadaqah,* and *waqf* (ZISWAF) purely for charitable purposes. In general, *zakat, infaq, sadaqah,* and *waqf* are only disbursed for consumption, social, and religious purposes. Few Muslims actually utilise ZISWAF Islamic social funds for wider economic benefit. Concerning the role of ameliorating quality welfare, therefore, ZISWAF funds could be exploited to accelerate economic development, particularly in terms of assisting small businesses. Islamic social funds must be developed to generate income, develop businesses, and expand the Islamic economy through the Sharia financial services industry.

5.2.2 Zakat *and Consumption Behaviour*

Fundamentally, consumption motives in Islam include *maslahah*, needs, and obligations. Consumption activities also aim to increase worship and faith in Allah SWT. Monzer Kahf (1992) introduced Final Spending (FS) as a standard variable to observe the maximum satisfaction obtained by a Muslim consumer to achieve *falah*. Kahf assumed that *zakat* is obligatory for *muzakki* and, therefore, was excluded from the final spending variable. From the following formula, an inverse correlation between s and FS is observable, where a higher value of s equates to a lower FS. Maximum satisfaction, therefore, is obtained based on the amount of income and level of wealth. According to Kahf, the final spending of a Muslim individual is described across three different groups, namely *mustahik*, middle income, and *muzakki*, in a two-period analysis as follows:

$FS = (Y - S) + (S - Sz)$
$FS = (Y - sY) + (sY - zsY)$ or
$FS = Y(1 - zs)$

→

$Max\ U = U(FS, s)$
Subject to:
$FS + S = Y$ dan $DW = S \geq z(W + S)$

U = Consumer Utility
W = Consumer Wealth
D = Time Derivative
s = Percentage of Saving
z = Percentage of *Zakat*
$FS + S = Y$
$FS = Z; Z = Co$
$FS = Y + Z; Y + Z = Co$

$FS + S = Y$
1. $FS = Z;\ Z = Co$
2. $FS = Y + Z;\ Y + Z = Co$

Mustahik:

FS = Final Spending
Y = Income
S = Saving
Co = Autonomous Consumption
Z = Percentage of *Zakat*

Where Co is the consumption of basic necessities, Y is the income, and Z is the *zakat* received. In the first consumption model, consumption is sourced in its entirety from *zakat* funds, thus describing the primary source of consumption for *mustahik*, particularly *fakir, ibnussabil*, and *fisabilillah*. The second model illustrates the sources of consumption for poor *mustahik*, namely those with insufficient income to meet the primary needs, thus relying on *zakat* funds. Under such conditions, final spending exceeds income. According to Imam Ghazali, the amount of *zakat* distributed must be commensurate with the needs of the *mustahik*, implying that the *zakat* distributed to this *mustahik* group is used fully to consume basic necessities, particularly for the four categories of *mustahik* that have been mentioned. The final spending of the *mustahik*, therefore, is equivalent to their needs. The middle-income group is as follows:

$$\mathrm{FS} = Y - S$$

$$\mathrm{FS} = Cm + In + Sh$$

Where Cm is the total consumption of the middle-income group, In is *infaq*, and Sh is *sadaqah*. The middle-income group has sufficient income to meet its primary needs and consume secondary goods, yet their level of wealth has not reached the necessary criteria of *nisab*. Thus, *infaq* and *sadaqah* are required to maximise the final spending of this group.

Muzakki:

$$\mathrm{FS} = Y\text{–}S$$

$$\mathrm{FS} = Cz\text{–}(Zy + In + Sh + Wf)$$

Where Cz is the total consumption of the *muzakki* group, *Zy* is *zakat* income, and *Wf* is *waqf*. In the model above, *zakat* is assumed to originate only from income (excluding *zakat* on property/assets). It is important to note that *muzakki* are eligible to pay *zakat*, *infaq*, and *sadaqah*, as well as donate *waqf*. Though *zakat* is considered spending to attain success, happiness, and well-being (*falah*), the permanent nature (*mahdhuh* worship) excludes it from the final spending variable. The disparate roles of *zakat* are clearly evident between the *mustahik* and *muzakki* groups. According to Al Ghazali, Ihya Ulumuddin, and Asy Syifa, Vol. 2 (1990), *zakat* distributed to the eight *mustahik* groups (*asnaf*) determines their level of consumption of basic necessities or primary needs, with their final spending thus limited to the consumption of primary needs. Regarding the *muzakki* group, *zakat* will reduce their final spending, while *zakat* will not influence the final spending of the middle-income group.

In discussions concerning the consumption behaviour of individual Muslims, the characteristics of *zakat* are known as a vital economic instrument. Absence of the *zakat* mechanism within the economy will undermine the economic balance and lead to large social imbalances.

Logically, *zakat* appears to have an inverse correlation to consumption because the attention of the *zakat* discussion focuses on the mechanism of the *muzakki* community group, even though the most dominant group is *mustahik*, where consumption depends on *zakat* distribution. In other words, *zakat* has a positive correlation with consumption.

Essentially, the macro consumption model in Islam is no different from the conventional model, as determined by autonomous consumption for basic necessities and consumption derived from income.

$$C = Co + bYd$$

Where C is the total consumption, Co is the autonomous consumption, b is the marginal propensity to consume (MPC), and Y is the income.

Based on deeper analysis from a *mustahik* perspective, it is clear that *zakat* will logically increase aggregate consumption, or Co, due to the system accommodating market participants without purchasing power or economic access.

From a *muzakki* perspective, however, *zakat* would appear to reduce aggregate consumption because *zakat* payments reduce the amount of income available to consume. Naturally, therefore, the argument arises that even if consumption increases among the *mustahik* group due to *zakat*, the increase will be offset by a corresponding decrease in the *muzakki* group, leaving aggregate consumption relatively unchanged.

It should be remembered, however, that the surplus wealth of the *mustahik* group would not potentially be translated into consumption without the *zakat* mechanism. Potential consumption is greater if the excess wealth (as *zakat*) rests in the hands of the *mustahik* group because excess wealth in the hands of the *muzakki* group will be used to purchase secondary or luxury goods, while in the hands of the *mustahik* group, the funds will almost certainly be spent on primary needs.

When viewed in terms of potential consumption, excess wealth in the form of *zakat* is very effective or has greater potential in the hands of the *mustahik* group rather than the *muzakki* group. It may be concluded, thus, that *zakat* will affect consumption positively. In the long term, *zakat* funds are expected to improve the economy and increase per capita income (PCI), implying the concerns regarding the adverse economic effects of *zakat* are unwarranted.

Other economists have argued that *zakat* has a positive effect on MPC, a claim often refuted because of the assumption that the Islamic economy advocates frugal rather than luxurious consumption, leaving MPC at a low or reasonable level. Others may ask how *zakat* can increase demand when the morals associated with consumption encourage prudence and providence. In response, the motivation for consumption in Islam is not only driven by the desire or need to fulfil one's own requirements but is also driven by the motivation to perform good deeds (*amal shaleh*). Consequently, consumption can still increase, particularly as Islam only obliges *zakat* for wealthier economic actors. Therefore, the system forces excess (idle) funds to circulate in the economy through the *zakat* mechanism (refer to the subchapter on Islamic economic behaviour).

Therefore, the discussion on *zakat* and its relation to macroeconomics is inseparable from the main function of *zakat* as a primary demand-side variable of the economic system. This is also another characteristic of the Islamic economy, namely

Table 5.1 Zakat implications on consumption

Group	Implication on consumption
Mustahik	A. For the *Fakir*, *zakat* is the income to meet primary needs ($Y = Z = C$). B. For the Poor, *zakat* is additional or supplemental income to meet primary needs ($Y + Z = C$). C. For *Ibnussabil*, *zakat* is the main income to meet primary needs ($Y = Z = C$). D. For *Fisabilillah*, *zakat* is the family income to meet primary needs ($Y = Z = C$). E. For *Muallaf*, *zakat* is the main income to strengthen their faith ($Y = Z = C$). F. For *Amil*, *zakat* is the income to meet primary needs ($Y = Z = C$). G. For *Gharimin*, *zakat* is the income to repay debt ($Z = H$). H. For slaves, *zakat* is the income to be free from slavery ($Z = P$). Based on those assumptions, it can be concluded that *zakat* maintains the level of consumption to sustain the economy.
Assumption: *zakat* is distributed to *mustahik* based on their needs	
Notes: Y = Income, Z = *Zakat*, C = Consumption, H = Debt, and P = Price of Freedom	

equal attention paid to both the demand and supply sides along with comprehensive instruments that can be used to ensure a balance between the two.

An increase in aggregate consumption will precipitate an increase in economic performance, thus automatically supporting economic growth and development and confirming the revelations of Allah SWT in His words:

وَمَآ اٰتَيْتُمْ مِّنْ رِّبًا لِّيَرْبُوَا۟ فِيْٓ اَمْوَالِ النَّاسِ فَلَا يَرْبُوْا عِنْدَ اللّٰهِ ۚوَمَآ اٰتَيْتُمْ مِّنْ زَكٰوةٍ تُرِيْدُوْنَ وَجْهَ اللّٰهِ فَاُولٰۤىِٕكَ هُمُ الْمُضْعِفُوْنَ

> . . . But what you give in zakah, desiring the countenance of Allah—those are the multipliers. (Q.S. Ar Rum [30]: 39).

As explained previously concerning the effect of *zakat* on economic performance, *zakat* is a public instrument of demand-side economic policy (Table 5.1). Theoretically, *zakat* can raise the demand curve through increased aggregate demand due to the purchasing power of the *mustahik* community driven by *zakat* distribution. This will unequivocally raise prices in the short term, yet also increase revenue at the producer level (Total Revenue = Price × Quantity). Assuming that the information concerning higher prices is known to all market players (symmetric information), new market players will certainly enter the market. In other words, such a response will boost supply and correct prices. Though prices experience a correction, the general equilibrium of production increases rather than decreases, demonstrating how *zakat* stimulates economic growth in line with population growth. This is illustrated in the curve at Fig. 5.2.

From the explanation above, it can also be concluded that *zakat* as income for the *mustahik* community has a greater economic effect than *zakat* in the hands of *muzakki*. This can also be explained based on Fig. 5.3, which illustrates how increases in income boost demand among the *mustahik* and *muzakki*, the magnitude of which is larger for the *muzakki* group because of the sensitivity/elasticity of *mustahik* consumption (demand) to changes in income.

Fig. 5.2 Zakat in the economy

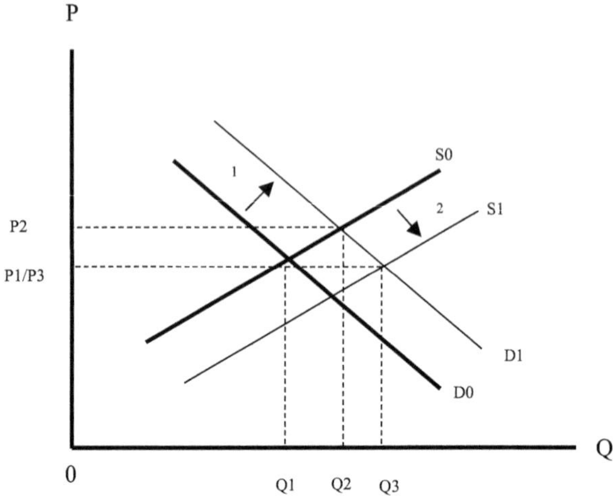

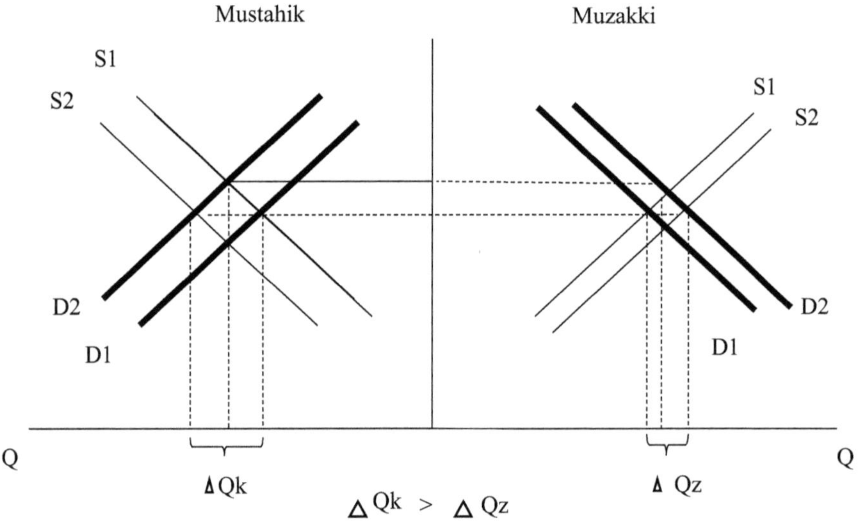

Fig. 5.3 Comparison of Mustahik and Muzakki demand

The macroeconomic effect of *zakat* can be determined in detail by calculating economic income using a conventional economic expenditure, output, or income approach. Calculating economic growth based on those three conventional approaches is also relevant for the Islamic economy. In general, the macroeconomic model based on an expenditure approach is as follows:

$$Y = C + G + I + (X - M)$$

$$C = Co + bYd$$

$$Yd = Y - Tx + Tr$$

$$Tx = tY$$

$$I = Io - gi$$

Where:

Y =Output
Yd=Disposible income
C =Consumption
Co = Autonomous Consumption
b= Marginal Propensity to Consume
Tx =Tax
t = Percentage of tax
Tr= Transfer
I= Investment
Io= Autonomous Investment
g= Sensitivity to interest
i = Interest
X= Export
M = Import

In Islam, consumption behaviour can be modified considering the characteristics of consumers/society based on the economic capabilities classified based on sharia law (*zakat* system). Therefore, consumption behaviour based on sharia principles can be expressed as follows:

$$C = Ci + Ck$$

Where:

$Ci = bYd$ (*muzakki* consumption)
$Yd = Y - Z - Nw$
$Nw = tY$
Z = *zakat*, the components of which are zY (*zakat* for income) or zW (*zakat* for wealth).

In this discussion, *zakat* is still expressed as Z to observe its macroeconomic role.

Nw = *Nawaib* (a temporary tax levied on the rich). Nw is levied on the rich (*muzakki*) when the economy enters a bust cycle and other government revenues are insufficient considering that the *mustahik* and *muzakki* groups may originate from non-Muslims and the economy is underdeveloped or underperforming.

$$Ck = Co = Z \text{ (\textit{mustahik} consumption)}$$

In the macroeconomy, *Ck* is more accurately categorised as government spending (G) because the state functions to safeguard the basic necessities of the needy (*mustahik*). This also implies that the main component is the provision of primary needs or consumption of primary needs for the community *mustahik*.

Based on Islamic principles and values, the following macroeconomic model of consumption behaviour is obtained:

$$Y = Ci + Ck + I + G + (X–M)$$

If elaborated based on consumption characteristics, the following models can be expressed:

$$Y = Co + b(Y - Z - tY) + Co + I + G + (X–M)$$

$$Y = 2Z + bY–bZ–btY + I + G + (X–M)$$

$$Y–bY + btY = 2Z–bZ + I + G + (X–M)$$

$$Y(1–b + bt) = Z(2 - b) + I + G + (X–M)$$

$$Y = \frac{Z(2 - b) + I + G + (X–M)}{(1–b–bt)}$$

Assuming that $0 < b < 1, 0 < t < 1; (1 - b - bt) > 0; (2 - b) > 0$, therefore *zakat* ($Z$) has a positive correlation with Y, implying that as Z increases, Y or national output/income also increases.

From the *mustahik* and *muzakki* consumption models, the MPC of *mustahik* is larger than that of *muzakki* because *mustahik* consumption is more sensitive to increases in income than *muzakki* consumption. From another perspective, this is explained by the fact that the distribution of *zakat* funds (including *kharaj, jizyah,* and *nawaib*) for *mustahik* must be equal to their primary needs, implying that their income from these funds is perfect (MPC equal to 1).

On the other hand, the MPC of *muzakki* lies between 0 and 1 because relatively, their basic needs have already been met. Based on such understanding from the *muzakki* consumption model, the variable bYd represents the secondary, tertiary, and even luxury needs of the *muzakki*. Based on this understanding, therefore, more faithful individuals or collectives will have an MPC value closer to 0 because the faithful tend to focus more on meeting only their primary needs. Notwithstanding, if MPC also contains all *muzakki* consumption preferences, including consumption for other individuals (motivated by good deeds—*amal shaleh*), it would be better to separate the *muzakki* MPC into two groups, namely MPC for self-consumption (real MPC) and MPC for others, such as *infaq—sadaqah* (MPC *amal shaleh*). Therefore, MPC can be expressed as follows: *MPCmuzakki* = *MPCriil* + *MPCamal shaleh*. The faith of a *muzakki* will dominate the MPC composition, with real MPC < MPC *amal shaleh*). In other words, the greater an individual's (*muzakki*) faith, the corresponding MPC will be dominated by good deeds (*amal shaleh*), as indicated

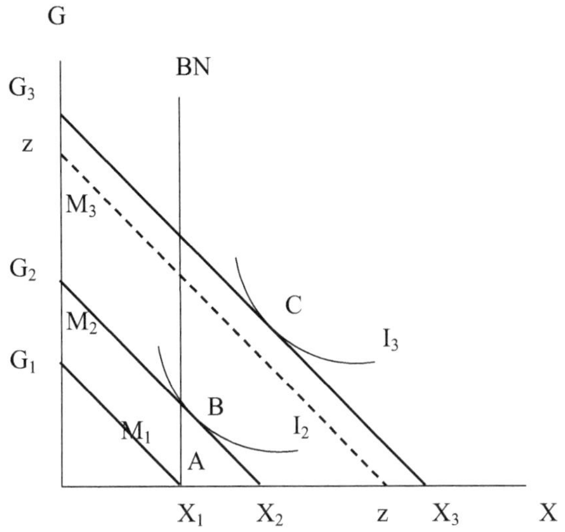

Fig. 5.4 Utility of Islamic consumers

by the dominance of MPC *amal shaleh*. By including good deeds, the *muzakki* consumption model can be expressed as follows:

$$\text{If } b = \text{MPCmuzakki}, c = \text{MPCriil and } d = \text{MPCamal shaleh};$$

$$\text{therefore } C = Co + (c + d)\ Yd\ C = Co + cYd + dYd$$

The *muzakki* consumption model above shows three components or motives for individual or collective consumption by *muzakki*, namely autonomous consumption for basic necessities (*Co*), secondary/tertiary/luxury needs (*cYd*), and consumption for *amal shaleh* (*dYd*).

The analysis shows that the faith factor influences individual consumption behaviour, especially the *muzakki*. Nevertheless, the same analysis cannot be used to determine the effect of faith on the consumption behaviour of *mustahik*, assuming that good deeds (*amal shaleh*) are beyond the remit of *mustahik* using income from *zakat*. Once again, this shows the suitability of potential *muzakki* behaviour to maximise their *amal shaleh* based on the teachings of Rasulullah SAW that all humans must strive to improve their economic circumstances and maximise the benefit for others.

This argument assumes that *amal shaleh* is carried out based on the amount of economic resources/wealth/income a person has access to, thus concluding that the ability to do good is greater for *muzakki* than *mustahik* (Fig. 5.4).

The curve above shows how the *mustahik* group reaches maximum satisfaction at point A, namely at the level of primary needs they receive. Possibly, their income is insufficient to obtain the basic necessities or perhaps no income is received, yet the *zakat* mechanism elevates their income to the X1G1 line. Meanwhile, the maximum satisfaction level of the middle-income group is at point B, and that of the *muzakki* group will be higher at point C. Islam teaches Muslims to strive for a state of sufficiency (*muzakki*) because such a condition not only removes economic barriers for Muslims to remain faithful yet also provides opportunities to perform *amal shaleh*.

The curve also illustrates how the *mustahik* group is unable to perform *amal shaleh* due to insufficient disposable income, while the middle-income group is still able to set aside a portion of income for *amal shaleh*, for instance through *infaq* or *sadaqah*, yet with insufficient income for higher levels of *amal shaleh*, such as *zakat* and *waqf*. Upon reaching the minimum wealth threshold (*nisab*), the *muzakki* group will perform *amal shaleh* through the *zakat* mechanism and, when receiving more income, the *muzakki* group are encouraged to perform more charitable deeds through *waqf*. Essentially, this satisfaction model is the same as that described by Monzer Kahf, yet with greater focus and detail on the three groups of consumers in society based on their economic capacity.

In conclusion, higher levels of satisfaction will be achieved in the community when economic conditions are better. This may also appear true in a conventional context, yet the element of *amal shaleh* as the parameter to measure satisfaction is the key difference between the Islamic and conventional models. Through the recipients (*mustahik*) and payers (*muzakki*), *zakat* plays a key role in levelling up economic performance. According to Khaf, the *zakat* received by *mustahik* will increase consumption and, therefore, aggregate demand from a macro perspective.

On the *muzakki* side, *zakat* serves to increase the savings ratio, assuming that each individual can maintain their level of wealth. This increment in the savings ratio, according to Khaf, represents compensation for paying *zakat* and bears a close correlation with increasing investment from *muzakki*. The bump in output due to higher *mustahik* consumption makes *muzakki* take investment decisions, hence simultaneously increasing aggregate demand.

The impact of *zakat* depends on the accumulation of *zakat* collected and subsequently distributed. *Zakat* effectiveness can also be measured based on the elasticity of the marginal cost function, with higher elasticity indicating greater effectiveness (Fig. 5.5).

5.2.3 Zakat *and Production Behaviour*

As described in the chapter on economic behaviour, *zakat* fundamentally helps to maintain economic performance through its impact on both consumers and producers. On the production side, the *zakat* mechanism essentially maintains market transactions to ensure the goods produced can be absorbed by the market.

By predicting such facts, producers, who are considered *muzakki* under the *zakat* mechanism, will maintain the rights of the poor through *zakat*. Consequently, producers simultaneously maintain a market for their products, while growing and developing their businesses in the long term. Furthermore, Monzer Kahf found that *zakat* has a positive correlation with the level of savings and investment. An

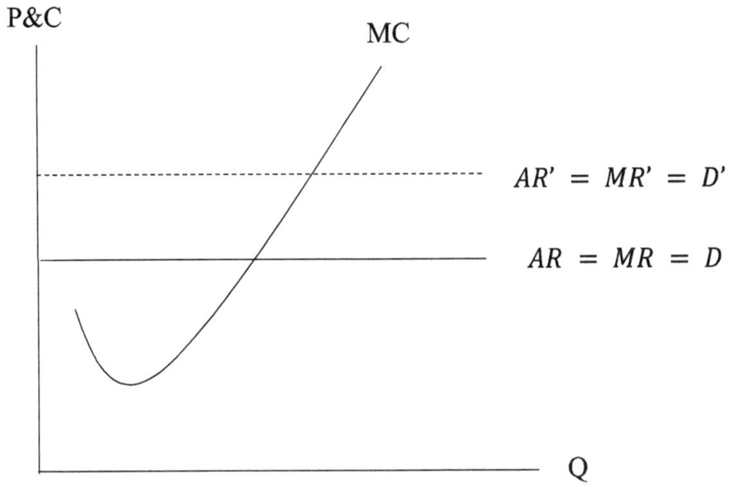

Fig. 5.5 Production in a perfectly competitive market

increase in saving due to higher income will also boost investment. The method for investing savings is known as *qardul hasan*, which is strongly recommended in Islam. This provides another motivation for Muslims to extend their wealth and property to producers. That way, production efficiency and consumer welfare are increased along with the satisfaction of the investor, which is considered productive activity considering the high rate of return. For a Muslim, *qardul hasan* is an investment with a clear and safe return.

During the classical period of Islam, the government provided various investment-oriented facilities to mobilise and utilise savings to the following ends:

1. Affording producers greater convenience in the production of goods.
2. Providing tax advantages for new production units. The tax methods used did not undermine the incentives or efficiency of economic units because tax was levied and collected proportionally based on the profit, rental income, and quasi-rental income obtained from various economic activities.
3. Enhancing private sector production efficiency and investment by introducing new production techniques and skills to Muslims.

A precedent was also set that *zakat* may be levied on savings based on a minimum threshold (*nisab*). By maintaining their savings ratio, investment became a solution for the *muzakki* group, thus automatically increasing the level of investment overall.

In addition, Kahf also found that *zakat* tends to reduce delinquency risk because *zakat* funds may also be allocated to assist indebted *mustahik*. In real terms, therefore, *zakat* reduces the unemployment rate and, according to Kahf, increases the number of active workers in the economy through two mechanisms. First, management of the *zakat* mechanism itself requires manpower. Second, by ameliorating the *mustahik* group to be economically active, who initially lacked economic access, the labour participation rate will increase.

5.2.4 *Zakat and Social Behaviour*

In conjunction with *amil zakat* (management) institutions, *zakat* maintains a good relationship between rich and poor without sacrificing the dignity of the poor by distributing social funds through *Baitul Mal*. The willingness and sincerity of the rich (*muzakki*) to apportion some of their wealth to their underprivileged brothers (*mustahik*) create a friendly atmosphere of warm social interaction, while maintaining calm and avoiding a less harmonious relationship between the two groups. In addition, the adverse effects of disparity between rich and poor, such as criminality, immorality, and other negative behaviours, will be significantly reduced. In other words, *zakat* has a positive correlation with dampening social and political turmoil. In his article,[2] Timur Kuran discussed this role and function of *zakat* critically, arguing that historical data shows *zakat* used more as a political rather than economic tool because of its efficacy in maintaining political stability rather than increasing productivity and driving economic development. Such rationale was refuted by Monzer Kahf (1992),[3] however, instead arguing that through the recipients (*mustahik*) and payers (*muzakki*), *zakat* stimulates economic performance. Kahf also argued that the *zakat* funds received by *mustahik* will boost their consumption and, hence, increase aggregate demand at the macro level. From a *muzakki* perspective, *zakat* helps to raise the savings ratio, assuming that each individual maintains their level of wealth, as a form of compensation for paying *zakat*. Furthermore, a higher savings ratio has a close correlation with more investment from the *muzakki* group. The improvement in output due to rising *mustahik* consumption increases the investment propensity of *muzakki*, simultaneously improving aggregate demand.

The basic necessities and primary needs were not only covered for Muslims yet also extended to non-Muslims, though not sourced from *zakat* funds. This was clearly illustrated by the peace agreement for the residents of Hairah in Iraq architected by Khalid bin Walid during the reign of Abu Bakr r.a. According to the agreement, *Baitul Mal* guarantees minimum living standards for every parent unable to work, the disabled, and *fakir*-poor, while exempting them from the obligation of paying *jizyah* while domiciled in an Islamic country.[4]

5.2.5 *Role of Zakat in Islamic Economy*

In the context of the overall Islamic economic system, *zakat* plays the following roles:

---

[2]Timur Kuran, "Islamic Redistribution Through Zakat: Historical Record and Modern Realities", http://www-rcf.use.edu/-kuran/ZAKAT-2002.pdf

[3]Monzer Kahf, op. cit., p. 101.

[4]Yusuf Qardhawi, op. cit., p. 421.

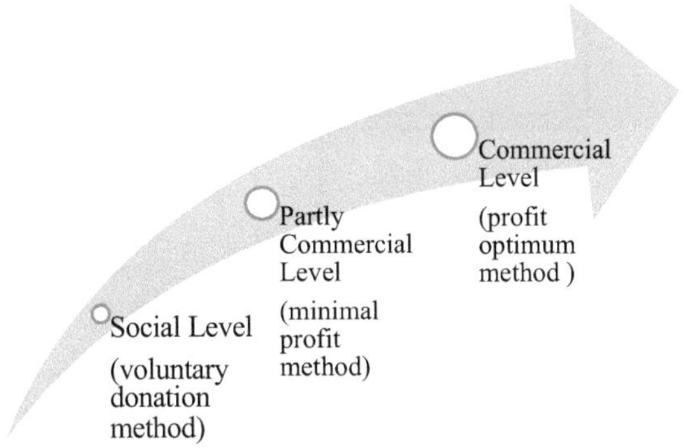

Fig. 5.6 Transformation of small enterprises. Source: Created by Author

1. Fulfilling the basic needs of the community, including sustenance, clothing, shelter, healthcare, and education.
2. Supporting independence, including work and skills training, overcoming unemployment and improving education or expertise (competencies), thus providing the opportunity to work and earn income.
3. Supporting economic development through business support at the social and semi-commercial levels, including entrepreneurial development, access to business capital, business assistance, and business consolidation.
4. Fulfilling important secondary needs, including legal defence, environmental conservation, *da'wah,* and advocacy to alleviate poverty and help the poor.

The primary focus of *zakat* utilisation aims to alleviate poverty and build the independence of the poor and needy to attain a decent standard of living. In the specific context of economic empowerment, namely by helping micro and small businesses, the position of *zakat* is to grow and support the development of micro and small enterprises, especially at the social level (Figs. 5.6 and 5.7).

Within a framework of realising efforts to create *zakat* as an instrument for strengthening the Islamic economy, the following measures can be taken:

1. Using *zakat* funds for business financing as the creation of a basic framework to mould strong entrepreneurs at the commercial level in preparation for transactions with Islamic banks.
2. Establishing and developing Islamic microfinance institutions (Social Trust Funds, Sharia Cooperatives, and *Baitul Maal wat Tamwil*).
3. Temporarily placing *zakat* funds, prior to distribution, in the Islamic finance sector to strengthen liquidity at Islamic financial institutions.
4. Channelling financing between Islamic banks, Islamic microfinance institutions, and community organisations assisted by *amil zakat* (management) organisations.

Efforts to manage and increase the role of *zakat* continue to face challenges and barriers in several Islamic countries, including Indonesia, which has the largest Muslim population in the world. Although *zakat* development in Indonesia

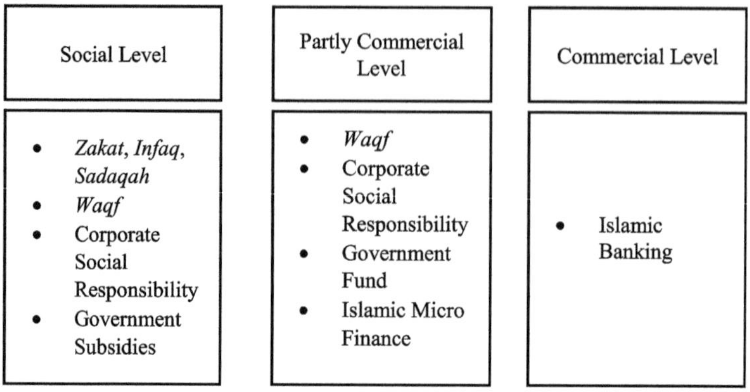

Fig. 5.7 Business level and source of funds. Source: Created by Author

continues in terms of both quantity and quality, numerous *zakat* management challenges and obstacles must be overcome, including:

1. There are still many Muslim communities in Indonesia today who do not understand the obligation of paying *zakat* on income and assets in a contemporary context (for example, professional *zakat, zakat* on stocks and shares as well as *zakat* on bank deposits). Consequently, there remains vast unexplored and untapped *zakat* potential from various types of income and wealth that exist in society today.
2. There are still many Muslim communities in Indonesia today who pay *zakat* directly to the beneficiaries (*mustahik*) without using a *zakat* management organisation, which makes it impossible to measure the amount of *zakat* received by beneficiaries in Indonesia overall or monitor the impact of sustainable community-based *zakat* empowerment.
3. There are still many *ulama* (Muslim scholars) in Indonesia who consider *zakat* distribution merely a form of consumptive charity, thus excluding *zakat* from utilisation for productive economic empowerment and development activities.
4. There are still many *zakat* distribution overlaps to the same beneficiaries (*mustahik*) by different *zakat* organisations or administrators in different regions of Indonesia, thus undermining optimal *zakat* distribution.

Several measures could be implemented to help overcome the various problems and challenges of *zakat* management faced today as follows:

1. Increasing *zakat* socialisation activities, particularly regarding *zakat* obligations in terms of the various types of assets that exist today.
2. Increasing socialisation activities concerning the importance of paying *zakat* through *amil zakat* organisations.
3. Improving *ulema* understanding of *zakat* jurisprudence (*fiqh*) and its evolution, particularly targeting the different forms of *zakat* that can be used to alleviate and overcome poverty.

4. Enhancing *zakat* management quality to ensure success in terms of helping the beneficiaries (*mustahik*) and overcoming poverty, thereby garnering public trust and confidence in *zakat* management organisations.
5. Increasing synergy between *zakat* management organisations to reduce overlap and accelerate successful *zakat* empowerment.

5.3 Implications of Utilising Non-*Zakat* Fiscal Instruments

As explained previously, the economic effect of *zakat*-based instruments is observable using macroeconomic models for consumption, government spending, and investment behaviours. Repeating the discussion on consumption, the impact of instruments, such as *kharaj, jizyah*, *infaq*, sadaqah, and *waqf* dan *nawaib,* can be observed through consumption models. The general macroeconomic consumption model is as follows.

$$C = Co + bYd$$

Where:
b = Marginal propensity to consume
Yd = Disposable income
Mustahik consumption:

$$C = Z = Co$$

Muzakki consumption:
$C = Co + b(Y - Z)$ *or* $C = Co + b(Y - Z - Nw)$.[5]
Where Nw stands for *Nawaib* (a temporary tax on the rich)

Nw is levied during an economic downturn when other government revenues are insufficient. Considering that *mustahik* or *muzakki* groups may contain non-Muslims and economic performance would be deteriorating, a variant of the consumption model above can be expressed as follows:

Consumption of Muslim/non-Muslim *mustahik*:

$$C = Za = Co$$

Where:

[5] In this equation, taxes are not included based on the assumption that taxes in Islam adhere to sharia law, such *as zakat, kharaj, jizyah, ushr, mawaib*, and so on. For a detailed discussion on these instruments, refer to the section on fiscal policy.

$$Za = Z + Kh + Jz \text{ or } Za = Z + Kh + Jz + Nw$$

Kh= *Kharaj* (individual tax similar to *zakat* on agricultural land payable by non-Muslims)

Jz = *Jizyah* (individual yearly tax similar to *zakat* historically levied on permanent non-Muslim subjects)

Consumption of non-Muslim *muzakki*:

$$C = Co + b(Y–Kh–Jz–Nw)$$

Meanwhile, the economic impact of *infaq, sadaqah*, and *waqf* through consumption can be modelled as follows:

$$C = Co + bYd$$

Where:

If b = MPCmuzakki, c = MPCriil, and d = MPCamal shaleh, therefore

$$C = Co + (c + d)\ Yd$$

$$C = Co + cYd + dYd$$

Based on the model above, the marginal propensity to consume (d) illustrates the propensity for *amal shaleh* in the form of *infaq, sadaqah*, and *waqf.* Notwithstanding, the implication of individual spending in the form of *infaq* (*In*) and *sadaqah* (*Sh*) in the consumption model tends to increase government spending (*G*), particularly for poverty alleviation programmes (government social spending—*Gso*).

$$G = Go + Gso;$$

$$Gso = In + Sh$$

$$G = Go + In + Sh$$

In terms of *waqf*, the implication lies on higher investment (I), particularly social investments (Iso) from *waqf* funds.

$$I = Ip + Ig + Iso; Iso = Wq\ (waqf)$$

$$I = Ip + Ig + Wq$$

Using the argument above and accommodating all variables in the Islamic economy, the Islamic macroeconomic model is expressed as follows:

$$Y = Ci + Ck + I + G + (X–M)$$

$$Y = Co + b(Y - Za) + Co + I + G + (X–M)$$

$$Y = Za + b(Y - Za) + Za + I + G + (X–M)$$

$$Co = Za$$

$$Za = Z + Kh + Jz + Nw$$

$$Y = 2Za + bY–bZa + Io + Ig + Wq + Go + In + Sh + (X–M)$$

$$Y–bY = 2Za–bZa + Io + Ig + Wq + Go + In + Sh + (X–M)$$

$$Y(1–b) = Za(2 - b) + Io + Ig + Wq + Go + In + Sh + (X–M)$$

$$Y = Za(2 - b) + Io + Ig + Wq + Go + In$$

Assuming that $\mathbf{0 < b < 1; (1 - b) > 0; (2 - b) > 0}$, therefore *zakat* (*Z*), *kharaj* (*Kh*), *jizyah* (*Jz*), *nawaib* (*Nw*), *infaq* (*In*), *sadaqah* (*Sh*), and *waqf* (*Wq*) have a positive correlation with *Y*, implying that as those instruments increase, *Y* or national output/income also increases. The macroeconomic model above simultaneously explains the model to calculate national output or income using the expenditure approach.

It can be concluded from the last equation that, specific to the Islamic economy, the element of faith has a positive correlation with economic growth. First, faith ensures that *muzakki* pay their *zakat* obligations, thus activating the *zakat* mechanism and improving *mustahik* purchasing power. Second, faith generates social funds that can be used for poverty alleviation programmes or the development of public facilities and infrastructure to reduce the social costs borne by low-income communities. Therefore, faith has a no less important role in stimulating economic growth.

Programmes to maintain and nurture faith by the authorities (in this case the state) must also receive attention. Thus, the variables that have a significant correlation with faith can be good indicators of faith in the community in general. And, if the success parameters of economic development can accommodate the level of faith in the community as an object of development, the variables of *zakat* (*Z*), MPC*amal shaleh* (*d*), social investment (Iso/*waqf*), and government social spending (*Gso*; *In* + *Sh*) can be used as indicators of individual or accumulative economic success. In fact, several variables can be modified to gauge economic progress in terms of faith in the community, such as the ratio of *zakat* collection to *muzakki*, the ratio of *zakat* distribution to *mustahik*, and others. Accommodating the faith factor in measures of economic advancement fundamentally ensures the human development process individually and collectively remains close to Allah SWT, by the grace of God who created the universe and the nature of His power.

5.4 *Waqf* Utilisation

Waqf is a social act of worship as an inalienable charitable endowment that is held in high regard in Islamic teachings. As a form of worship, *waqf* typically involves donating a fixed asset or other long-term asset. In the golden age of Islam, *waqf* was an important element of Muslim life. In general, *waqf* previously functioned to support the provision of social facilities and public facilities for the community.

Various social and public facilities have been provided using *waqf* assets. Buildings and places, such as mosques, madrasas, pesantren, orphanages, cemeteries, fields, and roads are examples of community needs fulfilled by *waqf* assets. To make *waqf* assets available, the community donates land, buildings, or money used to buy or provide land, buildings, or equipment in the public interest.

The aforementioned *waqf* management schemes are conventional, namely socially oriented, because *waqf* assets are used directly for the community or in the public interest. Based on this conventional *waqf* management model, the costs of daily operational *waqf* asset management must be subsidised using other funds, such as *infaq* and *sadaqah*. In this conventional sense, there are no economic processes or benefits on *waqf* assets.

The second model of *waqf* management entails the development of cash *waqf*, as popularised by M.A. Mannan with his famous Social Investment Bank in Bangladesh. In Indonesia, cash *waqf* are commonly known as *Wakaf Uang*, in an effort to collect *waqf* in the form of money that is typically deposited in Islamic financial institutions, such as Islamic commercial banks, sharia rural banks, and *Baitul Maal wat Tamwil* (BMT). The investment returns from those deposits are subsequently used to finance social activities, including helping the poor or financing mosque or pesantren operations.

In practice, cash *waqf* are also utilised by the broader monetary sector for investment purposes. In addition to sharia banks, investments are also made in sharia mutual funds, sharia bonds, sharia stock markets, and other sharia monetary sectors. The overarching requirement of *waqf* transactions is that *waqf* principles must not be lost but rather utilised as a reference for *waqf* investment in the monetary sector.

In the third model, *waqf* management applies a productive *waqf* mechanism, one of the potential uses of which is to facilitate the development of micro enterprises that play a critical role in terms of economic growth, employment, and productivity as well as social stability. In addition, *waqf* can also reduce government spending on education, healthcare, and other social services and lead to a more equitable distribution of wealth, which will boost the income of those languishing towards the bottom of the pyramid.

In the productive *waqf* model, *waqf* assets are intended for the provision of commercial assets for business activity or investment to generate income or profit, which is used to finance social activities, such as providing education services in a school, healthcare services in a hospital or medical clinic, food assistance for refugees, and support for orphans.

Waqf assets that can be used for investment purposes include shophouses, kiosks, markets, parking areas, factories, plantations, and so on. In the past, however, the full scope of *waqf* assets was rarely exploited. Nowadays, in addition to income or profit for social purposes, productive *waqf* assets also have numerous benefits, such as creating new job opportunities in the community, channelling benefits to *waqif*, providing jobs through business activities, and generating income in order to subsidise social activities.

5.4.1 Waqf *Management Independence from Wage Workers*

According to the Islamic jurisprudence (*fiqh*) practised in the economy of Umar, the following section explains the management and production elements of production activity, namely *waqf*. The *waqf* document written by Umar identifies land, *waqf* managers (*nazhir*), and slaves working on the land as essential production elements. A *nazhir* is mandatory if determined by the *waqif*. In the absence of a *nazhir*, however, *waqf* supervision becomes the responsibility of the endowed party or the government. On the other hand, the difference between a *nazhir* and (wage) worker is described as follows (Fig. 5.8):

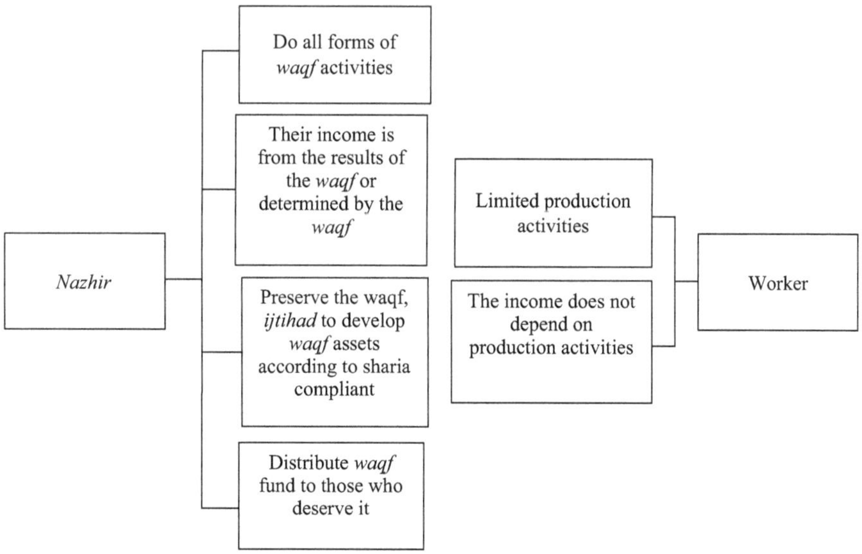

Fig. 5.8 The difference between a Nazhir and (Wage) worker

5.4.2 Waqf *for Agribusiness*

As an agricultural economy, Indonesia has been unable to attain food self-sufficiency from domestic production, thus with a high dependence on food imports. Indonesia continues to import rice, maize, soybean, and cassava. Breakthroughs are needed, therefore, through agribusiness innovation to achieve food self-sufficiency.

Non-residents are very interested in utilising and owning land in the territory of Indonesia, such as renting, buying, and cooperating to utilise land in Indonesia. On the other hand, there remain many untapped idle and unproductive land resources located in rural areas with vast potential for development into productive land, particularly in terms of supporting agribusiness activities. Instead of such land remaining idle or being sold to foreigners, it could be better utilised as a productive *waqf* asset.

1. The investment potential of *sadaqah* and *waqf* funds remains large in terms of empowering agribusiness activities that would improve quality welfare sustainably in rural communities.
2. Buying/selling productive and non-productive *sadaqah/waqf* land for sustainable agribusiness activity.
3. Massive, large-scale land management.
4. An agribusiness system model from an agro-ecosystem perspective through development of regional products with comparative advantage (priority commodities with high import dependence).
5. Agribusinesses that integrate on-farm (production/cultivation) and off-farm (post-harvest) processes.
6. Local community-based partnerships and assistance schemes.
7. Based on integrated management from planning to post-harvest.
8. Community empowerment integrated with business activities.
9. Profit distribution obtained through a sustainable social business process.
10. Land (from *sadaqah/waqf*) → (1) non-productive/idle (uncultivated) and (2) productive (cultivated).
11. Regional commodities with comparative advantage: food/horticultural crops (rice, cassava, maize, chilies, etc.) combined with ruminant livestock (cattle) and multi-cropping (annual crops: sengon, burflower-tree, rubber, and palm oil).
12. Diversified cultivation, polyculture, zero waste → integrated farming systems.
13. Management: Integrated management systems (production, post-harvest, and marketing).
14. Land management cooperation via partnership schemes in the community through labour in the short term and profit sharing in the long term.
15. Beneficiaries: Landless farmers or communities with a passion for farming → creating job opportunities.

In broad terms, there is a distribution of benefits from implementing the *waqf* system in the agribusiness sector as follows:

1. Farmer (wages/profit sharing)
2. *Waqif* (concern for the nation + *amal shaleh*)

3. Indonesia (maintenance and productivity)
4. Promoter/motivator (concern, participation, and motivation)
5. *Nazhir* (community help and capacity building)

Furthermore, the distribution of agribusiness outputs through the *waqf* system can be described as follows:

Selling Price – Cost Price = Gross Margin – Management Fee – Tax – Net Profit for Orphans and Needy

Consequently, there are several conclusions that can be drawn concerning the implications of *waqf* management in Indonesia as follows:

1. In general, Indonesians still understand and practice *waqf* in the form of social *waqf* (cemeteries, mosques, and madrasas).
2. Broader socialisation activities concerning productive *waqf* are required to increase public understanding and awareness.
3. Tangible implementation of productive *waqf* in the community with sound management is required, including through KJKS, to generate profits and benefits for the community, particularly taking advantage of the enormous potential afforded by *waqf* assets, such as *waqf* land.
4. There is also a need to improve regulations/policies/guidelines that facilitate the development of a broader range of productive *waqf* in the community.
5. *Waqf* management must be professional, accountable, efficient, and sustainable.

Breakthroughs and innovation are required in terms of productive *waqf* management to boost community enthusiasm for *waqf* as a daily practice (HAKI *waqf*, royalty fee, and franchise fee).

5.5 Supporting Infrastructure for Islamic Social-Public Finance

The support of appropriate infrastructure is necessary to guarantee successful policy implementation, including Islamic social-public finance policies. Infrastructure does not necessarily imply physical buildings, yet also includes institutions that contribute directly or indirectly to the goals of Islamic social-public finance. In this chapter, the authors describe which Islamic financial institutions interact directly with Islamic social-public finance practices and how the activities of such institutions have an impact on the desired goals.

5.5.1 Baitul Maal wat Tamwil *as a Soko Guru of Islamic Microfinance*

In 1994, Dompet Dhuafa Republika (DD) held a series of training sessions on *Zakat* Management and Islamic Economics. Upon completion of the training, each participant was granted Rp1–2 million to establish a *Baitul Maal wat Tamwil* (BMT). The skills acquired during the training coupled with steely enthusiasm to develop the sharia economy gave rise to numerous BMT entities serving unbanked small businesses. BMT are, therefore, part of the solution to various grassroots businesses that are unbanked or underserved by formal banking institutions.

DD efforts to develop BMT helped pioneer Islamic microfinance institutions in Indonesia. Beginning in 1984, ITB students at the Salman Mosque launched a sharia-based financing institution targeting small businesses known as the Baitut Tamwil Teknosa Cooperative. Subsequently, several activists in Jakarta also spearheaded pioneering development of BMT. Ikatan Cendekiawan Muslim se-Indonesia (The Indonesian Association of Muslim Intellectuals) (ICMI) strengthened BMT development as a movement accommodated by the Small Business Incubation Centre (PINBUK).

In terms of BMT development, from the beginning, DD considered BMT a tool of economic struggle for those towards the bottom of the pyramid. Not only does BMT aim to improve the economic independence of the poor and needy but also serve as a socialisation medium to instil Islamic economic practices and as a vehicle to ameliorate the living conditions of *duafa* socio-economically.

Conceptually, BMT has two functions, namely: (i) *Baitul Tamwil* (house of development) that develops productive businesses and investment to enhance the economic quality of micro and small entrepreneurs, specifically by encouraging a culture of saving, supporting economic financing, and investing for profit. In terms of BMT development by DD, this is implemented through savings and loan activities as well as productive businesses and (ii) *Baitul Mal* (house of money/wealth) that receives deposits in the form of *zakat, infaq*, and *sadaqah* funds, while optimising distribution to eligible recipients. The three main functional lines of BMT, assisted by DD, were previously referred to as the BMT Triangle.

BMT serves as a vehicle for community-based economic empowerment. Initially, BMT was a non-governmental organisation (NGO), in the sense that it was founded and developed by the community and run with resources, particularly capital, from the community itself. Over time, however, BMT has flourished into a sharia microfinance institution with the institutional arrangements based on a cooperative legal entity to serve the financial needs of feasible yet unbankable micro enterprises by providing business development financing and assistance.

During the next stage, BMT experienced significant economic development and growth, emerging as a viable business entity. The BMT group consolidated its position to become a standalone microfinance institution. Some of the BMT mentored by DD, which continued to serve the poorest socio-economic groups, realised they were solidifying and consolidating the group. On 14th June 2005, prominent BMT from throughout the Indonesian archipelago agreed to establish the Indonesia BMT Association, known as the BMT Centre, dedicated to continuous improvement through rules made based on mutual agreement with a firm commitment to strengthening and developing BMT as the Islamic microfinance industry, with a vision of driving a solid and robust BMT.

Through the BMT Centre, PT Permodalan BMT Ventura was born as an umbrella company to enhance business performance at BMT. Permodalan BMT was established to educate the community towards becoming more productive, cooperating with all exponents to perform socialisation activities and develop sharia-compliant economic infrastructure, educate stakeholders to understand and comply with sharia principles, invest in safe, professional, and profitable micro, small, and medium enterprises, and offer competitive profit sharing to investors, thereby creating and maintaining a healthy BMT business.

By the end of 2008, a total of 138 members joined the BMT centre with assets totalling Rp931.6 billion, averaging Rp6.75 billion per BMT. Furthermore, total assets expanded 41.14% on the previous year. In total, 343,289 customers were served by the members, with each BMC serving an average of 2487 customers, each of whom received an average of Rp2,048,481 in financing. That figure also shows that most BMT continue to provide financing to the micro and small business sector.

In addition to developing BMT Permodalan as an apex bank for its members, the BMT Centre has also developed the BMT Institute as a vehicle to develop BMT human resources. Consistent with the growing number of BMT and expanding business purview, human resources must always be ready for direct involvement in BMT development in order to maintain business continuity. Strategically, the BMT Institute exists to develop human resources in preparation to answer the new challenges that arise and resolve the problems faced by BMT.

BMT faces a number of issues as follows: (i) choosing the most appropriate institutional arrangements, use of a uniform and operational implementation to support future BMT development, (ii) the issue of BMT legality and legislation, including sharia microfinance issues, (iii) the lack of a liquidity guarantee institution, similar to the Bank Indonesia function available to banks, (iv) the availability of reliable human resources to manage and develop BMT, (v) the entry of (local and foreign) banks into the micro and small enterprise sector, thus increasing business competition, and (vi) the availability of sufficient capital and funds to keep pace with the dynamics of the BMT business.

Moving forward, BMT will also face the challenge of how to maintain BMT inclination to serve those towards the bottom of the pyramid amid a business vortex that tends to move vertically upwards. As BMT continues to accumulate and manage more and more funds from the public, the tendency and temptation are to place funds in the middle sector. Another challenge is how BMT can maintain flexibility, which may be eroded upon pivoting into a more regulated sector. Introspection is also necessary to ensure the transactions performed by BMT are not only profitable but also fulfil the ethos and contracts of sharia.

Finally, we are grateful that BMT has become an icon of Islamic microfinance, providing employment to many and quality welfare to the founders and managers, while restoring a love for sharia economics and practices and, ultimately, ameliorating the welfare of many poor people. It is appropriate to consider BMT a pillar of Islamic microfinance.

5.5.2 Islamic Social-Based Microfinance

Are there any financial institutions in Indonesia that specialise in serving the poor? There may be financial institutions that serve the poor but none that specialise in serving the poor. Typically, in Indonesia, financial institutions serve some poor and some non-poor customers. Even microfinance institutions only serve some of the poor because in its development, such institutions also serve non-poor groups.

Why do we need a financial institution that specialises in serving the poor? Because the number of poor people in Indonesia is still large. According to September 2015 data published by BPS-Statistics Indonesia, the number of poor people in Indonesia stands at 28.51 million, accounting for 11.13% of the total population based on the poverty line, which currently stands at Rp503,038 income per capita per month. Financial institutions specialising in serving the poor are also required because of the large unbanked population. In general, poor people do not have assets that can be used as collateral to secure loans from banks.

It is also imperative to pay attention to the fate of the poor because a country can only be considered prosperous if the poor are few. The level of quality welfare in a country is largely determined by the number of poor people. A large poor population implies less prosperity. Therefore, financial institutions must be developed that specialise in serving the poor because it is the duty of every person to help alleviate poverty.

What is the purpose of establishing a financial institution for the poor? The first objective is to provide an alternative financial institution that is devoted to serving the poor. The second objective is to prove that financial institutions specialising in serving the poor can exist and survive in the long term. There is a prevailing belief and opinion that financial institutions serving the poor cannot survive long term. It is a challenge, therefore, to disprove that commonly held belief. Ultimately, the goal of establishing a financial institution specialising in serving the poor is to reduce the number of poor people in Indonesia.

5.5.3 Islamic Microfinance

The Cambridge Business English Dictionary defines a revolving fund as:

> An amount of money that exists in order to finance something, but from which any loans must be replaced in order that the full amount is available again.

Meanwhile, Agvopedia defines a revolving fund as:

> Capital raised with a certain purpose which can be made available to the same users more than once, revolving represents that the fund's resources circulate between the fund and the users, meaning that each group member has the ability to borrow in turn, provided the others have repaid. Revolving funds are established with an intention that they should be self-sufficient and sustainable.

Fundamentally, the revolving fund method provides a means of lending funds to a group of beneficiaries, where each borrower repays the funds to be lent to another borrower. The goal of the revolving fund approach is to provide opportunities for as many beneficiaries as possible to experience the benefits of borrowing and increase business activity.

In addition to providing borrowing opportunities to more beneficiaries, another goal of the revolving fund is to build the mindset, ethos, and business capacity of the borrowers. By improving the mindset and business capacity, borrowers are better prepared to manage and develop their businesses towards becoming strong and independent entrepreneurs.

Implementation of the revolving fund approach is typically accompanied by business assistance/mentorship and business groups. Assistance not only functions to provide business motivation, yet also offers solutions to the business problems faced, while monitoring fund performance as well as circulation within the group of borrowers. This creates a more intense relationship between business players and those receiving assistance.

Though the revolving fund method has been adopted broadly in many countries to provide financing-based empowerment activities, there are unique characteristics in the context of *zakat* distribution because *zakat* has its own principles, mechanisms, and regulations. Some of the requirements, therefore, to use revolving funds as a means of *zakat* distribution are as follows:

1. **Training and Preparation**
   The goal of using a revolving fund for *zakat* distribution is to train and prepare *asnaf*, thus ensuring sound practices and stability to develop the business. *Zakat* distribution using a revolving fund and mentorship would mould the mindset and characteristics of the recipients (*asnaf*), while building a valid selection system for micro enterprises with adequate development capacity and potential.
2. **Maturity Limits**
   Fundamentally, *zakat* property belongs to the *mustahik*, implying that a revolving fund programme cannot run in perpetuity. *Zakat* funds cannot revolve continuously, thus the *zakat* funds appear to belong to the *amil*. By placing maturity limits, borrowers have demonstrated their discipline and business acuity to survive and repay the funds within a specific period. Such time limits also show that the process of mental strengthening and capacity building is an intermediate goal to prepare resilient borrowers.
3. **No direct fund management by the *amil***
   The funds should not be managed directly by the *amil* to avoid ambiguity concerning the ownership of *zakat* revolving funds. The revolving *zakat* funds must be channelled from the *amil* to the beneficiary group or organisation for further distribution to the beneficiaries as members of the group. The *amil* is, therefore, responsible for monitoring the funds and evaluating the beneficiaries. Consequently, it is critical to create an organisation that will be entrusted to hold and manage the *zakat* funds.

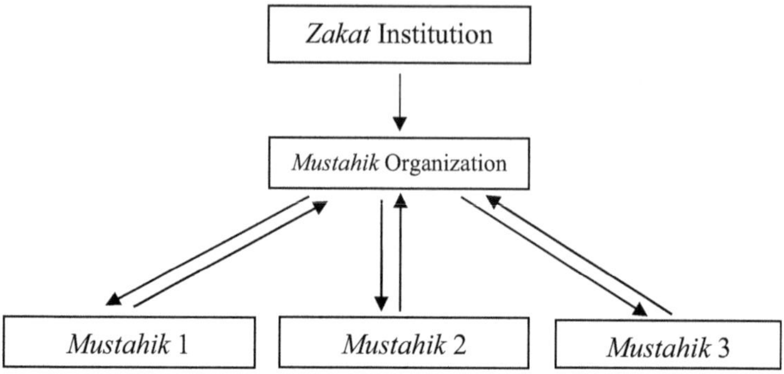

Fig. 5.9 Zakat distribution through revolving fund method

4. **Upon completion of the programme, the funds must be transferred to the *asnaf* (*mustahik*)**

   Upon completion of the programme, the revolving *zakat* funds must be transferred to the *asnaf* (*mustahik*) to ensure they are no longer managed or stored without clear ownership. Since the overarching goal of *zakat* distribution is the transfer of ownership of *zakat* assets from the *muzakki* to the *mustahik*, the assets are ultimately transferred at the end of the revolving fund programme to the *asnaf* (*mustahik*) who have proven to have a good mindset and business development capacity. By transferring the funds at the end of the programme, the *zakat* alms are successfully delivered to the entitled recipients, namely the *asnaf* (*mustahik*).

The requirements for distributing *zakat* through the revolving fund method help to ensure that the adverse effects of revolving fund activities do not impact *zakat* management. Furthermore, the requirements also facilitate *zakat* distribution via the revolving fund approach.

The mechanism for distributing *zakat* through the revolving fund approach is described as follows (Fig. 5.9):

Zakat distribution through the revolving fund method is based on *ijtihad* to optimise the benefits for the *asnaf*. Notwithstanding, *zakat* distribution via the revolving fund approach based on *ijtihad* has several of its own challenges as follows:

1. **Selecting the eligible *mustahik***

   It is important to ensure that the beneficiaries of *zakat* distribution through the revolving fund approach are specifically eligible in the *asnaf* or *mustahik* group. *Zakat* distribution is considered a form of worship. Therefore, all elements must be performed in accordance with the guidelines for *zakat* worship as stipulated in *zakat fiqh*, including accurately selecting eligible *mustahik* through a suitable selection process.

2. **Effectively establishing *mustahik* organisations**

   Another salient constraint of *zakat* distribution using the revolving fund approach is the effectiveness of establishing *mustahik* organisations. The *amil zakat* delegates the management responsibilities of *zakat* distribution to *mustahik* organisations; therefore, effective *mustahik* organisations will greatly determine the success of *zakat* distribution based on revolving funds. *Mustahik* organisations must have the requisite competencies to manage and distribute *zakat* funds effectively and efficiently.
3. **Effective mentoring and assistance process**

   The strength of a *zakat* distribution programme based on revolving funds lies in its ability to facilitate more interaction between the *amil zakat* and beneficiaries (*mustahik*). *Amil zakat* (mangers) must assign mentors to provide regular assistance to all beneficiaries, thus ensuring the transfer of independence and the ethos of spirituality, particularly in terms of increasing worship and piety to Allah SWT. Mentoring is also provided to ensure that the beneficiaries can repay outstanding funds back to the community organisations seamlessly, while providing broader opportunities for the *mustahik*.
4. **Handling loan arrears**

   An essential aspect of *zakat* distribution using a revolving fund approach is an appropriate handling mechanism if beneficiaries fall behind on their loan repayment. If unaddressed, unpaid loans would severely undermine the ability of the community organisation to maintain the revolving fund, possibly leading to failure and default. Prior to implementation, therefore, a *zakat* distribution programme applying a revolving fund method must prepare an adequate handling mechanism for unpaid loans and socialise the mechanism to the potential beneficiaries.
5. **Mechanism to transfer *zakat* funds to *mustahik* upon programme completion**

   Upon completion of the *zakat* distribution programme using a revolving fund method, the funds are transferred to the *mustahik*; therefore, it is necessary to prepare an appropriate delivery mechanism. Failure to transfer the *zakat* funds will undermine the previous successes of the programme. It is imperative to maintain the ethos and values built previously, along with sustainable business development and income-generating capabilities. Consequently, a mechanism to distribute *zakat* funds to the *mustahik* upon programme completion must be prepared and implemented correctly.
6. **Post-programme success and impact**

   Assessing programme success and impact is critical because a successful programme must be measurable. A *zakat* distribution programme based on a revolving fund approach must ameliorate quality welfare for the *mustahik*, both economically and spiritually. Such a programme must also prove its credentials in terms of impact beyond other *zakat* distribution methods.

5.5.4 Three Models of Islamic Microfinance

There are currently three basic models for a financial institution specialising in serving the poor. First, a financial institution with a pure social mission, operationally based on social services, applying *Qardhul Hasan* (benevolent lending) contracts and covering operating costs from subsidised funds. Second, a semi-commercial mission based on affordable financial services using *mudharabah/murabahah* contracts and covering operating costs from business profits with a maximum margin of around 6%. Third, a hybrid role that combines social services and affordable financial transactions based on *Qardhul Hasan* as well as *mudharabah/murabahah* contracts and covering operating costs from subsidised funds and business profits with a maximum margin of approximately 6%.

There are three main strategies of establishing a financial institution specialising in serving the poor. First is the product. In this case, a financial institution offers transaction services/products to the poor as an accessory to complement the commercial business. The second option is to implement a Window System, namely by providing a separate system to serve the needs of the poor, which is positioned to balance the commercial interests of the financial institution. The third option is a fully fledged financial institution specialised in serving the needs of the poor through its own office network, thus balancing the commercial industry.

Hopefully, financial institutions specialising in serving the poor can be realised and operational soon to improve productivity amongst the poor.

5.5.5 Social Trust Fund

In terms of financial practices, one of the most important entities used by modern society is the bank. From the beginning, however, banks have remained a profit-oriented commercial entity and, hence, selective lenders. Seeking to maintain financial sustainability and continuity, banks must select potential customers with adequate repayment capacity to generate income for the bank. Therefore, a series of requirements emerged for banks to effectively channel financing.

Unfortunately, the selective nature of banks precludes most poor people from formal financial services due to a lack of steady income or business assets that can be used as collateral. Consequently, banks consider the poor economically unfeasible and are reluctant to lend.

Overcoming such constraints, "banks" have emerged that were created specifically for the poor. Various financial entities for the poor have been created and put into practice, starting with rural banks, savings and loans cooperatives as well as microfinance institutions. The practices of Grameen Bank (from Bangladesh), which is widely considered a bank for the poor, have been imitated throughout Indonesia. In the storied development of Islamic financial institutions, *Baitul Maal wat Tamwil*

(BMT) was also developed to serve the needs of the poor, which has subsequently fallen under the legal auspices of the Sharia Financial Services Cooperative (KJKS).

Notwithstanding, due to the investment nature of the business and the overarching profit-seeking orientation, all financial institutions serving the poor slowly but surely strengthen commercial aspects. In fact, most have neglected social aspects in a minimalist financial structure, with social activities on average contributing less than 5% in financial ratios. Such conditions indicate a departure from genuinely helping the poor in favour of ambiguous corporate social responsibility (CSR) programmes in the pursuit of profit.

In reality, however, economic transactions in society are still needed to revive self-reliance in the community as the true spirit of assistance. In this context, lending and borrowing are purely social transactions due to the aspect of helping others. This is where the function of *Qardhul Hasan* (benevolent lending without an additional return) tends to dominate. Such financial practices are critical in the wake of a natural disaster, during extreme poverty or when attempting to establish a business for the first time.

A Social Trust Fund (STF) was developed by Dompet Dhuafa (DD) to fulfil the banking function with a focus on poor communities, dominated by *Qardhul Hasan* (benevolent lending) contracts. At the initial stage, during the first 2 years, the benevolent lending portion accounts for 100%, with funds sourced from *zakat, infaq, sadaqah*, CSR funds, or other social funds. The main strength of STF is the genuine trust built between the manager and the beneficiaries.

During the subsequent stage (after 2 years), the STF evolves beyond *Qardhul Hasan* contracts to generate income and support STF operations, targeting beneficiaries who have achieved socio-economic betterment through business development. The proportion of non-*Qardhul Hasan* financing must not exceed 40% of the overall financial ratio, however, to ensure the STF remains a social institution, while the institutional arrangements are based on a social cooperative to ensure the social function remains dominant. This represents a pioneering new genre of cooperatives in Indonesia.

STF is a form of ongoing socio-economic engineering and one of the biggest tasks is to ensure that STF remains a social-oriented entity.

Reference

Kahf, M. (1992). *A contribution to the theory of consumer behaviour in islamic society. Readings in Microeconomics: An Islamic Perspective*. Longman Malaysia.

Chapter 6
Islamic Social-Public Finance Practices During Early Islam

6.1 Introduction

Systematic and comprehensive studies of modern public finance are a relatively new phenomenon that only emerged at the end of the fifteenth century as the principles of modern public finance were applied. In his monumental book, The History of Economic Analysis (1953), Schumpeter noted that modern taxation practices first developed in Germany and Florence, Italy, based on the writings of various academics, including Carafa (Italy) and Bodin (France).[1] Nevertheless, studies of public finance only began to truly gain momentum when Adam Smith published his seminal work, The Wealth of Nations, in which one of the chapters is dedicated specifically to discussing the issues of public finance administration. In his book, Adam Smith recapitulates the thoughts proffered by various economists regarding public finance and presents his own views on tax regulations, the role of the state, public revenues and expenditures, as well as the issue of state debt. The book represents a steppingstone for other economists to provide further insight concerning the issue of public finance in contemporary economics.

Notwithstanding, public finance practices can be traced back much further than such studies. Historically, officials from the ancient world, including ancient India, Egypt, Greece, and Rome, managed government finances through the administration of public revenues and expenditures. Furthermore, public finance theories are also explained by the track record of social-public finance as developed during the time of Rasulullah SAW, the Rasyidin Caliphs and subsequent caliphs.

Historically, there has been a demonstrable tendency among Muslim rulers, from the Abbasid State to the Ottoman Turks, to manage social funds and support developmental activities, particularly education and madrasas. The Nizhamiyah Madrasa, for example, was built in the tenth and eleventh centuries in Baghdad using *waqf* funds donated by the rulers of the time. In addition, the modern Turkish

[1]Refer to Schumpeter (1953), page 197.

S. M. Juhro et al., *Inclusive Welfare*, https://doi.org/10.1007/978-981-96-0051-9_6

Ottoman Empire (eighteenth and nineteenth centuries) donated large *waqf* funds to cover education costs (Fauzia, 2003).

Islamic social-public finance practices are discussed over two chapters. In this chapter, Islamic social-public finance as practised in the early days of Islam is discussed, including public finance in the ancient world prior to the emergence of Islam, together with early works on Islamic public finance. This chapter also explains the instruments and institutions of public policy during early Islam. The discussions in this chapter are expected to provide greater understanding concerning social-public finance as practised in the early days of Islam as a reference for contemporary Islamic public finance management. From there, the application of Islamic social-public finance in Indonesia and several other countries is explored in the subsequent chapter.

6.2 Public Finance Practices in the Ancient World and Mediaeval Europe

6.2.1 Public Finance Practices in the Ancient World

In the annals of history, officials from the ancient world, including ancient India, Egypt, Greece, and Rome, instituted policies that could be considered public finance on the revenue and expenditure sides. In ancient India, public finance practices and policies were clearly found in the Mahabharata, Manusmriti, Arthashastra, and Brihaspati manuscripts and texts. The Mahabharata contains a poem stating that the ruler reserves the right to collect monies from the people, build a strong treasury, and use those funds to help the community. Furthermore, taxation must be a harmony with the prosperity and welfare of the people. Therefore, the imposition of land taxes should not burden or disincentivise the farmers. In addition, taxes must be levied progressively during each harvesting season. Another manuscript, Sukhranti, written by Shukra (Sharma, 1987), states that the monarch has the right to levy and collect taxes in order to provide protection and public services. Shukra also suggested that land taxes should be based on the availability of irrigation facilities. Therefore, farmland irrigated by a reservoir was subject to a land tax giving one-third of the agricultural produce to the crown. On the other hand, for farmland irrigated by wells, the tax was levied at one-quarter of the harvest and one-sixtieth for river-fed farmland. Another thinker and royal advisor, Kautilya, wrote in the Arthashastra that he supported a progressive tax system, with the king receiving one-sixth of the grain and one-tenth of the traded merchandise as compensation for the security and welfare provided.

On the public expenditure side, many ancient Indian thinkers did not specifically record aspects of public expenditure because the income side was considered much more urgent and important. Notwithstanding, several thinkers with opinions about public expenditure noted that most public expenditure focused on defence, civil administration, public facilities, and assistance for the poor. Shukra advocated for half of the income to be kept in the state treasury, with the remainder used for military purposes (one-quarter), remunerating village heads (one-twelfth), as well as charity, entertainment, remuneration, and personal expenses of the monarch. In general, Shukra's mindset indicates that public finance in ancient India had to run a budget surplus with larger state revenues than expenditures. In the case of a budget deficit, the government was permitted to borrow funds from wealthy citizens, but the loans had to be repaid with interest at a later date.

In ancient Greece, Egypt, and Rome, however, public finance practices were not as detailed as those recorded in ancient India because many records have been lost or were not documented. Nevertheless, public finance practices were confirmed by several empirical studies. As in ancient Greece, the state derived its main income from the management of crown land as well as profits from mining and tributes paid by the people to the state. In addition, donations were also provided by the rich during a state of emergency. In ancient Egypt, public finance entailed a tax on land producing grain, with an individual (head/poll) tax also levied on every male resident aged 14–62 years. In ancient Rome, public finance was also funded by individual taxes, but the tax object specifically targeted the foreign business community. Moreover, the Romans collected an inheritance tax levied at 20–100% on abandoned land, while also taxing animals, various commodities, and international trade.

In terms of public expenditure, spending on religious rituals dominated a large portion of public finance, including the construction of pyramids, temples, palaces, and tombs in ancient Egypt. In addition, other expenditures functioned to protect the citizenry from external aggression, maintain peace, and provide public services. More specifically, expenditures also targeted public welfare, including the construction of roads, irrigation channels, canals, dams, and so on. Governments in ancient Greece spent public funds on the construction of fountains, markets, sports facilities, and the great temples in Athens. In Rome, public expenditure included free grain distribution to the poor and orphans, particularly for those whose parents had enlisted in the armed forces.

6.2.2 Public Finance Practices in Mediaeval Europe

In addition to public finance as practised in the Ancient World, Europe in the Middle Ages implemented similar policies. Public finance in the Middle Ages can be divided into two distinct periods, namely the pre-Enlightenment era (AD 476–1200) and the Age of Enlightenment (AD 1200–1500). The beginning of the pre-Enlightenment era in Europe was marked by the collapse of the Roman Empire and formation of numerous barbarian kingdoms in its former territories under a feudal system based on social status, consisting of the monarch, nobles, knights, vassals, and peasants. Meanwhile, the Age of Enlightenment marked the beginning of opposition to an absolute monarchy and the fixed dogmas of the Church.

During the pre-Enlightenment era, the absence of a nation state meant also the absence of a financial management system or specialised bureau of public finance. Nevertheless, taxes remained the kingdom's primary source of revenue, including land taxes, property taxes, market fees, customs duties, fines, and various other sources of feudal income. In France, a special levy (*amal*) was used to support crown and church activities, charged at one-tenth of total income. Other taxes also existed in Europe at that time, including the taille (direct land tax on the French peasantry and non-nobles) as well as taxes levied on the consumption of tobacco, wine, salt, and other commodities. Of the various sources, however, state revenues in many European kingdoms were dominated by land taxes. On the expenditure side, almost no records exist to describe public spending in mediaeval Europe. Under the feudal government system, state expenditures appear arbitrary and dominated by the personal expenses of the monarch.

During the age of Enlightenment, a modern tax system began to emerge in England in the fourteenth century, levied on every (male and female) citizen, excluding beggars (head/poll tax). In France, however, a head tax was imposed based on social class as a measure of wealth owned and property ownership. Taxes were predominantly levied based on the living conditions of the individual, as measured by the number of stoves, house windows, and horse-drawn carriages owned. According to one source, taxes in France could reach 80% of total average income in the community, most of whom were farmers. On the other hand, state expenditures were still inefficient despite an allocation for public welfare, including the construction of public facilities. During the Age of Enlightenment, various authors emerged who were keen to offer their thoughts on public finance. One fifteenth-century Italian writer, named Carafa, suggested that public funds could be used to defend the nation, support those in power, and prepare for emergencies as precautionary savings.

6.3 Public Finance Practices in Early Islam

In addition to different civilisations of the ancient world and mediaeval Europe, public finance also appeared in the Arab region. During the Middle Ages, Arab nations achieved some of the most significant economic progress globally. A key driver of this progress was the emergence of Islam in the region in the seventh century, brought by the Prophet Muhammad SAW. Arab society, previously uncivilised, slowly transformed into a high-culture society due to the teachings of Islam. Islam not only teaches about human relationships with God and matters of faith, yet also about interpersonal relationships between humans, otherwise known as *muamalah*. *Muamalah* teachings contain guidelines concerning how the basics of public finance must be implemented in accordance with Islam. Such public finance practices emerged with the Prophet Muhammad SAW in Medina and were maintained by subsequent caliphs.

Table 6.1 State revenues and expenditures during the Reign of Prophet Muhammad SAW

Sources of state revenues	Sources of state expenditures
1. *Zakat*	1. National defence
2. *Waqf*	2. Remuneration of officials and volunteers
3. *Kharaj* (land tax)	3. *Zakat* distribution
4. *Fay'* (taxation of conquered peoples)	4. Assistance for travellers
5. *Amwal Fadhilah* (inheritance)	5. Servicing state debt
6. *Sadaqah*	6. Debt repayments for the poor
7. *Jizyah* (financial charge on permanent non-Muslim subjects of a state)	7. Entertaining religious delegations
8. *Ghanimah* (spoils of war)	8. Emergency provisions
9. Etc.	9. Etc.

At that time, guidance in *muamalah* matters, which included public finance issues, came from Al-Qur'an, as the holy book or central religious text of Islam, originating from the Sunnah of the Prophet Muhammad SAW. Public finance in Islam at that time consisted of the revenue and expenditure sides. The sources of revenue and expenditure during this period are presented in Table 6.1. On the revenue side, *zakat* dominated the underpinnings of Islamic public finance. The *zakat* instrument was introduced in the year 2H (AD 624) as a recommendation to donate part of one's wealth to those entitled. Not long after, other more universal instruments of public finance emerged, including *waqf*, *sadaqah*, and so on. Sources of Islamic state revenue became more diverse as Muslims obtained wealth and property from war, including *ghanimah, fay', kharaj*, and so forth. On the public expenditure side, spending was separated into primary or regular expenditure as well as secondary or situational expenditure. Primary or regular expenditure included the distribution of *zakat* to *asnaf*, national defence, and remuneration of state officials. On the other hand, situational expenditure included assistance to students studying religion in Medina, entertaining delegates from other countries, gifts for rulers of other countries, *diyat* payments (fines for manslaughter) for poor Muslims, allowances for the family of the Prophet Muhammad SAW, and emergency provisions for war.

State revenues apportioned for public needs were deposited in *Baitul Mal* (House of Money/Wealth) prior to redistribution. Storing public assets in *Baitul Mal* reflected the principles of Islamic public policy, which considers state revenues as public property that must be stored in a separate place. Public ownership is the full right of the public, while the ruler is considered merely a managing officer.

6.3.1 Public Policy of Caliph Abu Bakar Ash-Shiddiq

Abu Bakar Ash-Shiddiq was the first caliph of Islam after the passing of the Prophet Muhammad SAW in 11H (AD 632). Abu Bakar served as caliph for only 2 years. Consequently, his policy of public finance emulated that of the Prophet Muhammad

SAW. Abu Bakar maintained the *zakat* officer appointed by the Prophet Muhammad SAW to collect and distribute *zakat* in areas under Islamic rule. In addition, Abu Bakar continued to apply a budget balance policy. Funds deposited in the *Baitul Mal* were immediately redistributed to all those entitled, thus avoiding idle funds in the institution. The amount allocated by Abu Bakar was equal irrespective of the Islamic status of the individual.

Notwithstanding, despite the various public finance policies of the Prophet Muhammad SAW maintained by Caliph Abu Bakar, one new policy stood in stark contrast. While serving as caliph, Abu Bakar declared war on groups refusing to pay *zakat* (Ridda Wars) after the death of the Prophet Muhammad SAW. This policy garnered strong opposition from fellow companions because the Prophet Muhammad SAW never taught Muslims to attack other Muslims. Abu Bakar, however, provided a strong logical argument from a religious and social perspective, thereby convincing the companions to support his policy.

Of the reasons Abu Bakar provided to fight Arab groups unwilling to pay *zakat* after the death of the Prophet Muhammad SAW, one related to public finance. Abu Bakar considered *zakat* to play a crucial role in the socio-economic welfare of Muslims. With finite state resources to provide social security at that time, *zakat* became the primary instrument to overcome such constraints. Ultimately, Abu Bakar's actions were appropriate because he prevented disunity among Arab groups, while simultaneously reintroducing the *zakat* system, which provided a solid financial system foundation for subsequent caliphs.

Another policy of public finance that emerged during the brief tenure of Abu Bakar was to appoint the caliph as a state official. The task of the caliph was already sufficiently burdensome, divided with the personal duties of providing for the needs of his family. Therefore, the encumbrance of meeting the needs of the caliph's family was borne by the state during his reign and disbursed by *Baitul Mal*. Initially, Abu Bakar's remuneration as caliph was 2.5–2.75 dirhams per day plus lamb and ordinary clothing. Not long thereafter, however, the salary was considered insufficient to meet daily needs and, thus, increased to 2000–2500 dirhams per year. Before his death, Abu Bakar returned all income and facilities obtained from the state, totalling 8000 dirhams.

6.3.2 Public Policy of Caliph Umar bin Khattab

Umar bin Khattab replaced Abu Bakar Ash-Shiddiq, who died in 13H (AD 634), to become the second caliph. Under his leadership, many new public finance breakthroughs were discovered, with the innovations leading to a more orderly and efficient system of public finance in Muslim countries. Such innovations also strengthened the capacity of public finance in Islamic countries.

During the reign of Umar bin Khattab, the area under Islamic rule was vast, spanning the historic region of Syria (Syria, Palestine, Jordan, and Lebanon), Iraq, and Egypt. In terms of public finance, therefore, territorial expansion boosted state revenues. For the first time, Umar bin Khattab established a permanent *Baitul Mal* to accommodate the increase in state revenues. Umar constructed a central *Baitul Mal* in Medina, along with a regional *Baitul Mal* in each province. The establishment of permanent *Baitul Mal* was the result of careful planning between Umar and several Persians who had experience in recording state revenues and expenditures.

The surge of state revenues deposited in the *Baitul Mal* institution was inextricably linked to the aggressive policies implemented by Umar to control new areas. Under normal conditions, four-fifths of the spoils of war were distributed to the soldiers as *ghanimah*, which Umar amended to only include movable objects, such as livestock, jewellery, gold, and silver. Immovable property, therefore, such as land, belonged to the state and was managed by the original owner. In exchange, the landowner paid *kharaj* (land tax) and *jizyah* (individual tax) as a non-Muslim. Consequently, land in Islamic-controlled territories remained productive as it was managed by the original owners. During Umar's reign, a new type of tax was also introduced, known as *usyr*, which was levied on goods imported by foreign traders. This reciprocal policy was taken in response to similar measures imposed by rulers in other countries against Muslim traders.

With abundant funds in *Baitul Mal*, the public expenditures made by Umar were divided into three groups, namely social protection, remuneration, and investment. Social protection was provided to people in need. Remuneration was allocated to civil servants, including soldiers, governors, local treasurers, judges, and scholars teaching science. And investment was used to construct public facilities and infrastructure, including bridges, canals, irrigation systems, and road maintenance, while providing capital assistance to entrepreneurs.

The system of allowances implemented by Umar also differed to that of Abu Bakar. Abu Bakar distributed allowances equally irrespective of Islamic status, while Umar disbursed different allowances to each person based on when an individual embraced Islam. Individuals who embraced Islam earlier received a higher allowance than those who found Islam later. Umar adopted this policy solely because he appreciated the struggle of Muslims who fought alongside the Prophet Muhammad SAW since the beginning of his preaching.

6.3.3 Public Policy of Caliph Usman bin Affan

Caliph Usman bin Affan succeeded Umar bin Khattab in 24H (AD 644) to become the third Muslim caliph. In general, the public policies instituted by Usman were a continuation of Umar bin Khattab, including the policy of transferring the benefits of territorial expansion to the state for management by the local population. Most of the public expenditures allocated by Usman were the same as Umar, namely social protection, remuneration, and investment as well as providing allowances based on one's Islamic faith.

Notwithstanding, one of Usman's policies was never implemented by Umar, namely transferring the management of idle (*sawafi*) land to the Muslim community.

Though the policy created a lot of misunderstanding because many of the land managers belonged to Usman's own family, the policy proved very effective in terms of increasing state revenues. During Usman's reign, state revenues soared impressively from 4–9 million dirhams to 50 million dirhams. Usman also increased state revenues by replacing several governors with those more productive in collecting funds. Regarding taxes, Usman innovated by implementing a self-assessment system, thus conferring the authority to property owners to estimate the amount of wealth owned and *zakat* owed, which prevented unfair tax assessments by tax collectors when estimating *zakat* in the community.

With significantly larger state revenues, Usman could afford broader public expenditures. Therefore, Usman strengthened the existing system of allowances, pensions, and remuneration of state officials established by Umar, while boosting spending on national defence and building the first Muslim armada.

6.3.4 Public Policy of Caliph Ali bin Abi Thalib

Ali bin Abi Thalib succeeded Usman bin Affan to become the fourth rightly guided caliph of the Rashidun Caliphate from 35H (AD 656) and the last of the Rashidun Caliphs. During the reign of Ali bin Abi Thalib, the seat of government was moved from Medina to Kufa in Iraq for security reasons. In addition, *Baitul Mal*, which had become an integral government institution, was also moved to Kufa.

The public finance policies of Ali bin Abi Thalib more closely resembled those of Abu Bakar than Umar or Usman. Ali reinstated the system of public finance pioneered by Abu Bakar by distributing allowances equally irrespective of faith, while restoring the budget balance system, with *Baitul Mal* disbursing funds to those entitled immediately. Notwithstanding, Ali innovated the allowance system, with weekly disbursements every Thursday. In terms of taxes, Ali expanded the taxable objects that were subject to *zakat*, especially in the agricultural sector, to include fresh vegetables.

On the public expenditure side, Ali pursued a system similar to Umar and Usman, yet rescinded one of Usman's key policies, namely spending on the naval armada, which he considered unnecessary for Muslims at the time. On the other hand, Ali was the first caliph to establish a formal police/security system known as *shurta*. Though Umar had established a similar system, Ali tried to reorganise the security forces to effectively maintain the deteriorating security situation.

6.4 Early Works of Islamic Economics and Public Finance

During the emergence of Islam, public finance was an important concern of the Prophet Muhammad SAW and subsequent caliphs. Numerous verses of Al-Qur'an and the Hadiths stress the importance of managing public finance for quality social

Table 6.2 Early works on Islamic public finance

Al-Kharaj	Al-Amwal	Ahkam Al-Sulthaniyah	Compendiums
1. Kitab Al-Kharaj by Mu'awiyyah bin Ubaid Allah 2. Kitab Al-Kharaj by Abu Yusuf 3. Kitab Al-Kharaj by Yahya bin Adam 4. Kitab Al-Kharaj by Qudamah bin Abu Ja'far 5. Kitab Al-Kharaj by Hafsawaih.	1. Kitab Al-Amwal by Abu Ubaid 2. Kitab Al-Amwal by Humaid bin Zanjawaih 3. Kitab Al-Amwal by Abu Ja'far bin Nashr Al-Dawudi 4. Kitab Al-Amwal by Abdullah bin Muhammad Al-Ashfahani.	Kitab Al-Ahkam 1. Al-Sulthaniyah by Al-Mawardi 2. Kitab Al-Ahkam Al-Sulthaniyah by Abu Ya'la Al-Farra	1. Kitab Al-Muhalla by Ibnu Hazm 2. Kitab Al-Ghiyatsi Al-Umam by Imam Al-Haramain Al-Juwaini 3. Kitab Al-Tibr Al-Masbuk fi Nashihah Al-Muluk by Al-Ghazali 4. Kitab Ihya 'Ulum Al-Din by Al-Ghazali.

welfare in the community. Nonetheless, books specifically written about public finance in Islam only emerged in the second century Hijrah, driven by more complex issues of public finance that never existed during the time of the Prophet Muhammad SAW and his companions. In line with territorial expansion, coupled with burgeoning methods of work and land cultivation, the caliphs acknowledged the need to study public finance. In response, the Islamic jurists (*fuqaha*) performed various studies into different aspects of public finance. These early works can be divided into at least four topics as follows: (i) Al-Kharaj, (ii) Al-Amwal, (iii) Ahkam Al-Sulthaniyah, and (iv) the Compendiums (Table 6.2).

6.4.1 Al-Kharaj

Many books written by Islamic jurists (*fuqaha*) that discuss the earliest practices of public finance are explicitly entitled Al-Kharaj. Literally, the term *al-kharaj* translates to mean a burden levied on community wealth, yet *al-kharaj* is also defined as a burden levied on land and agricultural produce. In the early days of writing about Islamic public finance, however, the *fuqaha* used the term *kharaj* more broadly to encompass sources of state income generally collected through various existing means.

The first work of *fuqaha* dedicated to public finance under the auspices of Al-Kharaj was a book authored by Mu'awiyah bin Ubaidillah (d. AD 786). Mu'awiyah bin Ubaidillah was a prominent minister during the Caliphate of Al-Mahdi (d. AD 785) from the Abbasid Dynasty. In his book, Mu'awiyah advised the caliph to refine the *kharaj* system from fixed (*misahah*) to proportional (*muqasamah*). Proportional tax was applicable to land based on total production to avoid triggering fluctuations in seed prices and prevent injustice for the taxpayers. Unfortunately, the book has been lost to history.

Another piece of work under the Kitab al-Kharaj title, which is very well known and still exists today, is the book of Abu Yusuf (d. AD 789). Abu Yusuf was chief justice of the highest court (*Qadhi Al-Qudhaat*) during the Caliphate of Harun Ar-Rashid. As an expert of Islamic jurisprudence (*faqih*) under the direct tutelage of Iman Abu Hanifah, himself an expert in formulating laws based on reasoning, Abu Yusuf was flexible in his thinking of socio-economic development at that time. Abu Yusuf wrote Kitab al-Kharaj at the behest of the caliph, who wished to have taxation, revenue management, and public expenditure matters in accordance with religious laws and regulations. Therefore, Abu Yusuf wrote the book to offer recommendations to the caliph concerning his thoughts on public finance without any binding provisions because he also noted contrasting opinions concerning matters of public finance. The pragmatic approach applied by Abu Yusuf examined current policies, past policies as well as the legal provisions contained in Al-Qur'an, Sunnah, and Ijima, before ultimately describing his own personal opinion. Although the book written by Abu Yusuf is entitled Al-Kharaj, other types of state revenue, such as *kharaj, ushr, zakat, jizyah*, and *usyur* are also discussed alongside public spending. Abu Yusuf highlighted a problem regarding the ability and expediency of paying taxes for the taxpayer, which, according to Abu Yusuf, was critical to increasing state revenues. Abu Yusuf strongly opposed acts of injustice against taxpayers, including tax collection through coercion or involving third parties. In addition, Abu Yusuf also highlighted public spending, where the state has an obligation to provide equitable welfare for the public, partially in the form of allowances to those in need and partially in the form of infrastructure development in the public interest.

Another relatively well-known Al-Kharaj book was written by Yahya bin Adam (d. AD 818) and Qudamah bin Jafar (d. AD 932). In terms of the writing approach, Yahya bin Adam's book is quite different to that of Abu Yusuf, eschewing the current analysis of public finance at that time to highlight the hadiths relating to public finance, such as land status, income collection and reinstituting abandoned and idle land, as well as issues concerning the collection of *sadaqah* and *fay'* income. The book is considered special because of the large number of hadiths collected by Yahya bin Adam, totalling 640. Meanwhile, Qudamah bin Jafar opted to summarise the tax provisions practised at that time. As financial secretary of the Al-Mukhtafi and Al-Muktadir caliphs, Qudamah bin Jafar adopted the perspective and writing style of a government official, citing Abu Yusuf, Abu Ubaid, and Yahya bin Adam as the main sources for the book.

In addition to the four Al-Kharaj books mentioned, many other books entitled Al-Kharaj were also written, including the works of Hafsawaih (d. 789), Hasan bin Ziyad Abu Ali al-Lulu (d. 818), Abu Abdul Rahman (d. 824), Abdul Malik bin Quraibah al-Asmail (d. 831), Muhammad bin Mubasysyir al-Tsaqafi (d. 848), Ishaq bin Yahya al-Nasrani (d. 851), Abu Usman al-Jahizh (d. 846), and numerous others. Unfortunately, however, many of those books have been damaged or lost.

6.4.2 Al-Amwal

Many other works by *fuqaha* that discuss public finance have the same explicit topic and title, namely Al-Amwal. Literally, *amwal* (plural of *mal*) translates to mean wealth or finance. Nearly all writing by *fuqaha* that discusses the topic of *amwal* explores the sources of income available to Muslim countries. The main distinction from Al-Kharaj is the emphasis on sources of state revenue. Al-Kharaj discusses state revenue but with a focus on *kharaj* (land tax), while Al-Amwal discusses sources of state revenue more broadly.

At least six books are entitled Al-Amwal, of which only three have been published thus far. One of the earliest and most monumental works of Al-Amwal was authored systematically and comprehensively by Abu Ubaid (d. AD 838). Abu Ubaid's work differed from Abu Yusuf's Al-Kharaj in at least three ways. First, in Al-Amwal, Abu Ubaid discusses all sources of state revenue equally rather than focusing on *kharaj*, as in the case of Abu Yusuf in Al-Kharaj. Second, the study conducted by Abu Ubaid was not only based on Al-Qur'an and the Hadiths, yet also included letters written by the Prophet Muhammad SAW and subsequent caliphs to state officials, and Abu Ubaid researched the policy practices of the pious caliphs. Al-Amwal, therefore, provides a more comprehensive overview of different opinions concerning public finance. Third, Abu Ubaid's book also explains the various schools of thought juxtaposed against his own opinion. Despite significant advantages, the work of Abu Ubaid is limited in terms of explaining the practical application of public finance at that time, similar to the limitations experienced by Abu Yusuf. Nevertheless, the writing of Abu Ubaid remains one of the most quoted books by Islamic jurists (*fuqaha*) and authorities when formulating public finance.

Humaid bin Zanjawaih (d. AD 867) and Abu Ja'far bin Nashr Al-Dawudi (d. AD 1021) also produced works entitled Al-Amwal. Humaid bin Zanjawaih was a student of Abu Ubaid and used a similar style in terms of the content, closely resembling the work of Abu Ubaid, while providing additional opinions about public finance that were not mentioned by Abu Ubaid. Meanwhile, the book written by Abu Ja'far bin Nashr Al-Dawudi is considered special because it is the only work of that era from the Maliki school which discusses public finance. Compared with Abu Ubaid's work, Al-Dawudi's book provides a more focused discussion on land taxes in Iraqi, Sicily, and Spain. In addition, the book also reflects on the religious and political conditions of the time with many discussions devoted to the obligations of the authorities to control corruption amongst state officials in terms of financial issues. Ismail bin Ishaq Al-Qadhi (d. AD 896), Al-Khallal (d. AD 921), and Abdullah bin Muhammad Asfahani (d. AD 978) also authored books entitled Al-Amwal, which have been lost to history.

6.4.3 Ahkam Al-Sulthaniyah

Other works produced by Islamic jurists that discuss public finance were written under the title of Ahkam Al-Sulthaniyah. At least two *fiqih*, Al-Mawardi (d. AD

1058) and Abu Ya'la Al-Farra (d. AD 1065), wrote books entitled Ahkam Al-Sulthaniyah systematically and coherently. Neither book focuses solely on public finance, however, also discussing government administration.

Al-Mawardi's Ahkam Al-Sulthaniyah book has three main objectives. First, providing the rationale behind the application of specific laws to ensure better understanding and justice. Second, helping lawmakers understand sharia law to avoid infractions and violations. Third, helping judges and other jurists understand the fundamentals of prevailing laws, thus supporting the law-making process moving forward. In the book, Al-Mawardi discusses various administrative issues, including government regulations (appointment of imams, regional heads, and judiciary), before moving on to other aspects of public finance, such as *amil zakat*, distribution of *fay'* and *ghanimah*, *jizyah* and *kharaj*, as well as land management. One chapter is even dedicated to Al-Hisbah, as the supervisory authority overseeing the economy and market, which had not been discussed specifically by the *fuqaha* in previous works.

Many scholars have drawn similarities between the Ahkam Al-Sulthaniyah book of Al-Mawardi and the Al-Kharaj book written by Abu Yusuf. First, both books were written with the intention of providing opinions to the rulers concerning public finance. Although Abu Yusuf authored his book upon the explicit request of Caliph Harun Ar-Rasyid and Al-Mawardi did not, in terms of the goal, the books have many similarities. Second, both books provide practical guidelines for managing the state. Third, the authors were both chief justices (*Qadhi Al-Qudhaat*) at the time. Notwithstanding these similarities, the books also have significant differences. First, the request to author Abu Yusuf's book was explicit, while Al-Mawardi's book was not explicitly requested by the caliph. Second, Abu Yusuf presented his opinion from the perspective of the Hanafi school, while Al-Mawardi explained various *faqih* attitudes, including the Hanafi, Maliki and his own Shafi'i schools. Third, Al-Mawardi's book explained a broader scope of topics than Abu Yusuf's.

Another book entitled Ahkam Al-Sulthaniyah was authored by Abu Ya'la Al-Fara, applying a similar approach and presenting comparable content to Al-Mawardi's book yet with an emphasis on the Hanbali school of thought. The book discusses various issues of government administration and issues concerning market supervision. In addition, tax issues and the imposition of additional taxes, land management, aspects of public spending (including public loans), and other relevant financial issues were also discussed.

6.4.4 *Compendiums (***Rampai Bunga***)*

In addition to the three topics discussed on public finance during early Islamic civilisation, other *fuqaha* have expressed their opinions and thoughts relating to public finance that are not contained specifically in a *kitab*. Such writing is typically included in other books on broader themes. This collection of ideas in the classification of public finance works is known as a compendium. Such compendiums first emerged in the second half of the 5H century from renowned *fuqaha*, namely Muhammad bin Hazm, Imam Al-Haramain Al-Juwaini, and Abu Hamid Al-Ghazali.

In his book, Al-Muhalla, Ibn Hazm does not specifically discuss matters of state finance and government administration. Nonetheless, several chapters mention the responsibility of an Islamic state to eradicate poverty and guarantee social justice. Ibn Hazm provides an unambiguous view concerning the collective responsibility of Islamic society, namely that the poor have an inalienable right to a portion of the wealth of the rich and prosperous. In addition, Ibn Hazm also mentions the land tenure system, the characteristics of the tax collection system, and other related issues. On the other hand, Al-Juwaini presents his thoughts on public finance in a book entitled Al-Ghiyatsi Al-Umam, discussing the obligations of the ruler as well as the management of public revenues and expenditures. The book also contains ideas about permitting additional taxes after a natural disaster or during a food supply shortage.

Another compendium that discusses public finance is a collection of three books authored by Al-Ghazali, entitled Al-Tibr Al-Masbuk fi Nashihah Al-Muluk, Ihya 'Ulum Al-Din and Al-Mustashfa. Thoughts concerning public finance in this collection of books focus on the responsibilities of the ruling class, duties of the state as well as sources of public revenue and expenditure. Al-Ghazali emphasises the principles of taxation as well as the efficient and transparent spending of public funds. The hallmark of Al-Ghazali's books when discussing public finance is the concept of *maslahah* (public interest) in each of the issues presented. In the case of additional taxes collected by the state, for example, this is justifiable if there are problems with the policy. Al-Ghazali also argued for public borrowing in certain circumstances, including matters of national defence.

References

Fauzia, A. (2003). *Berderma untuk Semua, CSRC dan Ford Foundation*. Teraju Mizan.
Sharma, B. L. (1987). *Economic ideas in ancient India before Kautilya*. Ramanand Vidya Bhawan.

Chapter 7
Islamic Social-Public Finance Practices in Various Countries

Building on the previous chapter, the discussion in this chapter explores contemporary practices of Islamic social-public finance in several countries and different regions of Indonesia. Various aspects of history, motivation, form, and development are discussed in depth, supported by empirical examples in each country as the object of the study. After comparing current practices around the world, the discussion focuses on Islamic social-public finance in Indonesia and its development thus far, from the institutional arrangements to the existing services, regulations, and legislation, as well as supporting infrastructure.

7.1 Motivation for Disbursing Social Funds

Many verses explicitly and implicitly command Muslims to distribute wealth through *zakat*. The following Quranic verse for example:

(Q.S. At-Taubah [9]: 103)

خُذْ مِنْ اَمْوَالِهِمْ صَدَقَةً تُطَهِّرُهُمْ وَتُزَكِّيْهِمْ بِهَا وَصَلِّ عَلَيْهِمْۗ اِنَّ صَلٰوتَكَ سَكَنٌ لَّهُمْۗ وَاللّٰهُ سَمِيْعٌ عَلِيْمٌ

> Take, [O, Muhammad], from their wealth a charity by which you purify them and cause them increase, and invoke [Allah 's blessings] upon them. Indeed, your invocations are reassurance for them. And Allah is Hearing and Knowing. (Q.S. at-Taubah [9]: 103)

Zakat is considered the fourth pillar of Islam and, as such, a critical foundational teaching. Islamic scholars claim that 32 Quranic verses mention *zakat*, implying strong motivation for Muslims to distribute social funds throughout life.

Zakat constitutes a teaching of love bestowed by Allah SWT for all Muslims. *Zakat* teaches us that faith and the worship of God, as sole creator and owner of the universe, is not only achieved by bowing, prostrating, *dhikr*, praying, and reciting Al-Qur'an, yet also by paying attention to the condition of fellow humans in our

S. M. Juhro et al., *Inclusive Welfare*, https://doi.org/10.1007/978-981-96-0051-9_7

vicinity. *Zakat* contains a message that when a person professes to believe yet pays little attention to the lives of those in need around him, this is not a true form of faith.

According to *zakat* teachings, it is improper to rejoice or feel happiness when people nearby are crying due to hunger. Those who claim to believe yet do not show concern about the poor people around them (by not paying *zakat*) are known as religious hypocrites, as mentioned in Al-Qur'an (Q.S. Al-Ma'un [107]: 1–7).

اَرَءَيْتَ الَّذِيْ يُكَذِّبُ بِالدِّيْنِۗ(1)

فَذٰلِكَ الَّذِيْ يَدُعُّ الْيَتِيْمَۙ(2)

وَلَا يَحُضُّ عَلٰى طَعَامِ الْمِسْكِيْنِۗ(3)

فَوَيْلٌ لِّلْمُصَلِّيْنَۙ(4)

الَّذِيْنَ هُمْ عَنْ صَلَاتِهِمْ سَاهُوْنَۙ(5)

الَّذِيْنَ هُمْ يُرَاۤءُوْنَۙ(6)

وَيَمْنَعُوْنَ الْمَاعُوْنَ ࣖ(7)

> Have you seen the one who denies the Recompense? For that is the one who drives away the orphan. And does not encourage the feeding of the poor. So woe to those who pray. [But] who are heedless of their prayer—Those who make show [of their deeds]. And withhold [simple] assistance.

Zakat is a religious obligation for all Muslims who meet the necessary criteria (*nisab*) and ownership period (*haul*) to distribute wealth to help the eligible needy (*mustahik*).

Zakat also functions to cleanse the soul and purify the wealth of the rich. The miserly attitude that is sometimes inherent in the human soul must be set aside. By overcoming selfishness in terms of property ownership, a Muslim can separate a portion of wealth to which he is not entitled for the good of others. For some Muslims, *zakat* is also seen as part of the efforts to maintain wealth.

In the life of a Muslim, social charity is highly recommended. Charity using social funds has a very broad scope, including *zakat, infaq, sadaqah*, and *waqf* (ZISWAF). Even Rasulullah SAW applied social funds to fiscal policy, specifically to cover state expenditures, by asking Muslims for voluntary assistance to meet the needs of Muslim soldiers, borrowing equipment from non-Muslims at guaranteed returns and providing compensation in the case of damage, as well as increasing the labour force participation rate and production through incentives.

An interesting example is Al-Azhar University in Egypt, where the main funding sources were dominated by *waqf* along with other social funds, including *zakat, infaq,* and *sadaqah*, as well as other business proceeds. Consequently, Al-Azhar University was completely independent, boasting a budget that eclipsed the Egyptian state budget itself. In subsequent developments, however, the Egyptian Government, under President Gamal Abdul Nasser, nationalised all Al-Azhar's *waqf* assets in 1961. Al-Azhar University was incorporated into the state structure, with the budget determined and provided by the state. The President (*sheikh*) of Al-Azhar University was appointed a government official at the level of Prime Minister and remunerated by the Government. Therefore, Al-Azhar University is no longer an independent institution.

Zakat has developed differently in the Indonesian archipelago. Since the emergence of Islam in Indonesia (during the era of Islamic sultanates), *zakat* has become a part of Muslim life in Indonesia. Though few historical records of *zakat* in the context of Islamic society in Indonesia exist, academics believe *zakat* developed in Indonesia to characterise local Muslims. In the traditions of the Malay Kings, records were found that *sadaqah* and *zakat* were distributed by the king to the poor and needy during royal ceremonies, including birth ceremonies, haircutting rituals, and *nazar* paying ceremonies. *Sadaqah* was distributed by the king in the form of gold, silver, and clothes donated to the poor throughout the country. In Indonesia's own historical past, *zakat* was an important element of the existing legal system, including positive law and moral standards as socialised to the Islamic community.

During the era of Islamic sultanates in the Indonesian archipelago, no records have been found to show *zakat* as an obligatory activity involving the state (Fauzia, 2003). *Zakat* was never formally stipulated in the regulations of kings or sultans to be practised collectively by the Muslim community. Instead, *zakat* was seen as an individual activity in the context of performing religious duties, namely servitude to God, where the king or sultan supports and endorses the practice of worship as applied by the Muslim community.

In the traditions of the Acehnese people, an imam was appointed to lead the religious rituals at the mosque. In addition to imam, the titles of *qadi* or *penghulu* (headman/chief) were also used and always associated with religious duties, particularly in terms of jurisprudence and sharia law. Similar to the religious titles used in Java, *penghulu* was a term also known in Palembang to describe a religious officer under the sultanate administration charged with handling religious matters. In general, therefore, the *penghulu* also played a role in managing mosque finances (collected from *zakat, sadaqah,* grants, and *waqf* funds) as part of their leadership function in the mosque environment.

Based on writing by Christiaan Snouck Hurgronje, data shows that *zakat mal, zakat fitrah*, *sadaqah*, and other religious contributions were institutionalised in society in different regions of the Indonesian archipelago. The enforcement of *zakat* obligations and the objects of *zakat* differed from place to place. For example, *zakat* on livestock was never collected in Java or Madura.

Zakat on precious metals and traded goods was very rare. In Priangan, *zakat* was collected on the rice harvest, yet this was not the case in the Java region. *Zakat mal* was not often found in Java but the tradition of large-scale *zakat mal* distribution was popular on Madura. In the Java region, *zakat* was collected on a voluntary basis and never treated like a tax, differing from conditions in Priangan. Several important factors contributed to the differences in *zakat* collection in this region. In Java, tax pressures were intense, thus making it impossible to collect *zakat* on agricultural produce from local residents. On the other hand, according to Snouck, there was sufficient knowledge of sharia law in Priangan, along with persistent leaders, communal land ownership, and a faithful community, thus facilitating *zakat* collection on agricultural produce.

The tradition of *zakat fitrah* distributed in the form of cash, rather than rice, was already established by communities located in the Java region. Meanwhile, local residents felt no obligation to pay *zakat*, including to whom the *zakat* was provided. Most residents expected blessings from the *zakat* they distributed and only rich pious farmers were willing to pay *zakat* on agricultural produce and goods traded. To whom was *zakat* distributed? According to Snouck, there were no rules governing to whom *zakat* was distributed.

Some residents gave *zakat fitrah* to the midwife who delivered their children or to the teacher who successfully taught their child to recite Al-Qur'an. In addition, *zakat fitrah* was also given to *lebai* (prayer reciters), *modin, amil, kyai*, and *penghulu.* According to Snouck, residents believed *zakat fitrah* was distributed to the *kyai* in the hope that they would receive blessings from the *kyai* and the *mustahik* who received the *zakat.* Nevertheless, there was absolutely no supervision regarding how the *kyai* or *penghulu* managed the *zakat fitrah* funds. In Priangan, *zakat* management was professional. *Zakat mal* and *zakat fitrah* were collected by *kyai.* After deducting the *kyai's* share, the funds were accounted for and transferred to the regional *penghulu.* After a further deduction by the regional *penghulu*, the funds were forwarded to the *penghulu afdeeling* and referred to as "religious income". In this way, a vast amount of *zakat mal* and *zakat fitrah* was collected yet prone to corruption. In terms of the *mustahik*, or eight *asnaf* groups, according to Snouck, the *zakat* funds were ultimately distributed to *wong putihan* (white/religious people) in Java, *santri* (religious students), or *lebai* considered poor and needy in a broader sense.

Therefore, for *penghulu, naib,* all mosque officials, religious teachers, *pesantren* (Islamic boarding school) students, tomb guards, unemployed religious *fakir* and *amil* (managers), the *amil* or *zakat* collector/manager was appointed by Islamic officials and this title was widely used in West Java. After 1892, however, the position was no longer functional yet returned to prominence during the New Order era. The colonial government was reluctant to interfere in the management of *zakat mal* and *zakat fitrah*, a policy introduced long before Snouck became an Adviser for Indigenous and Islamic Affairs during the Dutch colonial period. The government issued a strict prohibition order on 18th August 1866 (Number 216) to remove all local government interference in voluntary religious levies. The policy was enacted due to fears the Government could be blamed for interfering in the structure of religious institutions/regulations. This concern was well-founded because most colonial government officials were ill-informed about Islam and the Muslim community in Indonesia. Though not comprehensively documented, it is quite clear that the institution and systems of *zakat mal* and *zakat fitrah* remained unchanged during the colonial period, with the colonial government merely supervising the implementation and management of *zakat* in Java and Madura, excluding the *vorstenlanden* (crown lands).

If change did occur, it was precipitated by reform of the Islamic institution itself, brought in by reformers or scholars from outside the archipelago, the Middle East in particular, via the Hajj pilgrimage, Javanese community or students. Notwithstanding, significant change was unlikely because *fiqh* discourse has faded over time. Possible changes exist in the modern interpretations of *mustahik* and *zakat* management. Although on the one hand, Snouck advocated for not interfering in the affairs of this voluntary religious donation, on the other hand he could not remain silent about the deceptive and corrupt practices plaguing such financial management, thus intervening in the oversight and management of mosque cash.

In practice, Karel A. Steenbrink observed that the *penghulu* was the official most entitled to collect *zakat*, yet not for the *mustahik*, merely for his own remuneration purposes. In several regions, the *penghulu* was considered an ordinary citizen living in a colonial environment and receiving a salary directly from Batavia. The distinction between a *kyai*/guru and *penghulu* was unambiguous. *Kyai*/guru typically taught at a *surau, langgar, madrasa*, or *pesantren*, living off donations and *fitrah* contributed by the students and local residents. Meanwhile, the *penghulu* was appointed and remunerated by the colonial government. Consequently, the tension that existed between the *penghulu* and local *kyai*/guru since the early days of the Islamic kingdoms resumed immediately. During the early Islamic kingdoms and sultanates, the *penghulu* was appointed by the sultan or king, yet during the colonial period, the *penghulu* was appointed by the colonial government. One of the "duties" of the *penghulu* was to monitor any potential local rebellion and suppress the popularity of the local *kyai*, as in the case of the dispute between Kyai Mutamakin and the Batang *penghulu*.

In practice, *zakat* in the Java region was used solely for the remuneration of mosque employees. This general community view is illustrated by a quote attributed to Steenbrink from Algemeen Verslag Regenstchaap Sumenep in 1811, namely that the *penghulu* only dealt with deaths and marriages, yet every holy fasting month received *zakat fitrah*, four katies of rice for each person or money, and every Hajj month received sacrificial (*qurban*) meat or livestock. In 1866, therefore, regulations were issued forbidding civil servants from intervening in *zakat* collection, with most residents no longer paying *zakat* to the *penghulu*, instead preferring to donate to the trusted and respected *kyai*. With a heavy heart, Snouck also acknowledged that the *penghulu* did not manage *zakat mal* and *zakat fitrah* matters. Worse still, Snouck also forbade other efforts by the *penghulu* to secure income from outbound Hajj pilgrims.

During that period, *penghulu*, religious teachers, and Hajj guides engaged in the illegal practice of collecting *zakat* at a rate of 2.5% of total Hajj monies, insisting that a pilgrimage where *zakat* has not been paid would be invalid and not halal. On the one hand, the return of this function benefited the *kyai* and *tariqa* gurus but was detrimental to the *penghulu* by reducing income. According to Snouck, however, this was important to restore the authority of the *penghulu* institution in the community. Consequently, the *penghulu* received remuneration from the large (marriage and divorce) monies deposited into the mosque's treasury.

In the early twentieth century AD, the practice of Islamic social funds flourished in Indonesia with the emergence of Muhammadiyah and Nahdlatul Ulama as well as other similar Islamic schools along with large social religious organisations, such as

Jami'at Khair and Sarekat Islam. The presence of Islamic educational institutions and social religious organisations in Indonesian Islamic society is inextricably linked with Islamic social funds and proves such institutions and organisations could support themselves independently.

The emerging spirit of generosity through the practice of charitable giving via Islamic social funds persisted until Indonesia's independence in 1945. In the ensuing period, particularly before Suharto stepped down from his presidency, Islamic social funds thrived and the situation could not be reversed. The practice of charitable donations using Islamic social funds in Indonesia has continued to develop. No longer is the use of Islamic social funds limited to the construction of madrasas, *pesantren* (Islamic boarding schools), or mosques, such funds are now used for economic empowerment, providing scholarships and other similar activities, which is very encouraging for the Islamic community in Indonesia.

Since the 1990s, the potential of Islamic social funds has continued to prosper. Trying economic conditions caused by multiple crises that have befallen Indonesia since the end of 1997 has not eroded social charitable work for Muslims in Indonesia. On the contrary, Islamic social fund continue to thrive in Indonesia. Billions in humanitarian and social funds have been collected through electronic and print media as well as philanthropic institutions. If such funds could be managed honestly and accountably, God willing, public trust will grow and develop.

Among Muslims in particular, the growth of charitable donations using social funds is reflected in the phenomenal growth of *zakat* funds collected by private institutions, such as Dompet Dhuafa, Pos Keadilan Peduli Umat (PKPU), Yayasan Daarut Tauhid, Rumah Zakat, and many more, led by professional management. Such institutions not only complement the existing BAZIS and LAZIS, managed under government auspices, yet also offer new breakthroughs and innovations in the collection, management, and distribution of social funds collected from the community.

Thus, it can be concluded that religious motivation, namely carrying out one's religious obligations, is the dominant motive for most Muslims to engage in charitable activities through social funds. Second, Muslims are motivated to disburse social funds to help alleviate poverty or ameliorate the living standards of the poor and needy. Third, social funds are used to provide peace, calm, and happiness to the contributors. Fourth, Muslims are motivated to disburse social funds to ensure protection for their property, increase good fortune, and grow their assets.

7.2 Islamic Social-Public Finance Practices Around the World

In terms of global application, Islamic social-public finance is represented by examples of management practices in secular countries with a strong religious influence, such as Indonesia and Malaysia, management practices in established

Islamic countries, such as Saudi Arabia and other countries in the Middle East, management practices in purely secular countries, such as in Europe, and management practices in Muslim minority countries, such as in Asia and Africa.

7.2.1 Zakat *in Saudi Arabia*

Saudi Arabia is a special country due to the Ka'bah, denoting the direction (*qibla*) towards which all Muslims around the world pray. Saudi Arabia is also home to the Great Mosque of Mecca (Masjid al-Haram) and the Prophet's Mosque (Masjid an-Nabawi), two of the holiest sites in Islam. The value of prayer at these two mosques is said to be much higher than at any other mosque in the world.

Every year, millions of Muslims from all over the world embark upon a pilgrimage to Saudi Arabia. Using various modes of transportation, Muslims flock to Saudi Arabia to perform the Hajj pilgrimage as the fifth pillar of Islam. In its entirety, the pilgrimage performed by all Muslims is closely tied to the state of Saudi Arabia.

In addition to the inbound pilgrims who generate massive income, Saudi Arabia is also endowed with abundant oil, the proceeds of which have made Saudi Arabia a rich country, also known as a petrodollar country. Nevertheless, poverty remains an issue in the country.

A wave of anti-government protests, uprisings, and armed rebellions that spread across much of the Arab World, known as the Arab Spring, demanded political reform and saw the downfall of rulers in several Middle Eastern countries. In anticipation, the Kingdom of Saudi Arabia issued a policy to provide subsidies for the unemployed. Therefore, every unemployed Saudi national receives a subsidy of SAR2,000 per month, equivalent to Rp4.5 million. In addition to subsidies, the Kingdom of Saudi Arabia also issued policy to cover the consumer debts of the population.

In Saudi Arabia, *zakat* is managed under one roof in the Ministry of Finance, known as Maslahtuz Zakat wad Dakhil. *Zakat* is an obligatory payment for Saudi individuals and companies owned by Saudi nationals. The government invites individuals to distribute *zakat* directly to *mustahik* or through social foundations, while corporate *zakat* must be paid to Maslahtuz Zakat wad Dakhil and managed by the Ministry of Finance.

Upon paying corporate *zakat* to the Maslahtuz Zakat wad Dakhil, the payer receives a certificate as proof *zakat* has been paid. Companies with such certificates are then able to extend business licences but companies without *zakat* payment certificates are unable to extend their business licence. Companies that are not owned by Saudi nationals are required to pay taxes. Therefore, *zakat* is paid by Muslim-owned companies and taxes paid by non-Muslim owned companies.

The *zakat* receipt system developed by Maslahtuz Zakat wad Dakhil is similar to the tax revenue system in Indonesia. *Zakat* collected by Maslahtuz Zakat wad Dakhil is redirected to the Ministry of Social Affairs for distribution to the *mustahik*. Currently, more than 400,000 Muslim-owned companies in Saudi Arabia pay *zakat* to Maslahtuz Zakat wad Dakhil, collecting more than Rp1000 trillion per year, equivalent to more than 70% of the State Revenue and Expenditure Budget (APBN) in Indonesia.

With huge amounts of *zakat* collected and a smaller poor population than Indonesia, *zakat* funds in Saudi Arabia are used to alleviate poverty in the country. In fact, *zakat* funds collected in Saudi Arabia are also distributed to other Muslim countries experiencing deprivation and hunger. Herein lies the importance of international *zakat* cooperation, where international organisations, such as the World Zakat Forum, are expected to help facilitate international *zakat* cooperation.

7.2.2 Zakat Management in United Kingdom of Great Britain

The UK Government has no involvement in the management of religious social funds despite allowing individual and collective practices. Furthermore, the UK Government has made no specific rules to regulate religious social funds, preferring broader regulations and permitting the management of religious social funds as contained therein (May, 2018).

The UK Government allows the establishment of organisations and institutions to manage religious social funds as charitable institutions or non-profit organisations. Consequently, each institution managing religious social funds (including Islamic) must obtain an official licence as a charitable institution or non-profit organisation to become a legal (recognised) institution.

There are several *zakat* management organisations in the UK, including the National Zakat Foundation, Islamic Relief, Muslim Aid, Muslim Hands, and several other organisations. In general, *zakat* is collected in the UK from Muslim professionals who have attained *nisab*. *Zakat* is paid via personal bank transfer from the individual account to the *zakat* management institution or directly at the *zakat* management office.

Zakat is distributed in the UK typically to construct places of worship and fund *da'wah* activities, provide scholarships, and disburse food assistance to the poor. A portion of the *zakat* funds collected is also sent to poor people in other countries, including several countries in Africa.

7.2.3 Waqf *Practices in Egypt, Syria, Turkey, and Kuwait*

During the Mamluk Sultanate, religious institutions in Egypt and Syria are said to have received nearly one million dirhams from *waqf* in Egypt. State development in Turkey at one time was also financed not only by the government, but also by *waqf* funds.

In Kuwait, *waqf* funds have contributed to glorious achievements in terms of education, healthcare, and agriculture, while improving spirituality in the community. Furthermore, *waqf* funds have also contributed to local economic development in the country along with other sources of income.

World history has shown that the proceeds obtained from developing *waqf* funds can effectively contribute to financing the construction of mosques, cemeteries, hospitals, schools, libraries, orphanages, warehouses, granaries, and businesses as well as other social, educational, health, and religious projects.

Waqf funds are also used to help meet the basic needs of the elderly and people living with disabilities, while alleviating poverty and financing animal care as well as agricultural, horticultural, and water management.

Waqf funds are collected from donations by ordinary citizens and those with privileged positions in society. Contemporary practices demonstrate that *waqf* funds can be utilised to develop ideas, culture, scientific development, and research and development (R&D), while strengthening social relations and increasing harmony within families, promoting environmental conservation as well as community development and empowerment.

In brief, *waqf* funds play a critical role in community development by improving the socio-economic status of Muslims and, thus, improving the dignity and prestige of Muslims themselves.

Current practices also show that *waqf* can increase private income by raising productivity in terms of investment and commercial activity. In Kuwait, for instance, cash *waqf* is placed in investment deposits in local banks, including shares of sharia-compliant businesses operating within and outside the country (Sulaiman & Hassan, 2016).

Investment in property is another good example, such as the residential centre project and Awqaf Commercial Complex in the 1960s. Establishment of the Kuwait Awqaf Public Foundation (KAPF) as a government body managing waqf in 1993 and diverse investment strategies designed to unlock sharia-compliant investment opportunities in modern applications have the strategic objectives of maintaining *waqf* assets, enlarging capital and generating income.

In 1996, the value of *waqf* assets reached KD4.2 million (USD12.1 million), representing an 18-fold increase on the value recorded upon KAPF establishment in 1993. The net value of *waqf* investment increased to more than KD10.1 million (USD28.9 million) in 1996, accounting for 294% of the value in 1994. Turkey, which has a glorious history of *waqf*, particularly during the Ottoman Empire, boasts a *waqf* bank known as the Waqf Bank & Finance Corporation.

Waqf funds have been mobilised to finance various business projects. Under the auspices of the Islamic Development Bank (IDB), the Awqaf Properties Investment Fund was established by world *waqf* ministers as members of IDB, the corresponding directorate and various Islamic banks in 2001. The institution aims to develop *waqf* internationally by applying *ijarah, istisna*, and *murabahah* financing mechanisms. In addition, IDB has also established the World Waqf Foundation, which is mandated to manage, maintain, and invest funds as well as channel the income to goals that are compliant with sharia principles.

In terms of *waqf* asset development, *muamulat fiqh* (Islamic jurisprudence) practices, such as *ijarah* (rent), *mudharabah* (profit-sharing), *syirkah* (joint venture), and other mechanisms, are available. Similarly, financing *waqf* development using *sukuk* is possible via other *waqf* mechanisms, including *waqf israd* (endowments by the government for public purposes), cash *waqf*, equity *waqf*, and other *waqf* assets.

Waqf practices should be encouraged, particularly among the more affluent upper-middle class. *Waqf* should be utilised as an alternative for the development of strategic economic assets.

7.2.4 Waqf *and Welfare in Australia*

On 15–19th April 2015, the Asia-Pacific Awqaf Congress was held, organised by Sydney University and Awqaf Australia, attracting participants from Indonesia, Malaysia, Pakistan, UK, Kuwait, Somalia, Fiji, Canada, New Zealand, and the host Australia. In general, the participants were *waqf* practitioners and academics or experts in the field of *waqf* from Asia-Pacific.

At the Congress, topics relating to the development of *waqf* and their uses were discussed, including *waqf* and economic empowerment, *waqf* for hospital management, *waqf* to finance research and innovation at universities, *waqf* to help former sex workers, *waqf* for business development, *waqf* management and *sukuk* for commercial financing, *waqf* for livestock businesses and the development of *nazhir* schools.

At the culmination of the event, the need for cooperation between *waqf* managers in different jurisdictions to facilitate *waqf* development was acknowledged, while recommending an expansion of the Asia-Pacific Awqaf Congress internationally. The International Awqaf Congress could facilitate an exhibition of the world *waqf* investment market, with each institution from each respective country presenting and offering *waqf* cooperation or investment opportunities to institutions from other countries.

In Sydney itself, mosques and Islamic schools have been built using *waqf* contributions from the community. For example, the Ali Bin Abi Thalib Mosque in Lakemba was built by a Muslim community of Lebanese descent. Currently, Awqaf Australia is developing *waqf*-based businesses, including the food sector, such as corned beef and honey, as well as manufacturing goods from cattle hides. The proceeds of such *waqf* investments are used to finance social and worship activities, including *da'wah*.

Compared with Indonesia, the use of *waqf* proceeds for social activities to help the poor in Sydney is very small because in Sydney, and Australia in general, quality welfare is of the utmost importance. The government provides subsidies for the poor in Australia to support their lives in the form of monthly benefits, exemptions from medical expenses at medical facilities, and free school tuition.

A colleague from Indonesia once recounted that, when a fellow Indonesian who was already a permanent resident of Australia had kidney failure and had to undergo routine dialysis three times a week at the hospital, all fees were waived. In fact, the patient was able to bring the kidney dialysis machine home to provide self-service after receiving a technical briefing. Dialysis machines are available at home to all Australian nationals with kidney failure.

Where do the massive funds required to provide health and welfare services come from? The source of funds is primarily taxes. Income tax in Australia is quite high, ranging from 30–60% progressively. Higher incomes incur higher taxes. Although wages in Australia are amongst the most expensive in the world, the taxes paid are also very high. Consequently, high income tax allows the state to provide high-quality welfare services to its citizens.

7.3 Islamic Social-Public Finance Practices in Indonesia: Suprastructure and Infrastructure

This subchapter focuses on how Islamic social-public finance is applied in Indonesia, particularly in terms of the supporting suprastructure and infrastructure. The institutional arrangements, types of service, regulations, and infrastructure are discussed in depth to comprehensively describe the overall development of Islamic social-public finance in Indonesia.

7.3.1 History of Zakat *in Indonesia*

Historically, *zakat* development in Indonesia can be divided into the following stages:

1. *Traditional Zakat Management (pre-1968)*
   Prior to 1968, *zakat* funds were managed traditionally and conventionally. At this time, *zakat* management was considered an individual pursuit, implemented by temporary *zakat* committees. In general, such *zakat* committees appeared a few days before Eid-ul-Fitr and were disbanded shortly thereafter. No formal *zakat* management institutions existed in this era.
2. *Proliferation of Zakat Managers (1968–1993)*
   This period was heralded by the establishment of BAZIS DKI Jakarta by the Provincial Government of Jakarta in 1968. The genesis of BAZIS DKI Jakarta was followed by the formation of Amil Zakat Boards (BAZ) in nearly all Indonesian provinces. Furthermore, BAZ were not only set up at the provincial level, yet also cascaded down to the subdistrict/village administrative level. On the other hand, BAMUIS BNI was established in 1967 to manage *zakat* within the community along with Yayasan Dana Sosial Al-Falah (YDSF) in 1987 in Surabaya.
3. *Zakat Management Professionalisation (1993–1999)*
   This stage was marked by the establishment of Dompet Dhuafa in 1993, which pioneered professional *zakat* management. The approach was exemplified by

professional *zakat* managers working full-time throughout the year (8 h a day, 5 days a week) with the primary tasks of collecting *zakat*, receiving adequate remuneration, and applying modern management practices. The *zakat* management approach pioneered by Dompet Dhuafa was subsequently replicated by many other *zakat* management organisations.

4. *Zakat Management Formalisation (1999–2009)*

   This era commenced with ratification of the *Zakat* Act (No. 38) of 1999, which mandated all *zakat* managers to be registered and recognised by the Government. The law architected *zakat* management by the government through Amil Zakat Boards (BAZ) and by the community through Amil Zakat Institutions (LAZ). Community-based *zakat* managers still required government approval/confirmation. At the time, numerous *zakat* managers in the community sought government approval in droves.

5. *Zakat Management Standardisation (2009–present)*

   The final stage of *zakat* management development in Indonesia was marked by ratification of the Amil Zakat Code of Ethics at the Musyawarah Nasional Zakat Forum in 2009. The Code of Ethics kickstarted *zakat* management standardisation in Indonesia. Subsequently, the Zakat Criteria for Performance Excellence was published as quality management guidelines for *zakat* management organisations. In conjunction with the National Amil Zakat Board (BAZNAS), the Indonesian Council of Ulama (MUI) also issued a collection of *zakat* fatwas as guidelines for *zakat fiqh* in Indonesia. In mid-2011, PSAK 109 was issued as accounting standards guidelines for *zakat* managers. Towards the end of 2011, Act Number 23 of 2011 was instituted as the amended *Zakat* Act, containing various *zakat* management standards applicable in Indonesia.

7.3.2 *Forms of* Zakat *Management Development in Indonesia*

As explained previously, *zakat* is the primary instrument of Islamic social-public finance. Therefore, *zakat* is the most discussed topic in terms of Islamic social-public finance. In Indonesia, *zakat* has been practised for a long time, stretching back to long before the Republic of Indonesia was proclaimed. Long-established *zakat* practices in Indonesia, coupled with the largest Muslim population worldwide, make Indonesia a laboratory for the global social sector. *Zakat*, as practised in Indonesia, has experienced significant development and innovative management over the years as follows:

1. *Defending the Oppressed (Legal Advocacy)*

   Toni is a village man who was stabbed by his neighbour due to trade-related jealousy. As the stabbing was perpetrated by an economically superior individual, the case failed to progress. Toni's protestations to the local police were largely ignored. Toni suspected the lack of police action stemmed from a bribe paid by the businessman.

Toni approached Dompet Dhuafa (*zakat* manager) in tears. Toni recounted his emotional story and provided evidence in the form of large stab wounds in his back. Toni also explained how eyewitnesses to the incident had been coerced into silence through fear of the businessman. Toni asked Dompet Dhuafa for assistance in his case.

Dompet Dhuafa requested legal recourse from a legal aid agency to defend Toni's case. The operational costs of defending the case were financed by *zakat* funds managed by Dompet Dhuafa because Toni was poor.

After months of litigation, from the investigation to the prosecution, trial and finally the verdict, the businessman was found guilty of stabbing Toni and sentenced to prison to atone for his mistakes.

Dompet Dhuafa also helped the case of a mother in a transmigrant area of Sumatra, whose land was seized by a businessman in collaboration with village officials. Aware of the case, Dompet Dhuafa cooperated with legal aid agencies to defend the mother along with several other cases.

Those examples show how *zakat* funds are used to defend the oppressed poor. *Zakat* funds can be utilised to protect the rights of the poor, oppressed by others. *Zakat* funds may be used to provide legal defence for the poor who are oppressed by usurpers. Defending the oppressed poor is also part of the effort to maintain the dignity of the poor and needy as human beings.

2. *Conserving the Environment with Zakat*

What is the relationship between *zakat* and environmental conservation? A valid question considering many people think *zakat* is only used to fulfil the basic needs of the poor and there is no direct connection with the environment. Consequently, environmental issues have not been touched by the issue of *zakat*.

Let us take the following example. There are 100 poor farmers and we ask them to plant 10,000 trees (each farmer planting 100 trees) and take care of them. We will pay maintenance for 1 year until the plants are productive, then the planted trees and fruit produced will become the property of the farmer to either eat or sell. If the cost of purchasing the trees and the cost of caring for the trees are paid using *zakat* funds, what is our opinion then?

In this case, in addition to using the funds as a source of income for poor farmers, *zakat* also serves as a vehicle to reforest the natural environs. In this context, *zakat* empowerment is also environmentally friendly. If this could be replicated more broadly, reforestation could be achieved.

In another example, there is one particular area that experiences drought annually. The local residents are struggling to keep fish in the pond, water the plants, and bathe themselves. The nearest spring is 5 km from the village. Under such circumstances, constructing a pipeline network to bring water to the village is a critical aspect of local development. Moreover, if the water is subsequently used for irrigation and aquaculture, the use of *zakat* funds to pipe the water would certainly be justified.

In reality, *zakat* utilisation boils down to creativity in terms of overcoming issues plaguing the poor within the sharia corridor. When *zakat* managers are creative, *zakat* empowerment will have an impact on environmental conservation. Diverse activities with a direct impact on environmental conservation are possible. Through innovative *zakat* empowerment programmes based on environmental conservation, poverty can be eradicated, the poor empowered, and the environment conserved.

7.3.3 Zakat *Regulations*

Though effective for 12 years, Act Number 38 of 1999 (the former *Zakat* Act) had many shortcomings and a narrow purview, and lacked the backing of a Government Regulation, with subsequent provisions subject to a Ministerial Regulation. An amendment or revision to Act Number 38 of 1999 has been a long time coming.

Initially, the notion to amend the former *Zakat* Act stemmed from the following ideas:

1. Sanctions for disobedient *muzakki* (administrative and financial sanctions).
2. The organisational arrangements of *zakat* management organisations, while separating the functions of regulator or supervisor, operator, and coordinator.
3. Recognising *zakat* as a tax deduction (according to Act Number 38 of 1999, *zakat* is recognised as a deduction on taxable income).

Drafting the new *zakat* legislation was a protracted affair, with the discussion starting in the People's Representative Council (DPR) during the 2004–2009 period. With the discussion incomplete, the new *zakat* law was delegated to the DPR for the 2009–2014 period. Through comprehensive discussions, the legal concepts have undergone several changes.

The new *zakat* law (Act Number 23 of 2011) was enacted on 27th October 2011, containing 11 Chapters and 47 Articles. The salient provisions of the new *Zakat* Act are as follows:

1. *Zakat* management comes under the authority of the state, with members of the public permitted to participate based on government approval.
2. *Zakat* management is the preserve of the National Amil Zakat Board (BAZNAS), which operates hierarchically from the central agency to the regency/city administrative levels (BAZNAS is authorised to establish Zakat Collection Units—UPZ).
3. BAZNAS members consist of eight public representatives and three government representatives. The public is represented by ulema, professionals, and public figureheads, while the government is represented by elements from the relevant ministries.
4. Zakat Management Institutions (LAZ) assist BAZNAS to manage *zakat* funds (LAZ are authorised to establish representatives).

Notwithstanding, Act Number 23 of 2011 contains several weaknesses as follows:

1. Article 15 concerning the formation of BAZNAS at the provincial as well as regency/city administrative levels, which fails to recognise the authority of the governor or regent/mayor.
2. Article 18 concerning the licensing requirements for LAZ, stipulating that LAZ must be an Islamic community organisation.
3. Article 29 concerning the coordination mechanisms between BAZNAS and provincial BAZ, regency/city BAZ, as well as BAZNAS and LAZ.
4. Article 38 and Article 41 concerning the threat of sanctions on unlicensed individual *zakat* managers.

Those articles, if the elucidation and implementation guidelines (government regulations and ministerial regulations) are ambiguous, could be counterproductive and negate some potential *zakat* development.

Article 43 of the new *Zakat* Act stipulates that existing BAZNAS, provincial BAZ, and regency/city level BAZ prior to enactment of the new law remain valid and are designated as central BAZNAS, provincial BAZNAS, and regency/city level BAZNAS. LAZ approved by the authorised government minister prior to enactment of the new law are still recognised as LAZ in accordance with the new *Zakat* Act. LAZ, as referred to in Paragraph (3), are required to modify their institutional arrangements no later than 5 years after enactment of this law.

Fundamentally, the new *Zakat* Act divides the community into four major groups. The first group are in full agreement with the law and willing to implement it completely. The second group agree with some of the articles and after the shortcomings have been corrected by government and ministerial regulations will be willing to implement the law. The third group partially reject the law and have conducted a judicial review of the articles therein, which may be implemented upon amendment. The fourth group fully reject the law in its entirety, submitting a judicial review to revoke and repeal the law.

The authors hope that the weaknesses in the law can be addressed without having to completely rescind the legislation. Whichever final form the new *Zakat* Act takes, it is expected to improve *zakat* in Indonesia in terms of collection, distribution, and impact on improving quality welfare for the people of Indonesia.

7.3.4 Indonesia **Zakat** *Blueprint*

In terms of how *zakat* practices will look in Indonesia moving forward, we need a natural and planned framework that allows *zakat* to evolve in accordance with development dynamics in Indonesia. Each party and element of the Indonesian state must have the freedom to move according to their respective views and aspirations. This will result in a melting pot where the desires and aspirations of all parties can collide and develop in harmony.

Within a planned framework, the future of *zakat* in Indonesia will be designed with a clear long-term plan concerning the direction of *zakat* development in Indonesia. In this context, a blueprint is required that lays out the future direction and orientation of *zakat* development in Indonesia.

A *zakat* blueprint will help guide those involved in seeking the realisation of *zakat* ideals, which are also described and explained in the blueprint, including the stages, processes, and milestones to achieve the desired goals. The blueprint also describes *zakat* development in Indonesia, the main constraints that have emerged, relevant laws and regulations, *zakat* ideals in Indonesia, and the stages or processes to achieve them.

The *zakat* blueprint must be prepared and formulated with the involvement of all stakeholders in Indonesia, representing the Government, People's Representative Council (DPR), *zakat* management associations, Islamic community organisations, centres of *zakat* study, *ulama*, and scholars specifically concerned with *zakat*, as well as members of the public. Ultimately, the *zakat* blueprint will be a culmination of *zakat* stakeholder agreements on the current state of *zakat* in Indonesia, the direction of *zakat* development moving forward as well as the stages and processes required to achieve the long-term goal/future of *zakat*.

The *zakat* blueprint will guide the formulation of regulations and policies, while providing a reference for standardising and developing the capacity of *zakat* management organisations. In addition, the blueprint will facilitate all components of the government and state when compiling guidelines to improve *zakat* management. It is more productive to spend time reaching an agreement that guides all parties rather than wasting energy seeking a solution to every problem as they emerge.

At the time of writing, the *Zakat* Forum (Indonesia Association of *Zakat* Management Organisations) was still formulating the Indonesia *Zakat* Blueprint, with several breakthroughs already achieved. Hopefully, the *zakat* blueprint will be realised and subsequently refined moving forward, with implementation expanded through the involvement of all *zakat* stakeholders in Indonesia.

7.3.5 Future Zakat *Scenarios*

Based on current developments and dynamics, the future of *zakat* development in Indonesia is expected as follows:

1. *BAZNAS to play a dominant zakat management role in Indonesia*
   The National Amil Zakat Board (BAZNAS) will function as coordinator and supervisor of *zakat* management in Indonesia. BAZNAS will continue integrating *zakat* nationally and, over time, centralise the hierarchical role from the central to provincial and regency/city administrative levels due to the increasingly harmonious relationship between BAZNAS and amil zakat institutions (LAZ).
2. *Enhancing the quality of Zakat Management Organisations (OPZ)*

The quality of zakat management organisations (OPZ) will be enhanced through appropriate regulations, capacity building, and standard setting. LAZ are suspected to merge or connect, which will strengthen OPZ. Licensed *zakat* managers in the community will be officially incorporated as *zakat* management units of BAZNAS or LAZ. With a healthier level of competition between OPZs and improving critical thinking in society, OPZs will set and implement higher *zakat* quality management standards.

3. *National mobilisation of zakat funds*

   Public awareness concerning *zakat* distribution through *zakat* management organisations will increase. In the next 10 years, approximately 50% of *zakat* payers will donate through *zakat* management organisations, totalling an estimated Rp50 trillion.
4. *Zakat will be tax deductible*

   Through various efforts, *zakat* will ultimately become tax deductible. The Government, through the Ministry of Finance, has finally realised that proper *zakat* management has the same goals as development policy. Therefore, trusted and professional *zakat* management by BAZNAS and LAZ in accordance with prevailing standards is a part of overall development implementation for quality public welfare.
5. *Development of a national zakat datacentre*

   Through close coordination, particularly in terms of data reporting and collection, a national *zakat* datacentre could be realised, especially if a fast, accurate, and reliable information system was used. The datacentre will collect data on *zakat* payers (*muzakki*), recipients (*mustahik*), managers (*nazhir*), poor people (*duafa*) and their location as well as various programmes for distributing or utilising *zakat* by BAZNAS and LAZ, including where the programmes are implemented.
6. *Increasing zakat synergy*

   Zakat synergy is increasing due to growing awareness of effective *zakat* management, coupled with the existing regulations and success of *zakat* coordination by BAZNAS. Synergy is increasing in terms of *zakat* collection, programme cooperation and implementation. Furthermore, *zakat* synergy is supported by the competencies of each respective OPZ, effective strategic programme allocation, and effective programme implementation.
7. *Increasing Zakat Utilisation Programmes*

   Zakat utilisation programmes have experienced remarkable growth in terms of creation, innovation, scope, depth, and distribution throughout Indonesia. Various management programmes implemented by zakat management organisations (OPZ) have improved programme planning and implementation along with the effectiveness and efficiency of *zakat* utilisation programmes.
8. *Numerous poor people helped by zakat*

   Success of the *zakat* utilisation programme in helping the poor has increased significantly due to improvements in *zakat* management quality. Over the next 10 years, the national *zakat* programme will help to alleviate 20% of the poverty in Indonesia.

9. *Stronger role for Indonesia in international zakat*

   Based on *zakat* developments and consolidation nationally, Indonesia will have opportunities to play a larger international role in *zakat* affairs. Indonesia could undertake various efforts to expand *zakat* internationally, while organising world *zakat* interaction and coordination forums, conducting various studies on international *zakat* and developing the capacity of *zakat* managers globally.

7.3.6 *Notes to Government Regulation on* Zakat *Act*

After the Judicial Review of Act No.23 of 2011 concerning *Zakat* Management was completed on 31st October 2013, the Government promulgated Government Regulation No. 14 of 2014 in February 2014 as follow-up legislation in accordance with the judicial review, implying that less than 4 months were required to issue follow-up regulations after the court rendered a decision. The Government should be commended for the speed at which the follow-up legislation was enacted.

Unfortunately, however, despite such rapid progress, the substance of the regulation raised at least three questions, known as the Notes to Government Regulation on the *Zakat* Act.

The first note deals with the requirements for establishing Amil Zakat Institutions (LAZ) as contained in Article 58 of the Government Regulation on the *Zakat* Act. Article 57 stipulates that only Islamic community organisations and legally incorporated institutions can establish LAZ. This means that Article 58 must contain an option for Islamic community organisations and legally incorporated institutions to establish LAZ, which is also in accordance with the Judicial Review of the *Zakat* Act by the Constitutional Court. Notwithstanding, Article 58 currently only states that Islamic community organisations can establish LAZ, without referencing legally incorporated institutions in the *Zakat* Act. Why are there inconsistencies between Article 57 and Article 58? Was this intentional or not?

The second note refers to the formation of national LAZ representatives, limited to one per province, who must also reapply for a licence at the local regional office of the Ministry of Religious Affairs as referred to in Article 62, Paragraphs 2 and 3. This raises a few issues because many LAZ have opened branch offices (defined in the Government Regulation as representatives), often with more than one representative in a province. Such institutional arrangements do not constitute a solid legal foundation in accordance with the *Zakat* Act and the Judicial Review of the Constitutional Court. Follow-up regulations must, therefore, prioritise the structure or institutional arrangements, rather than focusing on restrictions. Moreover, the *Zakat* Act and Judicial Review mandate a mission of distributing *zakat* services, *zakat* utilisation in particular, by BAZNAS and LAZ throughout Indonesia.

The third note refers to the mandatory sharia audit. Paragraph 2 of Article 75 stipulates that LAZ must consent to a sharia audit performed by the Ministry of Religious Affairs. To the limits of our understanding, the sharia fatwa authority in Indonesia is the Indonesian Council of Ulama (MUI) and *NOT* the Ministry of

Religious Affairs. Based on which rationale must the sharia audit be performed by the Ministry of Religious Affairs and not the Indonesian Council of Ulama (MUI)? Is it because the MUI has lost credibility in terms of appraising sharia compliance?

The Notes to the Government Regulation on the *Zakat* Act are an invaluable input for the relevant stakeholders to reconsider and amend the regulations appropriately. We certainly all hope that promulgation of the Government Regulation on the *Zakat* Act will improve the condition of *zakat* in Indonesia. The main orientation of *zakat* management in Indonesia remains the optimal mobilisation of *zakat*, proper utilisation in accordance with sharia law as well as *zakat* utilisation to alleviate poverty in a tangible and equitable manner.

Wallahu A'lam!

7.3.7 *Role of* Zakat *Regulator, Operators, and Supervisor*

Zakat is an Islamic teaching that has influenced the history of Islam since the time of the Prophet Muhammad SAW, including subsequent generations of companions and caliphs. Furthermore, *zakat* has proven itself in terms of alleviating poverty. During the reign of Caliph Umar bin Abdul Azis, *zakat* funds were used to eradicate poverty quickly.

As a massive economic resource of the people, *zakat* will remain present and robust when managed properly. Individual and transitory *zakat* management practices prevent the mobilisation and utilisation of funds for the strategic needs of the people.

Realising the enormous potential of *zakat* in Indonesia, all local Muslims must seek to optimise the power of *zakat*, working in cooperation to develop and strengthen *zakat* instruments.

In general, Muslims in Indonesia understand *zakat* payments in terms of *zakat fitrah*. Nonetheless, there are many Muslims in Indonesia who have met the minimum *zakat* requirements (*nisab*) of income and wealth yet are oblivious to their *zakat* obligations. On the other hand, some Muslims knowingly meet the *nisab* requirements yet are still reluctant or negligent to pay *zakat*.

Muslims in Indonesia who understand their *zakat* obligations typically prefer to pay individually and directly to the *mustahik*. This practice quickly depletes the funds and prevents mobilisation for the greater good.

Consequently, a First Effort is required to increase *zakat* mobilisation. The First Effort focuses on increasing *zakat* law enforcement by amending the *Zakat* Management Act (No. 38) of 1999 to include sanctions for *muzakki* failing to pay their *zakat* obligations. Such sanctions are expected to encourage more affluent Muslims to fulfil their *zakat* obligations.

Socialisation and education activities are also required concerning *zakat* obligations and assets. Such activities must provide detailed rationale for why *zakat* is necessary, including the fundamental arguments, how *zakat* is calculated, and when the payments are due.

More importantly, it is essential to ensure that *muzakki* always pay their *zakat* obligations through a legal *zakat* management organisation. *Muzakki* should only pay *zakat* through the official Amil Zakat Boards (BAZ) formed by the government or Amil Zakat Institutions (LAZ) formed by community groups and approved by the government. *Zakat* mobilisation through legitimate *zakat* management organisations will help optimise *zakat* collection, management, and distribution. In addition, all BAZ and LAZ must strive to improve *zakat* management performance to restore public trust and professional quality.

To revive *zakat* practices in Indonesia, an immediate Second Effort is required concerning the arrangements of *zakat* institutions in Indonesia. The existing institutional arrangements, as stipulated in prevailing ministerial laws and decrees, are considered inadequate in terms of regulating *zakat* institutions in Indonesia.

One of the fundamental weaknesses that has not been sufficiently addressed in prevailing *zakat* legislation is the legal position/status of the regulator, operators, and supervisor. Although the government has positioned itself as regulator, discharging this regulatory function remains ineffective.

In the context of regulation as an operator, the function of operator is mandated to BAZ and LAZ in accordance with prevailing laws. Nevertheless, the existing legal provisions as contained in prevailing laws have several inherent weaknesses, including ambiguity in terms of the relationships and jurisdiction between BAZ of different levels, and the relationship between BAZ and LAZ. Based on existing legislation, the coordinator role of *zakat* management in Indonesia is unregulated.

In the context of supervision, the oversight function remains dormant. Illegal *zakat* managers could potentially misappropriate or divert *zakat* funds due to a lack of supervision. LAZ approved by the government yet failing to meet eligibility standards and requirements are still unsupervised and free to operate. *Zakat* managers in violation of the law or flouting ethical norms are also left unsupervised. Such conditions point to the dire need for an immediate restructuring of the institutional arrangements of *zakat* managers in Indonesia.

A Third Effort is also required to strengthen *zakat* in Indonesia, namely programme synergy among *zakat* managers. The presence of different *zakat* operators with their respective skills and expertise necessitates synergy to hone the others' advantages. Furthermore, programme synergy would also exploit the advantages of each *zakat* manager to effectively negate the weaknesses of other *zakat* managers.

Programme synergy can be achieved in the context of collecting *zakat* funds by regulating the distribution area of *muzakki* in relation to the appropriate *zakat* management organisation. In terms of *zakat* utilisation and distribution, programme synergy includes coordinated programme implementation. During a disaster, for example, a *zakat* management organisation could establish a joint disaster management post.

Primarily, programme synergy involves implementing joint activities as part of a strategic programme, where the *zakat* management organisation in conjunction with guidance from the ulema and community representatives regularly determines what must be done to empower, prosper, and build the strength of the community.

Successful programme synergy will make *zakat* management more effective and efficient in Indonesia, while ameliorating quality welfare in the community more quickly. With the array of measures taken to improve conditions in Indonesia, *zakat* is expected to return stronger than ever. God Willing (*Insya Allah*)!

A field survey was also performed in the preparation of this rigorous study concerning various aspects of Islamic social-public finance in Indonesia. The field survey was conducted to describe the actual conditions and practices of Islamic social-public finance in Indonesia along with the distinct application dynamics and characteristics in each region. To that end, the survey was conducted in several Indonesian regions, namely Surabaya and Malang to represent East Java, Banjarmasin as part of South Kalimantan, Aceh, Yogyakarta and West Java, represented by Bandung. These regions were selected as the objects of the field study due to their specific characteristics in terms of Islamic social-public finance practices in Indonesia.

7.4 Islamic Social-Public Finance Practices in Indonesia: Regional Examples

7.4.1 Islamic Social-Public Finance Practices in Banjarmasin

Banjarmasin is the provincial capital of South Kalimantan. Known as the city of 1000 rivers, Banjarmasin is dissected by the Martapura River and located in the eastern part of the Barito River, with numerous smaller tributaries flowing throughout the region. For the city, the rivers not only provide clean water yet also shape the cultural system. Many houses were built on riverbanks by the people of Banjarmasin, with the river providing a major source of sustenance and numerous residents trading their agricultural produce and other wares by boats on the river. Such river trade is characteristic of Banjarmasin city, often referred to as the floating market. The area of the city itself spans 98.46 km^2, with a population of more than 800,000 in 2016. Of the total population, 95.54% are Muslim.

The Muslim community of Banjarmasin is known to be devoutly religious. The people of Banjarmasin have adopted a unique form of worship, where the spirit of individual worship is very highly upheld. This is reflected in the large number of Hajj and Umrah pilgrims sent from South Kalimantan, Banjarmasin in particular, every year. This uniqueness was confirmed by the respondents of the field survey, revealing that the Hajj and Umrah pilgrimages were a very high priority in the community. For example, many people from South Kalimantan, Banjarmasin in particular, undertake the Hajj and Umrah pilgrimages nearly every year, even though some do not own their own property or land assets.

The importance of Hajj and Umrah pilgrimages for the people of Banjarmasin is also reflected among university students, many of whom seek permission for college absence to undertake Umrah pilgrimages. For the people of Banjarmasin, high esteem is reserved for the title Haji or Hajah placed in front of the name. This implies that social status is an important aspect of cultural life in Banjarmasin. This is a departure from society more generally, where social status is acquired from position and wealth based on assets such as land, houses, or vehicles.

Corroborating the uniqueness of the Banjarmasin community, Muhaimin (2013) told of a tribe in the region that is known as hard-working merchants. Called the Halabiu, the tribe's motivation for relentless trading is to finance the Hajj and Umrah pilgrimages. In addition, the Halabiu is also said to have professional expertise in accounting.[1]

The steely enthusiasm of local people from Banjarmasin to undertake pilgrimages to the holy land should be consistent with other practices of worship, particularly worship with a social aspect. The ability of the local community to finance multiple Umrah pilgrimages, itself a significant financial burden, implies that local economic conditions are sound, as represented by high social awareness.

In reality, however, practices of social worship are far less developed in Banjarmasin than practices of individual worship. The local Muslim community still prefers donating *zakat* obligations directly to the *mustahik* rather than channelling the funds through *zakat* management organisations. In fact, Muslims in Banjarmasin also pay their *zakat* to local clerics, who continue to play a very important role in community decisions, including social worship, such as paying *zakat*. Public concern regarding *zakat* ineffectiveness due to ignorance about how the *mustahik* receive the funds is one of the reasons *muzakki* tend to prefer paying *zakat* to local clerics.

Such conditions are exacerbated by a low level of public trust in Banjarmasin concerning *zakat, infaq, sadaqah*, and *waqf* (ZISWAF) donations to official *zakat* management organisations. For example, the BAZNAS office in South Kalimantan received the largest *zakat* donation from civil servants, who were specifically advised to pay *zakat* via BAZNAS. In addition, the employees of Bank Kalsel Syariah also donate large *zakat* funds, totalling Rp2 billion per year, deducted at source. Despite representing the Government, BAZNAS has thus far failed to garner local community trust and support in terms of managing *zakat* funds.

Based on the local characteristics of social-public finance, the Muslim community in South Kalimantan, Banjarmasin in particular, pays *zakat* in accordance with *muqayyadah*, rather than *mutlaqah* principles. *Mutlaqah* principles afford the management organisation flexibility to manage and utilise the *zakat* funds, while *muqayyadah* principles allow the *muzakki* to determine limits regarding to whom and for which purpose the funds should be distributed and utilised.

Based on such characteristics, it can be concluded that the local Muslim community in South Kalimantan, in this case Banjarmasin, is devoutly religious.

[1]Muhaimin (2013). Secrets to Business Success of Halabiu Tribe. Yogyakarta: PT LKiS Pelangi Aksara.

Nevertheless, this piousness is reflected in individual worship rather than optimised for more social forms of worship.

The social characteristics of the local community in Banjarmasin are even more interesting from the perspective of a book authored by Clifford Geertz entitled "Islam Observed: Religious Development in Morocco and Indonesia", stating that South Kalimantan was a centre of the Islamic civilisation in Indonesia. Therefore, practices of Islamic social-public finance in the province should be in line with sharia law in terms of management, *zakat* in particular. South Kalimantan has long been considered a centre of Islamic civilisation in Indonesia since the arrival of Middle Eastern traders to coastal regions of the province. Islamic civilisation quickly developed with the help of Sheikh Muhammad Arsyad al-Banjari, a great scholar of the Banjar Sultanate who taught the Shafi'i traditional school of Islamic jurisprudence. The teachings and procedures for practising worship, including the obligatory payment of *zakat*, are already contained in the book written and taught by Sabilal Muhtadin, which has become a reference for many followers of Islam in Southeast Asia.

Unfortunately, the teachings of Sheikh Muhammad Arsyad al-Banjari were not practised after his death, not even by his descendants. The local community became inseparable from the direct guidance of local clerics, following the teachings of contemporary scholars, which do not fully reflect the teachings revealed in the book of Sabilal Muhtadin. Such teachings, especially in terms of social worship, are in accordance with sharia law. In fact, the book states that *zakat* must be managed by professionals or experts rather than individuals or local clerics.

Zakat distribution using local clerics as intermediaries, as practised in South Kalimantan, is motivated by convenience and the assumption of perfection in *zakat* worship. Local Muslims feel facilitated by the presence of a local cleric who can provide guidance to the *muzakki* when contributing *zakat*. It is this inherited religious culture that shapes the realisation of *zakat* worship, which is limited to merely a ritual.

Using Banjarmasin as an example, it can be concluded that Indonesian society is oral rather than written based, which explains why the teachings contained in the book of Sabilal Muhtadin are less studied and practised by the people of South Kalimantan, instead preferring to follow the direction of local clerics and contemporary scholars.

7.4.2 Islamic Social-Public Finance Practices in Aceh

Aceh province is a region of Indonesia famed for its implementation of sharia law. It is also considered a gateway for the spread of Islam throughout the Indonesian archipelago. Aceh has a long and illustrious history of Islamic rule. It is imperative, therefore, to include Aceh when reviewing the application of Islamic social-public finance in Indonesia, or even look to the province for best practices.

By observing the storied history of Islam in Aceh, including the Aceh Sultanate, which ruled for centuries as the richest, most powerful and prosperous sultanate in the Malacca Strait region, the discussion on Islamic social-public finance practices in Aceh is complete. Even now, Aceh is the only region of Indonesia with special dispensation to implement a sharia system of government. Therefore, it would be fair to assume that the practices of Islamic social-public finance in Aceh are already aligned in accordance with sharia law.

History also shows how the sultanates and kingdoms that once controlled Aceh used their own gold-based currency system, similar to dinar and dirham, which is actually recommended under sharia law. Observing the past greatness of the Aceh Sultanate has established the province as professional and competent in managing the state. In fact, it was the Acehnese Government that initiated the idea to form the National Development Planning Agency (Bappenas), based on the regional agency (Bappeda) already established in the area.

Unfortunately, those extraordinary facts and accomplishments have been eroded and set back over the course of history. Aceh has been subjected to various colonial interventions, including the Portuguese, British, and Dutch, along with Japanese imperialism that precipitated the collapse of the Aceh Sultanate, followed by civil conflict with the Indonesian Government after independence and the tragic tsunami that decimated large swathes of Aceh in 2004.

The field survey revealed how the civil conflict fought between the authorities in Aceh and the Central Government for independence from Indonesia through the Free Aceh Movement (*Gerakan Aceh Merdeka*—GAM) since 1975 has severely eroded various aspects of life in Aceh. Prolonged conflict has destroyed certain values, including the culture of respecting guests, as taught by Islam. A never-ending cycle of conflicts and political disputes in the region have made the current situation untenable because government level conflicts are highly detrimental to the community.

Regional conflicts are the main determinant of declining piety in Aceh. Typically, the local community, especially children, rush to the mosque (*meunasah*) upon hearing the *Maghrib* call to prayer to recite Al-Qur'an. During a conflict, however, strict curfews are enforced and the local community is reluctant to leave their homes, which disrupts the habit of reciting Al-Qur'an at the mosque. In addition, post-tsunami aid to the Aceh region further eroded religious values. The sheer abundance of aid created a culture of prodigality. In conclusion, such conditions have significantly altered the character and culture of Aceh. Now that the conflict has been resolved and the post-disaster recovery is complete, the people in Aceh have started slowly returning to their old habits, with local clerics and scholars inviting residents back to Al-Qur'an.

The conflict in Aceh was resolved and the peace process began in 2005, after the devastating tsunami in December 2004. The widespread physical and moral devastation caused by the tsunami created an environment more favourable to peace talks, with both parties preferring to seek peace and focus on post-disaster reconstruction and restructuring. Though the conflict and post-disaster recovery process are finally over, the moral and psychological scars are still felt in the lives of local communities.

Despite the numerous conflicts and experiences, the application of Islamic social-public finance in Aceh is still practised in accordance with sharia law, though not as extensively as during the period of Islamic leadership. This is understandable considering that Aceh is currently rebuilding a fully-fledged Islamic sharia system.

Since promulgation of Act Number 11 of 2006 concerning the Government of Aceh, *zakat* is a direct factor of tax deductions, stipulating that "*zakat* paid is deductible from the income tax (PPh) payable" and forms part of the locally generated revenue (PAD) in addition to local levies, the proceeds of separate regional asset management at the provincial, regency, and city administrative levels as well as capital investment at the provincial, regency, and city administrative levels.

The Aceh Government's decision to make *zakat* tax deductible represents affirmative progress for Muslims implementing sharia law. This action could potentially increase quality welfare in the community through facilities built using local government revenues and as a means of controlling tax payments through *zakat* data to determine the amount of income earned. There is a positive correlation, therefore, between taxes and *zakat* because a higher number of taxpayers and *muzakki* will increase *zakat* and tax revenues.

Obligatory payments to *Baitul Mal* by residents in Aceh also intend to establish payment compliance, eliminate possible conflicts of interest or other disputes between *muzakki* and *mustahik* as well as optimise *zakat*. Such conditions imply that *zakat* is a matter of the state. For example, *Baitul Mal* is authorised to manage the land, bank deposits, and other assets whose owners or progeny were not known after the 2004 tsunami for up to 25 years.

Specifically, one of the most fundamental aspects of Islamic social-public finance as practiced in Aceh is the existence of the *Baitul Mal* institution, as a government agency responsible for collecting and managing *zakat* funds from the Acehnese people. Basically, *Baitul Mal* is a type of BAZNAS at the provincial level, yet its authority is somewhat different to BAZNAS. The *Baitul Mal* institution in Aceh has considerable authority in accordance with *Qanun* Number 10 of 2007 concerning *Baitul Mal*. *Qanun* are Islamic laws established by the Aceh Sharia Government. *Baitul Mal* is the only official institution authorised to accept *zakat* payments. The regulation implies, therefore, that the public are not permitted to pay their *zakat* obligations directly to *mustahik* or through any institution other than *Baitul Mal*. The structure of the *Baitul Mal* institution in Aceh is divided into four administrative levels, namely provincial, regency/city, *mukim* (township), and *gampong* (village), regulated by gubernatorial and mayoral regulations.

On the other hand, the *Qanun* is equivalent to a regulation because of its failure to ensure *muzakki* pay *zakat* to *Baitul Mal*. This will impact *zakat* distribution on consumptive and productive needs.

Reluctance to pay *zakat* to *Baitul Mal* stems from the following factors:

1. Low law enforcement capacity concerning *qanun*, accompanied by increasing reluctance amongst *muzakki* to pay *zakat* to institutions.

2. Suboptimal implementation of the article "*Uqubat pada Qanun*", referring to the punishment for *muzakki* failing to pay *zakat* to *Baitul Mal*.
3. The culture of the Acehnese people who subscribe to Al-Qur'an and the Hadiths as interpreted through the words of ulema or *Teungku*, thus rejecting new and modern religious ideas.

In practice, therefore, many people in Aceh still pay *zakat* directly to the *mustahik* or through *Meunasah* (musalla or mosque). On the other hand, private *zakat* management organisations continue to receive *zakat* payments. The Aceh Government and *Baitul Mal* are unable to prevent this because privately owned social institutions contributed enormously to post-tsunami aid efforts in the region.

Zakat funds collected by *Baitul Mal* are managed separately through a special account, with utilisation reserved only for the eight *asnaf*, rather than other development costs. On the revenue side, *zakat* accounts for 1.2% of total provincial government revenues in Aceh, potentially totalling Rp1.4 trillion per year, with each regency/city averaging Rp38 billion.

In terms of compliance, nearly all residents of Aceh pay *zakat*. Farmers, for example, deduct *zakat* directly from the harvest. In fact, Aceh applies a rice *zakat*, which is not recorded by *Baitul Mal*, yet has been very effective and is paid directly to the village imam, despite the establishment of village level *Baitul Mal* as stipulated in the *Qanun*. Therefore, agricultural *zakat* is applied in Aceh. In terms of utilising *zakat* funds, not everyone wants to receive *zakat* funds. Uniquely, residents of Aceh who feel they do not deserve or are not eligible to receive *zakat* will refuse the donation, demonstrating a high level of public awareness in the region concerning *zakat* rights and obligations. Despite such high public awareness concerning the obligations and benefits of paying *zakat*, there are still many who do not understand how to calculate *zakat* correctly.

Higher public awareness and compliance in Aceh towards paying *zakat* it is also inextricably linked to the strong local Islamic culture. For Acehnese Muslims, obligatory social worship has been passed down from generation to generation. In addition, social worship is also practised widely in Aceh because the local community fears their businesses will not be blessed if *zakat* obligations are not paid. It becomes more interesting when we equate that to the contribution and struggle of the Acehnese people for Indonesia's independence. During the Indonesian National Revolution or War of Independence, the people of Aceh contributed most to help all Indonesians secure independence. For example, *waqf* donations from Aceh were used to purchase Indonesia's first aeroplane, the Dakota Seulawah RI-01, which helped win the war. In addition, the gold adorning the top of the National Monument (Monas) was donated by the people of Aceh. This is evidence of how socially aware the Acehnese people are, as a reflection of Aceh's glorious history, where the Aceh Sultanate ruled for centuries as the richest, most powerful, and prosperous sultanate in the Strait of Malacca. Various sources in this study stated that individual worship, such as praying, in Aceh is sometimes lacking. It is unequivocal, however, that enthusiasm for social worship on the other hand is massive and creates a sense of pride or shame if neglected.

In addition to *zakat*, the collection of *infaq* and *waqf* funds is also very high in Aceh. *Infaq* funds are also collected by *Baitul Mal* and in Aceh there is a SME management model that encourages business owners to pay *infaq* as part of their business or corporate social responsibility (CSR), levied at 0.5% on each government partner or contractor, which is paid to *Baitul Mal*. On the other hand, the practice of *waqf* is very well established in Aceh, where almost every village has *waqf* land. Unfortunately, the land is neglected and not certified. Despite high public acceptance, accurate and up-to-date records are lacking and the contracts ambiguous, thus preventing the *waqf* land from being utilised efficiently. Furthermore, the current high price of land has prompted a shift from land *waqf* to cash *waqf*.

In addition to the *zakat, infaq*, and *waqf* instruments described above, Aceh also practices *Galah* and *Mawah*, namely to pawn land and livestock. Both practices are currently widespread and customary in the region but not fully in line with sharia law and with no recordkeeping.

Another unique characteristic of Aceh that affects the application of Islamic social-public finance in the region is the distinct government structure that differs from the central government in Indonesia. Aceh applies a traditional administrative structure, where a *mukim* is situated between the regency and village administrative levels. The jurisdiction of traditional positions, such as *mukim*, is usually limited to implementing sharia law, including *zakat* obligations. The uniqueness of Aceh should be exploited to optimise cash *waqf* revenues and the utilisation of abandoned *waqf* assets.

7.4.3 Islamic Social-Public Finance Practices in Yogyakarta

In addition to Aceh, Yogyakarta is another region of Indonesia that has been accorded special autonomy status. Yogyakarta received special status due to its position as a sultanate when Indonesia unified, thus making Yogyakarta the only province in Indonesia that is managed through a combination of a sultanate system and Indonesian positive law. Furthermore, Yogyakarta is the only province of Indonesia ruled directly by its sultan as governor.

The Yogyakarta Sultanate has existed as a state since 1755, together with the Surakarta Sunanate, which split from the Mataram Sultanate, as one of the Islamic kingdoms in the Indonesian archipelago. History shows that both kingdoms, especially the Yogyakarta Sultanate, embraced the Islamic system. Furthermore, the use of "sultanate" also reflects the Islamic posture of the Yogyakarta Kingdom. In fact, ceremonies performed at the palace are based on Islamic culture, with a different taxonomy and methods considered unique, while not contravening sharia law. That is the basic rationale behind why Yogyakarta was selected as an object of study for the application of Islamic social-public finance in Indonesia.

Yogyakarta is the only active sultanate in Indonesia, with the culture permeating the daily lives of the local community. The sultan continues to maintain a strong influence over the Yogyakarta people, who also follow a sultanate state system. For example, if the Sultan is prosperous, the people will also prosper, and vice versa, if the Sultan experiences difficulties, the community will also suffer. The sense of belonging between the sultan and the people is very strong.

The level of local obedience in Yogyakarta to the sultan is also very high, as reflected by the will of the people to follow the instructions of the palace (*keraton*), including aspects of the economy.

The Islamic Sultanate of Yogyakarta and strong community culture to comply with the words of the sultan represent a solid entry point for sharia economic development in the province based on a top-down approach for greater efficacy. This is also supported by the powerful dual roles of the Sultan of Yogyakarta as head of state and head of government. In addition, the Sultan is supported by his Queen, as a beloved and important figurehead in the region. Yogyakarta, therefore, is a prime candidate to pioneer sharia economic practices due to its parallels with classical top-down Islamic leadership.

Islamic nuances in Yogyakarta are also reflected in the concept of urban planning, namely where the *keraton*, mosque, and market are situated in close proximity. This is the realisation of Islamic philosophy, stating that "the best places are mosques and worst are markets". In Islam, that is why the markets must be located adjacent to the mosque. On the other hand, similar examples demonstrate what happens when Islamic advice is unheeded. The fish market in Yogyakarta, which is devoid of visitors, is coincidentally located far from any mosque.

Land asset management in Yogyakarta is also noteworthy. Land in Yogyakarta that belongs to the Sultan is commonly referred to as Sultanate Ground or *Sultanaat Grond* (SG). Land ownership in Yogyakarta has conflicting definitions, however, with some statutes stating that all land in Yogyakarta is owned by the sultanate, yet other statutes stipulating that most (not all) land belongs to the sultanate.

Notwithstanding, anyone, particularly Yogyakarta residents, can utilise sultanate land by applying for a permit, which is represented and managed by Keraton Panitikismo. Fundamentally, the Palace will allow members of the community to use land for equitable welfare, such as trade, education, health, and so on, provided contract provisions are not violated and the tenant is prepared to return the land as required by the Palace. The specific contracts that stipulate land use rights are known as *Kekancingan*. Gadjah Mada University campus and Adi Sutjipto International Airport are examples of public (social) goods built on sultanate ground.

The land tenure concept applied by the *keraton* and the ease of land use by the community for welfare purposes are considered inherent components of an excellent system. Furthermore, the system prevents conglomerates from arbitrarily taking control of local assets, land in particular. The *keraton* is very firm on not allowing Indonesians or non-resident investors from owning land in Yogyakarta in accordance with Instruction of the Deputy Head of Yogyakarta Special Region Number K. 898/I/A/1975. The rationale is simple, to prevent excessive land conversion and ensure local land assets are utilised to the fullest extent for the benefits of all social strata in Yogyakarta. The policy also aims to protect land assets in the region and ensure agricultural sustainability.

The Sultanate Ground concept could theoretically replace the existing *waqf* land concept in Islam due to the various similarities. Consequently, the *waqf* nomenclature is rarely used in Yogyakarta. The *keraton* is not overly strict and allows the community to utilise land assets free of charge, providing the land is used for quality welfare in accordance with prevailing rules. This is considered a reward by the Sultan for himself and the *keraton*.

Though various policies of the Sultan have elicited a favourable public response and boosted equitable welfare, his kindness has also had negative development externalities in the region. By granting permits to use sultanate ground, local communities have been assisted economically, yet spatial and urban management has suffered in terms of neat and orderly urban planning. Street venders are free to trade on sultan ground, thus providing income, but clogging up pedestrian walkways and tarnishing the beauty of the city.

Financially, people in Yogyakarta, especially those in rural areas, tend to have less confidence in *Baitul Maal wat Tamwil* (BMT), which is also due to the institutional arrangements. There are currently around 130 BMT operating in Yogyakarta, yet inclusiveness and penetration remain low due to a lack of public literacy, even though 99% of local businesses are micro and small enterprises (MSEs). Notwithstanding, local people in Yogyakarta are active in the financial sector through communal institutions, such as the *arisan* community that provides savings and loan activities, often referred to as *selapanan*. This demonstrates how most social finance practices in Yogyakarta are informal yet continue to exist and remain sustainable.

In rural areas, communities implement a system of farmer contributions commonly referred to as "*uang tandur*". In addition, there is the practice of pinching (*jimpitan* or *jumputan*). Initially, pinching was applied to rice instruments, which has evolved in modernity into cash instruments. The contributions total at least Rp30,000 per neighbourhood association (*Rukun Tetangga—RT*) per evening, amassing approximately Rp700,000 per month. This is collected by the patrol officers and used to repair public goods. In addition to the *arisan* and *jimpitan* systems, vouchers are also used, primarily at Islamic boarding schools (*pesantren*), which prevents money from leaving that community or environment.

Reviewing the various examples of socio-public finance applications in Yogyakarta demonstrates that numerous alternative financial instruments exist in accordance with Islamic law.

7.4.4 Islamic Social-Public Finance Practices in Bandung

Representing West Java as another interesting area of Indonesia in terms of the discussion on how to manage Islamic social-public finance in Indonesia, Bandung is the capital of a region colloquially known as Tanah Pasundan or Priangan. Anthropologically, West Java is the most populous province of Indonesia. Economically, *Baitul Maal wat Tamwil* (BMT) emerged as a flagship of sharia economic development in Indonesia in the city of Bandung. BMT was first conceptualised and established in Bandung by activists from the Salman ITB Mosque in 1980 as the Technical Expertise Services Cooperative, which subsequently evolved into BMT in 1984.

According to Dr. Sofian Al Hakim, though the roots of Islam in East Java are considered stronger, the development of Islam in West Java has been rapid and diverse as a consequence of numerous Islamic groups, as reflected by the existence of various Islamic community organisations (*ormas*) in the province, particularly in Bandung. In fact, the local adage "if not Islam, then not Sundanese and, vice versa, if not Sundanese, then not Islam" is popular in the region. It is interesting to note, however, that the origins of the Sundanese Kingdom are rooted in Hinduism, not Islam, yet the arrival of Islam quickly usurped Hinduism amongst local tribes. Notwithstanding, differences emerged in the development of Islam between different regions of West Java. For example, elements of the kingdom are much stronger in the eastern part of West Java. Consequently, development of the Islamic economy and finance in Bandung can differ in approach quite significantly.

In one area of West Java there remains the Forbidden Kingdom of Sumedang, which has existed since the sixteenth century, in 1585, after separating from the Cirebon Sultanate. The Forbidden Kingdom of Sumedang is endowed with large swathes of royal land, yet ineffective land management has undermined a propitious impact on the welfare of local people. The royal land has been subdivided and a servant is responsible for managing 100 plots. This is a much less desirable condition compared with land asset management under the Ngayogyakarta Hadiningrat Sultanate, where sultanate ground is utilised for the welfare of the local people. The Forbidden Kingdom of Sumedang declared itself an Islamic sultanate, so asset management practices must be in accordance with sharia principles, such as the *waqf* asset management system.

In general, the current model for developing religious practices in West Java is heavily influenced by the past. For example, legacy issues from the Bubat War fought between the Pasundan and Majapahit Kingdoms continue to influence the Sundanese and Javanese peoples, leading to different religious practices in West Java and East Java.

Another characteristic of Islamic practices in West Java is that the level of piety tends to be more neutral, relatively fluid, and not fixed or centralised around one ulema. Muslims in West Java encapsulate modern Islam, especially in and around Bandung. This is reflected in the individualistic nature of the *zakat* payment model. The people of West Java, especially Bandung, prioritise rationality and modernity in terms of *zakat* payments. Initially, when only one BAZNAS was operating as an institution to collect *zakat* funds, for example, there was massive public mistrust because BAZNAS represented the government. When private institutions, such as Dompet Dhuafa and Rumah Zakat, entered the space, however, local communities began to entrust their *zakat* payments to such institutions based on rationality and modernity.

The rationale of some communities in West Java, especially in the city of Bandung, in terms of paying *zakat* is quite reasonable. During discussions with academics at a university in Bandung, a book was mentioned that discusses the efficiency of *zakat* management organisations, stating that various *zakat* institutions prioritise the empowerment of their own managers rather than the seven other *asnaf*. In addition, student field work also showed that *amil zakat* institutions were not professional, thus eroding public confidence in terms of paying *zakat* obligations to formal institutions.

At the institutional level, the application of Islamic social-public finance policies differs significantly depending upon the respective leadership. In West Java during the reign of Governor Ahmad Heryawan, for example, Muslim employees of the West Java Provincial Government had *zakat* obligations deducted at source from their government remuneration. Practices at the regency/city administrative level may differ, however. In addition, common practices at the university level are also quite different, including Padjadjaran University (UNPAD), which was established as a Sundanese and Islamic university. Nonetheless, policies relating to Islam tend to cause conflict, such as paying *zakat* to the *zakat* management organisation founded by UNPAD itself, where the number of payers is comparatively few.

7.4.5 Islamic Social-Public Finance Practices in Surabaya

The province of East Java, with Surabaya as the capital city, is another region of Indonesia with a large Muslim population. Islam in the province is very strong due to deep roots, with various institutional Islamic centres located in East Java, including educational institutions such as Islamic boarding schools (*pesantren*). East Java has the highest number of *pesantren* of any Indonesian province, totalling 6561 in 2013 and 1,040,391 human resources, including students (*santri*) and teachers (*ustadz*). Several *pesantren* in the region are very familiar in the Muslim community in Indonesia, namely Pondok Modern Darussalam Gontor, Pondok Pesantren Tebuireng, Pondok Pesantren Lirboyo, and Pondok Pesantren Sidogiri.

Pondok Pesantren Sidogiri is known for teaching its students to become entrepreneurs and engage in economic activity.

Islam is strong in East Java due inextricably to historical factors. In general, it is widely documented how Islam entered the Indonesian archipelago through trade routes with the Middle East. Middle Eastern Muslim traders are thought to have first entered Indonesia through East Java. Strong Islamic culture in the province was also influenced by five of the nine Wali Songo saints (propagators), who arrived and played decisive roles in the propagation of Islam in East Java, namely Sunan Ampel in Surabaya, Sunan Gresik in Gresik, Sunan Giri in Gresik, Sunan Drajat in Lamongan, and Sunan Bonan in Tuban.

A strong Islamic presence in East Java as the centre of Islamic proselytisation and propagation has raised the local level of Muslim understanding concerning Islamic teachings. This also extends to correct and appropriate Islamic social-public finance practices. Indeed, religious practices, including Islamic finance in East Java, have moved beyond the basic to enter the realm of innovation.

Although Muslims in East Java are considered to have innovated Islamic economic practices, including social-public finance, the strength of such practices actually emerged from the community itself and tends to lack integration. This has profound implications on the number of sharia financial institutions in East Java, including *Baitul Maal wat Tamwil* (BMT) and *zakat* management organisations. East Java is home to one of the highest numbers of BMT in Indonesia. In terms of *zakat* management organisations, the presence is at least commensurate with the amount of *pesantren* in the region that manage their own ZISWAF funds, thus making it easier for students to pay.

References

Fauzia, A. (2003). *Berderma untuk Semua, CSRC dan Ford Foundation*. Teraju Mizan.

May, S. (2018). *The best of deeds: The practice of zakat in the UK*. Journal of Church and State, 034.

Sulaiman, S., & Hasan, A. (2016). *Strategi Pembangunan dan Pelaburan Wakaf secara Lestari Menurut Perspektif Islam*. Jurnal Kanun.

Chapter 8
Islamic Monetary Economic Thought

8.1 Introduction

Economic management demands a series of optimal and measured policies to maintain macroeconomic stability. Among others, this is reflected in the control of several macroeconomic variables, such as the prices of goods and services, job availability, and unemployment as well as economic activity as a proxy of economic growth. Experience has shown that economic variables often perform uncontrollably in response to unforeseen economic shocks, changes in economic structure, or changes in terms of government policy, which can have a detrimental effect on the economy as a whole. The consequence of uncontrolled money supply, for instance, would undermine the performance of other major economic variables, namely production (output), prices, and exchange rates. Through synergic economic policies, therefore, a well-managed and integrated economic system provides a solid foundation to maintain economic stability and help optimise the utilisation of economic resources.

Seeking to deepen our comprehension of the view outlined above, it is essential to understand how the foundation of an economy works. As has been established, the economy comprises financial sector and real sector dynamics. In addition, the economy involves economic actors consisting of individuals and institutions, both public and private. In an open economy setting, there are cross-border interactions between economic actors in different countries. In general, there are four main actors integrated in the economy as determinants of income creation and expenditure, namely households, the government, firms, and the external sector. In the circular flow of funds as income and expenditure, corporate use of production inputs will channel income to households in the form of salaries/wages, rent, interest, and profit. Households subsequently use this income to meet their needs for goods and services, as produced by the corporate sector. In addition to consuming goods and services, households also pay income tax to the government. Therefore, households, firms, and the government can then purchase (import) goods and services from abroad. In

S. M. Juhro et al., *Inclusive Welfare*, https://doi.org/10.1007/978-981-96-0051-9_8

terms of production activity, a firm will import goods and services from abroad for investment purposes and to expand production capacity. In addition, firms also export domestic goods and services to the international market.

Despite a sectoral dichotomy between the financial and real sectors in contemporary economic practices, both must reach equilibrium, known in Keynesian economics as general equilibrium theory (Mankiw, 2009). The real sector incorporates the management of such matters as the production and distribution of goods and services. More broadly, the real sector is a productive economic sector where goods and services are produced and trade is facilitated. The real sector is influenced by two main markets, namely the market for factors of production (inputs) and the market for goods/services (outputs). Factor markets allocate factors of production, including raw materials, workers, capital, and natural resources. Output markets, on the other hand, produce goods and services for distribution to consumers, such as agricultural and manufacturing products as well as services. The outputs produced will generate value added in the economy, which reflects Gross Domestic Product (GDP). In addition, the real sector also encompasses pricing, including consumer prices, production factor prices and wages. Meanwhile, the financial sector includes the procurement of financial products and services through intermediation mechanisms. Similar to the real sector, there is also a balance between the supply and demand of financial products and services in the financial sector, comprising banking, insurance, pension funds, capital markets, microfinance, pawnshops, and such like. The financial sector plays a critical role in an economy as a key driver of the real sector through the accumulation of funds and technology. This dynamic interaction can be illustrated by the flow of income and expenditure in an economy as follows (Fig. 8.1):

Irrespective of whether there is a sectoral dichotomy between the financial and real sectors as well as the potential for achieving general equilibrium, the dynamics of economic development will continue regardless and become increasingly difficult to predict. In fact, rapid financial sector development is accompanied by potential instability. Such conditions, among others, underlie government and monetary authority efforts to maintain economic stability by controlling the main economic variables, such as money supply and interest rates. Therefore, these are the objects of discussion in this and subsequent chapters.

8.2 General Economic Equilibrium and IS-LM

General equilibrium theory attempts to explain the interactions between several markets in such a way that the overall economy is in equilibrium. The theory postulates that excess supply in one market must be matched or balanced by excess demand in another market, and vice versa. In other words, when three of four interacting markets have reached equilibrium point, the fourth market must also achieve equilibrium, which is generally known as Walras's Law. General equilibrium theory has been analysed rigorously, perhaps most famously by John Hicks and

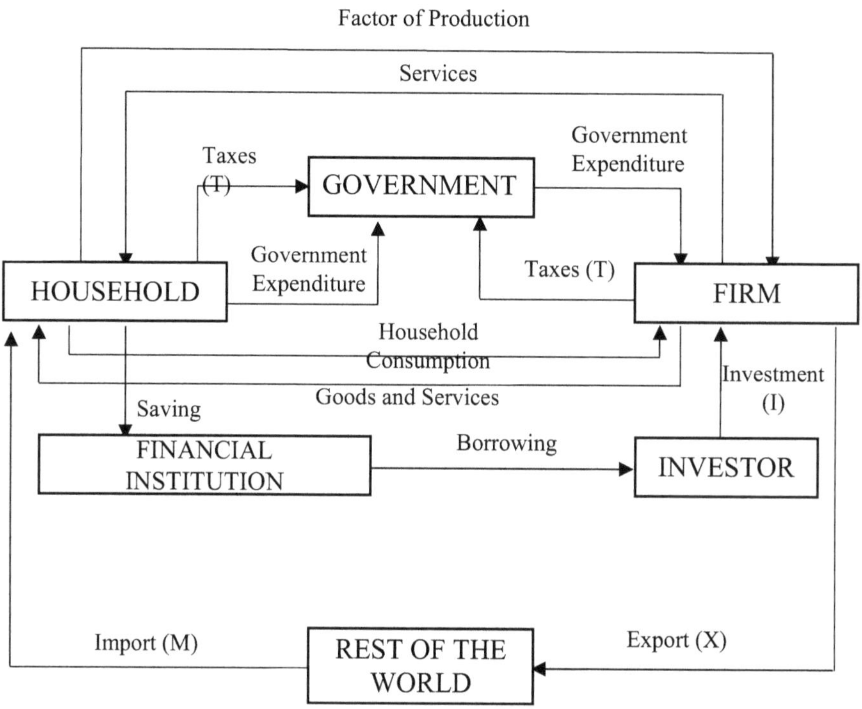

Fig. 8.1 Flow of income and expenditure. Source: Mankiw (2009)

Alvin Hansen through the Classical-Keynesian synthesis model to analyse equilibria in the goods market and money market (IS-LM), as reflected by the interaction between interest rates and real output in the goods/services market and money market (Gordon, 2009; Mankiw, 2009).

Keynesian economics, which embraces the conventional economic flow, formulates the relationship between the money markets and goods/services market in general equilibrium theory. General equilibrium describes the meeting point or intersection between the real sector and financial sector, as indicated by the interest rate, as the aggregate with the strongest influence when determining equilibrium. Macroeconomic general equilibrium applies the IS-LM concept. The IS (investment-savings) concept explains conditions in the real sector, while the LM (liquidity of money) concept describes conditions in the financial (monetary) sector. Ultimately, the IS-LM concept is used to reduce the equilibrium of aggregate supply and demand in an economy.

The economy's equilibrium simultaneously determined at the intersection of the IS curve and the LM curve, where both the goods and services market and financial market are in equilibrium. If goods and services market is out of the equilibrium and involuntary inventory decumulation or accumulation occurs, firms will step up or cut production and pushing the economy in the direction needed to reach the equilibrium. If the financial sector (money market) is out of equilibrium, there will be pressure to adjust interest rates. Regardless, the economy arrives at the equilibrium (Gordon, 2009).

In the IS concept, equilibrium in the real sector illustrates the equation between national income (Y) and aggregate expenditure (AE), which can be expressed as follows:

$$AE = C + I + G + (X - M) \tag{5.1}$$

Where Y is the national income, AE is the aggregate expenditure, C is the consumption (investment), G is the government, X is total exports, and M is total imports. As the aggregate expenditure component is influenced by income, interest rates, and other factors, equilibrium in the goods/services market can be expressed as follows:

$$Y = AE(Y, i, Z) \tag{13.2}$$

Where i is the interest rate, and Z is the vector of determinants of aggregate expenditure. Since interest rates are inversely correlated with aggregate expenditure, the point (Y, i) forms the equilibrium point of the goods/services market, namely the IS curve has a downward (negative) slope.

Meanwhile, the concept of LM equilibrium in the financial sector is expressed as follows:

$$Ms = Md \tag{13.3}$$

Where Ms and Md can be expressed as follows:

$$Ms = M_0 \tag{13.4}$$

$$Md = kY - hi \tag{13.5}$$

Based on Eqs. (13.3) and (13.4), Y can be expressed as follows:

$$Y = \frac{M_0}{k} + \frac{h}{k}i \tag{13.6}$$

Where:

Md	Money demand
Ms	Money supply
Mo	Autonomous money supply
k	Elasticity of money demand to national income
h	Elasticity of money demand to interest rates
i:	Interest rate

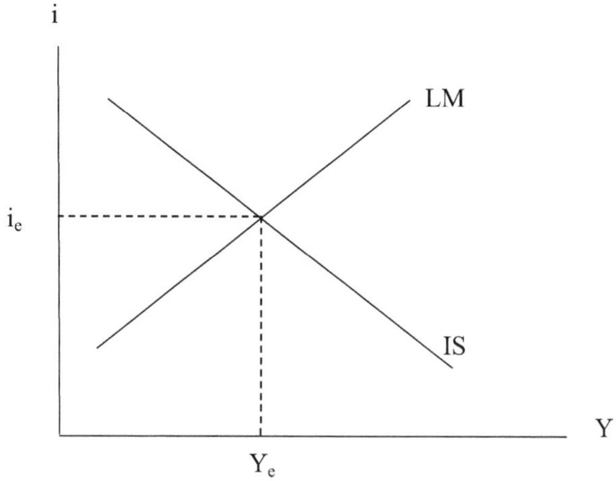

Fig. 8.2 General equilibrium curve. Source: Mankiw (2009)

From Eq. (13.6), the LM curve is observed to have an upward (positive) slope. The general equilibrium concept is illustrated in Fig. 8.2 as follows:

Based on the IS-LM concept, the equilibrium point between the money market and goods/services market is formed at the intersection of the IS and LM curves. At all other points, interest rates or national income will be adjusted to create balance between the two markets. In other words, interest rates play an important role in connecting the money market and goods/services market, where a shift in factors influences the money market and, therefore, interest rates are transmitted to the real sector.

With the focus in financial markets centred on interest rates, the goods/services market must also use the interest rate as a price indicator to ensure balance between the goods/services market and financial markets can be achieved. Notwithstanding, there is ambiguity concerning the definition of interest rates used in the two different markets. Consequently, conventional economists Joseph E. Stiglitz and Bruce Greenwald formulated a new theory to correct the previous general equilibrium theory.

Stiglitz and Greenwald redefined general equilibrium focusing on the supply and demand of credit or loanable funds. Thus, the equilibrium price formed is the lending rate. As a result, it is necessary to understand the important role of commercial banks here because interest rates in the loan market cannot be assumed to find a balance with the level of interaction between supply and demand of credit. There is a risk of bad credit, therefore, due to business failure or inaccurate lending by the banks. Hence, banks take on the role of risk-averse parties to minimise the risk of bad loans and maintain public trust in banks as intermediary institutions.

In addition, according to Stiglitz and Greenwald, in a situation of market imbalances due to high demand for credit, market imperfections, asymmetric information, and moral hazard measures will compel banks to pursue credit rationing. Under such conditions, the equilibrium interest rate represents the lending rate and expected

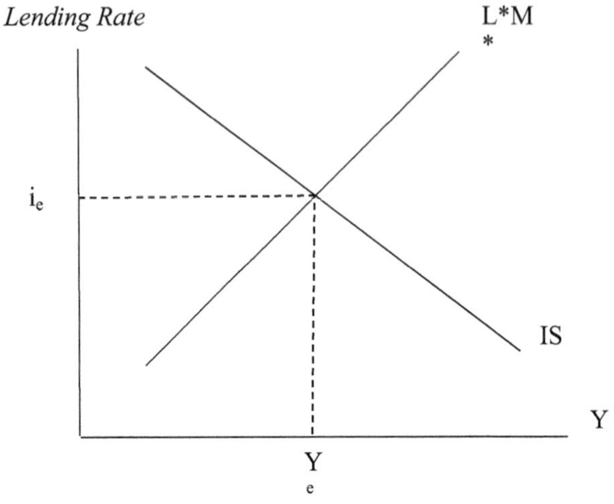

Fig. 8.3 General equilibrium by Stiglitz and Greenwald. Source: Stiglitz and Greenwald (2003)

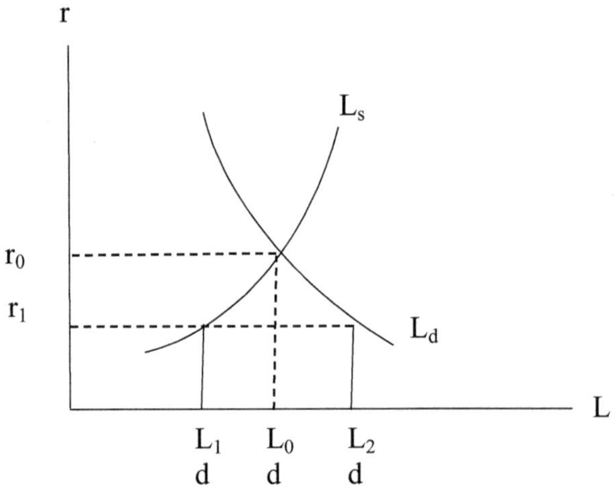

Fig. 8.4 General equilibrium of credit/lending market with credit rationing. Source: Warjiyo and Juhro (2019)

return. The general equilibrium curve developed by Stiglitz and Greenwald is illustrated in Fig. 8.3 as follows:

With credit rationing, general equilibrium in the credit/lending market can be illustrated as follows:

Where *r* is the interest rate and *L* is loanable funds or credit. The condition depicted in Fig. 8.4 illustrates a situation in which credit equilibrium has not been reached at the intersection between credit demand and supply (r_0,L_0), yet is achieved when demand for credit exceeds the supply of credit (r_1,L_2). Thus, the credit rationing that occurs is equivalent to $L_2 - L_1$.

In addition to credit rationing, there is also adverse selection bias in the lending, which occurs because banks may offer interest rates below the average rate for certain customers. Figure 8.5 describes the optimal interest rate offered by the banks.

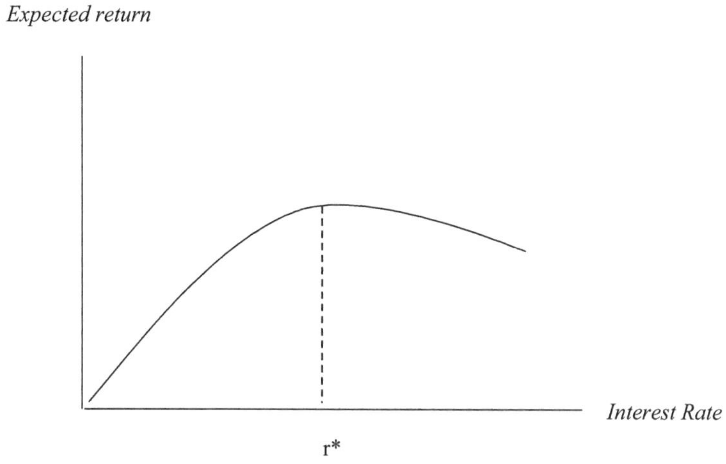

Fig. 8.5 Expected return and optimal interest rate. Source: Warjiyo and Juhro (2019)

The expected return is more rigid than lending rates (as shown in Fig. 8.5). At some point, however, the expected return will decrease. The optimal bank lending rate is formed, therefore, when the expected return reaches the maximum level, namely at a point just before the expected return decreases.

The model developed by Stiglitz and Greenwald was successful in correcting ambiguity in the interest rate variable as applied in the classical general equilibrium theory. Notwithstanding, the model cannot explain or define the nature of general equilibrium between the real sector and monetary sector. The model only explains equilibrium between the goods/services market and the credit market (not the financial market), which is insufficient to explain the overall economic condition.

8.3 Market Imperfection and Financial Instability

8.3.1 Market Imperfection

Market imperfection is a market characteristic that prevents economic agents from making optimal decisions. Market imperfections affect transactions and price formation in the market as a whole in various ways, such as by increasing transaction costs, influencing rational decisions by individuals, and creating asymmetric information in the market. Market imperfections can be defined as anything that can interfere with trade activity in the market. This can be observed from two perspectives. First, imperfections disrupt the rational behaviour of market participants. Second, the resultant market behaviour that deviates from the risks associated with the decision. Market imperfection is a phenomenon that continues to evolve over time, despite never reaching zero, implying that market imperfections will always exist.

On the other hand, however, market imperfections can provide profitable opportunities for entrepreneurs who successfully mitigate the associated risks, thereby achieving competitive advantage. Market imperfection, therefore, presents a challenge and an opportunity for entrepreneurs. Consequently, entrepreneurs must have the ability to identify and address the issues and problems relating to their business in terms of market imperfection (DeGennaro, 2005).

Why is market imperfection a phenomenon of such considerable concern? Market imperfections can increase transaction costs. By understanding the phenomenon of market imperfection, entrepreneurs can also understand the total transaction cost required to build and run a business. In addition, business players can maximise their allocation of funds based on priority and determine the most optimal business strategies. Furthermore, market imperfections also create business opportunities for entrepreneurs who can reduce the costs arising from such imperfections, thus achieving competitive advantage over other business players.

Market imperfection is an inexorable phenomenon that constantly changes over time. The level of market imperfection varies considerably as new imperfections arise and other imperfections can be overcome and eliminated. Examples of market imperfection include tax rates, asymmetric information, and moral hazard.

The tax rates levied on market participants have changed over time both in terms of the magnitude and types of tax. Meanwhile, information asymmetry largely stems from the rapid development of technology. Oftentimes, asymmetric information is overcome by utilising more sophisticated technology, big data management and utilisation in particular. In financial intermediaries, moral hazard explicitly forces lenders to be selective in terms of prospective borrowers. Moreover, lenders are risk averse and such conditions lead to the phenomenon of credit rationing, which presents a challenge itself for lenders (for example, banks). Notwithstanding, the use of technology and data processing can minimise such challenges.

Market imperfection is also a product of market structure, and market structure is affected by the risks facing market participants and the volume of trade transactions in the market. An ever-increasing volume of trade transactions will alter the market structure. Therefore, risk and trade volume are factors of market imperfection. Higher risk faced by market participants implies a higher degree of market imperfection and a larger trade volume also implies a higher degree of market imperfection.

8.3.2 *Financial Instability*

Financial instability encompasses anything that can disrupt the financial system and flow of information in financial markets, ultimately impacting investment stability in a country and thus undermining economic growth. Financial system stability is a critical issue that demands attention because it reflects the overall effectiveness of micro and macroeconomic performance. Shocks that occur in the financial system will impact economic balance, particularly in developing economies. The impact most felt in developing economies is when supply cannot meet high domestic demand, thus raising the prices of goods. In addition, national debt will increase along with capital outflow (Ekmekcioglu, 2012). Financial instability contains unsystematic risk and this condition is the ultimate culmination of the financial crisis phenomenon.

The phenomenon of financial instability has been explored in depth by Minsky (1992) in a theory known as The Financial Instability Hypothesis. Minsky's view is rooted in the basic concept that the capitalist system has the potential for instability. When the dominant actors in an economy are more prudent, the economy tends to move towards a better equilibrium point. Conversely, if the dominant actors are speculative or even Ponzi in nature, economic instability will ensue along with recession and crisis.

Financial system stability must be maintained because the financial system is the driving force of the real sector by providing funds for real sector needs. Consequently, financial system disruptions can spill over into the real sector as a corollary of the financial sector's inability to fund investment and other productive efforts in the real sector.

Indicators of disruptions or shocks in the financial system can be explained as follows. First, high market volatility caused by tighter market liquidity and suboptimal market infrastructure. Second, financial assets that are not utilised in accordance with their fundamentals. Third, higher non-performing loans, both domestically and abroad. And fourth, an increase in demand coupled with a decrease in supply. These indicators can be analysed to identify whether a country's financial system is experiencing instability.

Given that the impact can be debilitating, it is important to avoid and minimise shocks in the financial system by knowing and understanding which factors can lead to financial instability as follows:

(a) *Higher interest rates*. Increasing interest rates appear to risk the financial stability at present (Gros, 2018). Even a moderate shock in the financial system would disrupt credit transactions in the economy, as reflected by a decline in funds used for business loans or financing in the real sector. This would lead to higher interest rates that increase the probability of default among certain borrowers. Consequently, lending institutions tighten lending standards and become more selective when disbursing loans to contain the risk of default. The global financial crisis in 2007–2009 is the example of higher interest rate to financial instability.
(b) *Increasing financial uncertainty*. Financial markets must be monitored and supervised regularly to avoid elevated financial uncertainty. This is a natural phenomenon considering that the economy continues to develop and evolve over time, entailing a commensurate evolution in the framework and policies developed in line with current conditions and expectations of future conditions. Furthermore, technological development and innovation in the financial sector

have facilitated new uncertainty models in both developing and advanced economies (Smith, 2011). Notwithstanding, increasingly complex uncertainty issues also increase potential financial system instability in the markets, with uncertainty undermining lending as lenders refuse to lend to borrowers with uncertainty risk moving forward. Less lending implies less investment.

(c) *Deteriorating balance sheet performance of financial institutions.* Financial institutions have several ways to overcome difficulties in terms of raising sufficient funds to meet lending needs. Lending rates can be raised to reduce demand for loans and funds can be raised through third-party funds (deposits). This may be difficult, however, because capital is more expensive than third-party funds. Consequently, the balance sheet will deteriorate and potentially become unstable, thereby interfering with lending and investment activities and ultimately moderating economic growth. Shocks to banks' balance sheets reduce their capacity to hold aggregate risks and contracts the supply of loans. It implies a bigger increase in the loan rate, as the one happened in the recession in 2008 (Villacorta, 2018).

(d) *Deteriorating balance sheet performance in the non-financial sector.* The non-financial sector encompasses individuals, households, and firms as borrowers. As a factor of financial instability, borrowers contribute to higher interest rates in response to higher demand for loanable funds accompanied by a lack of such funds from the lender. During periods of high lending rates, borrowers have the option to avoid the loan if the lending rate is not appropriate. Subsequently, this erodes cash flow on the balance sheet of financial institutions (Canuto & Giugale, 2010). In addition, collateral (guarantees) in lending and borrowing transactions can also influence market stability because a guarantee will reduce the value of the lender's assets if a borrower defaults on the loan. In the event of a default, the lender will sell the guaranteed assets in lieu of the unpaid funds. Often, however, the price of such assets decreases, which further impacts the balance sheet and precipitates financial instability.

Furthermore, loans are not based on real assets in the conventional economy, instead applying interest rate mechanisms. If such loans exceed actual demand in the real sector, the level of output will decrease (Askari et al., 2010). If such conditions persist, financial instability will materialise. It can be understood that interest-based credit transactions contain high enough risks to trigger financial instability. It is necessary, therefore, to consider mechanisms in the Islamic economic system (which absolutely forbids interest or *riba*) to maintain financial system stability. In addition, there is an important role for policymakers to formulate appropriate policies to minimise such risks.

Financial instability in the practices of financial institutions that apply interest-bearing instruments, including conventional banks, is an endogenous phenomenon. In other words, interest rates themselves are a cause of financial instability. Furthermore, expectations of high returns with low interest rates can create a speculative credit boom phenomenon, followed sooner or later by bank failures. Even the existence of a central bank cannot reduce the risk of instability inherent to conventional banks. On the other hand, a central bank could exacerbate the risk of financial instability when using interest-bearing instruments or instituting expansionary policies that boost aggregate demand yet fail to prompt a commensurate increase in aggregate supply. In addition, the interest rate mechanism creates an avenue for speculators to speculate on interest rate fluctuations in financial markets, further contributing to financial instability (Askari et al., 2010). Consequently, the monetary authority plays an important role in harmonising the real and financial sectors to maintain financial stability and avoid sources of financial instability.

The key to avoiding financial instability is to position the real sector as the central focus of the economy, with the financial sector playing a supporting role in terms of providing funds for transaction activity in the real sector. This principle is central to the Islamic economy and finance and, therefore, it is important to consider optimising Islamic economic and financial practices towards achieving financial stability. In addition, policy support from the monetary authority is also required not only to regulate money supply from a financial sector perspective, yet also to regulate how funds in the financial sector can flow to the real sector in their entirety and boost the productivity of goods and services. This will minimise or even eliminate financial instability risk. Furthermore, because the real sector cooperates well with the financial sector, the prices formed are more stable and national output can increase.

The Islamic financial system tends to be more stable through the application of Islamic principles and sharia law orientated towards achieving quality justice and welfare (*falah*) socio-economically, economic efficiency as well as robust and stable economic growth. Therefore, all the mechanisms and methods applied are inextricably linked to that goal. Moreover, the Islamic financial system facilitates social financial mechanisms, such as *zakat*, which can ameliorate justice and the equitable distribution of income. Meanwhile, *zakat* also eliminates miserliness and greed and promotes economic behaviour that is not only profit-oriented. In addition, the Islamic financial system is based on equity (not liability), meaning that Islamic financial institutions own real assets and participate in real sector activity. Consequently, growth and development of the Islamic financial sector are determined by the real sector and not by the disbursement of loans (Askari et al., 2010). Therefore, application of the Islamic financial system can lead to the efficient allocation of resources, robust and stable economic growth, greater job availability, and maintained financial stability.

8.4 Balance in the Islamic Economy

According to Islamic economists, in addition to the absolute prohibition of *riba*, the Keynesian theory of general equilibrium also demonstrates inconsistencies. The definitions of interest rate variables as used in the IS and LM concept are not aligned because there are several types of interest rate in the economy, including lending rates and deposit rates. Theoretically, equilibrium in the real market is reflected through the IS curve using lending rates as a determinant of investment. On the LM side, however, deposit rates are used as a determinant of private motivation to hold or deposit cash in the bank as savings.

Thus, the types of interest rate used between the IS and LM curves lack parity. How can the two be related, or even intersect, if the types of variables used are different? It can be concluded, therefore, that general equilibrium between the real sector and monetary sector as described through general equilibrium theory is impossible. Even if the interest rate is assumed, it would still be irrelevant because it cannot explain the equilibrium phenomenon. In addition, the interest rate is not an appropriate economic variable because of its inconsistent function in explaining real and monetary sector equilibrium. In fact, interest rates make it increasingly difficult to successfully achieve balance between the monetary and real sectors in the economy.

Interest rates that act as the equilibrium price in an economy are the main cause of money creation that widens the gap between the real sector (goods/services market) and the financial sector (financial market). Using interest rates, the amount of money in the financial market will continue to increase beyond the ability of the goods/services market to absorb money. Consequently, transacting in the financial market is more attractive than the goods/services market. Ultimately, money that should be absorbed by the real sector is increasingly channelled to the financial sector, thus making it difficult to achieve balance between the real sector and financial sector. How can general equilibrium be achieved between the two sectors if the indicator variable is the interest rate when it is precisely the interest rate that causes imbalances between the financial and real sectors?

The theory developed by Stiglitz and Greenwald has failed to address several fundamental questions regarding general equilibrium between the real and monetary sectors. According to Sakti (2007), the questions include: (1) does general equilibrium between financial markets and goods/services markets actually exist or can it be achieved? (2) what exactly is the general equilibrium condition? (3) what is the general equilibrium transmission process? and (4) which kind of policies could encourage economic transition towards a state of equilibrium? Which economic assumption states that real and monetary sector equilibrium is the optimal condition for an economy?

According to Islamic economists, general equilibrium theory has become irrelevant for several salient reasons. First, there is no sectoral separation between the financial sector and the real sector in the Islamic economy. Islamic economics states that the real sector is the core of the economy, with the financial sector supporting the real sector. The financial sector cannot develop by itself without commensurate real sector expansion. Economic performance is gauged by real sector growth. Second, interest rates are considered *riba* under Islamic law and absolutely forbidden (*haram*). According to Islamic economists, therefore, IS-LM analysis should no longer use the interest rate variable, replaced instead by a monetary mechanism based on profit and loss sharing (PLS).

Financial market fluctuations as described by classical equilibrium theory or the general equilibrium theory developed by Stiglitz and Greenwald fail to fully depict actual economic performance due to separation between the real and financial sectors, implying the economy is not centred on the real sector. Moreover, interest leads to excess money creation and money concentration. These phenomena occur when interest rates readily facilitate money creation, which is concentrated in the hands of a few. If allowed to persist, this situation could damage the financial system and sustainable economic growth in the long term.

While interest rates and speculative practices are permitted within an economic framework, inflation and financial crises are inevitable. Although authorities continue to develop and implement various policy innovations, the overarching problems cannot be resolved. Policy innovation is just one part of efforts to minimise the damage. The Islamic economic system exists, therefore, to remedy the "diseases" afflicting the current economic system.

Additionally, conventional general equilibrium theory is plagued by several weaknesses beyond the *haram* status of *riba* as follows:

(a) The benchmark interest rate is determined by the monetary authority, yet for general equilibrium the rate should follow market interactions.
(b) The use of interest rates in the goods/services market and the monetary market tends to differ. The lending rate is used in the goods/services market, while the deposit rate is used in the monetary market. In theory, however, the lending rate will not reach equilibrium with the deposit rate. Consequently, the reliability of the equilibrium rate to be achieved in general equilibrium theory is questionable.
(c) Using both lending and deposit rates will incur economic losses. Lending rates will hinder the distribution of money to the goods/services market, while deposit rates can lead to a concentration of money in the monetary sector.
(d) The conventional general equilibrium model does not reflect actual market interactions because the application of interest rates encourages money creation and money concentration.

Within the Islamic monetary economic framework, the real sector is the primary focus. Moreover, total money supply is not the main concern, rather the distribution of money and other resources. Therefore, all apparatus in the Islamic monetary economy, encompassing the authorities, instruments, and policies, function to improve the orderly and equitable distribution of economic resources to all social strata.

Within the Islamic economy, the monetary sector manages the amount of currency in circulation, while regulating the mechanisms to finance real sector production. Hence, the monetary sector supports the real sector, the regulation of which is mandated to the state or monetary authority. Therefore, the state or monetary authority can transfer surplus money in the economy to the real sector as required. In addition, the monetary sector according to Islamic economics is not adorned with interest rates, instead preferring a profit-sharing mechanism, which is certainly more in line with business conditions in the real sector as it is based on actual profit. Such mechanisms help to uphold the value of justice in an economy and, ultimately, contribute to economic stability as a solid economic foundation.

The value of balance in Islam is an inherent part of human nature in every aspect of life, including the economy. This is written in Al-Qur'an, verse 3 of surah Al-Mulk as follows:

الَّذِيْ خَلَقَ سَبْعَ سَمٰوٰتٍ طِبَاقًاۗ مَا تَرٰى فِيْ خَلْقِ الرَّحْمٰنِ مِنْ تَفٰوُتٍۗ فَارْجِعِ الْبَصَرَۙ هَلْ تَرٰى مِنْ فُطُوْرٍ

> [And] who created seven heavens in layers. You do not see in the creation of the Most Merciful any inconsistency. So return [your] vision [to the sky]; do you see any breaks? (Al-Mulk [67]: 3)

Life in nature has been arranged naturally in such a way that balance or homeostasis is achieved. Humans themselves, however, create imbalances. In terms of economic life, humans tend to have a greater desire to prosper, thus justifying any means necessary to succeed.

Economically, it is important to achieve a balance between supply and demand. Interactions between the two occur within market mechanisms, thus creating an indicator of balance, namely prices. The prices formed can then accurately depict the condition of economic equilibrium.

Islamic economics recognises two primary markets, namely the goods/services market and the labour market. In the goods/services market, there is interaction between the supply and demand of goods and services. Factors that influence consumer demand include income, preferences, and the amount of *zakat* distributed, while the factors influencing supply from producers are the prices of input goods and the use of technology. The supply and demand curves can be illustrated as follows (Fig. 8.6).

The law of demand (D) states that the quantity purchased varies inversely with price. In other words, the higher the price, the lower the quantity demanded. Thus, the demand curve follows a negative slope. In contrast, the law of supply (S) produces a positive slope, implying that as prices increase, the quantity that

Fig. 8.6 Supply and demand curves for goods/services. Source: Lipsey (1999)

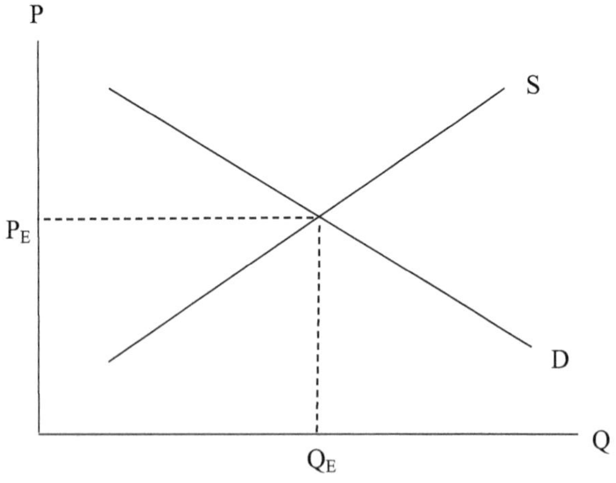

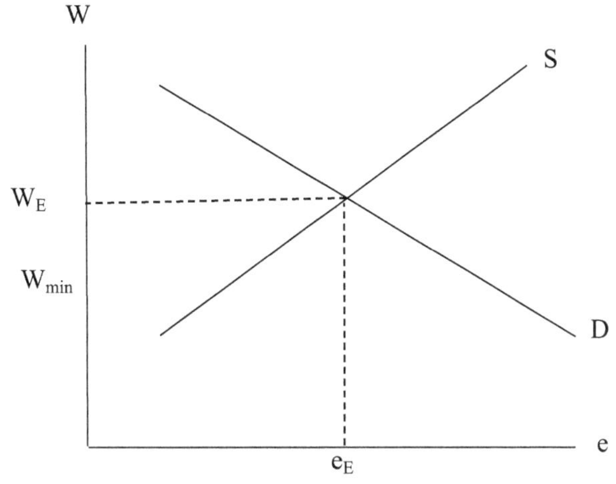

Fig. 8.7 Labour Market Equilibrium curve. Source: Mankiw (2009)

suppliers offer will also increase. The interaction between supply and demand will then form the equilibrium price (P_E) of goods and services in the market. The prices formed will reflect the value of justice achieved in society and the equilibrium quantity of goods and services (Q_E).

Demand for labour (D) will vary inversely with the wage rate because wages, as the price of labour, are a cost of production. Higher wages imply higher production costs. Consequently, corporate demand for labour is compressed to avoid higher production costs. Meanwhile, supply of labour (S) is directly proportional to the wage rate because higher wages attract more workers from the household sector. Therefore, interaction between the demand and supply forces of labour will form the equilibrium wage rate (W_E) and labour equilibrium (e_E). Interaction between the supply and demand of labour will occur when the equilibrium wage rate is at least equal or greater than the minimum wage (W_{min}). Thus, the minimum wage is the lower threshold for individuals to engage in the labour market (Fig. 8.7).

In the Islamic economy, there is a relationship between a decent wage rate and an instrument of Islamic social finance, namely *zakat. Zakat* distribution is a crucial indicator. Ideally, effective and maximal *zakat* distribution will raise the living wage to the same point or beyond the minimum living standards of the community. Consequently, members of the community, especially *mustahik*, are motivated to work rather than merely receive *zakat*, even though *zakat* funds could meet minimum living standards. This will also motivate the *mustahik* to elevate themselves towards a higher standard of living, thus advancing from the *mustahik* predicate.

Economic equilibrium in Islam differs from conventional general equilibrium theory hitherto understood. Several aspects are forbidden in Islam, including *riba, maysir*, and *gharar*. Therefore, general equilibrium indicators in Islam (including market mechanisms) are also different to conventional economic indicators.

Economic equilibrium in Islam focuses more on balance in the real sector as the core of the Islamic economy. Real sector equilibrium is formed through pure interaction between supply and demand in the goods/services market. This does not imply, however, that Islamic economics does not recognise the financial sector. Islam ascribes the financial or monetary sector a supporting role as a driver of real sector activity. According to Islamic economics, the financial sector plays a role in managing money supply as regulated by the monetary regulator. In addition, the financial sector is also reflected in investment activity, yet investment is tied directly to the real sector.

In Islam, the real sector and financial sector are considered disparate. Moreover, the financial sector cannot be compared or contrasted with the real sector as is the case with the conventional economy. The mechanism to establish general equilibrium in the Islamic economy, therefore, does not link the real sector with the monetary sector. Economic equilibrium in Islam is achieved through the interaction of supply and demand in the real sector.

The economy in Islam is broadly defined by interactions in the real goods/ services market. Thus, general equilibrium in Islam is understood in terms of a single sector, namely the real sector, unlike conventional equilibrium that is determined by two sectors, namely the real sector and monetary sector.

The success of an economic system can be reflected in the realisation of economic equilibrium in harmony with socio-economic development and quality welfare in the community. The plethora of issues currently blighting the contemporary economic system provides unequivocal evidence for the suboptimal nature of the system. Such problems could be minimised, however, through the application of an Islamic economic system.

The economic system would be stronger, more stable, mature, and steady if elements of faith and principles of sharia law were incorporated in terms of the participants and implementation. In addition, application of the Islamic economic system would be expected to resolve issues stemming from the contemporary economic system, for example the overarching issue of sectoral inequality. Inequality between the real sector and monetary sector is the most significant and acute problem, which could be resolved in an Islamic economic system due to the lack of sectoral dichotomy. In other words, core economic activity is based on the real sector, namely the production of goods and services.

8.5 Role of the Monetary Authority

As a subsystem of the Islamic religion, the Islamic economy runs optimally and provides maximum benefit when the authorities have jurisdiction to regulate, supervise, and develop the economy in accordance with Islamic principles. In this case, the authority is the government. A government that can uphold and maintain sharia law is an important prerequisite of implementing an optimal and maximal Islamic economic system. The function of maintaining sharia law is discharged by ensuring that the principles of justice are maintained in human economic interactions, thereby preserving balance at all levels of interaction or activity.

In carrying out its function, the state requires an independent and central institution to act as the economic authority, thus playing an essential role in maintaining economic balance. Such an institution can be established in the form of a central bank. In a monetary system, authorities such as the central bank play a significant and dominant role in safeguarding and maintaining the monetary sector. The central bank is responsible for printing and circulating currency, regulating the payment system and formulating monetary policy to achieve pro-growth monetary targets. In a conventional economy, the central bank is typically responsible for discharging these functions.

In the history of Islamic economics, however, the central bank concept is comparatively more obscure, particularly since the emergence of fiat money that is also a topic of debate in the Islamic economy. By absolutely forbidding the use of interest rates in the economic system, monetary policy for the Islamic economic and financial system focuses on optimising currency in circulation for productive economic activities. In Islam, the concept of a central bank has similar functions as a conventional central bank. In the execution of duties, however, an Islamic central bank must institute policies in accordance with Islamic principles and teachings, while rejecting anything contrary to Islamic teachings.

The discussion surrounding a central bank from the perspective of Islamic economic history refers to the concepts of *Baitul Mal* and *al-hisbah*, as introduced by the Prophet Muhammad SAW at the beginning of his leadership. In general, *Baitul Mal* is the state treasury, responsible for public finance, contributions, and expenditure. *Baitul Mal* is considered the first model of a state financial institution Islam. All state revenues are collected and subsequently disbursed according to the needs of the state. Meanwhile, *al-hisbah* performs a supervisory or oversight function for the economy, markets, and financial institutions.

8.5.1 Historical Function of Central Bank in Islam

As mentioned above, when the Islamic state was first formed during the time of Rasulullah SAW, there were no special authorities that could adjust the amount of currency in circulation through its policies. In addition, commodity money was used for transactions and there was no banking system. Furthermore, loans could not contribute to money creation because, at that time, only a few traders used credit and there were no money markets to provide funding, thus minimising speculative activities (Uddin, 2019).

At that time, the exchange of money only occurred during trade transactions in the goods/services market, which required the value added generated from the transaction. In this way, interaction between the goods/services market and money market towards equilibrium was achieved via cash transactions in the real sector. Total currency in circulation and the velocity of money, therefore, were always in line with the goods and services transacted, and conditions were consistently maintained in that way. Consequently, the velocity of money and economy remained comparatively stable.

During the time of Rasulullah SAW, monetary instruments, open market operations, and the sale and purchase of securities by *Baitul Mal*, which functioned like a central bank, were not known. In addition, interest-bearing instruments were absolutely forbidden in Islam due to inherent elements of *riba*. Notwithstanding, state institutions existed at that time mandated with economic governance, namely *Baitul Mal* and *al-hisbah*. The salient characteristics of both institutions are explained as follows.

Baitul Mal

In the historical literature concerning classical Islamic civilisation and economics, *Baitul Mal* was a dominant institution in the Islamic economy. Not merely economically oriented, *Baitul Mal* was also mandated with social responsibilities and maintained a strong position in the country, similar to the ruler or leader. Therefore, the *Baitul Mal* mechanism aligned closely with the function of the caliph as head of state. In other words, the various decisions and policies of *Baitul Mal* were instituted by the caliph.

In early Islam, the *Baitul Mal* institution had a similar mandate to contemporary central banks as a central finance house with branches in each Islamic state. The institution performed a similar function as contemporary central banks, namely issuing currency and maintaining price stability. The *Baitul Mal* concept is based on the belief that Allah SWT is the sole creator and sustainer of the universe. State leaders (caliphs) were created to implement the teachings of Allah SWT by maintaining prosperity and preserving the rights of the people to the goods. The *Baitul Mal* institution was subdivided into several types based on the funding sources available to discharge its function as follows:

(a) *Baitul Mal Zakat,* namely an institution mandated to collect *zakat* funds from the *muzakki*.
(b) *Baitul Mal Akhmas*, namely an institution mandated to collect and store wealth accumulated from taxes and *ghanimah* (spoils of war/plunder).
(c) *Baitul Mal Fa'i*, namely an institution mandated to collect and store wealth accumulated from *jizyah*, *kharaj*, and *'usyr*. *Jizyah* is an economic tax levied on affluent non-Muslims. *Kharaj* is an individual tax levied on productive land owned by the community. *'usyr* is a kind of import duty.
(d) *Baitul Mal Dhawa'i,* namely an institution mandated with storing abandoned assets or unclaimed inheritance.

Rasulullah SAW and subsequent caliphs unequivocally set out the function and existence of *Baitul Mal*, namely to simultaneously collect and distribute *zakat* funds. At the time of Abu Bakar, the *Baitul Mal* institution was deemed to function well if the officers could return from collecting *zakat* without any remaining funds. Circumstances changed under Umar Bin Khathab, however, when the collections became so large the decision was taken to deposit *zakat* funds for emergency purposes. Consequently, the *Baitul Mal* institution evolved to become responsible for managing such funds.

Baitul Mal emerged as evidence for the existence of specialised institutions to collect, manage, and distribute state funds in the national interest, the use of which was regulated by sharia law and development priorities. In the context of a modern economy, *Baitul Mal* is equivalent to the treasury or finance department as the Treasury House of the State. Fundamentally, *Baitul Mal* functioned to manage state finances by using the funds accumulated from *zakat*, *kharaj*, *jizyah*, *khums*, and *fay'* to implement social, defence, security, and economic development programmes, proselytise Islamic teachings through foreign diplomacy as well as execute all other development programmes as required by the state.

Al-Hisbah

The market is the central institution of the Islamic economy and even considered the heart of the economy. The market catalyses the circulation of economic resources among humans. In Islam, the benchmark of a well-functioning market is equitable prosperity and justice for all within the system. Good oversight, therefore, is required to ensure a well-functioning market.

Though during the time of Rasulullah SAW and the caliphs the *al-hisbah* institution had not been realised concretely or systematically in the state, the functions were nevertheless demonstrably carried out by the state, either directly by Rasulullah SAW and the caliphs or other companions appointed by Rasulullah SAW and the caliphs. The holder of the office of *al-hisbah* in classical Islamic administrations was known as a *muhtasib*.

There are numerous stories that recount how Rasulullah SAW, as head of state, visited the market to supervise all activities, including trade, debt, profit sharing, and the distribution of goods/services.

(HR. Muslim).

Rasulullah SAW also appointed a companion as *muhtasib*, a move that was emulated by subsequent Rashidun Caliphs. After the conquest and liberation of Mecca, Rasulullah SAW appointed Sa'id bin "Ash bin Umayyah as *muhtasib* of Mecca Market. Moreover, Rasulullah SAW also appointed the first female *muhtasib*, named Samra" binti Nuhaik al-Asadiyah.

The rationale behind the existence of the *hisbah* institution is also based on the argument that market participants naturally tend to behave deceptively and fraudulently. For example, merchants will lie and cheat in order to sell their wares at the market.

(Riwayat At Tirmidzi).

Despite focusing on market oversight, *hisbah* maintains a broader function. The *hisbah* institution provides facilities and infrastructure and will prosecute market participants in violation of Islamic principles.

In his book on *hisbah*, Ibnu Taimiyah states that the function of *hisbah* is to prevent wrongdoing (Chapra, 2001a, b). Not only an economic institution, therefore, *hisbah* also functions as a law enforcement institution similar to the police. In his study, Furqani (2003) mentions several *al-hisbah* functions as follows:

(a) Supervise the weighing scales, measures, and prices. In the context of a contemporary economy, *hisbah* oversees the business parameters or standards for goods and services in economic activity. This function is also part of the general agreement concerning what is permissible in the market in terms of quality, quantity, and halal. Therefore, *hisbah* operates as a supervisory body concerning general fluctuations in prices of goods and services in the market.
(b) Supervise prohibited trade, *riba, maysir* and *gharar* and fraud or deception. Economic activity must be free from actions prohibited by religion, thus requiring the harmonisation of practical activities and elucidation of prevailing laws. The *hisbah* institution reserves the right to apply limitations on economic activity contravening Islamic law, including the transactions, contracts, payments, settlements, goods traded, and information provided. This function creates transparency and justice in terms of economic activity.
(c) Supervise the halal status, health and hygiene of a commodity. The *hisbah* institution not only ensures that economic transactions are pursuant to sharia law, yet also ensures that the goods traded in the market are in accordance with what is permitted by Islam.
(d) Physically arrange the market and requisite facilities. Ultimately, this aims to ensure all parties can enjoy the freedom to participate in the market, while safeguarding the sustainability of a healthier and cleaner market with adequate facilities to create convenience when transacting.
(e) Help resolve complaints, disputes, and injustices and impose sanctions. The function of the state is to maintain socio-economic stability using sharia as a guide. If an incident occurs that could threaten the orderliness of market activities and relations from a socio-economic perspective, the *hisbah* institution, as representative of the state, reserves the right to regulate and resolve such disputes, including debt repayments by reluctant debtors with the means to pay. In addition, the *hisbah* institution is authorised to impose penalties and sanctions against those perpetuating illegal activities.

Operationally, *al-hisbah* not only focuses on market oversight yet also contributes to the provision of public facilities and infrastructure. Its presence does not raise concerns because *al-hisbah* does not intervene in the market through *Baitul Mal* or other institutions. *Al-hisbah* maximises its role in physically maintaining market stability based on sharia law (Chapra, 2001a, b).

Based on economic practices during the reign of Umar bin Khattab, *al-hisbah* had several important objectives as follows (Jaribah, 2003):

(a) Supervise and enforce Islamic rules and principles in economic activity to prevent economic actors deviating from Islamic principles.
(b) Create peace and security. During the reign of Umar bin Khattab, this was done to prevent crime and criminality in the market.
(c) Maintain the use of infrastructure to support economic and trade activity in order to improve orderly production and distribution activities.

8.5.2 Function of Central Bank in Islamic Monetary System

The modern monetary and financial system currently employed has begun to raise significant doubts, thus requiring evaluation and improvements must be considered (Toutounchian, 2009). Admittedly, the current system has various shortcomings, yet it is not the system which must be addressed initially, rather the policies that govern the system. Policy evaluation and assessment are fully the responsibility of the central bank, which must consider the application of Islamic principles in the implementation of monetary policy. Empirical evidence shows that by prioritising the principles of cooperation and sharing, an Islamic monetary system could provide the solution to many problems blighting the contemporary monetary system.

The main principles of economics are efficiency, justice, and equity. As the monetary authority, therefore, the central bank is obliged to uphold such economic principles. Justice and equity are the inalienable rights of every individual, such as the right to own assets in the form of money or other assets, the right to access financial institutions, and so on. Meanwhile, the principle of efficiency can be applied when determining the level of inflation, with the central bank expected to target a rate that minimises any adverse impacts.

The central bank plays an essential role in ensuring that money functions as it should, namely as a medium of exchange, and not as a commodity that can be traded like other goods and services in the real sector. According to Islamic principles, currency is not a tradeable commodity. The creation and volume of currency in circulation are best regulated by the central bank.

The central bank is obliged not only to regulate the amount of money in the financial markets, yet also maintain synergy and harmony between the financial sector and real sector. The central bank must formulate and institute an appropriate strategy to transform money in the financial sector into capital in the real sector (Toutounchian, 2009). The financial sector is not independent or separate from the real sector but serves to support real sector activities. Financial sector expansion, therefore, must be grounded by real sector growth. A higher velocity of money in the real sector will lead to stronger economic growth, which crucially must be maintained by the central bank.

Money supply is a tool used by the central bank to regulate monetary policy in a country. Even though the central bank has full jurisdiction over money supply, there is no justification to increase money supply beyond necessary levels or reasonable limits. Money supply should only be increased when production in the real sector expands, as characterised by an increase in demand for money in the productive sector.

In addition to maintaining synchronicity between the financial and real sectors, the central bank is also charged with disclosing accurate information to the public concerning the policy targets, strategies, and monetary instruments developed and applied by the central bank. Meanwhile, the central bank must also monitor and ensure all information concerning financial sector transactions is unambiguous and disclosed to each transacting party. The central bank, therefore, is legally responsible to provide symmetrical information to each individual as a preventative measure against moral hazard.

References

Askari, H., Iqbal, Z., Krichene, N., & Mirakhor, A. (2010). *The stability of Islamic Finance: Creating a resilient financial environment for a secure future*. Wiley.

Canuto, O., & Giugale, M. (2010). *The day after tomorrow: A hand book on the future of economic policy in the developing world*. The International Bank for Reconstruction and Development-The World Bank.

Chapra, M. U. (2001a). *The future of economics: An Islamic perspective*. (A. Amir, Y. Machmudi, F. Nur, L. Trialdi, E. Sudjono, & M. T. Ridho, Penerj.). Shari'ah Economic and Banking Institute.

Chapra, M. U. (2001b). *What is Islamic economics?* (2nd ed.). IRTI/IDB.

DeGennaro, R. P. (2005). Market imperfections. *Federal Reserve Bank of Atlanta Working Paper Series*, 1–31.

Ekmekcioglu, E. (2012). Problem of global financial instability. *International Journal of Academic Research in Economics and Management Sciences, 1*(2), 187–196.

Furqani, H. (2003). Institusi Hisbah: Model Pengawasan Pasar dalam Sistem Ekonomi Islam. *ISEFID Review: Journal of the Islamic Economic Forum for Indonesian Development, 2*(1), 36–50.

Gordon, R. J. (2009). *Ekonomi Makro* (11th ed.). Person Addison Wesley. ISBN 9780321552075.

Gros, D. (2018). *Financial stability implications of increasing interest rate. CEPS Policy Insight*. Centre for European Policy Studies.

Jaribah. (2003). *Fikih Ekonomi Umar Bin Al-Khathab*. Khalifa.

Lipsey, R. G. (1999). *Principles of economics* (9th ed.). Oxford University Press.

Mankiw, N. G. (2009). *Marcoeconomics* (7th ed.). Worth Publisher.

Minsky, H. P. (1992). The financial instability hypothesis. *Levy Economics Institute Working Paper* (74), 1–9.

Sakti, A. (2007). *Analisis Teoretis Ekonomi Islam: Jawaban atas Kekacauan Ekonomi Modern*. Aqsa Publishing.

Smith, D. (2011). *The age of instability: The global financial crisis and what comes next*. Profile Books.

Stiglitz, J. E., & Greenwald, B. (2003). *Towards a new paradigm in monetary economics*. The Press Syndicate of The University of Cambridge.

Toutounchian, I. (2009). *Islamic money & banking: Integrating money in capital theory*. Wiley.

Uddin, M. A. (2019). Islamic monetary economics: Insights from the literature. *Islamic Monetary Economics and Institutions: Theory and Practice* (hal. 39–53). Springer.

Villacorta, A. (2018). *Business cycles and the balance sheets of the financial and non-financial sectors*. ESRB Working Paper Series. European Systemic Risk Board.

Warjiyo, P., & Juhro, S. M. (2019). *Central Bank Policy: Theory and Practice*. Emerald Publishing Ltd.

Chapter 9
Basic Theory of Money in Islam

9.1 Introduction

Money has a very long and storied history, undergoing enormous changes since its inception. Consequently, money is not easy to explain or define in brief, clear, or precise terms. Money supply is one of the most important indicators underlying monetary policymaking and formulation. An excessive increase in the money supply could raise prices beyond expectations and disrupt economic growth in the long term. Conversely, prohibitively small increments in the money supply could prompt an economic downturn. If such conditions were allowed to persist, overall social prosperity would, in turn, fall into decline. Such dynamics, among others, underlie efforts by the government or monetary authority to control the money supply, which is commonly referred to as monetary policy and an integral part of the macroeconomic policies instituted by the relevant authorities.

In practice, monetary policy effectiveness depends on the relationship between the money supply and the main economic variables of output and inflation. In the literature, the salient findings regarding the relationship between the money supply, inflation, and output infer that, in the long run, the relationship between money supply growth and inflation is perfect, while the relationship between money growth or inflation and real output may be close to zero. Such findings point to consensus that in the long run, monetary policy will only impact inflation, with negligible effect on real economic activity. Despite the differing viewpoints, economic practitioners and academics generally concur that, in the short term, expansionary monetary policy can revive economic activity out of a prolonged recession. In contrast, contractionary monetary policy can slow the rate of inflation, which typically tends to occur during an economic boom.

Fundamentally, the money supply is the total stock of money held by the public at a particular point in time in an economy on the supply side. On the demand side, however, the public needs money to fund all economic activities. Ideally, the volume of money created or available must balance with the amount of money needed or

S. M. Juhro et al., *Inclusive Welfare*, https://doi.org/10.1007/978-981-96-0051-9_9

demanded in the community to avoid any excess or shortage of money in circulation. In practice, the demand for money is difficult to calculate because the people's needs are not only based on transactions but other motives as well, such as the precautionary motive or even speculation. In accordance with market law, if the volume of money supplied exceeds that demanded, the resultant excess supply could ultimately lower the price of money or interest rates.

Based on the relationship described above, changes in interest rates can occur as a result of changes in the money supply, which reflects interaction between the demand and supply sides. In this case, the motive to hold money is one of the fundamental aspects that creates imbalances. There are several motives that lead to unnecessary consumption and investment, such as prodigal consumption, non-productive and speculative investment as well as investment that is not linked to real sector activity. In Islam, speculation is forbidden because it violates the principles of Islamic economics. Controlling demand for money in Islam thus focuses on productive consumption and investment. Several aspects relating to the history, concepts, and basic theories of money are explained in this chapter from both the conventional and Islamic economic perspectives.

9.2 History and Concept of Money

Money was not directly conceptualised in the final form we see and use today but has evolved over time. Initially, there were no special objects or materials utilised as money, yet transactions were still possible using the simplest instruments, namely the barter system. Gradually, as the complexity and living standards of humans increased and the respective needs between people could not efficiently be met, the process of bartering and exchanging goods became increasingly difficult, thus eroding the effectiveness of the barter system. Consequently, people began to think about providing special tools for use in transactions, which became known as money.

Meanwhile, money also evolved in terms of its intrinsic value. At first, commodity money was used that had intrinsic value, which has been replaced by fiat money with no intrinsic value. In the past, people used commodity money as a medium of exchange, with gold and silver the most common forms. Over time, however, gold and silver reserves began to deplete, leading to other types of money, namely coins (copper at that time) and paper money. Coins and paper money were also used because the materials were easy to source, while incurring minimal cost and available in large quantities. Coins and paper money were the forerunner of fiat money that currently pervades the global community. In general, the evolution of money follows the following timeline (Fig. 9.1).

In the past, no specific object was called "money" as a medium of exchange. This does not mean, however, there was no trading activity at that time because humans, as social beings, rely on one another. Trade in those days applied the barter system, where participants in a transaction directly exchanged goods or services for other

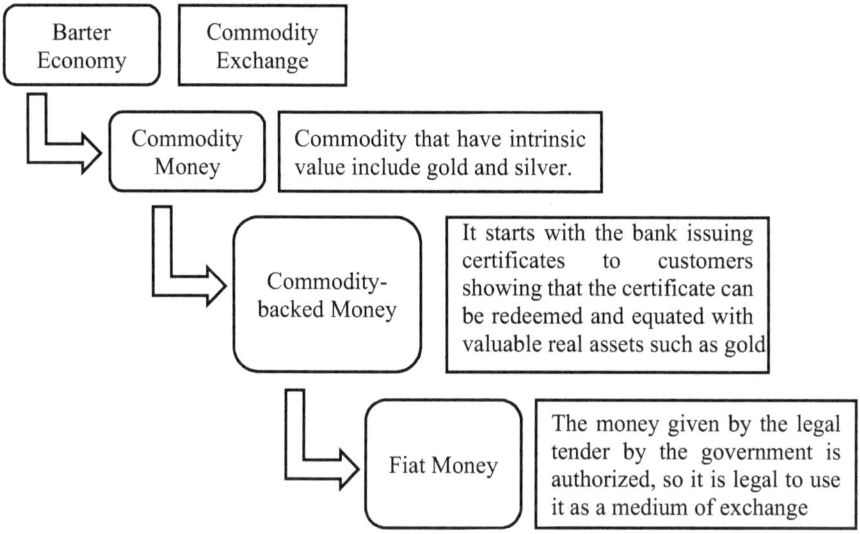

Fig. 9.1 Evolution of money. Source: Created by Author

goods or services without using a medium of exchange, such as money. For example, a driver could purchase rice using his services by taking the farmer from home to the rice field/market.

The gold standard was a monetary system in which gold and silver coins were used prior to the introduction and widespread adoption of fiat money. Gold and silver were used as currency due to their relatively stable intrinsic value. At that time, the global monetary system tended to be stable. Furthermore, the global application of the gold standard facilitated an orderly flow of international trade because all countries had similar needs and desires for gold.

Over time, however, difficulties and mistrust arose in the application of gold and silver coins. The high value of gold meant that carrying coins could attract the unwanted attention of nefarious criminals. The use of gold, therefore, became unsafe and a cause for concern in terms of personal safety. In addition, the high value of gold made it more difficult for those towards the bottom of the pyramid to divide the value of the money when purchasing cheaper items. Consequently, a new innovation in the form of a special "bank" was created to deposit privately owned gold (goldsmith).

Individuals depositing their gold in a bank for safekeeping received a certificate of ownership (paper money) for the amount of gold deposited, with the gold subsequently available for withdrawal (transferable) upon presentation of the certificate. In addition, the certificate itself could be used as a medium of exchange to facilitate trading transactions. As such, paper money allayed safety and security concerns because neither the buyer nor the seller held the gold/silver coins directly.

During this period, certificates of ownership backed by physical gold were approved by the competent authority as currency.

After World War I, money was no longer 100% backed by gold reserves, only partially. Banks began to approve issuing unbacked paper money without commensurate gold reserves. At the time, banks continued to create money not backed by gold and the central bank set the Statutory Reserve Requirement (SRR) as a percentage. The SRR demonstrated that banks could channel more money to the real sector. At the end of 1971, under the leadership of President Nixon, gold backed money was officially abolished and replaced with fiat money, which is 100% not backed by gold and remains legal tender to this day.

Money can be defined according to its function. Based on the fundamental theory of monetary economics, the function of money can be divided into four, namely two main and two supporting functions, as follows:

(a) Medium of exchange for goods and services. This is the main function of money. The primary activity of the real sector is the exchange of goods and services. Production would be futile, however, without consumers and money is crucial for maintaining the seamless exchange of goods and services. Therefore, producers can sell their goods and receive money, while consumers can purchase goods and services by handing over money to producers. This facilitates a convenient and efficient exchange process. For the function of money to serve as a medium of exchange, it must represent a standard of value that is accepted and recognised by the wider community as a means of payment. Any object could be used as a medium of exchange that has been recognised and agreed by the community depending on local beliefs and customs.
(b) A store of value. This is also the main function of money. People want to maintain the value of their wealth (purchasing power) by holding money. Therefore, money performs its role successfully if it can properly store purchasing power. The most important requirement of this function is maintaining stable value or purchasing power. Failure of this function diminishes the attractiveness of money as a store of wealth. During periods of high inflation, for example, the function of money as a store of value decreases.
(c) Standard unit of account. Though not a main function, this still plays an important supporting role for the medium of exchange. In the absence of this function, an item may still be considered money providing it can carry out its function as a medium of exchange. Nevertheless, this function makes it possible to measure the value of diverse goods, such as a mobile phone and a cup of coffee. Both goods can be standardised when expressed as a unit of money.
(d) Standard of Deferred Payments. This is not a requisite function of money yet money typically performs this function, which relates closely to debt or credit transactions. Money is a measure of certain payments when a transaction has not been cashed. For instance, a deferred payment on a purchase or a deferred payment on a cash loan.

Money is also subject to different types of value. According to Diwany (2002), the value of money includes the real value, intrinsic value, and extrinsic value (token). The real value reflects the amount of money that can be exchanged to receive the goods and services required by society, representing public purchasing power. The intrinsic value, or the actual value, measures the total cost of the production factors used to make and print the money, including the raw materials, labour, printing costs, and so on. This reflects the true value of the money itself. The extrinsic value, or token/nominal value, is the value legally authorised by the competent authority for a particular currency, which does not always align with the intrinsic value. For example, the real total cost of producing money worth Rp5000 is not Rp5000, indicating that the face value is higher than the intrinsic value.

Based on the functions of money described above, there are several types of money. In other words, money has more than one definition depending on its scope, from the narrowest to the broadest. This discussion will start from the narrowest sense of money, known as base money (M_0). Initially, when transactions between humans were simple, M_0 was the only term necessary, which included cash in the form of paper money and coins. This type of money became known as currency. As the role of banks in the economy expanded, however, M_0 as it is known today encompasses all physical currency held by the public, including coinage, and bank deposits held at the central bank. M_0 does not actually reflect real currency in circulation in the community or economy because part of the creation process is still on the balance sheet of the central bank as the monetary authority. On the supply side, base money will only become the money supply after completing a multiplication process as a corollary of interactions between the central bank, banking industry, and members of the public.[1]

As the complexity of human life increased, however, including the financial transactions, the notion of money expanded to cover the currency that actually circulates in the community, otherwise known as the money supply. We understand the money supply as narrow money (M1), the scope of which includes currency and demand deposits held by the members of public in banks. It is important to note that demand deposits also include balances belonging to members of the public deposited at a bank but as yet unused for consumption purposes. Owning demand deposits is equivalent to owning cash, yet a cheque or equivalent must be written to initiate a payment. The M1 equation can be expressed as follows:

$$M_1 = \text{Currency} + \text{Demand Deposits} \tag{9.1}$$

In addition to M1, broad money developed, known as M2, which is M1 plus quasi-money. The M2 equation can be expressed as follows:

[1]For a more detailed understanding of the definitions, creation process, and role of money in the economy, refer to Juhro and Suseno (2002).

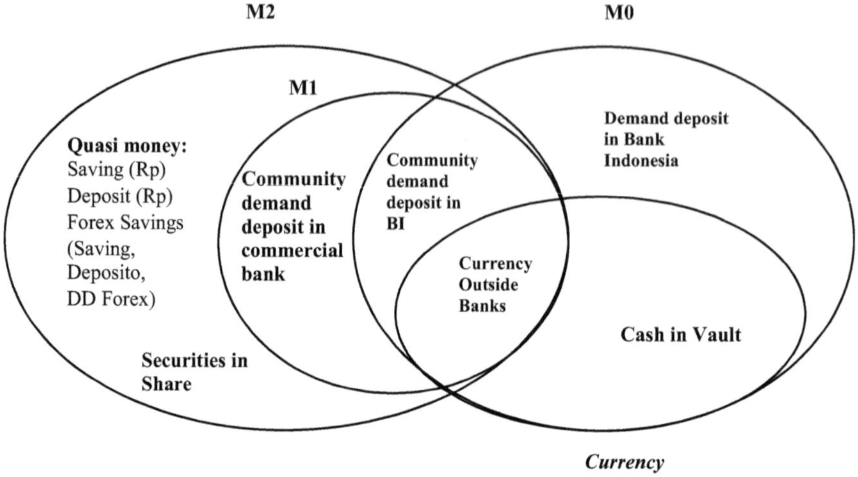

Fig. 9.2 Monetary aggregates. Source: Authors

$$M_2 = M_1 + \text{Quasi Money} \tag{9.2}$$

Quasi-money includes term deposits, savings deposits, and foreign currency demand deposits, which are non-transferable accounts that cannot be withdrawn at any time. Withdrawals are restricted to a specific period agreed between the customer and the commercial bank, for example 1 month, 3 months, and so on. Quasi-money, therefore, cannot be used directly as a means of payment until the maturity date when it can be converted into cash. In more detail, the money supply is categorised as follows (Fig. 9.2):

By explaining what conditions would occur without money, we can better understand its role in the economic system. The absence of money would impede the process of exchanging goods and services, thus severely hampering production and consumption activities. Consequently, society would only produce what it needs and only consume what it has produced, thus undermining progress and advancement in the real economy.

9.3 Supply and Demand of Money Theories

9.3.1 Demand for Money Theory

Currently, money is considered to have three main functions, namely as a medium of exchange, a standard unit of account, and a store of value. In Islam, however, the third function has a slightly different meaning as a store of wealth. Islamic principles teach that an object called money cannot "reproduce" or multiply by itself when merely stored. Saving, or holding money, is less attractive, therefore, as inflation renders the real value illusory. More so in Islam because of the obligation to pay *zakat* when savings reach the minimum threshold (*nisab*) that a Muslim must have before being obliged to pay *zakat*. Consequently, Muslims prefer to hold money only for transaction and investment purposes rather than as savings, with investment activities expected to generate a future return. The money demand function in Islam can be expressed in the following equation (Khan, 1986):

$$M^d/_P = l\,(r, Y), \qquad l_r < 0 \text{ and } l_Y > 0 \tag{9.3}$$

The money demand function closely resembles the liquidity preference function in conventional economics, where M is the total stock of money, P is the price level, and Y is the output. The difference lies in r, where r in this function is not the interest rate but the rate of return on assets from investment activity. It can be concluded, therefore, that demand for money in Islam is positively influenced by the need for transactions, as reflected in aggregate output, and inversely proportional to the rate of return on investment.

The demand for money referenced above is presented from an Islamic perspective, as adapted from conventional economic theories. Meanwhile, theories relating to money based on conventional economic teachings are explained below.

A compelling theory regarding money is the relationship between the quantity of money and price level. This is described by the well-known Quantity Theory of Money (QTM), stating that the general price level of goods and services is directly proportional to the amount of money in circulation, or the money supply. Notwithstanding, classical economists agree that this relationship occurs in the long run. In the near term, economic forces depend on increases and decreases in the money supply.

Based on notes written by Jean Bodin in 1568, another opinion states that the fairly rapid and significant increase of prices in Europe around the late sixteenth century was caused by an increase in imports of gold and silver, which functioned as money at that time. It can be said, therefore, that the proportional relationship between money and prices has been proven for centuries. This opinion was not disputed by Richard Cantillon in the eighteenth century, stating that an increase in money production resulted in an excessive quantity of money compared to what was actually required. To overcome this excess, big producers increase demand, especially for consumer goods, thus raising prices due to higher demand and eroding the real income (purchasing power) of the people.

Cantillon's findings were followed by the financial historian, David Hume, in his theory relating to money distribution. According to Hume, money follows a natural flow mechanism (natural law). If the natural mechanism is disturbed or shocked, a separate self-correcting mechanism will be formed. Price levels, therefore, are in a constant state of flux when money distribution is not in balance, similar to how the demand for goods increases to compensate for an excess quantity of money. The impact is an increase in the price of goods, including the prices of exported goods. This demonstrates how the trade balance deteriorates as exports decrease and vice versa if the quantity of money is lower than actually required. This mechanism will continue to repeat itself until the flow of money returns to its natural state. This theory did not apply, however, in the period after World War II, when the flow of money was not only influenced by economic forces alone, yet also by political and military forces.

In the nineteenth century, the opinion of Henry Thornton was slightly different, connecting the quantity of money to the banking system. Thornton believed that an increase in demand and an increase in the price level were indirectly related, with a mechanism involving the banking system at play. An increase in demand and price level would occur when an increase in the quantity of money was accompanied by an excess in terms of loanable fund sources in the banking system. An increase in reserves would largely be disbursed as loans, thus decreasing the interest rate. Low interest rates are an incentive for other customers to borrow from the bank. Therefore, the demand and prices will increase.

In the 1970s, Fan and Liu researched the money demand function in Asian countries. Contrary to prevailing opinion, the results were quite surprising because they showed that interest rates do not significantly affect demand in Asian countries. This was different to developed economies (Europe or United States) because capital markets in Asia remain underdeveloped so the demand for money is only influenced by transaction needs. Therefore, the demand function in Asian countries is affected by level of income.

A. *Orthodox Money Theory*

The public's ability to purchase goods and services and control the output of goods and services is influenced by stable monetary value. Changes in the value of currency affect public purchasing power. Low public purchasing power and currency exchange rates indicate high prices, while low prices point to higher public purchasing power and exchange rate appreciation. There is an inverse relationship, therefore, between the value of the currency and price level. With U representing the value of money and P the price level, the model can be expressed as follows:

$$U = \frac{1}{P} \tag{9.4}$$

Orthodox Quantity Theory of Money states that the price level is a multiple of the total money supply, which can be expressed as follows:

$$M = k * P \tag{9.5}$$

Where M is the total stock of money, P is the price level, and k is a constant representing a constant multiple. The formula states that for each increase in the quantity of money, the price level will also increase by a multiple of k multiplied by the quantity of money. In addition, as the quantity of money and price level changes proportionally, the elasticity of prices to the quantity of money is 1, otherwise known as unitary elastic.

Among others, the following assumptions are used to explain the orthodox quantity theory of money:

1. The economy is in a state of full employment and utilising all economic resources, leading to a stable amount of goods and services produced.
2. The velocity of money is considered constant. Public motivation to hold money does not change significantly.

   The theory omits speculative motives for holding money, instead focusing on transaction and precautionary measures. In addition, money does not function as a store of value according to this theory.

B. *Quantity Theory of Money*

Irving Fisher's research on the Quantity Theory of Money sought to correct the previous model. In his theory, Irving Fisher classified two types of money, namely M for banknotes and coins as well as M_1 for demand deposits so that:

$$M * V_T = P * T \tag{9.6}$$

Where M is the total stock of money, including banknotes and coins, demand deposits, and cheques. V_T is the transaction velocity of money. The size of P indicates the price level per transaction and T is the total of all transactions carried out using money in a given period. Irving Fisher formulated his Quantity Theory of Money in terms of the equation of exchange. The theory can be explained as follows:

1. Price level is directly proportional to the total stock of money and velocity of money and inversely proportional to the number of transactions in a given period. Equation (9.7) can thus be expressed as follows:

$$P = M\,\frac{V_T}{T} \tag{9.7}$$

According to Fisher, the price level is a passive variable because in the model, price level does not affect other variables, yet other variables influence the price level. The variables of the velocity of money and number of transactions are relatively constant and independent of total money and price level.

2. The amount of transactions in a given period (T) is described by the available resources, technology, and population size. The factors of T tend not to change in a given period, so T is considered constant in that period. In the long run, the number of T transactions may increase with changes in resources, population, and technological efficiency. In the short term, although the actual number of transactions tends to fluctuate in line with

the booms and busts of the national economy, the variables tend to quickly return to their original state (equilibrium level).

3. The velocity of money, V, is not determined by the total stock of money M. The factors affecting the velocity of money are relatively constant, including the payment systems, which mostly use cash or checks, the frequency of private income received, which is typically consistent, public propensity to use domestic currency rather than a foreign currency as well as relatively similar banking instruments. Notwithstanding, the velocity of money can change with a shift in public motivation to hold money, which is typically influenced by interest rates and inflation.
4. The ratios of demand deposits and currency tend to remain constant. Changes in price level, therefore, are influenced by increases and decreases in the total amount of both types of money in circulation. In addition, there are two salient points that must be noted concerning the total stock of money. *First*, people tend to stabilise the ratio of their cash and term deposits held. If the ratio is different, a self-correction mechanism will form to return to the original state. For example, when a person has excess cash available, it is typically stored as a bank deposit and vice versa. This fluctuation mechanism disrupts the ratio between currency and demand deposits, if only temporarily. *Second*, the statutory reserve requirement set by the central bank is relatively stable as a specific percentage of bank deposits.

   In actuality, difficulties still arise from the quantity theory of money as described above, namely in terms of measuring total transactions. Consequently, the quantity theory of money was developed further using an income approach, replacing the total transactions variable with the total output of goods and services produced in the country, while also substituting other variables based on an output-side approach. Equation (6.6), therefore, can be formulated as follows:

$$M * V_Y = P * Y \tag{9.8}$$

Where V_y is the amount of money transferred from person to person to obtain goods and services. P show the average price level per unit of final output produced and Y is the real output in a given period.

C. *Cash-Balance Theory*

In terms of formulation, there are no significant differences between the theories of Fisher and Marshall. There are differences, however, in the basic concepts. Fisher's theory is considered more traditional because it only pays attention to the role of money as a medium of exchange, implying observation from the supply side. On the other hand, Marshall's theory focuses more on the demand for money, including the function of money as a store of value. Furthermore, the determinants of money supply and demand are better explained using cash-balance theory.

Cash-balance theory is based on the demand for money. The aggregate demand for money model can be expressed as follows:

$$M_D = kPY \tag{9.9}$$

Where M_D is the demand for money, k is a multiple that shows a proportional relationship between demand for money and income, P is the average price level, and Y is the real output produced in a given period. In this model, the demand for money is assumed to have a proportional and constant relationship to the total products produced in a country. This is because people tend to stabilise the level of cash balance held based on a certain percentage of their income. When the desired cash balance does not match reality, the individual will strive to achieve the target. For example, if the cash balance is higher than the target, money will be spent until the desired cash balance is reached, and vice versa, when the cash balance is lower than expected, consumption is reduced.

The cash-balance approach assumes that the level of real output is inelastic to changes in the money supply. In the event of monetary imbalances (the quantity of money demanded is not equal to the quantity supplied), a self-correcting mechanism forms until equilibrium is reached between the two. For example, there are case studies observing the effects when the money supply is lower than the demand. People feel their cash reserves are being eroded, which is overcome by a lower propensity to spend in order to hold more cash. The impact is lower demand for consumer goods. Seeking to boost cash reserves further, people may sell securities, which will raise interest rates.

High interest rates compress the level of investment, accompanied by a decrease in general prices and private income. That way, demand for money can decrease in order to achieve equilibrium with the money supply, and vice versa if the demand for money is less than the money supply. This mechanism occurs continuously and alternately in order to achieve monetary equilibrium.

D. *Liquidity Preference Theory*

According to liquidity preference theory, demand for money is influenced by its liquidity. Relating to the demand for money, Keynes said that the public's motives for holding money extend beyond transactional or precautionary purposes to include speculative motives. In fact, it is the speculative motive that dominantly characterises the behaviour of money demand in the modern era. Departing from classical theory, which looks only at the role of long-term interest rates, Keynes explained the role of short-term interest rates. In this case, the interest rate is the price issued by the debtor to encourage a creditor to transfer their scarce and finite resources (money). Nevertheless, the money issued by the debtor incurs a possibility of loss in the form of risk of not receiving a certain interest rate. The theory assumes two kinds of investment, namely money and bonds. Money is the most liquid asset that can be used to make payments on liability obligations, whereas bonds must first be converted into cash. The demand for money, therefore, is a rational action and higher demand for money will raise interest rates.

Three motives for holding money have been identified as follows:

1. *The transactions motive*: The most basic motive for holding money is to settle transactions since money is a medium of exchange. This motive means that money is used by individuals to buy daily goods and services.
2. *The precautionary motive*: This motive is based on human nature to maintain precautionary savings to effectively deal with unexpected future events, such as sickness, accidents, and other disasters.
3. *The speculative motive*: This motive exists due to the interest rate system, thereby providing an incentive for the public to seek profit. These actions are carried out by speculators who observe interest movements intentionally to gain profit.

E. *Modern Quantity Theory of Money*

The quantity theory of money pioneered by Milton Freeman is known as Modern Quantity Theory, which refines and complements the classical and Keynesian theories. The similarities include the selection of assets that individuals wish to hold using profit and loss as the basis for consideration.

Friedman's theory is based on the assumption that people are motivated to hold money because money is the most liquid asset. In addition, more money held implies a lower Marginal Rate of Substitution (MRS), meaning that the additional benefit obtained from holding too much money decreases. Thus, a person will receive maximum total benefit by substituting a certain amount of money for other assets, such as bonds, securities, houses, and others.

The theory states that the owner of wealth will choose which assets and how much to hold depending on the benefits received, total wealth, and personal preference. Wealth as defined by Friedman is not limited to money yet also includes potential and valuable resources that can generate future income.

According to the theory, individuals can hold wealth in five types of asset, namely cash, stocks/shares, securities/bonds, physical wealth, and human resource wealth, while the affecting factors can be described as follows:

1. Total wealth of the individual: The total amount of an individual's wealth is directly proportional to the amount of cash one wishes to hold, implying that more wealth leads to more cash held by the individual.
2. Market prices of goods: Higher prices of goods increase the demand for cash.
3. Rate of return on other assets: The return on other assets has an inverse relationship with the demand for cash. When the return from holding stocks, bonds, and other assets increases, individuals will prefer such assets over cash, thus decreasing the demand for cash.
4. Ratio between human resource wealth and physical wealth (non-human): A higher ratio implies higher demand for cash.
5. Preferences (tastes): The last factor involves the subjectivity of each respective individual. This fact is abstract and cannot be explained from a quantitative perspective.

F. *Demand for Money in Islam*

A stable money demand function is key to successful macroeconomic activity and effective monetary policy. In Islam, several factors influence demand for money. First, real income. People hold money primarily to meet their daily (consumption) needs and consumption is determined by the level of real income. Higher real income increases demand for money. In addition, higher expectations concerning the possible rate of return will reduce demand for money. Therefore, the demand for money and expected rate of return are inversely proportional.

Stable demand for money will impact the stability of money velocity in the market. In Islam, the demand for money equation is expressed as follows (Chapra, 1996):

$$M_d = f\ (Y_S, S, \pi)(1) \tag{9.10}$$

Where, Y_s represents the goods and services required to meet daily necessities and productive investment purposes, S are the moral and social values in Islamic economics that influence the allocation and distribution of resources (*zakat* for example), π is the level of profit sharing in the financial intermediation system, and M_d illustrates the demand for money.

The following table explains some of the salient differences in the theory of demand for money based on conventional thinking and Islamic principles (Table 9.1).

9.3.2 Supply of Money Theory

After exploring the demand for money theory, it is necessary to study the mechanisms by which the aggregate supply of money can achieve equilibrium with the demand for money. In addition, we must pay attention to how much money in circulation is allocated in accordance with real sector needs. The central bank is the competent authority to determine the optimal level of money supply, when the demand for money is stable and optimal level of money supply can be achieved through zero interest rate policy (Uddin, 2019).

Currency in circulation plays an important role in greasing the wheels of the economy, analogous to the flow of blood through the human body or fuel through an engine (Ibrahim, 2020). Money supply, therefore, must be regulated to eliminate any surplus or deficit. Excessive money supply will drive up inflation, while a deficit could impede productivity and trigger deflation. Money supply is determined by policies instituted by the central bank as the monetary authority. Empirical results show that the money supply is determined in accordance with the monetary base (*MB*) as well as interactions with the banking system, as reflected by the money multiplier (*m*). The formula for the money supply can be expressed as follows (Ahmed, 2002):

Table 9.1 Comparison of demand for money theories

	Classical theory	Keynesian theory	Islam principles
Function of money	Main function as medium of exchange	Main functions as medium of exchange and store of value	Main functions as medium of exchange and unit of account.
Real-monetary sector relationship	Dichotomy between the real sector and the monetary sector, so both sectors are independent of each other	Nexus between the interdependent real sector and monetary sector	Real sector is main economic sector, with monetary sector playing a supporting role for the real sector.
Consequences of supply–demand interaction	Main interaction between the supply and demand of money is price setting	Main interaction between the supply and demand of money determines interest rates, while prices are formed by aggregate supply and demand	The money supply is adjusted to actual needs in the real sector
Motives for holding money	Transaction motive, precautionary motive	Transaction motive, precautionary motive, and speculative motive	Transaction motive and precautionary motive
Determinant factors	Demand for money is a given proportion of transaction volume, and transaction volume is a constant percentage of national income. Thus, the money demand function is influenced by the level of national income	With the speculative motive, demand for money is determined by interest rates as an individual consideration to hold money or purchase securities and bonds	Demand is determined by real sector needs. Business expansion will increase demand for money
Role of interest rates	The money demand function is not affected by interest rates, hence a vertical LM curve. Therefore, fiscal policy (reflecting the IS curve) will be ineffective at increasing national output. According to this theory, monetary policy can effectively increase national output	The implication of using interest rates as an individual consideration to hold money is demand instability, thus monetary and fiscal policies are harder to forecast	Rate of return as an alternative replacement to interest rates as an instrument to control demand for money. The rate of return is the yield on investor funds, in this case using profit and loss sharing principles or mechanisms
Money stability	Total money demand function is stable, while transaction volume changes slowly and incrementally	The speculative motive causes uncertainty and expectations that determine the money demand function, leading to instability in the total money demand function, with rapid shifts and fluctuations possible	Demand for money is grounded in real sector needs so the demand function in Islam tends to be stable

Source: Authors

$$MS = m * MB \tag{9.11}$$

In the implementation of an Islamic economic system, the central bank as the competent authority will not issue instruments containing elements of *riba*, so instruments such as bonds and shares that apply interest rates are absolutely forbidden. In addition, increasing the amount of money through domestic lending is also restricted, with only transactions based on underlying real assets that apply profit and loss sharing contracts permitted.

The monetary base consists of currency in circulation (C) and reserves (R), and the supply of money consists of currency and term deposits (D). Thus, the equation can be expressed as follows:

$$MB = C + R \quad \text{and } MS = C + D \tag{9.12}$$

Where m represents the prevailing banking system in a country, which can be described using the following model:

$$m = \frac{MS}{MB} = \frac{C + D}{C + R} \text{ with } R = R_r + R_e \tag{9.13}$$

Which can be rewritten as follows:

$$m = \left[1 + \frac{C}{D}\right] / \left[R_r + R_e + \frac{C}{D}\right] \tag{9.14}$$

Where C is the currency in circulation, D is the deposit rate, R_r is the statutory reserve requirement (SRR), and R_e is excess reserves. The direct impact of an increase in deposits will materialise in excess reserves, yet there is no direct correlation between increasing money supply and an increase in domestic lending. In an Islamic economic system, therefore, the banking sector cannot "create" money as easily as in the conventional economy.

9.4 Fiat Money

9.4.1 History and Concept of Fiat Money

In general, there are two classifications of money, namely commodity money and fiat money. Commodity money is money whose value is derived from the object (commodity) of which it is made, thus the nominal and intrinsic values of commodity money are the same. For example, commodity money during the time of Rasulullah SAW was represented by those commodities used as a medium of exchange, such as gold, silver, salt, wheat, and dates. Compared to fiat money, the value of commodity money is harder to change, even for the regulatory or monetary authority, because the value is pegged to market value. The absence of government regulatory intervention ensures greater stability concerning the value of commodity money.

On the other hand, fiat money or currency is the antithesis of commodity money. The nominal or face value of fiat money is determined by the regulatory/monetary authority of a country. Thus, the nominal value of fiat money is not the same as the intrinsic value. Fiat money has no intrinsic value yet is ascribed a nominal value by the competent authority. Nevertheless, fiat money is widely accepted and used as a standard to calculate the value of goods and services and as a medium of exchange for the goods and services required. This is possible because the nominal value of fiat money has been determined and set by the competent authority, thus serving as legal tender in its role and function as money for the public to use. Paper money (banknotes) and/or coins are examples of fiat money currently in use globally.

According to Jaribah (2003), there was precedent during the reign of Umar bin Khathab stating that money is essentially an object recognised as a means of payment and transacting in the community. In fact, Umar bin Khathab stated his desire to make dirhams (currency) from camel hide before changing his mind due to fear of camels becoming extinct. Meaning can be inferred from this anecdote, namely that the materials and form of money can be determined by the community leader, as long as benefits are provided, harm is not caused and Islamic principles are not violated. The contemporary implication of Umar bin Khathab's statement in terms of current monetary practices is that the use of fiat money should be permitted because it is regulated and authorised by state leaders. A deeper review is required, however, concerning whether the use of fiat money causes *mudharat* or harm in the monetary system.

Fiat money, which began as token money and is not backed by a real commodity, was first introduced by the Greek philosopher Plato. In modernity, all countries subscribe to their own version of fiat currency, which is not backed by real assets. Notwithstanding, fiat money has created ambiguity, beckoning the question of whether the nature of money is a form of commodity or, oppositely, could certain commodities be used as money because they meet the necessary criteria and functions?

Some monetary economists argue that money which can execute its function properly is a type of commodity money because of the primary function as a unit of account to establish the value of goods and services. Money must, therefore, have intrinsic value to discharge its function properly. Notwithstanding, empirical evidence demonstrates that fiat money can effectively carry out its function without the backing of any real underlying assets. Moreover, money was created to bridge and facilitate exchange activities, so the face value of the money does not have to depend on the raw materials used in the production of the money. Other factors are more important than the raw materials used, namely the ability to successfully function as a medium of exchange and unit of account. Starting with this mindset, fiat money is acceptable despite the lack of precious materials used therein, other than paper and copper coins. On the other hand, precious metals such as gold and silver could be used for other purposes and goals. Therefore, fiat money could be classified as commodity money.

Fiat money is legal tender but has weak value as it tends to depreciate easily as the total stock of money increases, particularly if the money supply exceeds actual real sector needs. In addition, the stability of the value of the currency against the value of domestic goods and currencies in other countries is strongly influenced by economic forces. Most developing economies tend to have lower value fiat currencies than their more established and advanced counterparts.

In addition to the predetermined nominal or face value, total currency in circulation or the supply of fiat money is regulated by the monetary authority, which can freely increase or decrease the money supply using various monetary policy instruments. Furthermore, the monetary authority (in this case, the central bank) can simply print more money if deemed necessary to increase the total stock of money in a country.

The first economic issue that arises from the use of fiat money is how easily and freely it can be created as required without underlying real assets. Consequently, the amount of money in circulation is rarely aligned with economic activity in the real sector. In general, the money supply tends to exceed real sector needs, which is why the real value of fiat money tends to decline, leading to a general increase in prices typically referred to as inflation (Rab, 2002).

Inflation is the root of several other economic issues. Inflation causes uncertainty in the value of goods and services required in society, making economic stability more difficult to achieve. Inflation also raises the cost of living, while simultaneously eroding public purchasing power. In addition, as inflation edges up the cost of living, people will try various nefarious methods to meet their daily needs, including through corruption.

High levels of corruption in countries with comparatively high inflation provide evidence that inflation creates heavier demands on the public regarding the cost of living. Corruption itself exacerbates the next adverse impact of lower state revenues, thereby slashing the budget available for national development in terms of public facilities and infrastructure, as well as leading to a suboptimal quality of life (QOL).

The use of fiat currency without the backing of real assets, coupled with the domination of interest rates in the monetary system, also causes other problems, such as speculation in the money market and the exploitation of resources (in this case money) from the upper class to those at the bottom of the pyramid.

From the beginning, the use of fiat money as a medium of exchange and a unit of account has been a mistake. Setting a nominal value of fiat money at odds with its intrinsic value is a form of currency manipulation. Ordinary paper and/or coins that are essentially worthless can be ascribed a high value due to the legal tender status afforded by the competent authority. In addition, the paper notes and/or coins are used as a unit of account for private wealth. The intrinsic value of paper notes and/or coins tends to be significantly lower than the nominal or face value legally designated by the monetary authority.

It can be said, therefore, that some of the wealth associated with fiat money issued without the backing of real assets and which is enjoyed by the community does not have significant value and is merely pseudo-wealth. The application of fiat money without the backing of real assets in the monetary system is the roots of various economic woes. Consequently, it would be almost impossible to fully resolve prevalent economic issues while fiat money is used in the monetary system as a unit of account and a medium of exchange for goods and services.

Printing money without a solid grounding in the real sector is a big mistake. The amount of money in the financial sector has become massive, far exceeding the amount required in the real sector. This implies that total money stock is accelerating beyond real sector productivity, leading to a bubble economy, where the value of real output in the real sector is much lower than in the financial sector. It may be inferred, therefore, that a bubble economy makes economic advancement illusory.

Using fiat money in the monetary system allows banks to readily channel money to the public, thus leading to a high level of money supply. Excess money in society increases the opportunity cost of holding cash. Consequently, such conditions incentivise members of the public, especially individuals with excess capital (investors), to deposit their money in banks, thus increasing bank deposits. When bank deposits exceed disbursed loans, deposit rates tend to be lower than lending rates.

If this occurs, some parties will benefit yet at the expense of others. Investors and banking institutions will benefit, while borrowers will suffer due to principal payments accompanied by relatively high interest payments. It can be said, therefore, that excess money supply tends to enrich the upper class to the detriment of the middle and working classes. This demonstrates how the flow of resources (in this case, money) is not equitably distributed with a concentration in the hands of a few. Such circumstances are an egregious violation of Islamic teachings.

Income inequality is not only rife between elites and non-elites but also between emerging and advanced economies. When depreciation drives up inflation, the prices of ready-to-use (finished) goods tend to be more elastic to higher prices in general, which are primarily produced by advanced economies. On the other hand, raw material prices are comparatively inelastic, which are produced in emerging economies. Consequently, advanced economies can generate higher profits than emerging economies, thereby exacerbating income inequality between advanced and emerging economies.

Islamic teachings reveal that money/capital must be distributed and flow evenly and fairly within the community. According to the word of Allah SWT as revealed in verse 7 of surah Al-Hasyr (59):

مَآ اَفَاۤءَ اللّٰهُ عَلٰى رَسُوْلِهٖ مِنْ اَهْلِ الْقُرٰى فَلِلّٰهِ وَلِلرَّسُوْلِ وَلِذِى الْقُرْبٰى وَالْيَتٰمٰى وَالْمَسٰكِيْنِ وَابْنِ السَّبِيْلِۙ كَيْ لَا يَكُوْنَ دُوْلَةً ۢ
بَيْنَ الْاَغْنِيَاۤءِ مِنْكُمْۗ وَمَآ اٰتٰىكُمُ الرَّسُوْلُ فَخُذُوْهُ وَمَا نَهٰىكُمْ عَنْهُ فَانْتَهُوْاۚ وَاتَّقُوا اللّٰهَ ۗاِنَّ اللّٰهَ شَدِيْدُ الْعِقَابِۘ

And what Allah restored to His Messenger from the people of the towns—it is for Allah and for the Messenger and for [his] near relatives and orphans and the [stranded] traveler—so that it will not be a perpetual distribution among the rich from among you. And whatever the Messenger has given you—take; and what he has forbidden you—refrain from. And fear Allah; indeed, Allah is severe in penalty. (Q.S. Al-Hasyr [59]: 7).

The verse explicitly states that Allah SWT commands his human subjects to maintain an economic system capable of distributing the flow of money equitably. Implicitly, the Quranic verse can also be interpreted to imply that Allah SWT forbids the hoarding or concentration of wealth in the hands of a few. To eliminate hoarding, Islam teaches Muslims to pay *zakat* at a rate of 2.5% when their level of wealth has reached the *nisab* threshold for more than 1 year.

Therefore, the hoarding or concentration of wealth in the hands of a few contradicts the Islamic principle of *muamalah*. Moreover, this is also contrary to human nature. According to Rab (2002), humans are not materialistic by nature, yet it is the surrounding environment throughout life that moulds such characteristics.

From an Islamic perspective, money used as a unit of account and a medium of exchange for goods and services should be aligned with the intrinsic value and not easily recreated, thus ensuring stability, while avoiding significant depreciation and other deleterious effects in the economic system.

Forms of money that tend to intensify price volatility should be reconsidered. In Islam, the application of fiat money, which is not backed by real assets, runs contrary to sharia principles. In this case, fiat money without the backing of gold or silver is forbidden in Islam, yet fiat money backed by gold or silver as the underlying asset would be permitted to circulate in the monetary system according to Islamic teachings.

9.4.2 The Issue of Using Fiat Money in the Economy

Islamic economists have stated that fiat money would fail to meet Islamic standards and principles if the purchasing power is not based on real assets. One implication of implementing fiat money is that the people are "compelled" to pay taxes at a higher value due to inflation. In Islam, however, the government is not authorised to "take" profit by force from rich or poor alike.

The application of fiat money, accompanied by interest rates, serves to further increase the wealth of the already affluent, thus widening the gap between social groups. Essentially, therefore, fiat money and interest rates combine to create poverty. The most significant impact readily felt by members of the public is in the form of higher real estate prices, thereby excluding those towards the bottom of the pyramid from purchasing assets in the form of houses, though shelter is considered a primary human need. The complexity of the issue is further compounded by other socio-economic problems stemming from poverty, such as crime and criminality.

The negative connotations associated with applying fiat money and interest rates also pose a threat to economic sovereignty, which can slowly and incrementally fall under the influence of other parties with more power. A real example is the economic sovereignty of developing countries, which is heavily influenced by advanced economies (United States) through a fiat currency (US dollar) that is stronger than other currencies.

The monetary system application of fiat money without the backing of gold/silver is a mistake from an Islamic perspective. As a unit of account and a medium of exchange for goods/services, fiat money is the root of other problems in the economic system.

The losses incurred from instability in the value of fiat money tend to exceed the advantages and convenience afforded by the creation of fiat money itself. Initially, this would be an issue in the financial sector, yet could eventually spill over into the real sector. If allowed to persist, the problems would extend beyond the economy to include environmental, social, and political issues (Meera & Aziz, 2002).

(a) *Economic Issues*

Fluctuating and unpredictable interest rates impact the flow of resources between economic actors, leaving movements in the economic system difficult to predict.

A salient economic problem that inevitably occurs in the application of currency is depreciation. Currencies in use today are the product of a worsening rate of depreciation, which is true in all countries, even the so-called superpowers. This is clearly demonstrable using the US dollar as an example. In 1971, 1 ounce of gold was equivalent to USD35. The lack of any gold backing, however, has seen the value of the US dollar plummet, with 1 ounce of gold equivalent to USD300 in 2002 (Rab, 2002). Depreciation occurs because fiat money can be created freely and easily as and when the monetary authority feels it necessary. What is even more dangerous, however, is when elites obtain the power to create demand for new money.

The ease with which new money can be created erodes the value of money and leads to instability, which brings into question the feasibility and suitability of using fiat money as a medium of exchange and unit of account. This is also contrary to the teachings of Islamic economics, which emphasise justice in all measures of value, which includes money in this context.

According to Al-Qur'an, currency that is used continuously and constantly subject to depreciation is tantamount to the destruction of earth (Chapra, 2000) and absolutely forbidden by Allah SWT, as revealed in verse 11–12 of surah Al-Baqarah as follows:

وَاِذَا قِيْلَ لَهُمْ لَا تُفْسِدُوْا فِى الْاَرْضِۙ قَالُوْٓا اِنَّمَا نَحْنُ مُصْلِحُوْنَ(11)

اَلَآ اِنَّهُمْ هُمُ الْمُفْسِدُوْنَ وَلٰكِنْ لَّا يَشْعُرُوْنَ(12)

And when it is said to them, "Do not cause corruption on the earth," they say, "We are but reformers." Unquestionably, it is they who are the corrupters, but they perceive [it] not. (Q.S. Al-Baqarah[2]: 11–12).

Hence, while currency without underlying assets is still used in the economic system, humans continue to damage the Earth as created by Allah SWT.

Inflation is the next issue that arises from the application of pure fiat money. Inflation occurs when price levels in general experience a continuous increase. Inflation demands special attention given its indirect impacts that are advantageous for some yet to the detriment of others.

When inflation occurs, the sectors affected more quickly, which therefore benefit, are those with access to bank loans, such as the property sector, financial sector, and other large enterprises. On the other hand, however, medium, small, and micro enterprises (MSMEs) are relatively unaffected and cannot reap the benefits of inflation. Consequently, the impact on those towards the bottom of the pyramid is a decrease in purchasing power or real income (Meera & Aziz, 2002).

Moreover, inflation that stems from the application of an interest rate system creates uncertainty in every economic decision. Allowing persistent inflation distances the economy from higher growth and full employment. The solution to attaining these targets is first to address the issue of inflation at its root. Ultimately, the inflation phenomenon serves as proof that fiat money fails in its functions as a unit of account and medium of exchange. Additionally, fiat money is also an unreliable store of value.

Inflation is not in harmony with Islamic teachings. Persistent inflation provides an incentive for creditors to apply interest rates on future loan repayments. As long as there is inflation, creditors will be unable or unwilling to forego the interest rate system. Under an interest-free system, creditors would experience injustice caused by inflation because the real value of the repaid debt would be lower than the real value of the funds lent. While such conditions persist, the monetary system will contain elements of *riba*.

(a) *Social Issues*

As a corollary of economic problems, in this case inflation, social issues can also emerge (Meera & Aziz, 2002). In the absence of a commensurate increase in nominal income, inflation erodes the level of real income, thereby increasing the demands on people's lives. High demands on people's lives are one of the factors pushing housewives into the labour market, namely to bolster the financial conditions of the household. This has increased the participation rate amongst housewives. Meanwhile, competition between male and female workers is a cause of gender jealousy, particularly when female workers hold a higher position than their male counterparts. In addition, occupying the same work environment increases the potential for sexual harassment against women in the workplace or even adulterous relationships between co-workers.

The social issues that can occur extend beyond the workplace to include the household or family environment. In general, workers have less time to focus on the household and their family, which could edge up the divorce rate though divorce is severely frowned upon in Islam. In addition, children can suffer from a lack of attention or concern when women enter the workforce, or even violence against minors.

The high demands on people's lives can also trigger childhood issues, such as dropping out of school, lower education levels, and malnutrition. In addition, children are often compelled to work to meet the basic necessities for their family, thus increasing child labour.

(b) *Socio-economic Issues*

The sectors most susceptible to the impact of inflation are those with broad access to bank loans, particularly large businesses in the property sector or capital market, where most investors are from the top of the pyramid. Prices in such sectors tend to be more sensitive to inflation, leading to comparatively higher profits because output prices increase faster than input prices. The nominal income of players in those sectors will increase beyond the rate of inflation, thereby strengthening real income (purchasing power). Ultimately, economic actors in those sectors will benefit more from inflation. It is clear, therefore, that inflation will allow greater capital ownership to be accumulated by those at the top of the pyramid.

Conversely, those towards the middle and bottom of the pyramid, the workers and small-scale business owners, do not benefit from inflation. Output prices do not increase faster than input prices. In addition, inflation erodes nominal income, hence decreasing the real income of the working class.

Ultimately, inflation can push a community into poverty, especially if real income drops below the minimum living standard. It can be concluded, therefore, that inflation disadvantages the working class. Moreover, absolute poverty occurs when real income decreases below the minimum living standard.

Inflation is a key determinant of lower real income among the working class and higher income for the upper class. This is an emerging issue, namely inequitable income distribution. Furthermore, the income gap is increasing with inflation annually, which clearly runs contrary to the values upheld in Islam, such as justice and brotherhood.

The issue of inequitable income distribution reflects how the current economic system has failed to achieve equitable justice and welfare for all (Meera & Aziz, 2002). According to Islamic teachings, the target of an economic system is not only economic growth but also achieving quality welfare in the economy. Realising robust economic growth would be futile, therefore, because the increase in consumption is only created by the upper class, with a significant gap in terms of income distribution between social classes.

The economic system set forth in Al-Qur'an and the Hadiths provides a viable solution to eradicate inequitable income distribution. Allah SWT guarantees sustenance for each of His servants and provides all the resources in the heavens and earth for humans to achieve quality welfare and fulfil the basic needs of human life. Notwithstanding, human actions deviate from His guidance and damage the earth, thus causing numerous issues that complicate and disrupt the balance of human life.

(c) *Environmental Issues*

Environmental issues can be classified as physical and social problems. According to Meera and Aziz (2002), the environment experiences physical damage through deforestation and the indiscriminate burning of forest land, illegal logging and sale of timber, massive degradation of water catchment areas, overfishing, the poaching of endangered species, and other exploitative actions. This is attributable to the application of an interest rate system that leads to inflation and higher production costs, resulting in nefarious producers chasing profit by any means necessary, irrespective of the harm that may be caused, to achieve the lowest production costs possible.

In addition, long-term social issues can also arise from the use of fiat money. The higher demands of life caused by inflation lead to desperation in terms of earning a living, with people forced to take shortcuts to meet their daily needs, including possibly criminal acts, such as stealing, robbing, human trafficking or murder. While inflation, poverty, and income inequality persist, criminality will be difficult to minimise.

Advantages of Fiat Money

The use of fiat money, which is not backed by real assets, faces the inherent risk of various negative problems. Notwithstanding, fiat money backed by real assets as the underlying has several advantages over gold and silver. During his reign, Rasulullah SAW did not place restrictions on which materials could be used to make money, implying that money could be made from materials other than gold and silver. In addition, Umar bin Khattab decided to make currency from camel hide before reversing his decision through fear camels may become extinct. This shows, however, that money does not have to be made from gold and silver. Umar bin Khattab proposed the idea of using camel hide to protect and maintain the value of the currency because gold and silver coins were regularly counterfeited at that time using alloys, such as copper. The implementation of fiat money backed by real assets is applicable to the Islamic economy based on the following advantages:

First, cheaper manufacturing and raw material costs. Paper as a raw material is easy to source and available in large quantities, thereby lowering prices. Furthermore, the manufacturing process for paper money is less complicated than minting gold and silver coins, thus allowing fiat money to be issued quickly and in large quantities.

Second, fiat money is easier to mobilise. The lighter weight and stackable nature of paper money make it superior in terms of mobilisation, contrasting the heavier weight and greater inconvenience of gold and silver coins.

Third, fiat money is easier to divide into smaller units or denominations. Fiat money is created in various units ranging from small to large denominations, thus ensuring fiat money is more efficient when purchasing lower value goods and services. In contrast, gold and silver coins tend to be of large denominations, making them less efficient when purchasing low-value items.

In addition to the salient advantages of fiat money over gold and silver coins as described above, there is also other corroborating evidence that strengthens the credibility of fiat money as a reliable medium of exchange because fiat money meets the following criteria (Ibrahim, 2020; Meera, 2018):

1. *Durability*: Constructed from strong and durable raw materials.
2. *Transportability*: Easily mobilised and transported securely and conveniently.
3. *Divisibility*: Can be divided into smaller amounts without losing value.
4. *Uniformity*: Uniform quality and design, also facilitating divisibility.
5. *Acceptability*: Accepted by the public as a medium of exchange.
6. *Limited Supply*: Available in limited quantities.

Fiat money successfully meets those criteria and is thus viable as legal tender and a medium of exchange.

9.4.3 Fiat Money According to Ulema

Despite the extreme opinion that gold and silver are the only acceptable forms of money, various contrasting arguments have been put forward. This beckons the question, however, regarding what would happen if gold and silver coins were reintroduced and fiat money abolished? Would a return to gold and silver be favourable or practical? Such questions provide the rationale behind why the monetary system continues to use fiat money to this day (Ibrahim, 2020).

In addition, there are compelling arguments for the continued use of fiat money. *First*, potential difficulties could arise if money was restricted to gold and silver. The total stock of gold and silver would gradually be depleted and, therefore, no longer sufficient for large transactions. *Second*, the practicality of using gold and silver is also questionable considering how interconnected the monetary system is at the global level. *Third*, declining value is not merely a phenomenon of fiat money, the value of gold and silver coins could also decrease if supply exceeds demand in the real sector.

Based on the various legal debates concerning the application of fiat money in terms of *muamalah* practices, it can be concluded that fiat money is in accordance with Islamic *muamalah* principles because the mandate to regulate the supply and circulation of fiat money is held by the central bank. The mandate is bestowed upon entities in the public sector (government apparatus) which are legally valid, official, and trusted by the community. The contemporary use of fiat money as legal tender, therefore, is valid.

Fiat money is widely accepted by those who use it. Under Islamic law, the use of fiat money has become customary, referred to as *'urf*. In addition, fiat money is permitted based on *muamalah* principles, stating that everything is permissible unless there is a valid legal argument (*dalil*) that prohibits it. In addition, Al-Qur'an contains no revelation that money other than gold and silver is forbidden or *haram*. This opinion was reinforced by the initiative of Umar bin Khattab to make currency from camel hide, thus demonstrating that money is not limited to gold and silver. Moreover, fiat money has a distinct advantage in terms of market liquidity.

In addition to the legal discourse debating the application of fiat money, the socio-economic consequences must also be considered. The overarching goals of the

Islamic economy are justice and quality welfare (*falah*) for all. If the use of fiat money brings justice and quality welfare to society, implementation is permissible in Islam providing that no interest-bearing mechanisms are involved, which are absolutely forbidden in Islam.

Meanwhile, the central bank has been mandated to regulate monetary policy using instruments that do not contradict Islamic teachings. In addition, the central bank is also authorised to regulate money supply in order to achieve monetary, inflation, and exchange rate targets for example. It is important to note, however, that fiat money issued by a central bank must be based on real underlying assets in accordance with market demand. Consequently, the fiat money issued should be channelled to the real sector in order to maintain stability as well as equilibrium between the real and monetary sectors.

The specific type of money used, therefore, is not important as both fiat money and coins have their respective advantages and disadvantages. The debate about whether to return to coins or persist with fiat money is no longer of concern to economists. It has become more important to identify the steps, mechanisms, and institutional frameworks that can ensure the proper management and control of money in order to maintain a stable value of currency.

9.5 Islamic Perspective of Money

9.5.1 A Brief History of Money in Islam

The history of money in Islam is divided into several eras, namely (i) Pre-Islam, (ii) Prophet Muhammad SAW and Rashidun Caliphs, (iii) Umayyad Caliphate, and (iv) Abbasid Caliphate.

(i) *Pre-Islam*

The use of gold and silver is as old as human civilisation. Before the emergence of Islam, gold and silver coins were minted by the Lydians during the period from 570–546 BC (Hasan, 2005). This practice was adopted by both the Jews and Greeks. In addition to commodity money, which circulated in the form of axes, transactions were also settled using gold and silver coins. The Romans also issued gold coins known as denarius in 268 BC to support the distribution of bronze. From 546 BC to AD 621, the Persians issued gold and silver coins but the civilisation began to decline as they issued coins minted from gold alloys and bronze, resulting in the loss of gold-based money.

Prior to Islam, Arabs used dinar and dirham to trade with neighbouring countries. When trading in Syria, Arabs bought golden dinars from the Romans (Byzantines). When travelling from Iraq, Arabs took silver dirhams from Persia (Sassanid Empire). Sometimes, Arabs also purchased Himyar dirham from Yemen. Such conditions imply that during the time of Rasulullah SAW, various currencies circulated amongst Arabs in the Hejaz and neighbouring countries.

(ii) *Money During Reign of Prophet Muhammad and Rashidun Caliphs*

The *da'wah* and Islamic teachings revealed by Rasulullah SAW during his time in Mecca focused on establishing monotheism and how to survive the treatment of infidels. After moving to Medina, Rasulullah SAW began to build an economy of Muslims in accordance with the revelations and guidance contained in Al-Qur'an. At that time, Rasulullah SAW focused on applying Islamic ethics and norms to economic practices, as well as achieving equity and justice for all. Therefore, economic resources were not allowed merely to circulate in the hands of a few.

To create such conditions, Rasulullah SAW took concrete measures to unite the Muhajirin (emigrants from Mecca) and Ansar (local inhabitants of Medina) in brotherhood. This aimed to establish good business relationships between the two groups, where the majority of Ansar had access to sufficient sources of wealth, which the Muhajirin lacked. Business cooperation intended to increase productivity and, thus, state revenue. In addition, *zakat* collection and distribution were managed well, thus optimising wealth distribution. Even in the ninth year of *hijrah, zakat* was obligatory.

Trade was the primary livelihood at the time of Rasulullah SAW and *Baitul Mal* existed as the state treasurer or financial management institution. In those days, trade was facilitated by a specific medium of exchange, namely money. Gold dinar and silver dirham were used for trade transactions with neighbouring countries to the north and south during the time of Rasulullah SAW. In verse 1–2 of surah Al-Quraisy, Allah SWT reveals:

لِاِيْلٰفِ قُرَيْشٍۙ(1)

اٖلٰفِهِمْ رِحْلَةَ الشِّتَاۤءِ وَالصَّيْفِۚ(2)

For the accustomed security of the Quraysh. Their accustomed security [in] the caravan of winter and summer (Q.S. Al-Quraisy [106]: 1-2).

The money used during this period was not in the form of coins, Arabs appraised of the value of the dinar and dirham by their gold and silver seed weight (*tibr*). As currency, the Heraclius dinar from the Byzantine Emperor and the Baqhli dirham from Persia were used.

The Prophet Muhammad SAW stated that the dinar and dirham would remain the primary currency in circulation. Rasulullah SAW and his companions relied on this currency to intermediate economic activities, such as *muamalah*, trade, and *zakat* (Zallum, 1983). Rasulullah SAW did not issue currency exclusively for the Islamic community, instead setting the Islamic dirham at 14 carats. This initiative distinguished the Islamic dirham from the Persian dirham, which had three weights and measures: 20 carats, 12 carats, and 10 carats. The number 14 comes from $20 + 12 + 10 = 42/3 = 14$.

The recirculated currency was not perfectly round like contemporary coins because coins were not minted in a mould. Furthermore, Arabs did not consider dinar and dirham coins according to face value, instead relying on weight, thus the currency was determined based on its value in gold and silver.

Currency minted from gold was not considered valid because the form and weight were subject to depreciation. It was possible to divide the coinage into halves and quarters, however, to obtain smaller value gold dinars and silver dirhams (Karim, 2006). After Muhammad SAW became Rasulullah SAW, he urged the people of Medina to adopt the Meccan tradition of circulating dinars and dirhams based on face value rather than weight. The Prophet stated, "Weight is weight for the people of Mecca, but measurement is measurement for the people of Medina," (Hasan, 2005).

After Rasulullah SAW, the first caliph was Abu Bakar As-Sidiq. Muslim society continued to use the Roman dinar and Persian dirham after Rasulullah SAW during the reign of Abu Bakar As-Sidiq and the beginning of Umar bin Khathab's rule. One of Abu Bakar As-Sidiq's initial actions as ruler was to rebuild the *Baitul Mal* institution and resume the wealth distribution system. Under Umar bin Khathab, *Baitul Mal* was developed permanently in the capital city, with branches in various provincial capitals. In addition, economic innovation flourished during the caliphate, with approximately 120,000 jobs created annually.

In 20 *Hijriyyah* (the eighth year of Caliph Umar's rule), Umar minted new dirhams based on the structure of the Persian dirham. Its weight, inner markings and letters, written in Persian Bahlawi remained unchanged. The only additions were words written in Arabic form, stylized in Kufic script, such as Bismillah and Bismillah Rabbi, placed on the corner of the coin. Muslims preserved this tradition of minting coins until the caliphate of Ali (Hasan, 2005). At the beginning of his administration, Umar had the idea to print money from hide, but his companions disagreed and the idea was abandoned.

During the rule of Usman bin Affan, Islamic territory expanded along with state revenues. The major breakthrough attributable to Usman was construction of the first port. During the reign of Usman bin Affan, the tradition of minting money followed the tradition initiated by Umar. During Ali's rule, however, limited edition coins were also minted (Karim, 2006). The measurement of the Islamic dirham at that time was weighed into 6 daniq and each 10 dirham was 7 mithqal, to correspond with the era of Rasulullah SAW. Starting from this period, Muslims had their own official Islamic dinar and dirham. As the last caliph, Ali bin Abi Thalib was very strict in terms of managing state finances.

(iii) *Money During Umayyah Dynasty*

Sasani and Byzantine coins inscribed with Islamic symbols were legal tender during this period. Minting coins was not the responsibility of any specific government party. Governors and regional rulers minted special coins for their respective regions. Other rulers during this era also minted their own coins. Al-Hajj minted baghli dirham. Abdullah bin Zubair minted an eponymous coin known as Abdullah Amir al-Mu'minin. While serving as Governor of Iraq, Mush'ab bin Zubair minted a special dirham. Several years later, Abdul Malik bin Marwan sought to unify the different currencies from all regions.

Abdul Malik bin Marwan minted a limited run of new gold dinars, and he is considered the first caliph to mint gold dinars. Overseeing significant monetary reforms, Abdul Malik bin Marwan instituted policy forbidding the use of non-Islamic currency and ordered the minting of Islamic money by a government institution. This policy was maintained by subsequent Islamic governments.

(iv) *Money During Abbasid Dynasty*

During the Abbasid dynasty, monetary policy reduced the weight of the dinar and dirham in circulation due to spiralling budgets. Since individuals tended to pursue life's luxuries, the money required did not fulfil overall circulation. Thus, the state needed to obtain additional resources. Unfortunately, it could not meet the required resources. Consequently, the minted gold and silver metal had to be mixed with copper, for the sake of profit in minting the coins (Hasan, 2005). Islamic legal experts and *fuqaha* disagreed with such practices as they would lead to inflation and gradual erode the value of the money. Inflation was precipitated by the growing number of dinars and dirhams in circulation.

9.5.2 Concept of Money in Islam

Islam states that money is a public good and follows the flow concept, contrasting capital which is a private good and follows the stock concept (Karim, 2002). In Islamic economics, money is a public good and follows the flow concept. Money has three basic functions as follows:

(a) Money as a measure of price
(b) Money as a medium of transaction
(c) Money as a store of value/wealth

In Islam, money is recognised as wealth, which must be protected. It should be noted, however, in terms of the relationship between money and the transaction value of goods/services, Ibn Taimiyah stated that money must be printed in accordance with the transactional needs of the community in order to achieve a fair price. Printing money in excess of the amount required for transactions will erode its value. In addition, a mismatch between the amount of money printed and transactional requirements in the real sector will create unfair prices and impact private wealth adversely, while opening the door for speculative actions by trading money. Trading currency has undesirable impacts on value and purchasing power. The basic functions of money are discussed in the following section. The concept of money is distinguished into two schools of thought (*madhhab*), namely precious metals and base metals (Haneef & Barakat, 2002). The concept of money in Islam is discussed as follows:

(i) Precious Metal Money School of Thought (*Madhhab*)

Two precious metals are recognised and permitted in Islam as money, namely gold and silver, with practices dating back to Rasulullah SAW. Precious metal was minted into money due to its comparatively stable value. The value of gold and silver does not fluctuate much. Second, gold and silver are naturally desirable and coveted by humans throughout their lives.

Money minted from precious metals has developed in line with the availability of the raw materials themselves. Precious metal coins can be classified and described as follows:

(a) Full-bodied money: Money that is minted using 100% raw materials of gold or silver, implying that the face value is the same as the intrinsic value. Dinar and dirham are examples of full-bodied money.
(b) Representative money: A type of precious metal money that is not actually minted from precious raw materials, instead applying the backup principle. Therefore, every paper note or coin printed or minted must be backed by gold or silver reserves. This money is further divided into two classifications, namely 100% reserve and partial reserve. Specifically, 100% reserve currency is fully backed by gold or silver, while partial reserve currency is only partially backed by precious metals.

(ii) Base Metal Money School of Thought (*Madhhab*)

In addition to money formed from precious metals, Islam also recognises the reliability and suitability of certain objects as transaction instruments, categorised according to *Amwale Rabuviah* and consisting of salt, wheat, dates, and barley, the values of which are stable. Rasulullah SAW, therefore, stated that such objects were reliable as money.

9.5.3 Motives for Holding Money from an Islamic Perspective

The motive to hold is said to be a determining factor for deciding the nominal amount of money held by the public, from which the demand for money can be derived. Based on conventional economics, the three salient motives for holding money are explained by the Liquidity Preference Theory, namely the transaction motive, precautionary motive, and speculative motive.

Islam subscribes to its own perspective for dealing with the motives to hold money. Fundamentally, interest rates are absolutely forbidden in Islam for containing elements of *riba*. In addition, speculation is considered a form of *maysir* (gambling) and, thus, also proscribed in Islam. The act of speculating in Islam is considered equivalent to gambling, or playing games of chance for money, where one party wins to the detriment of another. This is contrary to Islamic principles that forbid the taking of another person's property through *bathil* (falsehood). In terms of the motives for holding money, therefore, Islam only recognises two, namely the transaction motive and precautionary motive. In other words, there are no speculative motives recognised in Islam.

9.5.4 Function of Money from an Islamic Perspective

Based on conventional economic theory, there are generally three functions and criteria for an object to be recognised as currency as follows:

(a) A unit of account. Money must function as a consistent reference for the value of all tradeable commodities.
(b) Objects used as money must be recognised by the entire community without exception as a medium of exchange for transactional purposes to obtain goods and services. Here, it is the responsibility of the central bank to put the legal in legal tender.
(c) Money must function as a store of value. The purpose of holding money is not only to transact in the present but also to save for future needs. Objects viable as money, therefore, must have a stable value that does not depreciate easily.

Money is a standard for goods and services. Money can be defined, therefore, as a tool to measure the value of each good and service. Zallum (2002) stated that money is a medium of exchange used as legal tender in a specific region or country to create efficiency and provide flexibility when performing transactions to purchase goods or remunerate services.

Haneef and Barakat (2006) recapitulated the opinions of several experts concerning money. One opinion states that currency is limited to gold and silver, whereas the contrasting opinion states that currency is not limited to gold and silver. Islamic scholars from both the Salaf and Khalaf periods also proffered differing opinions regarding the use of gold and silver as currency. There are two salient schools of thought (*madhhab*) among the scholars (*ulama*). First, currency or money is limited to gold and silver. Second, currency or money is not only limited to gold and silver.

Both groups have provided evidence to support their respective opinions. Most support for the second opinion stems from contemporary scholars and Islamic jurisprudence (*fiqh*) boards. Though rejecting the idea that currency should only be limited to gold and silver, proponents of the second opinion agree that precious metals could fairly represent the value of other materials, such as copper. This differs from the contemporary practice of fiat money, which was created with no intrinsic value to back it up.

The estimated value of goods and services is expressed in specific units. This unit, therefore, is a standard that can be used to measure the value of benefit of the corresponding goods or services, hence becoming a medium of exchange known as money. According to Al-Ghazali, money plays a critical role in economic activity. Money is one of the blessings bestowed by Allah SWT to support life on earth. Consequently, money must be used in accordance with sharia law. In Ihya' Ulum al-Din (The Revival of the Religious Sciences), Al-Ghazali states that Allah SWT created the dinar and dirham as a blessing to maintain world order. Humans need dinars and dirhams to fulfil the bare essentials and basic necessities of shelter, sustenance, clothing, and so on.

According to Ibnu Taimiyah, money has two functions as a medium of exchange and a universally accepted unit of account. This was explained in more depth by Ibn al-Qayyim, stating that the function of money as a medium of exchange is to purchase goods and services, not as a commodity itself (Islahi, 2016). In other words, money should not be traded as a commodity. In addition, a stable value or purchasing power of money must be maintained.

An-Nabhani (1996) stated that Islam grants individuals the freedom to make exchanges at their own discretion. Nevertheless, Islam also reveals the best unit that can be used in the exchange of goods and services, namely gold and silver. This conclusion is based on various rationale, namely that Islam strictly forbids the hoarding of gold and silver as currency and a medium of exchange, as revealed in verse 34 of surah At-Taubah as follows:

يٰٓاَيُّهَا الَّذِيْنَ اٰمَنُوْٓا اِنَّ كَثِيْرًا مِّنَ الْاَحْبَارِ وَالرُّهْبَانِ لَيَأْكُلُوْنَ اَمْوَالَ النَّاسِ بِالْبَاطِلِ وَيَصُدُّوْنَ عَنْ سَبِيْلِ اللّٰهِ ۗوَالَّذِيْنَ يَكْنِزُوْنَ الذَّهَبَ وَالْفِضَّةَ
وَلَا يُنْفِقُوْنَهَا فِيْ سَبِيْلِ اللّٰهِ ۙفَبَشِّرْهُمْ بِعَذَابٍ اَلِيْمٍۙ

> O you who have believed, indeed many of the scholars and the monks devour the wealth of people unjustly and avert [them] from the way of Allah. And those who hoard gold and silver and spend it not in the way of Allah—give them tidings of a painful punishment. (Q.S. At-Taubah[9]: 34).

In Islam, gold and silver are intertwined in sharia law. For example, the financial compensation paid to the victim or heirs of a victim (*diyya*) for murder is 1000 dinars. In addition, for theft of property exceeding ¼ dinar, the punishment is hand amputation. Similarly, Rasulullah SAW prescribed gold and silver as the money standard. When Allah SWT obliged *zakat* on money, it was based on gold and silver, and the *nisab* threshold was also stipulated based on gold and silver. When laws were enacted on foreign exchange transactions (*sharf*), this was also based on gold and silver.

The function of money was explored by the scholar Ibnu Taimiyah, stating that if a ruler abolished the use of certain currencies and printed a new form of currency, this would be detrimental to anyone holding the old money, which would become invalid as legal tender and worthless. This would be considered an act of tyranny by rendering something of high value worthless. When Ibnu Taimiyah mentioned the two main functions of money, namely as a unit of account and medium of exchange, he stated that *atsman* (price/money) was intended as a measure of the value of goods (*mi"yar al-amwal*).

Ibnu Taimiyah was strongly opposed to all forms of currency trading because it detracted from the actual function of money. If two people exchange money and one of them pays in cash while the other promises to pay later, the first person cannot use the promised money in the transaction until he has actually been paid. Consequently, the first person loses the opportunity to use the money to meet his needs.

Meanwhile, Al-Ghazali had a very distinct view of money. As contained in his book, Ihya' Ulum al-Din (The Revival of the Religious Sciences), Al-Ghazali discusses the problems associated with money as used by humans as a blessing from Allah SWT based on the barter system. Furthermore, Al-Ghazali explains money as an important element of business regulations because money is a blessing from Allah SWT that must be placed in accordance with His rules.

More specifically, in Al-Ghazali's words, dinar and dirham are *khadimani wa la khadimun la huma wa muradani wa la yuradani*, namely tools to achieve a purpose or an intermediary tool only and not for other purposes. The definition put forward by Al-Ghazali, therefore, is consistent with other definitions. Al-Ghazali's opinion that money is only a unit of exchange and intermediary plays a significant role in today's modern economy.

In Islamic economics, money is money and not capital or a commodity to be traded. In addition, money is a public good and follows the flow concept. According to conventional economics, however, the concept of money is too broad, lacking specific rules. Money is simultaneously defined as money and capital, whereas capital follows the stock concept and is a private good. Money that flows is a public good, yet money that settles belongs to someone and becomes a private good.

In both the Islamic and conventional economic systems, money is considered a medium of exchange and unit of account, yet according to conventional economics, money has one more function as a store of value, which developed into "the money demand for speculation", thus changing the function of money to become a tradable commodity. This is despite the premonition of Iman Al-Ghazai that "trading money is equivalent to confining the function of money, if a lot of money is traded, little will be left to function as money".

The nature of money is mentioned several times in Al-Qur'an and the Hadiths as follows:

1. *Money in the form of gold and silver:* Before money emerged, Arabs at the time of the Prophet SAW used gold and silver as a medium of exchange for goods and services. Verse 4 of surah Ali-Imran in Al-Qur'an describes gold and silver as wealth and money in the form of dinar and dirham.

   مِن قَبْلُ هُدًى لِّلنَّاسِ وَأَنزَلَ ٱلْفُرْقَانَ ۗ إِنَّ ٱلَّذِينَ كَفَرُوا۟ بِـَٔايَٰتِ ٱللَّهِ لَهُمْ عَذَابٌ شَدِيدٌ ۗ وَٱللَّهُ عَزِيزٌ ذُو ٱنتِقَامٍ

   Before, as guidance for the people. And He revealed the Qur'an. Indeed, those who disbelieve in the verses of Allah will have a severe punishment, and Allah is exalted in Might, the Owner of Retribution. (Q.S. Ali Imran [3]: 4).

2. *Money as dinar and dirham:* At the time of Rasulullah SAW, dinar and dirham were considered currency. The decision to use dinar and dirham is also written in Al-Qur'an, verse 75 of surah Ali-Imran as follows:

   ۞ وَمِنْ أَهْلِ ٱلْكِتَٰبِ مَنْ إِن تَأْمَنْهُ بِقِنطَارٍ يُؤَدِّهِۦٓ إِلَيْكَ وَمِنْهُم مَّنْ إِن تَأْمَنْهُ بِدِينَارٍ لَّا يُؤَدِّهِۦٓ إِلَيْكَ إِلَّا مَا دُمْتَ عَلَيْهِ قَآئِمًا ۗ ذَٰلِكَ بِأَنَّهُمْ قَالُوا۟ لَيْسَ عَلَيْنَا فِى ٱلْأُمِّيِّـۧنَ سَبِيلٌ وَيَقُولُونَ عَلَى ٱللَّهِ ٱلْكَذِبَ وَهُمْ يَعْلَمُونَ

   And among the People of the Scripture is he who, if you entrust him with a great amount [of wealth], he will return it to you. And among them is he who, if you entrust him with a [single] silver coin, he will not return it to you unless you are constantly standing over him [demanding it]. That is because they say, "There is no blame upon us concerning the unlearned." And they speak untruth about Allah while they know [it]. (Q.S. Ali Imran [3]: 75).

3. *Money used to purchase goods and services:* From an Islamic standpoint, the functions of money are only a medium of exchange and unit of account. Money can be useful when exchanged for tangible objects or to remunerate a service. Verse 20 of surah Yusuf is as follows:

وَشَرَوْهُ بِثَمَنٍۢ بَخْسٍ دَرَاهِمَ مَعْدُوْدَةٍۚ وَكَانُوْا فِيْهِ مِنَ الزَّاهِدِيْنَ ࣖ

And they sold him for a reduced price—a few dirhams—and they were, concerning him, of those content with little. (Q.S. Yusuf [12]: 20).

4. *Money as a symbol of wealth:* Gold and silver are a form of property and represent wealth in the form of dinar and dirham currency as well as precious metals. The amount of property a person owns is also a symbol of wealth. Verses 33–35 of surah Az-Zukhruf reveals that gold was created as a blessing to be enjoyed in the world as follows:

وَلَوْلَآ أَن يَكُونَ ٱلنَّاسُ أُمَّةً وَٰحِدَةً لَّجَعَلْنَا لِمَن يَكْفُرُ بِٱلرَّحْمَٰنِ لِبُيُوتِهِمْ سُقُفًا مِّن فِضَّةٍ وَمَعَارِجَ عَلَيْهَا
يَظْهَرُونَ ٣٣ وَلِبُيُوتِهِمْ أَبْوَٰبًا وَسُرُرًا عَلَيْهَا يَتَّكِـُٔونَ ٣٤ وَزُخْرُفًاۚ وَإِن كُلُّ ذَٰلِكَ لَمَّا مَتَٰعُ ٱلْحَيَوٰةِ
ٱلدُّنْيَاۚ وَٱلْءَاخِرَةُ عِندَ رَبِّكَ لِلْمُتَّقِينَ ٣٥

And if it were not that the people would become one community [of disbelievers], We would have made for those who disbelieve in the Most Merciful—for their houses—ceilings and stairways of silver upon which to mount. And for their houses—doors and couches [of silver] upon which to recline. And gold ornament. But all that is not but the enjoyment of worldly life. And the Hereafter with your Lord is for the righteous. (Q.SAz-Zukhruf [43]: 33-35).

5. *Money as a medium of exchange:* The main function of money is as a medium of exchange. Using dinar and dirham, individuals can purchase goods/services to meet their daily needs. This is described in the Hadiths as follows:

وَعَنْ أَبِي سَعِيدٍ قَالَ: جَاءَ بِلَالٌ إِلَى النَّبِيِّ صَلَّى اللهُ عَلَيْهِ وَسَلَّمَ بِتَمْرٍ بَرْنِيٍّ فَقَالَ لَهُ النَّبِيُّ صَلَّى اللهُ عَلَيْهِ وَسَلَّمَ: «مِنْ أَيْنَ هَذَا؟» قَالَ: كَانَ عِنْدَنَا تَمْرٌ رَدِيءٌ فَبِعْتُ مِنْهُ صَاعَيْنِ بِصَاعٍ فَقَالَ: أَوَّهْ عَيْنُ الرِّبَا عَيْنُ الرِّبَا لَا تَفْعَلْ وَلَكِنْ إِذَا أَرَدْتَ أَنْ تَشْتَرِيَ فَبِعِ التَّمرَ بِبَيْعٍ آخر ثُمَّ اشْتَرِ بِهِ

Abu Sa'id said that Bilal brought the Prophet some barni* dates, and when he asked him where he had got them he replied, "I had some inferior dates, so I sold two sa's of them for a sa." He said, "Ah, the very essence of usury, the very essence of usury. Do not do so, but when you wish to buy, sell the dates in a separate transaction, then buy with what you get." (Bukhari and Muslim.)[2]

6. *Money as a measure of value:* At the time of Rasulullah SAW, gold and silver coins were used to measure the value of an object. Arabs used this type of currency based on weight rather than face value. The weight of this money

[2]Reference: Mishkat al-Masabih 2814. In-book reference: Book 11, Hadith 53.

served as a measure of value, including goods to calculate the *nisab* threshold for *zakat* collection. This is mentioned in the Hadiths as follows:

عَنْ أَبِي سَعِيدٍ الْخُدْرِيِّ قَالَ: قَالَ رَسُولُ اللَّهِ صَلَّى اللَّهُ عَلَيْهِ وَسَلَّمَ: «لَيْسَ فِيمَا دُونَ خَمْسَةِ أَوْسُقٍ مِنَ التَّمْرِ صَدَقَةٌ وَلَيْسَ فِيمَا دُونَ خَمْسِ أَوَاقٍ مِنَ الْوَرِقِ صَدَقَةٌ وَلَيْسَ فِيمَا دُونَ خَمْسِ ذَوْدٍ من الْإِبِل صَدَقَة»

Abu Sa'id al-Khudri reported God's messenger as saying, "No sadaqa is payable on less than five camel-loads (wasq) of dates, on less than five ounces of silver, and on less than five camels." (Bukhari and Muslim.)[3]

7. *Money to meet daily necessities:* The function of money is optimised when spent on daily necessities in ways revealed by Allah SWT and his Messenger SAW. The Prophet Muhammad SAW spoke of spending money wisely on the family and helping friends in need. This is contained in the Hadiths as follows:

وَعَنْ ثَوْبَانَ قَالَ: قَالَ رَسُولُ اللَّهِ صَلَّى اللَّهُ عَلَيْهِ وَسَلَّمَ: «أَفْضَلُ دِينَارٍ يُنْفِقُهُ الرَّجُلُ دِينَارٌ يُنْفِقُهُ عَلَى عِيَالِهِ وَدِينَارٌ يُنْفِقُهُ عَلَى دَابَّتِهِ فِي سَبِيلِ اللَّهِ وَدِينَارٌ يُنْفِقُهُ عَلَى أَصْحَابه فِي سَبِيل الله» . رَوَاهُ مُسلم

Thauban reported God's messenger as saying,"The most excellent dinar a man spends is one he spends on his family, one which he spends on his animal in God's path, and one he spends on his companions in God's path." Muslim transmitted it.[4]

8. *Money as a means of payment:* From an Islamic perspective, money is also used as a means of payment. With money, individuals can buy what they desire, which can be resold at a profit. A hadith narrated by 'Urwa is as follows:

حَدَّثَنَا عَلِيُّ بْنُ عَبْدِ اللَّهِ، أَخْبَرَنَا سُفْيَانُ، حَدَّثَنَا شَبِيبُ بْنُ غَرْقَدَةَ، قَالَ سَمِعْتُ الْحَىَّ، يُحَدِّثُونَ عَنْ عُرْوَةَ، أَنَّ النَّبِيَّ صلى الله عليه وسلم أَعْطَاهُ دِينَارًا يَشْتَرِي بِهِ شَاةً، فَاشْتَرَى لَهُ بِهِ شَاتَيْنِ، فَبَاعَ إِحْدَاهُمَا بِدِينَارٍ وَجَاءَهُ بِدِينَارٍ وَشَاةٍ، فَدَعَا لَهُ بِالْبَرَكَةِ فِي بَيْعِهِ، وَكَانَ لَوِ اشْتَرَى التُّرَابَ لَرَبِحَ فِيهِ. قَالَ سُفْيَانُ كَانَ الْحَسَنُ بْنُ عُمَارَةَ جَاءَنَا بِهَذَا الْحَدِيثِ عَنْهُ، قَالَ سَمِعَهُ شَبِيبٌ مِنْ عُرْوَةَ، فَأَتَيْتُهُ فَقَالَ شَبِيبٌ إِنِّي لَمْ أَسْمَعْهُ مِنْ عُرْوَةَ، قَالَ سَمِعْتُ الْحَىَّ يُخْبِرُونَهُ عَنْهُ. وَلَكِنْ سَمِعْتُهُ يَقُولُ سَمِعْتُ النَّبِيَّ صلى الله عليه وسلم يَقُولُ " الْخَيْرُ مَعْقُودٌ بِنَوَاصِي الْخَيْلِ إِلَى يَوْمِ الْقِيَامَةِ ". قَالَ وَقَدْ رَأَيْتُ فِي دَارِهِ سَبْعِينَ فَرَسًا. قَالَ سُفْيَانُ يَشْتَرِي لَهُ شَاةً كَأَنَّهَا أُضْحِيَّةٌ

Narrated 'Urwa*:*

That the Prophet gave him one Dinar so as to buy a sheep for him. 'Urwa bought two sheep for him with the money. Then he sold one of the sheep for one Dinar, and brought one Dinar and a sheep to the Prophet. On that, the Prophet invoked Allah to bless him in his deals. So 'Urwa used to gain (from any deal) even if he bought dust. (In another narration) 'Urwa said, "I heard Allah's Messenger saying, "There is always goodness in horses till the Day of Resurrection." (The subnarrator added, "I saw 70 horses in 'Urwa's house.') (Sufyan said, "The Prophet asked 'Urwa to buy a sheep for him as a sacrifice.")[5]

[3]Reference: Mishkat al-Masabih 1794. In-book reference: Book 6, Hadith 23.

[4]Reference: Mishkat al-Masabih 1932. In-book reference: Book 6, Hadith 157.

[5]Reference: Sahih al-Bukhari 3642, 3643. In-book reference: Book 61 Hadith 164. USC-MSA web (English) reference: Vol.4, Book 56, Hadith 836 (deprecated numbering scheme).

9. *Money as an instrument to be close with Allah SWT:* Money and property must be allocated in accordance with the rules and ways of Allah SWT. The goal is to use money optimally and beneficially, for example to free slaves or provide charity to the poor, while meeting the needs of the family. This is written in the Hadiths as follows:

وعن أبي هريرة رضي الله عنه قال: قال رسول الله صلى الله عليه وسلم : " دينار أنفقته في سبيل الله، ودينار أنفقته في رقبة، ودينار تصدقت به على مسكين، ودينار أنفقته على أهلك، أعظمها أجرًا الذي أنفقته على أهلك" ((رواه مسلم)).

Abu Hurairah (May Allah be pleased with him) reported:

Messenger of Allah (ﷺ) said, "A dinar you spend in Allah's way, or to free a slave, or as a charity you give to a needy person, or to support your family, the one yielding the greatest reward is that which you spend on your family". [Muslim].[6]

10. *Money to regulate transactions:* The following Hadith explains that buying and selling transactions must balance, for instance gold with gold, silver with silver, and cash with cash. Rasulullah SAW recommended that any excess should be returned. Failure to do so constitutes *riba*, which was strictly forbidden by Rasulullah SAW.

وَعَنْ أَبِي سَعِيدٍ اَلْخُدْرِيِّ - رضى الله عنه - أَنَّ رَسُولَ اَللَّهِ - صلى الله عليه وسلم -قَالَ: { لَا تَبِيعُوا 1اَلذَّهَبَ بِالذَّهَبِ إِلَّا مِثْلًا بِمِثْلٍ, وَلَا تُشِفُّوا بَعْضَهَا عَلَى بَعْضٍ, وَلَا تَبِيعُوا اَلْوَرِقَ بِالْوَرِقِ إِلَّا مِثْلًا بِمِثْلٍ, وَلَا تُشِفُّوا بَعْضَهَا عَلَى بَعْضٍ, وَلَا تَبِيعُوا مِنْهَا غَائِباً بِنَاجِزٍ } مُتَّفَقٌ عَلَيْهِ

The Prophet (ﷺ) said: "Do not sell gold for gold unless it is the same amount for the same amount, and do not make one amount greater than the other. Do not sell silver for silver unless it is the same amount for the same amount, and do not make one amount greater than the other. And do not sell that (cash money) which is not present (at the time of the transaction) for that (cash money) which is present." [Agreed upon].[7]

11. *Money to pay zakat:* Gold, silver, and money must be spent on *zakat*. *Zakat* on wealth and *zakat maal* have an inherent *nisab* of wealth acquired for a minimum period of 1 year (*haul*). If all *zakat* requirements have been met, the individual is obliged to pay. The Prophet Muhammad SAW narrated the following hadith:

[6]Reference: Riyad as-Salihin 289. In-book reference: Introduction, Hadith 289.

[7]Sunnah.com reference: Book 7, Hadith 65. English translation: Book 7, Hadith 835. Arabic reference: Book 7, Hadith 832.

وَحَدَّثَنِي عَنْ مَالِكٍ عَنِ ابْنِ شِهَابٍ أَنَّهُ قَالَ : أَوَّلُ مَنْ أَخَذَ مِنَ الأَعْطِيَةِ الزَّكَاةَ مُعَاوِيَةُ بْنُ أَبِي سُفْيَانَ . قَالَ مَالِكٌ : السُّنَّةُ الَّتِي لاَ اخْتِلاَفَ فِيهَا عِنْدَنَا أَنَّ الزَّكَاةَ تَجِبُ فِي عِشْرِينَ دِينَارًا عَيْنًا كَمَا تَجِبُ فِي مِائَتَىْ دِرْهَمٍ . قَالَ مَالِكٌ : لَيْسَ فِي عِشْرِينَ دِينَارًا نَاقِصَةً بَيِّنَةَ النُّقْصَانِ زَكَاةٌ فَإِنْ زَادَتْ حَتَّى تَبْلُغَ بِزِيَادَتِهَا عِشْرِينَ دِينَارًا وَازِنَةً فَفِيهَا الزَّكَاةُ وَلَيْسَ فِيمَا دُونَ عِشْرِينَ دِينَارًا عَيْنًا الزَّكَاةُ وَلَيْسَ فِي مِائَتَىْ دِرْهَمٍ نَاقِصَةً بَيِّنَةَ النُّقْصَانِ زَكَاةٌ فَإِنْ زَادَتْ حَتَّى تَبْلُغَ بِزِيَادَتِهَا مِائَتَىْ دِرْهَمٍ وَافِيَةً فَفِيهَا الزَّكَاةُ فَإِنْ كَانَتْ تَجُوزُ بِجَوَازِ الْوَازِنَةِ رَأَيْتُ فِيهَا الزَّكَاةَ دَنَانِيرَ كَانَتْ أَوْ دَرَاهِمَ . قَالَ مَالِكٌ فِي رَجُلٍ كَانَتْ عِنْدَهُ سِتُّونَ وَمِائَةُ دِرْهَمٍ وَازِنَةً وَصَرْفُ الدَّرَاهِمِ بِبَلَدِهِ ثَمَانِيَةُ دَرَاهِمَ بِدِينَارٍ : أَنَّهَا لاَ تَجِبُ فِيهَا الزَّكَاةُ وَإِنَّمَا تَجِبُ الزَّكَاةُ فِي عِشْرِينَ دِينَارًا عَيْنًا أَوْ مِائَتَىْ دِرْهَمٍ . قَالَ مَالِكٌ فِي رَجُلٍ كَانَتْ لَهُ خَمْسَةُ دَنَانِيرَ مِنْ فَائِدَةٍ أَوْ غَيْرِهَا فَتَجَرَ فِيهَا فَلَمْ يَأْتِ الْحَوْلُ حَتَّى بَلَغَتْ مَا تَجِبُ فِيهِ الزَّكَاةُ : أَنَّهُ يُزَكِّيهَا وَإِنْ لَمْ تَتِمَّ إِلاَّ قَبْلَ أَنْ يَحُولَ عَلَيْهَا الْحَوْلُ بِيَوْمٍ وَاحِدٍ أَوْ بَعْدَ مَا يَحُولُ عَلَيْهَا الْحَوْلُ بِيَوْمٍ وَاحِدٍ ثُمَّ لاَ زَكَاةَ فِيهَا حَتَّى يَحُولَ عَلَيْهَا الْحَوْلُ مِنْ يَوْمَ زُكِّيَتْ . وَقَالَ مَالِكٌ فِي رَجُلٍ كَانَتْ لَهُ عَشَرَةُ دَنَانِيرَ فَتَجَرَ فِيهَا فَحَالَ عَلَيْهَا الْحَوْلُ وَقَدْ بَلَغَتْ عِشْرِينَ دِينَارًا : أَنَّهُ يُزَكِّيهَا مَكَانَهَا وَلاَ يَنْتَظِرُ بِهَا أَنْ يَحُولَ عَلَيْهَا الْحَوْلُ مِنْ يَوْمَ بَلَغَتْ مَا تَجِبُ فِيهِ الزَّكَاةُ لِأَنَّ الْحَوْلَ قَدْ حَالَ عَلَيْهَا وَهِيَ عِنْدَهُ عِشْرُونَ ثُمَّ لَا زَكَاةَ فِيهَا حَتَّى يَحُولَ عَلَيْهَا الْحَوْلُ مِنْ يَوْمَ زُكِّيَتْ قَالَ مَالِك الأَمْرُ الْمُجْتَمَعُ عَلَيْهِ عِنْدَنَا فِي إِجَارَةِ الْعَبِيدِ وَخَرَاجِهِمْ وَكِرَاءِ الْمَسَاكِينِ وَكِتَابَةِ الْمُكَاتَبِ أَنَّهُ لَا تَجِبُ فِي شَيْءٍ مِنْ ذَلِكَ الزَّكَاةُ قَلَّ ذَلِكَ أَوْ كَثُرَ حَتَّى يَحُولَ عَلَيْهِ الْحَوْلُ مِنْ يَوْمِ يَقْبِضُهُ صَاحِبُهُ. وَقَالَ مَالِك فِي الذَّهَبِ وَالْوَرِقِ يَكُونُ بَيْنَ الشُّرَكَاءِ إِنَّ مَنْ بَلَغَتْ حِصَّتُهُ مِنْهُمْ عِشْرِينَ دِينَارًا عَيْنًا أَوْ مِائَتَيْ دِرْهَمٍ فَعَلَيْهِ فِيهَا الزَّكَاةُ وَمَنْ نَقَصَتْ حِصَّتُهُ عَمَّا تَجِبُ فِيهِ الزَّكَاةُ فَلَا زَكَاةَ عَلَيْهِ وَإِنْ بَلَغَتْ حِصَصُهُمْ جَمِيعًا مَا تَجِبُ فِيهِ الزَّكَاةُ وَكَانَ بَعْضُهُمْ فِي ذَلِكَ أَفْضَلَ نَصِيبًا مِنْ بَعْضٍ أُخِذَ مِنْ كُلِّ إِنْسَانٍ مِنْهُمْ بِقَدْرِ حِصَّتِهِ إِذَا كَانَ فِي حِصَّةِ كُلِّ إِنْسَانٍ مِنْهُمْ مَا تَجِبُ فِيهِ الزَّكَاةُ وَذَلِكَ أَنَّ رَسُولَ اللَّهِ صَلَّى اللَّهُ عَلَيْهِ وَسَلَّمَ قَالَ لَيْسَ فِيمَا دُونَ خَمْسِ أَوَاقٍ مِنْ الْوَرِقِ صَدَقَةٌ قَالَ مَالِك وَهَذَا أَحَبُّ مَا سَمِعْتُ إِلَيَّ فِي ذَلِكَ قَالَ مَالِك وَإِذَا كَانَتْ لِرَجُلٍ ذَهَبٌ أَوْ وَرِقٌ مُتَفَرِّقَةٌ بِأَيْدِي أُنَاسٍ شَتَّى فَإِنَّهُ يَنْبَغِي لَهُ أَنْ يُحْصِيَهَا جَمِيعًا ثُمَّ يُخْرِجَ مَا وَجَبَ عَلَيْهِ مِنْ زَكَاتِهَا كُلِّهَا قَالَ مَالِك وَمَنْ أَفَادَ ذَهَبًا أَوْ وَرِقًا إِنَّهُ لَا زَكَاةَ عَلَيْهِ فِيهَا حَتَّى يَحُولَ عَلَيْهَا الْحَوْلُ مِنْ يَوْمَ أَفَادَهَا

Yahya related to me from Malik that Ibn Shihab said, "The first person to deduct zakat from allowances was Muawiya ibn Abi Sufyan." (i.e. the deduction being made automatically) .

Malik said, "The agreed sunna with us is that zakat has to be paid on twenty dinars (of gold coin), in the same way as it has to be paid on two hundred dirhams (of silver)".

Malik said, "There is no zakat to pay on (gold) that is clearly less than twenty dinars (in weight) but if it increases so that by the increase the amount reaches a full twenty dinars in weight then zakat has to be paid. Similarly, there is no zakat to pay on (silver) that is clearly less than two hundred dirhams (in weight), but if it increases so that by the increase the amount reaches a full two hundred dirhams in weight then zakat has to be paid. If it passes the full weight then I think there is zakat to pay, whether it be dinars or dirhams". (i.e. the zakat is assessed by the weight and not the number of the coins.)

Malik said, about a man who had one hundred and sixty dirhams by weight, and the exchange rate in his town was eight dirhams to a dinar, that he did not have to pay any zakat. Zakat had only to be paid on twenty dinars of gold or two hundred dirhams.

Malik said, in the case of a man who acquired five dinars from a transaction or in some other way which he then invested in trade, that, as soon as it increased to a zakatable amount and then a year elapsed, he had to pay zakat on it, even if the zakatable amount was reached one day before or one day after the passing of a year. There was then no zakat to pay on it from the day the zakat was taken until a year had elapsed over it.

Malik said, in the similar case of a man who had in his possession ten dinars which he invested in trade and which reached twenty dinars by the time one year had elapsed over them, that he paid zakat on them right then and did not wait until a year had elapsed over them, (counting) from the day when they actually reached the zakatable amount. This was because a year had elapsed over the original dinars and there were now twenty of them in his possession. After that there was no zakat to pay on them from the day the zakat was paid until another year had elapsed over them.

Malik said, "What we are agreed upon (here in Madina) regarding income from hiring out slaves, rent from property, and the sums received when a slave buys his freedom, is that no zakat is due on any of it, whether great or small, from the day the owner takes possession of it until a year has elapsed over it from the day when the owner takes possession of it".

Malik said, in the case of gold and silver which was shared between two co-owners, that zakat was due from any one whose share reached twenty dinars of gold, or two hundred dirhams of silver, and that no zakat was due from anyone whose share fell short of this zakatable amount. If all the shares reached the zakatable amount and the shares were not equally divided, zakat was taken from each man according to the measure of his share. This applied only when the share of each man among them reached the zakatable amount, because the Messenger of Allah, may Allah bless him and grant him peace, had said, "There is no zakat to pay on less than five awaq of silver".

Malik commented, "This is what I prefer most out of what I have heard about the matter".

Malik said, "When a man has gold and silver dispersed among various people he must add it all up together and then take out the zakat due on the total sum".

Malik said, "No zakat is due from some one who acquires gold or silver until a year has elapsed over his acquisition from the day it became his".[8]

12. *Money must not be hoarded:* The hoarding of gold, silver, or money to generate a future profit is absolutely forbidden in Islam. Storing wealth is considered *bathil*, thus impeding the flow of wealth Allah SWT bestows on those in need. Verses 34–35 of surah At-Taubah in Al-Qur'an explains what awaits for those who hoard wealth as follows:

يٰٓاَيُّهَا الَّذِيْنَ اٰمَنُوْٓا اِنَّ كَثِيْرًا مِّنَ الْاَحْبَارِ وَالرُّهْبَانِ لَيَأْكُلُوْنَ اَمْوَالَ النَّاسِ بِالْبَاطِلِ وَيَصُدُّوْنَ عَنْ سَبِيْلِ اللّٰهِ ۗوَالَّذِيْنَ يَكْنِزُوْنَ الذَّهَبَ وَالْفِضَّةَ وَلَا يُنْفِقُوْنَهَا فِيْ سَبِيْلِ اللّٰهِ ۙفَبَشِّرْهُمْ بِعَذَابٍ اَلِيْمٍۙ(34)

يَّوْمَ يُحْمٰى عَلَيْهَا فِيْ نَارِ جَهَنَّمَ فَتُكْوٰى بِهَا جِبَاهُهُمْ وَجُنُوْبُهُمْ وَظُهُوْرُهُمْۗ هٰذَا مَا كَنَزْتُمْ لِاَنْفُسِكُمْ فَذُوْقُوْا مَا كُنْتُمْ تَكْنِزُوْنَ(35)

"O you who have believed, indeed many of the scholars and the monks devour the wealth of people unjustly and avert [them] from the way of Allah. And those who hoard gold and silver and spend it not in the way of Allah—give them tidings of a painful punishment. The Day when it will be heated in the fire of Hell and seared therewith will be their foreheads, their flanks, and their backs, [it will be said], "This is what you hoarded for yourselves, so taste what you used to hoard." (Q.S. At-Taubah [9]: 34-35).

[8] USC-MSA web (English) referenc: Book 17, Hadith 7
Arabic reference: Book 17, Hadith 587

13. *Money to avoid riba:* The Prophet Muhammad SAW recommended selling goods with similar goods, paid for in cash, as contained in the following Hadiths:

    وَعَنْ عُبَادَةَ بْنِ الصَّامِتِ قَالَ: قَالَ رَسُولُ اللهِ صَلَّى اللهُ عَلَيْهِ وَسَلَّمَ: «الذَّهَبُ بِالذَّهَبِ وَالْفِضَّةُ بِالْفِضَّةِ وَالْبُرُّ بِالْبُرِّ وَالشَّعِيرُ بِالشَّعِيرِ وَالتَّمْرُ بِالتَّمْرِ وَالْملح بالملح مثلا بمثل سَوَاء بسَواءٍ يَدًا بِيَدٍ فَإِذَا اخْتَلَفَتْ هَذِهِ الْأَصْنَافُ فَبِيعُوا كَيْفَ شِئْتُمْ إِذَا كَانَ يَدًا بِيَدٍ» . رَوَاهُ مُسلم

    'Ubada b. as-Samit reported God's Messenger as saying, "Gold is to be paid for by gold, silver by silver, wheat by wheat, barley by barley, dates by dates, and salt by salt, like for like and equal for equal, payment being made on the spot. If these classes differ, sell as you wish if payment is made on the spot." Muslim transmitted it.[9]

14. *Money not for debt:* The Prophet Muhammad SAW showed that getting into debt to buy or sell something is not recommended.

    وَعَنْ عُبَادَةَ بْنِ الصَّامِتِ أَنَّ رَسُولَ اللهِ صَلَّى اللهُ عَلَيْهِ وَسَلَّمَ قَالَ: «لَا تَبِيعُوا الذَّهَبَ بِالذَّهَبِ وَلَا الْوَرِق بِالْوَرِقِ وَلَا الْبُرَّ بِالْبُرِّ وَلَا الشَّعِيرَ بِالشَّعِيرِ وَلَا التَّمْرَ بِالتَّمْرِ وَلَا الْمِلْحَ بِالْمِلْحِ إِلَّا سَوَاءً بِسَوَاءٍ عَيْنًا بِعَيْنٍ يَدًا بِيَدٍ وَلَكِنْ بِيعُوا الذَّهَبَ بِالْوَرِقِ وَالْوَرِقَ بِالذَّهَبِ وَالْبُرَّ بِالشَّعِيرِ وَالشَّعِيرَ بِالْبُرِّ وَالتَّمْرَ بِالْمِلْحِ وَالْمِلْحَ بِالتَّمْرِ يَدًا بِيَدٍ كَيْفَ شِئْتُمْ» . رَوَاهُ الشَّافِع

    'Ubada b. as-Samit reported God's Messenger as saying, "Do not sell gold for gold, or silver for silver, or wheat for wheat, or barley for barley, or dates for dates, or salt for salt except equal for equal, kind for kind, payment being made on the spot; but sell gold for silver, silver for gold, wheat for barely, barley for wheat, dates for salt and salt for dates, payment being made on the spot, as you wish." Shafi'i transmitted it.[10]

15. *Money must not be misused or counterfeited:* Counterfeiting money is regarded as *dzalim*, it can cause national economic instability because the circulation of counterfeiting money will damage the country's foreign exchange. Al Ghazali is one of the ulama who pays attention to the problem that arises from counterfeiting dinar and dirham, such as smelting the dinar and dirham with low grade metals. Al Ghazali called the counterfeit currency as *zaif* (imitation). The counterfeit dinar and dirham could be mixture of copper, copper smeared with liquid gold or silver, or even just copper which does not contain elements of gold or silver.

    According to Al Ghazali, the circulation of counterfeit money (dinar and dirham) is not only a sin for individuals, but also a loss to the society. Circulating *zaif* or false dinars and dirhams is a great injustice and all who hold it are harmed. The counterfeit currency will continue to change hands, harm to everyone, and widespread economic damage. Passing a counterfeit dirham is worse than stealing a hundred dirhams, because the act of stealing is a sin that ends immediately after the sin is committed. But counterfeiting dinar and dirhams is a bad act whose sins will continue until the dirham disappears from

[9]Reference: Mishkat al-Masabih 2808. In-book reference: Book 11 Hadith 47.

[10]Mishkat al-Masabih 2819. In-book reference: Book 11, Hadith 58

circulation. It also bears the sin of destroying the economy of mankind as a result of counterfeiting dinar and dirham.[11]

However, Al Ghazali added that not all dinars and dirhams counterfeits such as copper metal plated with gold silver are included crime. If the copper mixed currency is officially printed by the state and known by all levels of society, then the currency is permitted to be circulated, although in fact scholars differ on this matter.

16. *Money used to pay cash:* Rasulullah SAW revealed that it would be better to trade using money than the barter system. Rasulullah SAW believed that the barter system contained the inherent risk of *riba*.

حَدَّثَنَا أَبُو نُعَيْمٍ، حَدَّثَنَا شَيْبَانُ، عَنْ يَحْيَى، عَنْ أَبِي سَلَمَةَ، عَنْ أَبِي سَعِيدٍ ـ رضى الله عنه ـ قَالَ كُنَّا
نُرْزَقُ تَمْرَ الْجَمْعِ، وَهْوَ الْخِلْطُ مِنَ التَّمْرِ، وَكُنَّا نَبِيعُ صَاعَيْنِ بِصَاعٍ فَقَالَ النَّبِيُّ صلى الله عليه وسلم
" لاَ صَاعَيْنِ بِصَاعٍ، وَلاَ دِرْهَمَيْنِ بِدِرْهَمٍ "

We used to be given mixed dates (from the booty) and used to sell (barter) two Sas of those dates) for one Sa (of good dates). The Prophet (ﷺ) said (to us), "No (bartering of) two Sas for one Sa nor two Dirhams for one Dirham is permissible", (as that is a kind of usury). (See Hadith No. 405). [HR. Bukhari][12]

17. *Money to repay the debt of the deceased:* When a Muslim dies and leaves a debt behind, dinars and dirhams (money) are no longer used upon the day of resurrection in the afterlife, the debt is repaid with kindness, as is written in the Hadiths:

وَعَنْ جَابِرٍ - رضى الله عنه - قَالَ: { تُوُفِّيَ رَجُلٌ مِنَّا, فَغَسَّلْنَاهُ, وَحَنَّطْنَاهُ, وَكَفَّنَّاهُ, ثُمَّ أَتَيْنَا بِهِ رَسُولَ اَللَّهِ
- صلى الله عليه وسلم -فَقُلْنَا: تُصَلِّي عَلَيْهِ؟ فَخَطَا خُطًى, ثُمَّ قَالَ: " أَعَلَيْهِ دَيْنٌ؟ " قُلْنَا: دِينَارَانِ،
فَانْصَرَفَ, فَتَحَمَّلَهُمَا أَبُو قَتَادَةَ، فَأَتَيْنَاهُ, فَقَالَ أَبُو قَتَادَةَ: اَلدِّينَارَانِ عَلَيَّ، فَقَالَ رَسُولُ اَللَّهِ - صلى الله عليه
وسلم -" أُحِقَّ اَلْغَرِيمُ وَبَرِئَ مِنْهُمَا اَلْمَيِّتُ؟ " قَالَ: نَعَمْ, فَصَلَّى عَلَيْهِ } رَوَاهُ أَحْمَدُ, وَأَبُو دَاوُدَ,
وَالنَّسَائِيُّ, وَصَحَّحَهُ اِبْنُ حِبَّانَ, وَالْحَاكِمُ

A man from among us died, so we washed, embalmed and shrouded him. We then brought him to Allah's Messenger (ﷺ) and asked him to pray over him. He went forward some steps and then asked, "Does he have any debt against him?" We replied, "Two Dinars." He turned away, but Abu Qatada (RA) took upon himself the bearing of them. We then came to him (again) (ﷺ) and Abu Qatada (RA) said: "I shall discharge the two Dinars." Allah's Messenger (ﷺ) thereupon said, "[Will you be responsible for paying them as] a right to the creditor; and the dead man will then be free from them?" He replied, "Yes." So, he prayed over him. [Reported by Ahmad, Abu Dawud, and an-Nasa'i. Ibn Hibban and al-Hakim graded it Sahih (authentic)].[13]

[11] Muhammad Ibn Muhammad al Ghazali, 2013. Ihya' Ulumiddin. Beirut: Dar al Kutub. j 2. h 93

[12] Reference: Sahih al-Bukhari 2080. In-book reference: Book 34, Hadith 33.

[13] Sunnah.com reference: Book 7, Hadith 120. English translation: Book 7, Hadith 881. Arabic reference: Book 7, Hadith 877.

9.5.5 *Dinar and Dirham*

The issue concerning whether fiat money is acceptable in Islam remains a topic of considerable debate and discussion. Opinions from both perspectives can be quite extreme (Ibrahim, 2020). There is a prevailing opinion amongst Muslim scholars that only gold and silver are acceptable as money in Islam and a monetary system that applies fiat money represents a form of economic deception and manipulation enveloped in legality. In fact, the strongest proponents of gold and silver coinage criticise contemporary scholars who accept the use of fiat money. The rationale behind this strict interpretation of Al-Qur'an is due to several Quranic verses stipulating explicitly that money is dinar and dirham, as stated in verse 34 of surah At-Taubah, verse 91 of surah Ali-Imran, and verse 20 of surah Yusuf. From those verses, an issue arises concerning the reapplication of gold and silver coins, known as dinar and dirham.

Dinar and dirham are a form of commodity money, where the nominal or face value matches the intrinsic value. It can be said, therefore, that dinar and dirham involve no deception or manipulation when determining their nominal value because it is based on the market forces affecting gold/silver. The amount of dinar and dirham in circulation cannot be adjusted arbitrarily based on the whims of the monetary authority, instead depending on actual transactions in the real sector. Consequently, the real value of the dinar and dirham tends to be stable without the need for intervention. Dinar and dirham function as a stable and reliable unit of account as well as a fair medium of exchange. Dinar and dirham, therefore, are more suitable and feasible in their function and role as money than currency.

In reality, the goal of the economy in general and Islam in particular is to achieve equitable welfare for the community and eliminate the income gap. To that end, a reliable and stable currency is vital because volatility is the root of poverty and income inequality (Meera & Aziz, 2002).

The stability of gold as currency can be demonstrated by the price of camels in dinar, which has not changed significantly since the time of Rasulullah SAW. In addition, the unit of account in society must also be taken into consideration due to the impact on all economic aspects and activities. A unit of account for wealth must be unambiguous, standardised, universally accepted, and difficult to manipulate. By returning to an economic system in accordance with Islamic principles using gold/silver as currency and eliminating the interest rate system (*riba*), the current economic woes could be resolved and eliminated at the root. According to the revelations of Allah SWT in verse 14 of surah Ali-Imran:

زُيِّنَ لِلنَّاسِ حُبُّ ٱلشَّهَوَٰتِ مِنَ ٱلنِّسَآءِ وَٱلْبَنِينَ وَٱلْقَنَٰطِيرِ ٱلْمُقَنطَرَةِ مِنَ ٱلذَّهَبِ وَٱلْفِضَّةِ وَٱلْخَيْلِ ٱلْمُسَوَّمَةِ وَٱلْأَنْعَٰمِ
وَٱلْحَرْثِ ۗ ذَٰلِكَ مَتَٰعُ ٱلْحَيَوٰةِ ٱلدُّنْيَا ۖ وَٱللَّهُ عِندَهُۥ حُسْنُ ٱلْمَـَٔابِ

Beautified for people is the love of that which they desire—of women and sons, heaped-up sums of gold and silver, fine branded horses, and cattle and tilled land. That is the enjoyment of worldly life, but Allah has with Him the best return. (Q.S. Ali-Imran [3]: 14).

That Quranic verse emphasises the urgency for using dinar and dirham. By nature, humans have a fondness and deep affection for gold and silver. It is almost impossible, therefore, for individuals to stop seeking or desiring gold and silver.

The characteristics outlined above make gold and silver suitable candidates for use as currency, implying that gold and silver are consistently deemed valuable to the human eye. In addition, gold and silver are precious metals that contain a superior physical and chemical composition. This view was supported by the Islamic scholar Ibn Khaldun, stating that Allah SWT created two precious metals, namely gold and silver, for use by humans for transactional purposes. A student of Ibn Khaldun, Al-Maqrizi, subsequently reinforced the opinion that only gold and silver were viable or worthy of use as money (Rosly & Barakat, 2002).

Dinar and dirham discharge their function as money well. Restrictions placed on the creation of dinar and dirham prevent currency depreciation (Rab, 2002). Furthermore, money supply is not determined by artificial demand for money or the arbitrary wishes of the monetary authority. Instead, money supply is determined by the real sector, thus an increase in the money supply reflects a tangible increase in the real sector. Consequently, there is no longer a gap between the real and financial sectors and the amount of money in the financial sector reflects that in the real sector. The relationship between the real sector and the financial sector is interdependent and not mutually exclusive.

By preventing currency depreciation, the use of dinar and dirham could also prevent the next economic issue, namely inflation. Eliminating inflation has positive economic implications. In the business community, any increase in real profit would be felt in real and true terms due to a lack of contamination by inflation. Furthermore, equitable income distribution could be achieved more quickly as no part of an economic sector would be more profitable to the detriment of others.

Price stability is a key consideration for investors planning to place capital in the real sector. Investment aims to turn capital into real assets for business purposes, with the hope that these real assets will generate future profits for investors. With no inflation, the investment returns are pure and real. For consumers, no inflation would have a positive impact on real income (purchasing power), which would not decrease arbitrarily but could increase in line with nominal income. Consequently, the poverty rate would not deteriorate.

Dinar: An Alternative to Fiat Money

Dinar is known as the most stable currency. The nominal value of the dinar represents the intrinsic value of gold itself. The dinar reflects its nominal value and the nominal value is determined based on the value of gold as the raw material. This is different to fiat money, which uses low-value raw materials yet has become a "symbol" with legitimate value as legal tender as conferred by the competent authority. Fundamentally, that is the basis of the opinion concerning fiat money as *haram* due to the lack of backing by an underlying real asset. Furthermore, currency fluctuations create economic uncertainty, inflation, depreciation, and speculation.

From an Islamic standpoint, gold is the most appropriate medium of exchange because the value of gold tends to be constant and stable. With a comparatively high value and good reliability, using dinar would maintain economic stability and help to contain risk in the financial sector. In addition, sharia law stipulates that gold is the most appropriate object to function as money, which has been proven to function optimally and effectively. Gold remains a secure store of value, even when economic conditions become unstable and the prices of other real assets decline.

Important Role of Dinar

The use of dinar as a single currency would confer many benefits and advantages. The dinar functions as money very competently. Furthermore, international cooperation between Muslim countries using the dinar would benefit by obviating the need for currency conversion. Solidarity between Muslim countries using the dinar, the intrinsic value of which affords stability, would signal to other countries concerning the urgency of using the dinar as a single currency, which would gradually move towards adoption.

Assuming the use of a single currency, namely gold, international trade between Muslim countries would be very convenient, thus providing greater impetus to increase trade between Muslim countries. Furthermore, closer international ties would strengthen the brotherhood (*ukhuwah*) between Muslim countries, thus reducing the level of dependence on non-Muslim countries and potentially accelerating domestic national development.

Countries in the Middle East are the largest exporters of oil globally. This dominance could be used to demand payment in gold, thus boosting the potential for gold to be adopted as a global currency. Ultimately, this would financially strengthen Muslim countries and reduce some of the common issues prevalent today.

Implications of Dinar and Dirham Adoption

The dinar and dirham could become a stable global currency because they are minted from precious metals, namely gold and silver, thus making it impossible to create or manipulate the value freely. This would create a stable monetary system and value of money (Meera & Aziz, 2002). In addition, the adoption of dinar and dirham could reduce the level of counterfeit currency in circulation. Meanwhile, the nominal value of the dinar and dirham is measured based on the intrinsic value of gold and silver, implying that the dinar and dirham could function better as a store of value. More importantly, adopting dinar and dirham and abolishing the interest rate system would overcome inflation more effectively than fiat money system because any increase in money supply would be in line with real sector conditions. In the corporate sector, the absence of inflation could reduce occurrences in the business cycle.

Gold and silver are precious metals, the desirability of which will never fade. For example, given the choice between receiving cash or gold bullion of equivalent value, most people would choose gold. In addition, the nominal value of dinar and dirham is the same as the intrinsic value, and dinar and dirham are easy to divide into smaller units. Dinar and dirham, therefore, would perform very competently as a medium of exchange.

The diverse range of currencies in use around the world today serves as an incentive for traders to seek profit from this situation. Various forms of speculation and arbitrage target foreign exchange transactions between currencies. This could be minimised through discourse to establish a single global currency, based on gold and silver coins for example. This would eliminate speculation in terms of profiting from fluctuations in currencies between different countries.

Dinar as a Global Trade Currency

Malaysia has already announced plans to adopt dinar and dirham similar to the time of Rasulullah SAW (Othman, 2002). The Malaysia Government hopes to gradually introduce dinar and dirham and replace the use of paper money. In fact, the Malaysia Government has acknowledged the urgent need to use dinar and dirham as a means of payment, including international trade. Despite hoping that the dinar and dirham will replace paper money universally, the Malaysia Government will not impose its will on other countries, instead preferring a bilateral approach to international trade.

Dinar as a Means of Payment in the Real Sector

Business transactions in the real sector involve at least two parties in mutual agreement, backed by a contractual agreement underlying the business activity. The contract regulates all aspects of the agreement in detail, including the means of payment. The use of gold as a means of payment, therefore, is possible between the transacting parties providing an agreement has been made. There are several other aspects that must be considered when using gold as a means of payment for business transactions as follows (Othman, 2002).

The first aspect relates to the ownership of gold used as a means of payment. The party responsible for making the payment must have full and uncontested ownership of the gold, either physically or deposited at an authorised institution with the respective certificate of ownership held by the transacting party. Ultimately, a separate specialised institution (goldsmith) could be established to regulate the storage of privately owned gold, like a saving deposit in a bank.

Second, the effectiveness of payments using gold coins must be considered. Physically moving gold coins could potentially create security issues, inconvenience, and impracticality in transit because gold is a high-value tangible asset. It would be necessary, therefore, to design payment methods using gold that are practical, secure, and convenient but allow for greater mobility and convenience.

Third, the ease of transferring ownership of gold coins is equally as important. The payer can transfer ownership of the payment instrument in two ways, namely: (1) physically handing over the gold coins or (2) transferring the benefits of the gold commensurate to the transaction value (for example, certificate of ownership), with the physical gold stored in a specialised institution. If the second method is preferred, however, the new owner must not be encumbered by complications when liquidating the certificate.

Barriers to Dinar Use as Means of Payment in Real Sector

In its original form as a gold coin, the use of dinar was beset with issues as a medium of exchange and means of payment. Moving large amounts of dinar was difficult, with the mass far outweighing paper banknotes. In addition, holding dinar as cash in sufficient quantities was inconvenient in terms of security. Physically speaking, therefore, dinar is very inconvenient to carry around or mobilise in large amounts as a means of payment.

When there are only two transacting parties, it is possible to agree payment methods alternative to cash within a binding agreement. This becomes more difficult, however, when the transacting parties do not have a black-and-white agreement, or between parties with one-off transactions. For example, shoppers do not have a specific agreement with the supermarket regarding the payment method.

Fortunately, however, technology is now advancing with rapidity. Communication and information technology has not only advanced rapidly but has also penetrated the economy. Technological advances offer potential solutions to constraints concerning the mobility of gold coins (dinar). Transaction payments no longer depend on cash systems but can be processed and settled electronically, and the reach of electronic payments is much wider.

With the backing of real dinar, e-Gold, GoldMoney, and OSGold are viable forms of electronic dinar (Meera & Aziz, 2002). The implementation of electronic money has a significant impact on economic actors, namely households, companies, and the government. Meanwhile, e-money minimises transaction costs between parties, is more efficient, convenient, secure, simple, and accepted by all. Therefore, all transacting parties using the dinar can feel confident regarding security.

9.5.6 Controlling Money Supply in Accordance with Sharia Law

Money supply in society is balanced as a result of interaction between demand and supply. Controlling the money supply tends to focus on controlling the demand for money because money supply is the jurisdiction of the central bank. In addition, money supply is comparatively fixed in a given period of time. The demand for money, however, is influenced by several motives, namely the transaction motive, precautionary motive, and speculative motive. The transaction and precautionary motives tend to focus on consumption activities, such as the daily necessities and unexpected needs of the community. In addition, these motives can also stem from productive investment activity in the real sector.

In contrast, the speculative motive leads to prodigal consumption as well as unproductive or speculative investment without underlying real sector activity. Islam does not recognise the speculative motive because it violates the principles of Islamic economics. Controlling the demand for money in Islam, therefore, focuses on productive consumption and investment.

Chapra (2001a, b) mentioned several aspects that must be considered when controlling the demand for money as follows:

1. *Price mechanism*: Fairly created prices can increase the equitable distribution of economic resources, while minimising economic inequality. Based on market

mechanisms, the prices formed are more affordable to the average consumer rather than the prices formed in a monopoly or through market intervention.

2. *Rate of return*: Given that interest rates (*riba*) are absolutely forbidden in the Islamic economy, the rate of return is used as an alternative means of controlling the demand for money. The rate of return refers to the return on investment funds. A higher rate of return discourages individuals from holding money, thus decreasing demand. In contrast, a low rate of return encourages individuals to hold money, thus increasing demand. According to sharia law, the rate of return is not based on interest rates, instead preferring a profit and loss sharing mechanism. That way, the investment is productive and tied to real sector activity.
3. *Moral values*: In this context, moral values aim to regulate consumer propensity to spend and avoid excessive (wasteful) consumption. This intends to control the demand for money because high demand for money leads to inflation.

If the demand for money is regulated within the Islamic corridor, the result is more controlled, stable and with a closer relationship to the needs and welfare of the public in general (Uddin & Halim, 2015). When the demand for money is based on actual transactional needs in the real sector, any increase in the money supply will be accompanied by a commensurate increase in economic growth.

The same is true on the supply side. Money creation in the current monetary system relies on the central bank through reserve instruments or the statutory reserve requirement (SRR) and on commercial banks through lending rates. Based on such mechanisms, therefore, a monetary system based on fiat money can create conditions ripe for manipulation and exploitation to the benefit of a few.

According to proponents, gold and silver money has an advantage because the money supply cannot be controlled by the monetary authority. Furthermore, money in circulation is linked to the value of transactions in the real sector, thus the velocity of money is comparatively more stable and constant. Notwithstanding, this principle could also be applied to the use of fiat money, created in accordance with transactional needs in the real sector, thereby focusing and honing the control of fiat money, and maintaining a more stable value.

References

Ahmed, H. (2002). Money and exchange rate in an Islamic Economy. *International Conference on Stable and Just Global Monetary System* (pp. 303-317). Research centre International Islamic University Malaysia.

An-Nabhani, T. (1996). *Membangun Sistem Ekonomi Alternatif Perspektif Islam*. Risalah Gusti.

Chapra, M. U. (1996). Monetary management in an Islamic economy. *Islamic Economic Studies, 4*(1), 1–34.

Chapra, M. U. (2000). *Towards a just monetary system.* (I. A. Basri, Trans.). Gema Insani Press.

Chapra, M. U. (2001a). *The future of economics: An Islamic perspective.* (A. Amir, Y. Machmudi, F. Nur, L. Trialdi, E. Sudjono, & M. T. Ridho, Penerj.). Shari'ah Economic and Banking Institute.

Chapra, M. U. (2001b). *What is Islamic economics?* (2nd ed.). IRTI/IDB.

Diwany, T. E. (2002). History of banking: An analysis. *International Conference on Stable and Just Global Monetary System* (pp. 1–33). Research Centre International Islamic University Malaysia.

Haneef, M. A., & Barakat, E. R. (2002). Gold and silver as money: A prelimi survey of Fiqhi opinions and the implications. In *International Conference on Stable and Just Global Monetary System* (pp. 139–149). Research Centre International Islamic University Malaysia.

Haneef, M. A., & Barakat, E. R. (2006). Must money be limited to only gold and silver?: A survey of Fiqhi opinions and some implications. *Journal of King Abdulaziz University: Islamic Economics, 19*(1), 21–34.

Hasan, A. (2005). *Mata Uang Islami: Telaah Komprehensif Sistem Keuangan Islami* (S. Barito, & Z. Ali, Trans.). RajaGrafindo Persada.

Ibrahim, M. H. (2020). *Concepts of money.* Money and Banking's Unpublished Teaching Material.

Islahi, A. A. (2016). *Economic concepts of Ibn Taimiyah* (Reprint ed.). The Islamic Foundation.

Jaribah. (2003). *Fikih Ekonomi Umar Bin Al-Khathab.* Khalifa.

Juhro, S. M., & Suseno. (2002). *Uang: Pengertian, penciptaan dan Peranannya dalam Perekonomian.* Pusat Pendidikan dan Studi Kebanksentralan.

Karim, A. A. (2002). Ekonomi Islam: Suatu Kajian Ekonomi Makro. *The International Institute of Islamic Thought Indonesia (IIIT Indonesia)*, 19–22.

Karim, A. A. (2006). *Ekonomi Makro Islami.* PT RajaGrafindo Persada.

Khan, M. S. (1986). Islamic interest-free banking: A theoretical analysis. *Staff Papers (International Monetary Fund), 33*(1), 1–27.

Meera, A. K. (2018). Cryptocurrencies from Islamic perspectives: The case of bitcoin. *Bulletin of Monetary Economics and Banking, 20*(4), 475–492.

Meera, A. K., & Aziz, H. A. (2002). The Islamic Gold Dinar: Sosio-economic perspectives. *International Conference on Stable and Just Global Monetary System* (hal. 151–173). Research Centre International Islamic University Malaysia.

Othman, J. (2002). Application of the Existing Laws and Regulations in Malaysia Relating to the Proposed Usage and Impelementation of the Dinar from a Private Sector Perspectives. *International Conference on Stable and Just Global Monetary System* (hal. 251–279). Research Centre International Islamic University Malaysia.

Rab, H. (2002). Problems created by the fiat money, Islamic Dinar and other available alternatives. In *International Conference on Stable and Just Global Monetary System* (pp. 91–120). Research Centre International Islamic University Malaysia.

Rosly, S. A., & Barakat, E. R. (2002). The economic thought of Al-Maqrizi: The role of the Dinar and Dirham as a money. In *International Conference on Stable and Just Global Monetary System* (pp. 123–136). Research Centre International Islamic University Malaysia.

Uddin, M. A. (2019). Islamic monetary economics: Insights from the literature. *Islamic Monetary Economics and Institutions: Theory and Practice* (hal. 39–53). Springer.

Uddin, M. A., & Halim, A. (2015). Islamic monetary policy: Is there an alternative of interest rate? *MPRA Paper.*

Zallum, A. Q. (1983). *Al-Amwal fi Daulah al-Khilafah.* Darul Ilmi lil Malayin.

Zallum, A. Q. (2002). *Sistem Pemerintahan Islam* (Cetakan Ke-3 ed.). (T. Al-Izzah, Penyunt., & M. M. W., Penerj.) Al-Izzah.

Chapter 10
Inflation, Exchange Rates, and Interest Rates

10.1 Introduction

Chapter 8 explored the relational dynamics between macroeconomic variables within the concept of general equilibrium, as well as several factors that could trigger potential imbalances or instability. Chapter 8 implied the need for sound economic management through diverse yet integrated economic policies to maintain economic stability and support equitable welfare for all. Several variables play key roles in determining such dynamics, namely prices (inflation), exchange rates, and interest rates. This chapter rigorously explores the existence, roles, and underlying theories from conventional and Islamic perspectives.

In general, it is understood that the interaction between the supply and demand of goods in the market forms prices, with the best and fairest prices formed naturally due to market interactions and forces. In Islam, the market is a public not individual good and, thus, open markets are justified according to Islamic teachings. In contrast, prices formed through government or third-party intervention are not justified according to Islam. There are, however, special circumstances in which the government is permitted to intervene in price formation, namely when market prices are too high for consumers or too low for producers. In this case, government intervention should not directly determine prices yet seek to correct the root cause of unreasonable price increases/decreases.

Price performance is typically associated with changes in the value of currency against goods and services, known as inflation. Notwithstanding, the value of a currency can also be determined based on the value of another currency, known as the exchange rate. In the context of an open economy, therefore, price changes correlate with exchange rate fluctuations. As mentioned in the previous chapter, currency has three main functions, namely as a medium of exchange, a unit of account, and a store of value. The most appropriate form of currency available to discharge those three functions effectively is commodity money because it has intrinsic value. Similarly, at the time of Rasulullah SAW, *muamalah* transactions

S. M. Juhro et al., *Inclusive Welfare*, https://doi.org/10.1007/978-981-96-0051-9_10

applied commodity money in the form of dinar and dirham. Consequently, economic stability was maintained at that time. This is contrary to an economic system that allows the development of fiat money and its application as a commodity.

The third variable relating to prices and exchange rates is interest rates. The interest rate represents the price of a sum of money held by the public or a rental fee for using a certain amount of money within a given period. The interest rate is quoted as a percentage of the principal over a certain period, for example per month, per year, and so on (Boediono, 1988). Interest rates have become a key instrument in the monetary and financial systems of most countries around the world. Interest rates play a vital role in the formulation of economic policies, including monetary and fiscal policies. With a predetermined return, interest rates are of particular interest to economic sectors, particularly the monetary and financial sectors. Interest rates provide assurance to investors concerning the expected rate of return. Consequently, interest rates have become the lifeblood of the contemporary economic system. Almost all parts of the economy are inextricably linked to interest rate mechanisms, from local to international transactions. In fact, product innovation in the financial markets and monetary sector based on interest rates is developing beyond the purview of the capital market and money market to include the derivatives market, which is "derived" from the capital and money markets (Khan & Mirakhor, 1989).

Thus, it can be inferred that a stable value of currency, in terms of both goods and services as well as against other currencies, must receive considerable attention as the overarching goal of the economic system because this is key to preventing economic imbalances. Furthermore, it is important to note that growth in the money supply must be based on additional demand for money in the real sector. That way, the value of money remains stable, allowing it to execute the main functions and roles well. Therefore, the application of an Islamic economic system is considered in line with those interests. The development of an Islamic economic system requires sharia-compliant financial instruments that can accommodate international transactions within an open economy. Such instruments are required to replace conventional instruments that contain haram elements forbidden in Islam, such as *riba, gharar,* and *maysir.*

10.2 Inflation

10.2.1 Concepts, Determinants, and Control of Inflation

Concepts and Indicators

Inflation is defined as a general and progressive increase in the prices of goods and services. The keywords that stand out in that definition are general prices (not just one or two goods) and progressive (not seasonal or temporary). Inflation, therefore, corresponds to a reduction in the real value (purchasing power) of money. This condition not only impacts the economy but also the social and political sides. Inflation contributes to the income gap. Income distribution becomes skewed because real wages are eroded by inflation, while higher market prices without a commensurate increase in wages boost corporate profit.

In general, inflation is considered a monetary phenomenon. The measures taken to overcome inflation, therefore, include demand-side management by regulating the availability of currency in circulation. Monetary economists argue that the money supply must be regulated to ensure growth is consistent with higher demand for money at stable prices. Inflation will occur when growth of the money supply outpaces the demand for money, with higher demand for money projected as an increase in real income.

Nonetheless, various studies on inflation in developing economies have shown that inflation is not merely a monetary phenomenon yet also a structural phenomenon because structural issues in developing economies tend to intensify inflationary pressures from the supply side. Structural problems include domestic economic shocks, such as crop failure (due to external factors including weather patterns and natural disasters) and food distribution constraints, as well as international relations, namely a worsening terms of trade (TOT) that could create price fluctuations in the domestic market. Under such conditions, supply-side management policies are typically instituted, including sectoral economic policies, to foster supply-side improvements.

Inflation indicators are a collection of data and information observed and analysed to reveal the direction of future inflation fluctuations, facilitating more effective and efficient monetary policymaking. Inflation indicators include the inflation rate itself along with other macroeconomic aggregates, such as interest rates, exchange rates, price measures, inflation expectations, government bond coupon rate, and aggregate supply and demand. In general, the monetary policy framework contains two types of monetary policy indicator. *First*, leading indicators are economic and financial indicators that signal future inflation movements. *Second*, policy indicators, namely financial and economic indicators, which can be used materially to analyse and determine the direction of monetary policy. Inflation indicators are classified as leading indicators.

Three indicators are commonly used to measure inflation as follows: (1) consumer price index (CPI), which uses the public purchase price of a basket of selected goods to reflect consumer spending, (2) gross national product (GNP) deflator, which is a measure of the average price of all goods based on a number of items actually purchased, and (3) producer price index (PPI), which measures the average change over time in the selling prices received by domestic producers for their output, including production costs in the form of raw materials and intermediate goods.

Types of Inflation

Based on the source, inflation can be classified into two main types, namely cost-push inflation and demand-pull inflation. Cost-push inflation is also known as supply-side inflation because it originates in the supply side from producers, where inflation is generally caused by declining supply, thus edging up prices. Specifically, the decrease in supply may stem from an increase in input prices (production costs), which have a significant impact on supply-side movements. In this context, inputs include raw materials and labour costs. Higher wages tend to be influenced by the strength of trade unions. When unions exert pressure to raise wages, companies respond by hiking the prices of goods.

On the other hand, demand-pull inflation relates to demand-side dynamics in the economy. Demand-pull inflation is caused by an increase in aggregate demand, which pushes up the price of goods. In addition, higher prices are also often associated with fiscal and monetary expansion, namely an increase in government spending. Expansionary fiscal and monetary policies tend to increase the demand for goods significantly, with production unable to keep pace because more time is required to ramp up production than increase demand. Consequently, higher demand will pull up prices.

In addition, inflation can be classified into two types based on its origin from within the country or externally. Domestic inflationary pressures drive changes in supply and demand, particularly factors such as a budget deficit or an increase in the total stock of money supply. Inflation from abroad is channelled through the exchange of imported and exported goods between countries. When the prices of exported or imported goods rise, inflation is transmitted through contagion from partner countries. Open economies, therefore, are more exposed to this type of inflation. Nevertheless, the government and domestic monetary authority may attempt to prevent the impact of imported inflation on domestic inflation through specific policies.

Inflation can also be distinguished based on the prevailing rate as follows: (1) creeping inflation of less than 10% per year, (2) galloping inflation between 10 and 30% per year, (3) high inflation between 30 and 100% per year, and (4) hyperinflation exceeding 100% per year.

Inflation and the Phillips Curve

Theories concerning inflation and economic activity, in this case unemployment or economic growth, relate closely to the trade-off stigma between the two. Various theories in monetary economics show an inverse relationship between inflation and unemployment. If the government wanted to reduce inflation, it must be prepared to face the issue of rising unemployment. On the other hand, when a government targets unemployment, inflation will be difficult to avoid. This theory was proffered by various pioneering economists, namely Irving Fisher, A. W. Phillips, and Richard G. Lipsey. The relationship between inflation and unemployment was first illustrated in the form of a curve developed by A. W. Phillips, known as the Phillips Curve. In general, the relationship between inflation and unemployment is negative, where high inflation is usually driven by lower unemployment that, in turn, prompts an increase in aggregate demand, particularly in the near term. In specific cases, however, rising inflation may be accompanied by rising unemployment (Fig. 10.1).

It is important to note that with rapidly changing economic dynamics and advancements in economic theory, the relationship illustrated by the Phillips curve is valid in the near term. In the long run, however, unemployment will tend to move towards its natural state. Empirical facts also emerged, such as stagflation as experienced in industrialised countries in the 1970s, which not only contradict the

Fig. 10.1 Phillips curve. Source: Mankiw (2009)

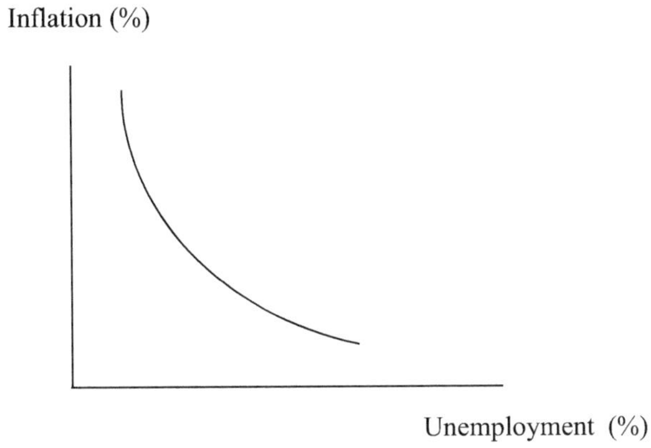

relationship depicted by the Phillips curve but also show the trade-off described in the Phillips curve is merely illusory in the long term. This idea, which is consistent with the neutrality of money or monetary policy in the long run, provides the basis for the need to set inflation as a policy target in the long term. Over the past decade, several studies have demonstrated a significant negative relationship between output growth and inflation. In other words, there is a positive relationship between inflation and unemployment.

Inflation Control

In general, the central bank is mandated with maintaining a stable value of money, both domestically (inflation) and internationally (exchange rates). The central bank strives to execute this mandate by formulating monetary policy oriented towards achieving a predetermined inflation target as announced to the public. This is achieved within a monetary policy framework based on the Inflation Targeting Framework (ITF). ITF has been adopted by various advanced and emerging economics, including Indonesia. ITF is a monetary policy framework oriented towards achieving the predetermined and published inflation target. ITF is defined as follows (Warjiyo & Juhro, 2019): (1) official affirmation that the central bank is mandated with achieving price stability (inflation), (2) publication of the medium-long-term inflation target, (3) monetary policy transparency towards good governance, and (4) central bank commitment to formulate monetary policy oriented towards achieving the predetermined inflation target.

Monetary policy implementation to control inflation using the ITF mechanism requires at least three supporting elements, namely inflation forecasting, rigorous studies of the monetary policy transmission mechanism, and implementation of effective monetary controls. Inflation forecasting plays an important role underlying monetary policymaking, particularly considering the lag between policy formulation and the impact on inflation. When implementing ITF, therefore, the central bank will assess various inflation indicators and rely on professional judgement based on qualitative information received in coordination with various economic sectors to formulate an effective monetary policy stance.

10.2.2 Inflation: An Islamic Perspective

Inflation demands vigilance. Inflation is a valid parameter to measure the success of public institutions, particularly the central bank as the first line of defence against inflation in a country. This phenomenon requires attention given the potentially devastating impact if allowed to spiral out of control. According to Zoellick (2011), inflation can cause the following issues: (1) a decrease in public purchasing power, (2) a greater public propensity to hoard resources, (3) higher unemployment, (4) a business downturn, and (5) deteriorating public welfare. Given the significant economic impact, policymakers strive to maintain a low rate of inflation.

High inflation indicates economic instability and reduces the attractiveness as an investment destination. The adverse impact of inflation on the economy from an Islamic perspective can specifically be explained as follows (Wulan & Nurfaiza, 2015): (1) reducing public propensity to save or deposit funds in a formal financial institution, (2) increasing public inclination to consume tertiary (luxury) goods, and (3) disrupting the function of money as a store of value.

Inflation remains an interesting topic of study. Inflation trends affect future economic development. Emergence of the Islamic economy is expected to resolve various issues in the economic system. The Islamic economic system tends to be more resilient to crises, thus providing hope of bringing real solutions to the shocks and problems that blight the economic system in general and the financial system in particular (Shahzad & Luqman, 2012). The Islamic economic and financial system plays a significant role in terms of advancing socio-economic development for all. The Islamic economy uses various tools to encourage participation in productive real sector activities, thereby ensuring that money does not concentrate in the financial sector.

According to Islamic economics, inflation is classified based on the causal factors, namely natural inflation and human error inflation. Natural inflation is caused by natural factors that cannot be prevented by humans, resulting in lower aggregate supply and higher aggregate demand. Natural inflation can also occur due to an increase in net exports, thus increasing the flow of money and aggregate demand. Other causes include drought, crop failure, and other large-scale disasters that erode aggregate supply. These things are beyond human control.

As the name suggests, human error inflation stems from human error. According to Karim (2010), human error inflation is caused by the following factors. *First*, the profit made by the authorities due to printing and issuing currency, otherwise known as seigniorage. The overprinting of money can result in significantly higher prices. Money must only be printed based on the transaction motivation or to develop business activity in the real sector, rather than seeking profit. *Second*, over-taxation encourages inflation by increasing production costs and diminishing aggregate supply. *Third*, complex bureaucracy will eventually reduce aggregate supply, similar to over-taxation, because the various levels of bureaucracy raise costs unnecessarily.

Islam recognises an economy bereft of inflation, which can be achieved when money is issued based on productive assets in the real sector. In this context, the overarching principle of the Islamic economy is harmony and balance between the financial sector and real sector. Aggregate demand is influenced by a private income, but aggregate supply may be unable to meet aggregate demand. This forms the basis of inflation. In Islam, harmony between the financial and real sectors can be achieved by only allowing humans to seek profit (money/wealth) in an equitable and justifiable way, namely through productive activities in the real sector. Money creation in the Islamic economy, therefore, must be based on increasing production in the real sector. Synchronicity between the financial sector and real sector can prevent or overcome inflation issues by increasing aggregate supply. In addition, Islam teaches moderation in consumption to avoid a *mubadzir* (prodigal) lifestyle.

Inflation is caused by sectoral inequality, particularly between the financial sector and real sector, namely imbalances between the money supply (public ability to spend money) and the ability of suppliers to produce goods, leading to higher prices. Islamic economic principles "force" financial sector transactions to be balanced with or based on real sector transactions, thereby reducing or even eliminating the gap between the financial sector and real sector. In the conventional system, however, there is a predetermined return in the form of an interest rate, which further increases the potential for inflation. Research conducted by Kia based on a sample of American countries showed that interest rates are directly proportional to inflation in both the near and long term.

The fundamental Islamic principle, namely the absolute prohibition of *riba* (interest), will reduce production costs and, therefore, fuel motivation to increase business activity. Empirical evidence is available from Japan and America, where very low interest rates were held until inflationary pressures were eliminated. Inflation can also be suppressed in Islam based on principles that forbid futures contracts and speculative transactions, thus reducing greed in humans and the hoarding of economic resources. It must be understood that the core tenets of Islamic economics encourage the equitable distribution of income and wealth between communities and sectors. Any increase in aggregate demand must be offset by a commensurate increase in aggregate supply. Meanwhile, all financial sector transactions must be based on value added in the real sector. Consequently, inflation can be suppressed or even eliminated completely.

10.3 Exchange Rates

10.3.1 Exchange Rate Concepts, Determinants, and Regimes

Concepts and Indicators

In an open economic system, exchange rates are an important indicator for the monetary authority. In general, the notion of exchange rates refers to the value of the domestic currency against a foreign currency. In this case, exchange rate fluctuations are influenced by supply and demand forces in foreign exchange markets driven by cross-border transactions (including international trade and capital flows), as recorded in the balance of payments (BOP) account. In addition, currency markets facilitate speculation, which can impact the value of currency.

According to Simorangkir and Suseno (2004), three main factors influence the demand for foreign exchange, namely import activity, capital outflows, and speculation. Higher imports of goods and services increase the demand for foreign exchange, which weakens the domestic exchange rate, and vice versa. In addition, higher capital outflows increase the demand for foreign exchange, which also weakens the domestic exchange rate, and vice versa. Meanwhile, more speculative activity increases the demand for currency and ultimately weakens the domestic currency.

On the other hand, export activities and capital inflows influence the supply of foreign currency. Higher exports lead to more foreign exchange and exchange rate appreciation. Conversely, declining exports tend to cause domestic exchange rate depreciation. Meanwhile, capital inflows have a positive impact on domestic exchange rate appreciation as the value strengthens, while lower capital inflows will prompt domestic exchange rate depreciation.

Exchange rate fluctuations in the market are influenced by several fundamental and non-fundamental factors. Fundamental factors include macroeconomic variables, such as economic growth, inflation, and exports-imports, while non-fundamental factors include market expectations concerning socio-political developments, market psychology in terms of processing information and rumours, and other developments that determine exchange rates (Syarifuddin, 2016). Exchange rate movements will change the relative prices of goods and services, thereby influencing the decision-making of economic actors regarding their economic activity. In addition, fluctuations of foreign exchange flows via the trade channel will also affect optimal monetary policy analysis for domestic monetary and financial stability. Therefore, there is a close relationship between exchange rates, foreign capital flows, and monetary policy formulation in an open economic system.

Exchange rates can be studied in terms of their relationship with other economic indicators, such as trade and inflation, thus allowing the formulation of effective monetary policy in an open economic system. *First*, the relationship between exchange rates and international trade can be explained as follows. Exchange rate depreciation is not always harmful because it can improve the trade balance as long as the exchange rate elasticity of exports is higher than the exchange rate elasticity of imports. Such conditions typically occur in countries where manufacturing sector exports exceed manufacturing sector imports, such as advanced economies (Warjiyo & Juhro, 2019). In his research, Rodrik (2008) found that exchange rate undervaluation in nominal or real terms could stimulate economic growth in developing economies.

Second, the effect of changes in the exchange rate on the prices of goods is one of the most important considerations when formulating effective monetary policy. According to Warjiyo and Juhro (2019), based on observations, changes in exchange rates in developing economies have a small effect on the prices of goods at the international level compared with changes in exchange rates in developed economies. This is also supported by research conducted by Frankel et al. (2005), showing that countries with a legacy of high inflation experience a greater magnitude of decline in the degree of influence exchange rate fluctuations have on international prices compared with countries with a history of low inflation.

Theories of Exchange Rate Determination

Regarding the behaviour of exchange rates, there are two salient theories concerning exchange rate determination. The first, purchasing power parity, is based on the flow concept to determine exchange rates for international trade activities. The flow concept occurs when the demand for foreign currency to pay for imported goods is equal to the supply of foreign currency for export purposes. In addition, omitting barriers to international trade, including foreign currency trade, the law of one price absolutely applies for different products traded internationally.

Based on the purchasing power parity (PPP) theory of exchange rates, the formula for determining the exchange rate can be expressed as follows:

$$E = {}^{P}/_{P^*} \tag{10.1}$$

where E is the exchange rate, P is the domestic price, and P^* is the international price.

From Eq. (10.1), the exchange rate reflects the value of domestic goods and services relative to the value of foreign goods and services. When the value of domestic goods and services is higher than the foreign value, the domestic currency will depreciate (an increase in the value of E or the exchange rate) because the competitiveness of domestically produced goods and services will decrease on the international market, thus reducing the level of exports and supply of foreign exchange in the country. This is subsequently accompanied by higher imports, leading to an increase in domestic demand for foreign exchange. Such conditions will appreciate the foreign currency and depreciate the domestic currency.

Another theory observes the behaviour of exchange rates from a financial perspective, namely the interest rate parity (IRP) theory, which depicts the relationship between the domestic foreign exchange market and international financial markets. The model is expressed as follows:

$$i = i^* + e \tag{10.2}$$

where i is the domestic interest rate, i^* is the international interest rate, and e is the expected exchange rate. From Eq. (10.2), it can be concluded that changes in the expected exchange rate are caused by the spread between domestic and international interest rates.

Exchange Rate Regime

Economic policy practices can be applied using one of three main exchange rate regimes (systems), namely a fixed exchange rate, floating exchange rate, and managed floating exchange rate (dirty float). Which regime to apply is determined based on the specific economic situation and conditions of the country concerned, including the level of foreign exchange reserves, economic openness, the foreign exchange system adopted, and the volume of the domestic foreign exchange market.

In a fixed exchange rate regime, the exchange rate of the domestic currency is pegged against a foreign currency at a certain value. For example, the exchange rate of the rupiah against the US dollar could be set at Rp15,000 per US dollar. Under such a regime, the central bank must be prepared to buy or sell foreign exchange reserves to maintain the predetermined exchange rate.

According to a floating exchange rate regime, the domestic exchange rate fluctuates over time, depending on the level of supply and demand of a foreign currency against the domestic currency. Therefore, any fluctuations in demand and supply will affect movements in the domestic exchange rate. When the demand for foreign currency against the domestic currency increases, the exchange rate of the domestic currency will decrease (weaker domestic currency). Conversely, when demand for foreign currency against the domestic currency decreases, the exchange rate of the domestic currency will increase (stronger domestic currency). On the supply side, when the supply of foreign currency against the domestic currency increases, the domestic exchange rate will increase, and vice versa. Notwithstanding, the central bank is authorised to intervene in the foreign exchange market, if necessary, to avoid excessive exchange rate shocks. Market intervention, however, does not seek to achieve a specific exchange rate target.

A managed floating exchange rate regime combines the fixed and floating regimes. The central bank determines a currency band as a range of upper and lower acceptable exchange rates for the national currency to fluctuate between. The exchange rate is determined by market mechanisms providing the fluctuations remain within the currency band. When the exchange rate falls outside of the currency band, the central bank will automatically intervene in the foreign exchange market to return the exchange rate to within the currency band.

10.3.2 Exchange Rates: An Islamic Perspective

The concept of exchange rates exists in response to the emergence of various currencies. During the time of Rasulullah SAW, for instance, two types of currency were in common use, namely dinar and dirham, along with three other types of commodity money, namely dates, wheat, and salt. During the Mamluk Dynasty (AD 1260–1382), three types of money were used, namely dinar, dirham, and copper coins (*fulus*). Exchange rates between different currencies were already known during that period. Teachings concerning the Islamic monetary system also regulate the concept of exchange rates. In this case, the exchange rate between two currencies must be of the same amount and executed in cash without any deferred payment. Rasulullah SAW once said:

وَعَنْ عُبَادَةَ بْنِ الصَّامِتِ قَالَ: قَالَ رَسُولُ اللَّهِ صَلَّى اللَّهُ عَلَيْهِ وَسَلَّمَ: «الذَّهَبُ بِالذَّهَبِ وَالْفِضَّةُ بِالْفِضَّةِ وَالْبُرُّ بِالْبُرِّ وَالشَّعِيرُ بِالشَّعِيرِ وَالتَّمْرُ بِالتَّمْرِ وَالْملح بالملح مثلا بِمثل سَوَاء بسَواءٍ يَدًا بِيَدٍ فَإِذَا اخْتَلَفَتْ هَذِهِ الْأَصْنَافُ فَبِيعُوا كَيْفَ شِئْتُمْ إِذَا كَانَ يَدًا بِيَدٍ» . رَوَاهُ مُسلم

'Ubada b. as-Samit reported God's Messenger as saying, "Gold is to be paid for by gold, silver by silver, wheat by wheat, barley by barley, dates by dates, and salt by salt, like for like and equal for equal, payment being made on the spot. If these classes differ, sell as you wish if payment is made on the spot." Muslim transmitted it.[1]

The hadiths above can be interpreted to mean that the exchange of similar currencies must be carried out with the same value, measure, time, and place. Meanwhile, exchanging different currencies was also based on the same principle, which must be done in cash with equivalent amounts exchanged. The hadiths also imply that buying and selling with different mediums of exchange is permitted in Islam, providing that the total value remains the same and is in accordance with the effective exchange rate at the time of the transaction (spot). This aims to avoid elements of *riba*.

There are four types of currency exchange transactions in the foreign exchange market, namely spot, forward, future, and swap. Islam, however, only permits spot transactions in the foreign exchange market, forbidding forward, future, and swap transactions. In addition to spot transactions, other principles must be considered in terms of the money market. *First*, it is imperative to remember the overarching principles of the Islamic economy, namely the absolute prohibition of *riba, gharar,* and *maysir*. Interest is considered *riba*, so all exchange rate transactions used in interest-bearing loans or bonds are clearly forbidden in Islam. *Gharar* appears when there are transaction conditions, in terms of quality and quantity, unknown to both transacting parties because transactions in accordance with Islamic teachings must be clear and unambiguous to all those involved.

Gharar can also manifest as *maysir*, or speculation, for example by delaying the exchange of foreign currencies in pursuit of a better future exchange rate to increase profit. Therefore, money market participants differ in the conventional economy and Islamic economy. In a conventional economy, market participants include traders, investors, and speculators. Notwithstanding, speculation is not permitted in Islam, so money market participants in an Islamic economy are limited to traders and investors.

The next Islamic economic principle concerns the prohibition of trading debt (including bonds). Buying and selling debt gives rise to the derivatives market, which runs contrary to Islamic teachings. *Third*, delaying the settlement of currency exchange transactions is not permitted, including deferring the purchase of currency until a future period despite paying at the current value or purchasing the currency at the current rate but deferring payment to secure a lower price.

The concept of exchange rate determination can be formulated through a monetary approach similar to conventional theory, such as the interest parity model. In the

[1] Reference: Mishkat al-Masabih 2808. In-book reference: Book 11, Hadith 47.

application of Islamic economics, however, the rate of return on investment is used instead of the interest rate system based on the following model:

$$r = r^* + e \tag{10.3}$$

where r is the domestic return on investment and $r*$ is the international return on investment.

To derive a model for calculating the exchange rate, the models in (10.1), (10.2), and (10.3) are substituted as follows:

$$\frac{M}{EP^*} = l\,(r^* + e, Y) \;\; l_{r^*+e} < 0 \text{ and } l_Y > 0 \tag{10.4}$$

The money supply model is subsequently included (Eq. 9.13) to illustrate equilibrium conditions in the money market as follows:

$$\frac{m\,(Q + F + G)}{EP^*} = l(r^* + e, Y) \tag{10.5}$$

Model (10.5) can be substituted again to obtain the exchange rate equation from an Islamic perspective, expressed as follows:

$$E = \frac{m\,(Q + F + G)}{P^*\;l(r^* + e, Y)} \tag{10.6}$$

where m is the money multiplier, financial transactions based on real assets (Q), foreign exchange reserves (F), and gold reserves (G).

The model shows how the application of Islamic teachings in the economic system can overcome the problem of exchange rate stability. One of the most important fundamental principles to achieve exchange rate stability is that the money supply and the demand for money must increase commensurately.

Exchange Rate Stability

The main goal of an Islamic economic system is currency stability, as reflected in a stable value against domestic goods and services as well as foreign currencies. Domestically, currency stability is reflected by the absence of significant inflation. Internationally, currency stability is evidenced by the exchange rate against foreign currencies. Stable exchange rates can be achieved by applying the supply and demand of money in accordance with the currency's fundamental value.

Islamic principles are adequate to achieve financial system stability, thus contributing to exchange rate stability. Fundamentally, Islamic principles prohibit *riba, gharar,* and *maysir*, transactions in the derivatives market and trading debt, while also requiring underlying assets in the real sector and applying a profit and loss sharing system for investment activity. Each of those principles could undoubtedly benefit the economic system of a country because they are already on a path that is in accordance with sharia law.

The application of interest rates actually represents a disruption in the economic system. In conventional economics, interest rates have a significant influence on investment stability, particularly in the near term. When interest rates fluctuate, investors can trade their short-term investment instruments freely, creating demand and supply shocks. Conversely, the incentive to invest, according to Islamic principles, is the rate of return.

Investment activities in accordance with sharia law must be based on actual transactions in the real sector. A shock in the level of return, therefore, would not impact the investor's liquidity as significantly as in a conventional economy. The elasticity of investment is lower in an Islamic economy than a conventional economy. In an Islamic economic system, there is a lag between changes in the rate of return on investment and the impact on capital mobility in the money market. Consequently, the exchange rate tends to be stable because the money market is not vulnerable to shocks. The prohibition of interest in the Islamic economic system, therefore, will help to overcome the problem of exchange rate fluctuations.

The absolute proscription of *maysir*, or speculation, in an Islamic economic system also has a favourable impact on exchange rate stability. The law of speculation is haram in terms of the action and the instruments. Speculators and their actions are a key factor in the occurrence of shocks in the money market, leading to exchange rate volatility. It can be concluded, therefore, that the absence of speculative actions will resolve the issue of exchange rate instability.

Profit sharing is the next sharia principle with implications for exchange rate stability. The return on funds from Islamic banks to depositors depends on the assets position, namely the profits generated by business operations, contrasting conventional banks that fix the rate of return at the beginning of the agreement. Consequently, the rate of return may not necessarily fall in line with the outcome of business activity, be it a loss or profit, because the return does not depend on the actual situation. During an economic downturn, depositors wishing to withdraw funds from conventional banks will receive a predetermined return that is not influenced by their asset position. In an Islamic economy, however, the probability of capital flight is lower, thereby underpinning exchange rate stability.

The monetary policy stance adopted by the central bank also influences exchange rate stability, specifically through regulation of the money supply. The exchange rate will remain stable providing money supply growth is commensurate with demand. This can be seen from an increase in the demand for money, which is caused by an increase in aggregate output. If the increase in the money supply is lower than the demand, the value of the currency would appreciate as money feels more valuable. Conversely, if the money supply outpaces the demand for money, the price of money will become "cheaper", leading to exchange rate depreciation. Limiting increases in the money supply based on Islamic principles, therefore, would reinforce exchange rate stability by only increasing the money supply when the demand for money increases, as evidenced by actual output in the real sector. Consequently, the supply and demand of money would remain in harmony and the exchange rate relatively stable (Khan & Mirakhor, 1989).

The impact of applying sharia economics on currency stability can also be projected from the fiscal side. By applying sharia economics, the central bank cannot freely disburse loans (financing) to the government, as the fiscal authority. Loans can only be allocated for purposes relating to capital expenditure. A government applying Islamic principles would ensure the operational expenditures are in line with the revenue received to avoid debt as much as possible. Restrictions on the allocation of capital loans from the central bank to the government can prevent imbalances between the money supply and demand for money. The provision of such loans is limited to productive real sector activities. Thus, the money supply, as regulated by the central bank, will remain in line with the demand for money, and exchange rate stability is maintained.

10.4 Interest

Interest rates play a significant and unavoidable role in the application of modern economics. Interest permeates every economic activity (Toutounchian, 2009). In fact, interest is taught as a return on one of the factors of production in a capitalist economy, namely capital. The interest rate, therefore, is the price for a certain amount of money that is channelled into the productive sector or for speculative actions. Meanwhile, the money disbursed is not necessarily transformed into capital in the real sector.

In general, interest rates reflect the cost of a loan. On the monetary side, the main affecting factor of interest rates is the interaction between the demand and supply of money. According to Keynes, the demand for money can be explained through three approaches. *First*, the demand for money is influenced by the transaction motive. Income is the variable that influences the transaction motive, so the demand for money is a function of income. *Second*, the demand for money is influenced by the precautionary motive, which is also a function of income. Notwithstanding, the background of both motivations is somewhat different, where the precautionary motive is based on holding cash balances for unforeseen circumstances. *Third*, there is the speculative motive, where money is considered an asset on the financial side. Money can be formed into a portfolio, where it is referred to as a bond.

The relationship between bonds and the demand for money can be explained as follows. Individuals have an opportunity to hold bonds rather than cash when interest rates rise because bondholders will receive a return based on the interest rate, while holding cash will not earn interest. When interest rates are high, individuals tend to hold less cash. According to Keynes, therefore, the relationship between interest rates and the demand for money is inversely proportional. This is known as the liquidity preference (LP) function.

In the near term, Keynes found that the money supply does not change significantly. It is merely a function of interest rates, so the shape of the curve is a straight vertical line (Boediono, 1988). To understand the interaction of money supply and demand equilibrium, Fig. 10.2 illustrates money supply and demand equilibrium.

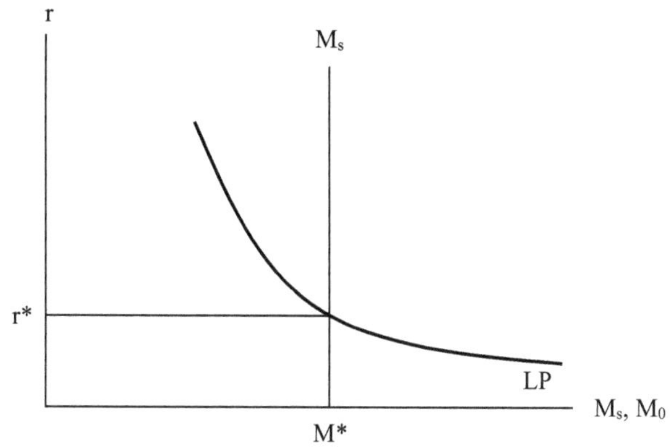

Fig. 10.2 Money supply and demand equilibrium. Source: Mankiw (2009)

Monetary policy can be applied to overcome an economic recession through interest rates. Interest rates affect investment and investment affects national output directly. Therefore, monetary policy is no longer effective when investment is inelastic to interest rates.

Interest and Investment

Interest rates influence national output through their relationship with investment. According to conventional economics, investment is dominated by physical capital for the production of goods and services. This relationship is depicted by the Marginal Efficiency of Investment (MEI). The MEI curve follows a negative slope, indicating an inverse relationship between interest rates and investment. This implies that when interest rates increase, investment will decrease and, vice versa, when interest rates decrease, investment will increase.

Conventional economics states that the goods/services market and money market are connected through interest rates. In the money market, interest rates influence changes in the money supply originating from the money creation process by commercial banks and shifts in the demand for money. This shift in the demand for money is a result of changes in the preferences of economic players concerning the ownership of financial assets and monetary assets (money for example). The relationship between the money market and the goods/services market is a channel for monetary policy transmission by changing interest rates to influence output in the goods/services market.

Interest and the Time Value of Money

The time value of money is an interesting concept in finance, broadly illustrating that a sum of money is worth more now than the same sum will be at a future date. It is also important to note, therefore, that the value of money yesterday is higher than the value of money today. This concept justifies the application of interest rates in conventional economics, particularly for financial transactions. Several theories underlie the time value of money as follows:

1. *Opportunity cost of money*

   The opportunity cost of money implies that an individual with money today has the opportunity to invest that money for future profit, but if the sum of money is lent to another party, the opportunity to generate that profit is lost. According to conventional economics, therefore, the interest rate is one determinant of the opportunity cost. Notwithstanding, interest rates are absolutely prohibited according to Islamic teachings.
2. *Uncertainty Concerning the Future of Flow of Money*

   Future cash flows cannot be determined with certainty. Individuals can only assume that the current flow of money is higher than the flow of money in the future.
3. *Decreasing Value of Money over Time*

   The diminishing value of money over time is indicative of lower public purchasing power. In this context, for example, Rp5,000 could buy a slice of cake in 2005, but in 2019, Rp5,000 will no longer buy a slice of cake due to inflation.

The time value of money is used as a justification for the application of interest rates. This does not mean the concept is not recognised in Islam, however. When studied in more depth, the time value of money concept is acceptable in Islamic economics. Muslim economists argue that in conventional economics, interest rates are just one opportunity cost. Therefore, the time value of money concept is acceptable as long as interest rates are omitted as one of the determinants of the opportunity cost.

This concept has made it legally justifiable to charge different selling prices for cash and credit transactions. This is allowed because there is an opportunity for the seller to lose out if the payment is deferred using an instalment mechanism. Nevertheless, Islam does not recommend transacting using instalments/debt, except in emergency circumstances. In the case of disbursing a loan based on a *qardh* contract, however, the value of the loan cannot exceed the amount of repaid funds.

10.4.1 Interest: An Islamic Perspective

Interest rates are an important instrument in contemporary financial transactions. Interest rates were introduced by conventional economists yet run contrary to the teachings of Islamic economics. At the time of Rasulullah SAW, no instruments explicitly known as interest rates were implemented, but Rasulullah SAW made it clear that transactions containing elements of *riba* were absolutely forbidden. Over time, however, economic practices have developed and interest rate instruments have emerged.

Interest rates are forbidden because of their resemblance to *riba*, which was prohibited by Allah SWT and His Messenger. Furthermore, the policy rate set by the monetary authority is used as a reference for the interest rates of commercial banks and the financial transactions therein. Therefore, various Islamic scholars assume that the contemporary interest rate mechanism is interchangeable with *riba*.

In Indonesia, this is supported by the official fatwa issued by the National Sharia Board of the Indonesian Council of Ulama (DSN-MUI), namely DSN-MUI Fatwa Number 1 of 2004 concerning Interest/*Fa'idah*. The fatwa explains that interest rates and *riba* are understood as an additional amount charged in financial transactions (loans in general) based on the principal without considering the value of benefits or outcome received from that principal amount. This interest rate has a maturity, and the value is predetermined at the beginning of the agreement as a specific percentage. According to the fatwa, interest rates are haram because they meet the criteria and characteristics of *riba* as appeared during the time of Rasulullah SAW, particularly *riba nasi'ah*. Furthermore, interest rates are considered haram for individuals and institutions, such as banks, insurance companies, capital markets, pawnshops, cooperatives, and other financial institutions.

Prohibition of Interest

Islam absolutely prohibits the practice of interest rates (*riba*), with the sin of *riba* considered more serious than adultery. This is explained in the Hadiths of Rasul, stating that the sin of an individual committing *riba* of just 1 dirham is greater than the sin of committing adultery 36 times. In addition, another hadith mentions the following:

وَعَنْ عَبْدِ اَللَّهِ بْنِ مَسْعُودٍ - رضى الله عنه - عَنْ اَلنَّبِيِّ - صلى الله عليه وسلم -قَالَ: { اَلرِّبَا ثَلَاثَةٌ وَسَبْعُونَ بَابًا أَيْسَرُهَا مِثْلُ أَنْ يَنْكِحَ اَلرَّجُلُ أُمَّهُ, وَإِنَّ أَرْبَى اَلرِّبَا عِرْضُ اَلرَّجُلِ اَلْمُسْلِمِ } رَوَاهُ اِبْنُ مَاجَهْ مُخْتَصَراً, وَالْحَاكِمُ بِتَمَامِهِ وَصَحَّحَهُ

The Prophet (ﷺ) said: "Usury has seventy-three categories, the least one in sin is as that of a man who marries (has sexual relations with) his mother, and the very essence of usury is the (violation of the) honor of a Muslim man." [Ibn Majah reported it in a short form and al-Hakim in a complete one. The latter also graded it Sahih (authentic)][2]

Riba is considered a sin not only to anyone committing it but also anyone facilitating, witnessing, recording, or involved in the implementation of *riba*.

Islam's opposition to *riba* is also reflected in numerous Quranic verses that explicitly prohibit the practice. In fact, Quranic verses prohibiting *riba* were revealed in four stages and explained as follows:

1. Verse 39 of surah Ar-Ruum

   The first verse belongs to the surah of Makkiyah, namely a Quranic verse revealed in Mecca. The verse reads:

[2]Sunnah.com reference: Book 7, Hadith 64. English translation: Book 7, Hadith 834. Arabic reference: Book 7, Hadith 831.

وَمَآ ءَاتَيۡتُم مِّن رِّبٗا لِّيَرۡبُوَاْ فِيٓ أَمۡوَٰلِ ٱلنَّاسِ فَلَا يَرۡبُواْ عِندَ ٱللَّهِۖ وَمَآ ءَاتَيۡتُم مِّن زَكَوٰةٖ تُرِيدُونَ وَجۡهَ ٱللَّهِ فَأُوْلَٰٓئِكَ
هُمُ ٱلۡمُضۡعِفُونَ

And whatever you give for interest to increase within the wealth of people will not increase with Allah. But what you give in zakah, desiring the countenance of Allah—those are the multipliers (Q.S. Ar-Ruum [30]: 39).

In that verse, Allah SWT does not explicitly forbid riba, explaining that riba is not something good or liked in the eyes of Allah SWT and will not receive the blessing of Allah SWT. On the other hand, zakat is pleasing to Allah SWT and zakat has the blessing of Allah SWT.

2. Verses 160–161 of surah An-Nisaa

These verses were revealed at the beginning of the *hijrah* to Medina. The words of Allah SWT in this verse were revealed as follows:

فَبِظُلۡمٖ مِّنَ ٱلَّذِينَ هَادُواْ حَرَّمۡنَا عَلَيۡهِمۡ طَيِّبَٰتٍ أُحِلَّتۡ لَهُمۡ وَبِصَدِّهِمۡ عَن سَبِيلِ ٱللَّهِ كَثِيرٗا ١٦٠ وَأَخۡذِهِمُ
ٱلرِّبَوٰاْ وَقَدۡ نُهُواْ عَنۡهُ وَأَكۡلِهِمۡ أَمۡوَٰلَ ٱلنَّاسِ بِٱلۡبَٰطِلِۚ وَأَعۡتَدۡنَا لِلۡكَٰفِرِينَ مِنۡهُمۡ عَذَابًا أَلِيمٗا ١٦١

For wrongdoing on the part of the Jews, We made unlawful for them [certain] good foods which had been lawful to them, and for their averting from the way of Allah many [people], And [for] their taking of usury while they had been forbidden from it, and their consuming of the people's wealth unjustly. And we have prepared for the disbelievers among them a painful punishment (Q.S. An-Nisaa [4]: 160-161).

The verse above describes *riba* as wrongdoing, while consuming wealth that contains elements of *riba* is an act harmful to others. In addition, the verse also likened those who commit *riba* with the behaviour of the Jews. The verse also contains the explicit threat of a painful punishment for anyone practising *riba*.

3. Verse 130 of surah Ali-Imran

The third stage of *riba* was revealed in this verse approximately three years after the *hijrah*. The words of Allah SWT in this verse were revealed as follows:

يَٰٓأَيُّهَا ٱلَّذِينَ ءَامَنُواْ لَا تَأۡكُلُواْ ٱلرِّبَوٰٓاْ أَضۡعَٰفٗا مُّضَٰعَفَةٗۖ وَٱتَّقُواْ ٱللَّهَ لَعَلَّكُمۡ تُفۡلِحُونَ

O you who have believed, do not consume usury, doubled and multiplied, but fear Allah that you may be successful (Q.S. Ali Imran [3]: 130).

In this verse, Allah SWT says "do not", implying that Allah SWT explicitly prohibits the practice of *riba*. Consequently, there is no longer any reason to justify the practice of *riba*. In addition, the verse describes how *riba* includes anything to do with doubling or multiplying money without specific effort, whether it is multiplied by small or large amounts.

4. Verse 279 of surah Al-Baqarah

This verse was revealed in approximately the ninth year of the *hijrah*. In the verse, Allah SWT reiterates that *riba* is something absolutely despised by Allah SWT. The verse reads:

فَإِن لَّمۡ تَفۡعَلُواْ فَأۡذَنُواْ بِحَرۡبٖ مِّنَ ٱللَّهِ وَرَسُولِهِۦۖ وَإِن تُبۡتُمۡ فَلَكُمۡ رُءُوسُ أَمۡوَٰلِكُمۡ لَا تَظۡلِمُونَ وَلَا تُظۡلَمُونَ

> And if you do not, then be informed of a war [against you] from Allah and His Messenger. But if you repent, you may have your principal—[thus] you do no wrong, nor are you wronged (Q.S. Al Baqarah [2]: 279).

In that verse, Allah SWT severely criticises those who consume *riba*. After explaining how bad *riba* is and its prohibition, the verse emphasises that anyone who insists on keeping outstanding interest must be prepared for war with Allah and His Messenger. A war against other humans may not necessarily lead to victory, let alone a war against Allah and His Messenger.

Another verse explains the behaviour of humans who already love their property despite origins in *riba*. Allah SWT also explains that *riba* is not equivalent to trade. This is contained in verse 275 of surah Al-Baqarah as follows:

ٱلَّذِينَ يَأْكُلُونَ ٱلرِّبَوٰا۟ لَا يَقُومُونَ إِلَّا كَمَا يَقُومُ ٱلَّذِى يَتَخَبَّطُهُ ٱلشَّيْطَٰنُ مِنَ ٱلْمَسِّ ذَٰلِكَ بِأَنَّهُمْ قَالُوٓا۟ إِنَّمَا ٱلْبَيْعُ مِثْلُ
ٱلرِّبَوٰا۟ وَأَحَلَّ ٱللَّهُ ٱلْبَيْعَ وَحَرَّمَ ٱلرِّبَوٰا۟ فَمَن جَآءَهُۥ مَوْعِظَةٌ مِّن رَّبِّهِۦ فَٱنتَهَىٰ فَلَهُۥ مَا سَلَفَ وَأَمْرُهُۥٓ إِلَى ٱللَّهِ وَمَنْ عَادَ
فَأُو۟لَٰٓئِكَ أَصْحَٰبُ ٱلنَّارِ هُمْ فِيهَا خَٰلِدُونَ

> Those who consume interest cannot stand [on the Day of Resurrection] except as one stands who is being beaten by Satan into insanity. That is because they say, "Trade is [just] like interest." But Allah has permitted trade and has forbidden interest. So whoever has received an admonition from his Lord and desists may have what is past, and his affair rests with Allah. But whoever returns to [dealing in interest or usury]—those are the companions of the Fire; they will abide eternally therein (Q.S. Al Baqarah [2]: 279).

The Quranic verse states that trade and *riba* are very different because trade is halal and *riba* is haram. Furthermore, Allah SWT likens humans who love *riba* to the devil, whose heart has been closed by an abundance of wealth.

An excessive love of wealth helps to sustain the practice of *riba* in an economy. Humans have become lost in their minds and dark in their hearts so as to justify all means of multiplying their wealth. This includes ways to cheat and deceive others through the application of *riba*. In fact, Rasulullah SAW warned of various ways that humans can become entangled in *riba*. Ultimately, *riba* will destroy mankind.

Interest and Economic Equilibrium

According to conventional economic theory, interest rates play an important role in balancing the goods/services market and money market. In Islamic economics, however, interest rates contain elements of *riba*, leading to economic imbalances. Interest rates make economic exploitation possible, thus widening the gap between rich and poor. In addition, interest can have a deleterious impact on economic indicators, including economic growth, productivity, equitable income and wealth distribution, unemployment, and economic stability.

The imbalances stem from the fundamental nature of interest rates, namely a predetermined return before any business activity in the real sector has been carried out. In addition, interest rates are always positive. Indirectly, this implies that the economy, or business activity in the real sector, must always experience positive change or remain profitable in other words. Clearly, this deviates from the nature of business itself, where profits may be generated or losses incurred, which cannot be ascertained in advance. The mechanism can be said, therefore, to violate market rationality. The predetermined nature of interest rates allows investors or financially advantaged parties to generate income through the financial sector irrespective of productive real sector activity.

In addition, there is a mismatch between money creation in the money market and the goods/services produced and transacted in the goods/services market within an interest-bearing system. Interest creates markets for money and financial assets, namely the money market, establishing separate financial investments. In this context, the meaning of investment is quite broad, encompassing deposits, bonds, and debt securities in the capital market, money market, and derivatives market. Nevertheless, this generalised classification of investment impairs economic policymaking at the advanced level. In addition, such investments intensify the risk of economic instability, where money creation leads to a bubble economy, in which growth of the money supply exceeds growth in the real sector, with economic progress thus illusory. Moreover, such money creation promotes exploitation, injustice, inequity, and economic inequality.

In the Islamic economy, however, investment is a form of business partnership (*syirkah*) performed in the real sector. From an Islamic perspective, therefore, investment has a close relationship with real sector conditions. The complexity of the modern economy is increasing, thus establishing investment activity as an important mechanism to distribute income and wealth. Investment activity can be seen as a catalyst of economic activity in the real sector. Consequently, investment must be driven by the real rate of return and rather than the interest rate.

Real Rate of Return Concept

The real rate of return is the percentage of profit earned on an investment, adjusted for price changes, such as inflation and other conditions. According to conventional economics, this adjustment compensates the tendency of price changes. The real rate of return concept is used extensively in conventional economics given that inflation will reduce the real value of a sum of money invested. The real rate of return is calculated by subtracting the inflation rate from the nominal interest rate. Conventionally, the real rate of return and nominal interest rate must be classified due to the inherent disconnect between the real sector and financial sector. This is not the case in Islamic economics.

All financial transactions in an Islamic economic system must be based on real underlying projects or assets in the real sector. The real rate of return in Islamic economics, therefore, is not an adjustment of the nominal interest rate to changes in prices, yet rather a mechanism that should be applied based on economic activity in the real sector.

10.5 Economic Activity and Monetary Control Without Interest Rates

The absolute prohibition of interest rates is part of the journey towards achieving a true Islamic economic system. Furthermore, interest rates are eliminated in the economy to achieve economic equity and justice. According to Chapra (2001a, b), the abolition of interest rates necessitates regulatory, institutional, and socio-economic reform. This entails a long and gradual process. Most importantly, an alternative financial system mechanism to interest rates must be prepared. The role of Islamic banking here is quite significant, considering that most financial intermediation is done in the banking industry. Therefore, Islamic banking innovation is important to maintain the existence of the Islamic economy.

The alternative mechanism in question is based on equity. Alternative solutions include sharia-compliant financial contracts at financial institutions, banks in particular, such as partnership contracts (*mudharabah* and *musyarakah*), lease contracts (*ijarah*), and sales contracts (*murabahah*, *salam*, and *istishna'*). The use of Islamic contracts will ensure that financial sector transactions are based on real sector conditions, thereby reducing the disconnect, or gap, between the financial sector and the real sector.

Concerning partnership-based contracts, the rate of return is not predetermined at the beginning of the contract. Instead, a profit-sharing ratio (*nisbah*) for future profit is mutually agreed. It is fair to assume that partnership-based contracts are higher risk due to the uncertain returns, which may be positive or negative depending on business conditions at the end of the agreement. The return is positive if the business generates a profit, and vice versa, the return will be negative if the business incurs a loss.

For risk-averse players, an alternative lower-risk mechanism is available for financial transactions without involving interest rates, namely lease or sales contracts. According to lease contracts, the rental fee (*ujroh* in Arabic) is determined and fixed at the beginning of the agreement and does not change during the term. For sales contracts, on the other hand, the selling price is mutually agreed between the seller and buyer at the beginning of the agreement and does not change. For a sales contract with deferred payments, the monthly instalments are fixed.

At first glance, lease and sales contracts may appear to resemble interest rate mechanisms as the rate of return is determined at the beginning of the agreement. There is a fundamental difference, however, namely that lease and sales contracts do not constitute lending or borrowing transactions, which apply an interest rate mechanism. In addition, the agreed rate of return for lease and sales contracts is not a percentage of the initial capital, as in the case of interest rates, but a fixed price that cannot be changed until the end of the agreement, even in the event of delays in payments or delivery.

In addition to the sharia-compliant contracts outlined above, Islam also justifies the existence of credit. There are differences, however, with conventional credit. Sharia-compliant financing must be related and tied to actual needs in the real sector. In other words, credit is based on real assets in the form of goods, services, or certain projects. Credit is absolutely forbidden for transactions deemed haram or speculative in nature and must be based on real underlying assets.

This beckons the fundamental question of how monetary control can be exercised if interest rates are prohibited? It is important to understand that, excepting interest rates, other conventional monetary control instruments can be adopted and used as Islamic monetary instruments, while adhering to sharia guidance, such as statutory reserves (SR), credit rationing, and selective credit. Notwithstanding, interest rates are still the main instrument for regulating conventional monetary policy, and even Islamic monetary policy still requires tools similar to interest rates in implementation. This is contrary to the teachings of Islamic economics, where the fundamental principle is the prohibition of *riba*. In this case, interest rates are considered *riba*. The Islamic monetary authority, therefore, needs to develop a new formula as an alternative to regulating monetary policy without applying interest rate instruments.

Islam prohibits interest rates for specific reasons. Considering that Islam brings blessings and mercy to all humans, anything that is prohibited must contain elements that are harmful. The most concrete evidence for failures in the current conventional monetary system is the previous crises triggered by interest rate fluctuations in the financial sector. Interest rate fluctuations create uncertainty in other economic variables, such as exchange rates, inflation, unemployment, savings, and investment. Another mistake is to determine interest rates not based on growth in the real sector, thereby failing to reflect actual real sector growth, which creates gaps between the real and financial sectors.

Returning to the nature of money, money should not be allowed to multiply without adding value to the real sector. Islamic economics, therefore, focuses specifically on real sector growth. Real sector growth leads to financial sector advancement. Money that is circulated must be based on an underlying transaction in the real sector. This is done to maintain balance and harmony between the amount of money in the financial sector and productivity in the real sector.

1. Alternative instruments to interest rates must be formulated to realise the fully fledged implementation of the Islamic economy. In addition, other urgencies in the creation of monetary control instruments without interest rates include (1) achieving optimal economic growth and full employment, (2) creating conditions for stability in the value of money domestically and abroad, (3) increasing mobility and the equitable flow of resources to achieve economic development, and (4) creating conditions for the equitable distribution of wealth and income among community groups. Regarding alternative instruments that are in line with Islamic principles to replace interest rates, Al-Qur'an points to the expected rate of profit in the real sector. Using the expected rate of profit as a benchmark in the monetary sector is one of the keys to achieving economic justice and stability (Supriyanto, 2019).

   Creating a special Islamic monetary benchmark that is separate from conventional monetary benchmarks is important when establishing an Islamic monetary system, considering the different characteristics of Islamic and conventional monetary economics, such as using the expected rate of profit. The expected rate of profit is a valid alternative instrument to interest rates for several reasons. *First*, the rate of profit is a measure of business activity to produce value added from a product. *Second*, transaction activities contain elements of risk-taking. *Finally*, there is responsibility and accountability for any losses that occur during the transaction.

In practice, however, there are differing points of view regarding the application of the expected rate of profit in various monetary instruments and operations. Some contracts use a post-determined rate of profit, while others prefer a predetermined rate. The post-determined rate of profit is used for *musyarakah* and *mudharabah* contracts, while the predetermined rate of profit is used for *murabahah*, *jualah*, *ijarah*, *wakalah*, and other similar contracts. This fundamental difference also affects the performance of monetary policy instruments in terms of controlling the money supply. Instruments with a predetermined rate of profit are generally more effective in controlling the amount of money in market circulation (Supriyanto, 2019). On the other hand, the predetermined rate of profit, as applied in Islamic monetary economics, differs from the predetermined nature of interest rate instruments in conventional monetary economics.

The operational target of Islamic monetary policy aims to influence liquidity in the Islamic banking system through expansionary and contractionary monetary policies. The expected rate of profit, therefore, is a valid instrument of Islamic monetary control because the rate of profit describes the level of profit at Islamic banks payable to investors at the end of each period. Thus, the operational target of monetary policy can be achieved effectively.

Expansionary monetary policy by the central bank increases the money supply by lowering the rate of profit in short-term transactions, specifically by lowering the rate of profit sharing for Islamic bank deposits. Consequently, individuals will be more inclined to allocate income for consumption rather than bank deposits, thus increasing aggregate demand. Ultimately, this will accelerate economic growth.

Monetary expansion using the rate of profit does not raise or lower asset prices because the instrument reflects the actual profits generated in the real sector. This is more consistent with the principles and rules of Islamic economics, which prioritises balance between the monetary sector and the real sector.

According to Islamic economics, alternative instruments to interest rates are required to control the monetary system. Such instruments should be formulated based on actual economic growth in the real sector. Research by Uddin and Halim (2015) showed that interest rates can be substituted by instruments that use GDP growth as a benchmark, yet no official name has been given to such an instrument.

The type of GDP growth that is applicable for use as a standard reference when determining instruments of monetary control is real GDP. GDP growth can be used as a benchmark because GDP measures the economic level of a country as well as performance. Furthermore, GDP accurately reflects conditions in the real sector. Real GDP is used for its ability to measure true output growth, unaffected by price increases (inflation). Using GDP growth as a reference for the rate of return in financial markets is appropriate and strategic because GDP growth describes the real value added of productivity in the real sector unlike inflation indexation, which describes the condition of rising prices rather than reflecting the conditions of output growth. Inflation indexation is also less accurate during periods of stagflation, when prices are rising but output decreases.

Using monetary instruments that are in line with real sector growth is expected to achieve healthy monetary conditions. In addition, this could also resolve the problems of declining economic growth, excessive inflation, and instability in the value of money while overcoming the main issue of achieving balance between the amount of money in the financial sector and what is actually required in the real sector. Meanwhile, unique alternative monetary control instruments are available that are in accordance with Islamic principles, namely the ratio of profit to capital in all investment projects undertaken by Islamic banks. The effective and efficient application of such instruments by the central bank could minimise the hoarding or concentration of money around just one point. On the other hand, money could be channelled effectively to the real economy. The overarching principle is that the central bank must be able to channel currency in circulation into the real sector for transformation into productive goods and services.

References

Boediono. (1988). *Seri Sinopsis Pengantar Ilmu Ekonomi No. 5: Ekonomi Moneter*. BPFE.

Chapra, M. U. (2001a). *The future of economics: An Islamic perspective.* (A. Amir, Y. Machmudi, F. Nur, L. Trialdi, E. Sudjono, & M. T. Ridho, Penerj.). Shari'ah Economic and Banking Institute.

Chapra, M. U. (2001b). *What is Islamic economics?* (2nd ed.). IRTI/IDB.

Frankel, J. A., Parsley, D. C., & Wei, S.-J. (2005). Slow passthrough around the world: A new import for developing countries? *The National Bureau of Economic Research Working Paper No 11199.*

Karim, A. A. (2010). *Sejarah Pemikiran Ekonomi Islam*. PT RajaGrafindo Persada.

Khan, M. S., & Mirakhor, A. (1989). The financial system and monetary policy in an Islamic economy. *Journal of King Abdulaziz University: Islamic Economics, 1*, 39–57.

Mankiw, N. G. (2009). *Marcoeconomics* (7th ed.). Worth Publisher.

Rodrik, D. (2008). The real exchange rate and economic growth. *Brookings Paper on Economic Activity.*

Shahzad, F., & Luqman, A. (2012). Impact of organizational culture on organizational performance: An overview. *Institute of Interdisciplinary Business Research, 3*(9).

Simorangkir, I., & Suseno. (2004). *Seri Kebanksentralan No. 12: Sistem dan Kebijakan Nilai Tukar*. Pusat Pendidikan dan Studi Kebanksentralan Bank Indonesia.

Supriyanto, T. (2019). Rate of profit as a monetary policy tool for financial stability. In *Islamic monetary economics and institutions: Theory and practice* (pp. 117–136). Springer

Syarifuddin, F. (2016). *Konsep, Dinamika dan Respon Kebijakan Nilai Tukar di Indonesia*. Bank Indonesia Institut.

Toutounchian, I. (2009). *Islamic money & banking: Integrating money in capital theory*. Wiley.

Uddin, M. A., & Halim, A. (2015). Islamic monetary policy: Is there an alternative of interest rate? *MPRA Paper*.

Warjiyo, P., & Juhro, S. M. (2019). *Central Bank Policy: Theory and Practice*. Emerald Publishing Ltd.

Wulan, E. R., & Nurfaiza, S. (2015). Analysis of factors affecting inflation in Indonesia: An Islamic perspective. *International Journal of Nusantara Islam*, 02(02), 67–80.

Zoellick, R. B. (2011). *The Middle East and North Africa: A new social contract for development*. The Peterson Institute for International Economics.

Chapter 11
Investment, Finance, and Monetary Policy

11.1 Introduction

Investment activity in the real sector provides an important and comprehensive economic contribution, particularly in the modern era of increasing economic complexity. The investment market is the primary driver of real sector activity because investment encourages the flow of resources and income. It must be remembered, however, that investment activity is in the form of capital investment. In Islam, capital must be channelled to stimulate productive activity and produce goods and services in the real sector. Investment plays an important role in economic growth. In fact, investment is one of the determinants of faster economic growth by creating new job openings, expanding the manufacturing industry, and increasing capacity in the corporate sector.

Investment patterns and trends are an important reference to understand the general financial and monetary landscape in Islam. Islamic economics does not recognise sectoral polarity between the financial and real sectors. Together, the financial sector and real sector form an integrated system. On the other hand, however, a financial sector that can multiply itself is indicative of superficial or illusory growth. Meanwhile, the real sector cannot exist without the support and impetus of real sector activities. In an Islamic economy, therefore, the financial sector fulfils that role by carrying out activities relating to the flow of money in real sector activities, including investment. Investment in the real sector aims to enhance the effective distribution and allocation of wealth and resources. Consequently, real sector growth will accelerate and productivity will increase.

From the description above, there is clearly a very close relationship between investment activity and the financial sector. The financial sector plays a consequential role supporting real sector activities. Nonetheless, the financial sector cannot "create" money by itself. The role of the financial sector is limited to providing funds for producing goods and services in the real sector to be traded in the goods market. According to Islamic economics, there is no sectoral dualism and, therefore,

S. M. Juhro et al., *Inclusive Welfare*, https://doi.org/10.1007/978-981-96-0051-9_11

investment in the real sector must be concurrent with the financial sector. In addition, the financial sector is not a producer of money but provides funds for real sector transactions. Furthermore, financial sector products are designed to increase the availability of funds for transaction activities in the real sector, including the production, distribution, and trade of goods and services.

Real sector investment activity driven by the financial sector will elicit changes in macroeconomic and monetary variables, such as the money supply, exchange rate, interest/return rate, economic growth, and inflation. Linkages, therefore, between real sector investment and the financial sector will have different implications for the monetary system. The monetary sector is thus required to maintain harmony between the real and financial sectors. Monetary instruments and policies are oriented towards maximising the flow of funds to the real sector. The money supply, for instance, would not increase without real demand in the real sector to ramp up the production of goods and services. Consequently, stable money supply conditions can be maintained in line with the level of demand for money in the community. With the supply and demand of money in harmony, prices tend to be more stable and inflation controlled. Such a mechanism, therefore, could ensure inflation or price increases are balanced by a commensurate increase in public purchasing power.

Monetary policy oriented towards linkages and harmony between the real sector and financial sector must not only focus on the monetary side or the money supply, but also focus on supporting the production of goods and services to increase aggregate supply to meet higher aggregate demand by facilitating the flow of funds into the real sector to bolster production activity. This also contributes to price stability because producers can meet higher demand by increasing supply. Stable prices also imply low and stable inflation. In addition to stable inflation, output will also increase due to stronger productivity, coupled with potentially greater public well-being and prosperity.

This is an essential chapter of the book as it seeks to bridge the readers' understanding from the previous focus on various fundamental Islamic monetary concepts and frameworks, including how several variables influence economic equilibrium and quality welfare, towards the practical and strategic substance of implementing Islamic monetary policy. The chapter explains the nature of the relationship between investment activity and the financial sector, as well as the Islamic monetary policy strategy to achieve the targets set. Finally, an explanation of monetary policy transmission from the conventional and Islamic perspectives enriches the discussion.

11.2 Concept and Types of Investment in Islam

Investment according to Islam differs from conventional economic theory. In Islam, investment encompasses the creation of goods and services. Investment in Islam, therefore, relates closely to the real sector, and investment instruments are transmitted and operationalised through the real sector. In conventional economics, however, the definition of investment extends beyond the creation of goods and services to include investment in financial assets that are detached from the real sector.

Investment and inflation are related because future inflation will decrease the value of assets currently owned. Asset value must be protected and increased, therefore, to hedge against the negative effects of inflation. That is the main motivation and goal for people to invest. Conventional and sharia-compliant investments are based on the basic concepts of risk management and the rate of return. Muslims, however, must not only consider the material and profitability aspects of the investment, yet also pay attention to the social benefits as well as compliance with Islamic principles and sharia law. Muslim awareness of sharia law is increasing, not only in terms of worship but also *muamalah* activities, including investment.

In an Islamic economic system, generating profit to hedge against inflation has different implications for real sector activities in terms of fixed capital formation. In a conventional economic system, interest rates create a credit market independently of the real sector. Though the credit market exists to finance real sector activities, the application of speculative interest rates has the potential to decouple the financial market from the real sector. Money creation and monetary concentration, as facilitated by the interest rate system, are sources of a bubble economy, leading to economic instability and fragilities. Interest and interest rates are absolutely forbidden, however, in an Islamic economic system, thereby obviating the existence of a debt market or a market for trading debt instruments. In Islam, the financial market exists to support the real sector and profits accrued from activities in the real sector are distributed based on a profit- and loss-sharing (PLS) mechanism. Investment in Islam, therefore, can be observed in terms of real investment and financial investment because the two are mutually related and interconnected.

Investment is a dominant Islamic economic activity due to the inherent wealth distribution aspects within the community. According to sharia law, it is reasonable to expect a return on investment, providing the return is generated in justifiable ways. Ultimately, investment can accelerate growth in the real sector by increasing business capital. Investment is also a component of wealth management, involving the development, distribution, and transfer of assets in the community. Consequently, investment activity in Islam is inseparable from productive business activity in the real sector.

Investment is a highly recommended *muamalah* activity in Islam. Investment can have a very beneficial impact on the overall economy by increasing the production of goods/services, social benefits received by the community, job opportunities, and job creation as well as mobilising idle funds. Rasulullah SAW exemplified this throughout his life. According to sharia law, investment is permissible (*mubah*) providing it does not contain any elements considered haram in Islam (Table 11.1).

The main Islamic principle concerning investment is the absolute abolition of *riba* (interest rates), *gharar*, and *maysir*. In addition, investment in haram businesses is not allowed, such as financial institutions applying interest rates, gambling companies, liquor companies, and food companies processing haram animals. Beyond that, Muslim investors must understand that sharia investment will contain the risk of loss. As with conventional investment, sharia investment also has the

Table 11.1 Examples of conventional versus Islamic investment

Conventional investment	Islamic investment
Savings investment. The profit accrued is the predetermined return on an initial sum of capital, as stated at the beginning of the agreement	Savings investment with *mudharabah* contract. From the outset, the contract states the profit-sharing ratio (nominal profit not stated at the beginning of contract)
Shares. Profit is obtained from dividend income and capital gain	Islamic shares. Profit is also obtained from dividend income and capital gain. Stock can only be purchased of firms operating in compliance with sharia principles
Bonds. Profit is obtained from a predetermined coupon rate, as stated at the beginning of the agreement	Islamic bonds (sukuk) must have an underlying translation for each sukuk issued. Income from profit ratio obtained in advance
Options contract	Islam does not recognise options contracts because the price is predetermined
Futures contract	Islam does not recognise futures contracts because the price is predetermined

Source: Authors

potential to incur losses. It is necessary, therefore, to mitigate investment risk. This can be achieved through diversification. The wide variety of investment options provides an opportunity for investors to diversify investment funds across several investment portfolios. Diversification mitigates portfolio risk.

Investment in Islam follows its own concept of supply and demand. The investment function in Islam is a function of expected return (*Er*). First, the concept of investment supply in Islam will be discussed. The total investment supply in Islam is inelastic to changes in the expected return because the investment supplier will initiate investment for any positive expected return. Any change in *Er* will not change the total investment supply. Investment supply, therefore, is said to be autonomous, thus creating a vertical supply curve.

In general, investment supply in Islam originates from several sectors, namely the private sector (I_P), government sector (I_G), and social sector (I_{Soc}). Therefore, the investment supply equation can be expressed as follows:

$$I_S = I_P + I_G + I_{\text{Soc}} \tag{11.1}$$

The investment supply does not depend on the expected rate of return, so changes are driven by business players, the government, and social actors.

The investment supply is also influenced by the motivation of Muslim investors to invest. First, optimal *zakat* implementation implies that individual assets, upon reaching a specific threshold, will become the object of obligatory *zakat* collection. In addition, there is the social motivation to help others lacking sufficient funds to operate a business yet with the requisite skills to carry out productive business activities (Sakti, 2007).

On the other hand, the demand for investment in Islam is categorised as autonomous or induced investment. Autonomous investment demand (I_O) is not

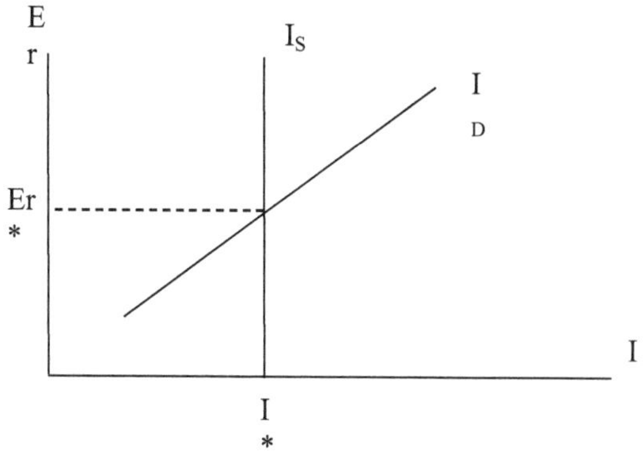

Fig. 11.1 Investment supply and demand equilibrium point. Source: Mankiw (2009)

influenced by other variables, including the expected rate of profit, rather by investor preferences based on individual/personal motivation and social motivation. On the other hand, induced investment demand is influenced by economic variables, such as higher demand and expected returns. This is typically motivated by investors trying to maintain or increase future wealth. Through investment, parties with requisite business skills but insufficient capital have the opportunity to implement their business ideas.

Having explained the two elements of investment demand, the complete investment equation can be expressed as follows:

$$I_D = I_O + f(Er) \tag{11.2}$$

where I_O is autonomous investment and *f(Er)* is the investment function against the expected return.

In addition to the equation for investment supply and demand as formulated in Eq. (11.2), the supply and demand curves for investment can also be illustrated as presented in Fig. 11.1, which can explain a shift in the curve and a shift along the curve. A shift in the curve occurs when I_O experiences a positive or negative change, while a shift along the curve occurs when *Er* experiences a positive or negative change, as depicted in Fig. 11.2.

Shifts in the investment supply and demand curves can affect the equilibrium point in the investment market. An increase, for instance, in the value of autonomous investment will precipitate a shift in the investment demand curve to the right (from I_{D1} to I_{D2}), and the supply curve is assumed to be constant; thus, the equilibrium point of the expected return will decrease (from Er* to Er_1). On the other hand, a shift in the investment supply curve to the right (from I_{S1} to I_{S2}), while the demand curve remains constant, will increase the expected return (from Er* to Er_2) and investment equilibrium will increase from I_1 to I_2. For greater clarity, refer to Fig. 11.2.

Investment and Savings

The concept of savings in conventional economics is defined as the difference between income and consumption. In other words, savings represent unutilised

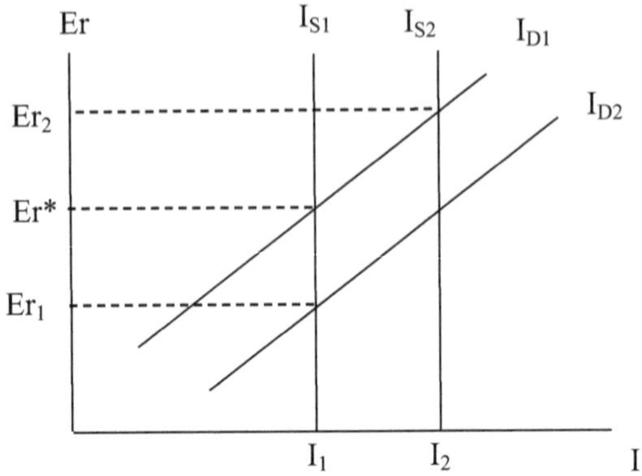

Fig. 11.2 Shifts in the investment supply and demand curves. Source: Mankiw (2009)

income. In contrast, Islam has a different perspective. Saving activity in Islam reflects moral values in accordance with Islamic religious guidance. In this case, moral values imply that humans are taught to live within their means and without excessive luxury, which nevertheless does not mean living in poverty. Humans must strive to meet their daily needs. In addition, the motivation to save is consistent with Islamic principles, namely for the benefit of all.

In terms of investment from an Islamic perspective, savings do not have a close correlation with investment. This is different from the conventional perspective, where savings and investment have a close economic relationship through interest rates, which is the root cause of fluctuations in investment and savings. When lending rates and deposit rates rise, investment will decrease and savings will increase, and vice versa, when interest rates decline, investment will increase and savings will decrease.

There is a fundamental difference between savings and investment from the perspective of Islamic economics, namely in terms of orientation. Investment activity is oriented towards profit seeking, accompanied by the risk of loss that may occur. Meanwhile, saving activity reflects a simple and frugal life, as a precautionary measure against unforeseen exigencies. Financial product innovation, however, has blurred the line between savings and investment. Savings products are now bundled with investment contracts, such as *mudharabah*, thus affording savings products investment potential by meeting the transactional motive for primary needs and the precautionary motive for unforeseen circumstances.

Private Investment

The private sector is oriented towards maximising profit, financed through external parties, including funds from investors. The private sector consists of goods and services that people need in their daily lives, such as vehicles, waterways, electronic goods, food, transportation, telecommunications, and others.

Given the profit orientation, the private sector strives to maximise profit, including through investment. In fact, private sector investment is the dominant contributor to overall investment in a country. Private investment enriches the private sector through returns on investment, which can be exploited to increase capital accumulation and production capacity.

For the recipients, investment funds provided by the private sector can be used to expand businesses or increase productivity, thus contributing to real sector growth. In addition, an increase of direct investment would boost national income because investment is one of the components.

Government Investment

Departing from the private sector, the government is not motivated by profit. Instead, the government is oriented towards providing public services and is accountable to the public. The government receives funds from taxes, levies, debt, profits of state-owned enterprises, a government investment. The government sector is used by the community to receive benefits at low cost or free.

The public sector is not oriented towards maximising profit; instead the government strives to progress national development. Therefore, the government also invests as part of the efforts to expand sources of income, thus contributing to increase national income through the investment component.

Social Investment

Social investment, otherwise known as socially responsible investment (SRI), unifies two usually disparate dimensions, namely generating profit and helping the social environment. This is achieved by expanding the orientation from 1P (profit) to 3P (profit, people, and planet). Social investment applies the principle of social responsibility to the environment, including the community and physical environment. Social investment, therefore, fundamentally aligns with the principles and values of Islamic economics, which uphold the tenets of justice and equity in life. One of the best-known forms of social investment is corporate social responsibility (CSR).

Social investment does not necessarily always entail disbursing funds directly to the surrounding community or environment; there are various other forms as follows: (1) creating job opportunities in the local community; (2) establishing social institutions for community empowerment, building hospitals, enhancing education facilities, establishing worship facilities, and training in agricultural cultivation techniques; and (3) providing assistance to victims of natural disasters, providing scholarships, improving the quality of public facilities and infrastructure, and providing capital assistance to micro and small enterprises.

Regarding the profit orientation of investment, social investment is also a source of long-run profit. Operational, financial, and reputational gains are unlocked through social investment. Operationally, the local community will increase its support for a company engaged in social investment, thus eliminating potential barriers to conducting business.

Reputationally, a company can maintain a good public image through social investment, thus bringing its own advantages by eliciting public sympathy. Public sympathy increases the bond between the company and the community and ultimately leads to greater public acceptance of the company's products. Finally, social investment can also reap financial benefits by raising the company's stock price, increasing productivity, or increasing corporate sales.

Types of Investment in Islam

The real sector is the spearhead of the Islamic economy. In the real sector, individuals can carry out productive activity by producing goods and services. According to Islam, the financial sector is not itself a separate or self-sufficient entity, instead serving to support the real sector. In this case, the financial sector executes an intermediary function that supports productive activity in the real sector. Consequently, every addition in the financial sector must be based on value added in the real sector. The nature of investment in Islam, therefore, is capital investment in productive activity or the production of goods and services in the real sector. Although investment exists in the financial sector, the ultimate target is productive activity in the real sector. Investment cannot merely generate or multiply income unless based on productive activity in the real sector.

Investing in Islam is subject to various rules and assumptions as follows:

1. Investment funds provided by investors are allocated as capital to produce goods and services, either directly to potential projects or via financial institutions.
2. Direct investment activity between investors and investment projects is based on a sharia-compliant (profit sharing) contract rather than a predetermined return as a fixed percentage of the funds invested because future profits or losses are uncertain or impossible to ascertain.
3. Investment activities channelled through a financial institution by financing potential projects apply profit- and loss-sharing contracts, *mudharabah* and *musyarakah* for instance. Though channelled via the financial sector, the investment funds must still be used to assist and support productive activities in the real sector, such as producing goods and services.
4. Financial institutions act as a bridge between investors and potential investment projects through a pre-agreed contract that does not violate Islamic principles. The task and role of the financial institution, therefore, is restricted to an intermediation function rather than multiplying investment funds without an underlying transaction in the real sector.
5. The profit-sharing mechanism must be applied to both sides of the contract, namely between the investor and financial institution and between the financial institution and the investment project.

Investment in Islam is facilitated by various instruments available in the financial sector, the real sector, or a securities portfolio. Investing in the financial sector is the preserve of investors with idle funds yet lacking sufficient time to invest directly in the real sector. Islamic financial sector investment involves the choice of various securities portfolios, namely the Islamic money market, sharia bonds (sukuk), sharia stocks and shares, and sharia investment funds.

(a) *Money Market*

Investment in the money market focuses on short-term securities or portfolios, typically with maturities of up to 1 year. Despite investing via the money market, the invested funds are ultimately channelled to the real sector. The risks associated with this type of investment are the lowest because of the short-term nature of the investment, yet the returns are also low. Such investments are typically used to maintain stable liquidity, capital, and income. Examples of money market instruments for investment include bank deposits, banker's acceptances, T-bills, and commercial papers.

(b) *Sharia Bonds (Sukuk)*

Conventional bonds are certificates of debt, differing slightly from sharia bonds (sukuk) as certificates of ownership interest in a current project. Each sukuk issuance is evidence of a productive project in need of development capital. It should also be emphasised that every sukuk purchased indicates that the investor supports the success of the underlying project. This is a medium- to long-term investment vehicle, and the return is in the form of profit sharing from the ownership interest of the sukuk as well as capital gain.

(c) *Sharia Stock*

A share represents part ownership of a company. By purchasing the shares of a corporation, the buyer assumes part ownership of the company. The funds invested to purchase the shares are subsequently used by the company for business expansion, for instance to increase the production of goods/services, build new facilities, and open new branches/offices, and for other expansionary activities. Therefore, the size of the company is usually directly proportional to the share price.

Ordinarily, equity investors have long-term goals. Moreover, long-term stock tends to generate higher returns. Equity investments are considered the highest risk but also generate the highest return. Returns from share ownership are realised in the form of dividend payments and capital gain. In Islam, there are two familiar markets in the world of share trading, namely the primary market and secondary market. In the primary market, shares are traded for investment purposes, with investors prepared to take a profit or loss. In the secondary market, however, income is generated from differences in fluctuations in the value of the shares traded. According to Islam, therefore, it is permissible to invest only in the primary market, with the aim of helping and supporting the real sector, and not the secondary market, which is solely profit oriented and speculative in nature.

Based on investor preference concerning the level of risk and return, shares are categorised into two types, namely growth funds and income funds. Growth funds prioritise share price appreciation by maximising income from capital gain, while income funds prioritise stocks that provide more competitive dividends rather than relying on share price appreciation.

(d) *Sharia Investment Funds*

Mutual funds or investment funds are in the form of collective investments managed by an investment manager. Investment funds are allocated to diverse portfolios, including deposits, sukuk, and shares. The management of sharia-compliant investment funds is oriented towards the real sector, allocated to increase productivity. The main advantage of investment funds is diversification while not requiring large funds and managed optimally by a professional. Investment diversification is a crucial part of risk management.

Though each type of investment, including investments in the financial sector, will ultimately be channelled to the real sector, some investors prefer to invest directly in the real sector without a financial intermediary. Foreign direct investment (FDI) and domestic direct investment (DDI) are examples of this. FDI is used to accelerate the economy. According to the World Development Indicators (WDI), FDI is the sum of equity capital, reinvestment of earnings, and other long-term capital and short-term capital as shown in the balance of payments. Based on direction, there are FDI inflows and outflows. FDI inflows are recorded as liabilities and FDI outflows as assets. FDI inflows play an important role in the economy when used optimally and on target. Moreover, foreign capital flows from advanced economies are crucial to accelerate economic growth in developing economies. In addition, higher FDI motivates domestic investment.

Securities portfolios are another form of investment, namely a collection of financial instruments, such as securities and other instruments, as investment options in the financial sector (Achsien, 2000). The choice of portfolio investment is influenced by how an individual views risk. In general, there are three ways an individual can look at risk, namely risk averse, risk neutral, and risk lover. When selecting an investment portfolio in line with Islamic teachings, sharia compliance must be considered, including the prohibition of *riba, gharar,* and *maysir*, coupled with the application of contracts that do not violate Islamic principles (*mudharabah*, *musyarakah,* and *murabahah*).

Risk averse is understood to mean a fear of risk and, thus, risk avoidance. Someone who is risk averse tends to choose an investment portfolio with a certain rate of profit, for instance a *murabahah* sales contract with a fixed sales margin that is higher than the purchase price (capital). Contrasting risk averse is the risk lover. As individuals, risk lovers tend to take investments with uncertainty in the contract, *mudharabah* and *musyarakah* for example. In such contracts, the profit-sharing ratio is predetermined, but the profitability of the business remains unknown. Furthermore, it is also impossible to ascertain whether a profit will be generated or a loss incurred. The choice of such an investment portfolio, therefore, requires mental fortitude and courage in the face of profit or loss.

11.3 Monetary Policy Transmission

The monetary policy transmission mechanism has become an interesting and important focus in the discussion of monetary economics. Monetary policy transmission encompasses the entire monetary policy process in terms of influencing all economic and financial activities towards ultimately achieving the stated objectives of price stability and economic growth. This is fairly complex because the process involves interactions between various parties, namely the central bank, financial sector, economic players, and other (national and international) authorities. In addition, the process must accommodate integration with other government policies, such as fiscal policy. Furthermore, global financial integration is gaining momentum due to various financial innovations that have intensified the complexity of the contemporary financial sector. It is necessary, therefore, to develop a more effective mechanism of monetary policy transmission.

The monetary transmission mechanism tends to change in line with economic and financial behavioural patterns. In fact, the transmission mechanism is relatively difficult to predict and is replete with uncertainty according to changes in the behaviour of economic actors, such as households, the government, central bank, and private entities in the financial and banking sectors. In addition, the development and growth of Islamic economies in various countries has triggered the emergence of studies on Islamic monetary policy and the transmission of Islamic monetary policy in particular. Consequently, there are now two major classifications of monetary policy transmission, namely conventional and Islamic monetary policy transmission.

11.3.1 Conventional Monetary Policy Transmission

In conventional monetary economics, monetary policy transmission affects the economy through two channels based on the dominant roles of money and credit, namely the money view and credit view.

Money View

According to the money view, monetary policy influences the economy, in this case consumption and investment, through long-term interest rates, exchange rates, and asset prices. Several theories underlie the money view of monetary policy transmission, including the neoclassical theory of investment, IS-LM analysis, the permanent income theory of consumption, and the life-cycle hypothesis (LCH). An important assumption from this perspective is financial market efficiency, namely that monetary policy does not have a distributive effect on price setting behaviour or various segments of the real sector. In addition, the financial system is considered efficient. The money view works through several channels, including the interest rate channel, asset price channel, and exchange rate channel.

1. *Interest Rate Channel*

   The interest rate channel influences investment and consumption, yet through different transmission mechanisms. *First*, monetary policy affects investment through the interest rate channel as it transmits the cost of capital to investment. This is based on neoclassical theory, stating that the cost of capital is the main factor influencing the demand for investment. In addition, several other factors must be considered in this analysis, namely long-term interest rates that have a stronger influence on investment, and the effectiveness of this transmission mechanism, which is influenced by the term structure of interest rates that links long- and short-term interest rates. *Second*, transmission through the substitution effect on consumption. In other words, interest rates influence consumption through the intertemporal substitution effect. Interest rates also affect public propensity to consume.

2. *Asset Price Channel*

   This transmission mechanism allows monetary policy to influence the economy through investment and consumption. Transmission is caused by investors not only investing their capital in bank deposits or the money market, but also placing funds in bonds and stocks. Thus, changes in market rates affect the prices of bonds and stocks. *First*, monetary policy influences investment by analysing the ratio between a firm's market value and the replacement cost of capital. Corporate demand for investment will increase if the market value is high and the replacement cost is low, and vice versa. *Second*, the effect of monetary policy on consumption, if analysed using the asset price channel, is through the wealth effect on consumption. Higher asset prices trigger consumption as wealth increases.

3. *Exchange Rate Channel*

   The transmission mechanism via the exchange rate channel influences inflation and international trade. Transmission of the exchange rate to inflation can be explained as follows. The exchange rate has a direct impact on inflation because fluctuations in the exchange rate affect public inflation expectations and corporate price formation. Meanwhile, transmission of the exchange rate to international trade occurs because interest rates cause currency depreciation, and exchange rate depreciation increases exports and decreases imports.

Credit View

The main assumption underlying the credit view is the existence of asymmetric information and moral hazard in various financial transactions, leading to an imperfect financial market. The transmission channels used in the credit view, namely the bank lending and capital channel, balance sheet channel, and risk-taking channel, can be explained as follows:

1. *Bank Lending and Capital Channel*

   This channel works through the supply of bank credit in the face of asymmetric information concerning the financial condition of borrowers and the requirements for submitting a bank loan. In this case, prospective borrowers could retain personal information that is not disclosed to the bank. Banks need to be selective, therefore, in terms of the loan applications submitted by prospective borrowers, specifically in terms of business feasibility. In addition, regular monitoring of the loan is required to avoid the risk of bad credit (loss). That is what affects the sustainability of the monetary policy transmission mechanism through credit supply from the banking industry.

2. *Balance Sheet Channel*

   This channel focuses on analysing the relationship between lenders and borrowers, which is vulnerable to moral hazard. For example, a borrower may be unable to meet repayment obligations. This may occur given the high cost and complex nature of verifying the borrower's business feasibility. The balance sheet channel offers two solutions to prevent or overcome the moral hazard issue, namely collateral provided to the bank in the form of valuable assets as well as external financing premiums.

3. *Risk-Taking Channel*

   This channel focuses on looking at the effect of monetary policy on risk management and financial product innovation. Risk in the financial system can increase as a corollary of several factors, including financial product innovation, risk tolerance, strong global financial integration, ease of funding, and the valuation methods used for capital and accounting. As such, higher risk in the financial sector is inextricably linked to monetary policy. Monetary stability can foster financial product innovation, financial vulnerabilities, and risk-taking behaviour. The risk-taking channel in the financial system works through the influence of interest rates on income and cash flows from investment, as well as the link between interest rates and the target rate of return on capital, which is often used to evaluate financial investments.

11.3.2 Islamic Monetary Policy Transmission

In addition to conventional monetary policy transmission, which has already enjoyed broad implementation worldwide, studies concerning the transmission mechanisms of Islamic monetary policy are flourishing to complement Islamic economic theories, especially Islamic monetary economics. Understanding Islamic monetary economics and the policies therein requires specific attention concerning the types of economic activities that are aligned and do not contravene Islamic moral values and sharia law. Compliance to Islamic values and principles will facilitate a righteous path towards achieving the main goals of the Islamic economy, namely justice and the equitable distribution of wealth and resources. Considering the main goals of the Islamic economy, the focus of Islamic monetary policy must also align to facilitate the equitable distribution of resources, including money. Towards that goal, the main economic activity is creating (productive) goods and services in the real sector, with the financial sector merely serving to support that main activity, including savings and investment as activities with tangible links to the real sector.

In terms of Islamic monetary policy, an equitable price formation process is imperative. Price stability must be maintained to avoid disrupting the allocation of economic resources and restricting the access of market players. Price must only fluctuate in response to changes in the demand and supply of goods and services. In general, excessively high prices will limit public access to economic resources, thus reducing public purchasing power. From a religious perspective, limiting public access to resources will disrupt the process of worship, thus contradicting the idea that economic resources should be used as an instrument of worship to Allah SWT. Monetary policy, therefore, must safeguard the uninterrupted interaction between demand and supply of goods/services, with the prices created accessible to the public. If the prices formed become so high as to disrupt public purchasing power, policies must be formulated to create accessible prices. In this context, such conditions could occur due to low supply caused by inadequate capital at the producer level. Thus, monetary policy is tasked with distributing the accumulated funds to the production of goods and services, thus eliminating the supply-side barriers.

In broad terms, monetary policy serves as a facilitator to link the financial sector and the productive (real) sector. In this case, Islamic monetary policy in financial activity is investment. From an Islamic perspective, investment is associated with the real sector.

A salient issue in terms of Islamic monetary policy is the use of commodity money, particularly precious metals. Admittedly, however, the use of precious metals is extremely difficult. Consequently, the Islamic monetary system continues to adopt the conventional use of fiat money. Notwithstanding, existing Islamic monetary instruments must be implemented optimally to ensure the objectives of Islamic monetary policy remain on target.

Expansive Islamic monetary policy must be maintained at an optimal level to achieve quality welfare for all. The money supply, therefore, is the key variable and focus of Islamic monetary policy rather than the interest rate. The money supply is a passive instrument, however, so regulation is required by the competent authority. The money supply must be maintained at a level commensurate with real sector demand. As the highest monetary authority, the central bank is responsible for expanding the money supply through appropriate monetary policymaking to support corporate financing, with the potential to increase output growth in the medium and long term, providing price stability is maintained.

It should be acknowledged that, thus far, Islamic monetary policy transmission has not been formulated comprehensively, ideally or rigorously. Chapra (1996), however, proposed several assumptions to establish an ideal set of Islamic monetary policies as follows:

1. Availability of diverse investment options at different levels of risk in the short and long term.
2. Abolition of the interest rate system, which contains elements of *riba* according to the Islamic perspective. Investors can invest funds based on a profit- and loss-sharing mechanism and must be prepared to accept a profit or loss. An investor with a low risk appetite can instead choose to hold the money to avoid the risk of loss. It is important to remember, however, that investments entail an opportunity to generate a profit and a risk of incurring a loss. If a potential investor instead opts to hold money, there is no risk of loss or opportunity for profit.
3. Investor propensity to invest in profitable instruments. Investors prefer profitable instruments to maintain their level of wealth despite paying *zakat* or inflation decreasing the value.
4. The rate of return on investment is not predetermined like interest rates. Only the profit-sharing ratio (*nisbah*) is determined at the start of the agreement and subsequently fixed for the duration of the contract.

Although the interest rate channel is not recognised as a transmission mechanism of Islamic monetary policy due to the inherent elements of *riba*, application of the asset price channel and credit channel is still possible. In addition, Islamic monetary policy can be transmitted through the profit- and loss-sharing channel. The transmission channels are described as follows:

Asset Price Channel
This channel works through two mechanisms, namely the impact of exchange rates and equity prices. *First*, asset prices react to exchange rates. Increasing world trade and international market integration have precipitated shifts in monetary policy influenced by exchange rate fluctuations. When an expansive monetary policy stance is pursued, domestic assets for investment become less attractive, leading to a capital outflow. Consequently, the domestic exchange rate depreciates, thereby making foreign products more expensive. As a result, exports increase along with real sector growth.

Second, the asset price channel also works through its effect on equity prices. When there is excess money in the monetary system, the demand for money adjusts to the new level. One way is through the stock market. The demand for shares will increase, thus edging up stock prices. The stock price reflects the value of a company, which will also increase. As the value of a company increases, it will pique the interest of financial intermediaries for mutually beneficial cooperation to expand the company's activities, leading to real sector growth.

Credit Channel (Credit View)
This channel includes the bank lending channel and the corporate balance sheet channel. The effectiveness of outstanding loans disbursed by commercial banks is influenced by symmetric information and the perfect substitutability of financial assets in the market. There are two important assumptions to ensure an effective credit channel through bank lending. *First*, monetary policy must have a significant impact on the credit supply from commercial banks and corporate dependence on commercial bank financing. Second, monetary policy transmission mechanism works effectively.

During a crisis period, Islamic banks outperform conventional banks due to higher capitalisation and liquidity reserves. Therefore, monetary policy transmission through the Islamic banking industry poses a viable alternative. The profit- and loss-sharing mechanism applied in Islamic banking ensures more effective transmission of Islamic monetary policy through the credit channel (Uddin, 2019).

Profit- and Loss-Sharing Channel
Conceptually, this channel works in the same way as the interest rate channel in conventional economics. The interest rate channel, which targets output, works through the following transmission mechanism. An increase in the reference rate for Bank Indonesia Certificates (SBI) will raise conventional interbank rates as well as lending and deposit rates. Higher interbank and lending rates restrict borrowing. Output, therefore, will decline because the higher SBI rate is not channelled to the real sector, instead remaining in the financial sector (Ascarya, 2012). Meanwhile, the

transmission mechanism for final inflation can be explained as follows. An increase in the SBI reference rate will raise lending rates and, thus, lower the demand for credit.

On the other hand, Islamic monetary policy transmission using Sharia Bank Indonesia Certificates (SBIS) relies on the return rather than the interest rate. In addition, Islamic economics does not recognise an interest rate mechanism for Islamic monetary policy, instead preferring a profit- and loss-sharing mechanism. Monetary policy transmission that targets output can be explained as follows. A higher SBIS return will increase returns in the sharia interbank money market (PUAS), and the profit- and loss-sharing (PLS) return will increase Islamic finance and output. Islamic finance is directly linked to the real sector; therefore, an increase in financing will increase output. Monetary policy transmission that targets inflation is not sustainable because the Islamic economy is not based on interest rates, rather focusing on the real sector, which is not inflationary (Ascarya, 2012).

11.4 Islamic Monetary Policy: Urgency and Goals

Policy is defined as the rules and actions taken by leaders striving to achieve predetermined goals. Similarly, in the context of economic activity, policies that regulate and coordinate economic activities are required. Various economic policies appear in the literature, oriented towards controlling the demand and supply sides. Examples of demand-side management policies are fiscal policy and monetary policy, while supply-side management policies are sectoral and structural economic policies.

Monetary policy controls the money supply using specific monetary instruments through monetary transmission to achieve the overarching goal of price stability. The central bank is the highest level of monetary policymaker, tasked with regulating the monetary sector by maintaining economic stability through the stability of currency in circulation. The main instruments used by the central bank are typically based on liquidity (such as the money supply and credit) and interest rates.

Implementation of a dual financial system requires an adjustment or further development of the rules relating to finance and the monetary sector, not only based on conventional economic practices but also in terms of Islamic finance and monetary policy. In Indonesia, for example, Bank Indonesia as the central bank has been mandated with formulating monetary policy to maintain price stability using conventional and Islamic principles. The concept of formulating rules relating to finance and the monetary sector, therefore, must be developed in the form of Islamic monetary policy.

The primary focus of Islamic monetary policy is maintaining the flow of economic resources in accordance with sharia law, obviating the need for interest rates, to dissuade potential investors from holding their money in the financial markets. Financial market deepening has increased the amount of money in financial markets, thus widening the gap between the monetary and real sectors. It can be said, therefore, that instruments alternative to interest rates are required to resolve existing economic issues.

Islamic monetary policy compels the regulator to reduce the gap in money stock between the real sector and monetary sector by eliminating transactions and products in the financial markets without underlying transactions in the real sector. Expanding productive businesses in the real sector can increase the velocity of money. Monetary regulation, therefore, should not only focus on the money supply, or interest rates, but on the circulation of resources (money) in the economy.

Fundamentally, Islamic monetary policy implementation must align with the overarching goal of the Islamic economic system, namely equitable welfare in this world and the afterlife (*falah*). The semi-objective of Islamic monetary policy is maximising human welfare. Meanwhile, Chapra (2000) explained that the primary target of monetary policy in the Islamic economy consists of three parts as follows:

1. *Full employment and economic growth*
   Full employment implies the full use of economic resources, including natural resources, human capital, and money. Money must remain in use and not left idle. Monetary policy, therefore, must provide instruments for economic actors to channel their money to the real sector. In this way, full employment and optimal economic growth can be achieved.
2. *Socio-economic justice and the equitable distribution of income and wealth*
   Socio-economic justice and equitable wealth-income distribution means providing opportunities for all socio-economic groups to engage and benefit from the economy, especially to fulfil individual and collective needs.
3. *Stability in the value of money*
   Stability in the value of money must be maintained domestically and internationally. Domestically, a stable value of money is reflected in the prices of goods and services that tend not to fluctuate, or low inflation. Internationally, stability in the value of money is reflected in the exchange rate.

Monetary policy implementation is expected to create conditions conducive to the smooth and orderly distribution of money, thus encouraging productive economic activity. Public access to economic activity will increase, therefore, ensuring the target of monetary policy is the same as the target of the Islamic economy, namely quality welfare in this world and the afterlife (*falah*).

Achieving those targets will ultimately meet the needs of the people, both physically and intellectually. Through economic adequacy, individuals can devote more resources and maximise worship as the main priority of life in this world as revealed by Allah SWT in surah Adz-Dzariyaat, verse 56 as follows:

وَمَا خَلَقْتُ الْجِنَّ وَالْإِنْسَ إِلَّا لِيَعْبُدُوْنِ

And I did not create the jinn and mankind except to worship Me. (QS Adh Dhariyat [51]: 56)

It can be concluded, therefore, that there are three main targets of Islamic monetary policy, namely full employment, social justice, and stability in the value of money.

This differs from conventional monetary policy, which is only oriented towards stability in the value of money using logical concepts and financial mechanisms based on prevailing principles. Though able to overcome the issues of full employment, optimising economic growth and stability in the value of money, conventional monetary policy has failed to address inequality and social economic imbalances, as reflected by equitable wealth-income distribution. It is necessary, therefore, to develop Islamic monetary policy (Uddin, 2019).

11.5 Islamic Monetary Policy Strategy and Instruments

Conventional monetary policy generally uses the amount of liquidity in the money market as a regulatory instrument in accordance with the money supply target. In practice, monetary policy effectiveness depends on the relationship between the money supply and macroeconomic variables, including inflation and output. Notwithstanding, the relationships between total money supply, inflation, and output work in opposing directions. Expansive monetary policy (increasing the money supply) stimulates production, which has a positive impact on output growth. On the other hand, however, an unregulated increase in the money supply will create inflationary pressures. There is a trade-off, therefore, between the disparate goals of controlling inflation and increasing national output. Instability in the relationship between the money supply and macroeconomic variables also encourages the use of interest rate-based monetary instruments. Nonetheless, such instruments do not necessarily enhance monetary policy effectiveness due to other core issues, such as the depth of the financial markets and the behaviour/perception of investors in the money market. The monetary authority, therefore, must determine the most appropriate strategy to formulate targeted, effective, and efficient monetary policy.

When selecting the most appropriate policy strategy for implementation, the monetary authority typically has several options (preferences): (1) the final target of monetary policy, either stabilising output or stabilising prices (inflation); (2) the policy instruments used to achieve the final target, either monetary aggregates or interest rates; and (3) the policy response. In general, monetary policy has the same overarching goal as other policies, namely to achieve and improve equitable and quality public welfare (Warjiyo & Juhro, 2019). As an integral part of macroeconomic policy, monetary policy can have multiple targets, for instance economic stability, price stability (inflation), job creation, and the balance of payments. Nevertheless, the focus of monetary policy as instituted by a central bank tends to prioritise the dual targets of economic growth and inflation. The history of monetary policy shows different targets in each period. During the 1950s and 1960s, central banks focused on price stability (inflation), before moving on to output stability and growth in the 1970s and 1980s. Since the 1990s, however, debates have raged between academics and central bankers, with academics more inclined to orient strategy towards inflation stability and real output, whereas central bankers prefer price stability as the overarching goal of monetary policy.

In theory, the impact of each monetary policy target can be analysed from the perspective of policy application in the near term and long term. In this context, long term implies the neutrality of money, namely when the economy is no longer affected by demand or supply-side shocks in the money supply. In the long term, monetary policy tends only to influence inflation, with a minimal impact on economic growth. In the near term, however, shocks triggered by monetary policy will cause fluctuations in real sector activity. It can be said, therefore, that monetary policy has a greater impact on economic growth in the near term, with the effect fading in the long term. Consequently, determining the strategic priorities of monetary policy, whether oriented towards price stability or output, is based on the horizon applied. Output stability is better targeted in the short term, while price stability is more appropriate in the long term. Recognising the inherent dilemma when determining monetary policy targets, the central bank must choose which policy targets to pursue. Currently, however, central banks tend to focus on a single target, namely to create and maintain inflation within a reasonable predetermined range or tolerance band.

Islamic monetary policy is viewed in the context of a dual financial system. How, therefore, does the monetary authority determine the direction, strategy, and instruments of monetary policy? In addition, there are contradictory fundamental principles between conventional and Islamic finance, which can be explained as follows. Conventional finance embraces the interest rate system and speculation, allowing the financial market to form its own sector, separate and parallel to the real sector. Conversely, interest rates and speculation are absolutely forbidden in Islamic finance. Islam considers financial activity a part of investment that is tied to the real sector. With different fundamental principles, the perspective for dealing with the main monetary issues (price stability or stability in the value of money) is also different.

From an Islamic perspective, the speculative motive for holding money is not recognised because it is considered haram, or unlawful. In addition, the absence of interest rates, as the basis for analysing speculative action, makes it possible to suppress and eliminate speculative actions. Without interest rates, the key variable of monetary policy is the money supply. The total money supply must be regulated to meet real sector needs to achieve economic growth. The total stock of money must be appropriate to manage economic capacity to supply goods and services optimally in accordance with the needs of the community. A monetary authority operating within an Islamic monetary framework will regulate the monetary supply for optimal and maximal use to turn the economic wheels of the real sector.

When prices increase due to lower supply than aggregate demand, the monetary authority is tasked with formulating policies to increase the productivity of goods and services, thereby raising aggregate supply. Consequently, Islamic monetary policy tends to be expansionary. Meanwhile, contractionary monetary policy, in principle, contradicts sharia law. Contractionary policies withhold resources, namely money, similar to *ihtikar* (hoarding).

Juhro et al. (2018) stated that the central bank, particularly in Indonesia, as the monetary authority responsible for implementing monetary policy in a dual financial system, can take the following strategic measures:

1. Determining Islamic monetary policy instruments within a dual financial system framework and under one monetary authority. The instruments must direct the signals of conventional and Islamic monetary policies in one unified direction, while remaining within a corridor that does not conflict with Islamic principles.
2. Formulating innovative monetary policies, not only focusing on the money supply, but also focusing on real sector activities. Achieving financial stability, therefore, will be consistent with output stability in the real sector.
3. Redoubling efforts to discover a series of policies and instruments suitable for conditions in a dual financial system, for example by adding scientific knowledge through discussions with relevant experts and practitioners.
4. Developing supporting infrastructure for Islamic monetary policy implementation with instruments that are in accordance with sharia principles.
5. Taking an approach to formulating laws and regulations that supports Islamic monetary policy sustainability.
6. Increasing the scale of Islamic finance and sharia banking to ensure the effectiveness of Islamic monetary policy.

Islamic Monetary Policy Instruments

In an Islamic economic system, in addition to the policy objectives, the formulation and determination of monetary instruments must also consider strategies that are in accordance with Islamic principles and rules, which can be explained as follows (Uddin and Halim, 2015):

(a) Interest-bearing assets are forbidden in the economy.
(b) Long-term financing opportunities are the same as short-term opportunities.
(c) There is no hoarding of assets.
(d) The rate of profit is distributed based on the profit-sharing ratio.

Islamic monetary instruments, therefore, specialise in the following functions: (1) maintaining balance between the real sector and the financial sector in the economy, (2) preventing the excessive accumulation of money in the financial sector, (3) preventing the multiplication of money without underlying productive activities in the real sector, (4) increasing economic resilience during crisis periods, (5) channelling excess funds in the economy, and (6) optimising the allocation of economic resources.

As stated previously, the goal of Islamic monetary policy is to create and maintain monetary stability by regulating the money supply. The goal is similar to conventional economic concepts, yet the instruments used differ. Fundamentally, Islamic monetary theory absolutely prohibits the use of interest rates as an instrument. According to Karim (2006), Islamic monetary instruments can be distinguished based on three schools (*Mazhab*) as follows:

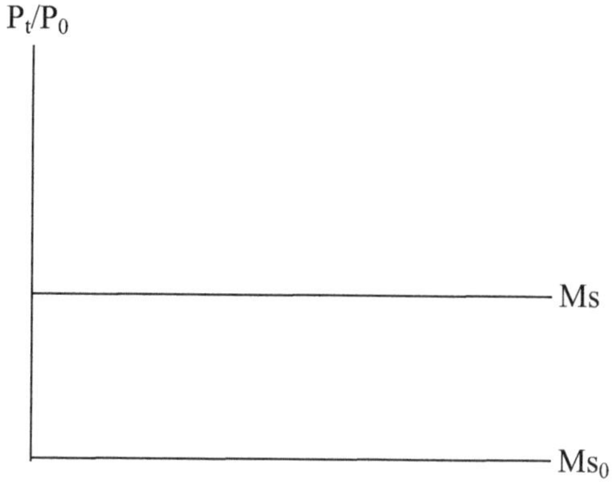

Fig. 11.3 Supply elasticity curve of Mazhab Iqtishaduna. Source: Created by author

1. *First Mazhab (Iqtishaduna)*

   In the early days of Islam, minimal banking practices or use of money rendered monetary policies unnecessary. Total money supply was perfectly elastic and the government, as the highest monetary authority, was unable to intervene in the money supply (Hasani & Mirakhor, 2003). Such conditions reflect the time of Rasulullah SAW, when dinar and dirham were circulated as currency (Fig. 11.3).

The curve also demonstrates how the velocity of money during a given period is equal to the value of goods and services produced in the same period. In addition, money is exchanged for something that adds value to the economy.

2. *Second Mazhab (Mainstream)*

   To maximise existing resources, Chapra opined that funds could be allocated to productive economic activity through the use of "dues of idle funds" as an instrument to influence the demand for money in accordance with the allocation to increase overall economic productivity.
3. Third *Mazhab* (Alternative)

   Choudhury described monetary policy as a *syuratiq* process, namely a policy taken by the monetary authority based on previous deliberations and consensus decision-making with real sector authorities. This aims to create harmony between monetary policy and the real sector. In addition, Chaudhury also proposed endogenous money (100% reserve).

Regarding the role of the central bank, the Islamic economy places more emphasis on regulating the money supply. In addition, the central bank also regulates the distribution of financing from commercial banks to remain at the most appropriate proportion. It can be concluded, therefore, that the central bank is obligated to facilitate a safe and controlled banking system. The central bank uses monetary policy instruments to discharge its mandate. According to research undertaken by Uddin and Halim (2015), Islamic monetary policy instruments can be categorised into two types, namely conventional monetary policy instruments that are in accordance with Islamic principles and new types of instruments. As an overview, the instruments of Islamic monetary policy are described in Fig. 11.4.

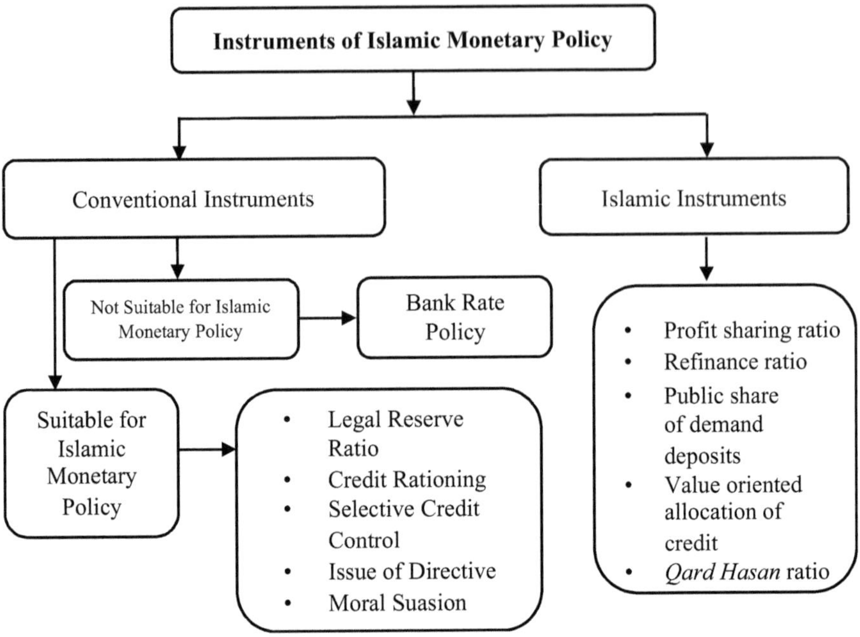

Fig. 11.4 Islamic monetary policy instruments. Source: Uddin and Halim (2015)

The absolute prohibition of interest rates in the Islamic banking system has strong implications for monetary policy that targets the Islamic economic and financial system, which is focused on the production of goods and services in the real sector. Though several Islamic monetary policy instruments are similar to conventional policy instruments, use is permitted in compliance with sharia law. Based on expert opinion and a review of the literature, the preferred monetary instruments are as follows:

1. *Money Supply Growth Targets (M_s and M_0)*

   Periodically, the central bank determines growth of the money supply (M_s) based on national economic targets. From a monetary economics perspective, one target of national economic policy is stability in the value of money. The money supply growth target must be reviewed regularly, on a quarterly basis for instance, in line with prevailing economic trends, related variables, and the income velocity of money estimated for a number of periods. This is inseparable, however, from the overarching principle of Islamic economics, namely the abolition of the interest rate system. After setting several updated targets, the money supply growth target must be reviewed regularly.

   In the monetary sector, the term high-powered money or M_0 is defined as the monetary base, namely the value of currency in circulation and commercial bank deposits held in the central bank's reserves. M_0 exists due to the central bank's power to create money, which must be used to achieve Islamic goals, namely prosperity and quality welfare for the community (*ummah*). The benchmark of quality welfare in the community is based on equitable income distribution and a narrow income gap.

M_s is obtained from the government, commercial banks, and financial institutions. M_s growth is monitored closely by the central bank to ensure allocations remain on target, including allocations to the government, central bank, and financial institutions in proportions determined by economic conditions. The M_s allocation for commercial banks is disbursed through a *mudharabah* financing mechanism and used by the central bank as the main qualitative and quantitative instrument to control credit. Similarly, the portion allocated to non-bank financial institutions is disbursed through a *mudharabah* financing mechanism and used for productive activities, such as farming, entrepreneurship, and others.

This instrument aims to foster real sector activity and prevent the hoarding of idle funds so individuals can invest their money in productive investments, which can be turned into capital for trade activity.

2. *Statutory Reserve Requirement (SRR)*

The statutory reserve requirement (SRR), or reserve ratio, is a monetary policy instrument that is also suitable for an Islamic economic system. The SRR system requires commercial banks to maintain a certain level of mandatory reserves placed at the central bank.

The statutory reserve requirement helps to provide a deposit guarantee and adequate liquidity for commercial banks. In addition, the SRR can be used to control the total money supply. Based on the following simulation, if commercial banks are required to maintain balances in their statutory reserve accounts (SRA) equivalent to 5% of deposits, yet the central bank feels it necessary to reduce the money supply, the central bank can institute policies to raise the reserve ratio to 20%, for example, to manage the build-up of liquidity.

The funds received by the central bank through statutory reserve requirements can be utilised for several purposes. First, as a last reserve for individuals with deposits in the banking industry. Islamic banking applies the principle of profit sharing, making future profits difficult to predict. Under such fragile conditions, Islamic banks require a backup or reserve for certain exigencies. In this context, the central bank functions as a last resource with the reserves that have been collected from Islamic commercial banks. In addition, the funds can be used during a financial crisis, which both the central bank and commercial banks can be susceptible to. Meanwhile, statutory reserves are also used to determine the distribution of financing by banks.

The statutory reserve requirement is a direct instrument that is considered appropriate for application in a dual banking system. Though several central banks in the conventional economic system have abolished the use of statutory reserves, such as the Bank of Canada, the instrument remains relevant and effective in terms of managing liquidity in the banking system. In addition to measuring the liquidity to be absorbed, reserve ratios can be used to overcome long-term liquidity imbalances.

According to Chapra (2000), the reserve ratio is a fundamental instrument of monetary policy that is also suitable for application in an Islamic economic system.[1] Notwithstanding, the conventional application of statutory reserve requirements focuses on the transaction account, whereas in Islamic banking, *wadiah* (safekeeping) contracts for demand deposit accounts are used. Term deposits in the form of an investment account, which apply *mudharabah* contracts in Islamic banking, are not subject to the statutory reserve requirement. The SSR is an important instrument and must remain in the Islamic economy to regulate liquidity.

Though the debate on applying statutory reserve requirements in Islam continues, Ariff argues that it is more important to apply statutory reserves to *mudharabah* contracts rather than *wadiah* demand deposits because, in practice, banks maintain most demand deposits in the form of liquid assets. Such conditions reflect the prudent behaviour of banks concerning the possible withdrawal of deposits by members of the public.

3. *Public Share of Demand Deposits*

The public share of demand deposits is a monetary policy instrument to mobilise funds collected as demand deposits in commercial banks.

The main advantage of this instrument lies in its social application by diverting a portion of demand deposits to the state treasury to finance productive, beneficial, and high-value social projects without burdening the community. For instance, the government must bear a proportion of the total cost of mobilising the demand deposits, providing all deposit services to the depositors and financing deposit insurance schemes.

Such funds are specified as a certain proportion of commercial bank deposits (up to 25%) and intended for the government as another revenue stream besides taxes that can be used to finance social welfare projects. Therefore, the overarching goals of optimising output or gross domestic product (GDP) and stability in the value of money can be achieved. In general, the regulation of this fund will be left by the government to the central bank to expand the monetary base from the M_0 side.

A ratio of 25% is considered the maximum during normal conditions yet can be adjusted to country-specific conditions, such as during an economic downturn. During a recession, banks tend to maintain loose liquidity conditions and larger deposits from the government as a buffer, with government deposits dominant.

The rationale behind this instrument is that commercial banks contribute as agents within an institutional framework to regulate the flow of idle resources in the community. *Second*, commercial banks do not bear the return on demand deposits. *Third*, the community does not need to bear the additional burden of demand deposit risk if deposit guarantee schemes are in place.

[1] Choudhury (2001) stated that the concept of an Islamic economy applies a 100% reserve requirement monetary system to maintain the money supply in line with demand towards price stability (zero inflation). That argument is in line with the opinion presented by Chapra (1985).

4. *Credit Ceiling*

   Limits on disbursed financing can be in the form of direct credit controls, credit ceilings, or credit directing. The main structure of such instruments is designed to restrict credit and ensure the central bank maintains control over the growth of financing disbursed by Islamic banks. The policy of setting credit limits available to commercial banks provides assurance that credit creation is in accordance with monetary targets, while simultaneously creating and maintaining healthy competition between commercial banks. Direct credit controls are known by several terms, including credit ceilings, financing limits, or open market operations (OMO).

   Open market operations (OMO) are used for more specific purposes, namely to influence bank liquidity by buying and selling securities on a profit-sharing basis. Securities are at the core of OMO implementation.

   Chapra (2000) advocates the use of credit controls, arguing that the relationship between bank reserve ratios and credit creation is not precise, so credit controls can be used as the monetary policy target. Meanwhile, credit directing aims to maximise credit allocation and achieve optimal production and distribution of goods and services.

   Instruments that control lending aim to create financing targets that are adjusted to the monetary policy target. Such instruments can also direct financing to burgeoning economic sectors. On the other hand, controls on the disbursement of bank financing can also limit banks from extending high-risk financing.

   Instruments that control the allocation of financing also aim to focus the disbursement objectives on the target of funds from the unemployed for transformation to business projects with socio-economic benefits, such as micro and small enterprises (MSEs). Fund allocations, therefore, can support production and distribution activities, including the goods and services needed in the community, to support the structure of the national economy.

5. *Value-Based Credit Allocation*

   Value-based credit allocation is credit realisation for the betterment of public welfare. Credit allocation can optimise the production and distribution of goods and services needed by most of the community. Proceeds derived from credit disbursements are also intended for the benefit of the community. It is necessary, therefore, to have credit guarantees agreed by the government and commercial banks to reduce the risks and costs borne by the banks.

6. *Sukuk*

   Sukuk are sharia-compliant bonds that also serve as a safety net against inflation. The government will issue sukuk to attract currency flows to the central bank and reduce the money supply. Sukuk, therefore, have the ability to increase or decrease the money supply.

   Sukuk issuances are an investment vehicle in the real sector. Sukuk can also absorb currency in circulation for distribution in national economic development projects. Furthermore, sukuk can also overcome the condition of full employment in the private sector when public finance fails, implying the government must step up to address the market failure.

Treasury bills, which imply the sale or purchase of central bank certificates, are a short-dated, interest-bearing instrument that can be issued by the government through financial institutions or the Ministry of Finance and sold by the central bank to brokers. Clearly, treasury bills are not appropriate or acceptable in an Islamic economic system. Instead, the government can issue interest-free instruments known as Government Instrument Certificates (GIC) as an alternative to treasury bills. When a central bank wishes to reduce the money supply, the certificates can be sold to commercial banks. Conversely, the central bank can purchase the certificates to increase the money supply.

The monetary instruments mentioned above are the most common instruments featured in the Islamic monetary literature and are also in accordance with sharia principles. Several Muslim countries and other countries implementing a dual monetary system apply monetary controls using securities with underlying transactions based on the principles of *wadiah, musyarakah, mudharabah, ar-rahn,* and *al-ijarah.*

In addition, several other monetary instruments are available for use in the Islamic banking industry as follows (M. N. Siddiqi in Banking Without Interest (Leicester, UK: The Islamic Foundation, 1983), pp. 110–25, M. Ariff, op. cit., pp. 36–7, and M. Akram Khan, ibid., pp. 251–4):

(a) *Common Pool*

A common pool is a monetary instrument that requires commercial banks to allocate a certain percentage of funds based on common agreement as a tactical fund to overcome liquidity issues. The pool is used by the central bank to control bank credit on the quantitative side. The instrument is very similar to the discount facility, which can be used by the central bank to help commercial banks overcome liquidity imbalances. The central bank requires commercial banks to contribute to the common pool as a certain percentage of their deposits through a cooperative arrangement between the two parties to overcome a liquidity mismatch.

(b) *Government Deposit*

A government deposit is also a quantitative control. Government deposits are deposits from members of the public used by the government to fund projects. The concept is similar to public deposits, yet the intermediaries through which government deposits pass are the public, commercial banks, the central bank, and the government, whereas public deposits are channelled directly to the government.

The government confers authority to the central bank to channel demand deposits from the government to commercial banks, thus directly influencing their reserves. In Saudi Arabia, this instrument has proven very successful in terms of monetary policy, with a similar function and effect as open market operations (OMO). In other countries, this instrument could indirectly affect the reserves of commercial banks.

(c) *Lending Ratio*

In this context, the lending ratio is a term from *qardhul hasan* (benevolent loan). In Islamic economics, lending is not a recognised term. *Qard hasan*, therefore, is not commercially oriented but a charitable loan without interest or profit sharing. The role of *qard hasan* is to help the underprivileged with financial difficulties meet urgent needs or start a small business.

(d) *Refinance Ratio*

The refinance ratio represents the proportion of interest-free loans from the central bank. The refinance ratio refers to the extension of funding or restructuring the calculation of funding (Chapra, 1985). The value of financing is directly proportional to the level of the refinance ratio. If the refinance ratio increases, disbursed financing also increases, and vice versa. Commercial banks, therefore, must be prudent because excessive and uncontrolled lending carries greater risk. The refinance ratio is used by the central bank for commercial banks applying *qard hasan* contracts. The calculation is adjusted based on the needs of commercial banks to alleviate liquidity shortfalls under certain conditions.

(e) *Profit-Sharing Ratio*

The profit-sharing ratio can be applied to the purchase and sale of shares and profit-sharing certificates to replace government securities in open market operations. The central bank can use the profit-sharing ratio as a monetary instrument. To increase the money supply, the central bank can institute policies requiring commercial banks to increase the profit ratios for customers. This equity-based instrument cannot be used for open market operations due to several reasons. *First*, the central bank does not buy and sell shares with private sector companies, only state-owned enterprises. *Second*, equity-based instruments do not have the same proportions as government securities and open market operations as they can significantly affect prices unless used for non-monetary purposes due to the limited value. *Third*, variations in equity-based instruments, if applied to open market operations, would be detrimental to shareholders. This is totally avoided because the purpose of the instrument is to help reduce liquidity at financial institutions in the private sector and stock market.

7. *Moral Suasion*

Moral suasion plays a very strategic role in the application of Islamic principles through formal and informal communication as well as consultation. The central bank can discern the issues faced by commercial banks and provide clear and precise suggestions to overcome the problems.

It is the responsibility of the central bank as an adviser to commercial banks to increase the demand for credit when the economy is in a state of depression. This aims to ensure that disbursed credit, as additional funds in the community, remains in sync with the economic cycle in the real sector.

The central bank can also utilise moral suasion to motivate the banking industry or members of the public to take actions that support monetary policy targets, such as banks channelling more financing to export-oriented businesses to strengthen the exchange rate. Through moral suasion, the central bank can even persuade relevant institutions outside of commercial finance sector, including the social finance sector, to increase spending for the poor and needy (*dhuafa*). By increasing social spending on the poor, the implication is that an increase of real sector transactions will be felt evenly across different social strata.

References

Achsien, I. H. (2000). *Investasi Syariah di Pasar Modal: Menggagas Konsep dan Praktek Manajemen Portfolio Syariah*. Gramedia Pustaka Utama.

Ascarya. (2012). Alur Transmisi dan Efektifitas Kebijakan Moneter Ganda di Indonesia. *Buletin Ekonomi Moneter dan Perbankan, 14*(3), 283–315.

Chapra, M. U. (1985). *Towards a just monetary system* (Vol. 8). International Institute of Islamic Thought (IIIT).

Chapra, M. U. (1996). Monetary management in an Islamic economy. *Islamic Economic Studies, 4*(1), 1–34.

Chapra, M. U. (2000). *Towards a just monetary system.* (I. A. Basri, Trans.). Gema Insani Press.

Hasani, B., & Mirakhor, A. (2003). *Essays on Iqtisad: The Islamic approach to economic problems*. Global Scholarly Publications.

Juhro, S. M., Darsono, S. F., & Sakti, A. (2018). *Kebijakan Moneter Syariah dalam Sistem Keuangan Ganda: Teori dan Praktik*. Tazkia Publishing.

Karim, A. A. (2006). *Ekonomi Makro Islami*. PT RajaGrafindo Persada.

Mankiw, N. G. (2009). *Marcoeconomics* (7th ed.). Worth Publisher.

Sakti, A. (2007). *Analisis Teoretis Ekonomi Islam: Jawaban atas Kekacauan Ekonomi Modern*. Aqsa Publishing.

Uddin, M. A. (2019). Islamic monetary economics: Insights from the literature. *Islamic Monetary Economics and Institutions: Theory and Practice* (hal. 39–53). Springer.

Uddin, M. A., & Halim, A. (2015). Islamic monetary policy: Is there an alternative of interest rate? *MPRA Paper*.

Warjiyo, P., & Juhro, S. M. (2019). *Central Bank Policy: Theory and Practice*. Emerald Publishing Ltd.

Chapter 12
Islamic Monetary Policy Practices

12.1 Introduction

As discussed in previous chapters, the orientation of Islamic monetary policy implementation is focused more on developing economic activity in the real sector rather than the financial sector. The financial sector is considered a catalyst of real sector activity. Through the application of Islamic monetary policy, transactions in the financial sector must be linked directly and based on underlying transactions in the real sector, such as investment and trade. Islamic monetary policy does not recognise the money multiplier as in conventional monetary policy practices. Optimal implementation of Islamic monetary policy is expected to confer various benefits as follows: (1) maintaining harmony and compatibility between the real sector and financial sector, (2) improving the seamless flow and distribution of money resources to avoid the hoarding of money, (3) avoiding the money multiplier effect without commensurate real growth in the real sector, (4) increasing the resistance and resilience of the economic and financial system against potential crises, (5) providing another channel for surplus funds in the economic sector, and (6) maximising the distribution of resources in the economy.

From a microeconomic perspective, the application of Islamic monetary policy will also change the governance and orientation of business actors in the financial sector, financial institutions in particular as the active players. Hamid and Nordin detailed five foundational aspects of governance and orientation in financial institutions under the umbrella of Islamic monetary policy, explained as follows:

First, Allah SWT is the absolute owner of all wealth and property on earth and financial institutions are merely human representatives in this world tasked with managing assets in accordance with Islamic teachings. As representatives, financial institutions must maintain the trust bestowed upon them. This is in accordance with Quranic verse 165 of surah Al-An'am as follows:

S. M. Juhro et al., *Inclusive Welfare*, https://doi.org/10.1007/978-981-96-0051-9_12

وَهُوَ الَّذِيْ جَعَلَكُمْ خَلٰۤىِٕفَ الْاَرْضِ وَرَفَعَ بَعْضَكُمْ فَوْقَ بَعْضٍ دَرَجٰتٍ لِّيَبْلُوَكُمْ فِيْ مَآ اٰتٰىكُمْۗ اِنَّ رَبَّكَ سَرِيْعُ الْعِقَابِۖ وَاِنَّهٗ لَغَفُوْرٌ رَّحِيْمٌ ۝

> And it is He who has made you successors upon the earth and has raised some of you above others in degrees [of rank] that He may try you through what He has given you. Indeed, your Lord is swift in penalty; but indeed, He is Forgiving and Merciful. (Q.S. Al-An'am [6]: 165)

Those guidelines must be adhered to by every actor in a financial institution, namely that the assets under management are not the property of the financial institution, merely a deposit for safekeeping from which the individual would not be justified to derive a profit. The implication is that the financial system operates in accordance with Islamic guidelines as the actors and players therein apply Islamic teachings as guidelines.

Second, the primary focus of financial institutions is real sector growth, rather than simply prioritising financial sector gains. This is in stark contrast to what actually occurs in the contemporary conventional system, where financial institutions prioritise financial sector growth rather than real growth in the real sector. Islamic monetary policy exists to overcome the problems associated with modern financial practices. Through Islamic monetary policy, financial institutions are encouraged to serve as a catalyst for the real sector, rather than multiplying money in the financial sector. Therefore, an economic environment is created in accordance with the values of socio-economic justice.

Third, Islamic monetary policy compels the business actors in financial institutions to increase contracts based on profit sharing, such as *mudharabah* or *musyaraka*, instead of debt-based contracts or receivables. As Islam does not condone profiting from debt, financial institutions cannot maximise profit through the application of debt-based contracts. Furthermore, Islam strongly discourages its adherents from incurring debt or owing money, as revealed in the Hadith of Rasulullah SAW as follows:

عَنْ عَائِشَةَ قَالَتْ: كَانَ رَسُولُ اللهِ صَلَّى اللهُ عَلَيْهِ وَسَلَّمَ يَدْعُو فِي الصَّلَاةِ يَقُولُ: «اللَّهُمَّ إِنِّي أَعُوذُ بِكَ مِنْ عَذَابِ الْقَبْرِ وَأَعُوذُ بِكَ مِنْ فِتْنَةِ الْمَسِيحِ الدَّجَّالِ وَأَعُوذُ بِكَ مِنْ فِتْنَةِ الْمَحْيَا وَفِتْنَةِ الْمَمَاتِ اللَّهُمَّ إِنِّي أعوذ بك من المأثم والمغرم» فَقَالَ لَهُ قَائِل مَا أكثر مَا تستعيذ من المغرم يَا رَسُول الله فَقَالَ: «إِنَّ الرَّجُلَ إِذَا غَرِمَ حَدَّثَ فَكَذَبَ وَوَعَدَ فَأَخْلَفَ»

> 'A'isha said that God's Messenger used to make supplication during the prayer saying, "O God, I seek refuge in Thee from the punishment in the grave, I seek refuge in Thee from the trial of the antichrist, I seek refuge in Thee from the trial of life and the trial of death. O God, I seek refuge in Thee from sin and debt." Someone said to him, "How often you seek refuge from debt!" He replied, "When a man is in debt he talks and tells lies, makes promises and breaks them."[1] (Bukhari and Muslim.)

[1] Reference: Mishkat al-Masabih 939, In-book reference: Book 4, Hadith 362.

It may be concluded, therefore, that a key implication of Islamic monetary policy on the behaviour of financial institutions is to minimise debt-based activity.

Fourth, financial institutions must contribute to society and facilitate members of the community in terms of operating businesses that underpin real sector growth. The role of financial institutions, therefore, is to provide public access to funds, with the expectation of increasing productive businesses in the real sector. This is consistent with Islamic teachings, namely that 9 out of 10 doors of fortune, or opportunities, come from business activity.

Fifth, beyond providing capital, the role of financial institutions is also to provide consultancy services for entrepreneurs. As financial institutions focus on the real sector, the orientation is towards enhancing productivity in the real sector.

In summary, the impact of Islamic monetary policy from a microeconomic perspective is the growth of productive businesses in the real sector in terms of quantity and quality. The micro-economy focuses on the development of individuals to establish and grow productive businesses in the real sector.

From a macroeconomic perspective, however, Islamic monetary policy seeks to reduce the amount of idle money for utilisation in the real sector. In addition to regulating the circulation of money to maximise growth in the real sector, Islamic monetary policy also regulates money management in the real sector to effectively enhance productivity.

By changing the supply of money through *mudharabah* financing as an intermediate target, monetary policy will affect macroeconomic variables. For example, monetary policy that increases the money supply will reduce the rate of return, thus increasing output. The transmission mechanism of Islamic monetary policy works through the rate of return because Islam absolutely forbids predetermined interest rates. The implementation of policy instruments based on interest rates increases the speculative motive, particularly in the derivatives market. Speculation disrupts the flow of money to the real sector and, hence, impacts macroeconomic variables, such as economic growth and inflation. Research by Herianingrum and Syapriatama demonstrated that Islamic monetary policy instruments have greater potential to foster economic growth as well as maintain low and stable inflation. The principle of profit and loss sharing can reduce production costs by eliminating the costs stemming from the application of interest rates. Furthermore, Islamic monetary policy, which prioritises the flow of funds to the real sector and increases production, also helps to maintain price stability.

12.2 Monetary Policy in a Dual Financial System

Emergence of the modern Islamic financial industry has led to the application of dual financial systems in a number of countries, simultaneously embracing conventional and Islamic systems. The birth of Islamic finance has generally been implemented in conjunction with the conventional financial industry that has existed for much longer. In fact, the conventional financial industry is often used as a benchmark for the application of Islamic finance. In general, the rules and regulations governing the Islamic financial industry are inspired by conventional finance. This is typically due to the shared pool of human resources as practitioners and regulators.

The dual financial system emerged with the development of Islamic finance, spurred by growing public demand for financial services in accordance with Islamic principles. Consequently, the Islamic financial system, as adopted in most countries, was developed based on a bottom-up mechanism, with a minority of governments in other countries taking a top-down approach. Most countries with an Islamic financial system began with Islamic banking. To this day, Islamic banking continues to dominate the overall Islamic financial industry. Indonesia, Malaysia, Saudi Arabia, Bahrain, Pakistan, the United Arab Emirates, the United Kingdom, and Singapore are examples of jurisdictions operating a dual financial system, along with many more. In the case of Indonesia, the development of Islamic finance was primarily driven by Islamic banking, with the first legislation concerning the Islamic financial industry contained in Act Number 7 of 1992 on Banking. The law specifically mentions Islamic banking business activities, though the diction used refers to profit-sharing banks.

The urgent need to establish and strengthen Islamic finance stems from the following reasons. *First*, in response to growing market demand. Public demand for sharia-compliant financial products and services is increasing. The Islamic finance industry, therefore, represents an optimal response to the financial system variations and innovations demanded by the market. *Second*, in response to the ever-present need for a financial system that is resistant and resilient to economic and financial crises, considering past crises that have shocked financial systems nationally and internationally. In other words, the Islamic financial industry can create and maintain a healthy and robust Islamic financial system.

Despite awareness concerning the urgency of Islamic financial industry development and application, implementation in many jurisdictions continues to face various challenges and obstacles, including the comparatively small size of the industry, the non-conducive financial industry environment, inadequate and insufficient infrastructure, and underdeveloped Islamic principles for the Islamic financial industry overall. Consequently, in countries where a dual financial system is applied, the size of the Islamic financial industry is comparatively small against the conventional financial industry in terms of volume. Nevertheless, Islamic finance, Islamic banking in particular, has become quite large in several countries. Data from the Islamic Financial Services Industry Stability Report (IFSB, 2020) revealed the market share of Islamic banking institutions in several countries that have adopted a dual banking system.

Islamic finance plays an important role in the overall financial system nationally, thus affecting monetary policymaking. Monetary policy formulation must be optimal to help create an environment conducive to Islamic finance. Islamic monetary policy is formulated paying due consideration to the alignment with conventional monetary policy while adhering to Islamic values and principles. In the case of Indonesia, Bank Indonesia, as the central bank, is the sole monetary authority mandated with regulating both the conventional and Islamic financial systems.

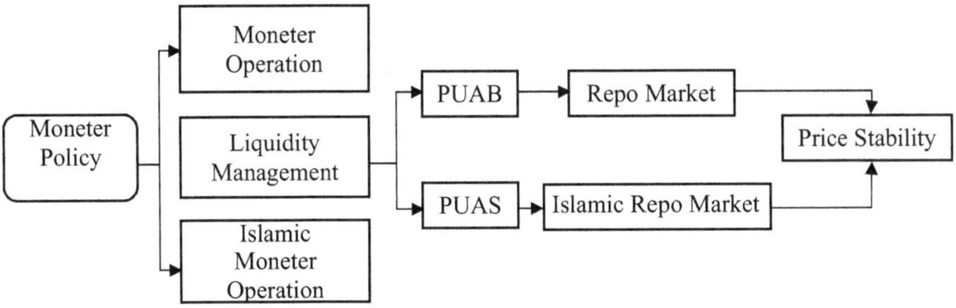

Fig. 12.1 Islamic and conventional monetary policy landscape. Source: Juhro et al. (2018)

Given its status as the sole monetary authority in a dual financial system, the central bank must be knowledgeable and informed in terms of monetary policymaking to ensure both systems remain mutually compatible and avoid discord. The monetary policy formulation strategy must be regulated to create and maintain a financial system that can contribute optimally to stable and sustainable economic growth. In addition, the central bank is mandated by law to facilitate the provision of Islamic monetary instruments to achieve price stability through monetary transmission in accordance with Islamic principles. Comprehensive understanding is required, therefore, to synergise financial aspects with Islamic principles.

Monetary policy practices within a dual financial system are generally formulated and implemented under the auspices of the same authority, namely the central bank, as in the case of Indonesia. Islamic and conventional monetary policy shares the same goal, namely price stability. When implementing monetary operations to achieve that goal, and to accommodate the needs of both monetary systems, the monetary authority must combine the two through liquidity management. Liquidity management can facilitate policymaking at the central bank using conventional and Islamic instruments. In general, the monetary policy landscape within a dual monetary system can be illustrated as follows:

In theory, the monetary authority must orient conventional and Islamic monetary policy in a congruent direction as monetary policy consistency dictates. This is imperative to avoid public confusion regarding the direction of monetary policy. Both conventional and Islamic monetary policy use liquidity as a tool of monetary management. In terms of liquidity management, the monetary authority targets banks. Regarding the pooling of funds, conventional and Islamic banks play a similar role. As a result, Islamic banks also face liquidity risk, thus necessitating instruments from the monetary authority to manage liquidity.

From the perspective of the authorities, liquidity regulation in the banking sector is a transmission channel of monetary operations, with the ultimate goal of price stability. The monetary authority can implement conventional and Islamic monetary policy with a shared direction and common goals through liquidity regulation in the banking sector. As shown in Fig. 12.1, however, the measures taken operationally between conventional and Islamic monetary policy are quite different. Islamic monetary operations are channelled through the sharia interbank money market

(PUAS) and Islamic repo market, while conventional monetary operations use the conventional interbank money market and conventional repo market.

Islamic monetary policy practices have distinctive characteristics as part of the Islamic monetary and economic system. Islamic monetary policy is designed on the premise that the role of the financial sector is limited to financial intermediation between those with a surplus and those with a deficit of funds in the productive business sector. The financial sector in Islam is not permitted to create its own markets with money as a product and interest rates as the price of that product. The existence of a separate market in the financial sector, distinct from the goods/services market, demonstrates a sectoral dichotomy between the financial and real sectors, which contradicts the principles of Islamic monetary economics.

Islamic monetary policy is formed, therefore, to channel potential funds that have become idle. Idle funds can delay real sector activity and impede the productivity of goods and services in the real sector. Consequently, aggregate supply will decrease, leading to higher prices (inflation). Financial intermediation, therefore, is critical to stimulate sustainable economic growth while maintaining price stability of goods in the market.

Acknowledging the various inherent advantages, the Islamic economic and monetary system is applicable in all countries, particularly Muslim countries. This includes monetary policy. With the overwhelming dominance of the conventional monetary system, however, implementing a full-fledged Islamic monetary system (such as in Pakistan and Iran) will face a number of barriers and challenges. A transition period is necessary, therefore, during which Islamic and conventional monetary systems are applied simultaneously within a dual system.

In practice, the conventional monetary system remains dominant and, consequently, the Islamic monetary system must adapt to the existing system. For example, interest rates are the main policy instrument in the current monetary system. Islamic monetary policy tends, therefore, to use interest rates as an operational benchmark. Furthermore, Ascarya and Yumanita found that the current Islamic monetary system mimics the conventional system in terms of applying fractional-reserve banking. Notwithstanding, it is important to maximise the use of Islamic monetary instruments to ensure the money supply follows the demand for money.

There is one salient difference between the conventional and Islamic monetary systems that can be applied in a dual monetary and financial system. On the conventional side, interest rates are the main policy instrument in the current monetary system, which are absolutely forbidden in Islam. Instead, the Islamic economy applies a profit- and loss-sharing mechanism and real sector return index to replace interest rates. Meanwhile, other theoretical differences have not been applied maximally between the two systems in countries embracing dual financial systems.

In the contemporary era, therefore, the main difference between Islamic and conventional monetary systems, as applied in dual monetary and financial systems, is the concept of profit and loss sharing to replace interest rates. Interest rates and profit sharing are fundamentally disparate concepts. Profit sharing entails the real rate of return in the real sector as a fixed ratio (profit-sharing percentage).

Transactions based on profit sharing, therefore, are in line with real sector conditions. The concept of interest rates, on the other hand, follows a predetermined return as a percentage of the principal. Movements in interest rates can be regulated by the authorities. Interest rates, therefore, do not consider or reflect actual conditions in the real sector (Hasanah et al., 2008).

Beyond the dominance of conventional teachings in the contemporary monetary system, the current implementation of Islamic monetary policy is suboptimal due to several other factors, according to Juhro et al. (2018), as follows:

1. In terms of monetary, financial, and social aspects, the foundation and framework of the Islamic economic system are not solid, even in countries that apply a dual economic system.
2. Development of Islamic finance has not been maximised, thus remaining secondary or subordinate to conventional finance in the national financial system.
3. Formulation of an ideal Islamic monetary system remains a subject of study by Islamic monetary experts, including the mechanisms, tools, and instruments of Islamic monetary policy. In addition, the Islamic monetary system remains a comparatively new concept in contemporary economic practices, with no settled formula in the application of Islamic monetary policy.

Through a range of instruments, Islamic monetary policy aims to increase the velocity of money to the real sector, including the use of idle funds. Even today, in countries embracing a dual monetary system, the contribution from the Islamic monetary side is primarily oriented towards integrating the financial sector with the Islamic socio-economic sector to strengthen and drive the real sector and avoid sectoral imbalances. Notwithstanding, implementation of a dual monetary system could give rise to a trade-off between the conventional and Islamic financial systems. Furthermore, the market share of Islamic finance is significantly smaller than conventional finance.

In addition, Islamic monetary policy aims to maintain supply and demand mechanisms and, thus, market price stability. If the prices formed in the market increase beyond accessible levels, the government, through monetary policy, must intervene to bring prices back to an affordable level.

Goods prices may rise due to constraints in the flow of funds from individuals with a surplus to the real sector, thus impeding the supply of goods in the real sector. In this case, monetary policy plays a key role in resolving such issues. As the competent authority, the monetary authority must formulate policies that provide channels to mobilise funds to productive sectors as capital to increase production, thereby restoring the supply side. That way, the characteristics of monetary policy in terms of financial transaction are consistent with Islamic principles, namely investment.

Beyond increasing the supply of goods in the real sector, the Islamic monetary authority is also obliged to formulate policies that can increase the money supply to meet potential financing needs. This is done to boost output growth in the medium and long term within the corridor of a price stability framework. It is important to note, however, that monetary expansion must remain consistent with the desired portions, not excessive or insufficient. Expansive policy must support economic capability and capacity to supply productive goods and achieve quality welfare for the community, as is expected in the goals of the Islamic economic system.

Contrasting conventional monetary policy, interest rate tools to control the demand for money are not recognised in terms of Islamic monetary policy. In addition, the conventional monetary policy framework was constructed on the understanding that money is a commodity that can form its own market, with interest rates as the price of that commodity. This is also supported by human nature based on conventional teachings, namely that individuals can maximise their satisfaction with the money they have, which ultimately leads to the multiplication of money through interest rates. According to Islamic teachings, however, monetary policy serves to bridge the financial and productive (real) sectors through investment and savings (Juhro et al., 2018).

In Islamic monetary policy, the quantity theory of money is more applicable than the price approach using interest rates as the main tool in the monetary policy transmission mechanism. Notwithstanding, Islam permits use of the price approach using the expected return as an instrument in the monetary transmission mechanism. Islamic monetary policymaking, therefore, focuses on the money supply rather than the interest rate. In addition, Islamic monetary policy has several primary objectives to support the successful implementation of the Islamic economic system. As mentioned previously, the main objectives of Islamic monetary policy include achieving full employment and economic growth, socio-economic justice, the equitable distribution of wealth and income, and stability in the value of money (Chapra, 1996).

Excepting the benefits, Islamic monetary policy implementation continues to face considerable barriers, particularly in countries with long-established and mature conventional monetary systems. The Islamic monetary system is comparatively new in most countries that have adopted a dual monetary system. One of the most binding constraints in terms of formulating Islamic monetary policy is a severe lack of data concerning Islamic monetary implementation, making it difficult to know which monetary policy instruments are effective and efficient at achieving the monetary policy targets.

Data relating to the Islamic economy, specifically Islamic monetary and financial data, are insufficient for use as substantive material in policy analysis to determine how effective and efficient Islamic monetary policies and instruments are. Despite the data limitations faced, efforts can be taken to maximise the consistent implementation of the Islamic monetary system. Consistency will increase the analysis material available for appropriate and effective policymaking in the Islamic monetary system, such as by consistently and maximally applying the profit-sharing system, *zakat* policy, and commodity money (gold and silver), which are in line with the objectives of Islamic monetary policy.

Conventional monetary system data are not applicable to Islamic monetary policy analysis and there are significant differences between the characteristics of the profit-sharing system and conventional interest rate system. The profit-sharing system requires information concerning business performance in the real sector, so granular field data are imperative to analyse the appropriateness and effectiveness of Islamic monetary policy.

12.3 Islamic Monetary Policy Practices in Indonesia

Fundamentally, the goals of monetary policy based on Islamic principles are the same as conventional monetary policy, namely maintaining financial system stability and stability in the value of money to achieve the desired level of economic growth (Chapra, 2000). That argument was reinforced by Ibn Qayyim, a mediaeval Islamic jurisconsult, who stated that stability must be maintained in the value of money. As economic practices continue to develop, therefore, monetary policy to achieve those goals is required. The main difference between Islamic and conventional monetary policy stems from the motives for holding money. Islam recognises transactional and precautionary motives for holding money, while the speculative motive based on the assumption that money is a commodity is considered a violation of Islamic principles, namely *maysir*. Increasing the amount of liquidity beyond what is required for production in the real sector can erode stability in the financial system and distort the economic development process.

Despite interchangeable goals, there are technical differences in monetary operations to achieve those goals. The basic difference lies in the types of instruments. The instruments of Islamic monetary policy must not deviate from Islamic principles or contravene sharia law. For example, debt cannot be bought or sold (*ba'i dayn*) nor the rate of return based on interest rates. The formation of monetary instruments based on sharia principles is very important, therefore, in the pursuit of Islamic monetary system implementation. The policy instruments formed must comply with Islamic principles yet maintain a high transmission effect for the implementation of monetary policy.

In the context of Indonesia, the Islamic finance industry has grown and developed rapidly on the back of sharia banking. Formally, Islamic banking practices were legalised with promulgation of Act Number 7 of 1992 on Banking, which implicitly paved the way for Islamic banking activities through profit-sharing banks. In 1998, however, Act Number 7 of 1992 was amended by Act Number 10, which provided a solid legal foundation for the Islamic banking system. The amendment triggered exponential growth of Islamic banking in Indonesia, as reflected in the number of Islamic bank branch offices, sharia business units at conventional commercial banks, and deposits recorded on the balance sheets of Islamic banks. Such conditions compelled Bank Indonesia to pay more attention to the development of Islamic banking in Indonesia (Juhro et al., 2018).

As the central bank for commercial banks in Indonesia, Bank Indonesia has also issued a number of instruments specific to Islamic banks as follows:

(i) Statutory reserve requirements (SRR), as the minimum amount a commercial bank must maintain in their statutory reserve accounts at the central bank set by Bank Indonesia as a specified portion of deposit liabilities. SRR is mandatory to ensure bank survival. In addition, statutory reserves are a monetary instrument that function to control the amount of money in circulation.

The precursory statutory reserve requirement system was fixed, implying that all primary reserves had to be fulfilled at the end of each day, which was later changed to average reserve requirements over a given period. Currently, rupiah reserve requirements for conventional commercial banks stand at 6.5% of deposits and average reserve requirements for conventional commercial banks are 2% (since 16th July 2018). Furthermore, of the total foreign currency reserve requirements applicable to conventional commercial banks at 8%, average reserve requirements of 2% were introduced on 1st October 2018. For sharia banks and sharia business units, total rupiah reserve requirements stand at 5% of deposits, with 2% average requirements introduced on 1st October 2018. Sharia bank deposits consist of (i) *wadiah* demand deposits, (ii) *mudharabah* savings deposits, (iii) *mudharabah* investment term deposits, and (iv) other liabilities.

(ii) Interbank Mudharabah Investment Certificates (SIMA) are used by Islamic banks with excess funds seeking to profit as a means to extend funds to Islamic banks with a 90-day agreement period.

(iii) Bank Indonesia Wadih Certificates (SWBI) are a sharia-compliant Bank Indonesia instrument used for open market operations. The instrument is based on a *wadiah* contract. SWBI can also be used by sharia banks to absorb excess liquidity and as a short-term safekeeping contract.

(iv) SukBI, or Bank Indonesia Sukuk, are issued by Bank Indonesia using Government Sharia Securities (SBSN) and global sukuk held by Bank Indonesia as the underlying assets.

(v) Foreign Currency Sharia Term Deposit (TD) is a fund placement instrument at Bank Indonesia available to participants of sharia open market operations. Foreign currency sharia term deposits are available for various maturities, with tenors of one week, two weeks, one month, and three months. In 2020, foreign currency sharia term deposits were dominated by tenors of one month and two weeks.

(vi) Sharia-Compliant Liquidity Management (PaSBI) provides funds to participants of sharia open market operations for liquidity management with sharia-compliant securities used as collateral. The instrument applies *wakalah bi al-istitsmar* contracts. Through such contracts, Bank Indonesia authorises participants of sharia open market operations to manage an amount of funds without compensation. Sharia-compliant securities are used as collateral to guarantee this instrument with tenors ranging from 1 week to 12 months. In addition, this instrument uses an auction mechanism and transactions are denominated in rupiah. Recently launched in 2020, this innovative new instrument is expected to support liquidity management in the sharia banking industry.

(vii) Sharia-Compliant Liquidity Facility (FLiSBI) is a sharia standing facility (SFS) available in rupiah through a mechanism to disburse funds from Bank

Indonesia to SFS participants guaranteed by sharia-compliant securities. The instrument uses *qard* and *rahn* contracts. *Qard* contracts refer to an interest-free loan, where the borrower repays the principal in one instalment, while *rahn* contracts require a guarantee from the SFS participant to Bank Indonesia as collateral to secure the loan. The term structure of FLiSBI is overnight. Nevertheless, this instrument does not apply an auction mechanism. FLiSBI was introduced to strengthen sharia monetary operations sustainably. In addition to enriching the sharia monetary instruments available to Bank Indonesia in the context of monetary control, this instrument also strengthens liquidity management in the sharia banking industry.

(viii) Sharia-Compliant Interbank Fund Management Certificates (SiPA) are a new instrument of the sharia interbank money market (PUAS). The sharia interbank money market facilitates short-term interbank financial transactions based on sharia principles to maintain adequate liquidity in the banking system. This instrument is available in rupiah and foreign currencies.

SiPA are issued based on *wakalah bi al-istitsmar* contracts. This contract authorises sharia commercial banks, sharia business units, and/or conventional commercial banks to manage an amount of funds without a fee (*ujrah*). During SiPA issuance, PUAS participants authorise and are authorised to manage funds. Conventional commercial banks are permitted to transact in the sharia interbank money market only as lenders, whereas Islamic commercial banks and sharia business units may participate as borrowers and lenders. SiPA are collateralised, thus entailing lower risk.

SiPA are issued scripless and denominated in rupiah, with tenors ranging from overnight to 1 year and are non-transferable prior to maturity.

Though a solid legal base to support the advancement of Islamic finance in Indonesia already exists, efforts to establish strong fundamentals for developing a robust Islamic financial system and ecosystem must be continued. This can be achieved through operational freedom, upholding the principles of fair treatment and fully transparent market information. Therefore, the Islamic Development Bank (IDB) and Islamic Financial Services Board (IFSB) developed a systematic framework to accelerate Islamic financial system development globally, known as the Ten-Year Framework for the Islamic Financial Services Industry. The framework serves as a guide for authorities, particularly in IDB member countries, when preparing a masterplan and platforms for Islamic finance industry development. Furthermore, the framework is expected to help realise the development of an efficient, competitive, resilient, sustainable, and integrated Islamic finance industry in the world financial system as a single unit.

In general, the initiatives encompass the development of policy instruments issued by the central bank as well as state financial instruments. Policy instruments issued by the central bank include SWBI and the requisite repo facilities, while the policy instruments issued by the government are regular issuances of Government Sharia Securities (SBSN). As the monetary authority, Bank Indonesia will stock an amount deemed sufficient to balance the money supply through open market operations based on sharia principles. The new monetary operations also follow the same expansion and contraction mechanism used by Bank Indonesia for existing monetary operations.

In the long term, the monetary operations implemented must be dynamic to adapt to the concept of monetary stability, which is constantly evolving. For the Islamic financial system to reflect its true identity as a system that balances financial transactions with production and productive activity, intensive efforts are required, such as determining indexes to reflect real productivity and their relation to financial activities. Strong correlation between the financial sector and productive sectors has become the goal of financial sector development, as stated in the roadmaps for the banking and non-bank sectors.

In its function as the monetary authority, Bank Indonesia can take the following measures:

(a) Formulating monetary policy using appropriate Islamic monetary instruments within the framework of a dual financial system under the auspices of one authority, with one policy signal that does not conflict with the philosophy of Islamic economics and finance. This must be accompanied by other efforts to enhance the effectiveness of policy formulation, such as determining industry preferences and adequate volume.
(b) Formulating monetary policy that initially focuses on controlling the money supply and then linkages between the total stock of money in the monetary and real sectors. Therefore, monetary policy formulation to achieve financial stability is inextricably linked with efforts to create and maintain stability as well as orderly activity in the real sector.
(c) Prioritising scientific exploration by inviting monetary experts to formulate monetary policies and instruments in accordance with prevailing conditions in the financial environment of Indonesia, particularly the dual financial system.
(d) Refining and amending prevailing laws and regulations to ensure that sharia-compliant monetary policies and instruments can be implemented in line with Islamic philosophy.
(e) Developing complementary and comprehensive infrastructure to optimise the implementation of Islamic monetary policies and instruments.
(f) Pursuing various efforts to expand the scale of Islamic banking and finance in the national economy.
(g) Enhancing the implementation effectiveness and efficiency of Islamic monetary policies and instruments.

The strategic measures that can be taken to develop the concept of Islamic monetary policy include examining the relationship between conventional and Islamic monetary policy while adopting aspects of conventional monetary policy that do not contravene Islamic economic principles. The BI 7 day Reverse Repo Rate, for example, depicts inflation caused by the credit, exchange rate, and asset pricing channels. With the development of real asset-based transactions, the portion of asset channelling has become more dominant in the composition of BI Rate formation. This is consistent with Islamic economic concepts that prioritise real transactions in the real sector. In the medium term, Bank Indonesia could perform studies on real sector benchmarks to better understand the proxy for differences between the BI Rate and real sector productivity.

Money is the most efficient means of exchange. In addition, money can reduce the uncertainty associated with exchanging goods. Money plays a significant role in economic development through its circulation in the monetary sector, implying that the regulation and supervision of money circulation must be rigorous and orderly to ensure its role does not deviate. This is inseparable from the role of institutions and authorities when carrying out monetary activities. According to Sanusi, there are several aspects that need to be considered in relation to the development of a monetary system based on Islamic principles: (1) determining gold and silver currencies, for example the use of dinars that are equivalent to 4.25 grams of gold; (2) adjusting export price standards for Muslim countries, which are dominated by raw materials; (3) applying Islamic principles when managing excess funds in the form of savings in Islamic banks, namely the absolute prohibition of *riba*, maximising the utility of wealth and audits, and annual *zakat* deductions from savings; (4) using dinar as the main currency, particularly in Muslim countries given the stable intrinsic value of gold; (5) liberating Muslim countries from their dependence on foreign currencies; and (6) using the gold dinar as an international trade currency.

12.4 Islamic Monetary Policy Practices in Other Countries

12.4.1 Malaysia

The Islamic finance industry in Malaysia is one of the most established and developed in the world. The highest monetary authority in Malaysia is Bank Negara Malaysia (BNM). Islamic finance in Malaysia began with the establishment of the first Islamic bank, namely Bank Islam Sdn. Bhd., in 1984. The Government of Malaysia is a strong proponent and supporter of Islamic finance and banking by providing various incentives and encompassing industry development comprehensively in national programmes. The main incentive offered by the Malaysian Government is a supportive tax system, coupled with special laws for the Islamic finance industry, known as the Islamic Financial Services Act (IFSA), promulgated in 2013.

Like Indonesia, Malaysia embraces a dual financial system. Malaysia's monetary policy framework has evolved in line with the changing environment of the domestic financial industry. Monetary policy formulation differs slightly from Indonesia, however, with Malaysia implementing the following monetary measures:

(a) No special deposit facilities for commercial banks other than statutory reserves.
(b) No return on statutory reserves.

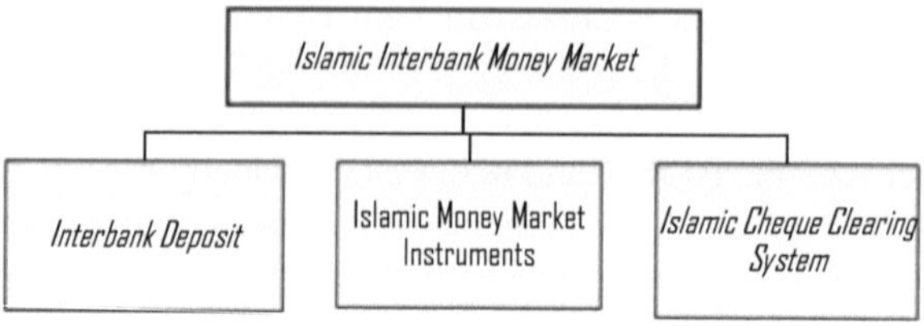

Fig. 12.2 Structure of the Islamic Interbank Money Market in Malaysia. Source: Batcha (2008)

(c) Short-term securities, such as Islamic Treasury Bills and Islamic BNM Notes, are available to Islamic banks.
(d) As the central bank, Bank Negara Malaysia (BNM) also provides deposit facilities for Islamic banks using Commodity *Murabahah* (*tawarruq*) or the Commodity *Murabahah* Program (CMP).
(e) Several instruments are also available for Islamic banks to secure financing from the central bank through various deposits, including *wadi'ah*, *rahn*, and *mudharabah* contracts.

Malaysia is one of few countries that has successfully developed an Islamic money market (Uddin & Halim, 2015). The Islamic money market is part of the Islamic banking system and serves as a source of funding through short-term portfolios for Islamic financial institutions and as a transmission channel for Islamic monetary policy.

Malaysia has successfully implemented various instruments to regulate liquidity in the banking system and other financial institutions in accordance with sharia principles. Through the Islamic Interbank Money Market, Islamic banks and banks participating in the Islamic Banking Scheme (IBS) can match the funding requirements effectively and efficiently. The Islamic Interbank Money Market (IIMM) was first implemented in Malaysia on 3rd January 1994 after Bank Negara Malaysia, as the central bank of Malaysia, issued guidelines to facilitate proper implementation of the Islamic Interbank Money Market on 18th December 1993. The structure of the Islamic Interbank Money Market in Malaysia is depicted in Fig. 12.2 (Batcha, 2008).

Malaysia applies several monetary instruments for use in the Islamic interbank money market as follows (BNM, 2020):

(i) *Mudharabah Interbank Investment (MII)*

MII refers to a mechanism whereby a deficit Islamic banking institution (investee bank) can obtain investment from a surplus Islamic banking institution (investor bank) based on *Mudharabah* (profit sharing). The period of investment is from overnight to 12 months, while the rate of return is based on the rate of gross profit before distribution for investment of 1 year of the investee bank. The profit-sharing ratio is negotiable between both parties. The investor bank at the time of negotiation would not know what the return would be, as the actual return will be crystallised towards the end of the investment period. The principal invested shall be repaid at the end of the period, together with a share of the profit arising from the use of the fund by the investee bank.

(ii) *Wadiah Acceptance*

A *Wadiah* Acceptance is a transaction between BNM and Islamic banking institutions using a mechanism whereby the Islamic banking institutions place their surplus funds with BNM based on a *wadiah* (safekeeping) contract. Under this concept, the acceptor of funds is viewed as the custodian for the funds and there is no obligation on the part of the custodian to pay any return on the account. However, any dividend paid by the custodian is perceived as *hibah* (gift). Under the liquidity management operation, BNM uses the *Wadiah* Acceptance to absorb excess liquidity from the IIMM.

(iii) *Government Investment Issue*

This is a non-interest-bearing certificate issued by the Government of Malaysia known as Government Investment Certificates (GIC). The GII was introduced in July 1983 under the concept of *qard al-hasan*. Nevertheless, the *qard al-hasan* contract did not satisfy GII as a tradable instrument. On 15th June 2001, therefore, a 3-year GII of RM2.0 billion was issued under a new *bay al-inah* contract. GII tenors start from one year with securities as the underlying asset. The instrument is a source of funds for the government.

(iv) *Bank Negara Monetary Notes*

BNMN are Islamic securities issued by Bank Negara Malaysia. The maturity of these issuances has been lengthened from 1 to 3 years. New issuances of BNMN may be issued either on a discounted or a coupon-bearing basis depending on investor demand. Issuance of this instrument also requires an underlying asset.

(v) *Sell and Buy Back Agreement*

A Sell and Buy Back Agreement (SBBA) is an Islamic money market transaction where the bank and central bank agree to trade assets at a pre-agreed price, in which an SBBA seller sells assets to an SBBA buyer, and subsequently, both parties enter into a separate agreement in which the buyer promises to sell back the asset to the seller at an agreed price. In summary, a Sell and Buy Back Agreement is an overnight financing facility from the central bank.

(vi) *Cagamas Mudharabah Bonds*

Cagamas *Mudharabah* Bonds were introduced on 1st March 1994 by Cagamas Berhad to finance the purchase of Islamic housing debts from financial institutions that provides Islamic housing financing to the public. The bond is structured using a *Mudharabah* contract, where the bondholders and Cagamas share the profits according to the agreed profit-sharing ratios.

(vii) *When Issue*

A When Issue is a transaction of sale and purchase of debt securities before the securities are issued. The National Shariah Advisory Council viewed that the WI transaction is allowed based on a licence for the sale and purchase transactions.

(viii) *Islamic Accepted Bills*

Islamic Accepted Bills were introduced in 1991. The objectives are to encourage and promote both domestic and foreign trade by providing

Malaysian traders an attractive Islamic financing product. The IAB is formulated on the Islamic principles of *murabahah* (deferred lump-sum sale or cost-plus) and *bay ad-dyn* (debt trading). *Murabahah* refers to the selling of merchandise at a price based on cost-plus profit margin agreed to by both parties. *Bay ad-dyn* refers to the sale of a debt arising from a trade transaction in the form of a deferred payment sale.

(ix) *Islamic Negotiable Instruments*

The INI covers two instruments. *First*, Islamic Negotiable Instruments of Deposit (INID). The applicable concept is *mudharabah.* It refers to a sum of money deposited with Islamic banking institutions and repayable to the bearer on a specified future date at the nominal value plus declared dividend.

Second, Negotiable Islamic Debt Certificate (NIDC). The transaction involves the sale of a banking institution's assets to the customer at an agreed price on a cash basis. Subsequently, the assets are purchased back from the customer at principal value plus profit to be settled on a future date agreed by both parties.

(x) *Islamic Private Debt Securities*

Islamic Private Debt Securities (IPDS) were introduced in Malaysia in 1990. Currently, the IPDS which are outstanding in the market were issued based on the concepts of *bay bithaman ajil, murabahah,* and *mudharabah. Bay bithaman ajil* contracts apply the following mechanism. Financial institutions purchase assets from the borrower and subsequently sell back the asset at a higher price. The higher price consists of the principal cost and margin (profit).

(xi) *Ar-Rahnu Agreement (RA)*

Under RA, the lender will provide a loan to the borrower based on the concept of *qard al-hasan.* The borrower will pledge its securities as collateral for the loan granted. However, in the event where the borrower fails to repay the loan on the maturity date, the lender has the right to sell the pledged securities and use the proceeds from the sale of the securities to settle the loan. If there is surplus money, the lender will return the balance to the borrower. BNM uses RA as a liquidity management tool for its money market operations. Return from the RA will be in the form of gift (*hibah*) and is determined based on the average interbank money market rates.

(xii) *Sukuk Bank Negara Malaysia Ijarah*

This sukuk is based on the *ijarah* concept. BNM Sukuk Berhad was established to issue sukuk *Ijarah.* The proceeds from the issuance are used to purchase Bank Negara Malaysia's assets. The assets will then be leased to Bank Negara Malaysia for rental payment consideration, which is distributed to investors as a return each period. Upon maturity of the sukuk *Ijarah*, which will coincide with the end of the lease tenure, BNM Sukuk Berhad will then sell the assets back to Bank Negara Malaysia at a predetermined price. The inaugural issuance took place on 16th February 2006 with an issuance value of RM400 million. Bank Negara Malaysia issues this instrument on a regular basis with subsequent issues ranging from RM100 million to RM200 million.

Malaysia also has separate infrastructure to regulate dinar, namely a special intermediary institution (dinar bank). The institution must be trustworthy and uphold the values of Islamic principles. The implementation of depositing dinars in several institutions in Malaysia is as follows:

Bank Negara Malaysia

Bank Negara Malaysia is subject to special laws known as the Central Bank of Malaysia Act (CBMA). In terms of dinar currency transactions, Article 30, Paragraph 1 of CBMA stipulates the following points:

(a) BNM may accept and sell gold coins.
(b) BNM may sell and purchase currency.
(c) BNM may accept securities from consumers.
(d) BNM may undertake on behalf of customers the purchase, sale, collection and payment of securities, currencies and credit instruments in and outside Malaysia, and the purchase or sale of gold and silver.

It can be concluded from the CBMA that BNM is a form of infrastructure with the capability and legal authority to maintain, safeguard, and regulate dinar currency transactions (as a custodian). In addition, BNM also has the authority to purchase gold from members of the public requiring cash liquidity, and vice versa. There is still a slight contradiction, however, because BNM is already mandated with the challenging responsibilities inherent to a central bank. Perhaps a separate specialised institution could be established or appointed as a custodian of the dinar currency, regulated and supervised directly by BNM.

In addition to the CBMA, several other laws and regulations govern the implementation of finance in Malaysia, including the Exchange Control Notices of Malaysia (ECM Notices) of 1953, Banking and Financial Institutions Act (BAFIA) of 1989, and the Money Changing Act (MCA) of 1998.

12.4.2 Iran

In Iran, the central bank is Bank Markazi Jomhouri Islami Iran, otherwise known as the Central Bank of Iran (CBI) in English. Established in 1960, CBI is mandated with designing and implementing monetary policy, credit policy, and general economic policies in Iran. The functions and responsibilities of CBI can be described as follows (CBI, 2020):

(a) Issuing notes and coins
(b) Supervision of financial institutions, including banks and other intermediary institutions
(c) Formulation and regulation of foreign exchange policies and transactions
(d) Regulation of gold transactions
(e) Formulation and regulation of transactions and inflow/outflow of domestic currency

In addition, CBI also acts as a bank for the Iranian Government, mandated with maintaining the government's balance sheet and providing loans/credit to state-owned companies. Meanwhile, CBI also functions as a lender to commercial banks, as well as buying and selling government securities.

The main functions and responsibilities listed above are implemented to achieve the main goals and objectives of CBI as follows (CBI, 2020):

(a) Maintaining the value of the national currency
(b) Maintaining equilibrium in the balance of payments
(c) Facilitating trade-related financial transactions
(d) Improving the economic growth potential of the country

In terms of money, monetary policy, and banking institutions, after the Iranian Revolution, the design and implementation of monetary policy focused on complying with the principles as regulated in the Constitution of the Islamic Republic of Iran. Currently, the CBI designs and formulates monetary policy in line with the government's five-year development plan and annual budget. In addition, monetary policy is formulated and implemented without deviating from the country's constitution, including the Bank Administration Act of 1979, Bank Nationalisation Act of 1979, and Interest-Free Banking Act of 1983.

Discharging its mandate as the monetary authority, the Central Bank of Iran (CBI) implements monetary policy using several instruments. Furthermore, the CBI has instituted a number of modifications to the Islamic banking system in order to maintain competitiveness in this era of global competition, while remaining compliant with the main principles of Islamic economics, namely the absolute prohibition of *riba* and *gharar* (uncertainty). The monetary authority in Iran utilises the following sharia-compliant monetary instruments:

(i) *Reserve Requirement Ratio*

The reserve requirement ratio (RRR) is an indirect monetary policy instrument, with the CBI authorised to set the RRR between 10 and 30% in order to absorb excess funds in the banking system and maintain liquidity at commercial banks.

(ii) *Adjusted Open Market Operations (OMO)*

Fundamentally, OMO are ineffective in countries with underdeveloped financial markets. Adjustments are required, therefore, for OMO to be effective. In addition, predetermined interest-based operations must be avoided and commercial banks are not permitted to purchase government bonds.

(iii) *Discount Rate*

Given the absolute prohibition of *riba*, this instrument cannot be used as freely as in the conventional banking system. Notwithstanding, the central bank's functions as lender of last resort and ultimate source of liquidity imply the need to provide liquidity when banks need it most, thus justifying the use of this instrument.

(iv) *Credit Ceiling*

This instrument is used by the monetary authority to control money creation and maintain liquidity by allocating credit facilities to specific sectors.

(v) *Minimum Expected Profit Ratio of Bank and Bank's Share of Profit in Various Contracts*

The Central Bank of Iran sets the minimum ratio of expected profit from banks in joint ventures and *mudharabah* activities for each economic sector or business field.

12.4.3 Saudi Arabia

The highest monetary authority in Saudi Arabia is the Saudi Central Bank, previously known as the Saudi Arabian Monetary Authority while retaining the same acronym (SAMA). Established in 1952 (1372 Hijriah), the main mission of SAMA is to maintain monetary and financial stability in Saudi Arabia. In addition, SAMA is mandated with stimulating balanced and sustainable economic growth. To achieve that mission, SAMA has the following duties and responsibilities (SAMA, 2020):

(a) Issuing and managing banknotes
(b) Formulating and implementing monetary and financial policy
(c) Regulating and supervising financial sectors
(d) Managing foreign exchange reserves
(e) Ensuring the provision of innovative and secure payment systems
(f) Providing banking services to the government
(g) Compiling monetary and financial data and conducting economic analyses and research

In addition, SAMA performs many functions pursuant to civil laws and regulations. The most important functions are as follows:

(a) Dealing with the banking affairs of the government
(b) Minting and printing the national currency, namely the Saudi riyal
(c) Strengthening the Saudi currency and stabilising its external and internal value
(d) Managing the Kingdom's foreign exchange reserves
(e) Managing the monetary policy for maintaining the stability of prices and exchange rates
(f) Promoting the growth of the financial system and ensuring its soundness
(g) Supervising commercial banks and exchange dealers
(h) Supervising cooperative insurance companies and the self-employment professions relating to the insurance activity
(i) Supervising finance companies
(j) Supervising credit information companies

Concerning the supervision function, SAMA focuses on the following aspects:

1. *Consumer Protection*

   The main responsibilities of SAMA in terms of consumer protection include providing detailed information concerning the rights and obligations of consumers who have agreed to interact with financial institutions (banks). This includes laws, rules, regulations, news, and market information relating to financial institutions. SAMA regulates the rights and obligations of consumers under the auspices of consumer protection as follows (Table 12.1):

2. *Bank Control*

   SAMA is responsible for ensuring the health and effectiveness of the banking system in carrying out its functions. Discharging its responsibilities, SAMA has a separate department, the Banking Control Department, tasked with supervising and controlling the banking sector in Saudi Arabia. This includes granting licences, establishing effective policies and regulations, performing inspections and oversight to ensure the banking sector complies with the rules, and enforcing justice against violations. The functions and responsibilities of the Banking Control Department are explained as follows:

   - Develop a regulatory and supervisory framework for banking by establishing guidelines on supervisory responsibilities and inspection procedures

Table 12.1 Rights and responsibilities of bank customers in Saudi Arabia

Consumer rights	Consumer obligations
Fair and equitable treatment	Provide accurate personal data
Disclosure and transparency	Carefully read all information provided by the bank
Adequate financial education and awareness	Ask questions to clarify any ambiguous conditions
Protecting privacy and information	Understand appropriate complaint submission procedures
Protection against fraudulence	Update personal data and information at the bank in the event of change
Access to dispute settlement	Be prudent when giving power of attorney
Access to search and compare various bank products and services	Immediately report unauthorised transactions in personal bank accounts
Receive the best banking services	Keep confidential information regarding bank accounts private from others
Receive information on conflict settlement	Discuss with the bank if experiencing financial difficulties
	Financial products and services based on financial conditions, customer risk appetite, and the needs of the individual
	Keep copies of all documents and receipts relating to the bank

Source: SAMA (2020)

- Develop and issue policies relating to the banking sector, including rules for granting bank licences
- Supervise the activities of banks to minimise risk potential
- Perform inspections on domestic and foreign banks

3. *Insurance*

   In addition to supervising the banking sector, SAMA also supervises and regulates insurance activities, including laws, regulations, news, and insurance markets in Saudi Arabia. This information is intended for insurance companies, insurance service providers, insurance customers, and policymakers.
4. *Regulatory Sandbox*

   The regulatory sandbox was designed to prepare national and international companies for testing digital technology under the umbrella of financial market development in Saudi Arabia. In addition, the regulatory sandbox is used to assess the impact of the latest technologies adopted in the financial sector in Saudi Arabia. The expectation, therefore, is for the financial markets in Saudi Arabia to develop into a more efficient financial centre.
5. *Payments*

   The payment system is an essential financial market infrastructure that regulates payments at the retail, wholesale, capital market, money market, and foreign exchange market levels. Discharging its supervisory function, SAMA established a set of rules, as contained in regulations known as the Criteria for Systemically Important Payment Systems in the Kingdom of Saudi Arabia. The criteria for a systemic payment system include one or a combination of the following:

- Any system that facilitates payments between banks and customers that may pose a risk to financial stability
- A main payment system in terms of aggregate daily value and volume
- Any system used to resolve issues affecting other financial market infrastructures
- Any system at the centre of payment system infrastructure

  The following systemically important payment systems operate in Saudi Arabia:
- *Saudi Arabian Riyal Interbank Express (SARIE)*

  SARIE is a real-time gross settlement (RTGS) mechanism that facilitates interbank payments denominated in Saudi riyal in the Kingdom of Saudi Arabia. In addition, SARIA provides settlement functions for all other payment systems operating in Saudi Arabia.
- *Saudi Payments Network (SPAN/MADA)*

  SPAN is the national routing switch for cross-bank ATM transactions and POS transactions connecting all banks in Saudi Arabia. In addition, SPAN allows bank customers to access their funds electronically from anywhere within the territory of the Kingdom of Saudi Arabia at any time.

- *Electronic Bill Presentment and Payment System (SADAD)*
  A national electronic bill presentment and payment system for the payment of one-off and recurring bills via banks, ATMs, electronic banking, and mobile banking.

Monetary Policy in Saudi Arabia

Monetary policy in Saudi Arabia is influenced by the price of oil produced (Al-Jasser & Banafe, 2008). Liquidity in Saudi Arabia is abundant due to the high oil price along with other determinants, such as increasing loans from domestic banks to individuals and business customers. One of the biggest challenges, however, is how to overcome asset price inflation.

The monetary policy framework in Saudi Arabia relates closely to the fixed exchange rate regime. The exchange rate is used as a benchmark to stabilise the expected exchange rate and maintain low and stable inflation. It is also expected to attract capital inflows for domestic investment. The primary objective of monetary policy in Saudi Arabia is to regulate the liquidity system and maintain Saudi riyal stability against the US dollar.

The monetary policy instruments consist of the policy targets, policy strategies, operational framework, and policy transmission mechanism.

(i) The monetary policy targets in Saudi Arabia are to achieve price and exchange rate stability.
(ii) The policy strategies are the processes used to achieve those policy targets. The Inflation Targeting Framework (ITF), exchange rate, monetary aggregates, and statutory reserve requirements are part of the monetary policy strategy process.
(iii) The monetary policy operational framework aims to determine appropriate measures to achieve the desired exchange rate.
(iv) The monetary policy transmission mechanism is a series of monetary policy processes that impact the economy in general and policy targets specifically.

In the case of Saudi Arabia, the exchange rate is used as an instrument of monetary policy. In addition, statutory reserves, SAMA Bills, and the repo rate are also used as policy instruments. The statutory reserves set by SAMA tend to be constant and have not been adjusted since 1980, while SAMA Bills were introduced in 1984. Since then, SAMA has used the repo rate to regulate daily liquidity and signal the overnight rate in the money market. Ultimately, the repo rate and reserve repo are the most effective instruments of monetary policy control.

Saudi Arabia is an emerging market that is more susceptible to financial market uncertainty than more advanced economies. By implementing a fixed exchange rate regime, therefore, Saudi Arabia can suppress domestic interest rates through capital inflows. In addition, investment will increase by a larger portion than domestic savings.

Under a fixed exchange rate regime and near-perfect asset substitution, monetary policy cannot stand alone. In Saudi Arabia, therefore, proceeds from oil exports and their impact on fiscal policy greatly influence the monetary policy scheme. Monetary policy, as regulated by the Saudi Central Bank, is critical for liquidity management without disrupting free market competition. According to Al-Jasser and Banafe (2008), over the past few decades, the ratio of government debt to gross domestic product (GDP) initially increased and then fell dramatically, with SAMA playing a crucial role as central bank and manager of government debt.

12.4.4 Sudan

The Central Bank of Sudan (CBOS) first instituted Islamic monetary policy in 1984. Initially, Sudan relied heavily on conventional monetary instruments, such as interest rates, credit ceilings, a statutory liquidity ratio, and discount rate. In the beginning, those instruments were very effective but gradually created distortions in the allocation of bank resources, disrupted the price mechanism, and stifled competitiveness due to restrictions on bank asset management. Ultimately, Sudan opted for sharia-compliant instruments, namely reserve requirements and open market operations. The Central Bank of Sudan subsequently issued policy to all banks requiring the implementation of Islamic principles for banking activity.

The policy reform was not immediately successful as the Central Bank of Sudan confronted the challenge of substituting conventional monetary instruments for Islamic monetary instruments. Nevertheless, the policy reform did not supersede the central bank functions of supervising commercial banks, expanding or contracting the money supply or credit, formulating monetary policy, and safeguarding the public interest.

The CBOS is mandated to discharge the following duties and responsibilities (CBOS, 2020):

(a) Achieving stability of prices, maintaining stability of the exchange rate and efficiency of the banking system, and issuing currency, while organising, controlling, and supervising the circulation of currency.
(b) Formulating and implementing monetary policy, depending on market forces, in such a way to achieve the national objectives of the national macroeconomy in consultation with the Minister of Finance and National Economy.
(c) Organising, monitoring, and supervising banking business, striving to promote and develop as well as raise the efficiency of the banking industry to achieve balanced economic and social development.
(d) Act, in its capacity as the government banker, as an advisor and agent thereof, in monetary and financial affairs.
(e) Abide in the discharge of the duties, achievement of the objectives, exercise of the powers, and supervision of the dual banking system by the ordinances of Islamic sharia and conventional banking customs.

The CBOS discharges its responsibilities to achieve the following vision and mission. The vision is to become one of the leading central banks at the regional and international levels in maintaining financial and monetary stability in such a way that may contribute to the realisation of sustained economic growth and reinforce international confidence in national banking credibility. Meanwhile, the mission is to maintain monetary and financial stability under a dual banking system consistent with the volume of economic activity in Sudan and to realise an attractive investment environment together with securing soundness and strength of the banking system by adopting effective financial and monetary policies and exerting the required efforts to disseminate financial and banking knowledge (CBOS, 2020).

In addition to upholding its vision and mission, the CBOS has the following core values (CBOS, 2020):

(a) Consolidation of the spirit of association
(b) Reinforcement of the principles of integrity, credibility, and transparency
(c) Perform with high professionalism and excellence
(d) Effectiveness and efficiency
(e) Work with team spirit

In practice, the Central Bank of Sudan applies a number of rules concerning monetary policy and the instruments therein in compliance with Islamic values as follows:

(i) *Reserve Requirement*
Commercial banks should maintain cash balances with the Central Bank of Sudan in the form of statutory cash reserves of 20% of total deposits (10% of total deposits in the local currency and 10% of total deposits in foreign currencies), excluding investment and savings deposits based on the final monthly balance sheet of the banks.
(ii) *Central Bank Musharaka Certificates (CMC)*
Central Bank *Musharaka* Certificates are a source of liquidity for the financial sector, including banks and non-banks.
(iii) *Ijara Certificates (Sukuk)*
A type of security used to mobilise short-term deposits for the development of long-term infrastructure projects through the securitisation of tangible assets, such as airports, roads, buildings, factories, schools, hospitals, power plants, oil refineries, and others.
(iv) *Finance Window*
A facility available to banks experiencing liquidity shortfalls or requiring additional sources for investment financing.
(v) *Foreign Exchange Operations*
A tool of the central bank to maintain exchange rate stability.
(vi) *Government Musharaka Certificate (GMC)*
Securities issued by the government to raise funds with a mutually agreed return to investors. Investment is in the form of ownership in public companies or the provision of financing for certain projects that will generate future profit.
(vii) *Other qualitative and quantitative rules and regulations as follows:*

    (a) 50% minimum requirement of total credit disbursed to rural areas.
    (b) Bank groups can form loan portfolios for priority sectors with the knowledge of the Central Bank of Sudan.

(c) Credit will not be extended to persons/institutions that fail to meet their obligations in the banking system unless approved by the Central Bank of Sudan.
(d) A certain percentage of income will be taken from banks that fail to settle late payments of customer credit, with the value added to the bad debt provision.
(e) All credit must meet sharia principles.
(f) Certain sectors are prioritised to receive credit, including agriculture, manufacturing, mining and energy, transportation and storage, exports, professionals, craftsmen, micro and small enterprises, public housing, and stock market investment. At least 90% of bank credit must be allocated to these priority sectors, with the remainder disbursed to non-priority sectors.
(g) The minimum profit margin for *murabahah* contracts ranges from 10 to 50% based on the sector and currency used.

12.4.5 Bahrain

The Central Bank of Bahrain (CBB) is a public corporate entity established on 6th September 2006, succeeding the Bahrain Monetary Agency, which had previously carried out central banking and regulatory functions since its establishment in 1973, with the additional regulatory function for the insurance business and capital market added in 2002.

The main duties of the CBB are to regulate and supervise the entire financial sector in Bahrain. In addition, the CBB also licenses and supervises conventional and sharia financial institutions, including banks, insurance companies, investment companies, and other financial services providers. The CBB also regulates exchanges and clearinghouses and acts as the listing authority for financial companies and instruments listed on capital market exchanges.

The CBB vision is to strengthen the position of Bahrain as a major international financial centre through the application of sound monetary and financial policies consistent with international best practices. In addition, the CVB has the following missions (CBB, 2020):

(a) Providing central banking services to the government and financial sector which are cost-effective and reliable and that support national objectives and Bahrain's position as a major financial centre.
(b) Ensuring that the regulation and supervision of the financial sector of Bahrain meets the highest international standards.
(c) Facilitating market innovation, including the development of Islamic banking and finance, and encouraging the use of training and technology to enhance the competitiveness of Bahrain's financial sector.
(d) Encouraging an open and competitive financial sector, which welcomes new entrants, including from overseas, provided they pose no undue regulatory risks.

(e) Working with international organisations, such as the International Monetary Fund (IMF), Bank for International Settlements (BIS), International Organization of Securities Commissions (IOSCO), International Association of Insurance Supervisors (IAIS), and the Financial Action Task Force (FATF), to foster the stability of the global financial system.
(f) Promoting a culture of excellence within the central bank work environment which emphasises the highest standards of professionalism, integrity, prudence, teamwork, and innovation.

Bahrain has a free market economy, with no restrictions on capital movements, foreign exchange, foreign trade, or foreign investment. The Kingdom holds a leading position in the region as an open, free, transparent, and welcoming environment for investors. The monetary policy framework is geared to support the general economic goals of Bahrain.

Similar to Malaysia and Indonesia, Bahrain implements a dual financial system. The CBB is the monetary authority and regulates short- and long-term government bond instruments, such as treasury bills, *salam* sukuk, and *ijarah* sukuk. The issuance of government debt securities is executed in coordination with the Ministry of Finance and National Economy. Interestingly, Islamic monetary instruments in Bahrain are owned by the government, which relieves the monetary burden typically borne by the monetary authority. The Islamic monetary instruments used in Bahrain are as follows:

(i) *Statutory Reserve Requirement*

Similar to other countries, Bahrain also implements a reserve requirement system to maintain the money supply and day-to-day liquidity conditions in commercial banks.

(ii) *Open Market Operations*

The following instruments are used to implement open market operations:

(a) Islamic Sukuk Liquidity Instrument (ISLI)

The ISLI mechanism is based on sale and purchase transactions using *ijarah* contracts in the local currency.

(b) *Salam* Sukuk

Sukuk issued by the government using a parallel sale and purchase mechanism with a 3-month tenor and underlying assets.

(c) *Ijarah* Sukuk

Sukuk issued by the government based on the concept of *ijarah muntahiyyah bittamlik* (IMBT).

(iii) *CBB Wakalah Facility*

The *Wakalah* Facility was launched in March 2015 and the agreement was developed based on a standard contract of the International Islamic Financial Market (IIFM). The *Wakalah* is an investment opportunity for Islamic retail banks that wish to deposit excess liquidity with the CBB, overnight and for 1 week. Islamic retail banks need to sign a *Wakalah* agreement which appoints the CBB as an agent (*wakil*) to invest cash on behalf of the bank (*muwakkil*).

Accordingly, the *wakil* will invest these funds in the investment portfolio allocated in advance, containing international Islamic Sukuk in US dollars and cash in Bahraini dinars. The *Wakalah* expected profit rates are decided by the Monetary Policy Committee at the CBB and posted on a daily basis on the CBB website.

Chapter 13
Realising Inclusive Welfare: Lessons Learned

13.1 Introduction

Indiscriminately blighting advanced and emerging economies alike, economic and financial crises have prompted further exploration of more suitable, stronger economic concepts and systems. Furthermore, economic development has hitherto failed to manifest a significant impact on poverty alleviation and social inequality, thus fostering the application of an economic and development strategy approach that prioritises inclusive welfare. The global initiative of the Millennium Development Goals (MDGs), followed by the Sustainable Development Goals (SDGs), is a response to the failure of the outdated trickle-down theory approach to development. The MDG/SDG approach employs a modern development style with a direct impact on achieving poverty alleviation targets, reducing inequality, and ameliorating welfare for all through economic empowerment and financial inclusion programmes (microfinance).

Naturally, the concept of inclusive economic development has become a hot discussion topic, accompanied by research and discourse in scientific journals and global economic forums. Various financial inclusion strategies have been discussed and recommended in a virtuous effort to improve the living standards of the poor as well as support micro and small enterprises. Diverse economic development concepts are being recommended for the attention of economic authorities, including the notion of economic inclusion and inclusive growth. In general, a more inclusive view of economic development is one in which the benefits stretch beyond elevating income or expanding the number of products and services in an economy to encompass social aspects, such as quality-of-life improvements, social security, health, and the environment, which are the inviolable rights of all, irrespective of social standing.

Underpinned by the paradigm of economic inclusion and inclusive growth, experts are recommending holistic economic development concepts with the benefits felt by the entire population. Rather than focusing on the value of goods and services

S. M. Juhro et al., *Inclusive Welfare*, https://doi.org/10.1007/978-981-96-0051-9_13

produced (GDP), economic inclusion and inclusive growth are oriented towards increasing economic participation in the wider community and how many people will experience the benefits in the form of living standards, health, social security, food sovereignty, and other similar indicators. As recommended by Stiglitz, a comprehensive development strategy is required according to the concept of inclusive growth based on a new understanding of economic success and social transformation.

In general, the goal of economic inclusion and inclusive growth is to ameliorate welfare for as many people as possible, while supporting development strategies that prioritise the interests of the broader community, especially those languishing at the bottom of the pyramid (*dhuafa*), who traditionally have not experienced much prosperity or welfare. Referring to quality development, namely living standards, social security, health, economic participation, and similar indicators, this new paradigm of economic development aligns harmoniously with the overarching principles of the Islamic economy. Almsgiving based on *zakat* in Islamic social-public finance and the absolute prohibition of *riba* in the commercial financial sector (monetary economy), for example, facilitate an economy based on sharia principles that prioritises the interests of the poor and optimises resource allocation, thus maximising economic participation in productive activities. Islamic economic principles in the Islamic social-public finance sector and monetary economy characterise economic inclusiveness.

It can be concluded, therefore, that economic inclusion and inclusive growth are fully in line with the spirit and goals of the Islamic economy, particularly in terms of creating inclusive welfare for all, including material satisfaction and spiritual peace through the development of humanity and resources. In that context, the need to achieve equitable wealth distribution in the inclusive welfare dimension can be satisfied. Of course, this is contrary to the conventional notion of prosperity and welfare, namely a Pareto efficient or Pareto optimal condition. Pareto optimal is defined as a condition where it is no longer possible to change the allocation of resources to improve welfare of economic actors (better off) without compromising other economic actors (worse off). Under current conditions, society can only increase the optimal level of satisfaction to the detriment of others. Based on real experience, such conditions are clearly untenable as a basis for achieving true economic welfare and prosperity due to the lack of impartiality and overall benefit.

13.2 Islamic Economic Inclusion: On the Role of the Islamic Social-Public Finance Sector

The public sector involves government budget management as manifested in public or fiscal policy that aims to reduce unemployment, control inflation, and stimulate economic growth. Public finance is concerned with government revenue and expenditure activities. Conventional theories of public finance strive to achieve three goals, namely mobilising resources to meet government spending needs, moderating or dampening fluctuations in the business cycle, and reducing inequality in income distribution. Although the goals of conventional public finance appear economically beneficial, particularly for the community, the theories are built on a materialistic philosophy that prioritises the interests of the state or ruler above all. Occidental philosophy of public finance is inextricably linked to the history of taxation, which serves to mobilise funds from the people for the benefit of the ruler. Economic inclusiveness, therefore, has only emerged through issues in development policy.

The public finance sector exists to support the market (private sector) as the primary conduit of wealth and income distribution. From an Islamic perspective, however, the distribution of wealth and orderly flow of economic resources is not left entirely to the private sector. In fact, Islam institutes mandatory mechanisms that compel the equitable distribution of wealth and economic resources. Public finance in Islam not only complements the private sector but also serves as a safeguard, an ineluctable mainstay of the economy. Islamic social fiscal instruments, such as *zakat*, collected from the rich and distributed to the poor, are fundamental to the equitable distribution of economic resources. On the other hand, *zakat* functions as income for the poor, strengthening their purchasing power. In other words, the purchasing power afforded by *zakat* distribution to the poor enables economic participation and market access to the economic resources needed.

Zakat ensures that the economy (based on sharia principles), the social-public finance sector in particular, prioritises the interests of the poor and needy in economic development. *Zakat* represents a key characteristic of the sharia economy, focusing on *dhuafa* as the predominant policy line of the Islamic public sector. This attribute emerged as a consequence of *zakat* principles, demonstrating the inclusive nature of the Islamic economy. Through *zakat*, the Islamic economy has shown consistent inclusiveness from the beginning, with the poor positioned as the main priority of economic development. The sharia economy not only targets the poor for development policies but also serves as fundamental economic guidelines.

From an Islamic perspective, economic inclusion did not emerge due to policies as part of a paradigm shift towards inclusive growth yet has remained the overarching priority of development since inception. *Zakat* is a religious obligation and a pillar of Islam. In other words, inclusiveness has been a tenet of Islamic economics from the beginning as a consequence of *zakat*. Islamic economic inclusion *is* social inclusion and has been since the beginning, ensuring that the basic needs of the poor are met because of the purchasing power provided by *zakat*. This mechanism, therefore, also maintains economic participation among the poor. Without exaggeration, the Islamic economy is positioned as a viable alternative economic concept, answering the growing call for economic inclusion.

Beyond the dimension of inclusiveness, which has distribution implications in terms of wealth and income, Islamic social-public finance based on *zakat, infaq, sadaqah*, and *waqf* (ZISWAF) instruments has a spiritual dimension as the embodiment of its philosophical function, namely the preservation of moral values by maintaining the faith of the people and community collectively. Maintaining faith is the ultimate goal of all economic activities in Islam, not only social-public activities but also the activities of individuals, households, and corporations in the private (commercial) sector. Maintaining the flow of economic resources and distribution of wealth and income through the social-public finance sector, therefore, essentially strives to provide the basic needs of Muslims so that they may fulfil their obligations to God (maintaining faith). Qaradhawi (1988) stated that *zakat* serves as a guardian of the faith, especially for the poor and other *mustahik* groups in general. A combination of the material dimension in concert with the spiritual dimension represents a robust characteristic of the Islamic economy, including Islamic social-public finance activity.

A number of modern Islamic economists have stated that the application of public finance in Islam relates to the state function in terms of the economy. Siddiqi (1996) mentioned three functions of state: (1) implement the permanent mandate of sharia law, including the *zakat* mechanism, while prohibiting *riba* and *maysir*, (2) implement the mandate of sharia law in accordance with *ijtihad* based on specific needs or conditions at a certain time, and (3) implement the people's mandate based on the Consultative Council of Muslims of Indonesia (Majelis Suryo). This opinion is supported by Kahf (1995), namely that the most important function of the state is to maintain the religion and supremacy of the will or rules of Allah SWT. Kahf (1995) also stated that in terms of public policy, state spending should be limited to the following objectives: (1) safeguarding the internal and external security of the state, (2) minimising the administrative needs of the state, (3) meeting the basic necessities of the people, and (4) developing sectors that are not attractive to the private sector.

A characteristic of Islamic social-public finance is that each instrument has its own specific set of rules, implying that each instrument has its own target, which are nevertheless mutually reinforcing and complementary. For example, *zakat* targets the poor and needy (*dhuafa*), travellers in search of knowledge (*ibnussabil*), and preachers and teachers (*fisabilillah*). Meanwhile, *khums* are intended for the state (with a portion for Allah SWT, Rasul SAW, and His family), orphans, and the poor. In the Islamic public social-finance sector, *waqf* instruments are definitive and must be used in accordance with the intention of the donor (*muqoyyadah*). In addition, when the use of *waqf* assets is left to the discretion of the *nazhir*, the benefits are still directed in the interest of Muslims. *Waqf* for Muslims can reduce social costs and, for the economy, increase social investment, thus boosting economic volume on a macro scale.

Challenges and Opportunities

The development of *zakat, infaq, sadaqah,* and *waqf* (ZISWAF) in Indonesia is gradually demonstrating the usefulness and significance of Islamic social-public finance in the national economy. On a macro level, the Indonesian economy has a new sector to support development efforts and economic growth. It is no exaggeration, therefore, to say that if sharia economic development reaches beyond the social sector to also encompass the financial sector and real sector (halal industry), such development would have great potential as a new source of economic growth nationally. Realising inclusive sharia economic development in the application of

Indonesia's modern economy has a number of inherent challenges. In the context of Indonesia, the following challenges have been identified:

(a) Challenges in terms of regulation and development to ensure the sector maximises its role in the national economy, particularly efforts to alleviate poverty, reduce inequality, and improve welfare in general. In terms of government regulation, the application of Islamic social-public finance must be integrated with the existing legal or regulatory systems.
(b) Despite a dominant Muslim majority population, the application of Islamic social-public finance requires continuous education and socialisation efforts as well as constant refinement and improvement. The current culture of paying *zakat* individually, coupled with a lack of proper bookkeeping and financial accounting, has led to distribution overlaps, thus impeding optimal outreach to all community groups in need. For example, many Muslims in Indonesia pay their *zakat* obligations directly to the *mustahik*, rather than through official government or private sector institutions. This is part of the culture in Indonesia and requires education at the community level together with structural improvements in its application.
(c) Scientific exploration and insight must be nurtured concerning the development and implementation of Islamic social-public finance instruments that are relevant to current conditions. Innovative products, such as cash waqf-linked sukuk (CWLS), represent solid breakthroughs in terms of developing Islamic social-public finance applications in the modern era. Innovation in the form of social and commercial finance integration, targeting the instruments, programmes, and business models, must be fostered and developed continuously as the community requires a variety of applications to increase economic participation.
(d) The government and all relevant parties must continue to raise public literacy concerning the application of Islamic social-public finance. Enthusiasm for social funds beyond *zakat*, such as voluntary *infaq, sadaqah,* and *waqf*, must be exploited to increase willingness among Muslims to set aside a portion of their wealth to help others in need. This, in addition to educating the community, Muslims in particular, concerning their obligations to carry out religious principles, will also increase the sense of care and awareness in the community, which will maintain wealth and income distribution, assist in poverty alleviation efforts, reduce economic inequality, and ameliorate welfare. Fundamentally, building awareness in the community is akin to increasing faith, understanding *zuhud* values in terms of wealth and property as well as the values of solidarity. Maximising the socio-public finance sector in Islam requires government support in terms of public understanding towards religion.

Meanwhile, the opportunities afforded by the successful implementation of Islamic social-public finance and achieving the goals recommended by sharia are massive. In this respect, Indonesia is blessed with several endowments offering great potential:

(a) A prodigious Muslim population. Indonesia is the most populous Muslim country in the world, with Muslims dominating more than 80% of the

Indonesian population, totalling approximately 271 million in December 2020 (BPS-Statistics Indonesia). Such demographic conditions imply that economic practices, as carried out by most Indonesian people, should be influenced by sharia principles, including the application of Islamic social-public finance. Over the past few years, Indonesia has been recognised as the most generous country in the world, demonstrating huge capital to mobilise the Islamic social-public finance sector and contribute to national economic growth. Furthermore, the predominantly Muslim population in Indonesia will help the government and private sector facilitate development of Islamic social-public finance.

(b) Government regulatory support is required to increase Islamic social-public finance, which is slowly being internalised in the daily lives of the people. This is also inextricably linked to the state's function in terms of social-public finance. Currently, the opportunity is even larger due to the existence of the National Islamic Economy and Finance Committee (KNEKS), as a coordinating body for all sharia economic stakeholders in Indonesia. KNEKS will help focus and integrate sharia economic development.

(c) The development of Islamic social-public finance by private Islamic social-finance institutions is helping to raise public literacy and awareness. In addition, the emergence of Islamic social-finance institutions is spurring the application of structured Islamic social-public finance to the significant benefit of the community. Islamic social-public finance can, therefore, meaningfully assist government programmes to alleviate poverty and ameliorate welfare. This is also in line with growing awareness and understanding among the Muslim community towards religion, ushering in greater compliance with sharia principles and moral values when managing assets, including *zakat* obligations or heeding religious teachings and recommendations to set aside a portion of assets in the form of *infaq, sadaqah,* and *waqf.*

(d) Sharia rules that regulate the mobilisation and distribution of funds or assets in Islamic social-public finance tend to promote much greater transparency and accountability in terms of government budget management. This represents an attractive alternative form of public finance for the government because Islamic public finance policies offer a viable alternative to existing public policy options, while simultaneously improving the government's reputation and increasing public trust in the government as a result of greater transparency and accountability. Instruments of Islamic social-public finance, such as *zakat, kharja,* and *jizyah*, entail disciplined principles in terms of collection and distribution. Other instruments of Islamic social finance, such as *waqf*, also promote transparency and accountability because distribution is tied to the intentions of the donor (*muqoyyadah*).

The opportunity for applying the concept of Islamic social-public finance in Indonesia is growing in response to the keen interest shown in various alternative instruments offered through the Islamic economic system. In addition, the Islamic economy and finance have become a hot topic globally, discussed widely through international forums. In fact, several non-Muslim majority countries are implementing sharia economic practices in their economies, including commercial and social finance, such as the United Kingdom.

The public sector encompasses government budget management, as embodied in public policy and fiscal policy, which aim to reduce unemployment, control inflation, and stimulate economic growth. Public finance is an integral part of the public sector relating to government revenue and expenditure. Conventional (occidental) theories of public finance are used to achieve at least three goals, namely mobilising resources to meet government spending needs, moderating fluctuations in the business cycle, and reducing inequitable income distribution. Though the goals of conventional public finance activities appear beneficial for the economy and society in general, the underlying theories were built on the philosophy of materialism. This is reflected in the impact parameters and indicators of public finance policy. In the Western world, the philosophy of public finance is inseparable from the history of taxation, which serves to mobilise funds from the people for the benefit of the ruler or king.

The social-public finance sector serves to support the role of the market (private sector) in terms of discharging its function for wealth-income distribution. From an Islamic perspective, however, wealth-income distribution or the orderly flow of economic resources is not left entirely to the arbitrary whims of the private sector. Those towards the bottom of the pyramid, who are typically neglected in the modern economic model, are accommodated in the Islamic economic system. Disadvantaged community groups must be included in economic activity as the main participants of wealth-income distribution. Islam employs mandatory mechanisms that compel the equitable distribution of wealth and income and flow of economic resources. The public finance mechanism in Islam not only complements the private sector but is also a safeguard or guardian of and by itself. Fiscal instrument in Islam, such as the obligatory religious duty of *zakat*, which is collected from those with a surplus and distributed to those with a deficit, is a basic instrument that ensures the flow of economic resources is maintained.

On the other hand, *zakat* represents income for the *dhuafa*, thus affording greater public purchasing power. In other words, the purchasing power provided by *zakat* distribution prevents economic exclusion in favour of economic participation. Using *zakat* as income, the poor can maintain market access to obtain the economic resources required. In addition, *zakat* also ensures government policies in terms of public finance prioritise *dhuafa* as the mandatory focus of policy. This emphasis on the poor differentiates Islamic public sector policy from conventional.

In addition to the technical dimensions associated with wealth-income distribution, the mechanism of Islamic social-public finance also has a spiritual dimension as a goal, namely maintaining the faith of the Islamic community and society collectively. Fundamentally, maintaining faith is the ultimate goal of all economic activities in Islam, not only activity in the social-public sector but also the goals of individuals, families, and corporations in the private (commercial) sector. By focusing on the objective of maintaining the flow of economic resources and wealth-income distribution, the social-public finance sector essentially aims to provide the basic needs of the Islamic community in order to fulfil their obligations to God (maintaining the faith). Qardhawy argued that *zakat* is an instrument which functions as a guardian of faith, especially for the poor or *asnaf* groups of *mustahik*. The material dimension that goes hand in hand with the spiritual dimension is a robust characteristic of the application of the Islamic economic system, including Islamic social-public finance activities.

A number of modern Islamic economists have stated that the application of public finance in Islam relates to the state function in terms of the economy based on Islamic principles. Fundamentally, Islamic public finance must be in line with the goals of the government in Islam. Siddiqi (1996) mentioned three functions of the state: (1) implement the permanent mandate of sharia law, including the *zakat* mechanism, while prohibiting *riba* and *maysir*, (2) implement the mandate of sharia law in accordance with *ijtihad* based on specific needs or conditions at a certain time, and (3) implement the people's mandate based on the Consultative Council of Muslims of Indonesia (Majelis Suryo). This opinion is supported by Kahf (1995), namely that the most important function of the state is to maintain the religion and supremacy of the will or rules of Allah SWT. Kahf (1995) also stated that in terms of public policy, state spending should be limited to the following objectives: (1) safeguarding the internal and external security of the state, (2) minimising the administrative needs of the state, (3) meeting the basic necessities of the people, and (4) developing sectors that are not attractive to the private sector. This opinion was also held in the classical era, with the Islamic legal scholar Syatibi stating that sharia, as implemented by the state, must ultimately protect religion (faith), life (soul), family and progeny, wealth (resources), and reason (science) as stated in the maqāṣid al-sharīʿa legal doctrine.

A characteristic of Islamic social-public finance is that each instrument has its own applicable rules, implying that each instrument has its own target, which are nevertheless mutually reinforcing and complementary. For example, *zakat* targets the poor and needy (*dhuafa* and *faqir*), travellers in search of knowledge (*ibnussabil*), and preachers and teachers (*fisabilillah*). Meanwhile, *khums* are intended for the state (with a portion for Allah SWT, Rasul SAW, and His family), orphans, and the poor. In the Islamic public social-finance sector, *waqf* instruments are definitive and must be used in accordance with the intention of the donor (*muqoyyadah*). In addition, when the use of *waqf* assets is left to the discretion of the *nazhir*, the benefits are still directed in the interest of Muslims. *Waqf* for Muslims can reduce social costs and, for the economy, increase social investment, thus increasing economic volume on a macro scale.

The application of Islamic social-public finance must not be constrained by past understanding based on a significantly less complicated economic environment. Deep understanding is required along with innovations appropriate to the concept of Islamic public finance for application in the highly complex modern economic environment. Socialisation and education activities concerning the application of Islamic public finance must be continued, with the opportunity for inclusion in formal public finance curricula explored to enrich and expand insight, particularly among policymakers. Efforts to integrate Islamic public finance in the conventional public finance framework are equally important to develop alternative policy options for policymakers to achieve their objectives, namely stimulating economic growth, reducing unemployment, and alleviating poverty.

Meanwhile, another important thing is related how to accelerate Islamic social-public finance (ISF) in order to achieve falah according to maqasid alsyariah. One crucial and emerging thing to be implemented in Islamic social-public finance is digitalisation. The growth of digitalisation in finance has accelerated rapidly, especially due to the impact of the COVID-19 pandemic as a catalyst in 2020. Digitalisation brings various advantages to economic growth, corporate establishment, corporate financial performance, and resilience to external shocks. Digitalisation is also radically changing the business process, including the financial sector, to become more transparent, efficient, and effective. Islamic Social Finance (ISF), e.g. zakah, infaq, alms, and waqf, can also benefit from digitalisation. However, despite numerous studies on ISF, only a few studies further assess ISF as a whole and there is also a lack of research regarding digitalisation's impact on ISF.

Due to the nature of digitalisation, the usage of technology was found to be correlated with financial inclusion by reducing unbanked people through providing accessibility and raising purchasing power to alleviate inequality. Moreover, underutilised ISF potential in Indonesia as a country that has the most Muslim population, along with the enthusiasm of Muslims to implement digitalisation on ISF, create a potential for ISF development. Despite its potential, digitalisation brings several consequences. It requires a high upfront investment cost, including but not limited to brand new infrastructure, IT helpdesk, server, and so on. Aside from this, digitalisation raises concerns such as cyberattack issue, misuse of consumers' data, and inadequate legal frameworks. Furthermore, digitalisation is heavily reliant on electrical sources and Internet coverage, which may pose a risk of digital divide in remote areas.

The alternative technologies that could be implemented for ISF consist of artificial intelligence (AI), blockchain, cloud computing, big data, QR code, and digital platform. In brief, AI can be used in ISF to automate processes and improve fundraising through smarter segmentation and prediction of individual behaviour. Blockchain is a reliable technology which holds a list of immutable transaction records that can be seen by anyone in the ecosystem, so the accountability and transparency of ISF organisation will be better maintained. Next, cloud computing could further develop ISF with economies of scale, high scalability of IT investment, and minimisation of management cost. Big data that contains data from all ISF organisations can be analysed to produce accurate decision-making. QR code can be used for ZISWAF payment. Lastly, digital platform improved communication among donors, partners, and beneficiaries.

13.3 Sharia Economic Inclusion: The Role of Islamic Monetary Economics

Fundamentally, the implications of Islamic principles that absolutely forbid *riba* (interest) and *maysir* (gambling/speculation) serve to optimise resource allocation. The absence of *riba* and *maysir* nurtures financial intermediation in the financial sector, thereby supporting activity in the productive sectors as the real sectors of the economy. Financial intermediation through Islamic financial institutions, typically dominated by Islamic finance, can now apply sales and purchase contracts or investment (profit-sharing) contracts. The exclusion of *riba*, therefore, promotes close linkages between the financial sector and the real sector, where financial intermediation perpetually leads to the creation of goods and services in the real sector. Consequently, through the prohibition of *riba*, the Islamic economy encourages the optimisation of community involvement and economic participation. This represents the inclusiveness of the sharia economic system from an Islamic finance perspective. Once again, Islamic economic inclusion naturally exists in the system due to sharia principles that prohibit *riba*.

Such conditions depict the private commercial financial sector from an Islamic perspective. Meanwhile, private Islamic commercial financial intermediation activities are also supported by the presence of a competent authority, responsible for providing various instruments to facilitate financial activity, including instruments for liquidity management in financial institutions and policy instruments issued by the relevant authorities. In fact, alternative instruments of Islamic finance are currently being developed, such as Government Sharia Securities (SBSN), known as government sukuk. The underlying assets of government sukuk are infrastructure projects initiated by the state, including airports, toll roads, ports, and other similar projects, demonstrating that government sukuk are a viable financial instrument in the government sector with close linkages to productive economic activity. In theory, government sukuk can also be utilised as a policy instrument, offering a practical alternative when the private commercial financial sector experiences intermediation constraints to the real sector as a result of specific conditions. Government sukuk, therefore, provide an alternative channel to circulate liquidity to productive economic sectors, thus balancing supply with demand to maintain price stability. In general, the application of Islamic finance, in the private and public sectors, aims to support productive economic activity in the real sector.

Sharia values and principles towards money also strengthen Islamic economic inclusion in the financial sector. From an Islamic perspective, money is regarded as a medium of exchange rather than an asset that can be traded, such as in the conventional financial system where money is traded using interest as the price of that money. This also has implications for the absolute prohibition of *riba* and *maysir* in the Islamic economy. In accordance with sharia principles, therefore, the total stock of money in the economy will not increase excessively beyond additional productivity (creating economic value added in the form of goods and services) in the economy. Moreover, sharia principles tend to rein in the excessive printing of money by the competent authority. In theory, sharia principles tend to balance the amount of money in circulation with the amount of goods and services created, where the relevant authorities balance the creation of money with the addition of goods and services produced in the economy.

With the characteristics of Islamic finance outlined above, economic inclusion from an Islamic perspective is also evident in the monetary system or in the discipline of Islamic monetary economics. By optimising financial intermediation, the prohibition of *riba* and *maysir* unlocks more economic participation opportunities in the community. The absence of *riba* and *maysir* ensures that the Islamic monetary sector cannot decouple from the real sector. Consequently, financial activities that generate profit must have underlying transactions in the real sector. Echoing those sentiments, the prohibition of *riba* and *maysir* in Islamic finance moulds the characteristics of the sharia economy as an inclusive economy.

The role of the monetary system based on sharia principles is critical, especially in light of modern economic practices. Contemporary economic activity has become complex, compelling economic players to depend not only on private sector actors but also on the government and authorities. In the financial sector, it is the function of the competent authority to establish a monetary system that can direct orderly financial activities. From an Islamic perspective, the monetary system is not merely implemented to attain the overarching policy objectives; the health and equity of the system are also important metrics. Not only is knowledge of Islamic economic principles and theories required, but also the full support of the relevant institutions and regulators in order to achieve an effective, robust, and equitable monetary system. The application of the current monetary system can be evaluated based on the following aspects.

The alignment of conventional principles and Islamic principles, or even transformational principles, must be facilitated not only on an individual level but also collectively, accompanied by institutional transformation. Monetary institutions and authorities are expected to create regulatory and policy frameworks for the holistic application of Islamic values in the monetary system. The Islamic community and institutions have mutually supporting roles to create a climate and practices conducive to implementing a monetary system in accordance with Islamic principles. Institutions must formulate rules and regulations to ensure implementation within a corridor of Islamic values. In addition, institutions are also tasked with developing infrastructure for the implementation of their regulations. On the other hand, the role of the community certainly supports the institutional measures. The rules set by the authorities are futile if not applied and obeyed by the community. Moreover, the community must be able to maintain and make best use of the infrastructure that has been developed. Notwithstanding, the first step of this journey entails that both the community and relevant institutions must fully comprehend the urgency of implementing Islamic values and principles in the monetary system.

The next aspect that must be explored is the pervasive nature of interest rates in all forms of business capital. Interest rates undoubtedly guarantee an amount of profit received by the lender even though neither party can ascertain beforehand whether the capital will generate a profit or incur a loss. If a loss is incurred at the end of the period, however, inequality and injustice have been created because only the lender will receive a profit regardless of the hardship or losses suffered by the borrower. On the other hand, all losses are borne in their entirety by the borrower, who is still obligated to continue repaying the principal plus interest. Such conditions are unjust and inequitable as the lender, who already enjoys a superior economic position to the borrower, still receives additional profit irrespective of the outcome. Consequently, the rich get richer and the poor get poorer.

Ultimately, the role of the authority is to maintain stability in the value of money. Based on the contemporary monetary system, however, it is difficult to stabilise interest rates without adjusting the money supply and it is difficult to control the money supply without the support of setting interest rates. In Islam, there is no interest rate system, so price stability can be maintained because growth in the money supply is linked to consistent growth in the real sector. Consequently, inclusive welfare can be achieved in real terms.

The uninhibited creation (printing) of money beyond the needs of the real sector is a major cause of economic imbalances—imbalances because the amount of money in the monetary sector is incongruent with real sector requirements and imbalances due to the concentration of wealth in the hands of a few. Islamic economic principles, therefore, can overcome such problems associated with inequality. Furthermore, sharia principles facilitate wealth-income distribution in the community to ensure the basic needs are met.

The application of Islamic principles in the monetary system will precipitate a range of favourable effects. *First*, the total money supply will return to its natural state, only increasing in response to a tangible need for money in the real sector. *Second*, excessive or superfluous demand for money can be avoided because such characteristics are undesirable in Islam. *Third*, price instability triggered by the application of interest rates can be eliminated. *Finally*, and most importantly, the equitable distribution of wealth and income can be achieved.

In addition to the monetary authority, government support is also required. The government must participate in synergised policymaking and ensure policies do not conflict with Islamic principles. The goals and practices of government policy must be formulated in such a way to not conflict with Islamic values. The comprehensive inculcation of Islamic values can be achieved in a country if all stakeholders are aligned in their policy goals and objectives. This is also consistent with the inexorable fact and expectation that rapid growth and development of the Islamic economy and finance offers a solution for economic empowerment of the wider community, in turn fostering economic growth. Synergy between the government, central bank, and other relevant national and local authorities is required, therefore, to achieve the overall national development goals.

Additionally, the absence of interest rates will have an indirect impact on the spending behaviour associated with fiscal policy. Fiscal policy plays a strategic role in supporting economic activity in the real sector through the main policy instruments, namely taxes and management of state expenditures. Government spending intends to provide public facilities and infrastructure as well as other social programmes that support welfare in the community. The absence of interest-bearing financing, therefore, will increase government discipline in terms of managing expenditures to avoid a reliance on sources of finance. Furthermore, project implementation will be more controlled as projects without a significant social impact on community welfare can be ruled out immediately. Conversely, a focus on government projects that significantly ameliorate socio-economic welfare will also have a strong social impact by optimising government debt management.

Growing awareness that the current monetary system is the root cause of financial instability and crises that have shaken the very core of the financial system in both developed and developing economies has revived discourse concerning the application of a gold standard, as implemented under the Bretton Woods system of monetary management in 1944 but unilaterally terminated by the United States in the early 1970s. Economists have stated that successful implementation of the gold standard in the past was supported by a simpler financial system compared with the complexities of today, coupled with innovative economic activities. Furthermore, the contemporary economic and financial system relies on interest rates and *maysir* (speculation), thus rendering the reintroduction of gold money an even greater challenge.

Islamic monetary economics has developed a mechanism that compels the financial sector to avoid the accumulation or hoarding of money while ensuring an orderly flow of money as business capital to optimise the real sector. The prohibition of *riba* (interest rates) and *maysir* (speculation) is the main pillar of Islamic monetary and financial activity. By prohibiting *riba* and *maysir*, the primary objective of the financial sector shifts away from money creation, instead supporting activity in the real sector. Money is not a commodity to be traded. Al-Ghazali stated that money reflects the value of goods and services transacted with that amount of money. In the absence of *riba* and *maysir*, the reasons for holding money are limited to the transaction motive and the precautionary motive. According to Islamic principles, money cannot be held for the speculative motive.

In the absence of *riba* and *maysir*, the only profit-generating activities are transactions in the real sector. If an owner of funds, irrespective of reason, cannot generate income directly in the real sector, investing through an investment manager in real sector businesses provides an alternative opportunity. The proceeds of the investment are subsequently distributed to all parties involved based on a mutually agreed ratio. Underlying assets, therefore, from financial transactions in Islamic financial institutions are required. Underlying assets reflect the value added in the economy. Accordingly, changes in the financial sector depend on the real sector and the financial sector cannot grow without commensurate growth in the real sector.

With increasing economies of scale, economic players, and the complexity of economic activity, the financial intermediation function is essential to serve the investment needs of fund owners and the business capital needs of entrepreneurs. This function must be implemented by financial institutions effectively and maximally. Suboptimal mechanisms in financial institutions result in stagnant flows of money, leading to inflation caused by imbalances between production (supply) and consumption (demand) in the economy.

Fundamentally, the Islamic monetary sector is a catalyst of the financial sector in terms of facilitating the flow of resources. *Economic resources*, including money, as a lubricant and catalyst of economic activity, the *monetary authority* that determines monetary policy and the requisite instruments, and *financial institutions* must cooperate and coordinate in synergy to foster full employment in the real sector. Such conditions can overcome the issues associated with unemployment, currency instability, and suboptimal economic growth. With the characteristics of Islamic finance functioning to support the real sector, Islamic monetary instruments are accommodative in terms of achieving price stability and economic growth. At their core, Islamic monetary policy instruments provide a channel for excess money in the financial sector to flow to the real sector. Such Islamic monetary instruments ensure the efficient use of resources (full employment) and avoid idle funds.

The global economy and national economies around the world are currently facing massively complex challenges. The deleterious impact of the coronavirus disease (COVID-19) pandemic has not only claimed untold lives but also wreaked havoc on global, regional, and national economic performance. Consequently, the world economy, including Indonesia, faces extraordinary threats posed by economic, financial, health, and humanitarian crises, with rising poverty and unemployment. Interrelated health and economic crises have forced unprecedented constraints on authorities in every jurisdiction. Resolving the health crisis will require economic strength and, vice versa, resolving the economic crisis will require an expeditious end to the health crisis. Such an inauspicious outlook demands planned, measured, and integrated handling.

In general, the COVID-19 pandemic has accelerated existing international trends, including diminishing globalisation or deglobalisation. Brexit, as the name given to the United Kingdom's departure from the European Union, and the protracted trade war between the United States and China compelled various countries, particularly advanced economies, to implement inward-looking policies. Such conditions have eroded globalisation, a process that was expected to benefit all countries by increasing world trade volume and global economic interaction. The COVID-19 pandemic, which has forced many countries to isolate, or lock down, to break the domestic chain of transmission, will certainly reinforce the current deglobalisation trend.

In response to current conditions, efforts to identify and explore new sources of economic growth have become an important strategy for the Indonesian economy. Rapid growth of the Islamic economy and finance represents a potential new source of economic growth for Indonesia. As the most populous Muslim nation globally, this represents Indonesia's main capital to establish a more significant role for the Islamic economy and finance sector in the national economy.

Challenges and Opportunities

Development of the Islamic monetary economy moving forward faces a number of challenges as follows:

(a) The dominance of conventional economics and finance, coupled with a lack of well-established Islamic economics and finance, means that conventional economics is often used as a benchmark for the application of an Islamic monetary system. Likewise, the understanding and expertise of human resources serving in the monetary authorities of various countries is not fully anchored to Islamic economics, thus undermining the formulation and development of optimal Islamic monetary policy. For example, interest rates remain the primary benchmark for determining the prices of financial products and monetary instruments. Corresponding benchmarks for price setting in accordance with Islamic principles are not available. Consequently, the pricing of Islamic financial products and monetary instruments is still influenced by interest rates. Such tendencies are reinforced by pervasive public logic based on interest rates.

(b) Conventional and Islamic monetary policy implemented under the roof of one authority in a dual system demands harmony and alignment in terms of the policy direction and objectives, yet the principles, concepts, theories, and application of the two can be quite different. This is the biggest challenge for the authorities in terms of formulating the most optimal policies to achieve the target of stability in the value of money and economic growth. Meanwhile, the dominance of conventional finance over Islamic finance implies a trade-off between Islamic and conventional monetary policies. A dual monetary system regime, where the monetary authority applies conventional and Islamic principles in the monetary system, often creates a policy dilemma when determining what measures must be taken. The application of a dual monetary system must be optimised, therefore, to maintain balance and harmony between Islamic and conventional monetary systems.

(c) The dominance of conventional financial practices in the community prevents Islamic finance from appearing authentic in accordance with ideal Islamic principles. The public remain unfamiliar with Islamic finance. Education and socialisation activities targeting segments of the public concerning the urgent need to apply an Islamic monetary system are crucial. The successful application of an Islamic monetary system rests on public enthusiasm.

(d) US dollar dominance at the international level remains a challenge for the implementation of an Islamic monetary system. Since the end of the Second World War, the United States has remained a global superpower with significant influence on the world economy. The challenge, therefore, is how to mobilise a global lobby advocating the reintroduction of gold and silver currencies for international transactions. On the other hand, innovative change is required to bolster the level of security when holding gold coins and ensure greater convenience when using gold as a medium of exchange.

Meanwhile, there are a number of opportunities to be exploited for the development of an Islamic monetary economy as follows:

(a) Despite a generally low level of public literacy concerning Islamic finance, public interest in financial practices free from *riba* and *maysir* continues to grow in line with the spirit of community faith. The emergence of learning and research centres for Islamic economics and finance at various universities is helping industry players and regulators build knowledge and awareness. This will also serve to enhance the quality of human resources in the Islamic finance and monetary sectors.

(b) Existing legal and regulatory aspects (though not maximised) provide sufficient space for the development of sharia monetary and finance applications, such as the emergence of Islamic financial products and monetary instruments that can represent ideal Islamic finance and monetary practices. For example, Indonesia is currently developing the concept of indexing real sector returns as a reference for industry players to set prices for their financial products. For regulators in the near term, real sector return indexes can function as a reference for monetary policy instruments to replace interest rates.

(c) Technological development offers new opportunities to develop and use gold money. Gold money can be converted into electronic money, such as e-dinar and e-gold. In addition, educational, socialisation, and promotional activities regarding the application of gold money are possible through technological advancements. The rapid proliferation of online transactions via e-commerce platforms represents another opportunity to advance gold money as a medium of exchange. Classic gold money could be converted into electronic form, such as e-dinar and e-gold. In addition, the emergence of e-commerce has led to borderless transactions, obviating spatial and time restrictions that can impede the transaction process.

(d) Economic decline and other structural issues that continue to plague the most developed and advanced economies, including the United States, Europe, and Japan, have spurred various studies into the root of the problem. From such studies has emerged the idea of returning to a monetary system based on Islamic principles as a potential solution to the economic woes. Current discussions include the role of a universal currency to support the growing trend of international transactions. Gold has the largest potential of becoming a single currency because gold is recognised universally.

Therefore, various integrated efforts to support Islamic monetary system development through scientific exploration are required. Importantly, monetary authorities must formulate Islamic monetary policies and instruments that can function optimally in a dual financial system environment. Expanding insight and knowledge of the Islamic financial and monetary system in an ideal, comprehensive, and holistic way will help to determine the most appropriate Islamic monetary development strategy. Development of the Islamic economic and financial system in Indonesia, including the Islamic monetary economy, is expected to provide a viable alternative to the conventional monetary and economic system currently applied because the Islamic system offers a superior arrangement to improve public welfare (Juhro et al., 2019). Application of an Islamic economic system that priorisies *maqashid shariah* will achieve the overarching goal of the Islamic economy, namely inclusive welfare and socio-economic justice for all (*falah*) within a corridor that is in accordance with Islamic law. By applying Islamic values, mankind will find happiness in the economy in this world and the next.

The Islamic economic system has three comprehensive and complete sectors, namely the private sector, public sector, and social sector. In the private sector is the interaction of the real sector and financial sector, reflected by trade and investment, which must be conducted in accordance with sharia-compliant contracts. The public, or government, sector acts as the regulator and executor in managing the government budget in accordance with government instruments. Finally, the social sector is a special sector in the Islamic economy, where voluntary community social activities can occur with government assistance to help meet the needs of the community. Social sector instruments are also voluntary, including *infaq*, *sadaqah*, and *waqf*.

The social sector is an important component of the economic system because it can facilitate the equitable distribution of wealth and income.

The sectors that make up the Islamic economic system are appropriate to the needs of each economic class in society. The public sector, with *zakat*, and the social sector, with *infaq, sadaqah,* and *waqf*, play a crucial role in raising the standard of living of those languishing at the bottom of the pyramid, who desperately need "free" financial assistance without the obligation to pay back. As this group levels up to the lower-middle class, microfinance products are available to manage funds within micro or small enterprises. For the middle class, access to bank finance is possible by meeting creditworthiness requirements, while the upper-middle and upper classes serve as investors.

13.4 Emerging Issues in the Modern Monetary System

The modern monetary system has matured and become complex. The need for monetary management that can create a robust and resilient financial system based on the experiences and lessons learned from numerous financial crises raises various issues in terms of monetary system implementation. In addition, issues in the monetary sector are developing with rapidity, influenced by the relentless advancement of digital technology, particularly in the use of money, including digital currency and cryptocurrency. Some of the emerging issues relating to the use of such currency in the monetary system are as follows:

1. *Opportunity to Use Gold as a Global Currency*

   Growing awareness that the current monetary system is the root cause of instability and financial crises that have rocked the financial system in both developed and advanced economies has revived discourse concerning the application of a gold standard, as implemented under the Bretton Woods system of monetary management in 1944 but unilaterally terminated by the United States in the early 1970s. Economists have stated that successful implementation of the gold standard in the past was supported by a simpler financial system compared with the complexities of today, coupled with innovative economic activities. Furthermore, the contemporary economic and financial system relies on interest rates and *maysir* (speculation), thus rendering the reintroduction of gold money an even greater challenge.

   One of the difficulties using gold as currency is the limited availability of gold as a raw material, coupled with the total reform needed of the financial system in terms of regulation, structure, and operations. The constraints faced in the application of a gold standard are sufficiently complex, both systemically and situationally (Diwany, 2002; Meera & Aziz, 2002; Vadillo, 2002). The difficulties and constraints faced in returning to a gold standard as a currency and medium of exchange in the economy have led to the application of gold merely as a benchmark for the price of various financial portfolios. Moreover, in times of economic distress and uncertainty, many investors diversify and rebalance their portfolios towards safe-haven assets, such as gold, which is why gold is commonly used as a backup asset. Beyond its status as a safe-haven asset, gold prices also do not tend to decline in the medium-long term.

Reinstating gold as currency for all transactions is not impossible but only if decided and enacted by the regulator. In addition, the government would be responsible for ensuring whether other countries would reciprocate and receive payments in gold. In general, the acceptance and approval of other countries would be needed in accordance with Islamic law. Cooperation between all countries, particularly Muslim majority countries, would be critical, therefore, to establish a single currency for international trade. The most important first step would be for Muslim countries to unite through serious discussions to realise such a mechanism.

In terms of the discourse outlined above, a more pertinent and contextual question would be to ask what the opportunities are for the dinar and dirham as global currencies. Sharia law is absolute, as revealed by Allah SWT. The truth of His law is inevitable and indubitable. Sharia law does not need to adapt to the current human condition. On the contrary, humans are still subject to and bound by the laws stipulated in Islam under any and all conditions, including sharia law in the economy.

In economics, particularly the monetary branch, fiat money as used today is not fully in accordance with Islamic teachings. The existence of fiat money and exchange rates between currencies in different jurisdictions creates inequality in the value of money between countries, including the US dollar, as the dominant international trade currency. The United States endeavours to maintain US dollar dominance and rejects the use of other global currencies, such as the dinar and dirham. According to Vadillo (2002), even the International Monetary Fund (IMF) supports the continued use of US dollars and avoids the reintroduction of gold currency.

Dinar and dirham are viable global currencies. Between Indonesia and Russia, the dinar is the same, providing unequivocal reliability. Furthermore, the value of the dinar and dirham tends to be stable, as reflected in the price of a chicken at the time of Rasulullah SAW until now, both costing 1 dirham.

The market value of dinar and dirham is in accordance with the intrinsic value. By using dinar and dirham, money creation and lending could not function as freely as in the conventional system. The current economic system supports the application of a speculative economic system, creating a bubble economy. This is clearly evident by the fact that gross national product (GNP) is accelerating but the income gap is growing because financial sector transactions are not commensurate with real sector transactions. In contrast, the application of gold and silver currency is related directly to the real sector, thus reducing speculative actions and safeguarding monetary stability.

2. *Role of Electronic and Digital Money*

In line with rapid and broad-based technological development, economic transactions have also experienced significant evolution, including the types of money now available as a medium of exchange for economic transactions. Fiat money is evolving into electronic money (e-money), while technology and knowledge have been used to create cryptocurrency. Such innovations have simplified economic transactions and enhanced efficiency. Keeping up with modern advances, central banks are developing central bank digital currency (CBDC).

Based on Islamic teachings, Muslims must not merely focus on the innovation side, which is generally associated with greater efficiency and outcomes, but also pay attention to the compatibility with Islamic principles. Not all innovations are created in accordance with Islamic values and principles. As Muslims, we should not take innovation for granted; we must seek the truth (*tabayyun*) in line with Islamic principles. Innovation that is achieved in accordance with the principles and values of Islam is justifiable, but if found to contain any elements proscribed by sharia law, it must be avoided. Rigorous studies are required, therefore, into current development trends and innovations in terms of money.

Electronic Money (e-Money)

The rapid advancement of modern technology has accelerated all aspects of our mutually interconnected existence. Technology has also permeated economic transactions, such as through electronic commerce (e-commerce) transactions via online platforms. The emergence and proliferation of e-commerce has dramatically increased the urgency for electronic means of payment, such as e-banking, m-banking, and e-money. E-banking and m-banking are fairly recent banking industry innovations that provide convenient customer access to the banking system to check account balances, transfer funds, pay bills, and so on. Discussions concerning innovation in terms of money should thus focus on electronic money.

According to Bank Indonesia, electronic money is defined as a payment instrument that meets the following criteria: *issued based on the value of money paid in advance to an issuer, the value of money is stored electronically on a server or chip, used as a payment instrument to a merchant that is not the issuer of the electronic money, and the value of electronic money managed by an issuer is not defined as a deposit in accordance with laws regulating the banking industry*. In summary, electronic money is a payment instrument, the value of which is paid in advance to an issuer to be stored on a chip-based electronic medium.

Fundamentally, electronic money is similar to fiat money commonly used by the public, which has just been converted into digital form. Electronic money can be stored on certain media (such as a chip-based card) or in a payment system account. For example, card-based electronic money includes BNI Tapcash, BCA Flazz, and the Indonesian commuter train multi-trip card. On the other hand, electronic money that is stored in a payment system account includes GoPay, OVO, and so on. In conclusion, e-money is also known as a digital wallet.

Ownership of electronic money starts with the holder who exchanges cash for e-money with electronic money issuers. The issuer provides electronic money to the holder with an account balance commensurate to the cash exchanged. The holder can then use the electronic money as a means of payment at cooperating merchants. The electronic money balance is automatically debited for every transaction made. Furthermore, the holder can top up the electronic money balance at any time.

The discussion on electronic money from an Islamic perspective can begin with the benefits (*maslahah*) felt by the users of electronic money. If there is no *maslahah*, it is not in line with Islamic principles. In general, technological advancement can increase transaction efficiency from various perspectives. The time required to complete transactions is more efficient. Cash transactions are more time-consuming because the cash must be counted along with the change. Electronic money payments are faster because the balance is automatically debited according to the amount to be paid. This can drastically reduce queueing for cash payments on toll roads or at retail outlets.

Transactions using electronic money can also simplify the transaction process through the integration of agents, cards, applications, websites, and systems accessible online. Users are no longer required, therefore, to visit a bank branch. In addition, electronic money can heighten the sense of security and convenience by obviating the need to carry large sums of cash. Users can mobilise electronic money worry free, even when large sums are involved. Finally, electronic money transactions can minimise calculation errors that typically occur when using cash while avoiding the need to calculate or give change.

Additionally, whether electronic money is halal must also be discussed. According to Muamar and Alparisi (2017), the concept of electronic money is in accordance with the concept of money in Islam. This is indicated by the reliability of electronic money as a medium of exchange and unit of account in economic transactions. In addition, the use of electronic money can rein in excessive spending due to the maximum limits imposed on transactions and balances. Consequently, electronic money users are discouraged from excessive transactions and consumption while reducing losses from the misuse of electronic money.

In terms of security, electronic money offers different levels of security and protection based on the type. Registered electronic money is protected by a stringent security system, using biometric data, such as fingerprints and retinal scans, or a personal identification number (PIN) to obtain access. Such tight security helps to minimise theft, loss, and other misuse. On the other hand, unregistered electronic money does not employ the same level of security in the form of biometric data or a PIN, exposing it to misuse by a third party. Consequently, unregistered electronic money does meet the prerequisite security standards for use as money.

It is important to note that electronic money does not contain any element of *riba*. The amount of cash converted into electronic money is always of the same value, thus avoiding *riba fadhl*. In addition, the exchange of cash for electronic money is simultaneous, thus avoiding *riba nasiah*.

It can be concluded, therefore, that electronic money complies with Islamic principles, as evidenced by the absence of elements that are forbidden in Islam when using electronic money. On the other hand, electronic money can bring many benefits (*maslahah*) to human life. Certain aspects of the electronic money mechanism require further refinement, however, especially unregistered electronic money.

The level of security when using unregistered electronic money must be improved, for example by adding a password or PIN to obtain access.

Cryptocurrency

In contrast to e-money that is issued on a server or chip basis, cryptocurrency is digital money created by applying encryption techniques and cryptography (Bakar et al., 2017).[1] Cryptocurrencies do not have any real physical form and are not backed by real assets. This type of currency, therefore, has no intrinsic value. Cryptocurrencies are created and issued by private parties. Unlike fiat money, cryptocurrencies are not regulated or supervised by any government or central bank. Thus far, cryptocurrency has not been recognised by the central bank as a currency or legal tender.

Lacking central bank supervision, there are no specialised institutions to guarantee cryptocurrency, leading to uncertainty and potentially high risk. The advantage of cryptocurrency, however, is that it is difficult to counterfeit due to cryptography, unlike banknotes. This is also because cryptocurrency can only be created by solving complex mathematical problems, the value of which is stored digitally.

The price of cryptocurrency is determined based on an algorithm using blockchain technology to store the dataset. This data is calculated using complex algorithmic techniques, and it is this mechanism that forms the value of the cryptocurrency when it is first issued. The subsequent price is determined based on interaction between demand and supply. Cryptocurrency is a new component of sophisticated technology in economics and finance. This currency highlights the advantages of transaction cost efficiency resulting from technological innovation. In addition, the use of cryptocurrency can mitigate the risks associated with a single point of failure.

Notwithstanding, the absence of centralised supervision or oversight and the continued use of cryptocurrency will destabilise the value of money, even posing a threat to finance and banking. The position of cryptocurrency is strengthened by the fact that transactions are purely peer-to-peer, without approval required from an external source or third party. If performance continues to flourish, it is not beyond the realm of possibility to see government-issued fiat money usurped by cryptocurrency.

3. *Cryptocurrency: An Islamic Perspective*

   How Islam views the practice of cryptocurrency is an interesting topic. Cryptocurrency uses cryptographic technology and algorithms in a blockchain system, thus providing various advantages, such as security, long-term storability, complexity (difficult to counterfeit), and efficiency. To become

[1] Encryption techniques are used to manage currency units and verify the transactions. Meanwhile, cryptography is applied to limit the creation of cryptocurrency and provide system security when transacting. In addition, cryptocurrency is created through mining, namely using sophisticated hardware that solves extremely complex computational math problems. Each unit of cryptocurrency is mined based on a different computational math problem (Meera, 2018).

money, however, the following characteristics are preferable, stability, security, and effectiveness. Rigorous studies are required to ascertain whether cryptocurrency is compatible with the characteristics of money from an Islamic perspective. The following discussion is oriented towards the existence of cryptocurrency as a fair representation of cryptocurrencies in general, considering that cryptocurrency maintains a dominant market share among all cryptocurrencies.

Broadly speaking, Islam does not recommend the use of cryptocurrency given its lack of intrinsic value and backing by a reserve of real underlying assets. The intrinsic value or reserve of real assets fundamentally serves to maintain a balance between money creation and the increase of goods and services created in the economy. A device or mechanism that can maintain a balance between the creation of money and additional goods and services in the economy is important. Cryptocurrencies, however, do not employ a mechanism to control creation, stoking fears of disrupting currency stability and the financial system as a whole. Concerns also stem from the lack of regulation and supervision by the competent authority. Cryptocurrency creation is independent from prevailing monetary policy and national economic conditions, which could have a significantly adverse impact on the economy as a whole.

The criteria used for robust and reliable money must be reviewed to analyse the suitability of cryptocurrency in accordance with Islamic principles. In addition, elements forbidden in Islam must also be reviewed, namely the use of *riba*, *maysir,* and *gharar*. If cryptocurrencies are found to contain at least one of the proscribed elements, the use of cryptocurrency would be haram from an Islamic perspective. According to Meera (2018), money must have the following characteristics to carry out its role effectively and efficiently: (1) acceptability, (2) durability, (3) portability, (4) divisibility, (5) uniformity, (6) stability, and (7) limited availability.

Cryptocurrency is created through cryptography and encryption techniques to solve complex mathematical problems, known as mining. Cryptocurrency does not have a tangible physical form and is not backed by real assets. In addition, cryptocurrency has no intrinsic value because it is created using technology. Consequently, cryptocurrency does not even meet the first criterion above.

Cryptocurrency is stored in a system that is secure enough to maintain the durability and protect against counterfeiting. Cryptocurrency cannot be counterfeited; the only way to acquire cryptocurrency is through purchases and mining. In terms of this criterion, cryptocurrency is superior due to its lack of physical form, thereby meeting the second characteristic above. In terms of the third characteristic, cryptocurrency is highly portable and easily mobilised. Cryptocurrency has no physical form and, therefore, can be transported easily while requiring no physical space for storage. By simply having an account, cryptocurrency users can access their cryptocurrency from anywhere and at any time. Given its electronic form, cryptocurrency also enjoys uniformity in terms of the value of each unit and is easily divisible into smaller values for transaction purposes, thus meeting the fourth and fifth criteria above. On the other hand, cryptocurrency is very volatile, as reflected by the dramatic increase in value towards the end of 2017. Cryptocurrency instability stems from the absence of real underlying assets, exposing the currency to interaction between demand and supply. Consequently, cryptocurrency fails to meet the sixth criterion. Cryptocurrency is not easily obtained, with enthusiasts compelled to purchase cryptocurrency or mine cryptocurrency using powerful computers to solve complex mathematical problems. Cryptocurrency, therefore, satisfies the seventh characteristic of currency.

It can be concluded, therefore, that cryptocurrency fails to meet some of the criteria to be considered as a currency. The criteria not met by cryptocurrency are critical, however, thus bringing about a negative impact on the economy. A medium of exchange that has no intrinsic value creates a bubble economy and illusory economic growth. The purchasing power of a currency with no intrinsic value does not reflect the actual purchasing power of that currency, such as bitcoin. In addition, cryptocurrency is highly volatile, thus impacting the economy through uncertainty caused by price fluctuations affecting goods and services, possibly leading to inflation. Moreover, the complete absence of government oversight and regulation would lead to greater price uncertainty if cryptocurrency were used as a medium of exchange. Based on the aforementioned criteria of money, therefore, cryptocurrency is not in accordance with Islamic principles.

The use of cryptocurrency must also be explored in terms of whether the cryptocurrency contains elements of *riba*, *maysir,* and *gharar*. Concerning whether cryptocurrency contains *riba*, certain currencies are exchanged for cryptocurrency of commensurate value and in cash, with no deferred payment on either side. This indicates that cryptocurrency does not contain *riba*, providing currencies and cryptocurrency are exchanged of commensurate value and in cash.

Though cryptocurrency has been shown to not contain elements of *riba*, the application of cryptocurrency is not necessarily in line with Islamic teachings due to the potential elements of *maysir* and *gharar*. *Maysir* entails gambling and speculative activities, thus justifying an advantage for one of the transacting parties to the detriment of the other. In terms of using cryptocurrency, high volatility encourages *maysir* (speculation) due to fluctuations in the value of the cryptocurrency, with speculators poised to take advantage.

In addition to probably containing elements of *maysir*, cryptocurrency is also at risk of *gharar* (uncertainty). Uncertainty is an inherent characteristic of cryptocurrency according to Bakar and Rosbi. The inventor and creator of cryptocurrency is unknown. No regulator supervises or regulates the technical implementation of cryptocurrency. Where cryptocurrency comes from and what is behind it are replete with uncertainty. Similarly, there is no central competent authority to control, supervise, and confirm each transaction using cryptocurrency, making it harder to track and investigate cases of fraud or system errors. The mechanisms to create and use cryptocurrency are Internet-

and technology-based, which are vulnerable to hacking risk. Furthermore, the ability of hackers is increasing over time in line with technological advancement and sophistication, coupled with the lack of a central authority and oversight.

Lacking any physical form, cryptocurrency is only stored in a system. This shows that cryptocurrency also has no intrinsic value. Cryptocurrency is created by humans using sophisticated technology to mine the cryptocurrency by solving complex mathematical problems. In fact, cryptocurrency has not been recognised as legal tender or certified as an official medium of exchange, and cryptocurrency is not backed by real assets, such as gold. From an economic perspective, the status of cryptocurrency is ambiguous, whether it can be used as money or an asset, thereby containing elements of uncertainty. In addition, cryptocurrency is very unstable, with the value rising and falling dramatically. At the end of 2017, for example, the value of cryptocurrency skyrocketed 2000%. From an Islamic economic perspective, a currency that lacks stability is not suitable for use as a medium of exchange because unstable exchange rates are the root cause of various other economic issues. On the other hand, cryptocurrency users are anonymous, making it difficult to trace their identity in the event of unusual or suspicious transactions, which could endanger other parties. Such conditions evidence the ambiguity and uncertainty inherent to cryptocurrency.

Depending on the exchange transaction, the discussion above shows that cryptocurrency can be used without containing any elements of *riba*. Notwithstanding, *maysir* and especially *gharar* are intrinsic to cryptocurrency use. Consequently, cryptocurrency as a medium of exchange and currency is contrary to the principles and values contained in Islamic teachings. This argument was reinforced by Bakar et al. (2017), stating that cryptocurrency is not suitable for use as money due to the lack of intrinsic value, anonymous ownership and issuer, and instability of value. Furthermore, cryptocurrencies are issued without underlying real assets.

Islamic Cryptocurrency

The use of conventional cryptocurrencies, as described above, seems incompatible with sharia law. By changing several of the mechanisms, however, it may be possible to implement a cryptocurrency in accordance with Islamic principles. Not all mechanisms of conventional cryptocurrency violate Islamic principles. The use of cryptographic and blockchain technology are in line with Islamic teachings (Billah, 2019).

In general, Islamic cryptocurrencies could be applied after some changes in their mechanisms and operation are made. The changes include legal issuances, broadly accepted by the public, clear objectives, valid documents, official rules and frameworks, and operational mechanisms that are in accordance with Islamic principles. When Islamic principles are upheld, therefore, alternative Islamic cryptocurrencies become available. The blockchain mechanism, cryptographic technology, models, goals, operational functions, and all other activities relating to cryptocurrency must comply with Islamic rules and standards for use as an Islamic cryptocurrency, accompanied by the establishment of a legal regulator. An Islamic institution would be necessary to supervise and maintain sharia compliance concerning the use of an Islamic cryptocurrency. In addition, the overarching goal of implementing an Islamic cryptocurrency would have to be oriented towards achieving the welfare of all (*falah*) through the creation of a cryptocurrency platform based on the principles of cooperation and solidarity.

In addition to the main principles that must be built into the foundations of Islamic cryptocurrency, Billah (2019) put forward several principles that must be met in terms of cryptocurrency governance according to Islamic principles as follows: (1) all models used in Islamic cryptocurrency must be in accordance with sharia principles and standards, (2) all Islamic cryptocurrency operations using hybrid models must be in accordance with Islamic principles, (3) asset-backed and asset-based mechanisms of Islamic cryptocurrency must be within a sharia framework, (4) products and services must be based on underlying real assets with value, and (5) all Islamic cryptocurrency operations are accommodated by sharia-compliant contracts, such as *mudharabah*, *musyarakah*, *sharf*, *wadiah*, *wakalah*, and other contracts.

A number of products and services could be provided in the implementation of Islamic cryptocurrency. Halal cryptocurrency in the form of coins that have intrinsic value could be commercialised through a platform applying blockchain technology. The platform would facilitate international trade, as well as exchange and payment transactions using the coins. There are also services that could offer cashless payments through the issuance of cryptocurrency. This has become very important in today's society, where cashless transactions are usurping cash to become king. With such a service, in addition to being cashless, we can also become card-less. Meanwhile, there are many spaces or areas that could use Islamic cryptocurrency, such as *waqf* management, trading platforms, and corporate social responsibility (CSR) or charitable foundations established by companies that manage Islamic cryptocurrency. With the products and services that become available through the issuance of Islamic cryptocurrency, it is hoped that *maqashid syariah* will be maintained and inclusive welfare (*falah*) achieved. All products and services stemming from Islamic cryptocurrency must be backed by real assets. Such assets are in the form of an initial coin offering (Billah, 2019).

From the discussion above, cryptocurrency can be understood to have emerged as a prerequisite of development in the digital era and moving forwards. There is currently no standardised or legal operating system or mechanism, however, for cryptocurrency. Consequently, cryptocurrency requires further improvement in terms of management, regulation, and operation to align with Islamic values (Islamic cryptocurrency). Islamic cryptocurrency offers a solution in terms of applying technology to different forms and types of money without ignoring the principles and rules of Islamic teachings. The system, operations, code of ethics, and regulations of Islamic cryptocurrency, therefore, must remain in accordance with *maqashid syariah*.

Central Bank Digital Currency (CBDC)

Departing from cryptocurrency issued by private parties, central bank digital currency (CBDC) is a digital form of fiat money issued in accordance with the regulations of the monetary authority and prevailing laws. The concept of CBDC, also known as digital fiat currency, is being explored by central banks in several jurisdictions, including Canada, the United Kingdom, China, Switzerland, and Iran. In general, the authorities are applying a similar concept to digital currency, namely using distributed ledger technology (DLT).[2] What differentiates CBDC from other digital currencies is the issuer, with CBDC issued by the central bank. Moving forward, CBDC is expected to discharge the functions and roles of the existing fiat money as a medium of exchange, unit of account, and store of value. In addition, CBDC will enjoy status as legal tender.[3]

The CBDC concept has a number of advantages and benefits. One advantage of CBDC is increasing the accuracy and transparency of transaction recording using distributed ledger technology. Consequently, actual and accurate data and information will be available for optimal monetary policy formulation. According to Dyson and Hodgson, the central bank will reap the following positive impacts and benefits by issuing CBDC: (1) expanding the choice of monetary policy instruments to implement negative real interest rate policies, (2) enhancing financial system security using central bank money for transactions, (3) reducing liquidity risk in the payment system, and (4) supporting financial inclusion by expanding public access through companies providing digital cash accounts.

CBDC is also being developed with consideration to the implications for central banks, commercial banks, and payment systems. For central banks, the use of CBDCs could create a potential conflict of interest if the CBDC issued can also be deposited at the central bank given the central bank functions as supervisor and regulator. When CBDC becomes a perfect substitute for savings instruments and term deposits at commercial banks, a new monetary policy framework will be required that is quite different from the existing framework. In addition, CBDC could have positive implications for the monetary system by enhancing the effectiveness of low interest rate policies and economic efficiency. On the other hand, the role of commercial banks will be eroded in line with declining bank business. As CBDC converges with deposits and savings instruments in commercial banks, the

[2]Distributed ledger technology (DLT) refers to the technological infrastructure and protocols that allow simultaneous access, validation, and record updating in an immutable manner across all members in a network. Transactions between members, therefore, can be processed directly without the need for an intermediary, which has its own advantages, such as greater transaction cost efficiency and mitigating single point of failure (SPOF) risk. Notwithstanding, the technology also contains inherent weaknesses, including a protracted transaction process and potential fragmentation. After a transaction has occurred in the distributed ledger network, validation will simultaneously occur. A transaction cannot be changed once recorded and validated.

[3]China has become the first country to launch a digital currency (CNBC, 2019). The digital currency issued by China is the first digital currency issued officially by a central bank and could rival the US dollar, which remains the most dominant global currency. Other than China, several other central banks are also rumoured to be launching their own digital currencies.

possibility of commercial banks losing out to the central bank will become quite high. Customers will likely prefer to transact using accounts at the central bank due to the heightened security and lower risks compared with commercial banks. Consequently, a narrow banking system will emerge. In terms of the payment system, CBDC will reduce the risks associated with the centralised system, including credit risk, liquidity risk, and operational risk.

From the perspective of Islamic finance, CBDC has different implications than other digital currencies, including cryptocurrency. CBDC issued by a central bank will have an effective mechanism to regulate the money supply, which, based on sharia principles, must consider the additional creation of goods and services in the economy considering the main function of money is as a medium of exchange for goods and services. Money is not a commodity that can be bought or sold based on interest (*riba*) or speculation (*maysir*). In terms of Islamic finance, the seamless circulation of money is maintained as far as possible to avoid hoarding and idle funds, which would interfere with the allocation of resources and smooth production processes of the goods and services needed in the economy. As a digital currency, CBDC would certainly facilitate unimpeded circulation in transaction activities. In other words, (digital) technology will increase the velocity of money, in both commercial and social activities.

13.5 Linkages between Islamic Monetary Policy and Islamic Social-Public Finance

As explained in the previous section, the Islamic social-public finance sector and the Islamic monetary economy emphasise the inclusiveness of the sharia economy. There is a link, therefore, between the role of Islamic Monetary Policy and the role of Islamic Social Finance in terms of moulding the Islamic economy, particularly the equitable distribution of wealth, thereby significantly reducing inequality, ameliorating welfare, and expanding public participation in the economy. This relationship can be described in five dimensions as follows:

(a) *Spirit and Final Goal*

The mechanisms of Islamic monetary economics and Islamic social finance have a corresponding spiritual dimension, namely to maintain the faith of individuals and the community collectively. The focus, therefore, on the goal of maintaining an orderly flow of economic resources as well as the equitable distribution of wealth and income in the Islamic monetary sector and Islamic social finance essentially aims to provide the basic needs of Muslims and the community to fulfil their obligations to God (maintaining the faith). The goal of implementing an Islamic monetary economic system and Islamic social finance is to provide just and equitable distribution and facilitate the ultimate goal of effective policy. The full panoply of economic tools in the Islamic economic system function, therefore, to facilitate the distribution/circulation of economic resources for the benefit of all.

(b) *Regulatory Role*

In pursuit of this goal, the Islamic monetary sector and Islamic social finance require deep knowledge and understanding of Islamic economic principles and theories, with the full support and protection of the institutions and regulators. Similarly, poverty alleviation and equitable wealth distribution require a financial system as a regulatory conduit, with Islam, as a way of life, providing perfect guidance. Islam is a perfect and comprehensive guide covering every facet of life, including worship, social aspects, political aspects, and *muamalah*. In this case, the role of the government is necessary to establish institutions and regulations that support and grow Islamic monetary policy and Islamic social finance, which are expected to formulate regulations and frameworks for the overall application of Islamic values in both systems.

(c) *Public Participation*

Public participation is essential to ensure the policies and programmes formulated and implemented by the institutions and regulators are successful in supporting the ideal application of both financial systems. A preliminary step in implementing the two systems is comprehensive understanding regarding the urgency of applying Islamic values in both financial systems by the community and institutions. *Zakat* principles in the Islamic social-public finance sector, coupled with the absolute prohibition of *riba* and *maysir* in the Islamic monetary sector, will increase public participation in economic activities. Consequently, the economy is more dynamic, with higher transaction volume expected to foster prosperous economic growth. On the other hand, public participation is also a prerequisite for creating a sound and robust Islamic financial climate to optimise the equitable distribution of wealth.

(d) *System Balance and Economic Empowerment*

Economic inequality, the gap between rich and poor, is rising. This is due to economic imbalances caused by the unencumbered creation of money beyond real sector needs as well as imbalances precipitated by the concentration of wealth in the hands of a few. Seeking to overcome such gaps, the overarching role of the Islamic monetary economic system and Islamic social finance is fair and impartial distribution. In addition, both systems can accelerate the distribution of wealth between community groups while simultaneously meeting the social needs of the community. The Islamic monetary economic system and Islamic social finance also have a propitious impact on the economic system, including equitable wealth distribution and the money supply returning to its natural state, thus only increasing to meet the demand for money in the real sector. Furthermore, both Islamic financial systems can serve to increase economic empowerment in the wider community and revive economic growth, thus contributing to comprehensive national development with the support of synergy between the government, the central bank, and various relevant institutions centrally and regionally.

(e) *Optimising the Role of Money*

The Islamic monetary economic system and Islamic social finance could create a flourishing system that compels the financial sector to prevent the hoarding of wealth and ultimately facilitate the flow of money as business capital, thereby optimising the real sector. Fundamentally, the two financial systems (Islamic monetary economy and Islamic social finance) discharge their functions as drivers of the financial sector in terms of facilitating the flow of resources, including money. Money is an economic resource that functions as a medium of exchange to facilitate economic activity. Money in Islamic social finance and Islamic monetary economics helps to increase the velocity of wealth between humans (economic players). Money can be used to facilitate the unhindered flow of *zakat, infaq, sadaqah, waqf, jizyah, kharja*, etc. Furthermore, money can lubricate and accelerate economic activity in the private, social, and public sectors. If the Islamic monetary economic authority and Islamic social financial institutions can execute their policies in synergy with the corresponding instruments, they could simultaneously achieve full employment in the real sector.

Finite resources and the actualisation of the Islamic vision of *falah* and *hayatan thayyibatan* for every individual are two of the challenges faced by all Muslim countries. Such conditions encourage higher moral quality as well as brotherhood and socio-economic justice, which will remain but a fleeting illusion unless the finite resources can be brought to bear to alleviate poverty, provide basic necessities, and bridge the income gap. In fact, similar to other developing economies, most Muslim countries experience severe inequality, along with external imbalances and macro-economic hardships without progressing towards the realisation of their vision.

The material happiness of all individuals is impossible to achieve unless the available resources are used efficiently and equitably. Happiness, as it is now recognised, is a reflection of peace of mind or *an-nafs al-muthma'innah* in Al-Qur'an (al-Fajr:27), which cannot be achieved unless the individual is in harmony with inner peace. Happiness is only possible when the material and spiritual needs of the individual are satisfactorily met because material satisfaction and spiritual peace are mutually and inextricably linked, for which the fulfilment of both will only occur when the spiritual dimension is imbued into the material dimension to provide meaning and purpose.

A specific strategy is required, therefore, to facilitate the efficient and equitable allocation of finite resources according to the demands of *hayatan thayyibah*. Such a strategy is separate from the socially accepted filter mechanisms to distinguish the efficient and equitable use of resources. In addition, a system that motivates individuals to use resources in accordance with the filter mechanism requires socio-economic restructuring to enforce both components in their reallocation and distribution of resources, as demanded by *hayatan thayyibatan*.

In this regard, the financial system has a strategic role to play not only in the allocation and distribution of finite resources but also in terms of economic stability and growth. Consequently, financial institutions are also considered as national resources because the sources of finance available to financial institutions originate from deposits placed by a representative sample of the entire population, which must be used, therefore, for the welfare of society. Such financial resources are scarce, however, implying equitable utilisation and optimal efficiency.

To that end, the financial system also plays a major role by encouraging and facilitating the efficient allocation of financial resources and real resources for different purposes and targets. Islamic finance is a system that originated from Al-Quran and Sunnah, as well as the scholarly interpretations of the revelations. The aim is to provide halal financial services to the Muslim community while providing a tangible contribution to the achievement of Islamic socio-economic goals. The main goals also include economic welfare, job availability, robust and sustainable economic growth, socio-economic justice and equitable income distribution, reasonable wealth, stability in the value of money, and the mobilisation and investment of savings for economic development to offer profit sharing for the transacting parties and social security for the wider community. Through such ideas and strategic measures, underpinned by stronger brotherhood (*ukhuwah*), inclusive welfare can be maximised effectively.

References

Bakar, N. A., Rosbi, S., & Uzaki, K. (2017). Cryptocurrency framework diagnostics from Islamic finance perspective: A new insight of bitcoin system transaction. *International Journal of Management Science and Business Adinistration, 4*(1), 19–28.

Billah, M. M. (2019). *Islamic financial products: Principles, instruments, and structures*. Palgrave Macmillan.

CNBC. (2019). *CNBC Indonesia*. Dipetik November 19, 2019, dari CNBC Indonesia YouTube. https://youtu.be/OwwffUGK77w

Diwany, T. E. (2002). History of banking: An analysis. *International Conference on Stable and Just Global Monetary System* (pp. 1–33). Research Centre International Islamic University Malaysia.

Juhro, S. M., Syarifuddin, F., Sakti, A., & Suryanti, E. T. (2019). *Keuangan Publik dan Sosial Islam: Teori dan Praktik*. PT Rajagrafindo Persada.

Kahf, M. (1995). *Ekonomi Islam, Telaah Analitik terhadap Fungsi Sistem Ekonomi Islam*. Pustaka Pelajar.

Meera, A. K. (2018). Cryptocurrencies from Islamic perspectives: The case of bitcoin. *Bulletin of Monetary Economics and Banking, 20*(4), 475–492.

Meera, A. K., & Aziz, H. A. (2002). The Islamic Gold Dinar: Sosio-economic perspectives. *International Conference on Stable and Just Global Monetary System* (hal. 151–173). Research Centre International Islamic University Malaysia.

Muamar, A., & Alparisi, A. S. (2017). Electronic Money (*E-Money*) dalam Perspektif Maqashid Syariah. *Journal of Islamic Economics Lariba, 3*(2), 75–84.

Qaradhawi, Y. (1988). *Hukum Zakat*. Pustaka Litera Antar Nusa.

Siddiqi, M. N. (1996). *Role of the state in the economy: An Islamic perspective*. The Islamic Foundation.

Vadillo, U. I. (2002). The architecture of the gold Dinar economy: An academic perspective. *International Conference on Stable and Just Global Monetary System* (hal. 335–360). Research Centre International Islamic University Malaysia.

Glossary

'Aqd Contract or agreement

Akhlaq The practice of virtue, morality, and manners in Islamic theology and philosophy

Al-Hisbah An institution that existed throughout the Muslim history for implementing what is proper and preventing what is improper

Amanah Fulfilling or upholding a trust

Amar ma'ruf nahi munkar *Amar ma'ruf* means something is right, *nahi munkar* has the opposite meaning, something is wrong

Aqidah Belief or faith in the fundamental aspects

Ashir Collectors of custom duties and *zakat* stationed by the state on the public roads

Asnaf A party that is eligible to receive *zakat* aid collected for Muslims. The eighth member consists of poor, *amil*, *muallaf*, *riqab*, *gharimin*, *fisabilillah*, *ibnu sabil*

Astman Price or paid as price

Auqiyah Ounce, a general medieval commodity weight, equivalent to 40 dirham

Baitul Maal wat Tamwil A movement to help small traders in Indonesia. It is a non-governmental organisation that operates like a cooperative bank started in 1994. It focuses on very small business entities such as petty traders and hawkers who are too small to be bankable

Baitul Mal/Bait al-Mal An institution of early and medieval Islam, it functioned as the central bank of the state, state insurance company, and controller of domestic and foreign trade

Batil Falsehood. It can be used to describe a nullified or invalid act or contract according to the sharia

Bay' al-Istishna A contract of sale whereby the purchaser asks the seller to manufacture a specifically defined product using the seller's raw materials at a given price to be delivered at a specified place

Bay' as-salam A sale agreement that involves advance payment for goods that are to be delivered later

Bay' najasy Manipulating offers or request

S. M. Juhro et al., *Inclusive Welfare*, https://doi.org/10.1007/978-981-96-0051-9

Bay' A contract of sale of definite goods or property with the free consent of parties for a definite price. It involves proposal (*ijab*) and acceptance (*qabul*). The contract of sales has many types

Bay' al-inah A contract of sale where a person sells an object on credit and then buys back at a lesser price for cash

Bay' al-Ma'dun Sale of non-available goods

Bay' bitsaman ajil A sale deal with deferred payment. A person sells an object for cash but buys it back on deferred payment for a higher price. Thus, a person gets cash immediately which he has to repay with an increment later

Bay' tawarruq A sales contract in which the buyer obtains merchandise on credit and then sells it at a loss to the original seller for cash. The purpose of this transaction is to get cash and not to do business. It is condemned as a trick to give or to get an interest-bearing loan

Dalil The Arabic term for source in Islamic law

Duafa People who live in poor economic and social conditions

Dzimmi/Dhimmi A historical term for non-Muslims living in an Islamic state with legal protection

Fakir The poor that do not have access to income and cannot meet their basic needs

Falah To thrive, to become happy, to have luck or success. It implies success in the *Akhirah* (hereafter)

Fard A religious obligation or duty

Fardu Kifayah A legal obligation that must be discharged by the Muslim community as a whole

Fay' State income other than *zakat;* the collective wealth of Muslims derived from the taxation of conquered people

Fiqh Having knowledge in depth; having the knowledge of the rulings of Islamic law which are extracted from the legislative sources

Fuqaha Islamic jurists, an expert in *fiqh*, or Islamic jurisprudence and Islamic law

Ghanimah Wealth taken by force from an enemy in times of war

Gharar Sale of a thing that is not present at hand, or the sale of a thing whose consequence or outcome is not known, or a sale involving risk or hazard in which one does not know where it will come to be or not

Habluminallah The relationship between a human with The God

Habluminnannas The relationship between a human and other humans

Halal Permissible according to Islamic law

Haqq The Truth, is one of the names of Allah

Haram Forbidden or proscribed by Islamic law

Hawalah Bill of exchange, promissory note, cheque. A debtor passes on the responsibility of payment of his debt to a third party who owes the former a debt. Thus, the responsibility of payment is ultimately shifted to a third party

Hayatan Thayyiban A good life

Hibah Gift or donation. Transfer of a determinate property without any material consideration

Hurriyah Freedom or liberty

Ibadah The following of Islamic beliefs and practices, the obedience, submission, and devotion to Allah along with the ultimate love for Him

Ihsan A matter of taking one's inner faith and showing it in both deed and action, a sense of social responsibility borne from religious convictions

Ihtikar The hoarding of commodities of any kind, particularly foodstuff, with a view to creating artificial scarcity and rise in price

Ijarah Sale of usufruct of an asset in exchange for definite reward, but it is commonly used for wages

Ijarah Muntahiya bit Tamlik An *ijarah* financing, lease contract that ends with the transfer of ownership of leased assets to the lessee

Ijtihad Endeavour of a jurist to derive or formulate a rule of law on the basis of evidence found in the sources

Ikhtiyar Without control or authority, without choice or election

Infaq Spending to seek Allah's pleasure, whether to discharge a liability or voluntarily on the poor, needy, or to meet social needs

Islah Reform, to improve, to better, or to put something into a better position

Istisna A contract of sale whereby the purchaser asks the seller to manufacture a specific and defined product using the seller's raw materials at a given price to be delivered at a specified place

Jizyah A compensation for the security and protection that the non-Muslims have in the Islamic state without fighting for the defence of the country

Jualah Undertaking to pay specified fee or compensation for getting a specified service

Kafalah A contract of surety in which a person adds to his responsibility or liability on behalf of another person in respect of a demand for something

Khalifah In Islamic history the ruler of the Muslim community

Khamr Alcoholic drinks

Kharaj Land tax that is levied by the state on the state-owned lands whether the cultivator is a leaseholder or a permanent tenant

Khilafah An institution or public office governing a territory under Islamic rule

Khilkiyya Affirmed behaviour

Khums One-fifth or twenty per cent. In Islamic legal terminology, it means one-fifth of certain items that a person acquires as wealth must be paid to the state of Islam

Maqasid Syariah Objectives of the shariah, it refers to the protection of life, religion, reason (*'aql*), progeny, and property

Maslahah Utility or benefit. Exigencies which necessitate protection of faith, life, progeny, property, and rationality

Mafsadah Anything tending to disturb or corrupt

Maysir Speculation or gambling that is prohibited in Islamic finance because it creates wealth from chance instead of productive activity

Mazhab A division of thought or *fiqh* in Islam

Mi'yar al-Amwal Intended as a measure of the value of goods

MDGs The United Nations Millennium Development Goals; eight goals that United Nations Member States have agreed to try to achieve by the year 2015 that had been established following the Millennium Summit of the United Nations in 2000

Muallaf A call for individuals who are non-Muslims or non-Muslims who have the hope of converting to Islam

Muamalah Transaction or dealing. It is a part of Islamic jurisprudence including Islamic rulings governing commercial transactions

Mubah Permissible; an action for which people will neither be rewarded nor punished

Mudharabah A form of business contract in which one party contributes capital and the other personal effort

Mudharib In a *mudharabah* contract, the person who acts as a working partner or entrepreneur

Muhtasib A holder of the office of al-hisbah in classical Islamic administrations

Mujahid Those engaged in *jihad*

Mukhabarah An agreement to lease land on rent for cultivation with the condition to share the produce in a given ratio. In some cases, the agreement provides for the supply of seed by the land owner but it is not always the essence of the contract. It is also known as *khibr*

Murabahah Sale of goods with an agreed-upon profit markup on the cost

Musaqah A contract in which the owner (of the garden) shares its produce with another person in a predetermined ratio in return for latter's services in irrigating the garden

Musawah A global movement for equality and justice in the Muslim family and family laws

Mustahiq A person entitled to receive assistance from the *zakat* fund

Musyarakah A financing technique adopted by Islamic banks. It is an agreement under which the Islamic bank provides funds which are mingled with the funds of the business enterprise and others

Musyarakah Mutanaqishah A contract of partnership in an income-generating asset or venture, according to which one partner ends up owning that asset or venture at an agreed time schedule

Muzakki *Zakat* giver, the one who have paid zakat, purifier, the one who did purification

Muzara'ah A contract in which one person agrees to till the land of the other person in consideration for a part of the produce of the land

Nafal Reward granted by a state leader or field leader to a Mujahideen fighter as part of the *ghanimah* spoils, the total of which is above average

Najashy Concealment, rousing, and chasing the game for the purpose of snaring it. In business transactions, this term means to demand the sale of an article of merchandise for more than its price, not meaning to purchase but only to ensnare the innocent buyer

Nawaib Special tax that is levied depending on (transitory) economic conditions based on the state's prerogative to determine the rate of tax to apply

Nazhir Administrator or supervisor of *waqf*

Nisbah Percentage of profit sharing

Nisab Limit or certain minimum

Pesantren or madrasa Boarding school that teaches knowledge based on Islamic teachings

Qadi or penghulu Headman/chief were also used and always associated with religious duties, particularly in terms of jurisprudence and sharia law

Qard Loan or debt. Loan of mithl'I articles (such as money) with the stipulation to return them in the future. It is a general term for monetary loans without a deadline for repayment

Qardul hasan Interest-free loans or virtuous loan. A loan with the stipulation to return the principal sum in the future without any increase

Qibla The direction towards which all Muslims around the world pray

Rahn Readiness or immutability or durability. It also implies that a thing is inseparable from or tied up with its acquisition, earnings, and deeds. To pledge or lodge a real or corporeal property of material value, in accordance with the law, as security for a debt or pecuniary obligation, so as to to make it possible for the creditor to regain the debt or some portion of the goods or property

Riba An excess or increase. An increase which in a loan transaction accrues to the lender over time without giving an equivalent counter-value or recompense (*'iwad*) in return to the borrower

Riba nasi'ah Increment on the principal of a loan payable by the borrower. It refers to the practice of lending money for any length of time on the understanding that the borrower would return to the lender at the end of this period the amount originally lent together with an increment in consideration of the lender having granted him time to pay

Riba fadhl A sale transaction of the 'amwal al-ribawWyah (commodities where the injunction relating to riba is applicable) in which a commodity is exchanged for the same commodity but unequal in amount and the delivery of at least one commodity is postponed

Risalah Prophet Muhammad SAW is a messenger of God on earth

Rububiyyah Divinity. This philosophical foundation of Islam explains that everything created on earth by Allah SWT is perfect and within its own system

Sadaqah Charity. In its widest sense it means an attitude of mutual appreciation, affection, mutual assistance, an act of loyalty to God and to one's fellow beings, a sense of true human hood

Safi' Objects personally selected by the leader from *ghanimah* for himself

Sahur (suhoor) The meal that is eaten before daybreak during the *Ramadhan*

Salam A sale agreement that involves advance payment for goods that are to be delivered later. According to the general law, no sale can be effected unless the goods are in existence at the time of the bargain, but this sort of sale forms an exception to the general rule provided the goods are defined, price is paid in advance, and the date of delivery is fixed. The objects of this sale are mostly fungible things and cannot be gold or silver because they are regarded as monetary values

Santri Religious students who study in Pesantren or Madrasa

Sarf Sale of a monetary value for monetary value. Exchange of currencies

SDGs Collection of 17 interlinked global goals designed to be a "blueprint to achieve a better and more sustainable future for all people and the world by 2030.

Shaum (fasting) Hold from eating, drinking, and all actions that can break the fast, from sunrise to sunset, with certain conditions, to increase the *takwa* of a Muslim. Fasting is one of the five pillars of Islam

Shohibul maal Investors or person who give the capital

Siyasah al-ighraq Dumping to lower prices below the market price

Sunnah Practices of the Prophet Muhammad

Surau/Langar Place for pray or study

Syurthah Formal police/security system in Caliph Ali bin Abi Thalib

Ta'awun Character or attitude to help each other

Tabarru Gift, donation. Relating to the law of *mufawadah* partnership, it means the right of complete and unfettered disposition over joint property

Tabayyun Find the truth of fact

Tahsini Complementary human needs

Takaful Mutual or joint responsibility; solidarity; mutual agreement. An alternative of the contemporary insurance in the Islamic framework

Takaful ijtimai Social security refers to the obligation of Muslims to others in need by covering and realising their needs, caring for them, and avoiding harm befalling them. Social security also refers to the right of an employee to receive protection if disaster prevents gainful employment and protection for his family while at work or after death

Tawarruq A sales contract in which the buyer obtains merchandise on credit and then sells it at a loss to the original seller for cash. The purpose of such a transaction is to get cash and not to do business. It is condemned as a trick to give or to get an interest-bearing loan

Tawhid The absolute oneness or unification of God Almighty

Tazkiyah Sanctification and development. This implies that in the development process, humans must engage in purification of the self to ensure all developmental activities remain in line with the original goals, values, and aspirations

Thalabul 'ilm Demonstrated by the emphasis in Islam that commands the pursuit of knowledge

Tijarah/Tijari Buying something with the intention of selling it for profit, whether the profit is realised or not. This is distinct from *bai'*, which involves exchange of a valuable (*maal*) with another valuable, not necessarily with the intention of making a profit. But both the terms are often used interchangeably to denote sale transactions

Ujroh Wage that is given after finishing the work

Ukhuwah Brotherhood. Individuals to grow and develop economically through brotherhood, solidarity, and cooperation

Ushr One-tenth. A tax on the agricultural produce of land levied on the Muslims at the rate of 10 per cent if the land is irrigated by rainfall and at the rate of 5 per cent, if the land is irrigated artificially

Ushur One-tenth. Al-ushur imposed on goods of merchants who came to the Muslim lands from non-Muslim countries which had no treaty with the Muslims

Wadi'ah Deposit, trust. A contract whereby a person leaves valuables as a trust for safekeeping

Wadi'ah yad amanah A pure deposit contract

Wadi'ah yad dhamanah A safekeeping or deposit contract, where the funds can be used for specific business purposes

Wakalah Representation, agency. Contract of agency in which a person delegates his business to another and substitutes the other in his own place

Waqf Detention. Appropriation or tying up of a property in perpetuity so that no proprietary rights can be exercised over the corpus but only over the usufruct

Waqf Muqoyyadah *Waqf* where *waqif* establishes or donates his property or assets for a specific purpose

Waqif Relating to the law of waqf, refers to the person who establishes or donates his property by way of waqf

Zakat To purify. A tax that is levied on all persons having wealth above an exemption limit (*nisab*) at a rate fixed by the shariah to purify wealth and souls from impure love

Zakat fitrah Self *zakat* that is obligatory on every individual Muslim, male and female who is capable according to the conditions set

Zakat mal Obligation upon every Muslim man and woman having a certain amount of wealth kept for a (lunar) year, to pay a certain amount to deserving people

Zalim Cruelty or unjust acts of exploitation

Zina Any form of sexual intercourse which is prohibited under Islamic law, especially that between two people who are not legal spouses; adultery, fornication

Index

S. M. Juhro et al., *Inclusive Welfare*, https://doi.org/10.1007/978-981-96-0051-9

FSC
www.fsc.org
MIX
Papier aus verantwortungsvollen Quellen
Paper from responsible sources
FSC® C105338

If you have any concerns about our products,
you can contact us on
ProductSafety@springernature.com

In case Publisher is established outside the EU,
the EU authorized representative is:
Springer Nature Customer Service Center GmbH
Europaplatz 3, 69115 Heidelberg, Germany

Printed by Libri Plureos GmbH
in Hamburg, Germany